The Daily Telegraph

Chronicle of Cricket

The Daily Telegraph

Chronicle of Cricket

Edited by
Norman Barrett

GUINNESS PUBLISHING

Published in Great Britain by Guinness Publishing Limited
33 London Road, Enfield, Middlesex

Front cover illustrations: Michael Atherton by Simon Bruty/Allsport; W.G.Grace from the Hulton-Deutsch Collection.

Design and layout by John Mitchell

Printed and bound in Great Britain by The Bath Press, Bath, Avon

A catalogue record for this book is available from the British Library

ISBN 0-85112-746-0

Contents

Introduction

The coverage of cricket in The Daily Telegraph over the years has been second to none. The Telegraph first came out in 1854, and most of the reports in this Chronicle of Cricket since that date have been taken from the newspaper. Not that one has had the luxury of extracting complete reports for many of the matches featured in this book, such has been the extent of the coverage. It has usually been necessary to distil the words of the Telegraph correspondents, to include the important details without losing the flavour of the writing.

It was not until just before the First World War that by-lines were included in the Telegraph sports pages, so some sixty years of reports in this book must remain unattributed and unacknowledged. One can only admire the dedication, knowledge and attention to detail of those early correspondents and anonymous Reuter's reporters who provided the copy for the early Test matches overseas. Fortunately, as this tradition of quality writing continued in succeeding years, we were able to put a name to most of the copy penned for the paper at cricket grounds up and down the country and throughout the cricketing world - from Philip Trevor, through Jim Swanton and Michael Melford, to Christopher Martin-Jenkins, to mention just a few of the illustrious names that have appeared under the cricket headlines up to the present day. The writers' names have been acknowledged with all reports and articles except where a piece has had to be so summarised as to render the original purely reference material.

The language and idiom of the day has largely been retained, except where it might mislead or appear ambiguous, and it is hoped that not too many anachronisms have crept in when it has been changed. It has been necessary sometimes to take liberties with headlines, which at first were limited to 'Cricket' or the names of the teams, because it was felt that for a book of this nature it is more important that the reader is able to recognise the content of the reports. Likewise, it has also sometimes been necessary to fill in background detail, as contemporary reports assume a certain knowledge on the part of the reader of recent events, from the result of the previous Tests to the overnight scores. For reasons of space, scorecards have not been included, although summarised scores often appear at the end of a report, and 'sequels' are given in bracketed italics at the end.

A number of special articles have been inserted at the appropriate moments in the Chronicle to give an overall historical picture of long-running sagas such as the D'Oliveira and Packer affairs and the throwing and bodyline controversies. The chronologies featured with each year are intended to supplement the reports and articles, and repetition has been avoided. The inclusion of a Test series in the table for a particular year depends solely on the date the last Test of that series finished.

While the book has been compiled from an English viewpoint, with a bias towards English international and domestic cricket, the unrivalled coverage of overseas cricket in

'The Champagne of Cricket': A fine England side which defeated Australia at the Oval in 1896. Back row (l-r), Hayward, Lilley, Richardson, Hearne (J.T.); middle, A.C.McLaren, K.S.Ranjitsinhji, W.G.Grace, F.S.Jackson, Capt.Wynyard; front, Abel, Peel.

The Daily Telegraph has made it possible to include reports of many of the outstanding matches between other Test-playing countries and in overseas domestic cricket.

I have been fortunate in compiling this book to have had the services initially of Christine Forrest of Wisden, who pored over dozens of cricket books to provide the framework on which the selection of reports was based. If there are any omissions of important or momentous events, it is more likely to be for lack of space or an oversight of mine than for any lack of vigilance on her part. I have also been lucky in that the Cuttings Department of The Daily Telegraph numbers among its staff a cricket buff, namely Peter Warrington, and I am indebted to him for producing the bulk of the raw material, mostly in his own time. Thanks, also, to David Ward for supplementing the cuttings research and for his highly efficient extra picture research, to Robert Brooke for providing a mass of dates for the chronologies with his customary proficiency, and to Fred Gill for compiling the index. Finally, I should like to thank Simon Duncan and Charles Richards of Guinness Publishing for their patience.

Norman Barrett

April 1994

Early days

Organised cricket dates back to the mid-1600s in the south of England, although how it had developed from earlier stick and ball games is obscure.

Reliable references to the sport become more numerable in the late 17th century, when it was undoubtedly taking hold in Kent, Sussex and Hampshire. Matches began to draw spectators, and admission money to be charged. Many of the early, matches were played for large sums of money, and there was a great deal of betting associated with cricket.

The game began to attract the nobility, and even royalty, as patrons. Men who worked on the great estates were employed as much for their prowess with bat and ball as for their skills and ability as gardeners and gamekeepers. Labourers and landowners, artisans and aristocrats, all played together, and thus began the tradition of Players and Gentlemen.

Rules were drawn up, the earliest known Laws of Cricket dating from 1744. Early cricket was played with a curved bat something like a hockey stick. There were only two stumps, and the ball was bowled under-arm.

Cricket began to be played at White Conduit Fields, Islington, in the early 18th century. Later, the White Conduit Club was formed, and from this, in the latter part of the century, emerged the Marylebone Cricket Club, or M.C.C. Thomas Lord, a Yorkshireman, was a ground bowler at the White Conduit Club, and with the backing of the Earl of Winchelsea and others he opened a new private cricket ground on what is now Dorset Square. This was moved twice until the present Lord's Cricket Ground was opened in 1814.

Meanwhile the game had been taken abroad, most of the early 'missionary' work being done by the Royal Navy and British Army. It was played in the early settlements of Australia, and it took root in India in the days of the British Raj. Cricket was also taken to Canada and the United States, but other influences stifled its growth in North America. Indeed, the first touring team from England was to North America in 1859, and shortly after that there were tours to Australia and New Zealand, all organised privately, but with many of the leading cricketers of the day.

By the mid-1800s, truly representative county clubs were being formed and the leading players were travelling to all parts of the country with the All England XI. The concept of first-class cricket evolved in the 1860s.

As cricket developed into a game of subtle skills, so the first personalities won renown. Some of the best players of the latter half of the 18th century, as well as many of the biggest patrons and huge crowds of spectators, were attracted to a Hampshire village club, Hambledon (a few miles north of Portsmouth), where great matches were played on Broadhalfpenny Down. The inspiration of the Hambledon Club was Richard Nyren, the landlord of the Bat and Ball Inn, and the exploits of the players were recorded for posterity by his son, John - men such as John Small of the straight bat, wicket-keeper Thomas Sueter, long-stop George Leer, Richard Nyren himself, fast bowler Thomas Brett, the first off-spinner, Lambert the 'Little Farmer', and the 'swarthy gypsy', Noah Mann, one of the first exponents of swerve. These men could take on the rest of England without fear. David Harris joined the club after it moved to a new home, Windmill Down, and he set new standards in bowling, his accuracy, length, speed and leg-spin forcing batsmen to evolve techniques of batsmanship that laid the foundation of the skills of today. The move to Windmill Down meant that many Surrey players joined Hambledon, one such being 'Silver Billy' Beldham, the prince of batsmen, whose career continued long after the club went out of existence in 1796.

Other names appeared after Hambledon, among them gifted amateurs such as Lord Frederick Beauclerk, 'Squire' Osbaldeston and Edward Budd. The first half of the 19th century was blessed with professionals such as Nicholas Felix and Fuller Pilch, wonderful batsmen, and William Lillywhite, a slow, round-arm bowler whose accuracy and longevity earned him the nickname 'Nonpareil' and who played for Sussex till he was 61. And there was Alfred Mynn, a superb all-rounder, the greatest personality in cricket until the advent of W.G.Grace.

Born in 1848, 'W.G.' was 15 when he made his first hundred, 170 for South Wales against the Gentlemen of Sussex, and with Gloucester in the early seventies he began setting all manner of batting and bowling records, continuing to dominate the scene for two decades and more. It was W.G.Grace who put cricket on the map as a public spectacle.

Cricket in Marylebone Fields in the 18th century, depicted in a painting by Francis Hayman. Until 1775, there were only two stumps, and if the ball passed between them the batsman was not out.

Diary 1300-1875

1300 What is thought might be the first mention of cricket, or "creag", appears in the Wardrobe accounts of King Edward I at Newenden, in Kent, for expenditure for Prince Edward to play at "creag et alios ludos" with his friends.

1478 The first certain reference to cricket appears in a document in the Archives de France, specifically near St Omer, in northern France (then Flanders but not in the kingdom of France), as "criquet".

1523 First reference to "stool-ball", a term that covers rounders as well as cricket.

1598 Mention of "cricket" in a court case and inclusion in an Italian-English dictionary.

Early 1600s Cricket played in Sussex and Kent.

1621 Stool-ball played in Massachusetts.

1646 First recorded cricket match - at Coxheath, in Kent (betting involved).

1650s References to people being charged or fined for playing cricket on Sundays.

1668 Evidence of cricket as a spectator sport provided by references to sale of beer at cricket and the rating of a cricket field by an innkeeper in Smithfield.

1697 Report in a London paper of "great" cricket match played in Sussex.

1700 Notice in the Post Boy that a "Match at Cricket, of 10 Gentlemen on each side, will be play'd on Clapham Common, near Fox-Hall, on Easter Monday next, for £10 a Head each Game (five being design'd) and £20 the Odd one".

1709 First reference to a county match, in Postman newspaper of 25 June, proclaiming: "On Wednesday, the 29th instant will be play'd a famous match of cricket on Dartford Brimpth for £50 by Kent and Surrey."

1718 Cricket first played at White Conduit Fields, Islington.

1721 First reference to cricket in India, mariners of the East India Company playing an impromptu game at Cambay.

1720s Patronage of cricket by "principal noblemen and Gentlemen of quality" leads to the establishment of county cricket.

1725 First mention of cricket being played on the Artillery Ground in Finsbury.

1744 First recorded charge for admission, 2d, to the Artillery Ground, London, increased to 6d for the "greatest cricket match ever known" (according to the London Magazine), Kent v All England, which provides the first fully recorded score of an important match. First known issue of the Laws of Cricket.

1745 In the earliest women's match on record, the ladies of Hambleton beat the ladies of Bramley by 8 "notches" on Gosden Common, near Guildford, on 26 June.

1769 First recorded century is made by John Minshull, who scores 107 for the Duke of Dorset's XI v Wrotham on 31 August.

County of Kent against All England: 18 June 1744

Cricket as played at the Artillery Ground, London (*c.*early 1740s).

Kent defeat England by one wicket

From the Artillery Ground, London

THE greatest cricket match ever known took place at the Artillery Ground, between elevens of the County of Kent and All England. There were present their Royal Highnesses the Prince of Wales and Duke of Cumberland, the Duke of Richmond, Admiral Vernon and many other persons of distinction.

England batted first and scored 40 runs in their first innings. Newland was 18 not out. Kent then scored 53 to gain an advantage of 13 runs. In England's second innings, Newland again scored most runs, 15, before he was caught by Lord J.Sackville. Kent wanted 58 runs to win, which they got with their last batsmen at the wickets.

XI Women of Hampshire v XI Women of Surrey: 5 October 1811

A cruel depiction of the women's match of 1811 (from an engraving by Thomas Rowlandson).

Ladies' match for 500 guineas

From Balls Bond, Newington

THE ladies' match, made by amateur noblemen of Hampshire and Surrey for 500 guineas a side between elevens chosen from their respective counties, finished on the third day at three o'clock in a win for the ladies of Hampshire. Surrey's best bowler and fielder was Ann Baker, aged 60, and the youngest participant was a girl of 14. In view of the early finish, a single-innings match was played in which the Hampshire ladies confirmed their superiority.

A print purporting to portray the match between All England and Sussex at Darnall, near Sheffield, the first of three arranged as a trial for the new technique of 'over-cast', or round-arm, bowling.

First Experimental Match Sussex v All England: 4 June 1827

Victory for new style of bowling

From Sheffield

THE first of three matches to be played between the County of Sussex and All England, for 1,000 guineas a side, took place at Darnall, near Sheffield, and resulted in a win by seven wickets for the county eleven. Much feeling has been aroused by the new style (round arm) of bowling, and these matches have been organised as a trial of strength between the best hitters in the country and the leading exponents of the round-arm style, namely, William Lillywhite and Jem Broadbridge of Sussex.

Only three of England's batsmen scored more than 2 against these bowlers in their first innings, notably Fuller Pilch, whose innings of 38 was the highest score of the match. England reached a total of 81, to which Sussex replied with 91, Dale contributing 31 not out. Lillywhite and Broadbridge then had England out in their second innings for 112. Sussex scored the 103 runs wanted to win for the loss of only three wickets, the not out batsmen being Thwaites (37) and Broadbridge (15).

[Sussex won the 2nd match, at Lord's, by 3 wickets, but before the 3rd match took place, 9 England players threatened not to take part unless the Sussex players "bowl fair". In the event, they withdrew their declaration and England, despite being put out for 27 in their 1st innings, won by 24 runs.]

Grand Match North v South: 10, 11 July 1837

Jubilee match celebrates 50 years of the Marylebone Club

From Lord's

A Grand Match took place here between the North (with Box and Cobbett) and the South to celebrate the Jubilee of the M.C.C. The North were given the fine wicket-keeper Box, of Sussex, and the all-rounder Cobbett, of Surrey.

The North batted first and were got rid of for 64 runs, William Lillywhite of Sussex capturing six wickets. The South scored four fewer, and the successful bowlers were Redgate and Cobbett, with six and four wickets respectively.

When the North went in again, Lillywhite claimed eight wickets and a catch. North this time made 65, Garrat scoring 25. The South made the 70 runs wanted to win for the loss of five wickets, thanks to the scoring of Clifford (26) and Millyard (23).

A memento of the Grand Jubilee Match of 1837 (printed on silk squares).

1771 The Bourn Club beat the 22 of Dover by 2 wickets in the first known 3-day match.

1775 Third stump introduced.

1787 The Marylebone Cricket Club (M.C.C.) is founded, the first mention being a match against Islington C.C. In May, Thomas Lord opens his first ground (on what is now Dorset Square).

Cricket, as played on the celebrated Cricket Field, near White Conduit House, 1787.

1788 In the earliest recorded M.C.C. match, the White Conduit Club are beaten by 83 runs at Lord's on 27 June. The M.C.C. publish their first revision of the Laws.

1790 First mention of a county club, 'Essex Cricket Club', meeting fortnightly at the Green Man, Navestock, during the summer.

1792 (or earlier) India's first cricket club, Calcutta C.C., is founded, for Europeans only. Sussex & Surrey's 453 v England is the highest innings yet recorded.

1793 Season's batting averages recorded for the first time.

1795 First recorded lbw dismissal.

1803 First reference to cricket in Australia.

1806 First Gentlemen v Players match, staged at Lord's, is won by the Gentlemen. First reference to cricket in South Africa (in the Cape Town Gazette).

1811 The second Lord's is opened, at St John's Wood, with turf moved from Dorset Square so that "the noblemen and Gentlemen of the M.C.C. shall be able to play on the same footing as before".

1814 The present Lord's ground is opened nearby because of plans to cut the Regent's Canal through the second! The turf is again moved.

1817 The professional William Lambert becomes the first batsman to score a hundred in each innings of an important match, with 107 not and 157 for Sussex v Epsom at Lord's. But he is later "warned off the Turf" at Lord's for allegedly having "sold the match" - England v Notts - by not playing his best. (His record remains unequalled until Stoddart's 195 not out & 124 for Middlesex v Notts in 1893.) First mention of cricket in Tasmania.

1820 The amateur William Ward (Hants) makes the first double century ever recorded, 278 for M.C.C. v Norfolk at Lord's. (He later becomes MP for City of London.)

1825 The Lord's pavilion, with all its records, is destroyed by fire. (A new pavilion is built next year.)

Inter-colonial Match Victoria v NSW: 16 January 1857

New South Wales win again

From the Outer Domain Ground, Sydney

THE Grand National Cricket Match ended today at the Outer Domain with victory again for New South Wales over Victoria by 65 runs, the former having won the first match, which took place last year in Melbourne.

The match was commenced on the 14th January, and there was no toss, NSW batting first by arrangement. The bowlers had the better of the game in each innings, T.W.Wills of Victoria taking 10 wickets in the match for 65 runs in 64 overs. He will be remembered as a Cambridge Blue last year, even though he was not up at the University - he was formerly at Rugby School and was entered at Cambridge, and the University, being a man short, were allowed to play him.

The highest score in the match was 31, made by the NSW captain, G.H.B.Gilbert, coming in at No.7 in their second innings. He was born at Cheltenham, Gloucestershire. One unusual feature of the match that provoked discussion was the absence of a wicket-keeper when NSW fielded.

Scores: NSW 80 (Wills 6-25) & 86 (Wills 4-40), Victoria 63 (O.H.Lewis 4-13, E.W.Ward 2-23) & 38 (Ward 5-15, Lewis 4-21).

[Wills never went up to Cambridge; he was the first to train the aborigines to play cricket, and came to England with them on the tour in 1868; he stabbed himself to death in 1880. Gilbert was a cousin of the Graces.]

New South Wales v Victoria, at Sydney, in 1857.

County of Surrey v All England: 23 July 1859

England win by 292 runs: Mr Walker's fine performance

From Kennington Oval

THE match came to a conclusion today on the Surrey ground, England winning by 292 runs. England in their second innings yesterday had scored 281 runs for the loss of six wickets and today they finished their innings for 390, Mr V.E.Walker contributing the splendid score of 108. Surrey made a poor stand for their second innings, the whole of the wickets falling for 89 runs, Caffyn making the only double figure, 17. The bowling of Mr V.E.Walker and Jackson was very good indeed.

[Walker, indeed, accomplished the very rare double of a century and 10 wickets in an innings. His figures were 20 not out & 108 and 10-74 & 4-17. Jackson took the other 6 wickets.]

The England team just embarked on the *Nova Scotian* at Liverpool on 7 September 1859. Back row: R.Carpenter, W.Caffyn, T.Lockyer, J.Wisden, H.H.Stephenson, G.Parr, J.Grundy, J.Caesar, T.Hayward, J.Jackson. Front: A.J.Diver, John Lillywhite.

Tourist Match XII of Canada and USA v England XI: 24 October 1859

George Parr's team win last match in N.America: Unbeaten on tour

From Rochester, New York

ENGLAND'S first touring side, under the captaincy of George Parr (Notts) won their final match here, beating a combined twenty-two of Canada and the United States of America by an innings and 68 runs. The tour, organised by Mr W.P.Pickering, an old Cambridge Blue who has settled in Montreal, has been a great success, England winning all five of their matches and being royally welcomed everywhere they went. In this last match, John Wisden claimed the huge total of 29 wickets.

Scores:
Canada & USA 39 (J.Wisden 16-17) & 64 (J.Wisden 13-43), England 171 (T.Hayward 50).

Selection announcement: 7 September 1861

England v Australia

From Aston Park, Birmingham

THE English cricketers finally selected at Birmingham to play in Australia are - Bennett (Kent), Wells (Sussex), Iddison and E.Stephenson (Yorkshire), Thomas Hearne and Lawrence (Middlesex), and the following Surrey men: Caffyn, Griffith, Mortlock, Mudie, Sewell, jun, and H.H.Stephenson. The latter player was elected captain of the team, and a committee of four chosen - viz, Caffyn, Mortlock, Hearne and E.Stephenson. They are to have £150 per man and a free passage out and home, and are to steam from England on the 18th of October in the Great Britain.

[This first England tour to Australia was sponsored by the Australian catering firm Spiers & Bond. Their agent put the proposal to players during the North v South match at Aston Park. Ten leading players refused the terms, so the team was by no means fully representative. They enjoyed a splendid welcome and played 12 matches (W6, L2, D4), none of them first class, and apart from the first game which they won by 305 runs against 18 of Victoria, all against teams of 22.]

A scene depicting the arrival of the All England XI at the Café de Paris, Bourke Street, Melbourne, on 24 December 1861. England's first tour of Australia was a great success and they were welcomed by huge crowds wherever they went. ***[See also team picture on page 15.]***

1826 The first known cricket clubs founded in Sydney, New South Wales. Sussex, according to some sources, are the first champion county, but there is no solid evidence for this. Unofficial champions and tables are published by various sources until the official County Championship is inaugurated in 1890.

1827 Round-arm bowling is introduced. The first Oxford-Cambridge match takes place, at Lord's, and is drawn.

1832 Cricket club founded in Hobart, Tasmania. Colombo C.C. founded in Ceylon.

1837 William Lillywhite takes 120 wickets in important matches during the season.

1838 First mention of County Championship, in a Maidstone newspaper, referring to the Kent v Notts match.

1839 M.C.C. are bowled out for 15 by Surrey at Lord's. F.A.Paulett makes 120 in Melbourne, the first recorded hundred in Australia.

c.1840 Cricket first played in Georgetown, British Guiana, and in Antigua.

1842 Trinidad C.C. known to be of "very long standing". B.Taylor makes 110 not out at Wynberg, the first recorded hundred in South Africa.

1843 The Port Elizabeth C.C. is the first cricket club to be founded in South Africa.

1844 The first recorded cricket match in New Zealand, but there have been earlier references to the game being played there pre-1840. The professional Francis Fenner, fast round-arm bowler, is the first to take 17 wickets in a match, for Cambridge Town v Cambridge University. (Two years later he lays out the cricket ground at Cambridge that bears his name.)

1845 Professional William Hillyer, medium-paced round-arm bowler, generally regarded as the finest of his time, takes 208 wickets in important matches during the season.

1846 Touring All England XI organised by William Clarke. The last single wicket championship is played between Alfred Mynn and Nicholas Felix at Bromley, Kent, on 29 September.

Alfred Mynn (left) and Nicholas Felix.

E.M.Grace: Outstanding all-round performance.

XII Gentlemen of M.C.C. v XII Gentlemen of Kent: 15 August 1862

Mr E.M.Grace carries bat for 192 runs and takes all 10 wickets

From Canterbury

PLAY in this match was resumed today, Messrs Tredcroft and E.M.Grace (M.C.C.) continuing their innings to the bowling of Messrs Norton and Kelson. Mr Grace added 14 to his score yesterday of 102 when he received a smart thump on the left ribs from a ball bowled by Mr Kelson. and retaliated by hitting the next ball, for four, nearly over the scorer's monstrosity, whereupon Mr Barber took up the bowling at Mr Kelson's end. After bowling four overs Mr Barber turned it over to Mr Lipscombe, the score then being up to 276, when Mr Grace, in hitting a ball from Mr Norton, broke his bat, and with a fresh bat began by a fine forward drive for 4, and shortly after he made three more 4's from successively-bowled balls, and hit the fourth straight up a tremendous height, and it appeared all over with him, but it was badly missed by the wicket-keeper, Mr Kelson, who partly atoned for this mishap by very neatly having Mr Tredcroft at the wicket - the score standing at 316 runs for the loss of eight wickets; Mr Tredcroft having scored only 14, while Mr Grace scored 68. Mr Burnett took the vacant wicket, scored 6, and was then finely stumped by Mr Kelson - nine for 333. Mr Balfour was bowled off his pad by Mr Norton - ten for 340; and at half-past one the last of the M.C.C.'s, Mr Morse, was caught in the slip, the innings closing at 344, of which number Mr E.M.Grace contributed 192, and was 'not out'. He went in No.1, received the first ball bowled, saw the whole of his side out, and scored no less than twenty-six 4's, six 3's, twelve 2's, and forty-six singles. On the completion of his innings (the largest ever scored on the St Lawrence Ground), the Earl of Sefton, on behalf of the M.C.C., in a neat and appropriate speech, presented Mr Grace with a new bat, as a memento of the M.C.Club's appreciation of his finely played and extraordinary innings of 192 not out.

At a quarter to two the gentlemen of Kent commenced their second innings to the bowling of Mr Burnett and Mr Grace. The latter's underhands worked well, and four wickets went down for 34, all to Mr Grace's slows. After dinner Captain Taswell and Mr Barker brought the score up to 69, when Mr B. was caught 'mid on' for 24. Mr Fitzgerald made a fine catch mid wicket, that sent back Capt Taswell for a well-played 26. With few more runs added, the tenth wicket fell at a quarter-past five for 99 runs. This finished the match, and the Gentlemen of the Marylebone Club won in one innings, with 104 runs to spare. Mr Grace not only scored 192, not out, but in the second innings of the Kent Gentlemen 'took all their wickets' with his underhand bowling.

[As a 12-a-side match this does not merit first-class status, but that should not detract from E.M.Grace's performance. He took all 10 wickets to fall in the Kent 2nd innings for 69, one of the batsmen being absent. He also claimed 5 in their 1st innings.

It is interesting to note that this match, which finished on the Friday of Canterbury week, began at 4 on Wednes-day, following the 14 of Kent v 11 of England match, which ended at 2.15 and in which E.M. Grace also took part, top-scoring with 56 in England's 2nd innings as they went down by 170 runs. Only 4 of Kent's 14 took part in the second match, notable absentees being Willsher, Sewell and Bennett.]

The 1861-62 English team to Australia *[see page 13, Selection Announcement]*. Left to right (cricketers only): Wells, Bennett, Mortlock, Iddison, Caffyn, H.H.Stephenson (captain), Sewell, Griffiths, Mudie, E.Stephenson, Lawrence, Hearne. Behind the captain is Mr W.B.Mallam, the agent of the Australian sponsors.

Surrey v England: 26 August 1862

England score monster 503: Then walk off when Willsher is no-balled

From the Kennington Oval

UPWARDS of 5,000 visitors were on the Oval today to witness the continuance of, it is believed, the most extraordinary innings on record, and in which there were 9 hours and 55 minutes' play, 1,058 balls bowled, and the unprecedented number of 503 runs scored. The great innings by the Gentlemen of Berks in 1860 was 427; Sussex scored an innings of 445 against the Marylebone Club in 1817; in 1792 Surrey & Sussex combined scored 453 against England; and in 1820, in the memorable match wherein Fuller Pilch made his début at Lord's, and Mr Ward played his great score of 278, the Marylebone Club's first innings amounted to 473. This, we think, is the nearest to the monster innings of 503 made by the England Eleven at the Oval yesterday and today.

Hayward and Carpenter resumed their batting this morning with the England score on 244 for three, and it had risen to 338 before the two Cambridge cracks were parted, Carpenter being finely 'c and b' by Heathfield Stephenson. George Anderson then joined Hayward. The score quickly rose to 356, whereupon Lockyer went on to bowl and Griffith, who had enjoyed no success with his slows, kept wicket, and uncommonly well Old Ben kept it too. Lockyer's fast bowling did not pay at all, so he tried 'lobs', and in the second over of these he bowled the bails off Hayward's wicket, making five done for 402 runs, Hayward having scored an innings of 117 runs. Both Hayward and Carpenter were complimented at the Pavilion.

Anderson (42) and the Hon.C.G.Lyttelton (26) both played fine innings and were finely caught out at the wicket by Griffith, making 451 for seven. Iddison (33) and Jackson (21), by brilliant hitting, brought the score up to 497, and then Mr V.E. Walker had the honour of effecting a cricket coup de main such as never before fell to the lot of a cricketer, i.e., by a hit for a single making up an innings of 500 runs. It was his only run and the innings closed at exactly half-past five.

Everything had gone off merrily - at all events, for England. But then occurred a very unpleasant affair. Willsher (at the Pavilion-end) and Mr V.E.Walker began the England bowling; Sewell, senior, umpiring at Mr Walker's end, and John Lillywhite at Willsher's. Mr V.E.W. soon had a wicket down for 4 runs, Humphrey being very finely caught by Grundy. Then Willsher began his third over, "No ball," shouted John Lillywhite, and it was cut by Mr Burbidge for 4. The next ball was delivered by Willsher, and "No ball" called again by Lillywhite, who also "no-balled" the remainder of the balls bowled by Willsher, who then quietly turned round and walked off the ground. Several of the other England players immediately had a brief consultation, and then followed Willsher, leaving the two gentlemen, Mr V.E. Walker and the Hon. C.G. Lyttelton, on the field.

Immediately all was confusion; the great crowd of people present broke on to the ground; the play was stopped for the day, and strong opinions both ways were expressed. On inquiry, we learnt that, on bowling his second over, Willsher was cautioned by John Lillywhite that he was getting high in delivery, and that he should feel it his duty to 'no-ball' him if he continued to so deliver the balls.

No doubt some arrangement in the true spirit of cricket will in the morning be made that will enable play in this memorable match to proceed. One thing is certain, that today's proceedings are pregnant with important results to the national game, and after this season Rule 10 will either have to be carried out by umpires in its integrity, or struck out of the laws of cricket.

[A compromise was suggested that Willsher "on that occasion" be allowed to bowl in his usual way, but Lillywhite, much to his honour, declined to act unless he was entirely unfettered, so another umpire was appointed Willsher took 6 wickets and Surrey followed on, but the match was drawn. The restrictions on over-arm bowling were removed in 1864.]

1848 Professional Edmund Hinkly, a left-hand fast round-arm bowler, playing for Kent v England at Lord's, is the first to take all 10 wickets (in a first-class 11-a-side match), in England's second innings, having taken 6 in the first.

1850 John Wisden (Sussex), bowling fast round-arm, takes all 10 wickets for North v South at Lord's, all bowled.

John Wisden.

1851 A match takes place at Launceston Racecourse, Tasmania, between Van Diemen's Land (Tasmania) and Port Phillip District (Victoria), which is later recognised as the first first-class match in Australia; T.W.Antill takes 7-33 & 6-19 for Victoria but they lose by 3 wickets.

1856 In the first inter-colonial match, NSW (76 & 16-7) beat Victoria (63 & 28) by 3 wickets at Melbourne in what is regarded by many as the beginning of first-class cricket in Australia; fast under-arm bowler J.J.McKone takes 5-25 & 5-11 for NSW, and fast round-arm bowler G.Elliott 7-25 & 3-7 for Victoria. Fast round-arm bowler John Bickley (Notts) takes 8-7 for England v Kent & Sussex at Lord's.

1857 James Grundy, playing for M.C.C. v Kent at Lord's on 8 June, is given out 'handled the ball', the first instance recorded of this dismissal.

1858 G.Elliott takes 9 wickets for 2 runs in 19 overs (17 maidens) for Victoria (115) v Tasmania (33 & 62) at Launceston; in Tasmania's first innings there are 14 extras, no batsman reaching double figures.

1862 Fast bowler Tom Sewell, jun (Surrey), playing for H.H.Stephenson's team in Australia *(see picture on page 15)*, England's first tour there, takes 15-27 - all in the XXII of Geelong's 2nd innings, on 22 January. Fast round-arm bowler Joseph Wells is the first to take 4 wickets with consecutive balls, for Kent v Sussex at Hove on 26 June. William Caffyn, medium-pace round-arm, takes 7-7 for Surrey v Kent at Canterbury in 24 overs, 20 of them maidens.

The Australian Aboriginal cricketers who toured England in 1868.

Tourist match Surrey v Aboriginal Blacks: 25 May 1868

Successful début of Australian Black Eleven

From Kennington Oval

SUCCESS far beyond expectation has attended the début of the Australian cricketers at Kennington Oval. That famous cricket ground, which gloriously upheld its reputation as the dryest of all fields, despite long continued showers, also distinguished itself by a day's financial operations rivalling those of a large theatre on Boxing night. The sum taken at the gate during the day was £264 12s, by far the largest amount ever counted after any 'event' at the Oval. It would be grossly to understate the attendance at 5,300, however, because many persons entered without paying.

Mr Miller won the toss for the club and decided to take first innings. From the first moments of the blacks coming in sight, it was evident that the great mass of spectators had assembled with a determination to encourage, in hearty English fashion, the efforts of the strangers. There was, of course, a good deal of curiosity mingled with the desire to welcome these sable cricketers, not a man of whom knew bat or ball until trained by Mr Hayman, whom the whole eleven had served in the capacity of shepherds. They are stalwart fellows, of good average height, though they were today thrown into comparative shortness by their antagonists, the Surrey gentlemen, who ranged in stature from five feet ten inches to six feet four. Their skins are as black, or nearly, as the skins of African races; but instead of the closely matted wool they have glossy black hair, straight or curly, and they seem to take some pride in the arrangement of their whiskers, which are naturally of luxuriant growth.

The Australians are led by a noted English professional cricketer whose name - Charles Lawrence - will recall him to general remembrance as one of the All-England Eleven. His services were the more needful today inasmuch as the best bowler in his well-disciplined team has been laid on a bed of sickness.

The position taken by the blacks was in manner following (using the nicknames employed by the tourists): King Cole was at point, Jim Crow at cover point, Twopenny long-stopped, Dick-a-Dick and Tiger at long-off and leg looked like two lonely sentinels in their scarlet uniforms, white trousers with black stripe, and blue cap, in which costume all the Australian eleven, except their white captain, were dressed - with different-coloured scarves to distinguish them individually; Redcap was square leg, Bullocky was wicket-keeper, Peter was at slip, Charley Dumas was at mid-wicket, and Lawrence and Mullagh, by whom the bowling was commenced, took short slip alternately.

The Surrey innings ended at half-past five for 222 runs, Mr Baggally making a fine score of 68. Lawrence took seven wickets for 90, and Mullagh, who is a remarkably good bowler, three for 101, and the Australians showed themselves, by their fielding, to be worthy opponents to the best English cricketers.

The batting was commenced on the side of the blacks, but by the time stumps were drawn at seven o'clock, they had lost four wickets for only 34 runs.

[The Aboriginals made 83 and, following on, 132, Mullagh top-scoring, with 33 and 73, in each innings. King Cole died in June, and Sundown and Jim Crow went home in August because of ill-health.]

Surrey County v Cambridge University: 20 June 1868

Absolom given out 'obstructing the field' in exciting finish

From the Oval

1,012 runs were scored in this match, and yet Surrey were the victors by 14 runs only, and the match was otherwise excitingly finished. Surrey, who had followed on 160 runs behind yesterday, resumed this morning on 236 for the loss of five wickets. Splendid batting by Jupp (134) and Mortlock (66 not out) enabled Surrey to take their score to 334 all out by a quarter to three, 40 minutes having been lost because of a rain shower.

The University Eleven then had 175 runs to score to win. They had lost seven wickets, however, with only 90 runs made, when Mr Absolom joined Mr Warner and they proceeded to pull the match round in excellent style. Mr Warner was playing quite up to the form that won the match at Lord's last year, and Mr Absolom surprised us by the careful and very steady cricket he played. They had put on 48 runs together when there occurred an unfortunate incident that caused considerable excitement among the onlookers and seriously jeopardised the University success. Southerton was bowling from the lower wicket; he bowled to Mr Absolom a ball that gentleman drove in great form - in fact, this was one of the finest drives made on the Oval for many a season - they had run 6 for the hit when the ball appeared to be knocked out of Pooley's hand some few yards, and loud cries of "run", "run" induced the batsmen to start for the seventh run; Humphrey fielded the ball and, with "unerring instinct" and aim, threw the ball at the wicket that Mr Absolom was running to; that gentleman grounded his bat; the ball, "travelling in a direct line to the wicket, hit the bat," and on appeal, Tanner, the umpire, gave Mr Absolom out for 'obstructing the field'. Being given out, Mr Absolom returned to the Pavilion; there, being told he was not out, he returned to the wickets: but, being there again "told" he "was" out, Mr Absolom finally retired, having scored 38.

Such - so far as we could gather them - are the facts of this contretemps that, in all probability, lost Cambridge the match; nevertheless, we thoroughly believe the decision to be a conscientious one. Mr Warner was soon out for a well-played 50 and Cambridge lost by 14 runs.

[This is the first recorded instance of an 'obstructing the field' dismissal in first-class cricket.]

Yorkshire v Cambridgeshire: 13 July 1869

Easy win for Yorkshire: Emmett takes 16 wickets

By Telegraph, from Hunslet, Leeds

THE match came to a rather sudden conclusion at Leeds today. The Cambridgeshire team was very much weakened by the absence, through illness, of Tarrant, and other causes, and they only succeeded in scoring 86 runs in their two innings. Yorkshire, on the other hand, was strongly represented both in fielding and batting, Emmett, by his close bowling, taking sixteen wickets, while Iddison scored no less than 112 runs, for which he was rewarded by a £5 subscription. The total number of runs obtained by the Yorkshiremen in one innings amounted to 352.

[Tom Emmett, a fast, round-arm bowler, in accomplishing this feat, was the first player to take 16 wickets in a first-class match. His figures were 16-38 (7-15 & 9-23).]

Varsity Match: 28 June 1870

Cambridge win by 2 runs: First 100 and hat-trick

From Lord's

IF it be acknowledged that the genius of a nation may be inferred from the sports it enjoys or patronises, a foreigner visiting the Marylebone Cricket Ground during the last two days would certainly have surmised that we English were a very harmless set of 'muscular Christians' indeed. Instead of Roman matrons gazing on the fearful scenes of the arena, and simpering out "Habet" as some wretched gladiator lay weltering in his blood; instead of dark-eyed beauties calmly calculating the life-and-death chances of the matador against his taurine foe; he would have seen our Saxon maids and matrons forming the cloud-like circle of dark and light blue, in the centre of which 22 of the youth of England were contending in the mimic strife of the bat and ball. It is, perhaps, a spectacle which no other country but England could present; it is an occasion out of which certainly none but an Englishman could manage to extract a 'sensation'.

The sensation came right at the end, but the day commenced with the second innings of Cambridge being opened by Mr Dale and Mr Tobin, Cambridge being in the minority of 28 runs on the first innings. They lost wickets quickly, and were only 12 on when they lost their fifth batsman. At that point, Mr Yardley went to Mr Dale's aid, and the 'turn of the tide' was Cambridge-wards.

Excellent as was the Oxford bowling, it was fairly and finely mastered by these gentlemen. They were not parted until they had added 116 runs and the score had risen up to 168, a catch at deep leg ending Mr Dale's careful and correctly played innings of 67 which was the foundation of the success of his side. Mr Yardley continued with his fine hitting and increased his score to 100, the first century ever made in the university match, to a roar of cheers from the pavilion. Immediately after, a loud exulting Oxford cheer greeted Mr Francis having 'c and b' Mr Yardley; 195 for eight. Cambridge were all out for 206, Mr Francis having claimed seven wickets for 102.

Thus the Oxonians were set 179 to win. They lost a wicket before a run was scored, but then Mr Ottaway came in, and first with Mr Fortescue (44) and then Mr Tylecote (29) took the score to 153 for three - 26 to win and seven wickets to fall - it appeared simply a question of 'time' as to the success of the Dark Blues. Even when My Tylecote fell at this score and then Mr Ottaway for 69 seven runs later - after a rare display for one so young of careful and correct cricket - they wanted only 19 runs with five wickets remaining.

Then came the extraordinary end to this wonderful match. The sixth wicket fell at 165, the seventh at 175 - 4 to win. Then it was that Mr Cobden began his last over. A single was scored off the first ball - 2 wanted to tie the match, with three wickets to fall. From the second ball, Mr Butler was splendidly caught out at mid-off by Mr Bourne; with the third ball Mr Belcher was bowled, and with the fourth Mr Stewart was bowled, all three wickets falling with the score at 176; and thus, amid a scene of wild excitement, and tumultuous cheering, did Cambridge after all win the thirty-sixth match by 2 runs.

[Cobden's was the first hat-trick performed in the Varsity match; he took 4-35 (8-76 in match) and Harrison-Ward 6-29 (9-62). For Oxford, Francis took 5-59 & 7-102.]

1864 The first match in New Zealand to be recognised as first-class is played at Dunedin, where Otago (78 & 74) beat Canterbury (34 & 42) by 76 runs. Playing for M.C.C. v Oxford University on 10 June, Henry Bull is the first player to be given out 'hit ball twice' in a first-class match, dismissed by umpire Fennell when he starts for a run after the second strike. On the same day, over-arm bowling is legalised. First issue of John Wisden's Cricketers' Almanack published.

1865 The first inter-colonial match in the West Indies, Barbados v Demerara (now in Guyana), is played in Bridgetown. George Wootton takes all 10-54 for All England XI v Yorks at Sheffield (19 July). V.E.Walker takes all 10-104 for Middlesex in Lancashire's 2nd innings (22 July), and is the first bowler to perform the feat for a second time, having done it for England in 1859.

1868 The Australian Aborigines are the first side to tour England, none of their 47 fixtures in 5 months being first class but their opponents mostly being little below that standard; they win 14 matches and lose 14. The Surrey professional Edward Pooley, one of the great wicket-keepers of his day, dismisses a record 12 batsmen in the match against Sussex at the Oval (6-7 July), 6 in each innings (8ct, 4st). Edmund Tylecote, in a House match at Clifton, makes 404 not out for Classical v Modern, the highest score in any match to date.

1869 W.G.Grace, in his innings of 127 for M.C.C. v Kent at Canterbury, makes a hundred (116) before lunch, the first recorded instance of such a feat in first-class cricket.

1870 William Hickton takes all 10-46 for Lancs v Hants at Old Trafford on 23 July.

1871 W.G.Grace is first player to score 2,000 runs in a season - 2,739.

1872 The M.C.C. are all out for 16 v Surrey at Lord's, having been 0-7, 2-8 and 8-9. During Canterbury Week, James Lillywhite takes all 10-129 in 60.2 overs (22 maidens) for South v North, who nevertheless win by an innings (6-7 August).

1874 Henry Jupp carries his bat through the innings twice in a match, 43 not out and 109 not out, for Surrey v Yorks at the Oval. W.G.Grace scores a 100 and takes 10 wickets in a match five times during the season. A team of American baseball players tours England in August, giving exhibitions of their national game and playing 7 cricket matches, always fielding between 18 and 22 men against poor sides, and winning 4 and drawing 3 matches.

1875 The professional Alfred Shaw, slow-medium bowler renowned for his accuracy and economy, takes 7-7 for Notts v M.C.C. in 41.2 overs with 36 maidens.

Varsity Match: 26 June 1871

Great bowling feat: Butler obtains all ten Light Blue wickets

From Lord's

THE first innings of Cambridge was commenced at a quarter to four and will ever remain a famous one in the Universities' cricketing annals, from the great bowling feat achieved by Mr Butler, who obtained all ten Light Blue wickets, 'bowling' eight of the ten.

Oxford, who won choice of innings and went in at 11.30, scored 170 in their first innings, Mr Pauncefote making 50 and Mr Tylecote 42. Five wickets fell to Mr Bray for 38 runs, four to Mr Powys for 40. When Cambridge went in to bat, Mr Butler bowled from the pavilion end. An hour and thirty-five minutes later, the innings was at an end, Cambridge being all out for 65 and all ten wickets falling to Mr Butler. Only 3 runs were made by the last five wickets, and the last six wickets were had by Mr Butler in the last 14 balls he bowled. In all, he bowled 24 overs and one ball, including 11 maidens, and conceded 38 runs.

Of the Cambridge batsmen, only Mr Yardley (25) and Mr Money (23) reached double figures. When Cambridge followed on, 105 runs behind on first innings, Mr Butler bowled Mr Money with the score at 5. With the score at 57, Mr Hadow bowled Mr Tobin for 30, and when stumps were drawn Cambridge had surpassed their first innings score by one, without the loss of further wickets.

[Butler took 5-57 in the Cambridge 2nd innings (129) and Oxford won by 8 wickets.]

W.G.Grace: 100 before lunch.

Gentlemen v Players: 3 July 1873

Another big innings by Mr W.G.Grace: Gentlemen on top again

From the Kennington Oval

TO say that Mr W.G.Grace is far and away and beyond compare the best batsman that ever scored a run is to tell an old tale. Certainly this week Mr Grace's star has been fast rising to the zenith. On Monday and Tuesday he scored 163, and today 158. In the former innings he was caught at point from a no-ball when he was 63, and today, very early in his innings, he played a ball of Emmett's very hard on to his wicket, without, however, knocking off either of the bails. Both these accidents were terribly unfortunate for the Players. The Lord's match they lost by an innings and half a hundred runs, and the Oval match they seem destined to lose almost as badly. The Gentlemen made 330 runs in the first innings. Then the Players, tired and jaded from their long day's fielding, lost four of their best wickets for 34.

Mr Grace rattled the score along in the morning, putting on 93 for the first wicket with Mr Longman (24) and making 101 by dinner time, when the score was 159 for four wickets. When the score had reached 245, just after he had been missed at deep square-leg by Jupp, the great batsman was clean bowled by Alfred Shaw for another wonderful innings, made in three hours and a quarter and including a 6, two 5's and fifteen 4's. His last three innings have been 134, 163 and now 158, an extraordinary succession of grand batting displays of which even he may well be proud.

Mr Tylecote (of 404 not out notoriety) took the place of the 'champion' and made 49 in really first-class style, including a 6, a 5 and four 4's before being last out. Alfred Shaw took five wickets for 64 runs in 50 overs, J.C.Shaw three for 116 and Emmett two for 65. Buchanan took three of the Players' four wickets to fall before the close.

[The Players were beaten by an innings and 11 runs, Buchanan taking 7-52, G.F.Grace 3-39, in the 1st innings (106), and W.G.Grace, who did not bowl in the 1st, 7-65 and Buchanan 3-59 in the 2nd (213), in which Oscroft made 73, Emmett 49.]

M.C.C. v North: 1 June 1874

Alfred Shaw takes all 10 wickets

From Lord's

IN fine summer weather this match was commenced today at Lord's, the North playing a very strong eleven. The feature of the day's play was the bowling of the Nottinghamshire professional Alfred Shaw, who obtained all ten of the North's wickets when they were bowled out in their first innings for 175. However, the North finished the day on top, having got rid of the Marylebone Club for 154.

Play began shortly after twelve, and Shaw sent down two maidens before bowling Greenwood with the score at 11. Then Lockwood (38) joined Mr Hornby (53) in a long stand, which was not broken until Shaw returned to have Mr Hornby caught at slip with the score at 96. While, at the other end, Morley and Mr W.G.Grace bowled without reward, the wickets kept falling to Shaw, who finished up with all ten for 78 runs in 36 overs. His analysis was not as good as usual, in that he rarely concedes much more than one run per over, but after the fall of the third wicket he bowled in the fine form we naturally expect from the man who is beyond question the best bowler of the day.

Mr Grace opened the M.C.C. innings with Mr Coote, whom he lost with the score at 7. Mr Grace, however, began hitting very freely, and seemed likely to make one of his long innings when he was finely taken at long-on by Greenwood, who ran several yards to make the catch. Mr Grace made 43 of the 63 scored - a clear proof of the brilliancy of his hitting. The next three wickets added 70 runs, but then the last five were rapidly got rid of for only 21, the last falling at 154. Mr Buller, who had retired with a strained leg, came out again towards the close of the innings, with Mr Grace to run for him, and carried his bat for 24.

[North made only 106 (Morley 5-48, Shaw 3-43), but then dismissed M.C.C. for 82 (J.C.Shaw 5-44) and won by 45.]

The American baseball players: Exhibition at Liverpool after their first cricket match.

Tourist match Surrey v XVIII of America: 14 August 1874

Cricket gives way to exhibition of base-ball

From the Kennington Oval

THIS two-day match resulted in a draw, stumps being drawn at 4.30 in order to commence the base-ball match. The Surrey Club & Ground brought a very weak team into the field, and the game was all in favour of the American base-ball players. The visiting eighteen compiled exactly 100 in their first innings, although only two batsmen reached double figures. The northern professional Edward Barratt claimed 10 wickets for 63 runs with his left-arm slows, H.Wright scoring 23 and E.B.Sutton 18 not out. Then Surrey were got rid of for 27, only Mr J.Wood (16) scoring more than 4. In their second innings, the Americans compiled 111, and then had Surrey at 2 for the loss of four wickets before play was halted.

After the cricket match, scratch sides were formed for an exhibition of the national pastime of the Americans - sides being chosen by Mr Spalding (Boston Red Stockings) and Mr McMullen (Athletic Blue Stockings). Several of the Surrey side made their base-ball début for one side or the other. Mr Spalding's side eventually won by 14 to 11.

South v North: 17 May 1875

Southerton's bowling brightens dull day

From Lord's

AT least 8,000 visitors were present at Lord's today to witness the North and South match, which ended a few minutes past seven in a victory for the South by ten wickets. This lame and premature conclusion was due to the ridiculous weakness of the North eleven, of whom only two or three, in addition to the crack bowlers - Alfred Shaw and Morley - were at all worthy to play in a first-class match. The majority of the Nottingham men were playing for their county, while the Yorkshiremen were engaged in a gate-money match against odds in the North. It being thus impossible to get together a proper team, the better plan would have been to play another match, say M.C.C. & Ground, including W.G.Grace, against the South of England.

The match, however, served to amuse a good-humoured, if somewhat noisy, holiday crowd, though it was devoid of real cricket interest. The only noteworthy feature in the play was the really splendid bowling of Southerton, who obtained 16 of the 20 wickets, a grand performance, and one we hope to see him follow up by others equally as brilliant. In the North's first innings, he captured nine for 30 in 29 overs, while while Messrs W.G. & G.F. Grace shared 29 overs without success, the North being all out for 90 (Shaw 26 not out). The South, however, fared hardly better, making 123 against the bowling of Morley (5-55) and Shaw (4-52). But in their second innings, the North were got rid of for 73, Southerton taking seven wickets for 22 runs in 23.2 overs, assisted this time by Mr W.G.Grace, who took three for 47 in 23 overs. Having 40 runs to get, the South put in Mr W.G.Grace and Jupp, and Mr Grace pleased those of the spectators who had stayed for the finish by some very hard hitting, and the runs were got with all wickets in hand.

The late 1800s

In the last quarter of the 19th century, cricket was transformed both domestically and as a world game. Before the turn of the century, the matches between England and Australia were being followed with almost fanatical interest and excitement from both ends of the world.

In England, competition between counties continued to develop, with regular fixtures and a table of merit at the end of the season. This format crystallised into an official County Championship in 1890 for the eight first-class counties, a list that was augmented until there were 15 competing in the Championship by 1899. In the ten years, Surrey (six titles) and Yorkshire (three) were the dominant counties.

There was much more to first-class cricket in England than county competition. Players v Gentlemen, North v South, M.C.C. and All England XI's, the Varsity match, Canterbury Week, Eton v Harrow - all had their place, and all went to make up the panorama of an immensely popular sport in which rough-hewn professionals without initials rubbed shoulders (but not in the same changing-rooms) with the gentlemen amateurs who hailed mostly from the universities and enjoyed a 'Mr' before their names.

Linking the somewhat disorganised cricket at the beginning of this period with the structured sport of the 20th century was the formidable figure of W.G. Grace, who could be seen knocking up 400 against the '22 of Grimsby' in 1876 and still leading England out against Australia in 1899, at the age of 50! 'W.G.', 'The Doctor', 'The Champion' - Grace dominated the game for some forty years, and was said to be the most easily recognised figure in England along with prime minister W.E.Gladstone. He was not only an all-round cricketer whose feats became a legend in his own lifetime, but a man of striking personality who, by stamping his character on the game, helped to popularise cricket and greatly influenced its development. It was W.G. who scored England's first century against Australia, in 1880 at the Oval.

Three English teams had visited Australia in the sixties and seventies, but without playing a Test - a term, incidentally, that did not come into use until the mid-nineties. Tours were arranged privately in the 19th century, and when James Lillywhite's eleven of 1876-77 lost to teams of fifteen in both New South Wales and Victoria, the visitors were prevailed upon to play an Australian XI in Melbourne in what later became recognised as the first Test match. England lost this game and won a return. But despite the Australians' successes, and warnings of their prowess, they arrived in Britain in 1878, on their first tour, virtually unheralded and unsung. They were soundly beaten at a cold Trent Bridge in their first game, but in their next they thrashed a powerful M.C.C. team - W.G. and all - by nine wickets, Spofforth, the 'Demon Bowler', taking 10 for 20 and Boyle nine for 17. So in the space of less than five hours' play, on a sticky wicket at Lord's, the fame of Australian cricket was established for all time.

Inexplicably, no fixture with England was arranged on that tour. But regular, alternate tours were organised in the 1880s, and the legend of the Ashes, originating in 1882, served to intensify the competition between England and the 'Colonials' - for Australia was not, as yet, a Commonwealth, but a collection of colonies. Only New South Wales, Victoria and South Australia were strong enough to be rated as first-class, and because of the great distances involved in travel between the colonies, the cricketers enjoyed relatively little first-class cricket - the Sheffield Shield, for competition among the three colonies, was inaugurated in 1892-93. The getting together to play as an All Australian side against the Mother Country had some small contribution, it has been said, to the move towards federation, which came about just after the turn of the century.

South Africa joined the Test-playing fraternity in 1889, but made little impact. The England sides that went to South Africa were at best second elevens, yet they won all eight Tests played on four tours, while the South Africans were not to play a single Test in England, nor meet the Australians, until the 20th century. England regained the ascendancy in the 'fight for the Ashes' after their initial shocks, but not by very much. Out of 56 Tests played by the end of the century, they had won 26 and Australia 20.

Lord Sheffield's team that toured Australia in 1891-92: Players, standing (l-r), Attewell, Lohmann, Read (M.), Bean, Sharpe; seated, Briggs, G.McGregor, W.G.Grace (capt.), Peel, A.E.Stoddart, Abel.

1876

19-21 Jun An aggregate of 1,217 runs are scored in the match between Oxford University and Middlesex at Prince's.

Jul W.G.Grace scores 400 not out at Grimsby, with 22 fielding on a rather grassy and slow outfield.

15-17 Aug In between his two triple hundreds (against Kent and Yorks), W.G.Grace makes 177 against Notts.

2 Oct Agostini (75) and Wedekind (41) put on 110 for the 5th wicket for Trinidad against British Guiana at Georgetown, the 1st first-class 100 partnership in the West Indies.

Oxford University v Middlesex: 21 June

Record innings of 612: Oxford last-wicket pair take score past 600

From Prince's

OXFORD resumed their innings today at ten minutes after twelve in reply to Middlesex's 439, and when they were all out at seventeen minutes to five they had made 612, the highest score in first-class cricket.

Briggs and Game were in their overnight form and soon put the 300 up. The partnership was not broken until Briggs was sixth out at 422 for 71. Game put the 500 up at a quarter past three amid loud applause. He was caught shortly afterwards, at 506, for 141, far and away the highest and best innings he has ever played in a grand match.

With eight wickets down, it was thought that the innings would soon be over, but, as it turned out, the troubles of the Middlesex men were far from over. Royle and Lewis put on 56 for the ninth wicket, and then the last man, Tylecote, who has never scored much on London grounds, came in and soon began hitting the Middlesex bowlers.

The 600 came up at five and twenty minutes to five, amid a perfect roar of applause. When Tylecote was stumped for 26, Royle had made 67 not out and Oxford 612. There was, of course, not time to finish the match, and when stumps were drawn at 7 o'clock, Middlesex had made 166 for four wickets in their second innings. The wicket kept in splendid condition until the last.

Canterbury Cricket Week Kent v M.C.C.: 12 August

Phenomenal innings by Mr Grace: His 344 saves the game

From Canterbury, Saturday evening

Mr Grace at the wicket.

TODAY'S cricket was of a most sensational character, and brought the week to a fine conclusion. At the close of play last night the M.C.C., after following their innings with a balance of 329 runs against them, had scored 217 for the loss of four wickets, Mr W.G.Grace being not out 133. There being 112 runs to hit off, it was naturally accepted that Kent would be enabled to win by five or six wickets. Such expectations were completely falsified, thanks to Mr Grace's batting, and the match, at a little before six o'clock, had to be abandoned as drawn.

At 12 o'clock Grace and Crutchley resumed their places at the wicket, and despite all efforts to part them they stayed together until three minutes to four. During this really wonderful stand, Kent tried ten bowlers. But the score had been raised to 430 before the batsmen were separated. Crutchley, who was caught at the wicket, made 84 of the 227 scored during his stay.

Further stands were made with Turner and then Clarke before Mr Grace's splendid innings came to an end. From Harris's bowling, he was very well caught low down at mid-off by V.K.Shaw, for 344, the highest individual innings ever made in a match of importance.

Ordinary words of conventional praise would seem absurd when applied to such a stupendous achievement. This 344 is the second highest innings Mr Grace has ever made, the highest, of course, being his now famous 400 not out made at Grimsby some few weeks back against 22 in the field. He was at the wickets altogether six hours and 20 minutes. His hits were fifty-one 4's, eight 3's, twenty 2's and seventy-six singles.

In playing this phenomenal innings Mr Grace had two things in his favour, a superlatively good wicket and, on one side of the ground, easy boundaries. The innings may, perhaps, not count in first-class averages for the year, but nothing can gainsay the merit of such a score made for the leading club against a really good county team.

When stumps were drawn just before six o'clock, the M.C.C. total was 557 for nine wickets, a score which has only once been exceeded in a good match - namely, at Prince's this season, when Oxford University made 612 against Middlesex.

County match Hants v Derby: 25 July

Wonderful bowling by Mycroft in vain: 17 wickets but on losing side

From Southampton

THE return match between these two counties ended today in a victory for Hampshire by one wicket. Mycroft bowled wonderfully well for Derbyshire, taking in all 17 wickets for 103 runs. This is only the second time in the history of first-class cricket that a bowler has had so many victims in a match, the first being in 1844, when Fenner of Cambridge Town did so against the University.

In Hampshire's first innings, Mycroft obtained nine wickets for 25 runs, seven of them clean bowled, and he caught the tenth as Hampshire were bowled out for 63. Hampshire's most successful bowler was Mr Ridley, who took 11 wickets.

The finish today was very exciting, as Hampshire made the highest innings of the match, 145 for nine, to win. Mr Hargreaves took his bat out for 35, the highest individual score of the match.

County match Glos v Yorks: 18 August

Mr Grace carries his bat for 318: Another wonderful innings

From Cheltenham

MR W.G.GRACE (216 not out) and Mr Moberley (73 not out), resuming at one o'clock after a delay for rain, continued in their overnight form for Gloucestershire and the score rose rapidly. When Mr Moberley was caught for a splendid 103, Mr Grace had made 263. Three more wickets fell in quick succession before the last man, Mr J.A.Bush, made a lively 34. When he was bowled by Ulyett, the innings closed for 528.

Mr Grace, in first, carried his bat for a wonderful innings of 318. His chief hits were a 7, two 6's, three 5's and twenty-eight 4's. This is a far greater performance than his 344 at Canterbury last week, the bowling of Yorkshire, of course, being much superior to that of Kent. Twice within ten days Mr Grace has passed the previous best individual score in grand matches - 278 by Mr W.Ward at Lord's for M.C.C. in 1820 - and we heartily congratulate him on his triumphs indeed.

Representative match Australia v England: 17 March

Australian XI prevail: England beaten by 45 runs

From Reuter's, Melbourne

THE English cricketers have played and lost a match against the combined New South Wales and Victoria team.

In this first match between the English cricketers under the captaincy of James Lillywhite, representative of the best professional talent in the country, and an Australian side made up from Melbourne and Sydney players, the Australians prevailed by 45 runs after a keen contest. Tom Kendall, the Melbourne left-arm slow bowler, took seven wickets for 55 runs today, and England were bowled out for 108.

Charles Bannerman had laid the foundations for Australia's victory by scoring 165 in their first innings, before he had to retire hurt when a fast ball from Ulyett split his finger. None of his colleagues reached as many as 20.

Scores: Australia 245 (Bannerman 165 retired) & 104 (Shaw 5-38, Ulyett 4-39), England 196 (Jupp 63; Midwinter 5-78) & 108 (Kendall 7-55).

[This was the first time teams from England and Australia met on even terms, and the match was later the first to be accorded 'Test' status.]

Representative match Australia v England: 4 April

England win return fixture by four wickets: Honours even

From Reuter's, Melbourne

The English cricketers have played and won a match against the combined New South Wales and Victoria team.

In this second 'Test', G. Ulyett scored the only fifties of the match, 52 in England's first innings, 63 in the second, completing a splendid all-round performance in which he also took three wickets (2-15, 1-33). Needing 121 to win, England were at one stage reduced to 76 for five, but then Ulyett saw them to the verge of victory before A.Hill hit the winning runs.

George Ulyett: Splendid all-round performance.

Gentleman v Players: 4 July

Last-wicket stand sees Gentlemen through

From Lord's

IN a remarkable and exciting finish here today, the Gentlemen just made the 143 runs required to win thanks to a last-wicket stand of 46 between G.F.Grace and W.S.Patterson

At the start of play, the Players, who were six runs behind on first innings, had scored 100 for the loss of four wickets. Yesterday's rain had made the wicket very dead, and runs were got with difficulty. After an hour and a half, they were all out for 148. A notable feat in this innings was that of Mr Webbe, who made no fewer than six catches, four at short slip and two in the long field.

The Gentlemen's second innings was opened by Messrs W.G.Grace and I.D.Walker, the captain, who was bowled first ball. The Hon. Alfred Lyttelton joined Mr Grace and a good stand was made. Mr Grace cut and drove Mycroft with good hits, but both batsmen were got rid of with the score at 64. Mr Lyttelton was bowled by Ulyett for a plucky and useful 20, and Mr Grace was caught and bowled by Morley for 41. His innings was in every way worthy of his reputation.

Wickets now began to fall with regularity to Ulyett and Morley, and when Mr Patterson, the last man, came in to join Mr G.F.Grace, the Gentlemen had collapsed to 97 for nine wickets. The partisans of the Players looked upon the match as almost over. But each ball was watched with growing excitement, and every hit or good piece of fielding provoked immense cheering.

When the score reached 119, Daft changed the bowling at both ends. Watson sent down three maiden overs, but Mycroft came in for severe punishment at first. Runs then became more difficult to get as the bowlers found their form, but Mr Grace finally settled the match in fine style amidst great cheering. He hit Watson to leg to tie the scores, and from the next ball got the winning hit. Mr Patterson deserves every credit for his plucky and excellent innings of 24 not out, while for Mr G.F. Grace's batting no praise can be too high. He scored 23 not out, playing every ball that wanted playing with the greatest judgment, and he never threw away a chance of scoring.

It may be a long time before so fine a struggle is again witnessed. The third and last Gentlemen and Players' match for the season will be commenced tomorrow at Prince's.

W.G.'s round-arm style earned him 17 wickets.

1877

15 Mar England's fourth touring team to visit Australia play what is retrospectively the first Test against Australia, at Melbourne.

16 Mar Charles Bannerman's 165 out of Australia's 245 against England is 67.34% of the total, a Test record still standing in the 1990s. (He never scores another first-class 100.)

15 May William Mycroft takes 6-12 for MCC in England's 2nd innings to give MCC victory by 24 runs in a revival at Lord's of a fixture first played in 1792.

4 Jun Middlesex migrate to Lord's from their headquarters at Prince's.

TEST SERIES

England in Australia
E 1, A 1

County match
Glos v Nottm: 15 August

Mr W.G.Grace captures 7 wickets for 1 run: 17 wickets in match

From Cheltenham

GLOUCESTERSHIRE brought their match with Nottingham to a speedy conclusion today, the play being of a most extraordinary character. The visitors resumed their second innings on 69 for two, still 55 runs behind. They managed to add only another 10 runs while their remaining eight wickets fell, so Gloucester won by an innings with 45 runs to spare.

Mr W.G.Grace's bowling was, of course, the chief cause of their easy victory. This morning he bowled 10 overs and a ball, 9 maidens for 1 run and 7 wickets - an almost unprecedented achievement in first-class matches. He took eight wickets for 34 in this innings, nine wickets for 55 in Nottingham's first innings. Altogether his bowling in this match gives the following figures: 76.1 overs, 36 maidens, 89 runs and 17 wickets. If Mr Grace has not made any of his sensational scores lately, he has certainly been bowling better than he has ever bowled in his life.

1878

10 Jun R.G.Barlow, playing for North v South at Lord's, was put out for handling the ball twice, only the fourth instance of this rare dismissal recorded in first-class cricket.

20 Jun Gloucestershire-born all-rounder Billy Midwinter, on tour with the Australians, is 'persuaded' by W.G. Grace to travel by cab from Lord's, where he is due to play, to the Oval and play for Glos v Surrey. He does not play for the Australians again on tour. (He later represents England and Australia, again, in Tests, and commutes between Glos and Victoria.)

M.C.C. Resolution: 2 November

Gentlemen cricketers

THE committee of the Marylebone club has passed the following resolution: "That no gentleman ought to make a profit by his services in the cricket-field, and that, for the future, no cricketer who takes more than his expenses in any match shall be qualified to play for the Gentlemen against the Players at Lord's: but that if any gentleman feels difficulty in joining in the match without pecuniary assistance, he shall not be debarred from playing as a gentleman by having his actual expenses defrayed."

Tour match M.C.C. & Ground v The Australians: 27 May

M.C.C. (33 and 19) beaten in a day: Shock victory for Australians

From Lord's

The 1878 Australians. Top (l-r): Spofforth, Mr Conway, Allan; middle: Bailey, Horan, Garrett, Gregory (capt), A.Bannerman, Boyle; bottom: C.Bannerman, Murdoch, Blackham.

THE M.C.C. suffered today a humiliating and unexpected defeat at the hands of the touring Australian team, losing by nine wickets after only four and a half hours' play. After their innings defeat in their first match by Nottingham, the Australians have shown their mettle, bowling England out twice for an aggregate of 52 runs, and, while no Australian batsman scored more than 10 runs, they finished easy victors.

The M.C.C. won the toss, and at a very few minutes past twelve began batting with Messrs W.G.Grace and Hornby to the bowling of Allan (left hand, with a high delivery) and Boyle (right hand, rather above medium pace), the latter from the Pavilion wicket. From Allan's first ball Mr Grace made a square-leg hit for 4, but from his next he was easily caught at square leg, the downfall of the great wicket causing immense delight to the Australians.

Mr Booth followed, but after a single had been added, he was clean bowled by Boyle. Mr Ridley came to Mr Hornby's aid. When the score had reached 25, Spofforth (fast round-arm) replaced Allan at the Nursery wicket. There followed a remarkable spell of bowling in which England were all out for the addition of only eight more runs, Spofforth taking six wickets for four runs in 5.3 overs, including the hat-trick. Only Hornby (19) reached double figures, and six M.C.C. men were dismissed without scoring. Boyle took three wickets for 14 runs, and Allan one for 14.

The Australians commenced their innings after an interval of 20 minutes with Midwinter and C.Bannerman to the bowling of Shaw and Morley. They fared little better. Before a run had been scored, Bannerman was grandly caught at long-off by Hearne off Morley. Shaw was proving almost unplayable, but it was Morley who took the early wickets and by the luncheon interval the Australians were 17 for three. Up to this time Shaw had bowled 13 overs for one run.

The score progressed very slowly after lunch and the wickets fell regularly. Midwinter made their top score with 10, and the Australians had eight wickets down before they passed M.C.C.'s total. They were bowled out for 41, eight runs in advance of M.C.C. Shaw returned the superb figures of five for 10 in 33.2 overs. Morley had five for 31 in 33 overs. In contrast, M.C.C. had lasted less than 29 overs.

At four o'clock M.C.C. began their second innings, and Spofforth's second ball shattered Mr Grace's wicket, and the great batsman retired without making a run. M.C.C.'s second innings was all over in 17.1 overs. Boyle took six wickets for three runs in 8.1 overs (six maidens), and was deservedly cheered on his retirement for his magnificent bowling. Spofforth, with four for 16, had match figures of 10 for 20.

The Australians needed 16 overs to score the 12 runs needed, and they lost the wicket of C.Bannerman, who was bowled by Shaw for one. But at a quarter to six this extraordinary match ended in the victory of the Australians by nine wickets.

Tour match Players v Australians: 2 September

Barratt takes all 10 for 43, but Spofforth strikes back

From the Oval

AT least 10,000 persons were present at Kennington Oval to witness the first day's play in the long-expected match between the Australian eleven and an eleven of the Players of England. Considerable discussion has been indulged in as to the composition of the Players' team, and a good deal of feeling has been exhibited.

The game has already presented some remarkable features. Six Englishmen and seven Australians were out for nought. Barratt took all 10 Australian wickets, and Spofforth bowled seven of the Players, for whom James Phillips made 19 not out. But the batting feature of the day was Charles Bannerman's admirable 51, an innings played on a most difficult wicket, and with only one hard chance.

The Players won the toss and elected to send the Australians in to bat. Apart from Bannerman, who was last out, only Spofforth with 14 reached double figures, and the Australians were put out for 77. Barratt bowled unchanged and 10 wickets were captured at the cost of 43 runs in 29 overs. He had a wicket that suited him perfectly and his bowling is one of the greatest features of the season

Rigley opened the Players' innings with Barlow, and made 18 of the first 22 before being caught by the bowler Allan. Barlow was stumped for a patient 16 when the score was 44. Hearne was bowled by Spofforth for eight at 59, and three more wickets went down to the same bowler without further addition to the score. Soon it was 64 for nine, and it was only a last wicket partnership between the last man M'Intyre, who made 10, and J.Phillips, who took out his bat for 19, that carried the Players past the Australians score to 82, a lead of five. Spofforth took seven wickets for 37, a wonderful piece of bowling. The fielding of the Colonists was excellent throughout, and Murdoch's brilliant wicket-keeping was repeatedly applauded.

[Australia made 89 and beat the Players (76) by 8 runs, Spofforth taking 5-38]

Representative match Australia v England: 4 January

Spofforth's 13 wickets and hat-trick: England defeated in Australia

From Melbourne

Spofforth: 'The Demon Bowler'.

THE English team under the captaincy of Lord Harris have played a match with the Australian eleven which visited England last summer. The match, which lasted three days, resulted in the defeat of the English eleven by 10 wickets. The English went in first.

The 'Demon Bowler' Spofforth was once more the architect of the defeat of an English team. He performed the first hat-trick in the series of matches between England and Australia, capturing the wickets of Royal, Mackinnon and Emmett in England's first innings. England were reduced to 26 for seven wickets before lunch, and Spofforth had taken five of them. Harris (33) and Absolom (52) put on 63 together for the eighth wicket, but England were all out for 113. Spofforth took six for 48 in 25 overs.

Emmett bowled splendidly for England, capturing seven wickets for 77, but Australia gained a substantial first-innings lead, as they went to 256 all out on the second day. The chief scorer was Alec Bannerman, the younger brother of Charles, with 73. He added 64 for the fourth wicket with Spofforth, who made 39.

It was Spofforth again who devastated England when they went in again, taking this time seven wickets for 62 runs, to finish with match figures of 13 for 110 in 60 overs. England only just managed to stave off an innings defeat, their last wicket putting on 32, to leave Australia needing 18 runs to win. This they accomplished without losing a wicket.

[This was the only match (Test) played against Australia on the tour. A return was cancelled owing to a pitch invasion by spectators in the game with New South Wales.]

1879

25 Jan A cricket match is staged on ice between L.Wallgate's XI and C. Ullathorne's XI, and one D.Hearfield makes 105 not out, the first recorded instance of a century on ice.

8 Feb The England tour to Australia is marred by an incident in the second match against NSW, at Sydney, when Murdoch is given run out in the NSW 2nd innings. Their captain, D.Gregory, comes onto the field and raises a formal objection to Coulthard, the English umpire, but Lord Harris refuses to change him, at which Gregory calls his batsmen out and refuses to continue. The crowd rush on to the ground and amidst great confusion Lord Harris is assaulted. Gregory eventually relents and the game continues.

Lord Harris: Incident.

10 Feb The NSW opener W.L.Murdoch carries his bat for 82 out of 177 against Lord Harris's XI at Sydney.

Mar C.H.A.Ross makes the first recorded 100 in Ceylon.

TEST SERIES

England in Australia
Australia 1

Testimonial match Over Thirty v Under Thirty: 22 July

Presentation to Mr Grace

From Lord's

DURING the luncheon interval today of the match now being played in compliment to him at Lord's, the national testimonial to Mr W.G.Grace was formally presented. Among the earliest promoters of the testimonial were Lord Fitzhardinge and the Duke of Beaufort. The former nobleman made the presentation, the Duke not being in England.

Included in the long list of subscribers are His Royal Highness the Prince of Wales, several noblemen and a number of gentlemen well known in cricket circles. The Surrey, Yorkshire and Kent County clubs subscribed £50 each, the Cambridge University Cricket Club £25 and the Manchester Cricket Club 20 guineas. The M.C.C. gave a hundred guineas. Altogether the amount received is about £1,400.

The proceedings were of a brief and informal character. On a table in front of the Pavilion rails was placed a handsome timepiece in black marble and bronze, which has been purchased for Mr Grace out of the subscriptions, and which is intended as a memorial of the occasion, with a suitable inscription.

In making the presentation, Lord Fitzhardinge said that it had been intended for some time to buy Mr Grace a medical practice, but after full discussion it was arranged to put the Gloucestershire and the M.C.C. subscriptions together and hand the sum over to Mr Grace, leaving it to his judgment to get a practice for himself.

Mr Grace made a short speech of thanks, and then Lord Charles Russell said a few eloquent words in praise of Mr Grace's play and the earnestness with which he competed - he was not alone a good bowler, a fine fielder and an unapproachable batsman, but he played the game with all his heart and soul.

Play in the match was curtailed because of the weather. The Under Thirty team were bowled out for 111, Mr Grace taking three wickets for 54 and his younger brother Mr G.F.Grace taking his bat out for the top score of 34. The Cricketers Over Thirty innings commenced at ten minutes to six, but, with the third ball of the innings, Mr Grace was clean bowled by Morley without scoring. At stumps, the score had moved along to 79 for one wicket, with an elder Grace brother, Mr E.M., not out 33.

[It was being said of 'W.G.', now 31, that his powers were on the wane, that increasing weight and corresponding loss of elasticity must have a "sensible effect on his powers of batting". Nearly 20 years later, he was still going in first for England.]

Inter-County match Glos v Middlesex: 16 August

Over 1,000 runs scored in match: Mr Grace saves Gloucester from defeat

From Clifton

OVER a thousand runs were scored here in the return match between Gloucestershire and Middlesex. It looked likely this afternoon that Gloucester were heading for defeat, but a fine eighth-wicket stand between Messrs W.G.Grace and Cranston saved the day.

Gloucester were dismissed for 320 this morning and, with three wickets lost for only 37 runs when they followed on to Middlesex's 476, the chance of Middlesex winning seemed very great. Messrs Townsend (71) and Moberly (32) made matters look far better for their county. But they were 197 for seven when Mr Cranston joined his captain, Mr W.G.Grace. These two thwarted the Middlesex bowlers and were still together at the call for time, having added 70 runs and taken the aggregate of runs in the match to 1,063.

Despite this high scoring, there was only one hundred in the match, 122 by Mr A.J. Webbe in the Middlesex innings. However, Mr Gilbert made 99 in the Gloucester first innings, and Mr W.G.Grace had scores of 85 and 81 not out.

1880

18 May The noted Scottish soccer and rugby international Henry Renny-Tailyour scores 331 not out in 330 minutes for the Royal Engineers against the Civil Service.

1 Jul A.Browning scores 204 for Montreal v Ottawa, the highest individual innings on the American continent.

6-8 Sep In what retrospectively is the first Test played in England, the three Grace brothers are in the side, Drs W.G. & E.M and Mr G.F. 'Fred', the youngest. Fred is twice out for 0, but makes a famous catch off the giant Bonnor, from a ball hit so high that the batsmen are said to have run two before he catches it. Tragically, he dies 14 days later of congestion of the lungs, not yet 30.

E.M.Grace, senior brother

29 Sep England slow-medium bowler Alfred Shaw underlines his reputation for accurate and economical bowling, finishing the season with an average of 8.54 for 185 wickets.

TEST SERIES

Australia in England
England 1

Representative match First day: 6 September

Reconciliation effected between England and Australia: Then Dr Grace hits 152

From the Oval

IN the presence of between twenty and thirty thousand people the reconciliation between England and Australia, from a cricket point of view, was ratified today. And when England went in to bat in this first fully representative match against Australia in this country, they scored 410 for the loss of eight wickets, Dr W.G.Grace hitting a magnificent century.

No matter who was to blame for the soreness that was left after the visit of the last English team to Australia, there is now and forever an end to it, and this the hearty cheers that greeted the Australians, as with commendable punctuality they stepped from the Pavilion, abundantly proved.

It is difficult to overestimate the amount of interest in the event now in progress. The success of the Colonial team, who in 30 matches have lost but two, and who, among other notable successes, have lowered the colours of both Gloucestershire and Yorkshire, will in some degree account for it, while the feeling that we were bound to vindicate the honour of English cricket, and prove that we yet retained our supremacy, must also be taken into consideration by those who seek an explanation of the extraordinary scenes witnessed at the Oval. The official paying gate was 20,736, but thousands who could not get more than an occasional glimpse of the players stood throughout the day. There was not a point that was not occupied, even the tops of refreshment bars and the roofs of buildings.

When Messrs E.M. and W.G.Grace went out to open England's innings at five and twenty minutes to twelve, the one regrettable circumstance was the absence of Spofforth, Australia's best fast bowler, due to an injured hand. Without him, the Australians could not hope for victory against such a magnificent team as had been got together to oppose them.

Mr W.G.Grace played one of his great innings - such an innings, indeed, as no other batsman could equal. After a perhaps hesitant start, in which he missed a 'Yorker' from Palmer, he barely made a single error. He put on 91 for the first wicket with his brother E.M., who made 36, and completed his 100 on three o'clock. With Mr Lucas (55) he added 110 for the second wicket, and 58 for the third with Mr Barnes, who made 28.

His innings finally ended when he was bowled by Palmer with England on 281, out of which he made 152. He had played magnificent cricket, his hitting and defence being equally perfect. His innings included 12 fours.

Lord Harris was now playing brilliant cricket, and with Mr Steel (42) put up the 400 before being caught at slip for 52. Everyone in the England team scored except the third brother, Mr G.F. Grace, and he went in five minutes before time in a dreadfully bad light.

Representative match Last day: 8 September

Magnificent Murdoch innings in vain: England win by 5 wickets

From the Oval

IT is almost impossible to commence a notice of yesterday's magnificent struggle at the Oval without referring to 'the glorious uncertainty' of cricket.

The close of yesterday's play left the Englishmen with, to all appearance, a very easy task. With four wickets to fall in their second innings, the Australians wanted 101 runs to save a single innings' defeat. So marvellous a change, however, came over the game that in the end the Englishmen found it difficult to win by five wickets.

The last two wickets of the Australian innings put on no fewer than 140 runs, and this against capital bowling and superlatively good fielding. The credit of this great up-hill fight rests mainly with Murdoch, the Australian captain, who played an innings it would be impossible to surpass. Yesterday, without anything like a mistake, he had made 79 not out, and today, taking out his bat, he increased this to 153 - one more than Mr Grace scored on Monday.

Murdoch's ability was recognised with his first appearance with Gregory's team in 1878, but perhaps few judges thought him capable of withstanding for five hours the best bowling in England. This he did, however, and his name must rank henceforth among the greatest of batsmen.

The Australians' total was 327, leaving England only 57 runs to win. Then came some sensational cricket. The wicket was in capital order and it seemed as if the runs would be made with ease. But a panic appeared to seize the English batsmen. Mr G.F. Grace was bowled in the second over to be followed by so remarkable a series of disasters that five wickets were down for 31 runs.

With 12 runs still wanted, Mr Frank Penn was missed at slip. But he survived to score 27 and with Mr W.G.Grace (9) saw England home.

W.L.Murdoch (opposite): An innings to rank with the best.

Cambridge Univ v Gentlemen of England: 26 May 1880

Cambridge 37 runs short of Oxford record

From the University Ground, Cambridge

THE match between Cambridge and the Gentlemen ended today in a draw after the University, in reply to the Gentlemen's first innings 232, amassed the tremendous total of 593. Their innings, which started Monday and occupied the whole of yesterday and today, fell short by only 37 runs of the greatest score ever made in a first-class match, Oxford University's 630 against Middlesex four years ago.

Of the 12 men comprising the Cambridge team, only the last two batsmen failed to reach double figures. The first three batsmen scored between them more than half the total - Mr R.S.Jones (124), Mr H.Whitfield (116) and the Hon. Ivo Bligh (90).

Altogether, the game may be classed as one of the most remarkable ever played, 22 wickets falling in three days at an average of 37.5 runs per wicket. All 12 members of the Gentlemen's team had a go at bowling. The most successful was the veteran Mr D. Buchanan, who sent down 123 of the 338.1 overs bowled and captured five wickets for 146 runs, while the failure of Mr Rotherham, the Uppingham fast bowler, was conspicuous.

1881

27 Jun Three brothers, C.T., G.B. and J.E.K.Studd, play for Cambridge in the Varsity match at Lord's, Charles taking 10 wickets and scoring 62 runs in the match, won by Oxford (see below).

12 Jul William Roe hits 415 not out for Emmanuel Long Vacation Club v Caius LVC at Cambridge.

12 Jul Walter Forbes makes 331 for Fellowes' XI v Huntingdonshire.

18-19 Jul Wilfred Flowers takes 4 wickets in five balls (over two days) for A.Shaw's XI v T.Emmett's XI at Bradford.

10 Aug In James Lillywhite's benefit match, the Players beat the Gentlemen at Hove by 1 run thanks to Alfred Shaw (6-19) and Billy Bates (3-15), who bowl the Gents out for 111.

Dec In a minor match at Bendemeer, NSW, Spofforth takes 20 wickets (all bowled) for 48 runs.

27 Dec Victoria win the D.Long Trophy (the precursor of the Sheffield Shield) outright by beating NSW for the third time in succession.

31 Dec Billy Midwinter becomes the first player to represent both England and Australia when he turns out for England at Melbourne.

Billy Bates: 3-15 as Players defeated Gentlemen.

Inter-County match Lancs v Notts: 2 June

Notts weakened by dispute: Lancs on top

From Old Trafford

IN beautifully fine weather the first match of the season between these two counties was commenced today at Old Trafford, Manchester. Owing to the dispute that has taken place between the Nottinghamshire Committee and the seven professional players, Shaw, Shrewsbury, Scotton, Barnes, Flowers, Morley and Selby, all stood out of the match.

Only four members of the regular team therefore represented Nottingham, and, as was to be expected, Lancashire, with an almost full-strength side, had by far the better of the play. They batted first and totalled 239, Mr R.Wood making 50, and then bowled Notts out for the paltry total of 67 in an hour and 35 minutes. Watson and Nash bowled unchanged and took five wickets each, while only four Notts batsmen reached double figures.

[Gunn (49) averted an innings defeat, but Lancs scored the 4 runs needed without loss. The dispute was about remuneration, many professionals, aware of the financial arrangements of the Australians on their recent tours, feeling that their own services were undervalued. It was some time before the 'strike' was resolved.]

Varsity Match: 29 June

Oxford complete surprise victory: Cambridge dismissed for 123

From our own reporter, at Lord's

GLORIOUS weather today favoured the concluding day's cricket at Lord's, and there was another large attendance. But it must have been disappointing for the ardent admirers of the light blues that their champions did not make a better attempt at getting the 259 runs they needed to win the match. The Oxford contingent, attracted by the almost certain victory, were not disappointed.

Cambridge were bowled out today for 123 runs, and defeat by such a majority as 135 was totally unexpected. Indeed, before the match, it was said of the dark blues that they "had not the ghost of a chance". Nor did they appear to when they were dismissed for 131 on Monday. But fine fast bowling by Mr A.H.Evans, who took seven wickets for 74, restricted their first-innings deficit to 48, and it was Mr Evans who did most of the damage again today with six wickets for 56 in 42.2 overs. Mr Evans managed his side well and, in addition to his 13 wickets in the match, took three catches. As to the fairness of his bowling, there is a difference of opinion. Some of the best judges in the game see nothing to object to, while others, quite as competent, consider him an unmistakable thrower.

1882

3 Jan In the drawn 1st Test, at Melbourne, Tom Horan (124) and George Giffen (30) put on 107 against England for the 5th wicket, the first 100 partnership recorded for Australia.

10 Jan George Nash takes 8-14 in 15.3 overs (12-38 in match), including 4 wickets in 4 balls (one 4-ball over) as Lancs dismiss Somerset twice (29 & 51) in a day to win by innings and 157.

11 Feb NSW amass a world record score of 775 against Victoria at Sydney, Billy Murdoch making 321.

17-21 Feb George Palmer takes 11-165 in the 2nd Test v England at Sydney to help Australia win by 5 wickets and go one-up in the rubber. In England's 2nd innings, George Ulyett (67) and Dick Barlow (62) put on 122, the first 100 opening partnership in a Test for England.

10 Mar George Ulyett makes 149 for England in the drawn 4th Test at Melbourne, the first Test 100 by an Englishman in Australia.

11 Mar A.C.Bannerman (37) and Murdoch (85) put on 110 against England in the 4th Test, the first 100 opening partnership in a Test for Australia.

2 Jun Billy Barnes (266) and Billy Midwinter (187) put on 454 for the MCC & Ground 3rd-wicket against Leics (not first-class) at Lord's, MCC making 546.

TEST SERIES

England in Australia
A 2, D 2
Australia in England
Australia 1

Tour Match Sussex v Australians: 19 May

Australians set new scoring record in England: Murdoch unbeaten 286

From Brighton

AFTER their performance in the opening match of their campaign, at Oxford, the appearance of the Australian touring side at this popular watering place aroused much interest. Of course, their success against the Sussex team was felt to be assured before they took the field, but no one dreamt that they would so completely overmaster their opponents.

Having yesterday brushed aside the English county for a paltry 95 runs, the Antipodeans then scored 274 for two themselves before stumps. When they resumed today, the two not outs, Murdoch and Horan, had contributed 109 and 41 respectively. Not much fault was to be found with the fielding today, but the bowling was not very strong. Murdoch conquered it completely and carried out his bat for 286. All the visitors were not got out until they had credited themselves with the appalling number of 643 runs.

This total constitutes a new record for a first-class innings in England, beating the previous highest of 612, made by Oxford University against Middlesex in 1876.

Only Test Second day: 29 August

'Demon bowler' routs England: Colonials' first win over here - by 7 runs

From the Oval

The match at Kennington Oval today ended, not only in surprise, but also in a scene of excitement scarcely, if ever, equalled on any cricket ground. It had seemed no great feat for one of the most perfect batting elevens that England could select to score the 85 runs needed to win this match. But Australia, amidst mounting tension and drama, and with 'the demon bowler', F.R. Spofforth, to the fore, bowled them out for 77 and won by seven runs.

We ventured yesterday to say that the Colonials had played an exceedingly uphill game with such spirit as to give fine proof of their quality, and that, although the English team had 38 runs in hand on the first innings, the issue was still an open one. How well the Australians deserved this praise was shown when they went in for their second innings.

The wicket was even more decidedly against the batsman and in favour of the bowler than it was yesterday. Nevertheless our visitors nearly doubled their score, making 122 as against 63. There was, perhaps, some slight falling off in the English bowling. Barlow - who bowled almost the whole of yesterday afternoon with remarkable steadiness and success, taking five wickets for only 19 runs - was less effective, and even Peate, although he again captured four wickets, was not nearly as economical as before. Still, only three of the Colonials reached double figures, and of these, Massie's 55 was a major contribution to their eventual victory.

When Dr W.G.Grace and Mr Hornby came out to open the England innings, their appearance at the wickets was the signal for hearty cheering. The crowd, which had swelled to nigh-on 25,000 during the day, were confident of victory, although Spofforth's bowling in England's first innings (101) was obviously cause for concern.

Indeed, the 'demon' clean bowled Hornby and then Barlow with England's score on 15. Ulyett then came in and for a while the spell of the Colonial bowling seemed to have been broken. Runs came with fair rapidity; 20, 30, 40, 50 were successively exhibited on the board, and the hopes of an English triumph rose high. With eight wickets in hand, and Grace and Ulyett at the wickets, England required just 34 more runs for victory.

Suddenly, the demon bowler struck again: Ulyett caught at the wicket by Blackham, England 51 for three. However, it was not Spofforth, but Boyle, who attained the great prize, Grace caught by Bannerman at mid-off for 32. England now 53 for four - the Australians' elation naturally now knew no bounds.

The Hon A.Lyttelton now joined Mr Lucas, and it would be hard to name two more accomplished batsmen. But they found it difficult to play Spofforth and Boyle, and at one stage found themselves playing 12 successive maiden overs before the score reached 65.

This was the crisis of the game. Twenty runs wanted and to get them were Lucas and Lyttelton, with Read, Steel, Studd, Barnes and Peate to follow. At 66, Lyttelton was bowled by Spofforth for 12 - 19 runs wanted and five wickets to fall. The excitement now grew apace. It was visible everywhere - in the pavilion, on the stands, throughout the dense ring of spectators, and in the field itself. The Australians were congratulating each other openly, meeting in groups whenever a wicket fell, and displaying an eagerness and elation seldom seen in a cricket-field.

On the other side, there was delight when Mr Lucas played a 4 through the slips, but another accession of anxiety when Mr Steel was caught and bowled by Spofforth for nought - 15 runs wanted, four wickets to fall.

[contd. page 29, column 1]

Third Test Final day: 7 March

England beaten again in Sydney

From Sydney

AUSTRALIA beat England by 6 wickets at Sydney today in the third match to take an unassailable lead of two matches to none in the rubber, with one match remaining. Australia needed only 63 to win, but Peate made them work for it, taking three wickets for 15 runs. Alfred Shaw's men again failed with the bat. Only Shrewsbury (47) made a decent score, as he did in the first innings, when he scored 82 and no one else reached 20. For this, the credit should go to the Australian bowlers Garrett and Palmer, who each captured nine wickets in the match.

The result of the match, however, was determined chiefly by the record partnership between Alec Bannerman (70) and Percy McDonnell (147), who added 199 for the second wicket in Australia's first innings, having come together when the score was 16 for three. The importance of their stand is underlined by the fact that no other Australian reached double figures in that innings.

The fourth and final match with Australia starts at Melbourne on the tenth of March. England will be eager to gain some consolation from this series.

Maurice Read, the hope of Surrey, arrived at the wicket, fresh from his unbeaten 19 in the first innings and previous successes against the Colonials. The demon bowled him second ball for nought - 15 runs still wanted, three wickets to fall.

Barnes followed, presently drove the fast bowler for 2, and 3 were run for a bye. Then came another disaster. Lucas (5) played on to Spofforth - 10 runs were yet needed, and there were now only two wickets to fall.

The excitement reached a pitch which mere words can hardly convey, and it was not lessened when Barnes sent a catch to Murdoch off Boyle, and left Mr C.T.Studd and Peate, the last man, in face of the Australian bowlers, with still 10 runs to win.

Peate scooped the first ball to leg for 2, but this was the end. The last delivery of Boyle's over - Mr Studd never having had a single ball - disarranged the professional's wicket, and the English team were beaten by 7 runs.

The victors were warmly cheered by a vast and generous crowd. And so ended the most important of the contests between English cricketers and the Australians; a contest fought out with indomitable pluck by the winners, and which will long be remembered by those who had the fortune to witness it.

[Spofforth took 7-44 in England's 2nd innings, 14-90 in the match, an Australian record that was to stand for 90 years. This was the match that gave rise to 'the Ashes', for the next day a mock obituary "in affectionate Remembrance of English Cricket" was published in the Sporting Times, the body to be "cremated and the Ashes taken to Australia".]

Bowlers Spofforth and Boyle (bearded) flanked by Murdoch (left) and A.C.Bannerman.

1883

19-22 Jan Fred Morley, the Notts left-arm fast bowler, comes into the England team for the second Test despite rib injuries received on the way out when the team's boat was in collision with a sailing vessel at Colombo. His bowling is hampered, although he concedes only 20 runs in 25 overs and England win, and he goes on to take 8 wickets in the last two Tests. (He dies the following year.)

17-21 Feb For the 4th and final Test, at Melbourne, four wickets are prepared, a different one for each innings. Australia win by 4 wickets to square the rubber 2-2.

24-25 May Surrey make 650 v Hants, a new innings record for first-class cricket in England.

TEST SERIES

England in Australia
E 2, A 2

Second Test Final day: 22 January

England avenged: Triumph for Bates with bat and ball

From Melbourne

THE return match between the Australian Eleven and the Hon. Ivo Bligh's team has resulted in a victory for the latter, who won by an innings and 27 runs. England's victory was a triumph for Billy Bates, who made a fifty and captured 14 wickets in the match, including the hat-trick.

Coming in when England were on 199 for seven, the Yorkshireman scored 55 and helped Walter Read (75) add 88 for the eighth wicket. Then, in Australia's first innings, with four other bowlers having had little success, he came on with his slow-medium off-break bowling and took seven wickets for 28, including those of McDonnell, Giffen and Bonnor with successive balls - for which he was presented later with the traditional hat, made of silver, and £31. Australia lost their last nine wickets for 42 runs.

It was a similar story when Australia followed on, Bates taking seven wickets again, for 74 runs, as the Australian batsmen could muster only 153 to suffer defeat by an innings. The match figures of Bates, 14 for 102, represent the best bowling return of any Englishman in a match against the full Australian team.

Third Test Final day: 30 January

England beat the Australians again: The Ashes are born

From Sydney

The Ashes urn.

THE third match between the English cricketers, under the captaincy of the Hon Ivo Bligh, resulted in a victory for the English Eleven by 69 runs.

With a lead of 29 on first innings, England could make only 123 when they went in for a second time. Spofforth was again the destroyer, taking seven wickets for 44 to give him match figures of 11 for 117. But then, thanks largely to the brilliant slow-medium left-arm bowling of Dick Barlow, who with Morley (2-34) bowled unchanged and took seven for 40, England bowled out the Australians for 83. This was, indeed, a triumph for the Lancashire all-rounder, for he had opened England's batting, too, and made 52 valuable runs in the match.

England now take a 2-1 advantage in the rubber, and will return to Sydney in 18 days' time for the final match.

[It was after this Test that some Melbourne ladies burnt a stump, put the ashes in an urn, and presented it to the England captain, who later bequeathed it to MCC in his will. The urn stays in the Memorial Gallery at Lord's, whoever 'holds' the Ashes.]

Inter-County match Yorks v Surrey: 23 July

Surrey bowled out for 31: Peate takes 8 for 5

From Leeds

A most remarkable day's cricket was witnessed at Leeds today on a very dead wicket that greatly favoured the bowlers. Yorkshire won the toss and scored 116. Only Bates (55) and the opening pair, Hall (22) and Ulyett (21), got into double figures. But when Surrey went in to bat, none of the team could make any stand against the bowling of Peate and Bates, and the former obtained eight wickets at the cost of only 5 runs - a most remarkable performance - as Surrey were bowled out for 31 runs.

Seven Surrey batsmen were sent back without scoring, and only two - Maurice Read (12) and Mr Diver (11 not out) - reached double figures. Surrey fared little better when they followed on, making 33 for the loss of five wickets, four of them to Harrison, who did not bowl in first innings.

[Yorkshire won by an innings and 3 runs.]

1884

18 Feb George Giffen takes all 10-66 for Australia v the Rest in Sydney.

21 Apr The laws are revised and the new Code of Laws adopted by MCC.

5,7 Jun Giffen (113), playing for the Australians v Lancs at Manchester, is the first player to make a 100 and take a hat-trick in a first-class match.

10 Jul The first day of the first Test to be played at Manchester is washed out completely.

21-23 Jul In the 2nd Test, the first played at Lord's, Australia's 1st innings (229) is brought to an end when Scott (top scorer with 75), whose last-wicket stand with Boyle is worth 69, is caught by his own captain, Murdoch, who is substituting for the injured Grace! England, for whom Allan Steel makes 148, go on to win by an innings and 5 runs, George Ulyett taking 7-36 in the Australian 2nd innings.

12-16 Dec England win the 1st Test, the first played at Adelaide, by 8 wickets, although it nearly doesn't take place owing to the pecuniary demands of Murdoch's team (of supposed amateurs), just returned from England. Murdoch also vetoes umpire James Lillywhite, who is replaced by a local man with limited knowledge of cricket!

TEST SERIES

Australia in England
E 1, D 2

Tour match England XI v Australians: 26 May

The 'demon' takes 14 for 37 in day of 36 wickets

From Aston, Birmingham

JUST six years ago the Australians, on the occasion of their first visit to England, astonished British cricketers by concluding a match against the Marylebone Club, at Lord's, in one short afternoon. Today a somewhat similar collapse was witnessed. Six hours (inclusive of lunch and usual intervals between innings) sufficed to bring the contest to a conclusion, in which space of time no fewer that 36 wickets went down for a total of 217 runs.

The cause of this extraordinary cricket - for such it must be termed - is not hard to seek. No rain has fallen in Birmingham during the past fortnight, and the ground was therefore terribly dry. The authorities at the Aston Lower Grounds watered the space between the wickets, but nevertheless the sun baked the earth to a terrible extent, assisting the bowlers to such a length that the only wonder was how even the diminutive scores recorded were obtained.

The Eleven to whom the Colonials were opposed had been got together by Mr H. Rotherham, the well-known amateur, but owing to the number of first-class fixtures in course of decision, recourse was obliged to be had to Lancashire and a few unengaged amateurs. In the end, a fairly good eleven was got together.

But when the 'demon bowler' got to work, they were all out in their first innings for 82, F.R.Spofforth taking seven wickets for 34 and only Messrs Docker (19) and Walker (18) making double figures.

Even this total, however, proved too much for the Colonials on the fast-drying ground, and the deliveries of Barlow being dead on the wickets and breaking in the most perplexing fashion, the last man was out for 76, or six behind their opponents. Barlow captured seven wickets, Mr Rotherham three, and only McDonnell (21) reached double figures.

Then ensued a sensational performance, the English team being got rid of in three-quarters of an hour for but 26, Watson's 7 not out being the highest score. Spofforth proved perfectly irresistible, and obtained seven wickets at a cost of but 3 runs.

This left the visitors only 33 to get to win, but they lost six wickets in getting them.

Inter-County match
Notts v Glos: 1 August

Alf Shaw: Double hat-trick.

Shaw's unique feat: Second hat-trick of match

From Nottingham

TODAY, at Nottingham, Gloucestershire, in their second innings, again made so poor a showing against the bowling of Shaw and Attewell that Notts scored an easy victory by 10 wickets. And Shaw, by dismissing three of the Gloucester batsmen in successive balls for the second time in the match, achieved a feat unique in the history of first-class cricket.

The over-night records gave Notts, with one wicket to fall, an advantage of 52 runs over their opponents' first innings, and they added just four more before they were all out for 105.

In Gloucester's second innings, Shaw reduced the visitors from 17 for one to 17 for four, sending back Pullen, Townsend and Painter by as many consecutive balls. There was little further resistance, and the last wicket fell for 63, leaving Notts to make but 8 runs, which they accomplished in five minutes. Shaw took six wickets for 36 runs, 14 for 65 in the match, Attewell claiming the other six.

Third Test Last day: 13 August

Last Test drawn: England retain the Ashes after remarkable match

From the Oval

AT the end of the third and last day of the final match at the Oval, England have earned an honourable draw against the Colonials, which means they retain the Ashes[1]. Having followed on 205 runs behind Australia, they had made 85 for the loss of two wickets when stumps were drawn this evening.

This has been such a remarkable match, so full of incident, that it is worth recapitulating some of the events that took place since Australia went in to bat on Monday. Murdoch (211) made the first double hundred in matches between England and the Colonials and put on 143 with McDonnell (103) for the second wicket and 207 with Scott (102) for the third, a new record for any wicket in these matches. His innings lasted more than eight of the nine and a half hours Australia took to amass their record score of 551 in these matches, in which the scoring of three individual hundreds was also being performed for the first time.

Also for the first time in these matches, every player on the England side bowled. And the most successful was the wicket-keeper, the Rt Hon Alfred Lyttelton, who took off his pads and captured four wickets for 19 in 12 overs with his underarm lobs.

In England's first innings, the amateur W.W.Read, furious at Lord Harris for sending him in at No.10, proceeded to take out his ire on the Australian bowlers and hit a brilliant, match-saving 117 in just over two hours. Meanwhile, at the other end, the plodding Scotton, who had opened the innings, was steadily compiling his 90 runs, which took him five hours and 40 minutes, and their ninth-wicket stand of 151 was yet another record - for any England wicket.

[The Scotton-Read partnership remained an England 9th-wicket record until 1962-63, when Colin Cowdrey and Alan Smith put on an unbeaten 163 against New Zealand at Wellington.]

1 England were deemed to have won the Ashes when they beat Australia in the 3rd Test in 1882-83, at Sydney, even though another Test was arranged and Australia squared the rubber in Melbourne.

M.C.C. & Ground v Yorkshire: 2 June

Barnes and Gunn put on 330: Record partnership in first-class cricket

From Lord's

TODAY, at Lord's, this match, which is limited to two days owing to the Derby being set for decision tomorrow, was concluded, the result being a draw greatly in favour of the M.C.C. Yesterday, 21 wickets fell, M.C.C. being put out for 148 by Bates, Peate and company before Attewell and Flowers sent ten Yorkshiremen back to the pavilion for a paltry 69. Today, by contrast, saw the fall of only three wickets, and a stand between Barnes and Gunn unsurpassed in the history of first-class cricket.

Overnight, the Club, with one wicket down in their second innings, were 88 runs to the good. Continuing this morning at half-past eleven, in beautiful weather, Scotton and Hearne, the not-outs, were opposed by Peate and Bates. Runs came fast, as did bowling changes, before Scotton was caught at point off Peate, in his second turn, for a well-played 37, which took him 1hr 30min to compile. Hearne was bowled by Peate for 26, and then Gunn and Barnes got together, and a most extraordinary stand was made.

Billy Gunn: Double hundred.

Peel, Peate, Emmett, Preston, Bates, Ulyett and Louis Hall were tried, and interchanged over and over again, but the pair fairly mastered the Yorkshire bowling. Gunn's cutting and driving were grand, whilst Barnes played excellent cricket, his leg hitting and placing being especially fine. Gunn gave a hard chance to F. Lee in the long field, when he had made 80, and afterwards made one or two very queer strokes. On the whole, however, he played good cricket, outscoring his partner heavily, and once hit a ball right over the grand stand into the garden of one of the houses at the back.

The partnership lasted four hours and a half, and before Gunn was bowled by Peate, 330 runs had been put on since the fall of the last wicket, which is the largest number ever scored for one wicket in a first-class match. Of these, Gunn made 203. It was six o'clock when Flowers joined Barnes, and the pair kept their wickets intact till 'Time' was called, with the total 449 for four wickets, Barnes not out 140.

Fifth Test Final day: 25 March

England beat Australia by an innings to take rubber 3-2

From Melbourne

ENGLAND bowled Australia out for 125 in their second innings today to win the last match by an innings and 98 runs. In so doing, they have also won the rubber by three matches to two, having won the first two and lost the third and fourth.

They have been on top in this match from the start, reducing Australia to 99 for nine in their first innings before Trumble (34 not out) and Spofforth, the last man, added 64 for the last wicket.

Shrewsbury contributed a slow but invaluable 105 not out, the first hundred by an England captain, to the visitors' total of 386, with fifties from Billy Barnes (74) and Bates (61). Australia's second-innings wickets went down with, for them, sickening regularity, with Attewell, Ulyett and Flowers sharing the bowling honours for England.

And so a long and arduous tour - the first to include five matches with Australia - has come to an end for England, who will return with their triumph, perhaps, tempered a little in the knowledge that for some of the time, as a result of internal wranglings, Australia were somewhat under-strength.

1885

20-24 Feb In the 3rd Test, at Sydney, England reduce Australia's first innings to 101 for nine before the numbers 10 and 11, Garrett (51 not out) and Evans (33), put on 80 for the last wicket. Spofforth takes 10-144 in the match and Australia win by 6 runs to stay in the rubber (2-1 down).

16 Mar George Bonnor, at 6ft 6in and 16 stone known as the 'Australian Hercules', comes in at No.8 and makes 100 in 100min at Sydney in the 4th Test v England, 128 out of 169 in just under 2hr, to swing the match Australia's way.

Bonnor: 100 in 100min.

24 Mar Umpire J.Hodges refuses to continue after tea on the 3rd day of the last Test, at Melbourne, because of dissent at some of his decisions by England players, and his place is taken by one of the Australian players, Tom Garrett.

25 Mar Billy Barnes finishes top of England's Test batting averages (52.71), with most runs (369), and takes most wickets in the 5 Tests (19 at 15.36 apiece). Because of internal disputes, Australia use 28 players in the series.

24-26 Apr Louis Hall and George Ulyett (Yorks) are the first batsmen to make a 100 opening partnership in each innings (123 & 108) of a match, against Sussex at Hove.

Inter-County match Surrey v Sussex: 30 June

Roller scores 204 and takes the hat-trick: Unique feat

From the Oval

THE second day's play in this match at Kennington Oval was in keeping with its predecessor, the wonderful scoring being well maintained up to the close of the home county's innings. When stumps were drawn last night, Surrey had lost seven wickets for 462 runs, Mr Roller being not out 131. Before being dismissed today, he increased this to 204.

Roller had been at the wickets for over six hours without giving a decided chance. He went in fourth wicket down and was ninth out, and 418 runs were put on during his stay. He was well supported by other members of the team, initially by Mr W.W.Read, who made 163 yesterday.

When the last Surrey wicket fell, the total amounted to 631, which, with the exception of the 648 made by the same county against Hampshire in 1883, is the highest score in a single innings in a county match.

After their long outing in the field, and facing an almost hopeless task, the Sussex men made a creditable 168 before they were all out just before time was up. By way of supplementing his grand innings, Mr Roller performed the hat-trick, having Jesse Hide caught with the last ball of one over and clean-bowling Humphreys and Mr Brann with the first two of his next.

Only one player previously has made a 100 and done the hat-trick in a first-class match, Giffen for the Australians against Lancashire last season. Mr Roller's feat of 200 and a hat-trick is unique in first-class cricket.

[Roller's feat was still unique some 110 years later.]

TEST SERIES

England in Australia
E 3, A 2

Cricket in the 1790s: Under-arm bowling, curved bats, and three stumps, although the wicket is not yet upright.

William Lillywhite: Early champion of round-arm bowling.

The Evolution of the Laws

Many aspects of cricket had been regularised years before the first known set of Laws were drawn up in 1744. Matches were played for high stakes, with betting also involved, so if teams gathered from different counties, say, met each other, there had to be some common ground. We know that matches were played with double innings, that the ball was bowled along the ground and that a batsman could be caught (and at one time the batsman could charge down a fielder attempting a catch). The bat was club-like. but curved at the bottom like a hockey stick. The wicket had already evolved from perhaps a tree stump, and there were now two stumps, instead of the one as earlier.

The earliest known regulations were the Articles of Agreement drawn up in 1727 for matches between the teams of the second Duke of Richmond and a Mr Broderick of Peper Harow, in Surrey, and these provided, among other things, for a wicket-to-wicket distance of 23 yards. Rather than laws, these articles were more instructions for umpires and team managers, clarifying points that had presumably been in dispute. One of the articles stated that runs were not to be scored if a batsman was caught, so we may assume that the rule till then, in some places, was that a run made before the catch was completed was scored.

The 1744 Laws

In 1744, a full code of Laws was drawn up as a result of a meeting of 'the London Club', about which, strangely enough, little else is known. Eleven years later, with the help of other clubs, the code was revised at the Star and Garter Club, in Pall Mall, and was issued in the form of a pamphlet.

The Laws, of which there are several transcripts, were grouped under six headings. The first, general heading, "Ye Laws of ye game of Cricket", reads thus:

Ye pitching of ye first Wicket is to be determined by ye cast of a piece of money.

When ye first Wicket is pitched and ye popping Crease cut, which must be exactly 3 foot 10 inches from ye Wicket, ye other Wicket is to be pitched, directly opposite, at 22 yards Distance, and ye other popping Crease cut 3 foot 10 inches before it.

Ye bowling Creases must be cut, in a direct line, from each Stump.

Ye Stumps must be 22 inches long, and ye Bail 6 inches.

Ye ball must weigh between 5 and 6 ounces.

When ye Wickets are both pitched and all ye Creases cut, ye Party that wins the toss up may order which side shall go in first at his option.

From the content and the amount of detail contained in this first group of Laws, one can grasp the state of sophistication reached in the organisation of cricket at this stage in its development. The mixture of rustic language and more modern phrasing in this and succeeding groups would suggest also that the Laws of 1744 were clarifications of rules that had been in force for some time.

The second group, "Laws for ye Bowlers 4 Balls and Over", covers the bowler's delivery, requiring one foot behind the crease even with the wicket, and instructs the umpire to call "no ball" if this is infringed, and ruling that a player may not be out from a no ball. It also specifies the number of balls (4) before a bowler may change wicket (and only change once in an innings).

The Laws for strikers enumerate the ways a batsman may be out - bowled; striking, treading down or falling on his wicket (but not in running); a "*stroke or nip over or under his Batt, or upon his hands, but not arms, if ye Ball be held before she touches ye ground, though she be hug'd to ye body*"; and other carefully phrased definitions covering stumped, obstructing the field (only when "out of his ground"), hitting the ball twice, and run out.

A fourth set deals with the details of run-outs, dead ball, a player hindering a catch while "in his ground", not out, even when the ball hits the wicket and the bail is hanging from one stump, etc. The detailed content of this group of Laws, in particular, is evidence of their evolution as a result of a mass of experience of all kinds of incidents, many of them unusual, that occur in matches, and points to the existence of previous codes.

There are also laws to prevent the wicket-keeper putting the batsman off, and laws for umpires that cover the time allowed for a new batsman to come in (2 minutes) and between innings (10 minutes), marking of the ball (to prevent it being changed), and appointing them sole judges of outs and ins, fair and unfair play, hurts (real or pretended), hindrances, good or bad runs, etc. They also decree that a man may not be given out unless the umpire is appealed to by one of the players. Runs are always referred to as "notches", this being the original means used by the scorers to record them, i.e. the cutting of notches in wooden staves.

Revisions

So these were the basis of the Laws as they stand today, and they are a remarkable monument to the men of the Star and Garter Club who framed them. There was a revision in 1774, which incorporated, among other things, a decision of the Hambledon Club to limit the width of the bat to 4 1/2 inches. The weight of the ball was established at between 5 1/2 and 5 3/4 ounces, and an lbw law was introduced, making the striker out if he put his leg before the wicket with a "design" to stop the ball. The addition of a third stump, another Hambledon innovation (in 1775), was not found in the Laws until 1785, with the advent of two bails the following year.

Some of the Star and Garter members were to found the White Conduit Club in the early 1780s, which merged in 1787 with the newly formed MCC. Only a year later came the first revision of the Laws by the 'Cricket Club of Marylebone', which had, naturally, taken over the accepted custom as custodians of the Laws.

Alterations in the Laws were made regularly, and by the 1820s, the width of the bat had been reduced to 4 1/4 inches, the stumps increased to 26 inches out of the ground, the bails to 7 inches in length, and the popping crease to 4 feet distance from the wicket. Wides had been introduced (scored as byes), new bowlers were allowed a maximum of two balls for practice, a person stopping the ball with his hat would concede 5 runs (still called notches at this time), and rules had been framed for betting on the individual scores of players. "Design" had been removed from the lbw law in 1778, presumably to help umpires, and it now decreed that a player was out: "If with his foot or leg he stops the Ball, which the Bowler in the opinion of the Umpire at the Bowler's Wicket shall have pitched in a straight line to the Wicket, and would have hit it". One aspect of the Laws that would cause most controversy over succeeding years involved the bowler's action. At this time, it declared: "The Ball must be bowled (not thrown or jerked), and delivered underhand, with the Hand below the Elbow", otherwise the bowler would be no-balled.

From under-arm to over-arm

The first change in bowling was from rolling the ball along the ground (as in the game of bowls) to pitching it, and this came about some time between 1744 and 1773. We know little about the transition to what became known as 'lob' bowling, but it must have caused the striker, or batsman, considerable difficulty at first, as the curved bats of the time would have been inadequate for dealing with it. Indeed, this undocumented revolution in style gave the bowler two new weapons - length and direction - whereas before he had possessed only pace. And it forced batsmen for the first time to play forward or back. With the advent of the lob, the bowler also developed two more weapons, spin and pace off the wicket. But it was nearly twenty years before Tom Walker of the Hambledon Club appreciated that, with these variations in technique, it was no longer necessary to bowl fast, and he began bowling slow in 1792.

It was Walker who had been among the first to try round-arm bowling, for Hambledon in the 1780s, and he had been specifically warned against it. It gradually crept in, however, causing a great deal of friction, even after it was ostensibly prohibited in 1816. Its main practitioner was John Willes of Kent, who is said to have developed the style from practising with his sister whose voluminous skirt prevented her bowling under-arm properly. Willes was the first to be no-balled for bowling round-arm, playing for Kent against M.C.C. in 1822 - he promptly threw the ball down, left the ground in high dudgeon, and never played first-class cricket again.

The law was difficult to apply, however, and it would appear that umpires on the whole turned a blind eye to round-arm bowling. It gradually crept in, and two Sussex bowlers, William Lillywhite and Jem Broadbridge, became so proficient in the style that a series of three experimental matches against All England was staged in 1827, a year after which the Law was changed to allow the hand to be level with the elbow at the point of delivery - in effect, legalising round-arm bowling. In 1835, "shoulder" replaced "elbow" in the Laws.

Like round-arm, over-arm bowling was practised, if umpires allowed it, long before it was permitted by the Laws. The M.C.C. had by no means become a universally respected body, nor were their Laws absolute. The cricket in country districts, in particular, was practised with one or more modifications of the M.C.C. Laws (6-ball overs were in widespread use, for example). It was not easy for the umpire to spot a bowler with hand just above shoulder height, which is how over-arm bowling developed, but matters came to a head in 1862 with a notorious incident in which Willsher, bowling for Surrey against England, was no-balled six times by umpire John Lillywhite[1]. Two years later, over-arm bowling was legalised. From then, bowlers could raise their arm above their shoulder, but it would be 1878, with the first visit of the Australians, before over-arm bowling as we know it today was seen in England, and it took another ten years before the style prevailed. W.G.Grace was among the bowlers of the period who persisted with round-arm.

[1] The report of this match is to be found elsewhere in the book, but it does not quite convey the furore caused by the incident. A comment with the report began thus: "Willsher has been no-balled! To most of our cricketing readers the announcement may appear as stale and trite as the statement that her late lamented majesty Queen Anne was dead. The occurrence, however, is one of such moment and importance that it claims special record and comment at our hands...." The writer exonerates both Willsher and Lillywhite from all blame, and concludes: "... we cannot reprobate too strongly the conduct, utterly unworthy of Englishmen, of those who ventured to hiss and hoot at Edgar Willsher - as fine a cricketer and as good a fellow as ever handled a bat or trolled a ball."

1886

15 Mar George Giffen takes 17-201 for South Australia in the match against Victoria at Adelaide, bowling 116.2 overs with 41 maidens.

6 Jul K.J.Key (143) and W.W.Rashleigh (107) put on 243 in just under 3hr for the 1st wicket in Oxford's 2nd innings v Cambridge. No other Oxford batsman reaches double figures in their 304, but they win by 133.

4 Aug Middlesex batsman Andrew Stoddart, playing in a non-first-class match for Hampstead v the Stoics, amasses 485, the highest innings on record anywhere.

13 Sep Playing for an England XI v the Australians, W.G.Grace scores the first run at Lord's to be recorded on the new telegraph board, which alters the batsmen's totals as the runs are made.

TEST SERIES

Australia in England
England 3

Oxford University v M.C.C. & Ground: 22 June

'W.G.' scores a 100 and takes all 10 wickets

From Oxford

THE feature of today's play in this contest at Oxford was the wonderful form displayed by Dr W.G.Grace. To score a hundred in a match is always in itself a great performance, but to follow that up by securing every wicket in the innings of the opposing side is a feat which has very rarely to be chronicled.

Dr Grace has done many big things in cricket, but it is doubtful if he has ever surpassed or accomplished anything greater than his record of today. It will be remembered that at close of play yesterday the Champion and Mr E.J.C.Studd were not out 50 and 29 respectively, the total standing at 83 for no wicket. Resuming today, Mr Grace ran his score to 104; an innings made in his best style and without giving a chance. M.C.C. were all out for 260, a first-innings lead of 118.

On batting a second time, with the exception of Rashleigh and Page, none of the Oxonians could do anything with Mr Grace's bowling. He took all 10 wickets at a cost of 49 runs in 36.2 overs, while Wright and Attewell, who took seven wickets between them in the first innings, laboured through a combined 36 overs this time without reward. M.C.C. won by an innings and 28 runs.

Tour match M.C.C. v Parskes [sic]: 27 May

Indian cricketers in London

From Lord's

The Parsees, the first Indian team to tour England.

THE Indian cricketers made their first appearance on a metropolitan cricket-ground today, when they met a team of the Marylebone Club. Owing to the rain which fell during the early hours, however, play was not practicable until late in the day, and it was half-past three o'clock before a move was made.

The home team was a very strong one. W.G. Grace and I.D. Walker opened the batting for the M.C.C., who had won the toss, and after making a long stand, during which over 100 runs were scored, they were at last dismissed, Grace for 65, Walker 51. Several bowlers were tried before this was effected, all of whom performed creditably, Major being especially fortunate, the five wickets which fell being credited to him. When play ceased for the day, the score stood at 200 runs for the loss of those five wickets.

[The Parsees, a name obviously unfamiliar to the Telegraph sub-editor, began playing cricket in Bombay in the late 1700s and this was the first team from India to tour abroad. They were not a strong side and lost this match by an innings, but they were the pioneers of Indian cricket. Scores: MCC 313 (Major 5-91), Parsees 23 (Grace 7-18) & 66 (Walker 5-29, Grace 4-28).]

Second Test Second day: 20 July

Shrewsbury's batting and Briggs's bowling put England on top

From Lord's

SOMETHING like 20,000 visitors patronised the second day's play in the second match between England and the Australians at Lord's today, 15,663 paying at the gates. The play was again of a highly interesting character, and, as far as the Englishmen were concerned, very satisfactory, but the Australians' batting fell short of anticipation. Shrewsbury's batting and Briggs's bowling have been the great features of the match so far.

Arthur Shrewsbury's 164 is the highest innings ever played against the Australian Eleven in this country, beating W.G.Grace's record of 152 in 1880. The Nottingham professional will, indeed, take credit for playing one of the finest defensive innings ever seen against the Australian bowlers - among them, Spofforth, Garrett, Trumble, Giffen and Palmer - on a pitch made ideal for bowling by rain last night. He went in first wicket down, was tenth out, and was batting six hours and 53 minutes. Barnes, who helped Shrewsbury add 161 for the fifth wicket, also played very fine cricket for his 58 and England were all out for 353.

Briggs's performance when Australia went in was extraordinary against such a strong batting side. Scott and Jones put on 45 for the first wicket before Briggs (5-29) had them both out for 52. Steel (2-34) then captured the wickets of Bonnor and Giffen for the addition of only another eight runs, and with Barnes (3-25) also enjoying success Australia were eventually bowled out for 121 runs. This left the Australians under the necessity of following on, and when stumps were drawn for the day they had lost one wicket - to Briggs - for 12 runs.

[Briggs took 6-45 as Australia, whose overnight pair, the Nos.10 and 11, Palmer (48) and Trumble (20), put on 50 for the 2nd wicket, collapsed to 126 all out. England thus won by an innings and 106 runs to go 2-0 up in the 3-match rubber and retain the Ashes.]

Arthur Shrewsbury: Record innings.

First Test Third day: 31 January

Barnes and Lohmann bowl England to remarkable victory

From Sydney

England achieved a remarkable victory on the third day of the match with Australia, who needed just 111 runs to win but were bowled out for 97. Barnes (6-28) and Lohmann (3-20) did the damage, but they must share the credit with England's tail-end batsmen, Briggs (33), Flowers (14) and Sherwin (21 not out). When England were 103 for seven, a lead of only 29, defeat was staring them in the face, but the last three wickets put on 81 this morning to give their bowlers a chance.

So England have won this enthralling match after being put in and then bowled out in their first innings for 45, the lowest score they have ever made against Australia. Only Lohmann (17) reached double figures, and the wickets were taken by Turner (6-15) and Ferris (4-27), both making their first appearance for Australia, bowling unchanged.

Australia went ahead for the loss of only two wickets, but lost their last eight wickets for 55 runs, and were all out for 119. Barlow and Lohmann, with three wickets each, and Barnes with two, were chiefly responsible for keeping England in with a chance.

England took the lead for the loss of only one wicket, but Ferris, who took five wickets, caused another England collapse before the last English batsmen staged their great recovery.

George Lohmann: Best Test innings analysis yet.

Second Test Final day: 1 March

England win second match and rubber: Sixth successive victory

From Sydney

ENGLAND easily won the second and last match against Australia by 71 runs. It was their sixth successive win against the Colonials and they never looked in difficulties against a poor side.

This has been a poorly promoted tour, with no matches against Australia at Melbourne. The only Victorian in Australia's side for this match was Midwinter. Barnes was missing for England because of a damaged hand.

Australia can take consolation from the splendid bowling of their new opening pair in this rubber, Ferris and Turner. Each took nine wickets in this match. But the bowling laurels here must go to Lohmann, who took eight Australian first-innings wickets for 35, the best innings analysis for any bowler in matches between the two countries. Australia lost their last four wickets for two runs and never recovered from their first-innings deficit of 65.

Barlow made 42 not out in England's second innings, which was the highest individual score of the series, and Bates took four wickets for 26 today as Australia were dismissed for 150. Lohmann finished the match with 10 wickets for 87.

1887

1 Mar The low-scoring two-Test series finishes in Australia with some curious statistics. Wicket-keeper and No.11 Mordecai Sherwin tops the England batting averages with 30 (for only once out in 4 innings) and Barlow has their highest aggregate with 82 runs, including the highest score of the rubber, 42 not out. Harry Moses, top of the Australian averages with 29, is the only player to score 100 runs (116) and to reach double figures in all four innings, while McDonnell's 35 is their highest individual score. Conversely, of course, the bowlers return splendid figures. Lohmann takes 16 wickets for England at 8.56 apiece, Barnes 8 at 5.87 in his one match. Australia's new opening pair take 35 of the 40 England wickets to fall, Turner 17 (9.47) and Ferris 18 (13.50).

17-19 Mar The highest innings total in first-class cricket, and the first of over 800 is amassed by the Non-Smokers, who score 803-9 v the Smokers at East Melbourne, in a fixture between two sides composed of leading players. The 3rd-wicket stand of 310 between the English pair Shrewsbury and Gunn is also a first-class record

1-2 Aug The first Canadian team to tour England draw at Lord's with a fairly strong M.C.C. amateur eleven, their slow-medium bowler Dr E.R.Ogden taking 12-163, including the wickets of Walker, Webbe and Stoddart.

TEST SERIES

England in Australia
England 2

M.C.C.Centenary Match M.C.C. v An England XI: 14 June

Stoddart and Shrewsbury hit 150s against M.C.C.: England on top

From Lord's

INTEREST in this match was sustained throughout the second day's play at Lord's as Stoddart and Shrewsbury continued to hit the Marylebone bowling to all parts of the field as England built up a huge first-innings lead. Their stand was not broken until it had reached 266, after four hours and 40 minutes at the wickets, when Stoddart was out for 151. Shrewsbury, who had just reached his 100, went on to make 152, and England, in nearly seven and three-quarter hours, amassed 514 for a first-innings advantage of 339. Barnes took the last six wickets to improve his analysis to six for 126.

Seldom has a better wicket been found at Lord's Ground, and in the matter of weather so far the fixture has been especially favoured, the sun shining brilliantly all day. When stumps were drawn at seven o'clock, M.C.C. in their second innings had scored 58 in under two hours for the loss of one wicket, the two not out batsmen being Grace, with 34, and Gunn.

[England won by an innings and 117, dismissing M.C.C. for 222 in another 2hr 20min. Barnes was their top scorer again, adding 53 to his previous 61, and Bates and Briggs were the chief wicket-takers, with five and four respectively.]

Oxford University v Middlesex: 24 June

Oxford pair in record first-class stand: 331 and still batting

From Chiswick Park

THE feature of the first day of this fixture, which began in fine weather, was the batting of K.J.Key and H.Philipson for Oxford. Coming together after six wickets had fallen for 104 runs, they were still there when stumps were drawn, having added 331 runs, a new record partnership in first-class cricket by a single run.

The two batsmen were together for about three hours and a half, and both hit in fine style. Key, who was missed at third man when he had scored but 13, made no further error and had reached 214 by the close. Philipson, who gave a hard chance when 24 and another that should have been taken by the wicket-keeper when 104, will resume tomorrow on 150.

The previous best partnership was made in 1885, when Barnes and Gunn put on 330 for M.C.C. against Yorkshire for the fourth wicket.

[Philipson did not add to his score, but the stand had risen to 340 when he was out, Key going on to make 281. Their partnership for the 7th wicket beat the previous best by 128 runs and remained a first-class record for 15 years.]

1888

25 Feb A match at Sydney between the Australian XI going to England this year and the Shaw, Shrewsbury and Lillywhite team ends in an innings and 42 runs victory for the visitors, after Australia are put out for 75 and 56 in reply to their 173. (This match is historically not accorded Test status, although the teams are arguably no weaker than those of the only Test counted as such.)

28-29 May In the wettest summer on record, the Gentlemen v Australians fixture is limited to two days not because of the weather, which is fine, but so as not to clash with the Derby, on what would have been the third day. The Australian bowlers, Charlie 'the Terror' Turner and J.J.Ferris, are collared for once, the Gentlemen scoring 490 (W.G.Grace 165, W.W.Read 109; Turner 6-161), but the match is drawn, with Australia having made 179 and 213-1 (Bonnor 119).

21 Jul George Burton takes all 10-59 for Middlesex v Surrey at the Oval.

3-4 Aug Charlie Turner takes 17-50 (8-13, 9-37) for the Australians against an inexperienced England XI at Hastings, the best match figures ever returned in a first-class match. Having already taken a record 106 wickets for an Australian season (1887-88), the NSW fast-medium bowler goes on to take 283 wickets in England, a record by a long way for a tourist.

Only Test Fourth day: 14 February

Australia bowled out by Lohmann and Peel for 42 on rain-affected pitch

From Reuters, in Sydney

The match between the combined English teams[1] and All Australia was resumed today on a pitch soddened by the heavy rain that stopped all play on Saturday and yesterday. The wicket was in a very unsatisfactory state, and the ground generally so soft as to make fielding difficult. The Australians, who at the close of Friday's play had scored 35 for eight wickets as against the English first-innings total of 113, made only 7 more. Their score of 42 is the lowest innings total in the history of matches between the two countries.

The Englishmen then went in for their second innings and after a poor start managed to compile 137 as the wickets seemed to become more playable. Turner, again bowling unchanged, returned the creditable figures of seven wickets for 43 runs and a remarkable match analysis of 88 overs, 50 maidens, 87 runs 12 wickets.

The Australians again fared badly in their second innings, their score at the end of the day being 47 for five wickets.

[Australia were out for 82 and England won by 126 runs, their 7th successive victory. Peel took 5-18 and 5-40, Lohmann 5-17 and 4-35.]

1 A selection from the two English teams currently touring Australia.

TEST SERIES

England in Australia
England 1
Australia in England
E 2, A 1

Surrey v Oxford Univ: 26 June

Surrey's 650 equals their own record: W.W.Read's 338

From the Oval

THE Oxford University eleven will long remember their match with Surrey. Between noon yesterday and until nearly half past five today, eight hours and a half were spent by them trying to get rid of their opponents, and when they eventually accomplished this task it was only after a total of 650 had been made. Thus Surrey equalled their own highest score in first-class cricket in this country, made against Hants in 1883.

Another remarkable feature was the batting of W.W.Read, who failed by a mere six runs to equal the individual first-class batting record of 344 set by W.G.Grace for M.C.C. against Kent in 1876. Read batted six hours and a half while making his 338, a truly magnificent innings, which included one 5 and forty-six 4's.

First Test Second day: 17 July

England beaten at last: No answer to Turner and Ferris: Toss was decisive

From Lord's

Turner 'the Terror': Splendid bowling.

AUSTRALIA have beaten England at Lord's by 61 runs after seven successive reverses since they won at Sydney in March 1885. In the 10 years that have elapsed since their first visit to this country, it is only their second success, the other being the very sensational contest at the Oval in 1882.

Without wishing to detract from the merits of their win, it must be said that the Australians secured a great advantage by winning the toss and batting first on an easy wicket. A sage authority said previous to the start that, considering the surroundings, the wicket and the weather, it was, in effect, tossing for the match. And so it proved.

It will be remembered that play was impracticable yesterday, owing to rain, until three o'clock, and that when stumps were drawn England had made 18 for the loss of three wickets against a first innings 116 by their opponents. Resuming at 11.30, the side were all out in 55 minutes for the meagre total of 53. Grace (10) failed to increase his figures, and so rapidly did wickets fall that, with seven down for 26, England still required 11 runs to avoid batting again.

Briggs then came in to make England's top score of 17 and with Peel (8) avert the follow-on. These two had taken between them seven wickets in Australia's innings, and likewise it was Australia's chief bowlers, Turner and Ferris, with eight of England's wickets so far, who saved their side from complete destruction by Lohmann and Peel, coming together at 18 for seven and making the only double-figure scores of the innings, Turner 12 and Ferris 20 not out - although it has to be said that never in the annals of cricket has such a fortunate innings as that of Ferris been compiled, almost every other ball he received being put up just out of reach of a fielder.

England's task of making 124 to win proved beyond them. Grace's 24 was far and away the best batting display *[contd. page 37, column 1]*

Inter-County match
Surrey v Sussex: 11 August

Surrey's record win: Sussex beaten by an innings and 485

From the Oval

THIS extraordinary match ended today in a win for Surrey by an innings and 485 runs, the greatest margin of victory in the history of first-class cricket. It was anticipated that they would win easily, but the visitors were not expected to capitulate in the way they did. They added only 99 in their second innings to their 114 in the first, and Lohmann again took six wickets, for 22 runs, to earn match figures of 12 for 80.

Surrey's score of 698, of course, is the highest made in English first-class cricket, beating their own record of 650, achieved twice, in 1883 and again earlier this season. Two players made hundreds, M.P.Bowden (189 not out) and W.W.Read (171).

of the match, but Steel, the captain, with 10 not out, was the only other to reach double figures as England subsided to 62, again to the splendid bowling of Turner, who took five for 36 (10-63 in the match) and Ferris, who captured five for 26 (8-45).

Perhaps the outstanding performance with the ball, however, was done by Peel, whose eight wickets for 50 included four for 36 in the Australians' first innings, when the wicket was easier than at any other time in the two days.

Third Test Second day: 31 August

England assert their supremacy: Innings victory gives them the rubber

From Manchester

THE supremacy of English cricketers was well asserted today at the Old Trafford Ground, where the team, captained by W.G.Grace, defeated the Australian combination by an innings and 21 runs. This result goes far to prove that the victory scored by the Colonials in the first match of the series at Lord's was somewhat of a fluke, as in the second engagement, at Kennington Oval, the home side proved victorious by an innings and 137 runs, and England have now scored the rubber.

Today's play was remarkable for the double collapse of the Australian batting, which was as weak as could be conceived. Resuming at 32 for two in reply to England's 172 (Grace 39; Turner 5-86), they lost five wickets for 13 and were all out for 81 despite Lyons' (22) brave attempt to save the follow on, Peel taking seven for 31.

In their second innings, the Australians proceeded to lose their first six wickets for seven runs, so that across the two innings nine wickets had gone down for seven. Then Lyons (32) was missed at point by Read, and he and Turner (26) put on 48 for the seventh wicket to put off the evil moment, which came when they were all out for 70 just before lunch - victory for England in record time.

1889

12-13 Mar S.Africa play their first Test, against England at Port Elizabeth, and lose by 8 wickets. The England captain, C.Aubrey Smith (of later Hollywood fame), the Sussex slow-medium off-break bowler, takes 5-19 and 2-42 (in his sole Test appearance).

26 Mar Bernard Tancred (S.Africa) becomes the first player to carry his bat through a Test innings, albeit for just 26 out of 47 in the 1st Test against England.

26 Nov An England team (under G.F.Vernon) arrives on the subcontinent for the first tour of India and Ceylon

27 Dec A.E.Moss takes 10-28 for Canterbury v Wellington, NZ, a new record innings analysis in first-class cricket.

TEST SERIES

England in South Africa
England 2

Second Test Second day: 26 March

Briggs skittles S.African XI: 15 for 28 in second match

From the Cape

The second match between the English cricketers and the Eleven of South Africa was concluded today in victory for the visiting team by an innings with 202 runs to spare. In face of the total of 292 scored by the English team, for whom R.Abel made 120, the Colonial Eleven were bowled out for 47 and, after having to follow on, for 43.

The destruction of the South African batting was perpetrated chiefly by Johnny Briggs of Lancashire, a left-arm slow bowler who captured seven wickets for 17 in the first innings and eight for 11 in the second. This is the first time a bowler has taken 15 wickets in a match between teams of two countries, and his second-innings figures are the best for an innings. England win the series 2-0, on this, their first tour of South Africa.

Johnny Briggs: Record match analysis.

M.C.C. Annual Meeting: 1 May

M.C.C. vote for five-ball over

From Lord's

THIS afternoon the Marylebone Cricket Club held their annual meeting in the Pavilion at Lord's. There was a larger attendance than for some years past, due no doubt to the proposed alterations in the laws of the game and the proposition to erect a new, larger pavilion at a cost of £13,000, the latter being agreed to after some discussion.

The committee then brought under the notice of the meeting the alterations which they recommended should be made in the rules. These were, first, to substitute five balls an over for four; second, that a bowler may change ends as often as he likes, but cannot bowl two overs in succession; third, on the last day of a match, and in a one-day match, at any time the in-side may declare their innings at an end.

Mr Perkins reported that the whole of the first-class counties were in favour of the alterations with the exception of Surrey, who disapproved of them altogether, and Notts, who were divided as to the question of the number of balls an over. After an amendment failed to be passed, the proposed alterations were all carried unanimously.

It should be noted that these laws apply to the game in England. In Australia, there has been a six-ball over for some time.

Inter-County match Middlesex v Yorks: 22 June

O'Brien's hitting earns Middlesex famous victory

From Lord's

AT ten minutes to seven this evening, Middlesex beat Yorkshire by four wickets, having been set to get 280 runs in three hours and 35 minutes. A difficult target looked even more unlikely when they lost Webbe and Stoddart before 40 runs had been made.

Nevertheless, when O'Brien joined E.A. Nepean (62) at the fall of the fourth wicket and began to hit freely, there appeared a slight hope of the runs being obtained. But the dismissal of Nepean at 182 and Hadlow at 197 again altered the complexion of affairs. Now, with Vernon joining O'Brien, 83 were needed in a trifle over 45 minutes.

They made them in 35. The 200 went up at a quarter past six as O'Brien began to punish the bowlers. When he hit the winning run, which also brought up his 100, he had been in for 80 minutes, making his second fifty in 25 minutes. Vernon, while not scoring so rapidly, contributed a valuable 30.

Needless to say, the pair of them - heroes of the first innings, too, with 92 (O'Brien) and 86 - were cheered all the way back to the pavilion.

1890

12 May Fast bowler Jesse Hide takes 4 wickets in 4 balls for Sussex v M.C.C. at Lord's.

12-14 May Glos v Yorks at Bristol is the first match in the first official County Championship.

17 May Arthur Shrewsbury (267) and Billy Gunn (196) put on 398 for the 2nd wicket for Notts v Sussex at Trent Bridge, a world record stand for any wicket in first-class cricket.

Archie MacLaren makes 108 on his first-class début for Lancs v Sussex at Hove.

21-23 Jul At Lord's, J.J.Lyons gets the 1st Test against England off to a flying start with 55 out of 66 in 45min (50 in 36min) and takes 5-30 in England's 1st innings. Jack Barrett, on his Test début, is the first player in England-Australia Tests to carry his bat, scoring 67 out of Australia's 2nd-innings 176. W.G.Grace, after a duck in the 1st innings, makes 75 not out in the 2nd, the highest score in the match, and England win by 7 wickets.

25-27 Aug 3rd Test abandoned without a ball bowled because of rain at Old Trafford on all three days.

TEST SERIES

Australia in England
E2, Abandoned 1

Second Test Second day: 12 August

Martin sets up England win and rubber is safe: 12 wickets on début

From the Oval

RIGHT up to the finish it was 'anybody's' victory as England struggled to make the 95 they needed to win this second match against the Australians, but fortune smiled upon them and they won by two wickets. This also means that they win the rubber, two victories to the good with only one match remaining.

England started the day slightly on top, having captured two wickets last night for five runs, so the Australians were still three runs behind. On a wicket that gave the bowlers an immense advantage, England soon had the visitors in desperate trouble, with only 53 on the board at the fall of the seventh wicket. Trott (25) was again the only batsman to play the bowling with any success, and he helped to stretch the Australian score to 102.

There were remarkable similarities between Australia's two innings. Trott and Lyons were top and second scorers, and the three English bowlers took the same number of wickets in each - Martin (6-50, 6-52), Lohmann (3-34, 3-32) and Sharpe (1-8, 1-10). The performance of 'Nutty' Martin, the Kentish left-arm fast-medium bowler, in taking 12 for 102 on his first appearance for England was quite remarkable.

England were soon in trouble against Ferris and Turner, however, losing their first four wickets while moving from 24 runs to 32. Maurice Read (35) and Cranston (15) then changed the whole aspect of the game with a stand of 51, but England again lost four wickets in the space of 10 runs before Sharpe snicked Ferris to cover point for the tying run and returned on Barrett's over-throw for the winner.

[Martin played only once more for England, against S.Africa.]

County Cricket Championship: 1 September

Surrey are first official champions

Monday round-up

THE match between Lancashire and Notts at Old Trafford on Saturday terminated the list of first-class county fixtures of a summer that will long be remembered by cricketers for the frequent dismal and damp weather, which has greatly interfered with the majority of the games.

The Cricket Council have, for the first time in the history of the game, recognised the existence of a competition among the counties. At the meeting of delegates at Lord's last December, it was resolved that, in estimating the positions of counties, drawn games should be entirely ignored, and the positions ascertained by deducting the losses from the wins. Adopting this method, the following table shows the relative positions of the counties:

		Played	Won	Lost	Drawn	Points
1.	Surrey	14	9	3	2	6
2.	Lancashire	14	7	3	4	4
3=	Kent	14	6	3	5	3
3=	Yorkshire	14	6	3	5	3
5.	Notts	14	5	5	4	0
6.	Gloucestershire	14	5	6	3	-1
7.	Middlesex	12	3	8	1	-5
8.	Sussex	12	1	11	0	-10

As in previous years, the number of inter-county engagements was 54, as Sussex and Middlesex, as heretofore, did not meet. The new power to apply the closure on the final day of a match was taken advantage of on ten occasions, four of which produced a win for the team making the declaration, the other six being drawn.

As will be seen from the above table, Surrey are well to the front as champion county. They have been top of the unofficial listings for the previous three seasons, including last year's triple tie with Lancashire and Notts.

Surrey started this season with a defeat and suffered two more near the end, and have not proved quite so powerful in batting as in recent years. W.W.Read and Key hardly showed in their true colours, whilst Abel, until the last few weeks, had not been in anything like the form of a few seasons ago. To a certain extent, the county have relied on the efforts of two bowlers, Lohmann and Sharpe, who each took more then a hundred wickets at just over 12 apiece. In addition, Lohmann, who has developed into one of the best bats in the team, came second in their batting averages, with 29, to Abel (39.11)

Sussex v Cambridge Univ: 21 June

Cantabs 703 is new record: Sussex beaten by 425 runs

From Hove

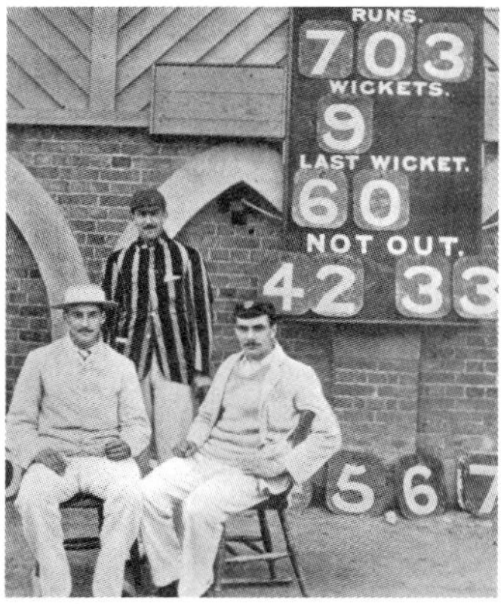

Foley, Ford, MacGregor and the historic Cambridge score.

IN a batting display of the most brilliant character, the Cantabs, after having had all the worst of the opening day's play, not only beat Sussex by the huge margin of 425 runs, but established a record in English first-class cricket by compiling the extraordinary number of 703 runs for nine wickets, thus beating the previous best of 698 scored by Surrey at the Oval two years ago, curiously against the same opponents.

The Light Blues began their second innings yesterday 91 runs to the bad. These were soon wiped off, and, chiefly by the aid of grand innings of 117 by Foley and 131 by MacGregor, the total had been taken to 494 for the loss of seven wickets when stumps were drawn for the day, Ford being not out 117.

This morning, Cambridge, with not only a win but also the record in their sights, hit out vigorously, and the result of an hour and a half's play yielded the extraordinary number of 209 runs, Ford taking his own score to 191 before being caught. At this point, on 703 for nine, the Light Blues captain declared the innings closed. Sussex were then got out for 187 by half-past five.

M.C.C. & Ground v Notts: 1 June

M.C.C. rout Notts for 21: Match over in a day

From Lord's

AN extraordinary performance with the ball was witnessed by those who were present at Lord's this morning. Ferris, the Australian, and Rawlin dismissed the Notts Eleven in an hour and five minutes for 21, the lowest total registered at St John's-wood in a fixture of first-class rank since Spofforth and Boyle disposed of a powerful M.C.C. team in 1878 for 19 on the first appearance of an Australian team in London.

The wicket was treacherous, bright sunshine having followed the heavy rains of last week, while the visitors, who were put in to bat, were without Shrewsbury and Mr Dixon. Yet their display was a very poor one. Only 15 were scored with the bat, the top score being made by opening bat C.W.Wright, who was an hour at the wicket for his 5. Ferris claimed six wickets for 7 runs, Rawlin four for 8.

When the M.C.C. went in, W.G.Grace and Ferris passed the Notts total before they both left at 37, and then Pope and Murdoch, another Australian, added 33. Pope was an hour and three-quarters for his 31 - a patient display of sound cricket - and M.C.C. made 127.

Notts went in a second time at half-past five, and Wright, top scorer again with 39, and Attewell (18) made 37 before a wicket fell. But after that a collapse almost as complete as that previously witnessed ensued as Ferris (5-25) and Phillips (5-30) finished off the innings for 69. Thus M.C.C. won by an innings and 37, and Ferris, who has joined Gloucester, finished with match figures of 11 wickets for 32 runs.

1891

14 Feb Monty Noble (227) and Syd Gregory (235), playing for Sydney against Warwick (Sydney) in a non-first-class match, put on 442 for the 8th wicket.

28 Mar W.T.Winyard is the first Maori to play first-class cricket, for Wellington v Canterbury at Basin Reserve.

4-11 Apr Transvaal v Griqualand West is first 1st-class match to last more than 5 days' play (7 days), and the aggregate (1,402 runs) is a record for S.Africa.

30 May Somerset make their County Championship début, against Middlesex at Lord's.

1-10 Sep The first Inter-Colonial Tournament takes place in the West Indies, between Barbados, Trinidad and British Guiana on the Wanderers ground, and is won by Barbados.

Varsity Match: 30 June

Close shave for Cambridge

From Lord's

OXFORD, the underdogs in this year's Varsity Match, and at one period staring an innings defeat in the face, came back pluckily and in the end made the Cantabs fight hard for their victory by two wickets.

The Dark Blues resumed this morning on 88 for seven in reply to the Cambridge first innings of 210. After three-quarters of an hour's play, they were all out for 108 and had to follow on. They made a better start to their second innings and were 66 for one before a collapse set in. Half the side were out and they still needed 21 to avert a single-innings defeat.

At this juncture, E.Smith and G.L.Wilson were associated, the former hitting with great power, the latter exhibiting fine defence, and they added 47 runs in 25 minutes before Smith was caught for 32. When Wilson was last man out, he had made 53 in an hour and 45 minutes while 117 runs were being made, including 55 for the last two wickets.

Cambridge went in to obtain 90 to win. They lost two wickets for 12, but Foley (41) put them in charge again, and when he was sixth out only 12 runs were still needed. When Berkeley (5-20) took another two wickets, however, the scores were tied. But down the pavilion steps strode the mighty Woods, capless, with no pads or gloves, and without further ado he smote the first ball he received to the boundary.

County Championship Notts v Sussex: 10 July

Bean averts Sussex follow-on with 100 before lunch: Notts pair in big stand

From Brighton

HOVE'S reputation for being the fastest run-getting ground in England was full upheld today in the match against Notts. With the wicket in admirable condition, the batsmen had matters largely their own way on the second day, three individual players exceeding the century, Bean of Sussex and two of the visitors.

Bean, who had made 45 overnight, carried his bat through the Sussex innings for a brilliant contribution of 145, which practically saved the home side from having to follow on. But when he ran out of partners, Sussex were still 56 behind. He was at the wickets for three hours and 25 minutes, during which period he hit twenty-eight 4's. At one time he sent the ball to the boundary on nine consecutive occasions. A collection on the ground afterwards realised £22 2s 6d.

Batting a second time, Notts soon lost Wright, but there ensued an extraordinary partnership between Shrewsbury and Gunn. For three hours and 20 minutes, both defied the bowling, and when play ceased for the day they were still together, with the total at 286 for one wicket, Gunn being not out 141 and Shrewsbury 136. Their performance upon this occasion calls to mind their memorable stand last year, when they established a record by scoring 398 for the second wicket at Nottingham, also against Sussex.

[The Notts pair did not break their record, but put on 312.]

George Giffen: Remarkable all-round feats.

Intercolonial Match South Australia v Victoria: 11 November

Giffen's unique all-round feat: 271 runs and 16 wickets

From Adelaide

The South Australian all-rounder George Giffen today completed a remarkable feat with bat and ball, unique in the annals of first-class cricket. In Victoria's second innings, he took seven wickets for 70 runs, making his match figures 16 for 166. Add this to the 271 runs he scored in South Australia's innings, and you have a performance far exceeding anything that has been accomplished by anyone else. South Australia (562), incidentally, beat Victoria (235 and 163) by an innings and 164 runs.

The closest comparable achievement belongs to Giffen himself, and again the victims were Victoria. In January of this year, at Melbourne, he made 237 and took 12 for 192 (5-89 & 7-103) as South Australia won by an innings and 62. Indeed, this veritable scourge of Victoria has produced other remarkable figures in previous matches between the two colonies, viz: 166 and 14-125 in February 1888, and 135 (and 19) and 13 for 159 in December 1888. In March '86 he captured 17 wickets for 201 runs, but scored 'only' 20 and 82.

1892

19-22 Mar England, with two former Australian Test players, Murdoch and Ferris, beat S.Africa at Cape Town by an innings and 189 runs in the only Test, while another English Test team are touring Australia. England's No.8, Surrey wicket-keeper Henry Wood, scores his maiden first-class century (134 not) in England's 369, and Ferris takes 13-91 as S.Africa are twice dismissed for under 100. Frank Hearne, who played for England against S.Africa on the last tour, is S.Africa's top scorer in both innings (24 & 23), playing against his two brothers, George and Alec, and cousin Jack Hearne!

27 Aug Surrey complete a hat-trick of official County Championships, having beaten Kent yesterday in two days, when Notts (2nd) lose to Lancs. Somerset, in their second season of first-class status, are 3rd.

13 Sep The Australian 'colonies' decide to purchase a trophy for intercolonial competition (Sheffield Shield).

Second Test Final day: 3 February

Australia win back the 'ashes': Well-deserved victory to go two-up

From Sydney

THE heroics of Lohmann, Abel and Briggs for England in this match have been in vain. The Colonials have emerged on this fifth and final day victorious after all, and for this they have to thank their heroes, especially Lyons, Bannerman, Giffen and Turner. In the end the winning margin was 72 runs, and this represents a remarkable recovery by the Australian eleven - or, more accurately, ten, because Moses was absent hurt during their uphill struggle against a first-innings disadvantage of 163. So to Australia go the "ashes", for they have won two matches now, with but one to play.

This morning, when England resumed their second innings, for the first time in the match it was they who were the under-dogs, at their overnight 11 for three wickets. Grace, their captain, returning to Australia for the first time in 18 years, was out, and blamed for not using nightwatchmen. Abel, who carried his bat right through the first innings for 132, the first Englishman to do so against Australia, was gone, too. And so was Bean. Stoddart was there, and he for a time revived the English hopes, before he lost J.M.Read at 64. The Middlesex amateur eventually went for 69 and there were no others to resist Giffen (6-72) and Turner (4-46) as they bowled England out for 156.

It had been so different last week when Lohmann ran through the Australians, taking eight for 58 as they capitulated for 144, and then Abel saw England right through to their 307. But it was J.J.Lyons who, having defied England for the top score of 41 in the first innings, now turned the tables on them, hitting 134 in magnificent style and with the greatest freedom. With Alec Bannerman, he put on 174 for the second wicket in two and three-quarter hours, before Bannerman soldiered on to 91 in seven and a half hours, adding only 24 to his overnight score. Bruce made a brilliant 72, before Johnny Briggs finished the innings off with a hat-trick - another English 'first' that was to be of no avail.

TEST SERIES

England in Australia
A 2, E 1
England in S.Africa
England 1

Third Test Fourth day: 28 March

Resounding England victory a consolation for lost Ashes: Briggs takes 12 for 136

From Adelaide

As was fully expected from the state of the game when stumps were drawn on Saturday in the final match between Lord Sheffield's Team and a representative Eleven of Australia, the visitors gained a brilliant single-innings victory with 230 runs to spare.

There was a marked improvement in the weather today, but, with the result a foregone conclusion, the attendance was meagre when Australia resumed their second innings at 124 for eight wickets. They managed to add another 35 before the inevitable overtook them. Briggs did not get another wicket today, but he takes the bowling honours with 12 for 136 in the match.

Scores: England 499 (Stoddart 134, Peel 83, Grace 58, J.M. Read 57, Attewell 43 not), Australia 100 (Briggs 6-49) & 169 (Briggs 6-87).

County Championship
Lancs v Somerset: 9 August

Briggs claims 12 as Lancashire win in a day

From Manchester

THE Old Trafford Ground today was the scene of some remarkable cricket, with 32 wickets tumbling at less than 10 runs apiece as Lancashire beat Somerset by eight wickets. As is so often the precursor of such freak results, a hot sun so affected a soddened wicket that the batsmen could practically do nothing. The ball at times got up in an alarming manner.

Somerset, who went in first, made 60 for two before the rot set in and the last eight wickets fell for the addition of only 28 more runs. Briggs took seven for 62, Mold three for 13. The home side, on the other hand, fared badly at the start, losing four wickets for 21 runs, but then recovered to aggregate 116, Woods and Hedley taking four wickets each. Somerset did even worse in their second venture, and the innings can only be termed a procession to and from the wickets, as in less than an hour and a half the lot were got rid of for the meagre total of 58, Briggs taking five for 21, Mold five for 27. With play extended to finish the game, Lancs scored 32 for two.

Lionel Palairet (left) and Bert Hewitt: Record for first wicket.

County Championship Somerset v Yorks: 26 August

Runs and records for Westerners: 346 for first wicket

From Taunton

SINCE their inclusion last season in the ranks of first-class counties, the Somersetshire eleven have accomplished some remarkable performances, but all these pale before their marvellous achievement today against Yorkshire. Not only did the team compile the huge total of 592, which is the highest so far this season, but the first pair of batsmen, Hewitt and Palairet, put on the remarkable number of 346 runs before being separated, which beats the first-wicket record of 283 established as far back as 1869 by W.G. Grace and B.B.Cooper for the Gentlemen of the South and the Players of the South at the Oval.

Resuming today at 78 without loss in reply to Yorkshire's first innings of 299 (Tyler 7-111), Hewitt (201) and Palairet (146) soon collared the bowling and runs came freely. Hewitt was first out, after three hours and a half over the two days, a brilliant innings that included thirty 4's. Palairet went 25 minutes later, with the score on 372, having hit one 6 and nineteen 4's. Then, as though Yorkshire's eight bowlers tried had not taken enough punishment, Hedley added 102 in dashing style, and, just before the time fixed for the drawing of stumps, the innings came to a close with Somerset 293 runs to the good.

Varsity Match First day: 3 July

Incident at Varsity Match: Follow-on 'plot' foiled

From Lord's

THERE were fine conditions at Lord's for the 59th encounter between Oxford and Cambridge, after the early outlook had been doubtful, and a crowd of nigh on 20,000 were present to enjoy the annual spectacle. At lunch-time and in the interval between the innings, the ground presented a brilliant spectacle during the customary promenade. But the talking point of the day - and, no doubt, of many a day to come - was an incident near the end of the Oxford innings, shortly before stumps.

The Light Blues, so determined to make up for last year's shock defeat, started as strong favourites again owing to a brilliant series of performances in their trial matches. They batted first, and although F.S.Jackson (38) got them off to a good start, the other batsmen failed to build on it. Especially disappointing to the Cambridge followers was Ranjitsinhji's early departure for nine. Oxford bowled them out for 182, Berkeley taking five for 38 in 30 overs.

The Oxford batsmen, however, fared not as well. Only L.C.H. Palairet (32), one of the brothers who opened for the Dark Blues, made any runs, H.Levenson-Gower and C.B.Fry, among others, being dismissed for a mere handful. When the last man came in to bat, Oxford, on 95, needed eight runs to save the follow-on. After scoring three of these, the two batsmen were seen to confer between the wickets.

It seemed uncertain whether they wished to secure the follow-on by bringing the innings to a close, or whether the Cambridge bowlers were purposefully careless in their deliveries in order to secure their innings for tomorrow. At all events, Wells bowled a no-ball and a wide, each of which went to the boundary for 4, running the Oxford total passed the number required. The last wicket fell without further addition, and Oxford were all out for 106, Wells taking five for 39.

[Cambridge won by 266 in two days, but the follow-on controversy continued - there were unprecedented scenes at the 1896 Varsity match following a similar incident - but the optional follow-on did not become law until 1900.]

Tour match Oxford & Cambridge (P & P) v Australians: 2 August

Australians continue their batting display: Record taken to 843

From Portsmouth

THE phenomenal scoring by the Australians during the first two days' play at Portsmouth, when they ran up the record total in first-class cricket of 805 runs for the loss of eight wickets, caused increasing interest to be taken in today's proceedings. Instead of declaring their innings closed, as was expected, they went on batting, presumably with the intention of beating the highest authenticated score known to have been made in any cricket match, namely, the 920 by the Orleans Club against Rickling Green in 1882.

William Bruce: 191 for Australians.

In this attempt, the visitors failed, as only 38 runs were added to the overnight score before the venture came to a termination for the total of 843. There had been little chance of bowling the opposition out twice as the wicket continued to wear well, and, although Turner and Giffen ran through them once for 191, stumps were finally drawn with the Universities Past & Present on 82 for one in their second innings.

The new innings total is only the second 800 in the history of first-class cricket, beating by 40 runs the record of 803 set by the Non-Smokers against the Smokers at East Melbourne in 1887. Bruce (191), Alec Bannerman (133) and Trumble (106) scored hundreds, and there were five other fifties - a record eight in the innings.

1893

3 Jun Frank Shacklock (Notts) takes 4 wickets in 4 balls v Somerset at Nottingham.

22 Jun C.W.Wright becomes the 4th player in first-class cricket out 'handled the ball', playing for Notts v Glos at Bristol.

17-19 Jul Shrewsbury (106 and 81) becomes the first player to reach 1,000 runs in Tests, for England in the draw against Australia at Lord's; Stoddart, captain in place of the absent Grace, makes the first declaration of a Test innings (previously not permitted); and Henry Graham (107) makes a match-saving hundred in 140min on his Test début, the first for an Australian at Lord's.

15 Aug An unusual hat-trick, all stumped, by W.H.Brain off the bowling of C.L.Townsend, is performed for Glos v Somerset at Cheltenham.

23 Aug Yorks win their first official County Championship, while Surrey slip to 5th place.

24-26 Aug Fast bowler Tom Richardson, replacing his injured Surrey team-mate Lockwood, takes 10-156 on his Test début, and the draw gives England the rubber, their fifth consecutive winning series at home.

Richardson: Test début.

TEST SERIES

Australia in England
E 1, D 2

Second Test Third day: 16 August

Briggs and Lockwood bowl England to victory: Australians beaten by innings

From the Oval

Australia put up much sterner resistance today in their second innings, but in the end Briggs and Lockwood repeated their first-innings performances with five and four wickets again, respectively, to earn England victory by an innings and 43 runs. Thus England go one up in the rubber with one to play.

Resuming on 158 for two, the Australians showed something like their true form. Instead of only staying in an hour and three-quarters for 91, as in the first innings, they remained at the wickets for four hours and 20 minutes, and scored during that time with such extraordinary rapidity that before the last wicket fell they had put together the fine total of 349 - giving an average of 80 runs per hour. Trott (92), Giffen (53), Bannerman (55) and Graham (42) were the most successful batsmen, and Lyons (31) hit in a fashion just after the Oval crowd's heart. But Briggs went through the last three men in a way that belied the proud Australian assertion that their eleven has no tail.

The England eleven was an exceptionally strong one, and they never looked back after the partnership between Stoddart (83) and Grace (68) put on 151 for the first wicket. Four other fifties followed, including F.S.Jackson's maiden century (103) for England. Then after taking their score yesterday to 483, they dismissed Australia for a meagre 91, Briggs taking five for 34, Lockwood four for 37. And although this pair had to work harder for their wickets today, they emerged at the end with splendid match figures - Briggs 10 for 148, Lockwood eight for 133.

1894

22 May South Africa begin their first tour of England (at Sheffield Park), but it is not first-class. It will be 13 years before they play a Test in England.

29 Dec Fast bowler Arthur Coningham (Australia) becomes the first bowler to take a wicket with his first ball in Test cricket, dismissing Archie MacLaren (ct Trott) with the first ball of the 2nd Test against England, at Melbourne. He takes 2-17 in the innings (and never takes another Test wicket nor plays in another Test).

Inter-county match Notts v Warwicks: 3 May

Warwicks make good impression: Hill 100 on first-class début

From Trent Bridge

THE fact that Warwickshire, by recent action of the M.C.C., have with others of last season's second-class counties been practically admitted into the ranks of the first-class caused exceptional interest to be taken in their match at Nottingham, which commenced today.

The home team were without such sterling cricketers as Shrewsbury, Gunn, Barnes and Sherwin, and the visitors were seen to decided advantage. Going in at noon on a true though slow wicket, they kept possession during the whole of the time available for play, and scored 282 for the loss of eight wickets.

The feature of the cricket was the brilliant form displayed by J.K.Hill, who, on his first appearance at this level, batted for three hours and a half and was still not out at the close with a grand 103 to his credit. He was sixth in and, although he started slowly, his play subsequently was of a masterly character. Hill is the first Warwickshire batsman to score a hundred against Notts, and the achievement so early in the season is one to be proud of. The Notts bowling was also thoroughly collared by both W.Quaife and Law, the latter contributing a well-played 53.

[Hill went on to make 139 not out. Warwicks became one of the five new counties admitted to the Championship the following season, when they finished a creditable equal 6th.]

First Test Sixth day: 20 December

Brilliant England victory by 10 runs after follow-on: Rain came at right time

Daily Telegraph Editorial

Rarely, if ever, has a more exciting contest been fought in the cricket field than that between Mr Stoddart's team of Englishmen and a representative Eleven of Australians, which has just resulted in a hard-won victory for the former side. It is a triumph of which the visitors have every reason to be proud, because it was one obtained by sheer dogged refusal to acknowledge that they were beaten, and by the indomitable pluck with which they played an almost desperate game.

The weather, no doubt, finally put victory within their grasp. All the earlier part of the match had taken place under brilliant skies and on a faultless wicket, and the Sydney cricketing ground is famous for the unrivalled pitches which it affords. It was just at the close of the struggle, and when the match looked a certainty for the Australians, that a night of heavy rain, followed by a bright sun in the morning, changed the whole aspect of affairs. The wicket became extremely difficult, so that even such a player as Giffen could do nothing in the way of scoring; and there are not two more dangerous bowlers under such conditions of turf than Peel and Briggs. The result was a most remarkable collapse on the part of the Australians, and their defeat by the very narrow margin of ten runs.

In the state of the weather, the proverbial 'luck' of cricket made its appearance in this particular game; but the credit of the English team is not thereby diminished. It was the splendid uphill fight that they made in their second innings, under the depressing influence of a 'follow-on,' that rendered it possible for them to take advantage of the changed conditions. Apart from the grand finish, the match is worthy of remembrance for at least two other good reasons: The total runs secured, 2,514, is a new record, and the large score, 586, compiled by the Colonials [especially after losing their first three wickets for twenty-one] in their first venture in the field.... Hearty congratulations over a splendidly-contested match are due to both sides in this historic cricketing tourney.

Left-arm spinner Bobby Peel: 8 wickets in match.

From Reuter's Special Service, in Sydney: Australia resumed on a bright and sunny morning needing 64 runs to win, having made 113 for two with little trouble before the close yesterday evening. But the pitch had suffered in consequence of the heavy rain that fell during the night. The wicket was sticky and was cut through in the first 20 minutes. Later in the day it became quite unplayable.

Darling (53) and Giffen (41) did not add many to their overnight score. On their dismissal, the batting of the home team utterly collapsed against the bowling of Peel and Briggs. Intense excitement prevailed until the last wicket fell at 166 and it was seen that the Englishmen had won by 10 runs.

Scores: Australia 586 (Gregory 201, Giffen 161, Iredale 81, Blackham 74; Richardson 5-181) & 166 (Darling 53; Peel 6-67, Briggs 3-25), England 325 (Ward 75, Briggs 57; Giffen 4-75) & 437 (Ward 117, Brown 53; Giffen 4-164).

[This was the first Test to be won by a side following on. It would not happen again until England repeated the feat over Australia in 1981 at Headingley.]

Inter-county match
Surrey v Essex: 18 June

Richardson terrorises Essex: 10 for 45 in first innings

From the Oval

BECAUSE of the showers, only 70 minutes' play was possible at the Oval, but it was long enough for Tom Richardson to bowl Essex out for the moderate total of 72. The pitch was slow after overnight rain, and the England fast bowler proved a terror to the visitors and took all 10 wickets for a personal cost of 45 in 15.3 overs.

Essex put their full strength into the match, but only Burrell (31) and Mead reached double figures. Surrey have a strong side, even without Key, Read and Lockwood. Stumps were finally drawn at half-past five, with the rain set in.

Fifth Test Final day: 6 Mar

Great English victory: Hard-fought rubber won 3-2

From Reuter's Special Service, in Melbourne

At a quarter past four this afternoon the great match between Mr Stoddart's Eleven and the All Australia team ended in a victory for the Englishmen by six wickets. Australia fought back from two matches down to level the series at two-all, and this was the deciding match – the 'match of the century'.

To win, England needed to score 297 in their second innings, of which total they scored 28 yesterday for the loss of Brockwell. They made a disastrous start this morning when Henry Trott bowled Stoddart first ball. But Yorkshire's Jack Brown came in to join Ward in the middle, and England had her two heroes. Brown took 11 off Giffen's first over and continued to hit the bowling to every part of the field. He was out at 238 after making 140 memorable runs. Ward departed at 278 for an invaluable 93. MacLaren, the hero of the first innings, and Peel hit off the last few runs.

Scores: Australia 414 (Darling 74, Gregory 70, Giffen 57, Lyons 55) & 267 (Giffen 51; Richardson 6-104), England 385 (MacLaren 120, Peel 73, Stoddart 68) & 298-4 (Brown 140, Ward 93).

[Brown's innings included the fastest 50 and 100 in Tests, and his 3rd-wicket stand of 210 with Ward was a record for any wicket in Tests.]

County Championship Glos v Somerset: 17 May

W.G.Grace scores his 100th century

From Bristol

TODAY will long live in the memory of cricketers as the day upon which W.G.Grace, the greatest exponent of the Summer pastime that the world has ever seen, accomplished the remarkable performance of scoring his 100th 'century' in first-class matches. To a man only two months short of his 47th birthday the feat is nothing short of marvellous.

He has done many wonderful things during his career as a cricketer, which extends over a period of 31 years, but at no time in his life has he displayed a better command over the ball than in the compilation of his magnificent innings of 288 at Bristol today. This is the tenth score of 200 or more he has made, although the last time he scored a double hundred was seven years ago.

Overnight, Gloucester were 58 for two in reply to Somerset's first-innings score of 303, with Grace on 38 and

The Champion: Still magnificent at 47.

Townsend 20. On resuming, the pair treated the spectators to a splendid display. Grace's progress was watched with the greatest of interest as he approached the hundred mark, and when he had got 98 Woods bowled him an easy ball to leg, which was promptly sent to the boundary amidst deafening cheers from the crowd.

Townsend went for a highly meritorious 95, having stayed with his captain while 223 runs were added. Grace was at the wickets for five hours and a half, hitting thirty-eight 4's, and at no time did he give anything like a chance until he was caught at extra mid-off for 288 made out of 463.

County Championship Middlesex v Glos: 30 May

Another milestone for 'W.G.': 1,000 runs in May

From Lord's

THE opening day's play at Lord's was notable for the climax of what has been another unique and remarkable performance from 'the Champion', W.G.Grace. It saw the completion of 1,000 runs by W.G. in first-class matches, a feat that has never before been accomplished by any batsman in the first month of the season.

Grace made his 169 in five hours and ten minutes, hitting twenty-one 4's, his timing and placing of the ball as accurate as ever. He needed 153 to complete his 1,000, and when within four of that number he received a 'long hop' on the leg side from Nepean, which he promptly dispatched to the boundary. The majority of spectators were aware of the achievement, and all round the ground they rose from their seats and cheered heartily.

The Champion performed his feat in 22 days, in ten innings from the 9th to the 30th of May at an average of 112.88, viz: 13, 103, 18, 25, 288, 52, 257, 73 not, 18, 169.

1895

29 Jan R.S.Lucas's team begins the first English tour of the West Indies.

16-17 May Notts compile 726 v Sussex at Nottingham, a new (but short-lived) county first-class record.

20 May Fred 'Nutty' Martin, left-arm medium, takes 4 wickets in 4 balls for M.C.C. v Derby at Lord's.

3 Jun Fast bowler Henry Pickett takes all 10-32 for Essex v Leics at Leyton.

18 Jun Fast bowler Arthur Mold takes 4 wickets in 4 balls for Lancs v Notts at Nottingham.

6 Jul H.K.Foster makes 121 out of 159 runs while at the wicket for Cambridge in Varsity match.

27 Jul Off-break bowler Walter Mead takes 17-119 (8-67, 9-52) for Essex v Hants at Southampton.

23 Aug Left-arm slow bowler Edwin Tyler takes all 10-49 for Somerset v Surrey at Taunton.

2-3 Sep Tom Richardson takes 15-155 (6-85, 9-70) for Surrey v Hants at the Oval and Surrey clinch their 5th official Championship in the first 6 seasons.

TEST SERIES

England in Australia
E 3, A 2

County Championship Somerset v Lancs: 16 July

MacLaren 424, Lancs 801: A day of records

From Taunton

After the huge score of 555 for three wickets made by Lancashire yesterday, with Archie MacLaren unbeaten on 289, it is perhaps not surprising that the records began to tumble today.

First and foremost, MacLaren scored the first 400 in first-class cricket. His 424 runs, made in seven hours and 50 minutes at the wickets, and containing one 6 (out of the ground) and sixty-two 4's, beat by 80 the previous record set by W.G. Grace in 1876 playing for M.C.C. against Kent. It also beat Grace's county record of 318 not out set in the same year, for Gloucester against Yorkshire. It is strange to relate that, in a season when Grace made his 100th 100 and 1,000 runs in May, he has also lost two of his oldest records.

This wonderful compilation by the young Lancashire amateur is even more remarkable when it is considered that he is not yet 24. When the Northerners' venture closed at 801, another record had been passed, as this is the highest innings total ever obtained in first-class county cricket, beating the 726 made by Notts at the beginning of the season.

Archie MacLaren: First 400.

1896

15 Feb England dismiss South Africa for 30 at Port Elizabeth in the 1st Test, a record low in Test cricket, Lohmann taking a record 8-7 (15-45 in match) and England winning by 288 runs.

2 Mar Lohmann takes 9-28 in S.Africa's 1st innings at Johannesburg in the 2nd Test, a record innings analysis in Test cricket. (He later finished with 35 wickets from the 3-match series at an average of 5.80.)

22 Jun In the Lord's Test, Ernie Jones's first ball to W.G., a short-pitched delivery that lifts sharply, passes through the great man's beard, deceiving the keeper, and goes through to the boundary - or so the story goes.

2-4 Jul Another follow-on altercation at the Varsity Match, more bitter than that of 1893, as Cambridge prevent Oxford going in again, but the Dark Blues, needing 330, win a famous 4-wicket victory as G.O.Smith makes his legendary 132.

G.O.Smith: Dark Blue hero.

18 Jul George Giffen (Aus) reaches 1,000 runs and 100 wickets in Tests on the same day, against England at Manchester. Ranji scores 113 (41 to 154) before lunch.

3-4 Aug W.G. scores 301 for Glos v Sussex at Bristol, at the age of 48.

10-11 Aug G.Davidson makes 274 for Derby v Lancs at Manchester, the highest first-class maiden 100.

TEST SERIES

England in South Africa
England 3
Australia in England
E 2, A 1

Tourist match M.C.C. v Australians: 11 June

M.C.C. avenge rout of '78: Australians all out for 18

By a Spectator, at Lord's

FEW of the 12,000 spectators who today witnessed the cricket at Lord's will forget the incidents attending one of the most sensational afternoons ever spent on the famous enclosure at St. John's-wood. Many will recall a similar event in 1878, when Spofforth and Boyle of the first Australian team bowled the M.C.C. out for 19. Now the tables are turned, and the M.C.C. have routed the Australians for one fewer.

There was no hint of the drama to come when W.G. Grace's side went in this morning on a wicket affected by rain and compiled 219. But Hearne had the Australians in immediate trouble at 18 for 3. W.G. then put on Dick Pougher for Attewell and not another run was scored. The medium-pace Pougher (Leics) took five wickets for nought in three overs, Hearne four for four in 11, Giffen being absent ill.

All out for 18! And this the side that have carried all before them, winning match after match with so much to spare, including comprehensive defeats of Yorkshire and Lancashire.

When the Australians, following on, went in again, they lost two wickets to Hearne for 8, but by the close had recovered slightly to 25 for two.

[An 8th-wicket stand of 112 by Darling (76) and Eady (42) averted another débâcle but not an innings defeat by 18. Hearne took all 9 wickets (Giffen still absent) for 73 in 50.3 overs. Pougher, 0-33, was never to play a Test against Australia.]

County Championship Warwicks v Yorks: 8 May

Yorkshire's 887 breaks all records

From Birmingham

WARWICKSHIRE spent a second full day in succession leather hunting at Birmingham while Yorkshire broke all records in putting together their innings of 887. This is the highest total ever made in first-class cricket, the previous best being 843, by the Australians against the Universities Past & Present in 1893, and it is a considerable improvement on Lancashire's county record of 801 made last July.

Perhaps the most remarkable thing about Yorkshire's achievement is that they added 435 today for the last three wickets. The overnight batsmen, Peel and Lord Hawke, put on 292, a new first-class record for the 8th wicket.

Scorers, in scorecard order: F.S.Jackson 117, Tunnicliffe 28, Brown 23, Denton 6, Moorhouse 72, Wainwright 126, Peel 210 not out, F.W.Milligan 34, Lord Hawke 166, Hirst 85, Hunter 5, Extras 15.

First Test Second day: 23 June

Australia come fighting back: Record 4th-wicket stand

From our cricket reporter, at Lord's

After yesterday had seen W.G., the grand old man of cricket, make his 1,000th run in international matches, today was Australia's day. Going into bat facing a deficit of 239 after being tumbled out for 53 in their first innings, they made a disastrous start, losing two wickets with but three runs on the board. They stumbled to 62 for three before Richardson bowled Giffen for 32. At this critical juncture Gregory came out to join his captain, Trott, and there followed the highest stand ever made in international cricket.

Before they were parted, these young Colonists, who had no idea what it was to be beaten, put on 221 runs for the fourth wicket. Trott, with a duck's-egg yesterday, played a brilliant innings, against the same bowling, of 143; Gregory, toiling by his side through the burden and heat of the day, found himself with 103 runs to his credit before he was caught by Lohmann off Hearne. Australia added only another 64 for their last six wickets and it left England with 109 to get.

[England, at one stage 42-3, won the next day by 6 wickets.]

Ranji: 154 not out on Test début.

Second Test Third day: 18 July

Australia square rubber: Ranjitsinhji and Richardson heroics in vain

From Manchester

AFTER one of the grandest finishes in cricket, Australia beat England by three wickets at Old Trafford today to square the series one-all, with one match to play. The defeat was made more bearable to England for the wonderful performances with bat and ball respectively, of K.S. Ranjitsinhji, who made a brilliant, unbeaten 154 on his first appearance for England, and Tom Richardson, surely the best bowler in the world today, who took six of the seven Australian second-innings wickets to fall for 76.

Two finer displays than those of the Indian Prince and the Surrey professional were never seen, and added to their first-innings exploits - 62 runs and seven wickets for 168, respectively - it is ironic that *[contd. page 45 column 1]* such deeds should in the end go unrewarded.

However, Australia have won. They made the 125 runs asked of them, but what a struggle it was: four wickets down for 45, seven for 100, before Trumble and Kelly saw them home. And so to the Oval.

['Ranji', nearly 24, made his début for England after for some time being considered ineligible by the authorities. He was the first Indian to play Test cricket. He topped the national averages this season with 2,780 runs (avge 57.91).]

1897

9 Aug Robert Abel (173) and Bill Brockwell (225) put on 379 for Surrey v Hants at the Oval, beating by 1 run the 1st-wicket record set by Brown and Tunnicliffe in July.

11 Aug S.H.Day, 18, makes 101 not out on his first-class début for Kent v Glos at Cheltenham while still at school.

16 Dec Charlie McLeod (Aus) is run out in the 1st Test after being 'bowled' by a no-ball, not hearing the umpire's call because of deafness.

Third Test Third day: 12 August

Peel 6-23 and Hearne 4-19, England bowlers clinch rubber: Sensational victory in deciding match:

From the Oval

FUTURE historians of our national game will rarely have to record so remarkable a match as the final encounter of the season of 1896 between England and Australia, which terminated today at the Oval in a triumph for the Old Country by the substantial margin of 66 runs. Given the weather conditions, the fact that the contest was played to a finish is remarkable in itself. Yet, in rather less than nine hours, four innings were completed and 40 batsmen were dismissed for 392 runs.

At the resumption of play this morning, England appeared to have the worst of the matter, with just 60 on the board - 86 runs on - and five wickets down. But when Trumble (6-30, 12-89 in the match) and McKibbin claimed the remainder of England's wickets in half an hour for the addition of only 24 runs, the manner in which they were making the ball do the most extraordinary of things did not bode well for the chances of their own batsmen.

And so it proved. Hearne, who claimed the first three wickets without cost to himself, and Peel were practically unplayable. Soon seven wickets were down for 14, and despite a plucky effort by last man McKibbin (16), the Colonials were all out for 44. Peel took six for 23 (8-53 in the match), Hearne 4 for 19 (10-60).

Gilbert Jessop: Wonderful hitting.

Gentlemen v Players: 14 July

Victory for Players but Jessop gives the crowd an afternoon to remember

From Lord's

ANOTHER memorable Gentleman v Players match at Lord's has ended, this time in victory for the Players. The startling part of today's cricket came after luncheon. Despite Grace's 66 - an innings that would have done him credit twenty years ago - the Gentlemen had six wickets down at two o'clock for 136, and as they still wanted 216 runs to win it seemed as if the finish of the match would be tameness itself.

In thinking thus, however, one reckoned without G.L. Jessop. That delightful young hitter proved to be in his most vigorous and aggressive mood. To him the reputation of a bowler is as nothing. He reached his 50 in 23 minutes, and in 35 minutes he scored 67 runs out of 83, hitting Richardson, J.T.Hearne and Hayward as though they had been the harmless bowlers of a college eleven.

It was an extraordinary innings. One can scarcely think of another batsman who could have played it. He lashed out at nearly every ball. Long hops, half volleys and yorkers were treated in an impartial manner that fairly delighted the onlookers. His 67 was made while 83 runs were being scored. It was not a story book ending, though, for the Gentlemen - they lost by 78 runs - but for the crowd of 9,000 it was an afternoon they will never forget.

County Championship
Yorks v Sussex: 13 July

Brown's 311 is Yorkshire record: Big stand with Tunnicliffe

From Sheffield

THE Tykes kept Sussex in the field all day today as they increased their lead to over 400 runs, and they still have five wickets left. Brown and Tunnicliffe, the opening batsmen, took their overnight partnership, which stood at 216, to 378 before they were parted. This is a new first-wicket record in all of first-class cricket, surpassing the 346 made against the county by the Somerset pair Palairet and Hewitt in 1892.

After Tunnicliffe's dismissal for 147, Brown, who had scored much faster than his partner, went on to make 311, a new Yorkshire record. At the close, Yorkshire had taken their score to 681, with Wainwright still there on 104.

[Yorks declared on their overnight score and won by an innings and 307 runs.]

First Test Second day: 14 December

Grand British batting: Ranjitsinhji's pluck - a century under difficulties

From Sydney

Not even the most enthusiastic admirers of Mr Stoddart's eleven could have been prepared for what happened today at Sydney. Everyone expected a substantial addition to the overnight score of 337 for five wickets, but a total of 551 exceeded all anticipation. This is the highest total ever obtained by England in a test[1] match.

The triumph of the team, however, did not end with their own innings, Ranjitsinhji's wonderful batting being followed up in such style by Richardson, Hearne and Briggs that in the latter part of the afternoon five of the best Australian wickets went down for 86 runs.

For Ranjitsinhji, today was a day of days. By making 175, he beat the best individual score ever before hit for England against Australia in a test match, that of 173 by Stoddart at Melbourne on the last tour. It was a superb, chanceless innings, climaxed - when the last man, Richardson, joined him - with 52 out of 74 made in half an hour, and all under the handicap of his illness, which needed medical treatment at the luncheon interval today.

Ranjitsinhji has quite won the hearts of the Australian public. Had he been playing today for Australia, he could not have had a more enthusiastic reception, and nothing is being talked about in Sydney tonight except his innings.

[England won by 9 wickets.]

[1] So-called in reports for the first time.

1898

4 Jan Ernie Jones (Aus) is the first bowler to be no-balled for throwing in a Test, at Melbourne.

14 Jan Joe Darling (178) reaches his 100 with the first 6 (ball hit out of ground) in Test cricket, at Adelaide in 3rd Test.

29-31 Jan Clem Hill (188) hits a Test record 182 on 1st day at Melbourne v England, and, after Australia are 58-6, puts on 165 with Trumble (46), a Test record for the 7th wicket which turns the match.

5-11 Feb 1,739 runs are scored in the NSW v Stoddart's XI match, a first-class record aggregate.

1 Mar Tom Richardson takes 8-94 in Australia's 1st innings at Sydney in the last Test.

2 Mar Darling (160) hits 100 in 91min at Sydney, the fastest yet against England and his 3rd 100 of the series.

19 Aug Although 88 runs short of the Peel/Hawke first-class record for the 8th wicket, the 204 of Tom Hayward (315 not) and Len Braund (85) for Surrey v Lancs at the Oval is made in 70min.

TEST SERIES

England in Australia
A 4, E 1

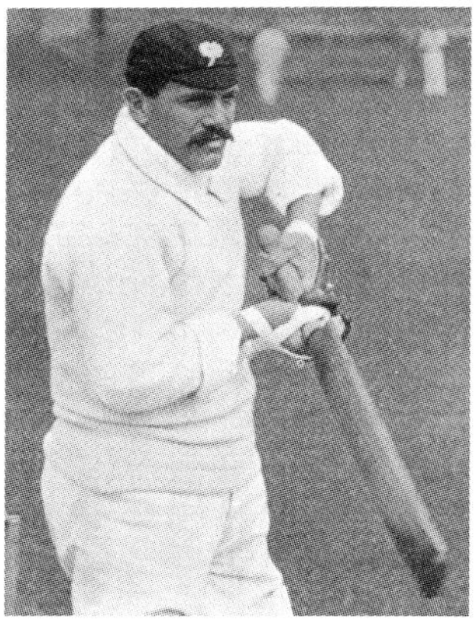

Brown (top) and Tunnicliffe: Stand breaks all records.

Fourth Test Fourth day: 2 February

Another Colonial victory: Australia take winning 3-1 lead in rubber

From Melbourne

NOTHING tamer could well be imagined than the finish at Melbourne today of the fourth test match. England's three outstanding wickets added only a paltry 9 runs to the overnight score of 254, and the Australians were left with 115 to get, which, with the pitch still in first-rate order, they made for an eight-wickets victory, at the same time winning the rubber.

The honours are with the Australians; in three matches out of four their superiority in both batting and bowling has been incontestable. For England the disappointment is extreme, especially after their convincing victory in the first test, when some Australian critics took quite a doleful tone as to the prospects of their own side. If the trip ended today, only MacLaren and Ranjitsinhji of Mr Stoddart's team would be able to look back on it with complete satisfaction.

[After a good start, England lost the last Test, too, by 6 wickets.]

Gentlemen v Players: 20 July

Tribute to the Champion

From Lord's

AT one time this afternoon the conclusion of the match at Lord's threatened to be so lame that a good many left the ground without waiting for the actual finish. When they learn what afterwards happened, they will bitterly regret their departure.

As everyone knows, the second annual Gentlemen and Players match took on a special aspect when it was arranged to start on Mr W.G.Grace's 50th birthday. As a result, the match has been a double attraction - the normal interest taken in one of the biggest fixtures of the cricketing season, combined with a national enthusiasm for the Champion, who for the best part of half a century has shown to his admiring compatriots with what unremitting zeal, energy and success the great game can be played. W.G. duly led the Gentlemen out on Monday, his birthday, bowled 12 overs and took a wicket as the Players compiled 335, and then yesterday opened for the Gentlemen and made 43, the third best score, in their reply of 303. But lameness and a hand bruised by a ball from Haigh meant that he could not field today.

The Gentlemen started their second innings at a few minutes past four, needing 296 to win. Though it had been arranged to play on till seven if necessary, the task was obviously impossible. The Old Man changed the batting order, because his hand was so bad that he did not want to go in unless it was absolutely necessary. And, thanks largely to the bowling of J.T. Hearne, it became so.

Hearne, who had taken 5 for 87 in the first innings, was even more deadly this time and W.G. found himself coming in at No.9 an hour and three-quarters after the start of the innings, and joined moments later by the last man, C.J.Kortright, with the score at 80 for nine. Between the two of them, they very nearly saved the match. Shrewsbury tried everything - Lockwood, Storer, Alec Hearne, Haigh, J.T.Hearne and Abel all had a spell with the ball. But it was not until Lockwood came back at the Pavilion end at 158 that he got Kortright magnificently caught by Haigh at cover-point for 46.

The Players thus won the match at two minutes before seven by 137 runs, Hearne six for 65. And as the Champion came off the field, 31 not out, 50 not out in years, he enjoyed a reception the like of which even he had rarely received before.

County Championship Derby v Yorks: 18 August

Brown and Tunnicliffe in 500 stand: Still there at the close

From Chesterfield

THE opening day's play in this match will undoubtedly stand for some time to come as one of the most memorable in the annals of the game. During the day an extraordinary record was established by Brown and Tunnicliffe, who opened the batting for Yorkshire on a good and fast wicket. The pair kept up their wickets throughout the whole of the day, and at the close had between them compiled the huge total of 503. No partnership in first-class cricket had even reached 400 before.

Prior to today the best stand in a first-class match, irrespective of wicket, stood to the credit of Gunn and Shrewsbury, who made 398 for the second wicket for Notts against Sussex in 1890. The previous best stand for the first wicket was claimed by Abel and Brockwell, who made 379 for Surrey against Hampshire at the Oval last August, beating Brown and Tunnicliffe's 378 made a month earlier

Today's display of hitting was a brilliant one, and although Brown gave four difficult chances, they scarcely detract from his grand efforts in keeping up his wicket all day for 270. Tunnicliffe's 214 has so far been made with only one fault. The receipts for the day amounted to £175.

[The stand reached 554 before Tunnicliffe was first out for 243, made in 5hr 5min and including 48 4's. Brown, acting under instructions, hit down his wicket when he had made 300, 5min later, having also hit 48 4's. The innings closed at 662 and Yorks won by an innings and 387.]

County Championship Surrey v Somerset: 30 May

High scoring at the Oval: Abel 357 not out, Surrey 811

From the Oval

AT the close yesterday, Surrey had made 495 for five, and they increased this today to 811. But for the failure of the tail, they might have passed the Yorkshire record of 887. Abel, who yesterday took part in a record first-class stand of 334 with Hayward (158) for the fourth wicket, took his overnight score of 227 to 357, when he ran out of partners, having carried his bat right through the Surrey innings. Only MacLaren's 424 in all of first-class cricket is higher. Surrey's and Abel's innings lasted 8hr 35min, and he hit a 6, seven 5's and thirty-eight 4's. At the close, Somerset were 165 for nine.

[Surrey won by an innings and 379 runs.]

County Championship Middlesex v Kent: 12 June

Middlesex 285 after losing 9 for 55: Record last-wicket stand

From Lord's

THERE were two sensations at Lord's today. First, the Middlesex batting - the same players who enjoyed the recent triumphs over Yorkshire and Sussex - collapsed as nine wickets went down for 55. And then, the Nos.9 and 11 defied all of Kent's bowlers for two hours and a half, during which time they put on 230 runs

This is a new 10th wicket record in first-class cricket, easily beating the 173 of Briggs and Pilling for Lancashire in 1885.

The two batsmen who so distinguished themselves were the local amateur Richard Nicholls, who came in when the score was 50 and hit 154, and Bill Roche, the Anglo-Australian professional, who arrived 15 minutes afterwards and was undefeated with 74. Kent were 75 for four at stumps.

[Middlesex won by 118 runs.]

Third Test Second day: 30 June

Hearne's test hat trick: Briggs unable to resume

From our own correspondent, at Leeds

J.T.Hearne: Test hat-trick.

Whatever the result of this game of fluctuating fortunes, both sides have already done enough for fame. For many a year, people who were at Headingley today will talk about Hearne's 'hat trick' and also about Australia's recovery from an almost impossible position.

The day started dramatically with the news that poor Briggs had been seized with an epileptic fit while he was watching the performance at the Empire Music Hall, and that he was unconscious in hospital. Thus England, 119 for four overnight in reply to Australia's 172, had now only five wickets to fall.

With Quaife and Fry bowled, however, without addition to the score, England were suddenly in trouble. But Hayward (40 not out) and Lilley (55) came to their rescue with a stand of 93 to give England a 48-run lead.

In a similar manner, Australia's innings collapsed dramatically, only to be revived by the later batsmen. Their first wicket went down at 34 and in the very next over, without addition to the score, Hearne achieved his hat-trick, capturing the valuable scalps of Hill, Gregory and Noble with successive balls. When Darling also went, five wickets were down for 39. England seemed to have the match in their hands, but three hours later they found themselves with the task of getting 177 in the last innings. It was Trumper (32) and Kelly (33) who tamed the rampant Hearne and Young, and Trumble (56) and Laver (45) who then put Australia back in the game - all in all, a splendid illustration of the courage that has always characterised Australian cricket.

[Rain prevented any play on the last day. The much-loved Johnny Briggs played little more cricket and died in an asylum in 1902.]

County Championship Surrey v Yorks: 12 August

Abel and Hayward beat their own record: 448 stand for 4th wicket

From the Oval

WHAT was in all senses a remarkable match terminated at the Oval today in a draw. Some 14,000 people witnessed the closing stages, and they will have good cause to remember the astonishing performance of the famous pair of professionals, Hayward and Abel, who had practically saved Surrey yesterday evening by adding 111 to the score at a critical time.

They became associated when the total stood at 58 for three wickets, and actually added 448 runs in six hours, thus eclipsing the fine stand of 340, by Wainwright and Hirst, in the Yorkshire innings of 704. It is the second best on record in first-class cricket, after the 554 of Brown and Tunnicliffe last season, and it beats their own record for the fourth wicket, set only this May.

In practically three full days' play, only one innings was actually completed, 1,255 runs being scored for the loss of but 17 wickets. In all, Abel was batting for 7hr 15min for 193, during which time the total was increased by 500, while Hayward occupied 6 hr 30min in compiling 273.

1899

16 Feb P.F.'Plum' Warner carries his bat for 132 in England's 2nd innings v South Africa at Johannesburg on his Test début, and England win by 32. A.E.Trott, the former Australian Test player also making his England début, takes 9-110 in the match.

1-4 April Jimmy Sinclair (106) makes S.Africa's first Test 100 and takes 6-26 and 3-63 v England at Cape Town, but Haigh (6-11) and Trott (4-19) bowl S.Africa out for 35; England win by 210.

23 May Middlesex (86) beat Somerset (35 and 44) in a day, at Lord's, after 3hr 5min play, the shortest first-class match on record.

23-27 Jun At Clifton College, in a junior house match, 13-year-old English schoolboy Arthur Collins carries his bat for a world record 628 (out of 836) for Clark's House v North Town (and then takes 7-33 and 4-30 as his side win by an innings and 688).

21 Jul Major R.M.Poore (304) and E.G.Wynyard (225) add 411 for Hants v Somerset at Taunton, a new first-class record for the 6th wicket (2nd highest for any wicket), Hants (672-7) making their highest score.

27-29 Jul W.L.(140 & 172 not) and R.E.Foster (134 & 101 not), two of seven brothers to play for Worcs, each hit two 100s in the same match, albeit against a weak Hants attack, but a unique achievement, nevertheless - and in Worcester's first season as a first-class county.

30 Aug Prince Ranjitsinhji (Sussex & England), playing against Hants at Portsmouth, scores his 3,000th run, the first time this has ever been done in one season. (He goes on to 3,159.)

TEST SERIES

England in South Africa
England 2
Australia in England
A 1, D 4

The early 1900s

The first decade of the 20th century marked the latter two-thirds of a period in English cricket often referred to as the 'Golden Age'. In the first years of the century the England side could choose batsmen of the calibre of MacLaren, C.B.Fry, Ranji, Tom Hayward, Abel, R.E.Foster, J.T.Tyldesley and latterly Hobbs, mighty all-rounders such as Hirst, Jessop, Rhodes, and Jackson, and bowlers Sydney Barnes - perhaps the greatest - Charlie Blythe and latterly F.R.Foster. Yet during the decade Australia were more than a match for them, and an analysis of the Test series played up to the war shows the rivals winning four rubbers each and Australia edging the Tests 15 to 14.

There were two main reasons for this. The first was a revival of the domestic game in Australia with its reorganisation into district cricket, which prevented all the best players falling into the hands of a few strong clubs and made cricket more competitive. The second was the presence in the Australian side of, among others, two great batsmen - Clem Hill and Victor Trumper. There are those who rate Trumper the greatest of all Australian batsmen, citing, in comparisons with Bradman, his ability to make big scores on even the worst wickets. There is no doubting Trumper was a genius. He was also wonderful to watch, an attacking player of consummate grace and skill, modest to a degree, and a popular hero in England as well as in his own country. Hill, a left-hander, was also an attacking player, a record-breaking batsman, at the peak of his skills at the turn of the century.

In truth, Australia was having its own Golden Age - Monty Noble, Warwick Armstrong, Joe Darling - all great captains, the first two outstanding all-rounders, Charles Macartney, another great batsman, and bowlers such as Hugh Trumble and 'Tibby' Cotter.

When England won back the Ashes in the 1903-04 series, it was their first winning rubber since 1896, under Grace. Four rubbers in succession Australia had won, three of them under the captaincy of Darling. Noble was to lead Australia to two further series wins in the first decade of the century, before Johnny Douglas, standing in for the sick 'Plum' Warner, skippered England to success on the 1911-12 tour, when England for the first time won four Tests. A rugged all-rounder and former Olympic boxing champion, he could defend obstinately at the crease and in Australia his initials were converted to reflect this characteristic - 'Johnny Won't Hit Today'.

In 1912 in England, a Triangular Tournament for the three Test-playing countries was staged for the first - and last - time. It was not a success for various reasons, among them the weakness of the South African side and the poor English summer. The Australians were also weakened by a domestic dispute that left them without six leading players, including Trumper, Hill, Armstrong and Sep Carter, their leading wicket-keeper, and they succumbed to England in the decisive match at the Oval.

The County Championship was notable for the decline of Surrey, whose only title in the first 20 years of the 1900s (15 seasons) came in 1914, while Yorkshire won it seven times and were only twice out of the first four. Kent had a purple patch in the nine seasons before the War, winning the Championship four times and only once falling below third. Yorkshire were a powerful, all-round side, bristling with great names, from, in the earlier period, the great opening pair Tunnicliffe and Brown, Lord Hawke, who led them to the Championship in 1900-02 - with only two defeats in three seasons - to the supreme all-rounders F.S. Jackson, Rhodes and Hirst. It was an all-rounder, Frank Woolley, who was the cornerstone of the Kent side, and they also had slow-bowler Blythe. Surrey lost several key players at the turn of the century, which even the advent of Jack Hobbs in 1905 could not compensate for.

The Championship was augmented to 16 counties in 1905 with the promotion of Northants, although Worcester withdrew for the 1919 season for financial reasons. After an abortive method of reckoning in 1910, based on the percentage of wins in all matches played, a new method of points scoring was introduced in 1911 - 5 for a win and, in drawn games, 3 for first-innings leaders and 1 for the other side. The 1919 season saw two-day matches and a reversion to the percentage system.

In 1900, 6-ball overs were legalised for all matches in England, and the follow-on became enforceable after 150 runs in a three-day match. Australia made the 8-ball over law in 1918-19.

Of course, the Great War cast a huge shadow over the game, as on every facet of life, towards the end of the first 20 years of the century. Most competitive cricket stopped, and many players were lost in action, including Charlie Blythe and Tibby Cotter.

Yorkshire in 1901: Top (l-r), Wainwright, Whitehead, Rhodes, Hunter; middle, Hirst, E.Smith, Lord Hawke, Mitchell, Tunnicliffe; bottom, Denton, Taylor, Brown.

Scene at the Adelaide Oval in January 1902, on the last day of the third Test, with Trumble and Darling batting for Australia and Jessop making a quick return from cover.

1900

May The 6-ball over replaces the 5-ball over in England.

8 May Yorks (99) beat Worcs (43 & 51) in a day, the first of the season, at Bradford, Rhodes taking 11-36.

19-21 Jul C.B.Fry (Sussex), with 125 and 229 against Surrey, is the first player to make a 100 and a 200 in the same match.

30 Aug Ranji completes his 5th 200 of the season, 220 for Sussex v Kent at Hove.

Tom Hayward: A merry month.

County Championship
Surrey v Glos: 31 May

Hayward emulates W.G.: 1,000 runs in May completed against his old county

From the Oval

WHILE the veteran W.G. Grace was scoring 86 for his London County team at Cambridge against the Light Blues, Tom Hayward was emulating the Champion's feat accomplished exactly five years ago of scoring a thousand runs by the end of May. The Surrey professional needed only 18 runs and, having evidently set his heart on reaching the 1,000 before the month was out, he played with extreme caution until, after 50 minutes, he reached the target.

His object once attained, however, he promptly altered his methods and played a free, vigorous game. He and Abel (101 not out) put on 201 for the first wicket, in reply to Gloucester's 212, before Hayward was out for 92, at which point stumps were drawn.

Inasmuch as Hayward played an innings of 120 at Easter, he has not quite rivalled W.G.'s feat of scoring 1,000 runs in May itself, but his 1,074 runs by the 31st of May has not been surpassed.

Gentlemen v Players Second day: 17 July

Gentlemen pulverise Players: R.E.Foster's brilliant second 100

From Lord's

MR R.E.FOSTER, by following his 102 not out yesterday with 136 today, became the first batsman, amateur or professional, to make two separate hundreds in a Gentlemen and Players' match. The Oxford captain also equalled a record belonging exclusively to Mr W.G.Grace - that of scoring two centuries in a match for a third time.

On a wicket that was just as good for one eleven as the other, a more one-sided day's play has not often been seen. The Gentlemen did not merely get the best of the game. They simply pulverised the Players, beating them at every point, and putting them in at the end of the afternoon to get just over 500 runs in the last innings.

After bowling the Players out for 136 and obtaining a first-innings lead of 161, the Gentlemen had lost two wickets for 43 when Foster joined C.B.Fry and began his memorable innings. So far during the day, the ball had been too much for the bat, and there was nothing to suggest the wonderful hitting that was to follow. Foster, however, immediately began to score freely, and after reaching his fifty let himself loose and gave a dazzling display. Rhodes, Trott, Mead and John Gunn were all tried, all being treated alike.

Foster did not alter his game in any way as he approached the coveted 100, and when at last, with a 4 to leg off Trott, he settled the matter, there was a demonstration the like of which is not often seen at Lord's. He continued to hit away in tremendous style for ten minutes or more before he was out to a fine catch in the deep field for 136. He batted in all for barely 105 minutes, hitting twenty-four 4's, while the total put on with Fry (who went on to make 72) was 195.

After Foster left, the Gentlemen went hard for more runs, and left the Players to get 501 to win, a target that has only once been achieved before in first-class cricket. At the close, they were 44 for one.

Sheffield Shield South Australia v NSW

Hill's unbeaten 365: New Australian record

From Reuter's, in Adelaide

IN the match against New South Wales at Adelaide today, South Australia ran up a total of 575, to which Clement Hill contributed 365 and took out his bat. This is a record for Australia. Hill gave only two sharp chances in eight and a half hours. The previous best Australian innings was Murdoch's 321 in 1882, and in all first-class cricket only MacLaren's 424 stands above it. Hill's ninth-wicket stand of 232 with Edwin Walkley is a new first-class record, beating the 193 of W.G.Grace and S.A.P.Kitcat made in 1896.

Clem Hill's record antipodean score.

Gentlemen v Players Third day: 18 July

Players win by two wickets: 501 target reached in last over

From Lord's

WITH the result, it seemed, a foregone conclusion, Lord's was only about a third full for the last day of this match to see the Players continue their uphill task of scoring 501 to win. But as soon as Abel joined Brown on 81 for two, it was evident that the Players would not go down without a fight.

In two hours, the partnership produced 165 runs before Abel was out for a splendid 98. They had broken the back of the task and now wanted only 255 more runs to win. Hayward, recovered from the touch of sunstroke that upset him yesterday, continued with Brown to give the Gentlemen a very bad time. They added 102 runs for the fourth wicket before Brown was out at 348. His 163, made in about 4hr 50min, is the highest ever made for the Players against the Gentlemen at Lord's, and only W.G. Grace, with 169 in 1876, has made a higher score in this fixture. Tea was taken - only 153 runs wanted to win.

Hayward lost two more partners before he went himself for 111, to the great relief of the Gentlemen. Now there were three wickets left and 32 to get. At 485, Kortright shot down John Gunn's wicket, and Rhodes joined Trott. Eleven runs were scored in one over from Kortright, a cut for 4 by Trott making the game a tie. It was half-past six, the time for drawing stumps, but Woods decided to bowl another over, without demur from the umpires. Whatever his reasons, it lost him the match, for Rhodes hit a 2 to take the Players to victory - 502 runs in the fourth innings, a remarkable achievement.

County Championship Notts v Yorks: 21 June

Notts dismissed for 13, new county record: Yorks win by innings

From Nottingham

WONDERFUL indeed are the effects of rain upon cricket. At the beginning of the week Notts scored 642 for seven against Sussex at Brighton. Today, at Trent Bridge, the same side (albeit with J.A. Dixon replacing the injured Shrewsbury) were put out by Yorkshire for 13 - the lowest total ever obtained in a county match, and, with one exception (Oxford University, batting one man short, dismissed by M.C.C. for 12 in 1877), the lowest in first-class cricket.

Notts had lost Hallam's wicket for a single yesterday in reply to Yorkshire's 204, and, after a delayed start today, the remaining nine wickets went down in fifty-four minutes. It was, of course, an inglorious display, but Notts had everything against them. The night's rain was followed by a sunny morning, and they had to play Rhodes and Haigh on a wicket made for them. Rhodes, bringing his aggregate of wickets this season up to 103, bowled seven overs and five balls for 4 runs and six wickets, and Haigh seven overs for 8 runs and four wickets.

When Notts followed on, Jones (47) and Iremonger (55 not out) made a brilliant start, putting on 82 runs in an hour for the first wicket and demonstrating that the Yorkshire bowling could be hit. At five o'clock, Notts were only 40 runs to the bad with seven wickets in hand. But suddenly the whole position underwent a change. Hirst, on being put on again, bowled in irresistible form and in nine overs and a ball he took six wickets for 11 runs. The match was finished off just after six, giving Yorks victory by an innings and 18, their tenth in county cricket this season.

County Championship Yorks v Somerset: 16 July

Setback for Yorks: Somerset 549 for 5 after following on

From Headingley

THE Yorkshire eleven have at last met with a very decided check in their triumphant career. They went into the field at Leeds this morning with a first innings lead of 238, having dismissed Somerset for 87, and no one would have been greatly surprised if they had finished off the match in two days. For once, however, their all-conquering bowlers have proved harmless. Somerset began their second innings soon after half-past eleven, and when the time came for drawing stumps they had scored 549 for the loss of only five wickets.

Having regard to the size of the Headingley Ground, the rate of scoring all through this day was astonishing. For sustained brilliancy there can scarcely have been such hitting this season. L.C.H. Palairet (173) and Braund (107), both with duck's-eggs in the first innings, sent up 200 in two hours and put on 222 for the first wicket.

The Yorkshire bowlers, accustomed this year to carry everything before them - never recovered. Braund was brilliant, but at times lucky. Palairet played a magnificent innings, F.A.Phillips (122) was not far behind and S.M.J. Woods made a useful 66.

The unbeaten Yorkshire men will strain every nerve to avoid defeat tomorrow, but whatever the result Somerset have done themselves proud.

[Somerset made 630 (a county record), bowled Yorkshire out for 113 and won by 279. This was Yorkshire's only defeat in 27 Championship matches and they easily retained their title.]

1901

8 Jan Two new records are set by NSW at Sydney against S.Australia - 918, highest first-class score, and 5 separate 100s in innings (Iredale 118, Noble 153, S.E.Gregory 168, Duff 119, Poidevin 140 not).

2 May A 259-188 majority - but not the requisite two-thirds - at the M.C.C. meeting is in favour of a proposed change in the lbw law that would have included any ball that would have hit the wicket, whether or not it pitched in line with the wickets.

11 Jul Fast bowler Arthur Mold (Lancs), who played for England in 1893, is no-balled for throwing 16 times in 10 overs v Somerset at Old Trafford. (County captains later vote to condemn his delivery, and he retires from first-class cricket.)

6 Aug Tom Straw (Worcs) makes his mark in the record books, given out 'obstructing field', only the 4th instance of this rare dismissal in first-class cricket, having previously been the victim of the 2nd instance - both of them against Warwicks. (The 3rd instance occurred this season on 7 June, when Leicester's J.P.Whiteside was dismissed v Lancs, and it did not happen again for 50 years.)

15-16 Aug Essex are dismissed by Yorks (104) for 30 and 41 at Leyton.

13-16 Dec England, led by MacLaren but without Fry, Ranji, Jackson and the Yorks bowlers Hirst and Rhodes (who are refused permission by their county to tour), beat Australia by an innings and 124 runs in the 1st Test, in Sydney, MacLaren scoring 116 and Blythe (7-56), Braund (7-101) and Barnes (6-139) sharing the wickets.

County Championship Sussex v Kent: 30 August

Record day for C.B.Fry: 5th successive 100 and 3,000 runs

From Brighton

C.B.Fry: A memorable day.

THE chief feature of a day's heavy scoring at Brighton was the great achievement of C.B.Fry, who eclipsed all earlier records by scoring his fifth consecutive century - no batsman had before scored more than three hundreds in a row. He also equalled Abel's record of 12 centuries in a season, made last year. And to cap a memorable day for the old Oxonian, he reached his 3,000 runs for the season.

Against Hampshire last Friday week Fry made 106, and his two innings at Brighton last week were 209 against Yorkshire and 149 against Middlesex, equalling the old record of which there have been numerous instances. He then beat the record two days ago with 105 against Surrey at the Oval, and his 140 today against Kent has extended it.

Only team-mate Ranjitsinhji (twice) had made 3,000 runs in a season before, and today we had two rivals striving to emulate him, Fry and, playing for Surrey against Middlesex at the Oval, Abel, who reached the coveted figure half an hour later.

[Fry went on to make a sixth successive 100, 105 for the Rest of England v Yorks at Lord's, his record 13th of the season. Fry's 3,147 runs was 12 fewer than Ranji's record, but Abel beat this with 3,309 runs, and Tyldesley (Lancs) also passed the 3,000 mark.]

1902

14-18 Feb James Kelly makes a record 8 dismissals (all caught) for Australia against England in the 4th Test, at Sydney.

3-5 Jul Australia win Sheffield's only Test by 143 runs (Hill 119 in 145min, Noble 11-103).

24-26 Jul Victor Trumper (104) hits 100 before lunch and with Duff puts on 135 in 78min for the 1st wicket, an Australian record, and, after Lockwood takes 11-76 for England, Trumble (6-53) and Saunders (4-52) gain a famous victory for Australia by 3 runs to win the rubber.

31 Jul-1 Aug M.A.Noble (284) and W.W.Armstrong (172 not) put on 428 for the Australians against Sussex at Hove, the highest ever 6th-wicket stand and the 3rd highest for any wicket

11-14 Oct Playing S.Africa for the first time, Australia have to follow on, but thanks largely to Hill's 142 they easily draw.

21 Oct Armstrong carries his bat for 159, the exact measure of Australia's victory over S.Africa in the 2nd Test, at Johannesburg.

5-6 Nov Bill Howell takes 17-54 for Australians v W.Province.

10 Nov Jimmy Sinclair (104) hits S.Africa's first 100 (in 80min), including 6 6's, in vain effort to avert defeat.

TEST SERIES

England in Australia
A 4, E 1
Australia in England
A 2, E 1, D 2
Australia in South Africa
A 2, D 1

Second Test First day: 1 January

25 wickets fall on first day: Remarkable bowling on both sides

From Reuter's Special Service, in Melbourne

ENGLAND made a sensational start to the second test after MacLaren put Australia in on a rain-affected wicket. Barnes had Trumper caught second ball, and with Blythe had five wickets down for 38 runs.

Australia made a partial recovery but were all out for 112, Barnes taking six for 42, Blythe four for 64. However, England made just as poor a start - five wickets down for 36 - and failed to make any kind of recovery as Noble (7-17) and Trumble (3-38) bowled them out for 61 in 15 overs and 4 balls.

When Australia went in again, the wicket was evidently improving, but Barnes put England right back in the game, taking four wickets, and Australia were 48 for five at the close - albeit with their best batsmen still to come.

[Hill made 99, Duff (coming in at No.10) 104 on his Test début and Armstrong (No.11) 45 not out, the last pair putting on 120, a Test record. Barnes took 7-121, his match figures 13-163. Noble took 6-60 (13-77) and Australia won by 229 runs.]

First Test Second day: 30 May

Australia collapse for 36: Remarkable bowling by Rhodes

From Birmingham

HISTORY was made at Edgbaston's first test today, when the Australians were bowled out for 36, the smallest total ever in a test game. They were batting for 85 minutes, and fell to the Yorkshire bowlers Rhodes (7-17) and Hirst (3-15). Only Trumper (18) scored more than 5.

Much rain had fallen last night, and the start was delayed until a quarter to three. MacLaren allowed the last-wicket pair of Lockwood (52 not) and Rhodes (38 not) to put on another 25 runs before declaring at 376 for nine, their unbroken stand being worth 81 runs.

After following on, Australia were 8 for no wicket in their second innings at the close.

[Rain came to Australia's rescue, and they advanced to 46-2 in what little play was possible.]

County Championship
Yorks v Lancs 20 May

Jackson's all-round performance: War hasn't dulled skills

From Sheffield

F.S.JACKSON has lost no time in proving that he is just as great a cricketer as he was before he had to give up the game for sterner business in South Africa. Last Saturday week he made a hundred for Yorkshire at Leyton, and today he had the chief share in a truly remarkable innings victory over Lancashire at Bramall-lane.

He played very finely on a drying wicket, staying in an hour and a quarter for 33, but though his was the highest score in the game, his success in batting was nothing compared with what he did as a bowler. At the end of Lancashire's first innings (72), he took three wickets for five runs. Then, after inspiring Yorkshire to a 76-run lead, he took five for 8 in their second (54), quite putting Rhodes in the shade.

F.S.Jackson: Back from the wars.

Fifth Test Final day: 13 August

Jessop and Hirst the heroes in epic England win

From the Oval

ENGLAND'S remarkable one-wicket victory over Australia in the last test provided some consolation for the lost rubber. One hears much of the tedium and slowness of present-day cricket, but the game at Manchester last month, where England ought to have won but lost by three runs, and this match at the Oval, where the opposite occurred, will make the year immortal to everyone who loves cricket.

With 263 runs wanted to win, five of the best England wickets fell on a pitch considerably damaged by rain for the wretched total of 48. Then the sound play of F.S.Jackson, who made 49, and the hurricane hitting of Gilbert Jessop in a wonderful innings of 104 (out of 139) put England back into the game with a stand of 109. But even after Jessop left, 76 more runs were required with only three wickets to go. The credit for winning the match belonged finally to Hirst, whose unbeaten innings of 58 showed immense nerve and fine judgment, and to his Yorkshire team-mate Rhodes, who, amidst ever-increasing tension and excitement, helped him make the 15 needed from the last wicket and hit the winning run.

[Jessop's 100 was made in 75min (75 balls), the fastest in Tests.]

County Championship
Essex v Sussex: 30 June

Amazing transformation in Sussex innings: Ranji and Newham on verge of record

From Leyton

A remarkable day's cricket at Leyton saw Sussex, going in first, lose six wickets for 92. But then Essex were kept in the field for the remainder of the afternoon and did not succeed in getting down another wicket. Ranjitsinhji, who had gone in fourth wicket down at 82, was joined by Newham, and the pair successfully resisted all endeavours to part them. As the result of four hours' batting, they added 332 runs, the score at the close of the day standing at 424.

Ranjitsinhji played delightful cricket. In making his 184, he was handicapped by a strain in the right calf and had to have a man to run for him from 123. Newham made 146 runs with hardly a bad stroke. They need just 9 more runs tomorrow to beat the first-class record for the seventh wicket, set in 1887 by Key and Philipson of Oxford University.

[They made 12 more (Ranji 230, Newham 153), and their world record stood until 1955.]

County Championship Surrey v Warwicks: 6 May

Just off the boat, Hargreave takes 15 for 76

From the Oval

WARWICKSHIRE had mainly to thank Sam Hargreave for their 126 runs victory at the Oval - he took 15 wickets for 76 runs as Surrey were twice bowled out for under a hundred. Yet their medium-slow bowler could not have taken part in the game had rain not washed out Monday's play, for he only arrived back from Lord Hawke's tour of Australia and New Zealand on Monday evening!

Play started at 12 o'clock yesterday, and Warwick, somewhat luckily, made 222, after which Hargreave - just off the boat, so to speak - got to work. He took six for 41 and Santall four for 33 as the two of them bowled Surrey out for 82, the last nine wickets falling for 26. Stumps were drawn, after which more rain fell heavily.

After another late start this morning, Warwick made 55 for four before declaring, leaving Surrey to get 196 in two hours and three-quarters. There was never a chance they would accomplish this and, again with Hargreave and Santall bowling unchanged, they were all out for 69 in the 33rd over. Hargreave capped a remarkable home-coming by taking nine wickets for 35.

Gentlemen v Players: 8 July

Extraordinary scoring by Fry and MacLaren

From Lord's

ONE of the most wonderful things in the history of cricket was done at Lord's today, the Gentlemen who, after following on, had made 74 for one yesterday, actually increasing their score to 500 and losing only one more batsman. The feat is without precedent in Gentlemen v Players matches.

The honours were divided by C.B.Fry and MacLaren. Fry's 232 not out is the highest score obtained in the Lord's fixture, and is second only to Abel's 247 for the Players at the Oval in 1901. He put on an unbeaten 309 for the third wicket with MacLaren (168 not out), who declared at 500 for two, leaving the game to tail off in anticlimax as the Players made 55 for one in the hour remaining.

1903

1-2 Jan Wicket-keeper Tom Hastings (106 not), playing for Victoria v S.Australia, makes the highest score for a No.11 in first-class cricket and shares in a stand of 211 with Mathew Ellis (118) a record Australian last-wicket partnership.

20 May M.C.C. (150 & 10-1) beat London County (72 & 87) in a day at Lord's.

1 Jun Gilbert Jessop hits 286 in under three hours for Glos v Sussex at Brighton. He takes 70 minutes to get his first 100, but doubles his score in another 50 minutes. His innings, the highest of his career, includes 41 fours. With Board (71) he puts on 320 runs for the sixth wicket in two and a half hours.

4 Jun P.F.'Plum' Warner (Middlesex), whose only Test cricket has been against S.Africa in 1899, is asked to captain the first official M.C.C. touring side, to visit Australia in 1903-04, and eventually accepts.

First Test Third day: 14 December

R.E.Foster 287 on Test début: England's record score

From Sydney

Foster (left) and Trumper: Memorable innings for respective sides.

The Englishmen did wonders here today, their total of 577 being the second highest ever obtained in a Test match. Moreover, R.E.Foster, with an innings of 287, easily beat all records in the whole series of Test games between England and Australia.

England resumed this morning on 243 for four wickets in reply to Australia's 285, with Foster on 73 and Braund 67. Foster, who had shown much self-restraint on Saturday and played a very safe game, adopted quite different tactics today, batting with great dash and freedom. His fourth-wicket stand with Braund (102) reached 192 before Braund was bowled by Howell on 309, both batsmen having just completed their hundreds.

Relf (31) helped Foster to add 115 for the ninth wicket, and Foster was last out after Rhodes, unbeaten with 40, had helped him add a record 130 for the last wicket in just 66 minutes.

Foster's marvellous display extended over seven hours and included forty-five 4's. His score of 287 is not only without precedent on a Test début, but is far and away the highest individual innings ever made in a Test match, beating Bill Murdoch's 211 for Australia at the Oval in 1884, and is the first double hundred scored for England. England's total is their highest in Tests, and surpassed only by Australia's 586 here in December 1894.

At the close, Australia had made 16 without loss.

[England won by 5 wickets despite a magnificent 185 not out by Trumper. Over the six days 1,541 runs were scored, a Test record. There was a notorious crowd demonstration against the umpire when Hill (51) was given run out, and England's captain, Warner, considered taking his side off.]

1904

Jan Advisory County Cricket Council set up by M.C.C.

25-27 Jan Victor Trumper and Reggie Duff are the first Australians to make two opening 100 stands in the same match, for NSW v Victoria.

5-8 Mar Australia, having lost the rubber, dismiss England on a damaged wicket at Melbourne for 61 and 101 and win by 218 runs, Hugh Trumble taking 7-28 including the hat-trick in England's 2nd innings, in his last match. Braund takes 8-81 in Australia's 1st innings.

4-6 Jul Another fine Gents v Players match at Lord's sees the Gents make 412 runs in the last innings to win with 2 wickets and 10 minutes to spare. J.H.King (Leics), called in to replace Tyldesley at the last moment, scores two 100s (104 & 109 not) for the Players, emulating Foster's feat of 1900.

16 Jul The touring South Africans, not given a Test, beat a good England XI by 189 runs at Lord's.

TEST SERIES

England in Australia
E 3, A 2

Second Test Fourth day: 5 January

England victory: Another great day for Rhodes

From Melbourne

Wilf Rhodes: Record match figures despite dropped catches.

ON a wicket utterly ruined by rain, Australia were bowled out in their second innings for 111, Wilfred Rhodes taking eight wickets for 68, and England won by the very substantial margin of 185 runs to go two matches up in the rubber. The Yorkshire slow left-arm bowler completed match figures of 15 for 124, more wickets than any bowler has taken in an England-Australia Test before.

Of course, Rhodes had a pitch that thoroughly suited him, but there are probably not more than three or four other bowlers in the world who would have been so difficult to play. Apart from Rhodes' splendid bowling, however, England were, in the last innings of the match, far indeed from covering themselves in glory. Never probably on an occasion of so much importance has there been such an epidemic of dropped catches, and who knows how much better Rhodes' figures might have been were it not for such wretched fielding.

Overnight rain had delayed the start today until 3.25, when England resumed their second innings on 74 for five, 267 runs to the good. The wicket was in a wretched state, but Tyldesley, 48 overnight, continued what has been a magnificent innings in the conditions, making 62 of the 85 runs scored in the 78 minutes he was at the wicket. He was top scorer in the first innings with 97, and in the absence through illness of Foster held England's second innings together.

Australia's task of getting 297 runs on such a wicket was hopeless. Only Trumper (35) provided any cheer for the Australian crowd, as he did with his 74 in their first innings.

Tour match Victoria v England XI

Remarkable bowling by Rhodes: Victoria all out 15

From Melbourne

THERE was a sensational finish here today, the Englishmen getting Victoria out for 15 - the smallest score on record in a first-class match in Australia - and winning by eight wickets.

Victoria began their second innings this morning with a lead of 51 runs. Four wickets fell without a run being scored, two each to Rhodes and Arnold. Rhodes should have had a hat-trick but Bosanquet missed Trott in the slips. Trott went on to make Victoria's top score - 9 runs. Despite two more misses, the innings was over in 12 overs and one ball, Rhodes taking five for 6, Arnold four for 8, while Sanders was kept away by illness.

Heavy rain delayed the start of England's innings until after lunch, when they knocked off the 67 runs needed for the loss of two wickets.

Fourth Test Sixth day: 3 March

Warner's XI win rubber: Australia fall to Bosanquet

From Sydney

ENGLAND beat Australia here this afternoon by 157 runs and thereby won the rubber in the Test matches. The Australians made a plucky effort at the finish, but it came far too late, and the result was never in doubt.

England, nine wickets down for 155 overnight, continued their innings this morning and Warner (31 not) and Rhodes (29) put on 55 for the last wicket, the biggest stand of the innings. Wanting 329 to win, Australia lost nine wickets for 114, Bosanquet doing most of the damage with a spell of five wickets for 12. Like England, however, Australia's last wicket caused a good deal of trouble, putting on 57. Noble, the captain, took out his bat for 53, while Cotter spoiled Bosanquet's average (6-51) with 34 in a little over half an hour.

County Championship Derby v Essex: 20 July

Wonderful win for Derby after Essex score 597 in first innings

From Chesterfield

IN beating Essex by nine wickets at Chesterfield today, the Derbyshire team accomplished what, in its way, was the most phenomenal performance ever recorded at the game of cricket. They went in yesterday against a total of 597, succeeded today in getting to within 40 of that number, then dismissed Essex in an hour and 50 minutes for 97, and finally hit off the 147 runs necessary to give them a victory in an hour and 20 minutes for the loss of only one wicket.

Such an achievement is quite without parallel. The nearest approach to it occurred in that famous Test match when England beat Australia at Sydney in 1894, after fielding out a first innings of 586; but they enjoyed the benefit of a follow-on and then caught Australia on a 'glue pot'. In the match at Chesterfield, Derbyshire did all their magnificent work in three days, had no follow-on to tire out the Essex bowlers, and were helped by no rain.

After Derbyshire were all out for 548 this morning, Essex, leading by 49, had three-quarters of an hour's batting before lunch, and although the wicket had certainly worn to some extent, there appeared not the slightest chance of anything but a draw. So finely did Bestwick (3-34) and Warren (4-42) bowl, however, that six batsmen were actually dismissed before the interval for 27 runs. Subsequently, the innings was all over for 97, with Curgenven taking two wickets for 7 at the finish.

Derbyshire had two hours and five minutes in which to get 147. Ollivierre, whose 229 was the corner-stone of the first innings, and Storer batted with the utmost freedom and confidence, and Derbyshire gained their glorious victory with three-quarters of an hour to spare. Ollivierre, who had hard luck in not being able to get another hundred, made an unbeaten 92.

[In Essex's 1st innings, Percy Perrin made 343 not out, the 5th highest score in first-class cricket, and hit a record 68 4's.]

B.J.T.Bosanquet, the Middlesex all-rounder.

County Championship Middlesex v Sussex: 27 May

Unique all-round feat of Bosanquet: Two 100's and 11 wickets

From Lord's

WINNING decisively at Lord's today by 324 runs, Middlesex gained their first victory this season. With a lead over Sussex of 284 runs and eight wickets in hand, they entered upon the last stage of the game with an easy victory in prospect, but no one was prepared for the rapid and overwhelming manner in which they forced the result. For the startling finish, Bosanquet was almost entirely responsible as he completed a unique all-round feat by scoring his second century of the match and taking his eleventh wicket.

Middlesex resumed this morning at 174 for two, with George Beldam 72 not out, and Bosanquet, who made 103 in the first innings, joined him first thing as runs were wanted quickly. In just an hour and a quarter, Bosanquet scored 100 out of 142, Beldam going for 94. Then, with only three men out for 318, the closure was applied.

Without Fry, Sussex had no hope of getting the 427 necessary to win, and so badly did they fare that they were all out in an hour and twenty-five minutes for 102. Rarely pitching short enough to be hit with safety, Bosanquet got a lot of spin on the ball, and no one played him well except Vine (31), who was fifth out at 63. Bosanquet took eight wickets for 53 to achieve match figures of 11 for 128. To dismiss a side on a hard pitch for 102 - and that is practically what Bosanquet did - was a remarkable performance. The small company present, if disappointed at the match ending early on such a glorious afternoon, were delighted at Bosanquet's success.

1905

May Northants become the 16th first-class county.

20 May Yorks all-rounder George Hirst scores 341 against Leics, at Leicester, including 54 boundaries.

30 May Archie MacLaren (140) makes his 5th Test 100, a new record, against Australia at Nottingham.

13 Jul Australian all-rounder Warwick Armstrong scores 303 not out against Somerset at Bath, and by the end of the season achieves a double of 2,002 runs (48.82) and 130 wickets (17.60).

24 Jul F.S.Jackson (113) makes his second consecutive Test 100 and equals MacLaren's record of 5 Test 100s, England winning the 4th Test at Manchester to take the rubber and retain the Ashes.

14-16 Aug England captain F.S.Jackson wins the toss for a record 5th time in a series, at the Oval. The 5th Test against Australia is drawn, and Jackson finishes top of both batting (70.28) and bowling (15.46) averages for both sides.

TEST SERIES

Australia in England
E 2, D 3

Tour match Essex v Australians: 24 June

Australians go down to Essex, but not without a fight

From Leyton

AFTER an exciting finish at Leyton today, Essex gained a victory by the narrow margin of 19 runs, and in so doing earned the proud distinction of being the first county to overcome the twelfth Australian team. Although hard pressed at the finish in consequence of a determined effort on the part of the Colonials, Essex thoroughly deserved their success.

The whole Essex eleven fielded admirably in both innings, Buckenham and Tremlin bowled in great form, and, if some of the batsmen accomplished little, the plucky work of the tail this afternoon turned what appeared at the time to be an impending defeat into a memorable success.

When the Australians resumed this morning with six men out for 119, they still wanted 103 more runs to win, on a pitch that had shown some signs of wear. In just ten minutes, they had lost two more wickets to Buckenham for the addition of only seven runs. Then McLeod joined Hopkins and scored 23 out of 31 for the ninth wicket before Tremlin had him caught at slip.

When Laver, the last man, came in, 65 runs were still needed. He at once began to score and, with Hopkins enjoying some narrow escapes, Essex were becoming extremely anxious. The pair had put on 45 in 40 minutes, and needed only 20 more runs, when Laver was finally caught on the boundary off Buckenham for 18, Hopkins taking his bat out for 67, the highest innings of the match.

For their victory, Essex are, of course, enormously indebted to Buckenham (6-92) and Tremlin (4-81), who between them took all 20 wickets, Buckenham obtaining 12 for 137, Tremlin eight for 135. For the Australians, Laver claimed 10 for 130. Essex have now played six matches against Australian elevens, winning two and losing only one, an impressive record.

[Essex are the only county to beat the 12th Australians.]

County Championship
Lancs v Somerset: 4 July

Brearley's remarkable feat: 17 for 137 and 4 wickets in 4 balls

From Old Trafford

WALTER BREARLEY began in sensational style this morning, taking the first two Somerset wickets with his first two balls. Having claimed their last two first-innings wickets on Monday with his last two balls, the Lancashire fast bowler brought off the rare achievement of capturing four wickets with consecutive balls. This is only the ninth instance of such a feat in first-class cricket, and the first to be performed over two separate innings.

Lancashire are heavily indebted to Brearley for their victory by an innings and 136 runs. He took nine wickets for 47 when Somerset were bowled out for 65 on Monday, and eight for 90 today, giving him the splendid match figures of 17 for 137. Only seven other bowlers have taken as many wickets in a first-class match before.

Fourth Test Final day: 26 July

England's victory by an innings: The rubber won

From Old Trafford

THE fourth Test Match came to an abrupt and unexpected end at Manchester this morning, England winning by an innings and 80 runs. Play was only in progress for an hour and 20 minutes, the last Australian wicket falling just at lunch-time. Following the victory at Nottingham and the drawn games at Lord's and Leeds, the win gives England the rubber.

With one wicket down for 118 and still 131 runs wanted to save a single-innings defeat, the Australians had a heavy task which was made impossible by the rain that fell before play started. But the state of the ground did not wholly account for Australia's collapse - nine wickets went down for 51 runs. Brearley's bowling kicked a good deal and was obviously very awkward to play, but the feeling that the rubber was lost no doubt took the heart out of the last few batsmen. Brearley took four wickets for 54 and had match figures of eight for 126.

1906

24-27 Mar Colin Blythe takes 11-118 (6-68, 5-50) at Cape Town in the 4th Test, in England's sole victory over S.Africa.

31 Mar Bert Vogler, with 62 not, is top scorer in S.Africa's 333 v England at Cape Town, going in at No.11.

18 Jul W.G.Grace, on his 58th birthday, playing his last big match, scores 74 for the Gents at the Oval to avert defeat by the Players, having bowled and taken 1-23, 41 years after his first match for the Gents.

9 Jul Fast bowler Arthur Fielder takes all 10-90 for Players v Gents in match celebrating present Lord's Centenary (Gents win by 45).

12-13 Nov D.W.Gregory hits 383 (318 on second day) for NSW v Queensland at Brisbane, the highest Australian score and second only to MacLaren's 424 in first-class cricket.

TEST SERIES

England in South Africa
SA 4, E 1

First Test Third day: 3 January

England's first defeat in S.Africa: Thrilling one-wicket win

From Reuter's Special Service, in Johannesburg

IN a thrilling finish here today, South Africa beat England for the first time in a Test match. When their captain, Sherwell, joined Nourse with nine wickets down, they still wanted 45 to win. But they made them, Sherwell scoring 22 and Nourse taking his bat out for an heroic 93.

Needing 284 in their second innings to win, South Africa resumed this morning in bright weather on 63 for two and immediately lost Shalders, run out for 38. By mid-day, they had lost six wickets for 105, with little hope left of winning. But Nourse came in and put on 121 for the seventh wicket before losing White, who had batted four hours and ten minutes for a faultless 81. Soon the score was 239 for nine, before the last two came together for a famous victory, Nourse having batted magnificently for three hours and 40 minutes. He scored 111 runs in the match without losing his wicket, and took two wickets for 7 runs in England's second innings.

Although the M.C.C. team, led by Plum Warner, was hardly representative of English cricket, it is considered to be a good side. This was the ninth Test played between the two countries, England having won the first eight.

Scores: England 184 & 190 (Warner 51; Faulkner 4-26), S.Africa 91 (Lees 5-34) & 287-9 (Nourse 93 not, White 81).

Third Test Fourth day: 14 March

England's third defeat: South Africa win rubber

From Johannesburg

ENGLAND suffered their third consecutive Test match defeat on their South African tour, by the considerable margin of 243 runs, so the Colonials have won their first rubber. The Englishmen resumed this morning in glorious weather having lost two wickets for 14 runs, and by lunch their score was 140 for six. They continued to struggle against the bowling of Snooke, and the last four wickets put on only another 56 runs.

There are still two Test matches to play, but England's tour must be regarded, in a strictly cricket sense, as a failure. The first match was close, but a nine-wickets defeat followed, and today they again failed dismally. It was felt before the tour that the English were not strong enough in batting, but that any deficiencies would be made up by the excellence and variety of the bowling. In this match, however, only Lees met with any success.

Inasmuch as only three members of the present side - Haigh, Denton and Blythe - played for England against Australia last year, the defeats need not be taken too seriously, but the recent form has been disappointing.

Scores: S.Africa 385 (Hathorn 102, Nourse 61; Lees 6-78) & 349-5 dec (White 147, Tancred 73, Nourse 55), England 295 (Fane 143; Snooke 4-57, Schwarz 4-67) & 196 (Denton 61; Snooke 8-70).

[England won the 4th Test by 4 wickets but lost the 5th by an innings and 16 runs.]

County Championship Glos v Essex: 6 August

Dennett takes all 10: Gloucester record

From Bristol

THE holiday crowd at Bristol had every cause for enjoyment, today's cricket going all in favour of Gloucestershire; while slow bowler George Dennett achieved a record performance for the county in taking all 10 wickets, and Jessop played one of his best innings.

Some rain had fallen, but it was not thought that the pitch would help the bowlers. However, Dennett, after having 11 runs hit from him, caused a complete collapse, and although one over of his yielded a dozen runs, he actually dismissed the whole Essex team at a cost of 40 - less than half the full total of 84. Thanks to Jessop, who scored 75 in an hour and a half, the home side secured a lead of 89. They then got rid of four of their opponents again for 63, Dennett taking three more wickets.

It is just four weeks since Fielder took 10 wickets in the Gentlemen and Players' match at Lord's, but previous to that it has been six years since the feat was performed.

[Dennett took 5-48 in Essex's 2nd innings, Roberts 5-69, the pair bowling unchanged throughout the match, which Glos won by 9 wickets.]

George Hirst: Emulates Bosanquet.

County Championship Somerset v Yorks: 28 August

Hirst and Rhodes sink Somerset with bat and ball

From Bath

GOING all in favour of Yorkshire, today's cricket at Bath was chiefly remarkable for the all-round cricket of Hirst and Rhodes. The two famous players bowled admirably early in the day, and were afterwards associated in a wonderful display of hitting.

Yorkshire had secured a lead of 243 on the first innings, and Ernest Smith let his side bat again, sending in Hirst first wicket down. He and Rhodes added 202 runs in 75 minutes without being separated, to put Yorkshire 523 runs in front. Brilliant in the extreme, the batting was scarcely marred by an error of any kind.

Hirst made his first 52 in 35 minutes, thus reaching his 2,000 runs for the season, and he went on to gain the distinction of scoring two hundreds in a match for the first time in his career, following up his 111 in the first innings with 117 (not out). Only one Yorkshireman had previously accomplished this feat - namely, Denton, at Trent Bridge in June. Hirst took 66 minutes to get his 100, while Rhodes was occupied half an hour longer over his. Before this terrible hitting, Hirst (6-70) and Rhodes (3-28) had combined to bowl Somerset out for 125.

[Yorks won by 389 runs, Hirst taking 5-45 to make it 11-115 in the match and rival Bosanquet's feat last season. He went on to make 2,385 runs and take 208 wickets, a unique 'double' double.]

County Championship Middlesex v Somerset: 22 May

Two 'hat tricks' in innings for Trott in benefit match

From Lord's

THOSE who were at Lord's today - they formed a crowd of very modest dimensions - saw some startling cricket, Albert Trott finishing off his benefit match with a truly astonishing piece of bowling, and gaining for Middlesex a victory by 166 runs.

Doing the 'hat trick' twice in one innings, he accomplished a feat without precedent in first-class cricket. To begin with, Trott took four wickets with four successive balls, and he wound up by getting the last three wickets with three successive balls - seven wickets for 20 runs in eight overs. The pitch was rather the worse for wear, it being possible to get a good deal of break on the ball, and the batting at the close was feeble to a degree, but that Trott bowled very finely can scarcely be questioned. Braund saw all 10 wickets fall, taking out his bat for 28. Though quite overshadowed by Trott today, Tarrant had a big share in winning the game for Middlesex, scoring 52 and 28, and taking in all nine wickets for 82 runs.

County Championship Northants v Kent: 1 June

Northants helpless against Blythe: Kent bowler takes 17 for 48

From Northampton

THANKS to some remarkable bowling by Blythe, Kent forced a victory in brilliant style at Northampton, beating Northants by an innings and 155 runs. Blythe took all 10 wickets in the Northants first innings, and came out with a record for the match of 17 wickets for 48 runs. The game ended at half-past four, but Kent only just won in time, for no sooner had the players left the field than rain fell heavily.

When play was resumed in the morning, with Kent only 212 for four, there did not seem much chance of a definite result. After the rain of Thursday and yesterday, the pitch was expected to be soft and dead. However, the remaining Kent batsmen added 42 runs.

Northants then gave a deplorable display. So helpless were the batsmen against the bowling of Blythe that the first seven wickets fell for 4 runs - two of them extras. The eighth should have gone down at the same total, but Vials was missed by Blythe. Profiting by this escape, Vials hit pluckily, and the innings was carried over the luncheon interval, the score in the end reaching 60, Vial 33 not out. Blythe took the 10 wickets at a cost of only 3 runs apiece.

Following on 194 behind, Northants fared even worse than before, the whole side being dismissed in an hour and a quarter for the miserable total of 39, Blythe taking seven for 18. Blythe's match figures are the best recorded in first-class cricket, albeit against the weakest of batting.

'Charlie' Blythe: Best match figures in first-class cricket.

County Championship Glos v Northants: 11 June

Northants out for 12, county record low: Dennett takes 15 for 21 in day

From Gloucester

ON a pitch that gave the bowlers great assistance, some startling cricket was seen at Gloucester today. Rain during the night was followed by bright sunshine, and in the first hour's cricket Gloucestershire, who had overnight scored 20 for the loss of four wickets, were dismissed for another 40 runs. The pitch was at the worst when Northamptonshire went in, and, bowling unchanged, Dennett and Jessop dismissed the whole side in forty minutes for 12 runs. Their score is the lowest ever obtained in county matches, and ties with the smallest on record in first-class cricket of any kind - Oxford University's 12 in 1877

Dennett, making the ball turn in an extraordinary way, was almost unplayable. Six runs were scored from him before he got a wicket, but for the remainder of the innings only 3 runs were obtained from his bowling while he dismissed eight batsmen. Jessop also bowled splendidly, keeping such a fine length that in sending down 33 balls he had only 3 runs scored off him and took two wickets

Dennett's good work did not end in Northants' first innings, as, after Gloucester, on going in for the second time, had been got rid of for 88, he obtained all seven wickets to fall at a cost of 11 runs. He accomplished the 'hat trick', and should have had four wickets in four balls, Wrathall dropping a catch offered by East. During the day Dennett took 15 wickets for 20 runs, and no bowler could possibly have made better use of the assistance given by the state of the wicket. When play ceased for the day Northants, with three wickets to fall, required 97 runs to win.

[Rain washed out play on the last day.]

Second Test Third day: 31 July

England beat S.Africa: Blythe's brilliant bowling

From Headingley

THE weather relented at Leeds this afternoon, and after all the delays and discomforts of the last two days the match was played out, England winning by 53 runs thanks to more fine bowling from Blythe. But one must guard against making too much of the victory. A match played between the showers on a wicket always affected by rain does not afford a very trustworthy test of skill.

England's last six wickets put on only another 52 this morning, leaving South Africa 129 to get, a heavy task the way the wicket was playing. And so it proved, as South Africa lost their first five wickets, either side of another heavy downfall of rain, for 18 runs. Thereafter, only Faulkner, Sinclair and Snooke got into double figures before Blythe finished off the innings for 75. The Kent slow left-arm bowler enjoyed match figures of 15 for 99 and joins the company of three bowlers, all English - Briggs, Lohmann and Rhodes - who have taken 15 wickets in a Test.

Scores: England 76 (Faulkner 6-17) & 162 (Fry 54), South Africa 110 (Blythe 8-59) & 75 (Blythe 7-40).

1907

May New ball permitted after 200 runs.

5 Jul A.W.Nourse (S.Africa) is out 'handled the ball' v Sussex, the first 20th-century instance.

3 Aug All-rounder Francis Tarrant takes 4 wickets in 4 balls v Glos at Bristol, the second Australian Middlesex bowler to perform the feat this season, after Trott (see report this page).

3 Sep Gilbert Jessop (191) hits the fastest 150 recorded in first-class cricket, in 63 minutes, for Gents of South v Players of South at Hastings.

13 Dec George Gunn (Notts), in Australia for health reasons, is called in to England's side for the 1st Test when Arthur Jones, captain of England (and Notts) becomes ill, and makes 119 and 74 on his Test début, but England lose by 2 wickets.

TEST SERIES

South Africa in England
E 1, D 2

1908

25 Feb At Sydney, in the 5th Test, Victor Trumper (166) makes his 5th Test 100 to equal the record of England's Jackson and MacLaren, and passes the 2,000 runs mark.

14 Jul The lunch interval at Leeds is extended for a presentation to Lord Hawke, at nearly 48, celebrating 25 years as Yorkshire captain.

20 Jul Middlesex (92 & 24-3) beat Gents of Philadelphia (58 & 55) in a day at Lord's.

TEST SERIES

England in Australia
A 4, E 1

Second Test Sixth day: 7 January

England square rubber after Titanic struggle: Last two wickets put on 73

By Major Philip Trevor, in Melbourne

ENGLAND scored a magnificent victory at 3.30 today by one wicket. Our batsmen failed in the morning, one after another, going from 159 for four to 209 for eight. Many people left the ground at the luncheon interval under the impression that England must be easily beaten. But Barnes, Humphries and Fielder, with good, intelligent batting, made the 73 runs needed to win.

Wicket-keeper Humphries (16) joined Barnes in a stand of 34 before Fielder came in, with 39 runs still wanted. Neither batsman showed the slightest trace of nervousness. Nor was any mistake, or even mis-hit, made all this time. The Colonial bowling was kept an accurate length, and the fielding was splendid. Barnes played better and better as the crisis approached, and Fielder never looked like failing.

Noble changed his bowlers around as the tension became extreme. At last, Fielder made the game a tie, playing Armstrong to mid-on. Then, amid intense excitement, Barnes, with a single in the direction of point, won the match. He took his bat out, after an hour and a half at the wickets, for 38, Fielder for 18. The aggregate attendance was 91,388, and the total receipts were £4,070.

[This was Jack Hobbs' first Test, and he scored 83 and 28.]

Third Test Fifth day: 15 January

Colonials' fine recovery: England field all day

By Major Philip Trevor, in Adelaide

ON a day of intense heat - 104 degrees in the shade and 152 in the sun at start of play - an unbroken, record partnership for the eighth wicket turned the third Test Australia's way. With seven second-innings wickets down for 180, Australia were only 102 runs to the good. Then Hill, batting at No.9 because of his indisposition, joined Hartigan before lunch, and when the stumps were drawn at six o'clock no other wicket had fallen.

The partnership has already yielded 217 runs, beating the eighth-wicket record of 154 set by Bonnor and Jones 23 years ago in Sydney, but both men should have been caught very early in the afternoon. Hill was not playing at his best when missed, and both presumed on good fortune with excellent judgment. Neither was unnecessarily rash, and they hit the ball with ease and confidence to all parts of the field. For once in this series the England bowling, though never really bad, was thoroughly mastered.

At the close, Australia had scored 397, and both batsmen had reached their centuries, Hartigan (on his Test début) on 105 and Hill on 106.

[The stand reached 243 before Hartigan was out for 116, but Hill (160) put on 78 with Carter (31 not) for the 9th wicket, and Australia made 506, winning by 245 runs after putting England out for 183.]

Fourth Test Fourth day: 11 February

England's disappointing display: Colonials win the rubber

By Major Philip Trevor, in Melbourne

AUSTRALIA beat England with the greatest possible ease at 5.30 today by 308 runs, and with their victory they also won the rubber, by three matches to one, with one match remaining. This morning the Australians were all out for 385 after the last two wickets added 27. Armstrong took his bat out for 133. England, wanting 495 to win, were all out for 186. There was nothing in the wicket or the bowling to account for such a poor display.

Australia owed their strong position this morning very much to Armstrong's fine defensive innings yesterday. Although they had an advantage of 109, after England, with the worst of the wicket, lost their last eight wickets for 17, they found themselves with half their wickets down for 77, a lead of 186 runs. But stands of 85 for the sixth wicket with Ransford (54) and 112 for the eighth with Carter (66) thoroughly justified Armstrong's cautious tactics and put Australia into an impregnable position.

Warwick Armstrong: Caution justified.

At the close of Australia's innings this morning, Armstrong had an overwhelming reception. His great innings included two 6's - hit from successive balls from Braund immediately after he had reached his first Test century - and fourteen 4's.

County Championship Northants v Yorks: 8 May

Hirst and Haigh bowl Northants out twice in afternoon: No batsman reaches double figures.

From Northampton

NORTHAMPTONSHIRE earned another unwelcome entry in the records of first-class cricket today when they were bowled out twice by Yorkshire in two hours and 20 minutes for scores of 27 and 15. Their aggregate of 42 in two completed innings is the worst ever. One needs to go back some 45 years to the previous worst, Wellington's 22 & 22 against Auckland in New Zealand, and 80 years for the previous worst in a county match, Sussex's 35 & 22 against Kent at Sevenoaks.

Rain had prevented resumption of the game until half-past two, but there seemed no reason to expect such a double débâcle, for Yorkshire added 23 quick runs without loss on the soft pitch before declaring at 356 for eight wickets. In the absence of some of their best batsmen, and further weakened by the inability of George Thompson to take any part in the cricket due to an attack of lumbago, Northants were not expected to fare well. But their utter collapse before Hirst and Haigh came as a complete surprise.

No batsman reached double figures, the highest score being 8 by W.H.Kingston in the first innings. Hirst and Haigh bowled unchanged throughout the two innings, and of the 18 wickets to fall, the stumps were hit 13 times and there were four cases of leg before wicket. Hirst had the remarkable match figures of 12 for 19 (6-12 & 6-7), while Haigh took six for 19 (3-11 & 3-8). They both bowled in their best form, their length being perfect, and they made the ball turn appreciably. Yorkshire's winning margin was an innings and 314 runs.

[Yorks went on to win the Championship, undefeated, winning 16 of their 28 matches. Northants finished 15th, above Somerset.]

First Test Third day: 29 May

England's great victory: Colonial collapse then Hobbs bats brilliantly

From Birmingham

ENGLAND'S victory by 10 wickets at Birmingham today was far easier than even the most sanguine English partisan had dared to predict. Indeed, there was a time early on, with Australia only two wickets down and 50 runs on, when the crowd was anxious and glum. But Blythe tempted Gregory when he was in full flow and then, with Hirst, ran through the rest of the Australian batsmen for only 54 runs. Hobbs, with the help of Fry, did the rest.

At the resumption of play this morning, the wicket, though slow, was more than fairly easy, and neither of the overnight batsmen, Gregory on 26 and Ransford on 28, seemed to be troubled either by Hirst or by Blythe. Then came the turning point, when Gregory, having just struck two over-pitched balls from Blythe to the boundary, was invited to try a third and skied a catch to short leg. Having broken the third-wicket partnership, which put on 91, Blythe and Hirst met with little further resistance. They finished with identical analyses for the innings, five for 58, giving Blythe match figures of 11 for 102, Hirst the other nine for 86.

England's task of making 105 runs to win, as against an average so far of just over 115 per innings, was arithmetically, at least, not an easy one. But Hobbs instantly raised the level of batting to a higher level than it had hitherto attained, and, with brilliant strokes and never the hint of a mistake, made 62 to Fry's 35 as the runs were made.

1909

26 Jul Australian player/manager Frank Laver, a medium-pace bowler, takes 8-31 in England's 1st innings at Old Trafford in the drawn 4th Test, record figures for Australia

3 Aug E.G.Arnold (200 not) and W.B. Burns (196) put on 393 for Worcs v Warwick at Birmingham, a new first-class record for the 5th wicket, beating the 340 of Wainwright and Hirst for Yorkshire in 1899.

9 Aug Australian captain wins the toss at the Oval, making it five out of five for the rubber.

26 Aug Gloucester (33 & 81) lose to Middlesex (145) at Bristol in a day.

TEST SERIES

Australia in England
A 2, E 1, D 2

Imperial Cricket Conference Inaugural Meeting: 15 June

The Imperial Conference: Triangular Tournament approved

From Lord's

REPRESENTATIVES of England, Australia and South Africa held a meeting at Lord's yesterday morning for the purpose of considering the rules governing Test matches and the interchange of visits. Rule 1, which defines the Test matches as being between England and Australia or England and South Africa, with matches between Australia and South Africa, was approved, as also was Rule 3, which deals with qualification by birth, and says that, subject to Rule 2, a cricketer is always at liberty to represent the country of his birth. The discussion of Rule 2, barring a cricketer from representing more than one country, was deferred, and this also affects Rule 4, as to qualification by residence.

The principle of triangular contests was approved, and it was agreed to aim for 1912 for the first of such competitions.

County Championship Worcs v Kent: 7 July

Record last-wicket stand by Woolley and Fielder: Kent win by innings

From Stourbridge

BATTING for Kent against Worcestershire at Stourbridge today, Woolley and Fielder put on no fewer than 235 runs for the last wicket, and in so doing beat by 5 runs the first-class record established at Lord's ten years ago by Nicholls and Roche for Middlesex against Kent.

The two batsmen came together yesterday afternoon, when Kent, going in against a total of 360, had nine wickets down for 320. During the last hour they increased the total to 439, and when they resumed today Woolley, who had come in after the fall of the third wicket, was on 136 and Fielder 67.

At once both settled down again to a brilliant, punishing game, and in an hour and 20 minutes, before the dismissal of Woolley brought the innings to an end, added another 116 runs.

Fielder had never before approached anything like a hundred in a county match, his biggest previous innings for Kent being 39. He gave nothing like a chance in his 112 not out, and hit fourteen 4's. Woolley, in putting together 185, also succeeded in making the highest score of his career. He was at the wickets for four hours and three-quarters, and his hits included a 6 and twenty-four 4's. Altogether, the Kent innings, which reached the formidable total of 555, extended over six hours and 55 minutes.

Irrespective of the record stand for the last wicket, the match was a memorable one, inasmuch as Kent, having to face a score of 360, proved victorious in a single innings. Worcestershire, on going in for the second time, speedily found themselves in a desperate plight. Just at six o'clock the last wicket went down for 162, and with only a quarter of an hour to spare Kent scored a famous triumph by an innings and 23 runs.

Fifth Test Third day: 11 August

Brilliant Colonial batting: Bardsley's record

By Major Trevor Philip, at the Oval

THE fifth and last Test at the Oval has ended in a draw, so the Australians have won the rubber by two matches to one. On the last day of Test match cricket, they certainly gave a magnificent display. Early failure on their part would have made an English victory a distinct possibility. Very quickly and very plainly, however, was any idea of initial failure on their part dispelled, and by lunch-time it was evident that Australia could not lose the game.

As Australia could not win either, the main interest, as their innings progressed, was in was in whether Bardsley would achieve his second hundred of the match, having scored 136 in the first innings. He was 33 overnight out of Australia's 76 for no wicket, and he and Gregory gradually made the match safe. Gregory (74) ran himself out on 180 (a record opening stand for Australia against England), at which time Bardsley was on 96. But the young left-hander did not make the crowd wait much longer before, at twenty-five past twelve, he completed his second hundred and became the first batsman to do so in a Test match.

Australia declared at 339 for five, Bardsley having made 130, leaving England to get 313 runs in two hours and a quarter. The series ended in anticlimax as England made 104 for three.

Bardsley: Two centuries.

1910

11-15 Mar England, having already lost their second rubber in successive tours to S.Africa, win the last Test, at Cape Town, by an innings, Hobbs (187) making his first Test century, Blythe taking 10-104 in the match and Billy Zulch carrying his bat through S.Africa's 1st innings for 43. Aubrey Faulkner sets a series best of 545 runs (60.55) for S.Africa, Hobbs 539 (67.37) for England, Faulkner also taking 29 wickets (21.89). Bert Vogler's 36 wickets is a series record for any country.

May A 6 is awarded for any hit clearing the boundary (hitherto only for hit out of the ground).

19 Jun Lancs make 403-8 to beat Notts at Old Trafford, with 10min to spare, their captain A.H.Hornby making 55 not out despite injury.

4-5 Jul Australian Philip Le Couteur performs the greatest all-round feat in the Varsity Match, making 160 and, with his googlies and leg-breaks, taking 11-66 (6-20, 5-46) as Oxford win by an innings.

9 Dec At Sydney, South Africa's introduction to Test cricket in Australia is greeted by a record 494 runs (for 6) in a day by the home side, Hill (191) and Bardsley (132) the chief scorers.

Australian captain Clem Hill: Stiff introduction for South Africa.

TEST SERIES

England in South Africa
SA 3, E 2

First Test Fourth day: 5 January

S.Africa beat England by 19: Faulkner & Vogler's match

From Johannesburg

ENGLAND made a good fight today in the concluding stage of the Test match, and in the end were only beaten by the narrow margin of 19 runs. Thompson, who was 25 when play resumed this morning, with England at 144 for seven wanting another 100 runs to win, made a fine effort. He was last out for 63 when Faulkner and Vogler finally bowled England out for 224.

The aforementioned players, both googly bowlers, took all 20 England wickets in the match between them, and were the chief architects of South Africa's victory. Faulkner completed the finest all-round performance in his country's Test history, with 211 runs (78 & 123) and eight wickets (5-120 & 3-40). Bert Vogler's match figures of 12 for 181 (5-87 & 7-94) have been surpassed only by his captain Snooke, who took 12 for 127 against England here four years ago.

County Championship Derby v Warwicks: 21 June

Record 9th-wicket stand for Derby: Warren and Chapman save match

From Blackwell

DERBYSHIRE saved their match with Warwickshire in remarkable style at Blackwell today, Warren and Chapman taking part in a record-breaking ninth-wicket partnership that left Warwick insufficient time to force a win. They put on 283 runs in two hours and 55 minutes, beating the previous best stand for this wicket of 232 set by Hill and Walkley for South Australia in 1900.

Derbyshire, having followed on, started the day with one man out for 51, still 191 runs behind. During the first 75 minutes' play, seven more wickets fell for the addition of only 50 runs, and thus, at ten minutes to one, when John Chapman and Arnold Warren came together, they still required 141 to avoid an innings defeat. When at length they were separated, Derbyshire were out of danger.

Playing the bowling with freedom and confidence, they scored 81 in 40 minutes before lunch, and then, after clearing off the arrears, both batsmen proceeded to three figures. Warren made 123, despite being handicapped by lameness, before a catch in the slips ended the stand. Chapman, who, like Warren, was at the wickets just over three hours, hit two 6's and nineteen 4's in his 165.

Schools match Harrow v Eton: 9 July

Fowler's match: Eton captain hits top score and takes 8 for 23

From Lord's

ONE can never tell what will occur at cricket, but the limit of the game's possibilities must have been nearly reached at Lord's this evening, Eton winning by 9 runs after having recovered from a seemingly impossible position. Following on 165 behind, Eton lost their ninth wicket soon after four o'clock, when they were only 4 runs ahead. Yet at six o'clock, their victory was an accomplished fact.

This will go down as 'Fowler's match', such was the Eton captain's all-round play today. Yet remarkable as his accomplishments were, it was Manners who extended the Eton total to give his captain something to bowl at, and it was Steel (2-12) who delivered the final coup de grace after Fowler had taken eight second-innings wickets for 23 (12-113 in the match).

Eton resumed this morning at 40 for five wickets. Fowler, with 21 the only player to reach double figures (there were 11 extras), made a few hits, but they were all out for 67 and followed on. At lunch-time, their second innings stood at 47 for four. But after the interval, Fowler, who had come in at 41, began to hit. He seized every chance, driving with fine power on the off-side, but was out for 64 just after the innings defeat had been averted.

The ninth wicket went down at the same score, 169, and the last man, Lister Kaye, joined Manners, with Eton 4 runs ahead. Encouraged by enthusiastic cheering, and gathering strength as he went on, Manners (40 not out) hit away with delightful freedom before Lister Kaye was finally out for 13. The pair had put on 50 runs in 25 minutes.

Nevertheless, one would not expect Harrow's task of making 55 to cause them much trouble. But when they went in to bat at five o'clock the atmosphere was highly charged. In the first three overs they lost three wickets, and were soon 21 for six, all to Fowler. Suddenly Eton were winning.

Fowler brought on Steel with his slows for Lister Kaye at the other end. This son of the famous England captain caught and bowled Blount for 5. Fowler claimed another two - 23 wanted and one wicket left. Graham and Alexander made a very plucky effort, and amidst a growing crescendo of sound added 13 runs before Alexander edged one to slips off Steel. Eton had won by 9 runs.

[Robert St Leger Fowler made his first-class debut for M.C.C. in 1913 but played in few matches because of his military career, and died in 1925, at 34. Allan Ivo Steel went to India, played for Calcutta and twice for Middlesex, and died in action in 1917. The Hon R.H.L.G. Alexander, described as "a sort of googly bowler", took 5-40 in the match; he became Field-Marshal, Earl Alexander of Tunis.]

Third Test Sixth day: 13 January

S.Africa's first victory over Australia: Exciting finish

From Reuter's Special Service, in Adelaide

AFTER six days' strenuous cricket in which a record number of runs (1,646) was scored, South Africa beat Australia by 38 to register their first ever victory over their fellow Colonials.

The heat was intense when play resumed at noon today, with the Australian second innings score standing at 187 for four wickets, and 191 runs wanted to win. The wicket was worn, with some nasty patches, and the wickets fell steadily in the morning. Just before lunch, Schwarz took two wickets with successive balls, leaving the Australians tottering at 285 for eight. Soon after, he claimed another, and the last man, Whitty, joined Cotter with 86 runs still needed.

The tension now grew as the score rose rapidly, and Cotter (36) brought great roars from the crowd for some terrific hits before Pegler had him caught at 339.

Scores: S.Africa 482 (Zulch 105, Snooke 103, Faulkner 56) & 360 (Faulkner 115, Llewellyn 80; Whitty 6-104), Australia 465 (Trumper 214 not, Bardsley 54, Ransford 50) & 339 (Kelleway 65, Bardsley 58, Hill 55).

County Championship 20 May

Extraordinary innings by Alletson: 189 in 90 minutes saves match

From Brighton

THE Hove ground at Brighton has been the scene of many brilliant batting performances, but probably nothing has been accomplished there more remarkable than that achieved today by the young Notts batsman Edwin Alletson, who gave a most extraordinary exhibition of rapid and fierce hitting. He has always been known as a batsman with strong punishing powers, but he entirely eclipsed anything he had ever before done in first-class cricket.

Going in when Notts, with seven wickets down in their second innings, were only 9 runs on, he accomplished the stupendous feat of scoring 189 runs out of 227 in 90 minutes. In 50 minutes before lunch he obtained 47 runs, but the 'pyrotechnics' came after the interval when he had Riley, the last man, as his partner.

Alletson began to treat Killick and Leach like a pair of schoolboys hitting 115 runs out of 120 from seven consecutive overs - 9, 9, 22, 13, 11, 17, and 34, the last including two hits off no-balls.

Robert Relf was then put on for Leach, and was hit for 15 in his second over, but Cox, after being twice sent to leg for four, got Alletson extremely well caught by Smith standing with his back to the grandstand. Alletson had scored his last 89 runs in 15 minutes. Twice he sent the ball over the grandstand, and his innings included eight 6's and twenty-three 4's. He made 142 out of 152 in 40 minutes after lunch, the latter figure being the amount of the last stand.

Sussex, needing 237, could still have won, but in the end they were satisfied to play for a draw, being at the close 213 for eight.

County Championship Yorks v Leics: 14 June

Wood's unique feat: Carries bat for 100 in both innings

From Bradford

C.J.B.WOOD, the Leicestershire opener, accomplished a wonderful batting performance in the match which ended at Bradford today, albeit in a victory for Yorkshire by five wickets. In Leicester's first innings he had carried his bat right through for 107, and today, when their second innings came to a conclusion, he was again not out with 117 runs to his credit. Only once before in first-class cricket has a player carried his bat through two complete innings, and that was Henry Jupp for Surrey against Yorkshire at the Oval in 1874. But this is the first time that it has been accomplished with a hundred in both innings.

Wood, batting with wonderful patience, was altogether at the wickets for eight hours and 40 minutes without giving a single chance. He is not new to the practice of carrying his bat, as Yorkshire should well know. He has now performed the feat on 15 occasions for Leicester, five of them against the Tykes. Only W.G.Grace has done it more, with 17, but even the Champion never did it twice in one match. *[Wood carried his bat twice more, in 1913, to equal WG's record.]*

Second Test First day: 31 December

Australians off to a poor start as Barnes takes 5 for 6: All out 184

From Reuter's, in Melbourne

SOME startling cricket was witnessed on the opening day of the M.C.C.'s second Test, the first six Australian wickets falling for the miserable total of 38 runs. After this, however, their reputed tail saved the innings from being an ignominious failure by adding 146 for the last four wickets.

Barnes bowled magnificently throughout, and in the early stages of the game he was well-nigh unplayable. In a devastating opening spell, he had Bardsley playing on first ball, and took four wickets in five overs for one run - Australia were reeling at 11 for four. He kept a perfect length, swinging in from the off and turning back.

After lunch, Frank Foster, the Warwickshire amateur, bowled Trumper for 13 - Australia 33 for five. Barnes soon had Minnett caught in the covers by Hobbs, at which point his figures read 10.1 overs, 6 maidens, 6 runs, 5 wickets - and Australia were 38 for six.

All of Australia's last five batsmen made runs, and Barnes did not take another wicket, finishing with five for 44 off 23 overs. The Staffordshire bowler was involved in an incident, however, when the crowd grew noisy as he changed his field. He threw the ball down and refused to bowl, and when he did resume, every run scored off him evoked great enthusiasm.

[England won by 8 wickets.]

1911

2-3 Jan Aubrey Faulkner (204) makes S.Africa's first Test 200, v Australia at Melbourne, in their 1st-innings 506, but they lose by 89 runs, Whitty taking 6-17 in their 2nd-innings 80.

17-21 Feb After losing to S.Africa for first time last month, Australia take revenge with a 530-run drubbing in the 4th Test at Melbourne, scoring a record 578 runs in 2nd innings.

9 Jun The first All India team to England lose by an innings and 168 runs to a strong M.C.C. side at Lord's.

3-5 Jul Another triumphant Varsity match for Le Couteur, with 11-179 (8-99 in 2nd) as Oxford win, but Light Blue captain J.F.Ireland does the hat-trick.

21-23 Aug Kent wicket-keeper Fred Huish makes a world-record 9 stumpings in the benefit match for his opposite number, Surrey's Herbert Strudwick, at the Oval, all off leg-spinners - Carr 5, Woolley 3 (plus a catch) and Blythe 1, but Surrey win by 9 runs.

29 Aug Warwicks beat Northants to become the first county outside original 8 to win the Championship.

15-21 Dec Trumper (113) makes his 8th Test 100 and passes 3,000 runs in Tests and Horden takes 12-175 for Australia as they go one up in the rubber v England.

TEST SERIES

South Africa in Australia
A 4, SA 1

Cecil Wood: Carried bat

1912

27 Jan Frank Woolley makes 305 not out for MCC v Tasmania at Hobart.

23 Feb-1 Mar England win the last Test, at Sydney, which extends over 7 days (not counting a rest day), there being no play on the 3rd and 6th days because of rain, by 70 runs, to take the rubber 4-1. Woolley (133 not) and Vine (36) put on 143, an English 7th-wicket Test record. Hobbs finishes with a record series aggregate for England, 662 (82.75).

10-12 Jun South Africa are all out for 58 v England in the 1st Test, at Lord's, 'extras' top-scoring with 17. Barnes takes 11-110 for England, who win by an innings and 62.

16 Jul Bardsley (164) hits 100 before lunch for Australia v S.Africa at Lord's.

13 Aug England beat S.Africa by 10 wickets before lunch on the 2nd day, the shortest completed match in the history of Tests. Barnes takes 13-57 (8-29 before lunch in 2nd innings) and finishes with 34 wickets at 8.29 for the 3 Tests, all won by England, in the Triangular Tournament.

TEST SERIES

England in Australia
E 4, A 1
Australia in England
E 1, D 2
South Africa in England
England 3
Australia v South Africa (in England) A 2, D 1

Fourth Test Second day: 10 February

Hobbs and Rhodes in record Test partnership: 323 for 1st wicket

From Reuter's Special Service, in Melbourne

Some startling batting was witnessed in the Test match here today. Hobbs and Rhodes, who were in possession overnight with their scores respectively at 30 and 23, put on together 323 runs for the first wicket. This is easily a record partnership for any wicket in a Test match, and both batsmen played grand cricket.

England resumed at 51 for no wicket in reply to Australia's first innings total of 191. One of the features of the stand was the splendid running between wickets. Hobbs reached his hundred in 2hr 23min soon after Rhodes had made his fifty. The Yorkshire all-rounder began to speed up now and after 3hr 40min hoisted his first Test hundred, out of 243, this figure equalling the Test record for any wicket, set by Hill and Hartigan at Adelaide against England (for the eighth wicket) four years ago.

This record was left far behind and when Hobbs was out for 178 after 4hr 28min, the new record stood at 323, Rhodes having made 132. At the close, Rhodes was still unbeaten on 157 and England were 179 runs to the good with only one wicket down.

Fourth Test Fourth day: 13 February

England's great victory: 'Ashes' recovered

From Melbourne

By their brilliant victory over Australia today in the fourth Test by an innings and 225 runs, England secured the rubber, and thus, once more, the mythical 'ashes' make their long journey from the antipodes. This success will tend still further to enhance the interest in the triangular tournament in which England, Australia and South Africa will engage in England during the forthcoming summer.

Their overwhelming victory, coming as it does after two previous successes and defeat in the first 'test', reflects immense credit on all concerned, and in every degree on Mr J.W.H.T. Douglas, the Essex skipper, who, owing to the regrettable illness of Mr P.F.Warner, has had to deputise as captain.

Several other members of the team have also rendered yeomen service with bat or ball, notably Hobbs and Rhodes, with their record stand and their contribution to a record total in Tests. The team as a whole, however, has proved its worth, and all its members are deserving of the highest commendation for their achievement.

Scores: Australia 191 (Minnett 56; Barnes 5-74; Foster 4-77) & 173 (Douglas 5-46) England 589 (Rhodes 179, Hobbs 178, Gunn 75, Woolley 56, Foster 50).

Triangular Tests Australia v S.Africa: 28 May

Two hat tricks in day by Matthews: Easy victory for Australia

By Major Philip Trevor, at Old Trafford

A most peculiar record was set up today at Manchester, when T.J.Matthews of Australia twice did the 'hat trick' in the Test match against South Africa, the first of the matches to be played in the Triangular Tournament. Probably such a performance will never be seen again. It is unique in Tests, and only Shaw (1884) and Trott (1907, in the same innings) have taken two hat tricks in any first-class match before.

Matthews is one of the change bowlers of the Australian team, a slow-medium leg-breaker who has effective command of a fast ball and is also a very useful batsman. Put on for the second time when Faulkner looked extremely like saving the follow-on, he got rid of Beaumont, Pegler and Ward with successive deliveries to bring the innings to a dramatic end.

Later, in the South African second innings, when there promised to be a third day's play, Matthews did the hat trick a second time, his victims on this occasion being Taylor, Schwarz and Ward. It was largely due to him that the Australians gained so easy a victory, although he did not take any other wickets. His figures were three for 16 in 12 overs and three for 38 in eight.

Scores: Australia 448 (Bardsley 121, Kelleway 114; Pegler 6-105), S.Africa 265 (Faulkner 122 not out; Whitty 5-55) & 95 (Kelleway 5-33).

Frank Woolley: 10-49 and a fifty.

Triangular Tournament England v Australia: 22 August

Australia bowled out for 65: England win Triangular Tournament

From the Oval

AS sunshine followed the heavy rain, it was inevitable that England should beat Australia in this final, play-to-a-finish Test, thus winning not only the rubber and retaining the 'ashes' but also winning the Triangular Tournament.

The three-country contest, the first of its kind, has not been a success, owing largely to the weather – the two previous England-Australia Tests were washed out - and to the weakness of the South African side. In addition, nine Tests provide possibly a surfeit of cricket, and contests between Australia and South Africa are not a great attraction to the British public.

England's triumph at the Oval today was comprehensive, albeit after the shock of losing their last five second-innings wickets to Hazlitt in 17 balls at the personal cost of one run. But then Dean and Woolley bowled in such form that Australia were all out in 80 minutes for 65, half an hour of brilliant hitting being followed by utter collapse and defeat by 244 runs.

Overall, England's was a hollow victory in the tournament, as Australia arrived with a far from representative team as a result of the Control Board dispute with six leading players. They sorely missed Trumper, Hill, Armstrong, Carter, Ransford and Cotter.

Scores: England 245 (Hobbs 66, Woolley 62; Minnett 4-34, Whitty 4-69)) & 175 (Fry 79; Hazlitt 7-25), Australia 111 (Woolley 5-29, Barnes 5-30) & 65 (Woolley 5-20, Dean 4-19).

[It was decided not to repeat the triangular experiment.]

County Championship Kent v Warwicks: 21 June

Unexpected Kent victory: Warwicks collapse for 16

From Tonbridge

IN the first meeting of these two counties since 1899, Kent, after appearing at one point this morning hopelessly beaten, gained an unexpected victory by the handsome margin of six wickets.

All the luck had gone in favour of the visitors in the early stages of the match and they had scored 262 on a perfect pitch and got rid of four Kent wickets for 104 before the rain yesterday. When Kent resumed this morning, with the sun shining out, the bowlers were likely to have an immense advantage. And so it proved. No fewer than 18 wickets went down in 100 minutes before luncheon and only 60 runs were scored.

In the first 45 minutes, the last six Kent batsmen were got rid of, five of them by Foster, for 28 runs, and Warwick were left with the apparently commanding lead of 130. Foster finished with six for 62, Jeeves four for 27.

Then came a performance by Woolley and Blythe that can have had few parallels in county cricket. The Midland county went in at 12.20 and by 1.05 were all out for 16 in 10.2 overs. None of the batsmen showed the slightest ability to cope with the wonderful work of the two famous left-handers, who both captured five wickets for 8 runs. Wicket-keeper Huish claimed four victims, three of them stumped, and no batsman scored more than five.

This state of affairs left Kent with 147 to make, and when they lost two for 16 before lunch, an exciting finish appeared likely. But Woolley, having taken 10 wickets for 52 in the match, completed an outstanding all-round performance, scoring an unbeaten 76 in 80 minutes and guiding Kent to victory.

Second Test

Barnes's great record: 17 wickets in Test match

From Reuter's Special Service, in Johannesburg

Sydney Barnes: Prince of bowlers.

ENGLAND gained a decisive victory in the second Test Match of the M.C.C. team's tour here today by an innings and 12 runs. The South Africans, who when stumps were drawn overnight had lost four wickets for 177, struggled gamely to avert the single innings defeat, but against the superb bowling of Staffordshire professional Barnes, who was in irresistible form, all their efforts were in vain, and the innings eventually closed for the addition of 54 runs.

Barnes's figures for today were 9.4 overs, 4 maidens, 21 runs, 6 wickets, and in the innings he took nine wickets for 103. This is a new Test Match record, no other bowler having secured more than eight wickets in an innings.

The Staffordshire League bowler, now 40, also broke the 'Test' record by taking altogether in the match 17 wickets, which is two more than the previous best, 15, shared by Rhodes (England v Australia, Melbourne, 1904) and Blythe (England v South Africa, Leeds, 1907). Barnes's feat is even more meritorious, accomplished as it was on a good matting pitch.

County Championship
Surrey v Lancs: 27 June

Hayward's 100th hundred

From the Oval

THOMAS Hayward accomplished a remarkable feat at the Oval today when he scored his 100th hundred in first-class cricket. Only W.G.Grace (the greatest of all cricketers) has a like record, but as the Champion played as many as 126 three-figure innings in important matches, his aggregate is not likely to be beaten. Only one other man is within measurable distance of emulating W.G. and Hayward, namely, C.B.Fry, who has made 92 hundreds.

For many years Hayward ranked as the best professional batsman of the day, and indeed it is only in the last two or three seasons that younger men have challenged his supremacy. His great performances have been many, notably his four consecutive hundreds in six days, in 1906, when he made 144 not out and 100 against Notts and 143 and 125 against Leicester. That summer he scored more runs in a season (3,518) than any other cricketer and made in all 13 hundreds, a record he shares with Fry. Facts like these speak for themselves, and it remains only to add that the great master of orthodox batting is now in his 43rd year.

Today, Hayward extricated Surrey from a very bad position as they began to lose wickets in reply to Lancashire's 558, including that of his opening partner Hobbs for 25. By the close they had made 197 for four, with Hayward 110 not out.

[Hayward made 139 and Surrey, following on, held out for a draw.]

1913

5-6 Jun W.B.Burns (102 not out) becomes only the 3rd player in first-class cricket to score a 100 and take a hat-trick in the same match, for Worcs v Glos, at Worcester.

4 Jul Hon Lionel Tennyson (110) makes 100 on his début for M.C.C. v Oxford University, at Lord's.

13-17 Dec In the 1st Test, at Durban, Staffordshire League medium-fast bowler Sydney Barnes takes 5-57 and 5-48 and becomes the first player to take 150 wickets in Tests. Both captains make 100s, Herbie Taylor (109) for S.Africa and J.W.H.T.Douglas (119) for England, who win by an innings & 157.

County friendly
Lancs v Yorks: 11 July

Dean's 17 wickets: Roses match in the balance

From Liverpool

BATSMEN had an unhappy experience on the Aigburth ground at Liverpool today in the special match arranged in connection with the King's visit to Lancashire. Hot sunshine following the rain gave the bowlers an opportunity that was not missed. In the course of little more than four and a half hours' cricket, 24 wickets went down for an aggregate of 236 runs. At the close of play, Lancashire had lost four second-innings wickets for 71 runs, and thus require another 88 for victory.

Yesterday, Harry Dean, the Lancashire left-arm fast bowler, took nine wickets for 62 runs - and that after missing play before lunch, having left the ground under the impression that, after all the overnight rain, there would not be a resumption until two. Today, he was there from the start, and in Yorkshire's second inning he secured eight for 29 as the Tykes were skittled out for 73, giving him the remarkable record of 17 wickets at a cost of only 91 runs.

Dean's feat, accomplished in 47.4 overs, has been bettered only four times previously, but no one has taken more than 17 wickets in a first-class match. In Lancashire's first innings Rhodes had five for 35, and he picked up another two when Lancashire went in again.

[Lancs won by 3 wickets.]

1914-15

18 Feb 1914 The 4th Test, at Durban, between South Africa and England, finishes in a draw, Sydney Barnes taking 7-88 (14-144 in the match). Barnes's series haul (he is unable to play in the last Test) is an unprecedented 49 wickets at 10.93 apiece - over 12 wickets per match.

26 Feb 1914 Victor Trumper (293) and Sir Arthur Sims (184 not out) set an extraordinary 8th-wicket record of 433 for the touring Australians v Canterbury at Christchurch, beating the previous best (Peel and Hawke in 1896) by 141 runs. It is only the fifth 400 partnership recorded in first-class cricket, and is a new Australian record, surpassing Armstrong and Noble's 6th-wicket 428 made against Sussex in 1902.

3 Mar 1914 England beat South Africa by 10 wickets at Port Elizabeth to take the rubber 4-1, Hobbs finishing with 443 runs at 63.28 without hitting a 100. The only consolation for South Africa is the magnificent overall performance of their 24-year-old captain, Herbie Taylor, who has been the only batsman consistently to withstand the formidable attack of Barnes and has outscored Hobbs with 508 runs (50.80). *[This was the last Test played for nearly 7 years.]*

18 Jul 1914 Alonzo Drake takes 4 wickets in four balls for Yorks v Derby at Chesterfield, the first time the feat has been performed for seven years.

22 Jul 1914 Sydney Smith takes 4 wickets in four balls for Northants v Warwick at Birmingham.

9 Aug 1914 The Oval is requisitioned for military use and Jack Hobbs's benefit match is transferred to Lord's.

13 Aug 1914 Tom Hayward makes his 104th (and last) 100 in 290 1st-wicket partnership with Hobbs for Surrey v Yorks at the Oval.

20 Feb 1915 Norman Callaway (NSW), 19, makes 207 in 210min (100 in 94min) v Queensland, in Sydney, the highest score on first-class début since Tom Marsden (227) in 1826, and, as it turns out, the highest innings for a player making his only first-class appearance. *[He is killed in action in France in 1917.]*

4 Apr 1915 Andrew Stoddart, former captain of England at both cricket and rugby, his health in decline, dies by his own hand at 52.

TEST SERIES

England in South Africa (1913-14) E 4, D 1

WHEN WAR BROKE OUT on 4 August 1914, county cricket struggled on to the end of the month against mounting criticism and the loss of several amateurs to the forces. A letter, however, from W.G.Grace, published in The Sportsman on 27 August, urging the cessation of cricket, had an almost immediate effect, but not before Alonzo Drake at Weston-super-Mare – who, like his namesake at nearby Plymouth more than three centuries earlier, when the Armada was looming large, continued bowling – had taken all 10 wickets in an innings the very next day for Yorkshire against Somerset.

The Oval was immediately requisitioned by the War Office, and Lord's was used during the War for various military purposes, from cadet training to military cooking classes. Services matches, however, were played there as well as M.C.C. XI's against public schools sides.

Many cricketers, of course, gave their lives in the war effort, and in 1915 cricket lost three giants – Grace, Trumper and Stoddart – from other causes.

In 1919, the first season after the war, county matches were played over two days, but the experiment was dropped for the following season. Yorkshire, who played 26 matches, more than any other county (some played as few as 12), won the title with a record of only 46.15%.

Capt. Gilbert Jessop (Glos) recruiting; he was later invalided out of the Manchester Regiment

County Championship: 5 August 1914

War declared: Cricket continues for the moment

DESPITE the declaration of war yesterday, county cricket continued today up and down the country, affected more by the weather than by the fighting on the Continent. Rain completely washed out play at Lord's, and the matches at the Oval, Birmingham and Bournemouth were abandoned.

One match that was affected by hostilities was at Northampton, where Leicestershire had to continue their innings without Aubrey Sharp. As German troops moved into Belgium, Capt Sharp left this morning to rejoin his regiment.

Meeting at Surrey C.C.C.: 31 August 1914

Surrey matches abandoned

AT the special meeting of the Surrey County Cricket Club, held today, to consider the propriety of continuing to play cricket during the present national crisis, it was unanimously decided to abandon all the remaining Surrey fixtures.

It was also learnt today that the Scarborough Festival has been abandoned, an almost inevitable result of the M.C.C.'s action in cancelling the two matches for which they had undertaken to send teams.

[Surrey, with a clear lead in the County table over Middlesex, had needed only one first-innings win from their remaining two Championship fixtures to clinch the title. It was argued by some, however, that they had forfeited their right to it. In the event, Middlesex had no objections and Surrey were awarded the 1914 County Championship.]

County Championship Somerset v Yorks: 28 August 1914

Drake's wonderful feat: First Yorkshire bowler to take all 10 wickets

From Weston-super-Mare

ALONZO Drake, who took four wickets in four balls last month against Derby, today performed another notable bowling feat, taking all 10 wickets in an innings, something no other Yorkshire bowler had previously done in a first-class match.

Although upwards of two dozen players have accomplished this before, only five could boast a better analysis than Drake's 10 for 35, in only 42 balls, in Somerset's second innings. The home side were all out for 90, and Yorkshire won by 140 runs.

Death of Victor Trumper

The death, from dropsy, is announced of Victor Trumper, the famous Australian cricketer – Reuter, Sydney, 28 June 1915.

A cricket correspondent writes: For some considerable time we feared that the days of Victor Trumper were numbered, and yet, now he has been called away in his 38th year, we who love our cricket, and by common consent regarded the famous Australian as the greatest batsman reared by his country, are shocked by the news of his death. Victor Trumper did not belong to Australia alone; he was of the whole world of cricket. He was just as popular in England as in his own country. The name of Trumper will endure for all time, for although we shall probably model our cricket differently in days to come than in other times, when life was less of a hustle and when our games were less commercialised, we shall always play cricket.

There have come to this country from Australia many men who were giants of the game, but it is doubtful whether any batsman who has visited us ever achieved the distinction and won the popularity of Trumper. It was essentially the way he had with him that made his charm; even in 1902, when it became a fashion to expect him to make runs under any conditions, he carried himself with the modesty, the quiet, of a youngster yet to win fame.

We spoke and wrote of him as 'the Ranji of Australia', for that was the highest compliment we could pay him. There was magic in his bat, a run in every stroke. Run-getting seemed to him a joy, a thing ridiculously easy, and it was a business, he made us believe, that must be all sparkle. Trumper was truly the champagne of cricket.

1919

22 May The Somerset versus Sussex match at Taunton is tied, as the visitors' last player, H.J.Heygate, who, having been injured, had not intended to bat, is controversially 'timed out' by the umpire - the only example of such a dismissal in first-class cricket.

26 Jun Andy Ducat makes 306 not out in a day for Surrey (523) v Oxford University at the Oval.

22 Jul Jack 'Farmer' White, the Somerset slow left-armer, takes 16-83 (8-36 and 8-47) in a day v Worcestershire at Bath.

Death of W.G.Grace: The greatest cricketer

WE regret to announce that Dr W.G.Grace, the famous cricketer, died early on Saturday morning [23.10.1915] from heart failure, at his residence, near Eltham, Kent, at the age of 67. He had been ill for some time past.

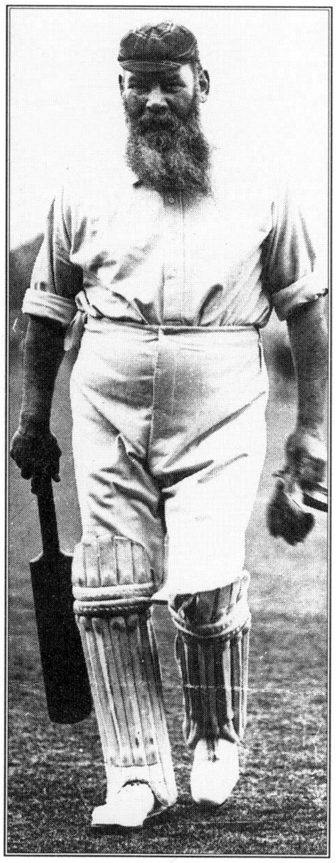

W.G., the Champion: a national figure.

W.G.GRACE[1]

"OUT!" and another master player retires from the wicket to the Great Pavilion, never to take the field again. Dr W.G.Grace is dead, and with him dies the finest all-round cricketer who ever donned flannels. For once there is no danger of over-praise. Giants of the game there still are; giants there were long before Grace's schoolboy name began to be known at Lord's more than half a century ago. But there has never been but one 'W.G.'

'W.G.' has been the hero of successive generations of English boys. He was for thirty years the outstanding figure of the cricket world. Others might blaze as the comets for a few brief seasons; 'W.G.' remained a fixed star of undiminished brilliance from his début in the middle sixties far into the nineties. Greater bowlers there have been, but no more formidable batsman, and certainly no shrewder captain.

The younger generation of men can scarcely realise what 'W.G.' was to those who were boys in the seventies, eighties and early nineties. England then was innocent of golf, and football was only just beginning to be what it is now. Cricket was not only the national game, but the game without a rival. To every boy who handled a bat, the name of 'W.G.' was not merely of a hero but of a demi-god. His scores were the chief thing that mattered in the newspapers during the sunny summer months, which seemed to last so much longer than they do now. A batsman who was reputed to play every ball hard for runs, even though it were the deadliest 'yorker', who strung his centuries together like beads on a string, and on his day could bowl out whole sides together – here was a hero indeed for the eager young enthusiasts of England. 'W.G.' stood for cricket, and for cricket at its best. That is why his passing will be regretted wherever cricket is played with a pang which those who know it not will find very hard to understand.

How many today in England, as they read the news of Dr Grace's death, will cast their memory back to the day when they first thrilled to see the big, black-bearded giant with a little red and yellow cap standing at the wicket. His bat looked a mere toy, a plaything, but with what vigour it descended to the ball; how clean and sharp the stroke; and how manifest the intention to send it just where it went. To see him open his shoulders for the drive, or, with the ball lost in that vast hand, to watch him lumber up to the wicket with that round-arm action. We have not been talking much about cricket this summer; on most of the county grounds hardly a ball has been bowled ; but a brighter day will come, sooner or later, and when it does, we wish nothing better than that the game may continue to be played in the spirit in which 'W.G.' played it for more than thirty years.

1 Extracts from the second leader (the first, 'Progress of the War', was shorter, at 15 column inches to 23!), which was published in addition to a 3,000-word obituary.

Advisory County Committee Meeting: 8 December 1919

Counties to revert to three-day matches

From Lord's

LORD Harris took the chair at the meeting of the Advisory Committee, with representatives present from the M.C.C., all the first-class counties and the Minor Counties' Association.

The proceedings were private, and at the end of the meeting information regarding the results of motions was supplied. The chief decision was that, for next season, three-day matches will be reverted to, so that cricket will carry on very much as it was before the war.

Scarborough Festival England XI v Australian Imperial Forces XI: 10 September 1919

Australians beaten: Close finish to representative match

THE closing match of the Scarborough Festival ended today in a victory for the England XI, but the honours rested to a large extent with the Australians, who, after being 106 runs behind on the first innings, only lost by two wickets.

Scores: Australians 81 (Hitch 6-24) & 296 (Willis 96, Taylor 71; Hitch 5-102), England XI 187 (J.M.Gregory 7-83) & 191-8 (Hobbs 93).

The 1920s

WHEN Test cricket resumed in the twenties, England had not recovered from the War. The MCC were reluctant to send a side to Australia in 1920-21, but it had been nine years since their last tour and Australia persuaded them to do so. It was a tremendous fillip for Australian cricket and huge crowds watched the matches, but England relinquished the Ashes and suffered an unprecedented 5-0 humiliation, losing every Test by substantial margins. Their run of defeats was extended to eight in 1921, and they did not beat Australia again until February 1925 in Melbourne, after losing 11 of 13 Tests.

England's biggest post-war problem was in bowling - Charlie Blythe had been killed in action, Frank Foster's career was finished by a motorcycle crash early in the war, and the great Sydney Barnes had retired from first-class cricket - and their fielding, compared with the brilliant Australians, was second-rate.

Yet cricket in England was more popular than ever. The post-Armistice Jeremiahs who were prophesying the decline of the game - some newspapers even predicted it would be superseded by baseball - could not have been more wrong. The best county matches drew huge crowds, gates at Lord's and the Oval double and even treble those of pre-War. And at Test level England recovered, winning back the Ashes in 1926 on a highly emotional day at the Oval and retaining them in comprehensive fashion in Australia in 1929, when Wally Hammond announced his greatness with 905 runs in a series that also saw the ominous emergence of Don Bradman for Australia.

For most of the decade, Jack Hobbs was still the best batsman in the world, as he had been from about 1910. And Hobbs and Sutcliffe were the best opening pair in Test cricket. Hobbs was the 'Master' on all wickets, and on sticky, difficult wickets there was no one to touch him. Everything he did was graceful, his fielding as well as his stroke-play, and he was just as popular and admired in Australia and South Africa as he was at home. Sutcliffe, more practical than elegant, shared Hobbs's appetite for runs and together they made 26 century opening partnerships. England also had the majestic left-hander Frank Woolley of Kent, who reached his 100 hundreds, and whose aggregate of runs in first-class cricket was topped only by Hobbs. Woolley regularly captured 100 wickets a season, and took more catches, mostly in the slips, than anyone else in first-class cricket.

Some of the counties after the war were very weak - Derbyshire lost all 17 of their matches in 1920 - but there was strong competition at the top. Middlesex, with Patsy Hendren's batting and the all-round performances of J.W. Hearne, won the first two titles of the decade, before Yorkshire reasserted themselves. The Tykes won the next four championships and were never lower than fourth in the twenties. Sutcliffe and Percy Holmes shared 69 century first-wicket partnerships, and Wilfred Rhodes, that greatest of all-rounders, continued his prolific wicket-taking into his fifties. Lancashire enjoyed a hat-trick of county titles in the late twenties, with Ernest Tyldesley their prime run-maker and Dick Tyldesley (no relation) a notable wicket-taker.

Interstate matches in Australia produced some massive scores, Victoria twice topping 1,000 runs to set new records, aided by the prolific scoring of Bill Ponsford, who twice topped 400 with world-record innings and made a couple of 300s, too. He was a thorn in England's side until Harold Larwood tamed him. For Australia, Charles Macartney continued his pre-War domination of England's bowlers for several years and Jack Gregory was a spectacular all-rounder, a fearsome fast bowler in tandem with Ted McDonald and in 1921 against South Africa hitting the fastest Test century ever.

South Africa had few successes in the twenties, although they did manage to share a series with England in 1927-28 and Herbie Taylor was a masterly batsman on matting wickets. The West Indies made their first tours to England since 1906, playing their first Tests in 1928, and although their overall play left much room for improvement, they produced some really sensational individual performers - George Challenor for his batting in 1923 and Learie Constantine for both batting and bowling in 1928.

A familiar and reassuring sight for England fans in the twenties, Hobbs (left) and Sutcliffe coming out to open the innings. Insets: Victoria's Bill Ponsford (top), and Patsy Hendren of Middlesex.

1920

15 May Percy Chapman makes 118 on his first-class début for Cambridge Univ v Essex.

22-24 May In their 543-4 dec, the first four Middlesex batsmen make 100s v Sussex: Warner 139, Lee 119, Hearne 116 not, Haig 131.

10 Jun K.A.Higgs (Sussex), at 33, scores 101 on his début v Worcs at Hove.

30 Aug Percy Holmes (Yorks) makes 302 not out v Hants at Portsmouth.

1 Sep G.J.Bryan (Kent) makes 124 on his début v Notts at Nottingham.

4 Dec Warren Bardsley (235) and Charles Kelleway (168) complete a world-record stand of 397 for the 5th wicket for NSW (802) v South Australia at Sydney, beating by 4 the Arnold/Burns (Worcs) mark in 1909.

22 Dec Wilf Rhodes, playing for England against Australia at Sydney, becomes the first to make 2,000 runs and take 100 wickets in Tests.

County Championship Northants v Surrey: 26 August

Tremendous hitting by Surrey: Fender's fastest hundred

From Northampton

GIVING a remarkable display of hitting, Surrey took their score from the overnight 12 for one to 619 for five wickets soon after the tea interval, before declaring. The innings reached an astonishing climax as Peach and Fender put on 171 runs in 42 minutes, the latter hitting the fastest century ever recorded in first-class cricket.

Fine weather and an easy wicket were all in favour of the batsmen. Before lunch runs came at a sedate pace, but after the interval the Northamptonshire bowlers came in for terrific punishment. Sandham played admirably, making 92 out of 160 in an hour and three-quarters. Then a brilliant stand was made by Peach and Ducat for the fifth wicket. The total stood at 213 at lunch time, and afterwards the bowling was hit all over the field, Peach having the satisfaction of scoring his first hundred for Surrey. Ducat joined Peach and, hitting still more freely, helped him put 200 runs on in an hour and a half. The partnership altogether realised 288 in two hours and a quarter, before a catch at the wicket dismissed Ducat, who had as his share 149, made without a serious mistake.

Percy Fender: Fastest first-class century.

With Percy Fender in, however, even the previous hitting was eclipsed. The amateur should have been caught at cover-point by Freeman when two, and for this bad mistake the home side had to pay a heavy cost. Fender actually made his 100 in 35 minutes, surpassing a memorable 100 by Jessop at Harrogate in 40 minutes. He hit five 6's and sixteen 4's in his 113. Peach completed 200, without giving a chance, in three hours and 10 minutes, striking twenty-six 4's.

Northants, 313 behind, made 59 for the loss of two wickets before the close, one of them to Fender.

[Northants made 430 and Surrey won by 8 wickets.]

County Championship Middlesex v Surrey: 31 August

Middlesex champions: Dramatic finish

By Colonel Philip Trevor, C.B.E., at Lord's

Middlesex won a magnificent victory over Surrey at Lord's today, and with it they won the Championship for the second time in their history after a gap of 17 years. The end came at 22 minutes past six, with victory by 55 runs. The crowd surged over the field, and gathered in front of the pavilion, loudly calling for "Warner", the Middlesex captain, a wonderful servant of both club and country, who came out to address them from the balcony.

This was Plum Warner's last match, and what a reward it was for his admirable captaincy and untiring zeal on behalf of the county. And what a climax for Middlesex, who had won eight matches in succession in August and had to win this one, Lancashire having beaten Worcester, if they were to take the title.

Warner himself, now nearly 47, had a big share in the victory gained. His steady batting for 79 on the first day averted a collapse. Then Lee (108) and Skeet (106), by their sound and skilful batting in the second innings, made victory at least a possibility, and finally, just when everything seemed to point to a win for Surrey, the googly bowlers Hearne (3-37) and Stevens (5-61) came to the rescue in the nick of time and pulled the match out of the fire.

Middlesex were 27 without loss when they resumed this morning, and Lee and Skeet put on another 172 runs in the two hours before lunch. Warner declared at 316 for seven, leaving Surrey to get 244 in three hours, not a very terrible proposition on such a wicket, but the Middlesex captain had to force a win.

Sandham, who carried his bat for 167 in Surrey's first innings, was again in his very best form, but Hobbs was not and went for 10. Sandham kept Surrey up with the clock, and found a good partner in Shepherd (26), before the latter was gloriously caught in the deep field, near the screen, by Hendren, swinging the game back to Middlesex. Sandham went on to make 68, but Fender, Peach and Ducat all failed, and when Stevens finally clean-bowled Strudwick, Middlesex were champions.

First Test Third day: 20 December

Australia 409 ahead with 5 wickets left: Collins 100 on début

From Sydney

BATTLING all day with ease and confidence, the Australians had secured a very strong position in the Test match when stumps were drawn this evening. At 332 for five, they were 409 runs on. A feature of today was the batting of Herbie Collins, who, at nearly 32, joined the select band of eight cricketers to score a century in their first Test.

England's bowling was weak and lacked sting. Douglas was criticised for not employing Rhodes, Woolley and Hearne more, and for not trying Hitch until after the tea interval. The fielding of the Englishmen was not so keen as on Saturday, and they appeared tired with the long day's leather hunting. Collins and Bardsley took their overnight opening partnership to 123, and Collins then enjoyed a further century partnership (111) with Macartney before he was out.

[Armstrong came in and it was another 187 runs before the next wicket fell, Australia winning by 377 runs. Scores: Australia 267 (Collins 70) & 581 (Armstrong 158, Collins 104, Kelleway 78, Macartney 69, Bardsley 57, Taylor 51), England 190 (Woolley 52) & 281 (Hobbs 59, J.W.Hearne 57, Hendren 56).]

Fourth Test Fourth day: 15 February

Mailey's brilliant bowling: Record 9 wickets puts Australia on top

From Melbourne

THANKS to some magnificent bowling by spinner Arthur Mailey, who took nine wickets for 121 runs in England's second innings, Australia have secured a strong position in the Test match. At the close of play this evening, they required another 119 runs to win with eight wickets still in hand. Mailey's performance in securing nine wickets in one innings establishes a new record for a Test match between England and Australia.

There was another large attendance today, fully 12,000 people witnessing the play after the tea interval. Warwick Armstrong, who made 123 not out in Australia's first innings, was still confined to his bed, suffering from the after effects of malaria, and Collins took his place as captain of the side.

At one stage, England were 200 runs ahead, on 305 for five. Rhodes gave a very sound and stylish display of patient cricket for his 73 in just over three hours, and Douglas and Fender both hit fifties in a sixth-wicket partnership that yielded 105 runs in 86 minutes. But as soon as Fender was out, the England innings suffered a dramatic collapse, only another 10 runs being added. Mailey, with his leg-breaks and googlies, claimed all five wickets, three of them stumped by 'Sammy' Carter. He finished with match figures of 13 for 236.

At stumps, Australia were 92 for two, having lost Collins and Bardsley.

[Australia won by 8 wickets. Over 70 years later, Mailey was still the only Australian to take 9 wickets in a Test innings.]

County Championship Glamorgan v Sussex: 20 May

Triumph of Glamorgan: Victory in first match

From Cardiff

GLAMORGAN began their career as a first-class county in a highly satisfactory fashion, defeating Sussex by 23 runs at Cardiff today.

They lost their remaining wicket this morning without addition to their overnight score of 213. But they had built up a strong position, leaving Sussex with the formidable task of making 334 runs to win. Sussex lost their first three wickets for 59, but a fourth-wicket stand of 166 between Bowley (146) and Jenner (55) put them right back in the match. After Jenner's dismissal, however, only Gilligan (33) offered Bowley much help and Sussex were all out for 310, Cooper and Creber taking four wickets apiece.

[Glamorgan won only one more match in the Championship and finished 17th and bottom.]

Third Test Second day: 4 July

Hobbs operated on: Tennyson's plucky batting saves follow-on

By Colonel Philip Trevor, C.B.E., at Headingley

Stirring stuff from captain courageous: Tennyson completes another 'forehand drive' with his one good hand.

England found themselves in desperate straits this morning, after losing three more quick wickets, having scored only 67 for five in reply to Australia's first-innings total of 407. The situation was, of course, even worse than the scoreboard suggested for, with Hobbs unable to bat - he was operated on this morning for appendicitis - and Tennyson able to use only one hand, another failure at this juncture could easily have meant the total collapse of the side. The left-hander Brown, England's new wicket-keeper, joined Douglas in a stand of 97 before he was out for 57, but White immediately followed, leaving England on 165 for seven, with only two wickets to fall.

That's when England's new captain, the Hon. Lionel Tennyson, came in to bat. Having badly split his hand trying to stop one of Macartney's drives yesterday, he could not grip his bat with the left hand, but he surprised and delighted everyone, hitting cleanly and keeping the ball on the ground. Douglas, the captain he had deposed, was as steady, stolid and reliable as ever, and the pair put on 87 runs before he was bowled by Armstrong for 75.

England still needed six runs to save the follow-on when the last man, Parkin, joined Tennyson, and, after two carefully made runs, he indulged in a mighty square-leg hit. It came off, and the crowd roared with delight. Half a minute later, Tennyson was caught at first slip for 63. Under the circumstances, his performance must rank as one of the best of its kind ever seen in a Test match. His fearless one-handed display against the fast bowling of Gregory and MacDonald will take its place in the folklore of cricket. England may well lose tomorrow, but they will not have been disgraced.

[Australia won by 219 runs. Tennyson made 36 in England's 2nd innings.]

1921

1 Jan Right-arm fast bowler Jack Gregory, having taken 7-69 in England's 1st innings, makes 100 (left-handed) in 137min at No.9, adding 173 for the 8th wicket with 'Nip' Pellew (116) to swing the 2nd Test, at Melbourne, Australia's way (they win by an innings).

14-20 Jan Australia win the 3rd Test at Adelaide to regain the Ashes, scoring 582 in their 2nd innings (beating by 1 their record in the 1st Test) in a match that produces the highest aggregate, 1,753 runs, in Tests. Mailey takes 10 for a record 302 runs conceded in a Test, and six 100s are scored.

1 Mar Australia chalk up their record 5th win in a rubber, whitewashing England 5-0. Gregory takes his 15th catch, a series record, and Mailey his 36th wicket, a record for an Ashes rubber.

22-24 Jun Vallance Jupp (Sussex) scores 102 and takes 12 wickets (6-61 & 6-78), including the hat-trick, v Essex at Colchester.

25, 27 Jun The Australians (675) beat Notts (58 & 100) by an innings and 517 runs, Charles Macartney hitting 345 out of 540 in 235min, the highest innings by an Australian in England and the most runs ever scored in a day.

13-16 Aug Phil Mead makes 182 not out in the 5th Test at the Oval, a record for England at home to Australia (beating W.G.Grace's 170 here in 1886), but the match drifts into a meaningless draw, with Australian captain Armstrong reading a newspaper in the long field - his comment on 3-day Tests. England used 30 players in the series.

23 Aug Mailey takes all 10-66 for the Australians v Glos at Cheltenham, the 5th player to perform the feat this season.

30 Aug The Australians (174 & 167) suffer their first defeat on tour, improbably by 'A.C.MacLaren's England XI' (43 & 326) by 28 runs, the 49-year-old former England captain having promised to produce a team of amateurs to beat the all-conquering tourists. The veteran South African all-rounder Aubrey Faulkner scores 153 and takes 6-63 (match).

12 Nov Gregory (119) makes the fastest Test 100 (70min) in the drawn 2nd Test in Johannesburg (and goes on to take 7 wickets).

TEST SERIES

England in Australia
Australia 5
Australia in England
A 3, D 2
Australia in South Africa
A 1, D 2

1922

17-18 Aug Fast-medium bowler George Collins takes all 10-65 for Kent v Sussex at Dover, and 16-83 in the match.

Nov The first ever wireless commentary on a cricket match takes place in Australia, on the NSW trial match for the benefit of former Test cricketer Charles Bannerman.

23-28 Dec In their first Test with England since before the war, S.Africa win by 168 runs at Johannesburg, thanks largely to 176 by their captain, Herbie Taylor, in the second innings.

County Championship
Sussex v Kent: 1 September

Freeman again: Kent win by an innings

From Hove

Thanks to the remarkable bowling of Freeman, who took 17 wickets for 67 runs in the match, Kent gained a brilliant victory over Sussex by an innings and 23 runs. After declaring on their overnight score of 196 for nine, a lead of 149, they dismissed Sussex for 126.

Freeman, it may be remembered, took all five Sussex wickets that fell during what play was possible on Wednesday for 10 runs, and then took four more yesterday at a personal cost of one run to finish with the remarkable analysis of nine for 11. He followed this up by taking eight Sussex second innings wickets today for 56 runs, which brought his record for the match to 17 wickets for 67 runs. He is only the twelfth bowler to capture as many as 17 wickets in a first-class match, and no one has taken more.

County Championship Warwicks v Hants: 16 June

Hampshire triumph: Remarkable transformation

From Birmingham

An altogether wonderful match at Birmingham ended this afternoon in an improbable victory for Hampshire by 155 runs. It is of interest to go over the ground of what occurred on the first two days.

Tennyson, it may be recalled, put Warwickshire in after winning the toss. But, having scored 223, the home side got rid of the Hampshire eleven for the paltry total of 15, in which Phil Mead was top scorer with 6 not out and eight batsmen failed to score. Howell, bowling very fast on a pitch that helped the bowlers, took six for 7, Calthorpe four for 4. From that point, Hampshire, following on, made such a marvellous recovery that when play ceased yesterday evening they had pulled the game completely round, having scored 475 for nine wickets. Such a transformation has rarely, if ever, been seen in first-class cricket.

Hampshire proceeded with the good work today, another 46 runs being added before the innings closed. Walter Livsey, who when not keeping wicket is his captain's butler, carried out his bat for 110, his first hundred for Hampshire. Having helped Brown (172) add 177 yesterday for the ninth wicket, he put on 70 with Boyes (29) for the last wicket.

So Warwickshire, despite their sensational bowling successes on the opening afternoon, found themselves left with no fewer than 314 runs to get to win. They never looked like making them, and by 4.20 were all out for 158. Hampshire had won a famous victory.

Phil Mead: Top scorer in Hampshire's first innings - with 6 not out!

Cricket in Australia 1923
Victoria v Tasmania: 5 February

Thousand runs in one innings

From Melbourne

VICTORIA second eleven playing against Tasmania here have made the remarkable score of 1,103 runs for nine wickets. Of this total Ponsford has contributed 429 runs, reports Central News.

This is the highest total of which there is any record for a match of any importance. But Ponsford's individual score has been beaten in England, A.E. Stoddart compiling 485 for Hampstead against the Stoics in 1886. The highest individual score in first-class cricket stands to the credit of A.C.MacLaren, who made 424 for Lancashire against Somerset in 1896. The highest total in England was also made in 1896 when Yorkshire scored 887 against Warwickshire. In Australia, New South Wales knocked up 918 against South Australia in January 1901.

[This match was accorded first-class status, and Ponsford's innings set a new world record. Victoria (not their 2nd XI as reported) went on to make 1,059 and win by an innings and 666 runs. This was only Ponsford's 4th first-class innings for Victoria. He came in at 200-3 and was out, 477min later, at 1,001-8.]

County Championship Notts v Hants: 1 September

Newman apologises: Great bowling by Richmond

From Nottingham

THE incident that marred yesterday's cricket, when John Newman was sent off by his captain, the Hon. Lionel Tennyson, was very happily closed today when the Hampshire all-rounder apologised to both captains. It will be remembered that Newman delayed before bowling an over and was barracked by the crowd, and when Tennyson ordered him to leave the field for "using offensive language" he kicked down the stumps as he went.

In response to an urgent request from the Hampshire Committee, he was permitted to resume his place on the field when cricket was proceeded with in the morning. And as the crowd had been largely responsible for provoking the incident, it was very pleasant to note that on going on to the field at Trent Bridge Newman had a very cordial reception from about 3,000 people.

Thanks chiefly to the spin bowling of Tom Richmond, who took nine wickets for 21, less than three hours' cricket proved sufficient for Notts to gain a capital victory by nine wickets and wind up the season second to Yorkshire in the County Championship.

County Championship Essex v Yorks: 1 September

Yorkshire champions: A few minutes' play at Leyton

From Leyton

YORKSHIRE became champions today for the eleventh time in their history, although it surely can never have happened in less dramatic fashion. A county match that does not begin till tea-time on the third day and then lasts only a few minutes comes rather near breaking a somewhat miserable record. Yet such was the state of affairs at Leyton today, it was only due to the desire of both captains to 'play the game' that there was any cricket at all. The weather outlook was already sufficiently ominous and the abandonment of the match in a very short time was practically a foregone conclusion.

During their brief time at the wicket Essex made 5 runs for the loss of Russell, and it was indeed a doleful end to the county cricket season in the London area. But in this way Yorkshire suffered no change in the percentage of points they had previously gained, and the title was theirs.

Second Test Fourth day: 4 January

Dramatic finish to Test: England win by one wicket

From Cape Town

IN a match that will go down in the annals of 'test' cricket as one of the most memorable ever played between the two countries, England today triumphed over South Africa at Newlands by the narrow margin of one wicket. It was a match of fluctuating fortunes, both sides collapsing in a greater or lesser degree in both innings. But when the last stage was entered upon, England's chance of victory was regarded as anything but favourable.

However, F.T.Mann and V.W.C.Jupp put on 68 for the seventh wicket before Jupp (38) left at 154, and the England captain, to whom the honours of the day must go, continued playing perfect cricket. It was not until England were within 6 runs of victory that he was out for 45, England's highest score in the match.

Even then, the game took another sensational turn as Brown was run out at 168 for a 'duck'. Macaulay, the last man, came in, and amidst great noise and excitement Kennedy pulled Blanckenberg to the boundary to equalise the scores. The fieldsmen closed in on the batsmen in a last desperate effort to stop the winning run, and Hall completely beat Macaulay with his second delivery. But the next ball the Yorkshireman got away for a single, and England had won.

Kennedy and Macaulay were loudly cheered at the close, while Alf Hall, who by his wonderful bowling (11-112) on his début almost won the match for his side, was chaired off the field in triumph. George Macaulay also had a notable début, for as well as hitting the winning run, he took a wicket with his first ball in Test cricket.

Scores: S.Africa 113 (Fender 4-29) & 242 (Catterall 76, Taylor 68; Macaulay 5-64, Kennedy 4-58), England 183 (Blanckenberg 5-61, Hall 4-49) & 173-9 (Hall 7-63).

1923

18-22 Jan Durban's new Test ground Kingsmead opens with a draw, Phil Mead making 181 in 8hr 20min for England.

16-22 Feb Charles 'Jack' Russell becomes the first English batsman to make two 100s in a Test (140 & 111) as England beat S.Africa by 109 runs at Durban to take the series 2-1.

24 May Fast bowler Henry Howell takes all 10-51 for Warwicks v Yorks at Birmingham.

13-15 Jun Middlesex compile their highest innings, 642-3d v Hants at Southampton, their first 4 batsmen making 100s: Dales 103, Lee 107, J.W.Hearne 232, Hendren 177 not, Nos.2 and 3 having participated in a similar feat in 1920.

21 Jun Fast bowler F.C.Matthews takes 17-89 for Notts v Northants at Nottingham.

17 Aug Yorks win their 13th county match in succession and, with 5 to play, are already champions again.

22 Dec Bill Ponsford (228) and Edgar Mayne (209) put on 456 for the first wicket for Victoria v Queensland at Melbourne, an Australian record for any wicket and surpassed only by the Brown/Tunnicliffe 554 stand of 1898.

TEST SERIES

England in South Africa
E 1, SA 2, D 2

County Championship Somerset v Surrey: 8 May

Hobbs's hundred centuries: Narrow victory for Surrey

By Colonel Philip Trevor, C.B.E.

Jack Hobbs made his hundredth hundred in first-class cricket at Bath today, and by so doing included himself in a select list of three, for W.G.Grace made 126 hundreds and Tom Hayward 104. It has, however, allowing for the war years, taken Hobbs far less time (13 years) than either of his distinguished predecessors. He was 21 when, in 1905, he played his first county match for Surrey - scoring, incidentally, 155 - and he has, of course, played much overseas cricket, including three trips each to Australia and South Africa. He played first for England in 1908 during the tour of Australia and, except by reason of illness or accident, has never been left out of an England eleven at home or abroad since. He has made 7 centuries for England, 70 for Surrey and the rest for the Players, M.C.C. and other representative teams. In 817 first-class innings, Hobbs has scored 34,534 runs.

It was under most anxious conditions that Hobbs accomplished his notable feat today, so badly had Surrey batted yesterday and again in their second innings today. But after some early setbacks, Hobbs found an invaluable partner in Hitch (67), and went on batting in masterly fashion to reach his coveted 100 in three hours and five minutes.

At 20 minutes past three, with the total at 216 for five and Hobbs not out 116, Fender declared, leaving Somerset plenty of time in which to make the 168 needed to win. But wickets fell regularly, and with play extended beyond half-past six, the Somerset innings closed for 157, Surrey thus gaining a sensational victory by 10 runs.

Tour match Surrey v W.Indies: 3 August

Surrey lose to West Indies: G.Challenor again

By Colonel Philip Trevor, at the Oval

THE West Indians won a magnificent victory this afternoon at Kennington Oval, where they beat Surrey, albeit without Hobbs, in hollow fashion by 10 wickets, the county's first home defeat this season. The story of this great win is the story of George Challenor's batting, and that story should be told in three parts. Challenor scored in all 221 runs, and his opponents did not get him out. On Wednesday he got 66 of those runs on a slow wicket, showing us that he was a very good defensive player. Yesterday he got 89 more on a nice easy-paced wicket on the fast side, showing us how to combine attack and defence, and carrying his bat for 155. And today he got 66 more runs by batting which, though exceptionally brilliant, was as faultless as his batting on Wednesday had been.

Challenor has got to be given very high ranking among the moderns. His timing of the ball is as nearly as possible perfect, and he never lifts it from the ground. Like most moderns, he is not at pains to do much straight driving, but his shots through the covers and behind point are superbly done, and I doubt if the best of our batsmen affect the leg glide with more certainty and precision than he does. Best of all, he makes batting look a joy, though he is undramatic in method and quite without mannerisms.

It was Challenor's match all through and his performance dwarfed everything else, even the fast bowling of team-mate George Francis, who took 10 wickets, and the dogged, faultless century of D.R. Jardine, fresh from Oxford, that gave the Surrey second innings some respectability.

Challenor: Perfect timing.

Scores: Surrey 87 (Francis 5-31, Browne 4-41) & 336 (Jardine 104, Abel 63, Shepherd 53; Francis 5-45), W.Indies 305 (Challenor 155 not; Fender 4-71) & 121-0 (Challenor 66 not).

1924

29 May Middlesex captain Frank Mann hits four 6's into the Lord's pavilion v Yorks.

6 Jun H.A.Peach (Surrey) takes 4 wickets in 4 balls v Sussex at the Oval.

28 Jun-1 Jul England (531-2d) beat S.Africa by an innings and 18 at Lord's for the loss of only 2 wickets, Hobbs (211) & Sutcliffe (122) putting on 268 for the 1st wicket.

3 Jul Dick Tyldesley takes 5-0 for Lancs v Leics at Manchester.

19-27 Dec Australia v England at Sydney, the 1st Test in the first series to use 8-ball overs, is the first Test to last into a 7th day. A record-equalling 6 hundreds are scored (3 each), Ponsford (110) on début; Hobbs & Sutcliffe make two opening century partnerships (157 & 110), and Tate takes 11 for 228 - but England lose by 193 runs in a match of 1,611. Mailey takes 7 wickets for Australia but concedes 308 runs, a record in Tests.

TEST SERIES

South Africa in England
E 3, D 2

County Championship Lancs v Glamorgan: 15 May

Parkin six for 6: Glamorgan put out for 22 runs

From Liverpool

AMPLE amends were made at Liverpool today for the loss of the cricket yesterday. The pitch proved most treacherous, and in the first 2hr 20min an innings apiece was completed. Lancashire were dismissed for 49, and Glamorgan, faring even worse, were disposed of in less than an hour for 22, the lowest score in their short first-class history. Subsequently, Makepeace and Hallows established a strong advantage for Lancashire.

In the Lancashire first innings, former Lancashire professional Helm Spencer, medium-pace right-hand, came on for Arnott and took five wickets for 9 in 10.1 overs. Mercer took three for 27 and Ryan two for 0 in two overs. Only Albert Rhodes (10) reached double figures.

For Lancashire, off-spinner 'Ciss' Parkin carried off the bowling honours. He actually took his first five wickets without having a run hit from him, and came out with the wonderful analysis of 8 overs 5 maidens 6 runs 6 wickets. Dick Tyldesley took the other four wickets for 16, and only Bates (11) made double figures for Glamorgan.

When Lancashire went in a second time the pitch was still very soft, but the heavy rollers eased it and Makepeace (41) and Hallows (49) gave them a good start. And although they lost five wickets before the close for 137, their lead of 164 puts them in a very good position.

[Lancashire won the match by 128 runs.]

First Test Second day: 16 June

Amazing collapse of the South Africans: All out 30

By Colonel Philip Trevor, C.B.E., at Edgbaston

Arthur Gilligan: Six wickets for 7 runs.

TODAY the South Africans gave us the extremes in batting on a good wicket, ranging in the space of a few hours from sheer rank bad in their first innings to some splendid hitting in their second at the end of the day as the England bowlers tired.

Replying to England's first innings total of 438, the South Africans were skittled out for 30, the lowest innings in a Test in England and equal to the lowest in Test history, also by South Africa against England, at Port Elizabeth in 1896 - when Lohmann took eight for 7 and Poore was top scorer with 10. At Birmingham today, it was a similar story, with England captain Arthur Gilligan taking the bowling honours with six for 7 - Tate's four for 12 reads quite tame in comparison - and 'Mr Extras' making top score with 11. No batsman reached double figures.

At ten minutes to one the South Africans, in the minority of 408 runs, followed on. By the close they had compiled 274 for four wickets and all the batsmen made runs. It is idle to speculate as to why several men in succession cannot face the music at noon or thereabouts, and then an hour or so later face it with confidence if not with ease, and one can only put it down, as is so often the case, to the 'glorious uncertainty' of cricket. Of the six batsmen who came to the wicket, three made fifties (two not out), and the least successful made 29 - only one fewer than the first-innings total. But they still need 134 to make England bat again.

[England won by an innings and 18 runs, Gilligan taking 5-83, Tate 4-103, and Catterall making 120.]

County Championship Glos v Middlesex: 26 August

Middlesex beaten: Triumph of Parker - another 'hat-trick'

By a Special Correspondent, at Bristol

Charlie Parker: Two hat-tricks.

WONDERFUL Gloucestershire! At Bristol today, after a match of astonishing fluctuations, they beat Middlesex by 61 runs. No better or more startling performance has any of the counties achieved in this especially wet season. To appreciate the full merit of their success against Middlesex, it is necessary that the match should be taken from its inception. Nigel Haig, making the ball do all manner of capers, played havoc with the Gloucestershire batting on Saturday, taking six wickets for 11 in 12 overs, the other four falling to Durston for 18. The whole side were out for 31, and no batsman reached double figures. Then Parker had Middlesex in great difficulties, taking seven for 30, including the hat-trick, his second this season, as they scraped together 74 by the end of a day that saw 20 wickets fall. Yesterday saw Gloucester lose two wickets for 12 before Hammond, the young professional, got them out of this seemingly hopeless position. Coming in first wicket down, he played a wonderful, almost faultless innings and carried his bat for 174. With such gallantry, confidence and freedom did he treat hitherto unplayable bowling that he recalled the days of Jessop with his back to the wall. His innings turned the whole complexion of the game, for Middlesex were set the task of making 252 runs to win.

Today, it was Charlie Parker with his left-arm slows who again did all the mischief; for the second time in the game, and for the fifth occasion in his career, he performed the 'hat-trick', dismissing Mann, Guise, and Haig with successive balls. And he did this when his fielders were given to missing catches. His total bag was 14 wickets for 131 - not bad for a man in his 42nd year.

Second Test Sixth day: 7 January

Sutcliffe's unprecedented feat: England's fine chance

From Reuter's Special Cricket Service, in Melbourne

THANKS mainly to the magnificent defensive tactics of Herbert Sutcliffe, who batted all day with stubborn determination and was still undefeated with 114 to his credit at the drawing of stumps, the Englishmen have an excellent chance of gaining a much-needed victory. In again reaching three figures, Sutcliffe performed the unprecedented feat of scoring three consecutive centuries in Test cricket and also equalled Warren Bardsley's record of two separate hundreds in an England-Australia match, made at the Oval in 1909.

Sutcliffe's masterly innings aroused great enthusiasm among the spectators, and was eulogised everywhere as the finest display of bulldog tenacity seen for a long time. The Australian bowlers kept a good length and the fielding was keen. The wicket was as hard as flint, and the ball used before lunch was found to be so cut about, with the hidden stitching exposed, that a new ball was requisitioned and frequently changed throughout the afternoon.

England resumed this morning at 51 for one, having lost Hobbs lbw yesterday, and it was rather an extraordinary fact that the next three batsmen were also given out in this way. The crowd shouted "What will they say in England?" after Woolley's dismissal for 50, and "Wait for the English newspaper comments". The Kent man stated he played the ball, a claim later corroborated by Oldfield, the Australian wicket-keeper.

When stumps were drawn, England were 259 for six, still requiring 113 for victory.

[Sutcliffe made 127 (303 in match), England, their tail failing again (last 4 wickets went down for 10), lost by 81.]

1925

17 Jan Coming in at 119-6 in the 3rd Test, at Adelaide, Jack Ryder makes 201 not and Australia go on to beat England by 11 runs and retain the Ashes.

13 Feb England's Herbert Sutcliffe (143) makes his 4th 100 in the rubber, at Melbourne in the 4th Test, England going on to win by an innings, their only success.

4 Mar Spinner Clarrie Grimmett (Australia) takes 11-82 on début at Sydney as Australia win last Test, while Sutcliffe's 734 (81.55) is a Test series record and Maurice Tate's 38 wickets, a record for Anglo-Australian series.

8 Jun Percy Holmes (Yorks) makes 315 not v Middlesex at Lord's.

28 Jul Charlie Parker (Glos) takes 17-56 (9-44 & 8-12) v Essex at Gloucester.

19 Aug Alfred Dipper (144) and 22-year-old Walter Hammond (250 not) add 330 for the 3rd wicket for Glos v Lancs, a record for Old Trafford.

3 Sep Hobbs makes 266 not for Players at Scarborough, a record for Gents-Players matches.

TEST SERIES

England in Australia
A 4, E 1

County Championship Notts v Middlesex: 23 June

Wonderful Middlesex, an unparalleled feat: Hendren's perfect batting

From Nottingham

MIDDLESEX, having to make no fewer than 502 to win, obtained them for the loss of six batsmen, and gained a brilliant and astonishing victory over Notts by four wickets. Such a performance is without parallel in county cricket. Indeed in first-class matches there are only three other instances of a side getting over 500 in the last innings.

Overnight, Middlesex had lost three good batsmen for 60 runs, while a fourth was dismissed first thing this morning for the addition of 6. Then came a splendid partnership by Hendren and Bruce, the latter of whom made 103 out of 154 put on in 95 minutes. But with six men out shortly before lunch for 231, the position certainly did not favour Middlesex. At that point, however, Hendren was joined by his captain, Mann, and the two men, establishing a complete mastery over a varied attack, stayed together until 20 minutes to six, and, by adding 271 in three hours and a quarter, hit off the balance without being separated. The whole innings took just 375 minutes.

The hero of the day was undoubtedly Patsy Hendren, who for the third time in a fortnight - in the course of which he has scored no fewer than 869 runs - put together an innings of over 200. Altogether he was five hours and a quarter at the wickets, hitting two 5's and nineteen 4's in his truly wonderful 206 not out.

County Championship Somerset v Surrey: 18 August

Hobbs excels the W.G.Grace record: 127th 100, fourteen in a season

By Colonel Philip Trevor, at Taunton

This afternoon, when Surrey beat Somerset by 10 wickets at Taunton, Jack Hobbs, with a score of 101 not out in the second innings, made the 127th hundred of his career, and so broke the record established long ago by W.G.Grace. His achievement was received with rapturous enthusiasm by the spectators, as was his 101 yesterday in Surrey's first innings when he equalled the record.

There was drama in the finishing stroke of his hundred today. When it was made, only half a dozen runs were wanted for victory. It follows, therefore, that Hobbs owed very much to Sandham (74 not out), who, despite the fact that he was at the top of his form, subordinated himself in order that his partner should do the great thing. At first both batsmen scored at about the same pace, but after he had got some 30 runs Sandham's unselfishness became increasingly obvious.

His record-breaking hundred was one of Hobbs's best, though not one of his most brilliant performances. He never gave the semblance of a chance, putting up his fifty in 65 minutes and reaching the coveted hundred in 141 minutes. Nor did he show a trace of nervousness, although at 95 he became for the first time what may be called extra cautious. At last, he pushed away to square leg a short-pitched ball, and the deed was done.

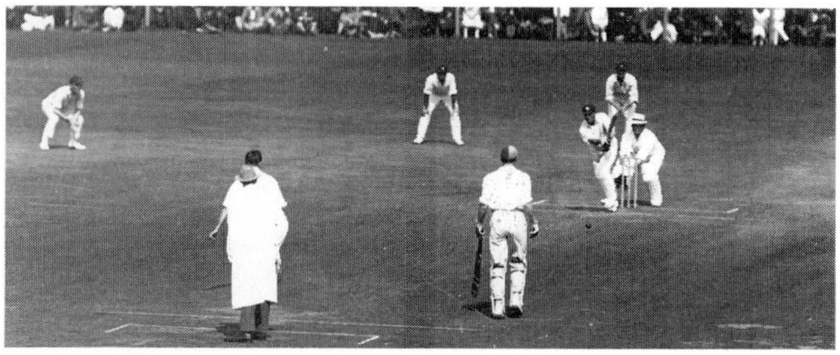

Jack Hobbs scores the run yesterday that brought up his 126th century to equal W.G.'s record.

The cheering continued for a minute and a half, and it seemed to grow in volume. The great batsman, who was evidently as delighted as everyone else, repeatedly waved his acknowledgments and, indeed, raised his cap in the air on the end of his bat.

Hobbs broke another record today, one, which he equalled yesterday, shared jointly by Hayward, C.B.Fry and Hendren, who have all made 13 hundreds in the course of one first-class season. Today's was Hobbs's 14th.

[Hobbs went on to make 16 100s this season, a record eventually beaten by Compton in 1947, but his career total of 197 100s, completed in 1934 at the age of 51, has never been surpassed.]

1926

5-8 Jun G.R.Cox takes 17-106 for Sussex v Warwicks at Horsham.

23-25 Jun Hobbs (261) and Sandham (183) put on 428 for Surrey v Oxford University, at the Oval.

28 Jun In the drawn 2nd Test at Lord's, Australian opener Warren Bardsley carries his bat for 193 and England opener Jack Hobbs makes 119, the two batsmen both 43, having been born within 9 days of each other in Dec 1882. The younger man, Hobbs, also passes the 4,000-run mark in Tests.

28 Jul India, New Zealand and West Indies are admitted to the ICC.

30 Aug Hobbs makes 316 not for Surrey v Middlesex at Lord's.

TEST SERIES

Australia in England
E 1, D 4

Third Test First day: 10 July

Australians sent in: Macartney's 100 before lunch

By Colonel Philip Trevor, C.B.E., at Leeds

THE England captain A.W. Carr won the toss at Headingley this morning and sent the Australians in to bat. The policy did not come off, and before the match was an hour old condemnation of him began. The brilliant Macartney scored a hundred before lunch, and at the close Australia had compiled 366 runs for the loss of only three wickets.

Personally, I think Carr was absolutely right. The sun had been shining several hours by the time the captains tossed, but ten minutes later it had sulkily retired. And how nearly the thing did come off. With the first ball bowled, Tate had Bardsley caught at first slip by Sutcliffe, and with his fourth ball he should have got another, but Macartney was missed at third slip, albeit not an easy catch, by Carr himself.

Macartney reached his hundred in 105 minutes, out of the 132 runs scored; at the luncheon interval, he had made 112, the most on the first morning of an England-Australia match; and when, with the total 235, he was caught at extra mid-off deep, his score was 151. It was a wonderful, dazzling innings. Without the suspicion of effort, he placed the ball between the fieldsmen time after time with unerring precision. I saw Macartney play his first Test innings in Australia nearly 19 years ago, and I then ventured to predict a great future for him. But I did not anticipate that I should see him, at the age of 40, as I saw him bat today. After due deliberation, I say that this is the most magnificent innings I have ever seen played in any Test match.

[Woodfull made 141, Richardson 100 and Australia 494, but the match was drawn.]

Charlie Macartney hits out.

Fifth Test Fourth day: 18 August

England triumph: Australia out for 125, Ashes regained after 14 years

By Colonel Philip Trevor, C.B.E., at the Oval

England won an overwhelming victory at the Oval this evening, for Australia were beaten by the huge number of 289 runs.

In the congratulations that follow, the Selection Committee should not be overlooked. They elected 'young' Chapman to captain, and they called on 'old' Rhodes to help. They were adversely criticised in consequence, but the laugh is with them now. Hobbs (100) and Sutcliffe (161), in a stand of 172, showed how to bat on a difficult wicket yesterday, and Rhodes and Larwood, the veteran slow left-hander at one end and the young fast right-hander at the other, showed how to bowl on one today. Rhodes bowled superbly and captured four for 44. Larwood, who claimed the early wickets of Woodfull and Macartney, took three for 34. And Australia were dismissed for 125.

Editorial: The scene at the Oval after the last wicket fell will be remembered by all who witnessed it. The spread-eagling of Mailey's wicket by Geary was the signal for a frantic outburst of delight and triumph from all over the enclosure. In the stands, erstwhile grave parsons sacrificed their hats, men hugged each other and danced madly, and women grew hysterical. Retired (and usually retiring) military men leapt the barriers and scampered gamely for the pavilion. The players were 'mobbed', friends and foes alike. And the result was received in the streets with an enthusiasm that became infectious. A forest of hats and handkerchiefs shot up in the air and waved for several minutes, accompanied by roar after roar of deafening cheers, which re-echoed along the Strand and over the bridges.

The Englishmen had suffered three humiliations on the cricket field since the war, losing 12 Tests while winning only one. But now the Ashes were back in England.

Sheffield Shield Victoria v NSW: 28 December

New cricket record, Victoria's total 1,107: Ponsford's great innings

From Reuter's Special Service, in Melbourne

CONTINUING their first innings against New South Wales today, Victoria, who at the close of play overnight had scored 573 for one wicket, batted all day before they were finally dismissed for 1,107, a new world record innings in first-class cricket, beating their own record of 1,059 made against Tasmania here in 1923.

Ponsford, who was 334 overnight, having put on 375 for the first wicket with Woodfull (133), soon had his magnificent innings brought to a close when he played on to Morgan for 352, only 13 runs short of Clem Hill's 26-year-old Sheffield Shield record. Shortly afterwards Hendry, who had helped him add 219 for the second wicket, was out for 100, made in 113 minutes.

Ryder now proceeded to flog the tiring NSW bowlers, rushing to a splendid 295 in 245 minutes, with six 6's and thirty-three 4's. The Sheffield Shield innings record of 918 (NSW v S.Australia, 1901) went, the 1,000 came up, and then, with one wicket left, Victoria passed their own world record. Their innings lasted altogether 10hr 33min. Mailey was the most 'successful' bowler with four wickets in 64 overs, but he conceded 362 runs, a world record for a single innings.

Only four members of the NSW side had previously played against Victoria. For one reason or another, Gregory, Macartney, Bardsley, Kelleway, Oldfield, Collins and Everett were not included in the side. When NSW go in to bat tomorrow, they will face a first-innings deficit of 886.

[NSW lost by an innings and 656 runs. An extraordinary reversal occurred a month later in the return match at Sydney, where Victoria, without 5 of the victorious side (including the chief run-makers, Woodfull, Ponsford and Ryder) were bowled out for 35! They made 181 in the follow-on and lost by an innings and 253 runs. A week later they lost to Queensland after scoring 86 in the 1st innings and 518 in the 2nd, and S.Australia won the Sheffield Shield.]

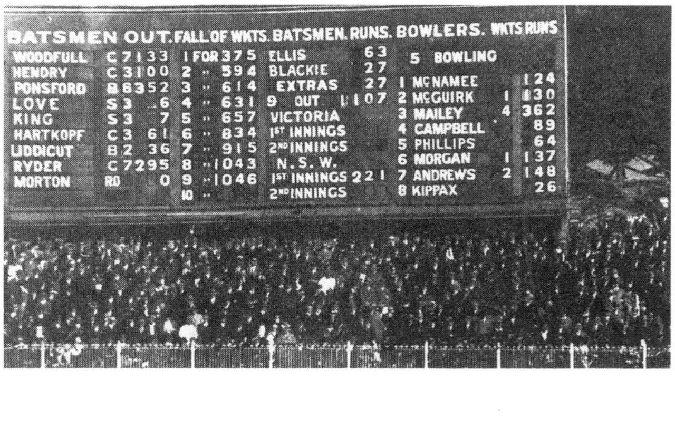
BATSMEN OUT. FALL OF WKTS. BATSMEN. RUNS. BOWLERS. WKTS RUNS
WOODFULL C 7 133 1 FOR 375 ELLIS 63 5 BOWLING
HENDRY C 3 100 2 594 BLACKIE 27
PONSFORD B 6 352 3 614 EXTRAS 27 1 McNAMEE 124
LOVE S 3 6 4 631 9 OUT 1107 2 McGUIRK 1 130
KING S 3 7 5 657 VICTORIA 3 MAILEY 4 362
HARTKOPF C 3 61 6 834 1ST INNINGS 4 CAMPBELL 89
LIDDICUT B 2 36 7 915 2ND INNINGS 5 PHILLIPS 64
RYDER C 7 295 8 1043 N.S.W. 6 MORGAN 1 137
MORTON RO 0 9 1046 1ST INNINGS 221 7 ANDREWS 2 148
10 2ND INNINGS 8 KIPPAX 26

The Melbourne scoreboard tells the story of Victoria's historic innings.

County Championship Hants v Glos: 28 May

WG's record equalled: Triumph of Hammond, 1,028 runs during May

From Southampton

W.R.HAMMOND, the young Gloucestershire batsman, put together against Hampshire today an innings of 192, and in so doing brought his aggregate for the present season to 1,028. He has thus equalled the achievement of W.G.Grace in 1895 of making a thousand runs during the month of May. The only other batsman to accomplish the feat before the end of May was Tom Hayward, in 1900, but he started with 120 runs made in April.

Apart from the special interest attaching to the performance, Hammond's batting was of a wonderful description, for he scored 192 out of 227 added during his stay in the course of 2hr 28min. He registered his first 50 runs in 45min, and completed his 100 in 85min. Travelling at such a tremendous pace, he naturally made mistakes, giving no fewer than five chances. But he batted in light-hearted fashion from start to finish, completing his 100 with a big off-drive for 6 from Boyes, and after his last escape, at 123, he struck three 6's in quick succession. Altogether 144 of his runs came from boundaries, six 6's and twenty-seven 4's.

[Like Grace, Hammond made his 1,000 in 22 days. His final innings, on 31 May, produced only another 14 runs, so he averaged 74.42.]

Walter Hammond in action.

1927

31 Jan-1 Feb R.E.S.Wyatt scores 124 and takes the hat-trick for MCC v Ceylon at Colombo.

14 May Essex v New Zealanders is the first wireless commentary broadcast in England.

8 Jul A.S.Kennedy (Hants) takes all 10-37 for Players v Gents at the Oval.

13 Sep The 1st New Zealanders wind up their tour at Scarborough, having played 26 first-class matches and 12 others, and having beaten 5 of the first-class counties.

26 Dec Herbert Sutcliffe and Ernest Tyldesley add 230 v S.Africa in the 1st Test at Johannesburg, a record for England's 2nd wicket.

County Championship Glamorgan v Notts: 2 September

Lancashire champions: Glamorgan outplay Notts

By a Special Correspondent, at Swansea

THE County Championship has, after all, gone to Lancashire, last year's champions. Notts, in their final match, with Glamorgan at Swansea, had only to avoid defeat to be certain of the Championship, which they have not won for 20 years, but Glamorgan, who had not recorded a single victory during the summer, created the surprise of the season by winning by an innings and 81 runs.

With two second-innings wickets down and still 119 behind at stumps yesterday, Notts lost any prospects of avoiding defeat when the overnight rain was followed by hot sunshine this morning. It was all over in just 50 minutes, as they were bowled out for 61. Mercer, medium-paced with spin and swerve, took four for 23 (6-31 in the innings) and Ryan, slow left-hand and turning the ball either way, four for 11 (4-14). At the end, the crowd rushed across the field to the pavilion and cheered their successful team for an hour - almost as if they had won the Championship instead of finishing 15th.

Sheffield Shield Victoria v Queensland: 17 December

Cricket record: W.H.Ponsford's big innings

From Reuter's Special Service, in Melbourne

PLAYING for Victoria against Queensland in the Sheffield Shield match today, W.H.Ponsford increased his overnight total of 234 runs to 437, thus breaking his own world's record for first-class cricket of 429 made for Victoria against Tasmania in 1923. Apart from giving a couple of very difficult chances, he batted in brilliant style. His hits included forty-two 4's and he occupied the wicket altogether 10hr 21min before he was caught and bowled by Amos in the last over of the day. The previous record score in a Sheffield Shield match was Clem Hill's 365 for South Australia.

[Victoria made 793.]

Sheffield Shield S.Australia v NSW: 17 December

Promising N.S.W. colt

From Reuter's Special Service, in Adelaide

CONTINUING their first innings against South Australia today, New South Wales carried their overnight total of 400 for seven wickets to 519. The innings lasted six hours and a half. Don Bradman, the N.S.W. colt, carried his unfinished 65 to 118. He thus earned the distinction of scoring a century on his first appearance in a Sheffield Shield match.

Alan Kippax, who retired ill yesterday after making 81, was able to resume today, and batted in brilliant style for nearly three hours, during which he compiled 143, including fifteen 4's. His partnership with Bradman realised 111. South Australia made a vigorous reply, scoring 208 for the loss of only one wicket.

First Test Third day: 27 December

England's easy victory: South Africa's collapse

From Johannesburg

THE first of the five Test matches to be played between England and South Africa ended today shortly after half-past four in a hollow victory for England by 10 wickets. The Englishmen were the superiors of their opponents in all departments except, perhaps, fielding.

At the close of play last night South Africa, with all their second innings wickets intact, were 117 runs behind, and there was every prospect of a dour struggle. But the magnificent bowling of Hammond and Geary had the South Africans in a tangle from the start, and they shared the 10 wickets equally between them. Hammond, in the course of 23 deliveries, got three wickets - Duminy, Taylor and Catterall - hitting the stumps each time without having a run scored off him. In all he bowled 21.2 overs for 36 runs and five wickets. Geary was only slightly less effective, his 'going-away' deliveries, judiciously mixed with well-concealed leg or off breaks, keeping the batsmen on tenterhooks, until they finally fell into his trap, either by edging one into the slips or by stepping in front of a straight-through delivery and getting out leg-before-wicket.

South Africa lost their first six wickets for 26 runs, and with two wickets to fall still needed 39 runs to equal the English total. But Vincent (53) and Coen (41 not out), the latter hobbling about on an injured ankle sustained while fielding, put on 80 in an hour to ensure England would bat again, setting a new ninth-wicket record for England-South Africa Tests in the process.

Scores: South Africa 196 (Catterall 86; Geary 7-70) & 170 (Vincent 53; Geary 5-60; Hammond 5-36), England 313 (Tyldesley 122, Sutcliffe 102, Hammond 51; Promnitz 5-58) & 57-0 (Sutcliffe 41 not).

1928

31 May Charlie Hallows (Lancs), in making 232 v Sussex at Old Trafford, emulates Grace and Hammond by scoring 1,000 runs (exactly) in May, with an average of 125.

18 Jun Aaron Lockett (Staffs) makes 154 on first-class début for Minor Counties v West Indies at Exeter, M.Counties winning after following on.

23-26 Jun W.Indies play their first Test, losing at Lord's to England by an innings and 58 runs.

27-28 Jun Leary Constantine scores 107 and takes 13-112 (7-45 & 6-67), including the hat-trick, as W.Indies beat Northants by an innings at Northampton.

11 Aug Les Ames (Kent) is the first to do the wicket-keeper's double, 1,000 runs and 100 dismissals in a season (he goes on to get 1,919r, 121 dis).

15 Sep Tich Freeman (Kent) becomes the first bowler to take 300 wickets in a season (setting a record 304).

30 Nov-5 Dec In the 1st Test, the first to be played in Brisbane, and the only one at the Exhibition Ground, England (521 & 342 dec) thrash Australia (122 & 66) by 675 runs. Woodfull carries his bat for 30 in Australia's 2nd innings (only nine bat).

TEST SERIES

England in South Africa
E 2, SA 2, D 1
West Indies in England
England 3

Tourist match Middlesex v W.Indies: 12 June

West Indies shock Middlesex: Wonder batsman and bowler

By Colonel Philip Trevor, C.B.E., at Lord's

THE West Indies beat Middlesex at Lord's this evening by three wickets, a result the outcome of some of the most amazing cricket I or anyone else has ever witnessed. L.S.Constantine won the match for his side by almost unbelievable batting and bowling, and I am sure I have never seen so signal an instance of a one-man victory. The spectators went wild with delight when he was in action, and at the end they crowded round the pavilion and cheered him to the echo.

When the morning's play began, Middlesex were 162 runs ahead with eight wickets in hand, and they added 58 for the loss of one wicket. Then fast bowler Constantine was shifted to the Pavilion end, and proceeded, in a spell of 6.1 overs, to take six wickets for 11 runs. Middlesex were all out for 136, leaving West Indies to get 259 runs at just over one a minute. But the early batsmen steadily fell further and further behind the clock, and half of them were out for 79. It was a miserable performance, but Constantine, who made 86 in their first innings, came to their rescue again, turning staring defeat into stirring victory. I scarcely know what to say of his innings. He was only batting an hour; he did not give the semblance of a chance, and he hit with a certainty and a ferocity that was worthy of the great Jessop himself.

Learie Constantine: Sent crowd wild.

West Indies were 5 runs short of victory when Constantine was caught in the slips for 103, and they lost another wicket while they struggled laboriously without him to get those runs.

County Championship Glos v Surrey: 17 August

Masterly Hammond: Two centuries against Surrey

From Cheltenham

HAMMOND, the brilliant all-round cricketer, enjoyed a personal triumph in the match at Cheltenham against Surrey, which ended in a substantial victory for Gloucestershire by 189 runs. Not out 64 overnight, Hammond carried his score to 143, having previously scored 139 in the first innings (he made two hundreds against Surrey at the Oval last season). In addition he brought off six splendid catches, and as he had already made four, he set a new world record with 10 catches - no one had taken more than eight before in a first-class match. Hammond gave one chance when 125, but otherwise his cricket was free from fault, and in a very fine display, which lasted for 3hr 25min, he hit a 6 and twelve 4's.

Another Gloucester player who contributed largely to the success of his side was Parker, who proved very difficult to play and took seven wickets today for 80 runs as Surrey were dismissed for 167, and had a record for the game of 13 for 197 runs.

Second Test Fourth day: 18 December

No England 'tail': Australia's feeble attack concede record 636 runs

By Clem Hill, in Sydney

ENGLAND, by scoring 636 runs, a record innings in Tests, have placed themselves in an unbeatable position in the second Test, as was foreseen at the close of play yesterday. It is now only a question of our *[Australia's]* batsmen having good practice - and I must confess that they need it badly.

Hammond, by his very first stroke today, promised that he would exceed R.E.Foster's record of 287, but, having made 251, he had the bad luck to play a ball from Ironmonger onto his wicket. Whereas England previously had a 'tail', it must be said that even Geary (66) and the highly promising wicket-keeper Duckworth (39 not out) seemed more at home than Hobbs and Sutcliffe when they opened the innings. The other English tail-enders all made runs - Larwood 43, Tate 25 and White 29. It was made obvious that our bowlers, even when fresh, are not dangerous: and when tired, whatever sting they might have disappears.

When Australia went in, Richardson was out for a duck, poking at a short ball from Tate and being caught by Hendren. At the close, Australia were 39 for one, 344 runs behind.

[Australia, with Woodfull and Hendry scoring 100s, made 397, but England's 'tail' knocked off the 16 runs for victory for the loss of 2 wickets.]

Sheffield Shield Victoria v NSW: 26 December

World's record 307 for last wicket

From Melbourne

NEW South Wales resumed here today on 367 for nine in reply to Victoria's first-innings total of 376, and the feature of the play was the completion of the magnificent innings of the Australian Test player Alan Kippax, who carried his bat for 260. His performance, compiled in 6hr 27min and containing thirty 4's, was the principal factor in raising the NSW first innings score from the bad start on Monday of 58 for seven - and then 113 for nine - to the very respectable figure of 420 all out and a first-innings lead of 44.

Alan Kippax: 260 not out.

The next-best scorer was Hal Hooker, the last man in, who in a remarkable last-wicket partnership of 5hr 4min with Kippax knocked up a useful 62. Their stand reached 307 before Hooker was out, and constitutes a world's record for the last wicket in first-class cricket, beating Woolley and Fielder's 235 made in 1909.

At stumps, Victoria had made 251 for six in their second innings.

[The match ended in a draw.]

Third Test Seventh day: 5 January

England retain the Ashes: Three-wicket victory in thrilling finish

From Melbourne

ENGLAND, for the first time since the tour of 1911-12, have won the rubber in a Test series in Australia. The Ashes, gained from the Australians at the Oval in 1926, are thus retained by the magnificent victory of three wickets at Melbourne in the third match.

Sutcliffe, having shared that wonderful opening stand of 105 yesterday with Hobbs (49) on a sticky wicket when no one gave England a hope of getting the 332 runs required, distinguished himself further today by completing a brilliant century - his fourth in consecutive Tests - before he was fourth out with the score at 318. Extraordinarily, England then struggled to get the remaining 14 runs and lost a further three wickets in doing so.

The aggregate attendance of 262,467 for the seven days, with receipts amounting to £22,561 18s, constituted a world's record for Test matches.

Scores: Australia 307 (Ryder 112, Kippax 100, Bradman 79) & 351 (Bradman 112, Woodfull 107; White 5-107), England 417 (Hammond 200, Jardine 62, Sutcliffe 58; Blackie 6-94) & 332-7 (Sutcliffe 135).

County Championship Sussex v Kent: 13 August

Match of 1,451 runs: Brilliant Duleep's double century

From Hastings

THE match at Hastings, which produced an aggregate of 1,451 runs for 36 wickets, ended today in Sussex beating Kent by 167. Only once before has a greater number of runs been obtained in a County Championship match (1,475, Surrey v Northants, 1920). Glorious weather made the annual Festival the most successful ever held at Hastings, and today another large company saw more superb hitting by Duleepsinhji, who, having scored 149 overnight, added 97 in 70 minutes before falling to a catch at long on.

He did not play quite so well as on Saturday, when he scored 115, or yesterday, giving two hard catches, but, for the most part, he was master of the Kent bowling, and, batting altogether for 3hr 15min, hit no fewer than five 6's and thirty-one 4's. Driving and strokes to leg were the outstanding features in a wonderfully fine display of free batting.

Sussex having carried their total of 215 for three wickets to 381 for eight, were able to declare soon after half-past twelve, 166 runs having been added in 90 minutes, and thus Kent were set the tremendous task of getting 412 in 3hr 40min. Any hopes that the visitors might have of saving the game were destroyed when Hardinge and Woolley both left to slip catches with 20 on the board, and soon after luncheon Kent had four men out for 66. There followed a most plucky partnership between Ames (118) and Todd (43), who put on 128 in 75 minutes, but after the tea interval Tate, with the new ball, clean bowled Ames, and shortly before five o'clock the innings closed for 244.

Tate, taking seven wickets for 58 runs, made his record for the match 13 for 194. Duleepsinhji's feat of scoring a hundred and double hundred in the same match has only been achieved on four previous occasions.

County Championship Glamorgan v Leics: 15 August

Record bowling feat: Geary's 10 for 18 in narrow defeat of Glamorgan

From Pontypridd

ON the day when he was chosen to fill the place of the injured Tate in the England team for the fifth Test match at the Oval tomorrow, George Geary accomplished the most remarkable bowling feat recorded in first-class cricket. He dismissed all ten Glamorgan batsmen at the small cost of 18 runs, and thus enabled Leicestershire to obtain an amazing victory by 15 runs.

The achievement of Geary, right-arm fast-medium, came as a climax to a series of fine performances on a pitch which always gave great assistance to bowlers - Ryan and Clay took eight and nine wickets respectively for Glamorgan, and Geary claimed 6-78 in their first innings. His figures in the second innings were 16.2 overs 8 maidens 18 runs 10 wickets. For the early instances of bowlers taking all 10 wickets, the runs conceded were not recorded, and the previous best analyses known are Bert Vogler's 10 for 26 in South Africa (1906-07) and, in England, 10 for 28 by Bill Howell for the Australians against Surrey (1899). Colin Blythe's 10 for 30 for Kent against Northants in 1907 was the previous best in the County Championship.

George Geary: Celebrated Test selection with record bag.

Glamorgan appeared to have the match well in hand, needing only 84 to win, but Geary, making the ball turn sharply, had half the side out for 19, and after Turnbull and Clay put on 36, accounted for the rest, too, sending the last four men back for just one run.

1929

25 Jan Don Bradman (NSW) makes 340 not out v Victoria at Sydney.

1-8 Feb England win 4th Test, at Adelaide, by 12 runs despite a brilliant début 164 by 19-year-old NSW opener Archie Jackson, Jack White taking 13-256 (5-130 & 8-126) in 124.5 (6-ball for this tour) overs. Hammond scores 100 in each innings to complete a run of 251, 200, 32, 119 not, 177 - in all, 779 in 5 innings. His stand of 262 with Douglas Jardine (98) is a Test record for the 3rd wicket.

8-16 Mar In the 5th Test, at Melbourne, the first ever to last 8 days, Australia chalk up their only win of the rubber, by 5 wickets, despite England's 1st innings 519 in which Hobbs, at 46, makes 142, his 12th and last 100 v Australia, and completes 5,000 Test runs. Hammond finishes with 905 runs (113.12), a record tally for a Test series.

9-10 May Dick Tyldesley (Lancs) takes 4 wickets in 4 balls v Derbys, spread over two innings.

15 Jun The amateur fast bowler G.O. Allen (Middlesex), playing on the understanding that his work at a department store would mean his missing the start of the match against Lancs at Lord's, takes all 10-40 in 25.3 overs, including the last 4 wickets in 5 balls.

29 Jun Frank Woolley (Kent) makes his 100th hundred, 131 v Yorks at Tonbridge.

Frank Woolley.

16 Jul 'Tuppy' Owen-Smith (129) completes a 100 before lunch for S.Africa in the 3rd Test at Leeds, and puts on 103 in 63min for the 10th wicket with 'Sandy' Bell (26), but England win by 5 wickets.

24 Jul Tich Freeman (Kent) takes all 10-131 v Lancs at Maidstone.

20 Aug In the 5th Test at the Oval, S.Africa declare at 492-8, their highest ever Test score, but Sutcliffe, with his 2nd 100 of the match (104 & 109 not) and Hammond (101 not) ease England to a draw.

TEST SERIES

England in Australia
E 4, A 1

South Africa in England
E 2, D 3

The 1930s

THERE were many great cricketers and fine achievements in the 1930s, but not since W.G.Grace in the 1870s has one cricketer so dominated his generation - and that man, of course, was Don Bradman. As the cricket historian H.S.Altham put it, "It may be that Bradman has not the sheer grace of Victor Trumper, the versatility on all wickets of Jack Hobbs, the annihilating unorthodoxy of Gilbert Jessop, but for ruthless efficiency no cricketer in the post-Grace era can compare with him. In the many pictures that I have stored in my mind of the burnt-out Junes of 40 years, there is none more dramatic or compelling than that of his small, serenely moving figure in the big-peaked green cap coming out of the pavilion shadows into the sunshine, with the concentration, ardour and apprehension of surrounding thousands centred upon him, and the destiny of a Test match in his hands."

That is a wonderful picture of the thirties, a decade dominated internationally by Australia, largely because of that little man in the big green cap. They won the Ashes in England in 1930, and held them - with one notorious exception - until the end of the decade, and beyond. The exception was the 'Bodyline' tour of 1932-33, when England's tactics to curb the run machine that was Bradman almost caused a split in the Empire. Never has there been such a controversy in sport, and although the laws were amended to eradicate such tactics from the game, the arguments have never diminished.

In almost any other era, England's Walter Hammond would have been the 'Colossus'. Having established himself in the late twenties with his batting feats at both Test and domestic level, he headed the first-class averages in England for an unprecedented seven successive seasons from 1933 until the war (and then again immediately after the war). In addition, he was a valuable medium-fast opening bowler, as his 83 Test wickets testify, and a brilliant slip fielder. If Hammond's batting record was overshadowed by the statistical achievements of Bradman, it is for the manner in which he made his runs that he is best remembered.

Near the end of the decade, there emerged in England two other batsmen who were to take their place among the world's finest - Len Hutton of Yorkshire and Denis Compton of Middlesex. Hutton, indeed, with his famous innings of 364 against Australia at the Oval in 1938, broke Hammond's Test record and set a mark that stood for nearly twenty years.

With the ball, Kent's 'Tich' Freeman continued to take over 200 wickets a season until he retired in the mid-thirties as the only bowler to take 10 wickets in an innings three times and 17 wickets in a match twice. Left-hand spinner Hedley Verity was a major influence behind Yorkshire's seven Championship titles, and he set a new first-class world record with 10 for 10 in an innings. He also took 14 Australian wickets in a day to bowl England to victory at Lord's in 1934. For Australia, Bill 'Tiger' O'Reilly, regarded by Bradman as the greatest bowler of his time, joined Grimmett to form the most formidable spin attack in Test cricket in the thirties.

West Indies won their first Test in 1930, beating England at Georgetown, where Headley, the 'Black Bradman', made a hundred in both innings, and they won their next home series, in 1935. Two more countries made their Test débuts in the early thirties, New Zealand and then India, but neither won a single Test.

The Bodyline Controversy erupted on England's 1932-33 tour of Australia. Here, the Australian captain Woodfull ducks to a rising ball from Larwood in the fourth Test, while an arc of six leg fielders wait expectantly. (Inset) Don Bradman bestrode the thirties like a colossus, the greatest run machine in the history of the game.

1930

25 Jan J.W.E.Mills (117) and C.S. Dempster (136) set a New Zealand record of 276 for the 1st wicket against England in the 2nd Test, at Wellington.

1-6 Feb England beat West Indies by 167 runs in the 2nd Test, at Port of Spain, thanks largely to a 2nd-innings score of 205 not out by Patsy Hendren followed by 7-70 by Voce. Hendren celebrates his 41st birthday by completing 1,000 runs for the tour (avge 168.6).

12 Feb Hendren's 254 not out against British Guiana is his 4th hundred (all double centuries) of the tour, taking his average to over 210.

18 Feb Hendren takes another hundred (171) off British Guiana.

21-26 Feb West Indies chalk up their first Test win over England, by 289 runs at Georgetown, Roach scoring 209 in their 1st innings and Headley making a 100 in each innings.

1 May The prolific Don Bradman makes his mark in England with 236 at Worcester in Australia's opening tour match.

14 Aug Kent slow bowler 'Tich' Freeman takes 10-53 against Essex at Southend, only the second player to accomplish the feat twice (V.E.Walker of Middlesex was the other).

22 Aug Despite scoring 405 in their 1st innings at the Oval (Sutcliffe 161), England lose to Australia by an innings for the first time on English soil. In what was a 'timeless' Test, Australia clinch the match and the Ashes on the 6th day. Bradman's 232 takes his series total to a record 974 runs (avge 139.14), passing Hammond's 1928-29 aggregate (905). His 4 hundreds included a triple century and two doubles. The Test also marks Jack Hobbs' retirement from Test cricket (5,410 runs, avge 56.94, 15 100s).

26 Aug Despite having been dismissed for 72 in their 1st innings, Gloucester tie with the Australians, Parker taking 7-54 in the tourists' 2nd-innings 117.

16 Dec Australia beat West Indies by 10 wickets at Adelaide in the first Test played between the two countries, Grimmett taking 11-183.

TEST SERIES

England in New Zealand
E 1, D 3
England in West Indies
WI 1, E 1, D 2
Australia in England
A 2, E 1, D 2

Sheffield Shield NSW v Queensland: 6 January

World record innings by Bradman

From Sydney

THE HIGHEST innings ever played in first-class cricket was compiled here today by Don Bradman, 21, who, playing for New South Wales against Queensland, made 452 not out.

Bradman's score was 205 when he resumed batting this morning. He was cheered by the Queenslanders when he was let off in the slips at 350, but there was no slackening in the efforts to dismiss him. As he approached Ponsford's record, the battle became more intense, but the batsman showed no sign of nerves, and took his score past 437 to one of the greatest bursts of cheering ever heard on the Sydney ground.

When Kippax declared the innings closed at 761 for eight wickets, Bradman was given another ovation. Queensland went in with a forlorn hope of getting 770 for victory. They lost half their wickets with only 23 runs scored, and finished the day at 72 for seven wickets.

Bradman scored his runs in 6hr 55min and hit 49 fours, compared with Ponsford's 10hr 21min and 42 fours two years ago.

First Test New Zealand v M.C.C.: 10 January

Allom's great bowling: Hat-trick against New Zealand

From Christchurch

NEW ZEALAND collapsed here today against England in the first of the four Test matches, and were all out for 112. England (who have another team currently on tour in the West Indies) had obtained a lead of 35 at the close of play with six wickets to fall.

The bowling of the Surrey and Cambridge player M.J.C. Allom put the New Zealanders to rout. Within half an hour of starting they had lost three batsmen for 15 runs, all to Nichols for nine. Then, at 21, Allom took four wickets in five balls in a maiden over, which also included the hat-trick. Allom bowled fast-medium to fast, but it was his ingenious slower balls that worried the New Zealanders.

Thus within an hour of the start New Zealand's score was 21 for seven wickets, Allom's share being four for 9. Blunt batted with resolution and carried out his bat for 45 as New Zealand recovered to 112 all out. Allom's final analysis was 19-3-38-5.

Fourth Test Third day: 5 April

Record Test match score: England total 849 against West Indies

From Kingston, Jamaica

ENGLAND made a Test match record here today, scoring 849 in their first innings against the West Indies. Of this total Sandham contributed 325, the highest score he has ever made. He was batting for ten hours.

The previous best total in a Test match was 636, made by England against Australia at Sydney in the 1928-29 tour.

The huge total destroys all chances of a West Indian victory. The match promises to end in a draw, a result which would mean divided honours in the rubber, in which each side have won one match with one drawn.

[The Hon. F.S.G.Calthorpe decided not to enforce the follow-on despite England's lead of 563, and the match appeared to have ended in a draw with England on 256-9 at the end of the 5th day. But it was then decided to play the Test to a finish, although it was finally abandoned on the ninth day because of continuous rain, with West Indies having scored 408 of the 836 runs they needed (George Headley making 223 at age 20) for the loss of 5 wickets.]

County Championship Sussex v Northants: 7 May

Record innings by Duleepsinhji: 333 in day

From Brighton

Sussex started badly in their first home match of the season, losing two wickets for 30 runs, but Duleepsinhji, always master of the bowling, completely changed the aspect of the game with a truly great innings.

Coming in with one wicket down for one run, he scored all round the wicket with delightful ease, and made 100 out of 141 in two hours and twenty minutes. It took him just over four hours to complete 200 out of 293, and he went on to beat the previous highest score for Sussex - 285 not out by his uncle K.S.Ranjitsinhji in 1901 - and reach his 300 in five hours and a quarter.

He batted without any mistake for five hours and a half, and was eventually stumped when going well down the pitch, the total then being 514. His great innings of 333 included one six and 34 fours.

Duleepsinhji.

Tour match Yorks v Australians: 10 May

Grimmett routs Yorkshire: All ten wickets

By B.Bennison, at Sheffield

CLARENCE GRIMMETT, at Bramall Lane today, took all 10 Yorkshire wickets, a feat only twice before accomplished by an Australian bowler in a match against a county - Bill Howell against Surrey in 1899 and Arthur Mailey against Gloucester in 1921. It was a truly remarkable performance, cheered to the echo by a crowd of some 5,000 people, generously applauded by his fellows and by the members of the Yorkshire side.

There could be no greater amplification of the glorious uncertainty of cricket than the change which this little man from South Australia brought about. Holmes and Sutcliffe had done much to strengthen the belief that there is little or nothing awe-inspiring in the bowlers at the command of Woodfull. Wall and Hornibrook, a'Beckett and McCabe, were all alike to these famous partners. Even Grimmett, who bowled for the first time when the total was 46, appeared to give them no serious concern.

He bowled Holmes for 31, but the interval score of 67 for one appeared decidedly satisfactory. The astounding fact is that Yorkshire were all out for 155. Grimmett's analysis was: 22.3-8-37-10.

From the moment that he got Holmes out, Grimmett was the master. With his leg-breaks, which he varied with a well-concealed googly, he had every man more or less in his clutches.

Sutcliffe, the exception, made a chanceless 69 before being caught at the wicket. Wood (17) was the only other batsman to make double figures. The deadly Grimmett dismissed the last seven men for 16. Rain later curtailed play, and by the close the Australians were 69 for one.

First Test Final day: 17 June

England triumph in the Test match: Bradman's brave innings

By Colonel Philip Trevor, at Nottingham

ENGLAND beat Australia this evening at Nottingham by 93 runs, but they had to work desperately hard for their victory, and there was a time when Australia looked likely to win the match.

Admittedly England were without Larwood, absent through illness. But Bradman and Ponsford settled in, and when McCabe, the baby of the side, joined Bradman, the pair soon edged ahead of the clock in the chase for the 429 runs required.

McCabe made 49, and Australia were still going well, at 296 for five, when Bradman was bowled by a googly from Robins, without playing a stroke. He had made 131 and given only one chance. The remaining four wickets added only 39.

Second Test Third day: 30 June

Australia's record score at Lord's: Bradman's great innings

By Col. Philip Trevor, at Lord's

TWO notable Test records were broken at Lord's today, one collective, one individual. By making 729 runs for six wickets, the Australians played the highest innings on record in the long list of Test matches between the two countries. The previous best was England's 636, at Sydney on the 1928-29 tour. R.E.Foster's 287, made at Sydney in 1903-04, still stands, but by scoring 254 Don Bradman has completed the highest Test innings made in England.

The Australians batted superbly. Bradman, who was finally caught by Chapman off White, had never looked like getting out. His bat was all middle and no edge. He gave a faultless display and even Tate never had him in the slightest trouble.

Australia had begun the day on 404 for two, having lost only the openers yesterday, Woodfull for 155 and Ponsford for 81 - just 21 runs behind England. They declared 304 runs ahead. By the close, England were 98 for two in their second innings, having lost Hobbs and Woolley to Grimmett. Duleepsinhji was still there on 27, but England will need a repeat of his brilliant 173 in the first innings on his Test début if they are to survive.

[Duleep was out for 48, but a splendid 121 by England's captain, A.P.F.Chapman, made Australia bat again They lost 3 wickets for 22, including Bradman's, but Woodfull and McCabe saw them safely to the 72 runs required.]

Third Test First day: 11 July

Triumph of Bradman: Record-making 309 and still undefeated

By B.Bennison, at Leeds

OUT of Australia's huge total of 458 for three at the end of the first day, Don Bradman has made 309. Coming in at two for one, he has defied the English bowlers for five hours and fifty minutes, and is still not out. This is the highest score in Tests between the two countries, beating R.E. Foster's 287 made in Sydney 27 years ago.

One cannot exaggerate the feat of the young man from New South Wales, or overstate the magnificence of it. As a maker of runs, he must be numbered among the phenomena of cricket. During the long hours he was at the wickets, he paid no respect to any of the bowlers. His perfect footwork, his unerring eye, his quick brain, enabled him to do almost what he willed.

This is the third three-figure innings Bradman has played against England in this country, and the fifth in all. He went to his hundred with a glorious boundary to leg off Larwood after batting for an hour and 36 minutes, and was 105 at lunch.

Bradman sparkled; he was care-free, joyous. When opener Woodfull was bowled by Hammond for 50, Bradman had made 142. He completed his 200 out of a total of 268 in three hours 40 minutes. At tea he was on 220, the only blemish a skier to mid-on which Tate was too slow to reach. With Kippax (77) he put on an Australian record third-wicket stand of 229.

When Bradman went on to record the highest score made in Test cricket, the game was held up for a couple of minutes so that the cheers might be prolonged. He waved his hand to express his joy, and for the first time indulged in a happy and expansive smile.

[Bradman extended his record to 334 out of Australia's 566 all out, but rain saved England from defeat after they followed on.]

Don Bradman completes a leg glance at Leeds on his way to another phenomenal score. Duckworth is behind the stumps.

1931

4 Mar West Indies gain their first Test victory over Australia, in the 5th Test at Sydney, after losing the first four Tests of the rubber. They win by 30 runs after a shrewd declaration by captain G.C. Grant leaves the Australians requiring 251 runs to win. They collapse to 220 all out on the final day with both Oldfield and Bradman out for ducks, Bradman having only once before been dismissed in first-class cricket without scoring - against Queensland during his first season.

26 Jun Oxford Blue the Nawab of Pataudi scores his 2nd hundred in the match against Surrey at the Oval, adding 100 to his first-innings 165.

27 Jun Pataudi's 138 for Oxford against Cambridge is his 4th 100 in succession, a record in University cricket.

27 Jun Herbert Sutcliffe, out of the England side against New Zealand because he was not considered quite fit by the Selection Committee, plays one of the finest innings of his career, making 230 for Yorks against Kent at Folkestone.

27 Jun Hampshire left-hander Philip Mead, 106 not out against Sussex, passes W.G.Grace's total of 126 centuries and now stands 2nd only to Hobbs (179 centuries).

23 July The Gentlemen of Ireland beat an M.C.C. side by an innings and 44 runs at Lord's, Dixon, the Irish captain, taking 8-54 in the match.

24 Jul Tich Freeman takes 15-144 (8-52, 7-92) as Kent beat Leics by 25 runs.

A.P. 'Tich' Freeman.

TEST SERIES

West Indies in Australia
A 4, WI 1
England in South Africa
SA 1, D 4
New Zealand in England
E 1, D 2

Fourth Test
Second day: 14 February

Australia outplay West Indies: Ironmonger 11-79

From Melbourne

AUSTRALIA won the fourth Test at Melbourne on the second day, beating West Indies by an innings and 122 runs. Ironmonger, who took seven for 23 in West Indies' first innings of 99, took another four for 56.

Declaring at 328 for eight (Bradman 152), Australia bowled out West Indies again for 107. Fairfax took four for 31 and Grimmett two for 10. Australia now lead 4-0 in the rubber with one more Test to play.

County Championship Yorks v Warwicks: 18 May

All 10 wickets for Verity: Remarkable feat on his birthday

From Leeds

THANKS to a great bowling performance from Verity, who took all 10 wickets in Warwickshire's second innings for 36 runs, Yorkshire beat the Midland county by an innings and 25 runs. Verity, who celebrated his 26th birthday today, made his first appearance in county cricket only a year ago.

Drake is the only other Yorkshire cricketer to take 10 wickets in an innings, a feat he accomplished against Somerset at Weston-super-Mare in 1914 at a cost of 35 runs.

Yorkshire passed the Warwicks first-innings total of 201 for the loss of four wickets. But Mayer (6-76) gave their later batsmen much trouble and they gained a lead of only 97.

Warwickshire were in trouble from the start of their second innings, losing four wickets for 51. Worse was to come, however, as Verity sent back four batsmen in one over and they were all out for 72. Verity finished with match figures of 13 for 97.

Left-arm spinner Hedley Verity.

Tour match M.C.C. v New Zealanders

New Zealanders' great win: M.C.C. twice dismissed in a day

By White Willow, at Lord's

EVERYBODY at Lord's today was aglow. We forgot that the chill grey of an English Maytime continued to mock our cricket fields as we sat absolutely still and stared. For in a single afternoon, the New Zealanders, who had given notice of fine things to come in the previous days of this match at headquarters, got the M.C.C. out twice and gained an innings victory.

Not since 1878, when the Australians dismissed them for 19, have the M.C.C. been humiliated on their own ground so thoroughly. Only Jardine, and White to a lesser extent, showed any fight whatsoever. Yet the New Zealand bowlers received little assistance from a turf so slow that every turn of the ball could be seen from the next township.

When, at the start of play, Lowry declared with the score 302 for nine, himself undefeated on 101, the Marylebone men immediately sniffed danger on all sides and proceeded to do everything but bat. They poked, they prodded - and they fell. Jardine (62 not out), who came in second wicket down, found himself deserted by batsman after batsman, as M.C.C. were skittled out for 132, Cromb taking six for 46.

It was not surprising, when the M.C.C. were asked to follow on, that Jardine, accompanied by Hearne, was sent in to continue his innings. That was at ten minutes past three. And, incredible though it might sound, Jardine and all the rest of them were back in the pavilion by a quarter past four! The whole side were out for 48, beaten by an innings and 122.

Merritt, who took two for 49 in the first innings, was the bowler this time, and Lowry did not even need to call on Cromb. Merritt was unplayable, with a ball that broke both ways and pitched more often than not on the 'blind spot'. He took seven for 28 in nine overs. Only Jardine (19) reached double figures, before being bowled by Blunt (3-13).

The spectators went home in time for tea, rubbing their eyes and asking themselves: "Suppose these New Zealanders win the only Test match that has been allotted to them when they come back to Lord's next month; what then?"

County Championship Worcs v Lancs: 19 May

Champions twice dismissed for under 100: Root's 9 for 23

From Worcester

LANCASHIRE, the champion county, have made a disastrous start to the season. They suffered their second reverse in their first three games today when Worcestershire overcame them by 126 runs.

The victory of the Midlands county was due chiefly to a magnificent bowling performance by Root, who in Lancashire's second innings took nine wickets for 23 runs. Lancs, however, contributed to their own undoing by feeble batting, altogether unworthy of their reputation.

During the day, 17 wickets fell for 154 runs. Root did not monopolise the bowling honours, for earlier in the day, when Worcs resumed with a lead of 142 and seven wickets in hand, Richard Tyldesley had most of the home batsmen in difficulties, taking six for 28, and returning a match aggregate of 11 for 59.

But Root went one better as Lancs were bowled out for 85, 10 more than their first innings, finishing with figures of 12 for 50.

County Championship Glamorgan v Yorks: 24 July

Great personal triumph for Verity: 5 for 7, 14–56 in all

From Swansea

ANOTHER wonderful bowling feat for Verity enabled Yorkshire to beat Glamorgan by an innings and 25 runs, the victory being remarkable for the fact that play during the three days was restricted to only seven hours.

Clever variation of pace and power of spin made Verity almost unplayable on a rain-damaged pitch, and he took eight for 33 to give him match figures of 14 for 56. He claimed the first five wickets that fell for only seven runs - including a hit for 6 by D.Davies! Yorkshire, who had declared their innings at 178 for eight (Leyland 77), now lead the County Championship by 30 points.

County Championship Notts v Warwicks: 24 July

Notts pass total of 511: Centuries by father and son

From Edgbaston

A REMARKABLE scoring match at Birmingham ended in a draw today, with the closing stages made exciting by Notts' great and successful attempt to gain the major points for a lead on first innings.

The game continued after they passed Warwickshire's total of 511 for three declared to enable G.V.Gunn, who batted so well in the important period, to complete his first hundred in first-class cricket.

This was an historic moment, as earlier his father, opener George Gunn, had made 183, a wonderful testimony to the fitness and ability of a man now in his 53rd year.

In the match no fewer than 1,032 runs were scored for the loss of only 10 wickets.

The Gunns: George (left) and son George Vernon.

First Test Second day: 29 June

Record eighth-wicket stand for England thwarts New Zealand

By Howard Marshall, at Lord's

THIS Test match swings from one extreme to the other. It was reasonable enough to anticipate that England, 190 for seven overnight, would pass the New Zealand total of 224, but who could have guessed that Ames and Allen would make an eighth-wicket stand of 246, an English record in Test matches, or that England's total would be 454?

Certainly, the New Zealanders did not expect to be 230 behind on the first innings, but after they had lost Mills in the first over, bowled by Allen with a full-pitch, they fought back so gallantly that by the close of play they had scored 161 for two.

That was good back-to-the-wall cricket, and it was characteristic of the game throughout the day. For a long time we shall remember that truculent English partnership, and then the sturdy Dempster, stolidly retrieving a desperate situation.

At the start of the day, with a perfect wicket, a fast outfield and glorious sunshine, everything suggested the possibility of high scoring - everything, that is, except the memory of Saturday's collapse. Ames, on 15, had been scratching at the spin bowlers, so Lowry brought Merritt and Blunt on immediately. But to our joyful surprise, Ames and Allen jumped out to them and punched them to the boundary.

Lowry then brought in Cromb with the new ball. But he was nowhere near as venomous or steady as on Saturday. By lunch, England had reached 385, with Ames on 105 and Allen, who had not batted on Saturday, just two runs short of his 100.

Wicket-keeper Ames, on his England début, went on to make 137, Allen 122, as the England innings ended at 2.55, and the prophets hinted at the possibility of an innings victory. But, after their early success, there was no sting in the England bowling. Dempster's innings of 86 not out confirmed the belief that he is a batsman of the highest class as he put New Zealand back in the match.

[New Zealand made 469-9 (Dempster 120, Page 104), and the match was drawn with England on 146-5, still needing 94 to win. This had been the only scheduled Test, but because of New Zealand's showing in preliminary matches, two more were arranged. England won by an innings at the Oval, the Old Trafford Test being washed out through rain.]

First Test Second day: 28 November

Bradman's Test record against South Africa

From Reuter, at Brisbane

DON BRADMAN set up another record at Brisbane today, his 226 being the highest individual score ever made in a Test match between Australia and South Africa. The previous best was 214 by Victor Trumper. Bradman's full Test match average is now over 100, as he has made 2,115 runs in 21 innings.

Bradman had reached his 200 by close of play yesterday, but not without incident. Early on, he was twice missed off Quinn's bowling, at 11 and 15. He was struck on the leg by a ball from Bell, which temporarily incapacitated him. And later, in attempting a big hit, he missed the ball and struck himself with his bat, collapsing at the crease!

Australia, thanks to Bradman, ran up a total of 450 today. South Africa started their innings badly, but had improved to 126 for three at the close. *[Australia won by an innings and 163 runs.]*

1932

5 Jan W.M.Woodfull (161) and Don Bradman (167) set a new 2nd-wicket world Test record with 274 for Australia against South Africa at Melbourne.

30 Jan Don Bradman completes his 1,000 runs against the current tourists when he reaches 109 in the 4th Test with South Africa, going on to make 170 not out by the close.

1 Feb Another record for Bradman as he takes his score in the first Test past R.E.Foster's 287 (1903) to record the highest Test score made in Australia, and he runs out of partners on 299.

2 Feb Clarrie Grimmett takes the last 6 S.African wickets for 9 runs in 9 overs, and Australia go on to win by 10 wickets and take a 4-0 lead in the series. His 7-83 gives him match figures of 14-199.

19-20 May At Southampton, 25 wickets fall for 217 runs on the 2nd day of the County match between Hants and Notts. Notts, resuming on 87-3 after a rain-affected first day, make 206 and then skittle Hants out for 57 (Staples 6-17). But they proceed to lose 8 wickets themselves for 41 on an increasingly worn pitch, Bailey taking 5-6. The next day, Bailey (7-7 and 11-47 in match) finishes them off with only 1 more run added, but Hants, with no-one reaching double figures, collapse again - for 30. Staples (4-4) finishes with match figures of 10-21, Voce (5-21) with 9-50.

14 Jun Jack Hobbs adds another record to his long list when he scores two 100s in a match for the 6th time, 113 and 119 not out as Surrey beat Essex by 9 wickets at the Oval. He previously shared the record with C.B.Fry. It is his 187th century, 59 more than any other player.

6 Jul Northants all-rounder V.W.C.Jupp takes all 10 of Kent's first-innings wickets for 127 runs off 39 overs at Tunbridge Wells, including the last 4 in 6 balls for 2 runs, the first Northants player to achieve the feat.

TEST SERIES

South Africa in Australia
Australia 5
South Africa in New Zealand
South Africa 2
India in England
England 1

Fifth Test Third day: 15 February

South Africa twice out for under 50: Remarkable bowling by Ironmonger

From Melbourne

MORE sensational cricket was seen in the last Test here today, when Australia dismissed South Africa in their second innings for 45, and won the match by an innings and 72 runs. Australia set up a new record by finishing off a modern Test match in a little over one day's actual play. Resuming this morning at five for one, after Saturday's complete wash-out, South Africa lost their remaining nine wickets in one hour 28 minutes. They were thus dismissed twice for an aggregate of 81 runs, another Test record.

Another feat which takes precedence over anything hitherto achieved in Test cricket between Australia and South Africa is the bowling of Ironmonger, who, at 45 years of age, took 11 wickets for 24 runs. Having taken five wickets for six runs in the first innings, he took six for 18 in the second.

That first day was also remarkable, 20 wickets falling for 194 runs. Australia bowled South Africa out for 36 in 90 minutes, Cameron (11) the only player to reach double figures. Then Australia, without Bradman, who twisted his ankle in the dressing-room, were dismissed for 153.

Only once before in any class of Test cricket has a side won all five matches in one rubber - Australia against England in 1920-21. The South Africans were 'caught out' in more ways than one, as not a single man was bowled - 18 fell to catches and two to stumpings.

County Championship Essex v Yorks: 16 June

Holmes and Sutcliffe in record stand: 555 for Yorks' first wicket

By White Willow, at Leyton

UNIQUE and thrilling deeds have made the match between Essex and Yorkshire at Leyton unforgettable, as Holmes and Sutcliffe, continuing their great first-wicket partnership, created a world record stand of 555. Yorkshire declared at this total and proceeded to bowl Essex out for 78 and take five second-innings wickets for 92.

Splendid bowling by Bowes (4-38) was succeeded by a deadly seven overs from Verity, in which he took five wickets for eight runs, and then the two bowlers shared the second-innings wickets to fall. Tomorrow, Essex require 385 to save defeat by an innings.

Prodigious figures! But they have arisen out of a prodigious game that took its place in cricket history at one o'clock precisely. For an hour and a half in the morning, Holmes and Sutcliffe had gathered runs majestically, soon carrying the overnight total of 483 into the fifth hundred, with Sutcliffe completing his 1,000 runs for the season and breaking his personal batting record of 255 - made, curiously, against the same county at Southend eight years ago.

He reached his 300 and then, to the accompaniment of enthusiastic applause, hit Eastman to the boundary twice in the same over - and the immortal names of Brown and Tunnicliffe - Yorkshiremen again - were relegated to second place in the annals of first-wicket partnerships after standing supreme for 34 years.

Sutcliffe straightaway played on to Eastman with a very casual stroke indeed, whereupon the Yorkshire innings was declared at 555 for one. The two openers - Holmes 224 not out and Sutcliffe 313 - were posing for their photograph in front of the scoreboard when, sensationally, the score was changed to 554. But, on further inspection of the score books, the original figure was found to be right, a no-ball having been overlooked when they were first checked!

All afternoon, telegrams of congratulation to the day's heroes poured into the ground. At first the messengers were allowed onto the ground, but eventually the telegrams were heaped up in the Yorkshire dressing-room and opened at close of play.

[Yorks went on to win by an innings and 313, Verity taking 10-53, Bowes 9-85, as they marched on in defence of their title.]

Holmes (left) and Sutcliffe in front of the historic scoreboard.

Only Test Final day: 28 June

England win by 158 runs: All-India's fighting finish in their first Test

By Howard Marshall, at Lord's

AFTER as good a game as anyone could wish to see, England beat All-India, in their inaugural Test, at Lord's by 158 runs.

Jardine was able to declare in the morning at 275 for eight, which gave England a comfortable lead of 345. There was just the outside chance that All-India might make the runs, and they did at least go down fighting. They lost seven wickets for 108, and then Amar Singh and Lall Singh put on 74 for the eighth wicket in 40 minutes, a most courageous partnership.

Amar Singh is an extremely attractive cricketer, for he is an uncommonly fine field, a really good bowler, and today his batting was superb. He drove Robins for three 4's and a 6 off successive balls in making his 51.

Everyone was delighted with his success, and there is no doubt that All-India have come out of their first Test with great credit. They have shown themselves to be excellent players, and popular players at that. They gave England a fright on the first day, sending Sutcliffe, Holmes and Woolley back to the pavilion with only 19 runs on the board and dismissing them for 259 by five o'clock. But perhaps the occasion was rather too much for their batsmen, who were never at ease against the English spin-bowlers.

All-India's splendid display led to the possibility that other Tests might be arranged, as with the New Zealanders last season, but it is understood that no further Tests will be played this year.

County Championship Yorks v Notts: 12 July

Verity takes all 10 Notts wickets for 10 runs: Record feat brings Yorks unexpected victory

From Leeds

AN AMAZING bowling performance, never before achieved in first-class cricket, was accomplished by Verity, of Yorkshire, at Leeds today. He took all 10 Notts wickets, including the hat-trick, for 10 runs. His analysis reads 19.4 overs, 16 maidens, 10 runs, 10 wickets. Ten wickets in an innings has been achieved on 45 previous occasions, but never for so few runs.

This remarkable feat enabled Yorkshire to gain an unexpected victory, which takes them to the head of the Championship table, two points above Kent. In the morning, they seemed to have no chance of success. But with the pitch still affected by the rain that had curtailed yesterday's play, and the start delayed until 12.30, Sellars declared on their overnight score of 163 for nine - 71 behind due mainly to the pace of Larwood and Voce.

It was a fine gamble, although the Notts openers were still there at lunch with 38 runs, neither batsman appearing to be in the slightest trouble. Yet in 70 minutes after the interval the whole side were out for the addition of only 29 more runs.

In his last two overs and four balls, Verity took seven wickets for three runs, including the hat-trick. Holmes and Sutcliffe then confounded the prophets by hitting off the 139 runs required in little more than an hour and a half - with a freedom that added to the wonder of Verity's achievement.

County Championship Kent v Warwicks: 30 June

Freeman takes 17 wickets for 92

By White Willow, at Folkestone

THE climax of the 'Freeman Festival' came at 5.15 this evening, when Kent's mighty atom among bowlers won for his county their fourth successive victory by taking his 17th wicket in the match and his 30th in four days during the Folkestone Cricket Week.

Warwickshire, apart from Wyatt, their captain, who was twice undefeated for 59 and 49, have been his helpless victims from start to finish, and they were beaten by 74 runs.

This is the second time in his career that Freeman has captured 17 wickets, a world record shared by others, but no-one has accomplished the feat more than once before. When he did it the first time, 10 years ago against Sussex at Hove, he conceded only 67 runs - the best figures stand to another Kent bowler, Blythe, 17 for 48 in 1907.

Freeman's figures for this match, albeit on a controversial pitch - were 41.4-12-92-17, eight for 31 and nine for 61. Added to the figures for the Lancashire débâcle on Monday, they give him 30 for 236!

Ironically, it was the Warwicks opening bowlers who prepared the way for Freeman's spin bowling by pounding the pitch - the marl and chalk villain of the piece - into powder during Kent's first innings. Mayer took nine for 73 in the match, Foster, playing his first match of the season, 11 for 163.

First Test First day: 2 December

Australians with backs to wall: Brave McCabe to the rescue

From Sydney

The defiant McCabe on the attack at Sydney, with Hammond and wicket-keeper Ames looking on.

AUSTRALIA, the conquerors of England in the last struggle for the Ashes, two years ago on English soil, are already fighting with their backs to the wall. Against the fiery bowling of Larwood and Voce today, when the new series of Tests began at Sydney, they lost four of the best batsmen for 87 runs. But a partnership by McCabe (127 not out) and Richardson (49) saved the side from disaster, and at the close of play Australia were 290 for six.

Without Bradman – 'run down' and controversially absent – and with Woodfull, Ponsford, Fingleton and Kippax all out for under 100, England began their challenge in wonderful fashion. But then McCabe and Richardson took the score from 87 to 216 for the fifth wicket.

It was a magnificent effort, especially on McCabe's part - only 22, the youngest in the team. He was the dominant partner, using his feet, wrists and shoulders superbly, scoring with strokes all round the wicket and with the most graceful batsmanship imaginable.

From the 'hill' came sounds of disapproval when Larwood and Voce sent down their bumpers, especially when Larwood hit Ponsford on the hip, and Voce's deliveries were seen to fly nearly head high. He bowled over the wicket with five short-leg fieldsmen. Voce took two for 76 and Larwood, attacking at terrific speed, four for 73, including a spell after lunch of three for 15.

[McCabe, with little support, went on to make 187 not out in Australia's 360 (Larwood 5-96). England replied with 524 (100s for Sutcliffe, Hammond and Pataudi on his début) and then Larwood (5-28) skittled the Australians, leaving England to get one run for a 10-wickets victory. But England's bowling tactics, employed first in the preliminary matches, would soon spark the Bodyline controversy.]

Don Bradman, caught by Allen off Larwood for eight on the second day of the Adelaide Test, in the leg-trap set by England captain Douglas Jardine (inset), villain of the piece. Bradman averaged a 'mere' 56.57 for the series.

The Bodyline Controversy

The 1932-33 MCC tour of Australia is still remembered as the 'Bodyline tour', and the debate it sparked rumbles on more than sixty years later. 'Debate' is too mild a word for it, for the controversy that sprang up is unparalleled anywhere else in the world of sport.

Cables began to fly across the world between the Australian Cricket Board and Lord's with the ferocity of the bowling that provoked them. British standards of sportsmanship were called into question, and the England fast bowlers were booed by the Australian crowds. Even the friendly relationship between the two countries was threatened.

Leg theory

What was - and is - all the fuss about? Well, some time after the great Don Bradman's demolition of the England bowling on the Australian tour of 1930 - in seven innings in the five Tests he scored 8, 131, 254, 1, 334, 14 and 232, a series record of 974 runs that still stands in the 1990s, at an average of 139.14 - the England captain Douglas Jardine got together with fast bowler Harold Larwood to devise a method for curbing this 'run machine' on the 1932-33 tour of Australia. They came up with 'leg theory' - bowling at or just outside the leg stump with a predominantly leg-side field, inviting the batsman to give a catch to the 'leg-trap'.

Leg theory was nothing new. But its method of employment by the England 'storm troops' immediately created a furore. However, before the first Test, 'White Willow', writing in The Daily Telegraph on 1 December 1932, said:

"To prevent them [Australia's 'forty to fifty an hour batsmen'] from finding their stride, Jardine will obviously call into action his storm troops. It was for this purpose that so many as five - Larwood, Allen, Voce, Tate and Bowes - were sent out, and the theory that speed rather than spin might be more effective on Australian wickets against such giants as Bradman has had really sensational support in the preliminary matches. Bradman, 103 runs in six completed innings; Woodfull, 48 in four, including a 'duck'; such meagre figures were not anticipated even in our wild dreams.

"The moral effect of this devastation must be tremendous. Shrewd observers on the spot have detected a loss of confidence in Bradman and his admirers....Unfortunately, it is not possible for Jardine and his co-selectors, Warner and Sutcliffe, to include more than three 'shock' bowlers in the side. The absence of spin-bowlers, especially a left-handed one, is not to be thought of...."

Bradman did not play in that first Test. He had a 'run-down condition', although a blood test revealed nothing organically wrong, and, much to the disappointment of the Sydney fans, he went off for a short holiday to recuperate. Meanwhile, despite a heroic unbeaten 187 by Stan McCabe, Larwood twice stormed through the Australian defences, taking 5 for 96 and 5 for 28, and England won by 10 wickets.

The argument erupts

In the second Test, on the slow Melbourne wicket, fast leg theory was less successful, and in a low-scoring match leg-spinner Bill O'Reilly (5-63, 5-66) and Bradman (0, 103 not out) helped Australia level the series.

It was at Adelaide, in the third Test, that the 'bodyline' argument erupted. Woodfull and Bert Oldfield were injured and the Australian Board of Control sent the following historic telegram to the MCC on 18 January 1933:

"Body-line bowling has assumed such proportions as to menace the best interests of the game, making protection of the body by the batsman the main consideration. This is causing intensely bitter feeling between the players, as well as injury. In our opinion it is unsportsmanlike. Unless stopped at once, it is likely to upset the friendly relations existing between Australia and England."

But the MCC Committee did not appreciate the full extent of the tactics being employed and the intense resentment they were causing. They backed their captain and manager and deprecated the charge of bad sportsmanship.

The former Surrey captain and Test player P.G.H.Fender sprang to England's defence with a long article in The Daily Telegraph the very next day, 19 January, headed THIS 'BODY-LINE BOWLING' IS NEW ONLY IN NAME: Form of Attack Australia's Batsmen Should Face Without Resentment.

Referring to what he termed the "acrimonious bickering", he went on:

"The main bone of contention, as officially noted in the cable from the Australian Board of Control yesterday, concerns what is described - whatever the term may mean - as 'body-line bowling'. It is a pity that so much time and thought have been wasted in finding new and insinuating names for something which is as old as the hills. Leg theory bowling, whether fast or slow, has been known and often used by the bowlers of both England and Australia. But never before has so much been made of it, and never has it been made the cause of such feeling."

He went on to criticise the use of the term 'body-line' as conveying an entirely erroneous impression of bowlers setting out to maim - an unsubstantiated, unimaginable and mischievous suggestion. He also stressed that it was the business of the bowler to discover a batsman's weakness and to direct his attack against it, charging that the Australian batsmen as a whole had a decided weakness on the leg stump. He continued:

"Why Jardine's determination to play on this weakness should 'cause intensely bitter feeling between the players' one can only guess. The complaint that it is dangerous and 'makes protection of the body the main consideration' can surely not be sustained without coupling with it the admission that their batsmen are unable to cope with fast bowling on the leg stump....Unless the Australians take the line that they cannot cope with it, and for that reason want it stopped, and the MCC agree to that for political reasons, there can be no ground for instructing our captain to discontinue their most successful form of attack."

He concluded that: "There can be no question about the legality of attacking the leg stump, and if there were the slightest question of a bowler going out more for the body than the wicket, the umpires are there on the spot, and would act without hesitation....The Press and the public, being 120 yards from the wicket, cannot see enough to warrant the belief that the success of our bowlers is due to anything more than that they have discovered a hole in the Australian batting, and are making full use of it."

A bold and forthright piece by Fender, which surely put the matter in perspective and those 'whingeing Aussies' in their place - or did it? The very next day, while Thomas Moult - a.k.a. 'White Willow' - was celebrating England's 338-runs victory in the third Test (and retailing the England team's joint statement, made to negate Press rumours of dissension in the camp, that they were to a man utterly loyal to their captain), on another page was a reader's letter (from a Mr Campbell Dixon of London) accusing Mr Fender of "shutting his eyes to the facts". Mr Dixon cited former England Test captain Sir Stanley Jackson and one of several cricketers noted for their sportsmanship, the Rev. J.H.Parsons, as among many who had stated that Larwood's tactics were new - not only new, but deplorable, according to the Reverend. The letter went on:

"The viciousness of the new attack lies in the fact that the batsman is deprived of the full use of his bat by fear of losing his wicket. Faced by a packed leg field, the batsman has to choose between playing a high-flying ball and being caught by the waiting ring of fielders, or letting the ball go and possibly being incapacitated.

"That Australians are not the only cricketers who see the risk is proved by Hobbs's vehement protest to Bowes last year (he prophesied that someone would be killed), and by Mr P.F. Warner's warning to Bowes at the time that his tactics were unjustifiable, and, if persisted in, would ruin his career. A voyage seems to have changed [team manager] Mr Warner's views, and this despite the fact that Bowes did not concentrate on the batsman's body to the extent that Larwood admittedly does, and is not nearly as fast."

Mr Dixon continues: "As an Australian, I ..." Ah, that explains it!

The debate continues

It is interesting to note that, while Larwood took seven wickets in the Adelaide Test, the amateur fast bowler G.O. Allen, who eschewed bodyline, took eight. Indeed, Allen took 21 wickets in the series, second only to Larwood's 33, as England went on to win the remaining two Tests.

The cables continued to flow - six each way - and more than once the tour was in jeopardy. It was only after England returned home that Hobbs, who reported the tour for the London Star, condemned bodyline (he had not wished to embarrass Jardine and the team while in Australia). And it was not until Warner, who was opposed to bodyline, made his report that the MCC took action. They published a resolution condemning direct attack on the batsman.

There were minor outbreaks of the tactics on less helpful English pitches - by the West Indians Constantine and Martindale (Jardine opened for England against them and made a hundred!) and by Larwood and Voce for Notts. But the controversy erupted again when the Australians toured England in 1934. Voce was taken off when he started bowling fast leg-theory against the tourists for Notts at Trent Bridge. The crowd blamed the Australians for this and booed them - an occurrence that for many warranted the cessation of Test cricket. At the end of the year, the MCC redefined "direct attack on the batsman" as "persistent and systematic bowling of fast, short-pitched balls at the batsman standing clear of his wicket" under the rules governing unfair play.

Stan McCabe (above), heroic batting for Australia in the first Test, and England's spearhead Harold Larwood (below), a great bowling performance.

So 'bodyline', as known in the unhappy and unpleasant tour of 1932-33, was in effect outlawed. Bradman, who had averaged a 'mere' 56.57 in that series, was never contained again in Test cricket. But the arguments and the acrimony continued.

Gilbert Mant, an Australian journalist who was recruited as a general reporter on the staff of Reuter's London office, was one of the very few reporters to cover the tour for English newspapers, and his pieces were syndicated to the whole national Press. These reported the cricket, with objectivity and accuracy, there being no time for opinionated writing. When he returned, he intended to write a book about the controversy, critical of the English tactics, but was refused permission by Reuter's, his employers. He did, nevertheless, write his book, and it was favourably reviewed by an eminent cricket correspondent in The Daily Telegraph, who agreed with his conclusions and was highly critical of the tactics of the England captain, Jardine - "a man with a paranoic *[sic]* antipathy to Australians".

Sure enough, a few days later, a riposte appeared in the Letters columns of the newspaper, from a Mr F.Cheeseman of Whitstable, Kent, headed "Bodyline: Aussies just bad losers". It deplored the attack by author and correspondent on "one of our greatest cricketers and certainly our best ever captain, D.R.Jardine". It continued:

"The Australians were annihilated by England during the 1932-33 tour. Their heroes were humbled, the country was in a state of economic depression and, not least, they cannot stomach defeat....The crowd's attack on Jardine and others was vile....They screamed so loudly that the King and Government thought we would lose part of the empire. The Establishment moved in!"

Other letters also took the article to task. Mr Geoffrey Griffiths, of Coggeshall in Essex, denied the reviewer's implication that Larwood and Voce bowled at the batsman's head - "the head was not in danger if the batsman did not duck into the ball". He quoted Arthur Mailey, "one of Australia's greatest bowlers and cricket journalists", who praised Jardine's captaincy and wrote in his book *And then came Larwood*: "England won the Tests because of superior play, and it is Australia's duty to settle down and find a combination capable of regaining the Ashes in 1934."

Why quote these particular letters? Well, it is for the fact that they appeared in The Daily Telegraph in October 1992, sixty years after the event! The author of the book in question, Mant, produced it in his nineties, and the reviewer and writer of the article was none other than EW Swanton.

1933

25, 27 Feb Harold Larwood, whose controversial fast leg-theory bowling brought him 33 wickets in the series, a record for a fast bowler, goes in as nightwatchman in the last Test, at Sydney, and scores 98 in 2hr 15min.

27 Mar A dust storm at Christchurch causes the first Test to be abandoned after New Zealand had followed on against England. Earlier Hammond (227) and Ames (103) had made 242 for England's 5th wicket.

2 Apr H.H.Shri Sir Ranjitsinhji Vibhaji, Maharaja Jamsaheb of Nawanagar - better known in the British Empire as Ranjitsinhji, or 'Ranji' - dies suddenly aged 60. The former Cambridge, Sussex and England player governed Nawanagar, a State covering 4,000 square miles, and his 26-year rule was marked by developments and reforms in all areas of the economy. He had also twice represented India at the League of Nations.

22 Jul Wicket-keeper Ivan Barrow (105) and George Headley (169 not) are the first West Indies batsmen to score hundreds in a Test in England, at Old Trafford in the drawn 2nd Test. Their 2nd-wicket stand is worth 200.

24-25 Jul England captain Douglas Jardine makes a dramatic reply to his critics with his first Test hundred (127) - against the 'body-line' bowling of West Indies' Martindale and Constantine.

24 Jul Patsy Hendren's 301 not out at Dudley against Worcs is the first triple hundred scored for Middlesex, surpassing the 285 not out played by Hearne v Essex at Leyton in 1929.

12-15 Aug England beat West Indies in the 3rd Test by an innings and 17 runs a few minutes into the 3rd day, Fred Bakewell making his maiden Test century (107) and leg-spinner Charles Marriott taking 11-96 on his Test début.

17-18 Dec England's Brian Valentine (136) and India's reserve wicket-keeper Lala Amarnath (118) make hundreds on their Test début at Bombay.

TEST SERIES

England in Australia
E 4, A 1
England in New Zealand
Drawn 2
West Indies in England
E 2, D 1

Third Test Sixth day: 19 January

England's overwhelming victory: Only Woodfull resists attack

By Thomas Moult ('White Willow')

ENGLAND gained an overwhelming victory by 338 runs at Adelaide yesterday in the third Test match. The end came tamely, Australia being all out in their second innings for 193. Only Woodfull, their captain, made any resistance, and he fought magnificently, carrying his bat for 73. England now lead 2-1 in the fight for the Ashes, with two Tests still to be played.

To dwell on the proud aspect of the Adelaide achievement is useful: it helps to relieve, in our case, at all events, an atmosphere over there which has become, in Reuter's words, "one of extreme bitterness, almost amounting to hysteria".

Indeed, so personal had the feeling become that before the final day's play began, the England team thought it fit to issue a statement, published in the later editions of The Daily Telegraph, denying Press rumours and pledging utter loyalty to their captain, D.R.Jardine, "under whose leadership they hope to achieve an honourable victory".

Then, the game being the thing, they went out and proceeded to do just that. The Australian batsmen were helpless against Allen and Larwood. Five wickets fell in 100 minutes for 73 runs, and as Oldfield was unable to bat, the finish of the match came soon after lunch.

Woodfull (pictured above), unbeaten at the end, was carried shoulder-high to the pavilion by the crowd. He had withstood the England attack for four hours, and when he reached his 50, the England captain made a gesture of goodwill by walking across and congratulating him.

Such an emphatic success as this of England's is a wonderful sequel to the dismay of the opening day when our leading batsmen collapsed to 30 for four.

Fourth Test
Sixth day: 16 February

England's great Test triumph: Ashes regained at Brisbane

By Thomas Moult

ENGLAND regained the Ashes today by beating Australia by six wickets in the fourth Test to take a winning 3-1 lead in the rubber. Nothing happened to snatch the honours of the game from their grasp on the sixth day, and the result was richly deserved.

The climax was swift and always sure. The 63 runs that England needed were scored in an hour and a quarter, and they cost two wickets.

That Paynter should have brought about the finish by making a winning hit for six was delightfully fitting. For it was Paynter, sent to hospital with tonsillitis on the second day and returning, clearly unfit, to play one of the pluckiest innings ever seen in a Test match - 83 in four hours - who gave England a narrow first-innings lead and paved the way for their eventual triumph.

England have won the Ashes by an all-round superiority that was not questioned even by their antagonists, but the outstanding factor in their memorable achievement has been the shock-bowling of Larwood. In the four Tests, he has taken 28 wickets, and it is significant that, in spite of all the sound and fury he has aroused, 13 of these were bowled, two lbw, and four caught on the off-side.

Second Test Second day: 1 April

Brilliant innings by Hammond: Bradman's 334 beaten

From Reuter, in Auckland

EVERYTHING else in the second Test between New Zealand and England at Auckland was overshadowed by a magnificent innings of 336 not out by Walter Hammond, which beat the previous record Test score of 334 by Don Bradman at Leeds in 1930.

England scored 548 for seven before declaring, and New Zealand replied with eight for none in their second innings. They are now 382 runs behind.

Hammond hit with great power and precision to all parts of the field, pulling, cutting and driving in a manner which can seldom have been equalled. His footwork was also superb, and the way in which he pierced the field left the New Zealanders bewildered. The bowling, with the exception of the two Otago men, Badcock and Dunning, was, however, generally mediocre, while the fielding was deplorable.

Both of those bowlers and Dempster were injured in trying to stop shots from Hammond, Dempster dropping a hot return and having to retire for a time. Hammond hit ten 6's - three off successive balls from Newman - and thirty-three 4's. He gave his first chance at 134, and was caught off a no-ball when 335. His 100 came in 134min, the 200 in 241min, the 300 in 288min and 336 in 318min.

[Heavy rain prevented a result for the second time and the MCC team sailed home, with Hammond, 227 in Christchurch, boasting a Test average of 563!]

County Championship Lancs v Yorks: 5 June

Yorkshire's amazing win at Old Trafford: Lancashire dismissed for 93 and 92

By Thomas Moult, in Manchester

A BATTLE of the Roses? No, indeed, not a battle, but a rout, probably unparalleled throughout the history of these two Northern counties. Twice in a single afternoon, a great Whitsun holiday crowd of 25,000 saw the bearers of the White Rose trample the Red flower of Lancashire into the dust, and win a most thrilling victory by an innings and 156 runs.

Lancs all out for 93 and 92 in three and a half hours; Watson, a leading batsman for the losers, knocked out of the game by a ball from Bowes; a hat-trick by Macaulay, and 12 wickets to the same Yorkshire bowler for only 49 runs - such is the stark story of Lancashire's first defeat of the season, and Yorkshire's seventh Championship win in their seven matches.

What will this amazing side do next? The majority of their games have been won on the second day. With this latest triumph was answered the criticism directed at one of their batsmen. That it was unjustified against Mitchell on Saturday has been proved today, for the wicket seemed so deplorable soon after the match began that his century, completed this morning at 123 in six hours altogether, was really a great one. And mainly through Mitchell, Lancashire had to face a total of 341 at one o'clock.

The pitch was already crumbling, especially at one end, the tropical heat having acted drastically on an over-prepared turf. They also knew they had the bowlers to make full use of such a condition, and this they proceeded to do magnificently.

Macaulay soon began to create havoc, and, despite being hit for 11 in one over by Parkinson (24), took seven wickets for 28. Four of these came in five balls, including the hat-trick, as Lancashire's last six wickets went for three runs.

It was a similar story in the second innings, Macaulay taking five for 21 and Verity, who had two for 27 in the first innings, four for 41 in this. Twenty-four wickets having fallen during the day for 239 runs, it was inevitable that the Lancashire rout should be followed by an inquest on the pitch, solemnly conducted by a whole host of officials.

County Championship Worcs v Glos: 4 July

Six centuries in match: Dacre and Hammond two each

From Worcester

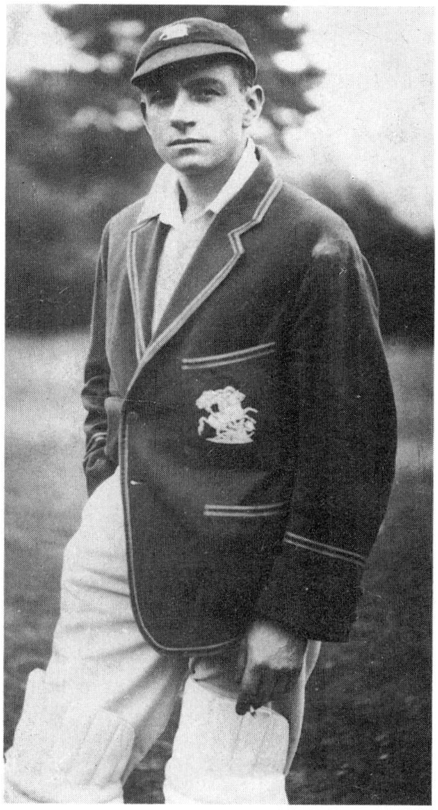

Hammond: Two centuries in match

Though no records were broken at Worcester as the game with Gloucester ended in a draw, six centuries were made, five by the visitors, for whom Dacre and Hammond made two each.

At Derby in 1898, four home batsmen reached three figures, as did two from Hants, and in 1928 at Coventry, four hundreds were credited to Notts, two to Warwicks.

Dacre (119 and 125 not out) and Hammond (122 and 111 not out) equalled the performance of R.E. and W.L. Foster in the Hants match at Worcester in 1899.

County Championship Essex v Yorks: 14 July

Verity takes 17 wickets in a day: Amazing Yorkshire triumph

By Thomas Moult, at Leyton

LEYTON was the scene today of a bowling achievement so remarkable that a record, 26 years old, was equalled, and another broken that had stood for 64 years. The havoc-worker and record-maker was Verity, backed up, of course, by the rest of the Yorkshire side, who were thus enabled to win another of their famous victories - the 14th out of 17 matches since the season began - by an innings and 172 runs over Essex.

Poor Essex. They put Yorkshire in on Wednesday partly to avoid batting on a pitch that Verity and perhaps Macaulay would make deadly. But all they did was put off the evil day. Yorkshire made 340 and, after yesterday was washed out by rain, they found themselves with no alternative but to go in on a wicket on which the sun had shone until it was really 'sticky', and between half-past eleven and ten minutes to four they were twice all out, for 104 and 64.

Verity was irresistible from the outset. He dismissed two batsmen with successive balls in his third over, and by the time he had completed the afternoon's devastation, his figures for each innings read: 1st 27-10-47-8; 2nd 14-3-44-9. In the whole of cricket history, only Colin Blythe of Kent has taken 17 wickets in a day before, in 1907. And the Yorkshire record of 16 in a day set by Emmett, has stood since 1869.

County Championship Sussex v Middlesex: 5 August

Sussex batsmen just miss world record: 490 for first wicket

By Our Special Representative, at Hove

THERE was some remarkable cricket at Hove today, where Bowler and John Langridge, batting for almost the whole day, scored 490 runs for the Sussex first wicket against Middlesex. The achievement broke, by huge margins, two records for the county for the first wicket (328) and for any wicket (385).

Both Bowley, with 283, and Langridge, 193, surpassed their previous highest scores, 280 and 142, respectively. From the very first, the Middlesex bowling was mastered, with Bowley, in his 44th year, scoring at a rapid pace. Had he not been continually deprived of the bowling at this stage, he would most certainly have attained his hundred before lunch. He did reach his second hundred before the tea interval.

All the bowling, on a wicket that seemed cruelly insensitive, was uniformly innocuous. The 400 was sent up after five hours' play, and just as it was becoming more and more likely that last season's world record (555) by Holmes and Sutcliffe would be beaten, Sims got Langridge lbw.

At the close, Sussex were 512 for three. Middlesex had shown commendable endurance and spirit, above all Hulme, whose tireless work on the boundary must have saved 40 runs.

1934

10 Feb Two pairs of brothers play for India against England at Madras in the 3rd Test, C.K. and C.S.Nayudu and Syed Nazir and Syed Wazir Ali.

1 Jun Kent beat Essex by an innings and 192 runs, having amassed, in 7 hours, 803-4 (Ashdown 332, including 307 on the first day; Ames 202 not; Woolley 172), the highest score in England this century and a record anywhere for the loss of only 4 wickets. Freeman takes 11-176 as Pope and O'Connor make 100s for Essex. Meanwhile, the Australians compile 629 at the Oval, with Ponsford (125) and McCabe (240) putting on 230, a new Australian first-wicket record in England - this after Sandham had scored 219 in Surrey's 1st innings. The match is drawn.

6 Jul Patsy Hendren (Middlesex) makes 132 for England against Australia at the age of 45.

Patsy Hendren

7 Jul Gubby Allen, opening the attack for England against Australia, sends down 3 wides and 4 no-balls in his first over, which comprised 13 deliveries, off which Brown scores three 4's.

4 Nov Madras (130) beat Mysore (48 and 59) at Madras in a day.

21 Nov A controversial major change in the lbw law is made, for a trial in both first and second class county competitions in 1935: the batsman may be given out lbw to a ball pitching on the off-side that would have hit the wicket. The M.C.C. Committee, in their continuing effort to rid the game of fast leg-theory, define "a direct attack by the bowler on the batsman" as "persistent and systematic bowling of fast, short-pitched balls at the batsman standing clear of his wicket".

28-31 Dec First women's Test held, England beating Australia at Brisbane by 9 wickets.

TEST SERIES

England in India
E 2, D 1
Australia in England
A 2, E 1, D 2

Third Test Final day: 13 February

England win rubber: India beaten by 202 runs

From Madras

ENGLAND have won the Test rubber. The first match of the series saw them secure a nine-wicket victory, the second was drawn, and the final game ended here today with India beaten by 202 runs.

Needing 452 runs to win after England declared yesterday at 261 for seven, and with two men out for 65 when play reopened today, the Indians set about their task spiritedly. No attempt was made to save the game - they just went for the runs.

There was some powerful hitting. Amar Singh struck eight 4's in his 48, made in 36 minutes, and the Yuvraj of Patiala, a young batsman new to Test cricket, followed by hitting 60 in as many minutes, including 10 boundaries, made with brilliant straight drives, off-drives and square cuts.

Verity, who took seven for 49 in the first innings, was now the chief victim, and his four wickets cost 104 runs. Langridge was the most successful bowler, with five for 63. At one stage, India were 209 for five, but they lost their last four wickets for 40 runs, Nacomal being unable to bat.

Second Test Third day: 23 June

Verity bowls Australia to innings defeat: 14-80 in a day

By P.F.Warner, at Lord's

ENGLAND beat Australia at Lord's today for the first time since 1896 - by an innings and 38 runs - to draw level at one Test each in the series. Rain during the weekend had affected the turf, and Verity seized his opportunity. Bowling magnificently, he equalled the feat of another great Yorkshire bowler, Wilfred Rhodes, who at Melbourne in 1903 obtained 15 wickets in a Test match.

Verity's figures were: First innings, seven for 61; second innings, eight for 43. His match analysis read: 58.3 overs, 23 maidens, 104 runs, 15 wickets. He was backed up by splendid fielding, Geary, Sutcliffe and Hammond forming a great semi-circle of slips, with Hammond shining as a star of the first magnitude.

The light was very bad when the players took the field at 11 o'clock, and an immediate appeal led to a cessation of play for 20 minutes. Australia resumed at 192 for two, 248 runs behind. Brown added only two more runs to his fine innings of 103 compiled on Saturday, caught at the wicket off Bowes. Verity took six of the remaining seven wickets, and Australia, all out for 284 just before lunch, were asked to follow on.

England struck an early blow in Australia's second innings, when Walters took a beautifully judged catch at long leg off Bowes to dismiss Brown for two. McCabe (19) came in next and was looking good when Hendren took a magnificent catch at silly point off Verity. Bradman joined Woodfull and made 13 out of 14 runs without looking confident. He had already mis-hit Verity, who had no outfield, over deep mid-on for two, when he skied a good-length ball and was caught by Ames in front of the wicket,

After tea, Verity was irresistible. Woodfull defended stubbornly, but after Hammond caught him off Verity for 43, Australia collapsed, subsiding from 94 for three to 118 all out. The crowd swarmed in front of the pavilion to cheer Verity. Wyatt, the captain, spoke a few modest words, and acknowledged the great part that the rain had played in England's success.

County Championship Lancs v Notts: 21 July

Voce uses fast leg-theory: Taken off after four overs

From Old Trafford

Voce: controversial.

FAST leg-theory bowling was used by Voce at Old Trafford in what may be the last fixture between Lancashire and Notts - that is, until the breach caused by the Notts fast bowler's methods is healed.

Voce had a 'leg-trap' of five fieldsmen, and made the ball get up shoulder-high at times. Bowling short of a length, the Notts left-hander twice in succession struck Iddon on the body.

The second time he was struck - the ball hit him over the heart - Iddon fell to the ground, and two ambulance men hurried to his assistance. After these incidents, and when he had bowled only four overs, Voce was taken off.

Returning to the Notts team after an ankle injury, Larwood bowled to an orthodox field, but took only one wicket while Lancs went to 387 for six wickets. Iddon, missed early on by Walker in the leg-trap, shared in three big partnerships and took out his bat for 144.

Fourth Test Second day: 22 July

Record Test stand of 388 by Bradman and Ponsford

By P.F.Warner, at Headingley

AS ONLY one wicket fell all day, Bradman and Ponsford completely changed the course of the fourth Test match at Headingley with a record partnership for any wicket. Their 4th-wicket stand of 388 beats the 323 of Hobbs and Rhodes for England at Melbourne in 1912, and with Australia 494 for four at the close, England are 294 behind.

At the close of play last night, Australia had lost Brown, Oldfield and Woodfull for 39 runs, all to Bowes. Ponsford was 22 not out and Bradman had not come to the wicket. Today, the England bowlers toiled from 11.00 to 6.30 and obtained only one wicket.

Ponsford (181) was not dismissed until five minutes to six, when he trod on his stumps while making one of the best strokes of his splendid innings - a hook to the boundary off Verity. He hit nineteen 4's and was at the wickets six hours and ten minutes.

Bradman hit two 6's and thirty-nine 4's, and, so far, has been batting six hours and five minutes for his unbeaten 271. From the first ball sent down to him by Bowes, which he forced by the bowler for four, Bradman was completely master of the bowling, his stroke play wonderful in its power, versatility and certainty.

[On Monday, Bradman was out for 304, bowled by Bowes, who took 6-142 as Australia compiled 584, but rain on the last day robbed them of certain victory.]

16 August

Let M.C.C speak out on leg-theory bowling

By Howard Marshall

DO WE want to save Test match cricket? A debatable question, perhaps, but one thing it seems to me is certain. Test match cricket is already in a critical state, and it will be as dead as a doornail if we have any repetition of the scenes at Nottingham on Tuesday, when the Australians were booed by the crowd.

Things have come to a pretty pass when an English crowd demonstrates against a visiting cricket team. It is an old boast of ours, and it can be substantiated, that there are no more sporting crowds in the world than English crowds. Something, then, was very wrong at Nottingham. Those spectators may have booed Test cricket out of existence.

We all know the bare facts of the case - how Voce bowled fast leg-theory with startling success against the Australians on Saturday, and how he was interviewed by the Notts secretary and took no further part in the match when he was due to bowl fast leg-theory again on the Tuesday.

On the face of it, we are bound to deduce that the Australians had protested against Voce's bowling, and that the Notts committee acted accordingly. But we do not know for sure, and as one of thousands of cricket-lovers in this country may I suggest it is high time we were given the facts.

I am not arguing the case for or against what has become known as body-line bowling. I am far more concerned to plead for wise handling of a situation that may seriously affect the friendly relationship between Australia and the Mother Country. I cannot believe that it is beyond the power of the M.C.C. and the Australian Board of Control to clear up the situation.

Fifth Test First day: 18 August

Bradman-Ponsford world record 451 stand: England's costly fielding errors

By P.F.Warner, at the Oval

IN a remarkable record partnership, Bradman and Ponsford put on 451 for the second wicket today, and unless this fifth and final Test match is destined to be the most extraordinary game in the history of cricket, Australia are on the high road to victory - and winning the Ashes.

England were kept in the field from twenty-five minutes to twelve until half-past six, in which time Australia made 475 for the loss of only two wickets. The second-wicket partnership broke the Test record of 388 established by the same pair at Leeds last month, and is a world record for the second wicket in first-class cricket, surpassing the 398 of Shrewsbury and Gunn in 1890.

Bradman gave not the semblance of a chance until he was caught by Ames off Bowes for 244. Ponsford, on the other hand, was missed five times - at 47, 57, 68, 115 and 116, but is still there on 205. The batting was magnificent. There is nothing new to be said about Bradman. He is the wonder of the cricket world. Ponsford may have been lucky, but he, too, played a great innings.

[Australia went on to amass 701 runs (Ponsford 266), and, as this was a timeless Test, did not enforce the follow-on when they bowled England out for 321 (Leyland 110). They made another 327 in their 2nd innings, and won back the Ashes when England collapsed, in the face of their 707 deficit, to 145 all out on the 5th day.]

Daily Telegraph Editorial: 23 August

AUSTRALIA have won back the Ashes with an overwhelming victory. At every point of every game, except one innings against Verity on a bad wicket, Woodfull and his men have been too good for ours. The Australians have always played like sportsmen and we cheer their triumph. Why is it then that the very crowds which have delighted to honour the Australians have gone home saying they have had enough of Test matches for a long time?

The answer is that the whole series has been played in an atmosphere of doubt and distrust. Anyone who knew anything about cricket could see that the English elevens did not represent England. The captain [Jardine] who led the team which won back the Ashes from Australia, the best captain England has had for a score of years and one of her classic batsmen, had reported himself not available for the season. His most brilliant bowler [Larwood] declared that he would not play against the Australians. Finally, the bowler [Voce] who took the other end efficiently in Australia, and who made an outstanding success against Woodfull's team here, was not asked to play in a Test.

The M.C.C. have only themselves to blame if the general public suspect and condemn their management of affairs. They answered the Australian protests with a cablegram that could be read to mean anything. The Australians took it to ban leg-theory. Yet the M.C.C. have never disowned the leg-theory that was bowled in Australia.

Before another team is sent to Australia, the M.C.C. must negotiate with the Australian Board of Control and reach a precise and public understanding as to what bowling is legitimate and what is not.

1935

7 Jan England's Myrtle Maclagan (119) makes first 100 in women's Tests, and next day England beat Australia to go 2-0 up in rubber with one to play.

18 May Harold Gimblett, aged 20, makes a sensational début for Somerset against Essex at Frome, scoring 123, with three 6's and 17 4's, his first 100 coming up in 63min.

3-10 Jun Old-stagers G.Geary, 41, and H.A.Smith, 34, bowl unchanged for Leics through 4 consecutive innings, dismissing Worcs (2nd innings) for 77, Glos (only innings) for 72 and Northants for 85 and 79, Smith taking 20-150 and Geary 18-148.

12 Jun Alf Gover takes 4 wickets in 4 balls for Surrey and 8-34 as Worcs are dismissed for 73 in their 1st innings.

15-18 Jun Geary and Smith continue to monopolise Leicester's wicket-taking, sharing the 10 Derby 1st-innings wickets at Leicester, and it is not until Derby's 2nd innings that another bowler, Marlow (5-69), achieves success. In between, Mitchell takes all 10 Leicester 1st-innings wickets for 64.

3-5 Jul Glamorgan record their first victory over Hants, by 10 wickets at Cardiff, and in their 1st innings Smart hits Hill for 32 (6,6,4,6,6,4) in one over.

6-9 Jul Hampshire's Hill, recovering from his thrashing at Cardiff earlier in the week, takes 14-146 as Hants beat Kent by 26 runs at Tonbridge.

9 Aug With Lancs 70-6, and with 20min left, against Somerset at Weston-super-Mare, needing another 32 to win, it is decided to take a tea interval of 10min. After this, to complete the farce, the captains decide not to continue, and stumps are drawn.

1 Nov H.B.'Jock' Cameron, wicket-keeper and vice-captain of South Africa on this year's tour in England, dies of enteric fever at the age of 30.

Jock Cameron.

TEST SERIES

England in West Indies
WI 2, E 1, D 1
South Africa in England
SA 1, D 4

First Test Third day: 10 January

Well, I declare! Remarkable win for England in West Indies

From Bridgetown, Barbados

ENGLAND won the race for runs here today and beat the West Indies in a thrilling finish by four wickets. The shocks of the first day, when West Indies' collapse was followed by Wyatt's declaration with the England total at 81 for five, were followed by more today.

After a four-hour delay due to rain, the West Indies, who had scored 33 for three overnight, lost three wickets for 18 runs within 15 minutes, Smith, the Middlesex fast bowler having taken five for 15. At that point, with the score at 51 for six, tea was taken, and George Grant, the West Indies captain, declared the innings closed.

England were thus left to score 73 for victory, not such an easy task as it might appear out of the context of this match, on a tricky wicket. The two West Indies express bowlers Martindale and Hylton opened the attack, and had England's openers Smith and Farnes back in the pavilion with only eight on the board.

Excitement was intense and the fieldsmen were on their toes, eager to press home the advantage. Fortunately for England, they had Hendren to call on, a great favourite with the crowd, and he promptly struck Hylton over the on boundary for 6. Martindale, however, accounted for Holmes and Leyland, both caught at square-leg, and yorked Hendren for 20 and had Paine caught, also at square-leg - six wickets down for 48 and 25 runs still needed, with Wyatt joining Hammond.

The captain defended with great skill and allowed Hammond to go for the runs. With a glorious drive for 6 off Martindale (5-22), Hammond (29 not out) carried the score to 75, and thus gave England victory by four wickets in one of the most amazing Test matches of recent years.

Headley, a brilliant unbeaten 270 against England.

Fourth Test Final day: 18 March

England routed in final Test: Innings defeat by West Indies

From Kingston, Jamaica

ENGLAND suffered a crushing defeat in the fourth and final Test match today, the West Indies winning by an innings and 161 runs. West Indies thus won the series, gaining two victories to England's one.

What hopes England had of batting all day and forcing a draw were completely dashed by the West Indies fast bowlers, Constantine and Martindale, who captured most of the wickets between them.

Still without the services of their captain, R.E.S.Wyatt, whose jaw was fractured in the first innings, England's batting broke down completely, and the side were all out shortly after lunch for 103, but not before Hammond (34) had defied the bowling for 135 minutes and Ames, the century-maker of the first innings, and Hendren had also batted stubbornly.

West Indies thoroughly deserved their win, which had become almost inevitable after George Headley, the 'Black Bradman' (270 not out), had steered them to 535 for seven declared on the second day.

Second Test Third day: 2 July

What's wrong with our cricket? South Africa's great triumph

By Howard Marshall, at Lord's

BY 5 o'clock this afternoon, South Africa had won their first Test match in England by 157 runs, and a generous Lord's crowd was cheering the players who thus made cricket history. A glorious victory, with blow after blow struck firmly home, and England must have felt as those in the lumbering Spanish galleons of the Armada did when they were harried and battered into amazed disaster.

In the morning, Mitchell (164 not out) and Langton (44) put on 70 invaluable runs and Wade declared at 12.35 on 278 for seven. There was a chance that England would save the game. They might even have won it, for they had 309 runs to make in four and three-quarter hours - by no means an impossible task.

I suggest that it would have been far more fitting for England to go down fighting for victory instead of fizzling tamely out in miserable defensive ineptitude. They chose to fizzle, however, and soon after tea were ignominiously routed for 151.

We may, perhaps, wonder what manner of devastating blight has fallen on English cricket, but that does not in any degree lessen the South African triumph. They are great-hearted players, dour and skilful and swift on the kill.

We shall remember this match mainly for the fine batting of Mitchell and Cameron, who made 90 in the first innings, and for the spin bowling of Balaskas, who today added to his reputation by taking four wickets for 54 runs in 27 overs, a great feat for a bowler of this type on turf that never became deadly. Added to his five for 49 in England's first innings, this represents a remarkable achievement.

County Championship Yorks v Essex: 1 August

Essex stun Yorkshire with innings defeat: Remarkable all-round performance by Nichols

From Huddersfield

MORRIS NICHOLS completed an outstanding all-round performance for Essex at Huddersfield. Having taken four for 17 yesterday in the rout of Yorkshire for 31, and then hit 146 out of Essex's total of 334, today he rounded off their humiliation with seven for 37 as the Championship leaders crumbled again to 99 and defeat by an innings and 204 runs. So ended an extraordinary match in which Yorkshire were all out in under an hour on the first day and Essex had first-innings points sewn up before lunch. Today Yorkshire were again dismissed before lunch.

Nichols was ably supported by Holcombe 'Hopper' Read, the fastest bowler in England today, who took six for 11 in six overs in Yorkshire's first innings and three for 51 in their second. This is the second successive season that Essex have beaten Yorkshire by an innings.

[This was Yorkshire's only defeat of the season and they went on to take the County Championship for the 18th time in 39 years. Two weeks later, Essex beat the South Africans by 7 wickets at Southend, and Read and Nichols opened the bowling for England in the last Test.]

Nichols (left) and Read: Deadly opening attack for Essex.

Fifth Test Final day: 20 August

More records fall but England fail to save rubber

By Howard Marshall, at the Oval

ENGLAND made a splendid attempt to win the last Test at the Oval today and save the rubber, but they failed as South Africa held on for a draw. Thus South Africa have won a Test series in England for the first time.

The game was alive and full of interest until late in the afternoon. First came a record fifth-wicket partnership of 179 by Leyland (161) and Ames (148 not out), and in 150 minutes England added 221 runs to their overnight total of 313. This was spirited batting, and at the luncheon interval, when England had made 534 for six wickets, their highest score against South Africa, Wyatt declared.

England led by 58 runs, and then South Africa lost three wickets for 67, four for 112, and it was not until Cameron came in at four o'clock to hit a succession of boundaries that hopes of an English victory really began to fade. In the end South Africa made 287 for six.

Well, South Africa, all honour to them, have won the rubber, by dint of their victory at Lord's in the second Test. A great achievement, and Wade and his men have shown themselves to be worthy opponents indeed. Our praise is unqualified, and we salute as pleasant and attractive a team of cricketers as ever came from overseas. If perhaps we may single out Mitchell, Cameron and Wade himself as their particular heroes, we must also agree that individually and as a team they have proved admirably capable of rising to the occasion.

England can look back upon this last match with some satisfaction, both individually and collectively. It was no small achievement to chase South Africa home so aggressively, particularly when faced with a first innings total of 476. Wyatt had put South Africa in and, after Mitchell (128) had given them a fine start, had the tourists at 333 for eight. But then Langton (73 not out) joined Dalton (117) for that remarkable record 137 ninth-wicket partnership in 75 minutes, and a draw seemed certain. Hammond (65) led England's fight-back, passing Hobbs's record total of 1,562 runs against South Africa when he had made 52, and his record fourth-wicket stand of 151 with Leyland took only 105 minutes. Then along came Ames to maintain the momentum. But it was not to be.

County Championship Yorks v Middlesex

Hutton century for Yorkshire: 19-year-old in brilliant form

From Headingley

NINETEEN-year-old Leonard Hutton, the Yorkshire colt for whom Sutcliffe predicts a big future, was in splendid form at Leeds, where the Championship leaders scored 272 runs for the loss of six wickets against Middlesex. Opening with Sutcliffe, he played a brilliant innings of 131 in four hours and three-quarters, and was fourth out at 247.

In the past, Hutton has been criticised for his stroke play, but on this occasion he combined a fine defence with judicious aggression. Hitting hard on either side of the wicket, he excelled with the off-drive and also used the hook shot with power and precision. He hit sixteen 4's, and not until he skied a ball and was caught at mid-on did he make the slightest mistake.

Sheffield Shield South Australia v Queensland: 26 December

Bradman back with a double century

From Adelaide

WHILE Australia's batsmen were struggling in Johannesburg in the second Test, Don Bradman was providing ample evidence of his return to health with a brilliant double century for South Australia, his new state, in the Sheffield Shield.

Bradman, who made 233, declared the innings closed at 642 for eight, only two runs short of South Australia's highest score in Sheffield Shield cricket, and by the close Queensland had been reduced to 115 for eight.

[South Australia won by an innings and 226 runs.]

Second Test Third day: 27 December

Record innings by Nourse gives South Africa a chance

From Johannesburg

A MASTERLY innings of 231 by A.D.Nourse - the highest ever made by a South African against Australia in a Test - gave South Africa a fine chance of beating Australia in the second Test. They took their overnight score of 254 for four to 491, and Australia, needing 399 to win, were 85 for one at the close.

Nourse completely collared the bowling, and delighted the 10,000 crowd. He drove powerfully on each side of the wicket, and his aggression caused even such a wily bowler as Grimmett to lose his accuracy. He hit 36 4's and batted 4hr 58min before being brilliantly caught at point by McCormick off McCabe at 440. The previous highest Test score by a South African against Australia was Faulkner's 204 at Melbourne in 1911.

Australia have all day tomorrow to get the remaining 314 runs, but the wicket is wearing and an interesting finish is in prospect.

[Australia scored 272-2, thanks chiefly to a brilliant 189 not out by McCabe, before rain robbed them of victory.]

1936

3 Jan Eddie Gilbert, the Queensland Aboriginal fast bowler, is no-balled by Test umpire Borwick in the Sheffield Shield match against NSW at Victoria for intimidating the batsmen. He becomes the first player to have the new law invoked against him, which was brought in by the Australian Board of Control to prevent 'bodyline' bowling.

3 Mar Clarrie Grimmett takes 13-173 (7-100, 6-73) as Australia beat South Africa by an innings and 6 runs in the 5th Test at Durban to wrap up the series 4-0. In his last Test, having made his début at the age of 32 and celebrated his 43rd birthday on the tour (Christmas Day), he finishes with an Australian record of 44 wickets (avge 14.59) in the series and a world record of 216 Test wickets (avge 24.21).

25 May Another monumental bowling performance from Hedley Verity, 9-12 (15-38 in the match) for Yorks against Kent, who are dismissed for 39 at Sheffield in their 2nd innings.

29 Jul John Mercer becomes the first Glamorgan bowler to take 10 wickets in an innings, with 10-51 against Worcs at Worcester.

31 Aug Hammond (Glos) scores 317 against Notts at Gloucester to complete 1,281 runs in August, beating W.G. Grace's 60-year-old record for the month by 3 runs. At Lord's, against Surrey, Patsy Hendren (Middlesex) also reaches 1,000 runs for the month, at 47, the oldest player to do so, and he scores a 100 in each innings for the fourth time.

7 Dec Jack Fingleton scores his 4th successive Test 100, for Australia in the 1st Test against England.

18-23 Dec England beat Australia by an innings and 22 runs to go 2-0 up in the series. Hammond's 231 not out, his 6th 100 on the tour, is his 4th century in his 4 Tests at Sydney, a record. He has now made 8 hundreds against Australia, 7 of them in Australia. England's bowling includes Voce 4-10 and Allen 3-19 in Australia's 1st innings of 80.

TEST SERIES

Australia in South Africa
A 4, D 1
India in England
E 2, D 1

Sheffield Shield
Victoria v S.Australia: 2 January

Bradman hits fifth triple century

From Melbourne

DON BRADMAN took his overnight score of 229 to 357 for South Australia against Victoria at Melbourne, and now stands alone as the only player to score five triple hundreds, overtaking his Australia team-mate Ponsford, who has four. Next on the all-time list is W.G.Grace, with three.

This is Bradman's second score of over 200 in consecutive matches, for an aggregate of 590 runs. It is the highest score ever made for South Australia against Victoria, beating C.E.Pellow's 271. He cut and drove brilliantly and hit forty 4's. His last 57 included 10 boundaries, and he was finally caught off a skier after batting for seven hours. South Australia made 569, and Victoria were 124 for three at the close.

[In S. Australia's 6 matches, Bradman scored 117, 233, 357, 31, 0 and 1 (avge 123.16), and they won the Shield without losing a game, C.L.Badcock scoring 325 in the last match, the return with Victoria.]

South Africa's Bruce Mitchell: Lone resistance.

Third Test Final day: 4 January

Test record for Grimmett as Australia crush S.Africa

From Cape Town

C.V.GRIMMETT established a new record for Test cricketers today when, taking five South African wickets, he brought his total of Test wickets to 193. This beat the previous record of 189 held by the English slow bowler S.F.Barnes, which has stood for nearly 25 years.

Clarrie Grimmett: New Test record

Grimmett's wickets today cost only 56 runs, and he played a big part in Australia's victory over South Africa by an innings and 78 runs, having taken five for 32 in the first innings. South Africa, who had followed on 260 runs behind and were 11 for nought overnight, were all out today for 182. After Wade (31) and Siedle (59) put on 87 for the first wicket, both Grimmett and O'Reilly (4-35) exploited a bad patch just outside the leg-stump and had the South Africans struggling for the remainder of the innings.

Fourth Test Second day: 17 February

Australia win rubber: Grimmett routs S.Africa again

From Johannesburg

AUSTRALIA won the rubber when they beat South Africa by an innings and 184 runs in the fourth Test here today. Of the five Tests, they have now won three and drawn one. Grimmett was again the destroyer, taking seven for 40 in South Africa's second innings, and becoming the first bowler to take 200 wickets in Test matches.

When play was resumed this morning, Australia had replied with 185 for three (Fingleton 108) to the South African first-innings score of 157 (O'Reilly 5-20, Grimmett 3-70). By tea, the Australians were all out for 439. O'Reilly, who came in at No.10, made 56 not out and put on 69 for the last wicket with McCormick (13).

This left South Africa needing 282 runs to avoid an innings defeat. They had no answer to Grimmett's guile, but there was some thrilling cricket before they were all out for 98 a few minutes after time on the second day, the captains having agreed to continue after the ninth wicket went down. Bruce Mitchell, alone, batted doggedly, coming in third wicket down and carrying his bat for 48.

South Australia v Tasmania: 2 March

More Bradman records and another triple hundred

From Adelaide

DON BRADMAN has once more resumed the role of record-breaker. Today he smashed the South Australia individual scoring record with a brilliant 369 against Tasmania - his sixth triple hundred. He raced through his third century in 40min - one of the fastest ever scored in Australia. He was also concerned in a third-wicket partnership with Hamence that realised 356 runs, another state record.

Hitting the bowling to all parts of the field, Bradman scored well over two runs a minute, and was mainly responsible for the partnership putting on its last 100 runs in 32min. He hit four 6's and 48 boundaries.

It was Bradman's farewell innings of the season, which he has finished with an average of 130.33 for nine innings. He had not been well enough to tour South Africa with the Australian team.

[At the same time, Australia were in the process of beating South Africa by an innings for the third time.]

County Championship Leics v Warwicks: 25 May

Geary's 12-12 in a day: What a benefit!

From Hinckley, Leics

FORMER Test player George Geary, nearly 43, celebrated his second benefit match by taking 12 wickets for 12 runs today for Leicestershire against Warwick. Not only that, he was top scorer in Leicester's first innings with 25.

Geary had taken one wicket on Saturday, when Warwick, having been put in by Dempster, made 60 for five before rain prevented any further play. Today he took their last five wickets for five runs as Warwick were all out for 133, and finished with six for 36. Only opener Croom could resist Geary, and he carried his bat for 69.

Leicester, however, lost half their wickets for 41 and with Mayer taking 5 for 19 and Hollies four for 19, were all out for 108. Then Geary, relentlessly exploiting a worn spot in Warwick's second innings, took seven for seven in 13.3 overs as they crumbled to 78 all out.

Needing 104 runs to win, Leicester had lost four wickets for only 41 runs by the close, to set up an exciting finish for tomorrow. In all, 29 wickets fell today for 300 runs.

[Hollies had Geary lbw for a duck and took 6-39, but Leics won by 1 wicket, with Dempster making an unbeaten 32 in 90min.]

First Test Final day: 9 December

England triumph as Australia are routed by Voce and Allen: All out for 58

By C.G.Macartney, in Brisbane

ENGLAND triumphed in the first Test by 322 runs. The Australian batsmen were routed today by Voce and Allen, bowling unchanged, for a second-innings total of 58, Australia's fifth lowest score in Tests. England's captain dismissed both Bradman and Badcock before they had scored and Australia were mown down without Verity handling the ball. But there was never any doubt after Bradman had gone that Voce and Allen would finish off the side, with McCormick absent .

Australia's batsmen, used to playing inter-State matches where wickets are covered, seemed to have no knowledge of conditions prevailing after rain. They were 20 for six at one stage; only Chipperfield (26 not out) showed any enterprise.

Allen never spared himself in bowling (3-71, 5-36), batting (35, 68) and fielding. Voce took 10 wickets for 57 in the match (6-41, 4-16). Leyland was England's batting hero, with 126 in their first innings.

England have won all three Tests in Brisbane, and this victory brings them level at 53 matches each, with 29 drawn.

Leyland (inset) straight-drives Chipperfield on the way to his hundred.

Second Test First day: 25 July

Hammond's brilliant century: All-India's attack tamed by master batsman

By Howard Marshall, at Old Trafford

HAMMOND has entered his kingdom again - that is the upshot of the first day's play in the second Test. The rest of the cricket was relatively unimportant, though it may be noted that All-India won the toss and were all out for 203; whereupon England proceeded to make 173 for two wickets.

Hammond 118 not out - that is what sets the pulse stirring. This is the first century Hammond has made in Test matches over here since 1930, when he pounded the Australian attack at Leeds. And how superbly he played today! There was the real Hammond, fit and confident, master of himself and the occasion. He reached his hundred in as many minutes, having hit 14 fours, and no batsman in the world more surely dominates the scene than Hammond in this mood. He forced the ball off his back foot to the boundary, he cut and drove with exquisite precision and controlled power.

The news of his innings may not be received with unalloyed delight in Australia, but our selectors must have watched its sure development with blissful rapture. The return of Hammond means a great deal to English cricket, and we may be excused, perhaps, this unrestrained jubilation.

[Hammond went on to make 167 and England 571-8 declared, but a marvellous 203 opening stand between Merchant (114) and Mushtaq Ali (112) earned All-India (390-5) a gallant draw.]

Third Test First day: 15 August

Hammond and Worthington dash All-India's Test hopes

By Howard Marshall, at the Oval

ENGLAND, one up in the rubber, won the toss in the final Test and made 471 for eight at the rate of over 80 runs an hour. In that plain statement, there is a mixture of triumph and tragedy. Triumph for the individual England batsmen, tragedy for All-India, who lost the rubber when they lost the spin of the coin.

All-India have had the luck running against them cruelly this summer. To come up against Hammond in form on a lifeless Oval wicket was perhaps the unkindest cut of all. I should be praising Hammond for his magnificent innings of 217, and Worthington for making 128, and both these players for their record fourth-wicket partnership of 266.

To my mind though, at least as much credit must be given to the bowling and fielding of All-India. That Oval wicket - as perfect as man could make it, was the official description - might well have broken the heart of a Tom Richardson. I have no use for these perfect wickets. They damp down the fires of cricket. They whittle away the subtle arts of the game.

Even so, with hopes of victory almost dead, All-India did not despair. Throughout the sunny day, they attacked as if they expected at any moment to shake England into disastrous collapse. They fielded brilliantly, they bowled wholeheartedly. Never did they wilt or falter.

What a great bowler is Amar Singh! With his late swing and variations of pace, he forced even Hammond himself into danger and hasty defence. C.K.Nayudu, a medium-paced spinner, also delighted us with his beautiful craft, and Mahomed Nissar was hurling down the second new ball with all the fine fury of a fresh opening bowler.

The great stand was broken at 422, when Hammond was bowled by Nissar, who soon repeated the exercise with Worthington. After that, the England batting faded away.

[England won by 9 wickets, Sims taking 5-73 in All-India's 1st innings, Allen 7-80 in their 2nd, and England won the rubber 2-0.]

1937

1 Jan P.E.Whitelaw (195) and W.N.Carson (290), a newcomer to Plunket Shield cricket, put on a world-record 3rd-wicket stand of 445 for Auckland against Otago in Dunedin, a New Zealand record for any wicket.

5 Jan Fingleton (136) and Bradman (248) set a world record 6th-wicket stand of 346, for Australia against England in the 3rd Test, at Melbourne, the only two higher Test partnerships both standing in the names of Ponsford and Bradman. Bradman is now co-holder of the record stands for Australia against England for the 2nd, 3rd, 4th, 5th and 6th wickets.

29 Jan-4 Feb Bradman (212) scores his 2nd 200 in successive Tests and Fleetwood-Smith takes 10-239 in match as Australia beat England by 148 runs at Adelaide to draw level 2-2 in the rubber.

25 June J.C.Clay takes 17-212 (9-66, 8-146) for Glamorgan against Worcs at Worcester.

15 July M.C.C. president Major Astor, in a speech at the club's 150th Anniversary dinner, at the Savoy, speaks of the cricketer's white flannel shirt as a badge of sanity in a vexed world, and of the calm deliberation of cricket as a hopeful sign amidst the distractions of modernity.

18 Aug Arsenal F.C. agree to release Middlesex's Denis Compton for cricket for the rest of the season. The sporting all-rounder, unluckily run out when backing up for 65 in his first Test, against New Zealand, yesterday, played in 14 matches for Arsenal last season and may be their regular outside-left this season.

20 Aug Hammond scores 52 for Gloucester at Dover to bring up his 3,000 runs for the season, but Kent, needing 218 in 115min, hit 219-2 in 71min for an improbable victory - Woolley 44, Ashdown 62 not, Ames 70 and Watt 39 in 10min with 3 6's and 3 4's to add to his 10-198 in the match.

TEST SERIES

England in Australia
A 3, E 2
New Zealand in England
E 1, D 2

Third Test Rest day: 3 January

Great battle of tactics in Test: How Verity gave away England's secret

By C.G.Macartney, in Melbourne

A DRYING wind today has improved the Test wicket, and if there is no rain before play begins tomorrow, Australia will resume batting with a big advantage.

The forecast is fine. As the game stands after yesterday's amazing cricket, during which both sides declared, England are in a dangerous position. Australia are 127 runs on with nine wickets in hand.

A great battle of tactics has been a feature so far. After the dismissal of Hammond in England's first innings, the batsmen evidently received instruction to throw away their wickets, but at the same time to disguise their intentions. This order was carried out with some considerable degree of subtlety until Verity, coming in, disclosed the secret by meeting Hardstaff half-way to the wicket.

Australia then wished to keep England in so that they would not be obliged to bat again on the same wicket. But Allen blocked the plan by declaring when the Australian bowlers were deliberately bowling wides to waste time. More subtle methods must be adopted if Australia expect to outwit players with greater experience of rain-damaged wickets.

Allen's effort to get an advantage was spoiled by bad light and rain. He would have gained more ground had he applied the closure after the fall of Hammond's wicket, thereby giving Australia an hour to bat and frustrating Bradman's reply of using tail-enders.

When England batted, the wicket was the worst yet experienced in the series, yet the batsmen showed superior form and knowledge of the conditions than the Australians had done at Brisbane and Sydney. Hammond's innings (32) was a masterpiece, and Leyland (17) and Barnett (11) also did well.

Hammond's clever defence for rising and turning balls was a sight worth seeing. More than that, his judgment in allowing balls to pass denoted his extraordinary eye and sense of spin. It is fair to say that Australia could well take a lesson from his exhibition.

Saturday's close of play: Australia 200 for 9 declared and 3 for one; England 76 for nine declared.

[After a rain-interrupted 3rd day, Australia had taken their score to 194-5, with Fingleton and Bradman having put on an unbeaten 97 for the 6th wicket. The next day they extended their partnership to a record 346 before Fingleton was out for 136, and their score to 500-6. Bradman went on to make 270, Australia 564, and on the 6th day England were all out for 323, losing by 365 runs.]

County Championship Leics v Glamorgan: 21 May

Century and hat-trick by E.Davies

From Leicester

GLAMORGAN gained their second win in the County Championship when trouncing Leicester by an innings and 49 runs. Emrys Davies was the outstanding player of the match, being top scorer with a sparkling innings of 139 in Glamorgan's 469 for seven declared and bowling a hat-trick in Leicester's second innings.

Davies, who scored 1,000 runs and took 100 wickets two seasons ago, played a big part in the Leicester collapse, taking four for 27 in their first innings and three - in successive balls - for 31 in their second.

Emrys Davies: Hundred and hat-trick.

Fifth Test Final day: 3 March

Australia retain Ashes: Series won from 2-0 deficit

From Melbourne

AUSTRALIA won the final Test by an innings and 200 runs, and retain the Ashes by three matches to two, after England had won the first two Tests.

It was unfortunate for England that they had to bat yesterday on a rain-damaged pitch in this final Test. But their fate was already decided, and if the fine weather had continued Australia's victory would only have been delayed.

Today, facing a hopeless task, England lost their last two wickets without adding to their overnight score, in just two balls from Fleetwood-Smith.

Australia's captain, Don Bradman, eventually appeared on the balcony to speak to the crowd, and every mention of his opposite number, G.O.Allen, was greeted with cheers. "Rain dealt England a very clear blow," said Bradman, "but I have yet to hear one word of complaint from any one of the players."

Allen, in reply, said how much Australia owed to their captain, "who has shown magnificent form, first with the bat and then with that infernal coin."

It was again Bradman who set Australia on the path to victory, coming in first wicket down and failing by only 31 runs to make his third double hundred in consecutive Tests. McCabe (112) and Badcock (118) also contributed centuries to Australia's total of 604 all out.

When the result of the rubber was known, the King sent a message of congratulation to Bradman and his team.

County Championship Derby v Warwicks: 17 July

Warwick routed by Copson: 8-11 and 4 in 4 balls

From Derby

AN AMAZING feat by Copson, Derbyshire's fast bowler, caused the collapse of Warwickshire for 28 runs in their first innings. He tumbled them out in an hour, taking eight wickets for 11 runs and sending back the last four in four deliveries - his second hat-trick of the season. He got tremendous pace off the pitch and made the ball swing either way, forcing the batsmen on the defensive and shattering the wickets no fewer than six times.

Then, going in at No.11, he celebrated his morning's success by hitting a dashing 30 not out, including seven fours, in Derby's 227, and took another two wickets as Warwick made 81 for two.

[Copson took only one more wicket (3-82) as Hill (105) and Dollery (98) put on 213 for the 3rd wicket, but Derby won by 5 wickets.]

Test Trial North v South: 25 May

Hammond tames North bowlers: Innings that will go down in cricket history

By Howard Marshall, at Lord's

A GLORIOUS century by Hammond and some fine fast bowling by Farnes enabled the South to beat the North by six wickets on the stroke of time at Lord's today. The South were left to make 156 in approximately three hours - allowing for the extra half hour - and after exactly 2• hours Compton hit the winning four.

A grand match, finished in glorious weather, was a most appropriate start to M.C.C's week of commemoration. Hammond yesterday (86) was good enough in all conscience, but today he was greater still, dominant, majestic, the master. He hit 11 fours and a six, and made his runs - 100 not out - out of 140 scored while he was at the wicket in just under two hours.

Whether he was driving - he nearly decimated Fleet Street with a prodigious hit into the Press box - or stepping back and forcing the leg-break like lightning through the covers, or placing the faster bowlers to leg with oceans of time for the stroke, he was supreme.

As for Farnes, he bowled in the grand manner, and during the day took five wickets for 33 runs - and good wickets at that.

For the North, Hardstaff (71) was a joy to watch in their first innings, and Hutton, having given two chances in his first over from Farnes, proceeded to make 102 in the thoughtful and entirely competent manner which encourages those who see him as England's opening batsman.

County Championship Surrey v Hants

Knight's classic innings: First county 100 for 16 years

By our special representative, at the Oval

D.J.KNIGHT, of whom a schoolmastering career robbed cricket for some years, stirred the memories of some of us and the pulses of all of us at the Oval today; took us back to the days when England's innings opened on a defiant, strident note.

Ten minutes of Mr Knight at the crease was worth hours of the fore-arm batting of which cricket is so largely made, these days. Here was a man with power in his wrists, and strokes that sent the ball flashing to the boundary with no apparent effort; a man with the true cricket strokes.

Sadly, it was all to no purpose: the rest of Surrey could not live up to this resplendent example. For Hampshire had declared and set them to score 308 runs in four hours.

Knight, assisted first by Sandham (24) and then by Squires (41), put Surrey well on terms with the clock. His 100 was one of the most delightful seen at the Oval for some years - his first in first-class cricket for 16 years.

He scored 105 out of 159 while at the wicket. But the last six wickets fell for 34 runs, Herman taking five for 18 with the new ball, and Hants won by 71 runs.

County Championship Sussex v Lancs: 28 July

Paynter's record-breaking innings: 322 in 5 hours

By Thomas Moult, at Hove

A MAMMOTH bonfire of runs was lit here today as Lancs scored 640 for eight, the season's highest total, and three of the batsmen who fed the mid-summer blaze heaped up 522 of them. Easily the biggest share of these was Paynter's record-shaking 322, which flashed from his bat so swiftly.

Lancashire's diminutive left-hander, who had come straight from the Test match at Manchester, filled the day with a brilliant glow, especially the morning hours when his batsmanship was fresh and untired. He hit 100 before lunch, and he and fellow-opener Washbrook, put on 175 - Paynter 108 - in the two hours before the interval.

They went on to 268 before Washbrook was caught a mid-on for 108. Following Iddon's dismissal, Paynter shared in another fine stand with Oldfield (92), which realised 271 before Paynter was finally lbw running down the pitch to James Parks at 546. He had made his 300 out of 513 in 290min and his complete innings took 300min and included 3 sixes and 39 fours.

County Championship Glos v Worcs:9 August

Goddard takes all 10: But Gloucester face uphill task

From Cheltenham

GODDARD, of Gloucester, joined the immortals of cricket who have taken all 10 wickets in an innings at Cheltenham today when he bowled out Worcester for 202. And how badly Gloucester needed some such achievement in this match. Their own innings was polished off for 196, the last six wickets going down for 83; and they were 114 behind. Even now their position is a perilous one. They still require 226 to win tomorrow and two wickets have fallen.

Goddard's wickets cost him 113 runs, and he bowled 28.4 overs. He has taken 16 wickets for 181 in this match with his off-spinners, and now needs only five more to become the first bowler to get 200 wickets this season.

[Hammond hit a remarkable 178 on a wearing wicket, sharing in a 3rd-wicket stand of 269 with B.O.Allen (78), virtually assuring Gloucester of victory, although the margin in the end was only 3 wickets.]

Tom Goddard: 10 for 113.

1938

14 Jun Bradman makes his 13th Test hundred to pass Hobbs's record.

24 Jun The Lord's Test is the first to be televised.

25 Jun In the Lancashire League, Indian Test all-rounder Amar Singh hits 120 in 68min and takes 8-22, including the hat-trick, for Colne against Rishton.

2-5 Jul 100th Varsity match is drawn (Cambridge lead 46 to Oxford's 38 matches won).

6 Jul Rain robs Yorks, needing 67 runs at lunch with only 3 wickets down, of inflicting the first defeat of the Australians by a county since 1912.

8-12 Jul The 3rd Test, at Old Trafford, is completely washed out by rain, without the teams even being announced (only other instance, also at Old Trafford, 1890).

13 Jul Hammond, turned amateur, captains Gents v Players, having captained Players last year - victorious both times.

23 Jul In the Central Lancashire League, West Indies Test star Learie Constantine hits a century in 33min for Rochdale v Middleton, with seven 6's and 10 4's in his 106, and then takes 5-21.

20-24 Aug In the record-breaking Oval Test, England's 5 Yorkshiremen score 612 of the 853 runs made from the bat and take 10 of the 16 Australian wickets to fall - Hutton 364 runs, Leyland 187 plus 1 wkt, Wood (wicket-keeper) 53, Verity 8 plus 2 wkts, Bowes 7 wkts. The next day, a large advertisement on the front page of the Telegraph quotes Hutton: "Like most Yorkshiremen, I always eat Bread for Energy."

24 Dec In Johannesburg, Hammond is first player to score 6,000 Test runs.

TEST SERIES

Australia in England
E 1, A 1, D 2

First Test Second day: 11 June

Hammond's great captaincy: Match of many records

By Howard Marshall, at Trent Bridge

THE outcome of today's remarkable play at Trent Bridge is that England, who declared at 658 for eight, have a reasonable chance of winning the first Test match. Before the close, Australia lost three wickets, Bradman's included, for 138.

Records were broken galore. England's total was the highest ever made against Australia. Paynter's magnificent 216 not out was the highest individual score ever made in England against Australia. Never before have four individual centuries been scored in one innings of a Test match, and Paynter and Compton put on the first 200 stand for the fifth wicket (206) in matches between the two countries.

Whatever happens now, England, with two days in hand, have made a wonderful and most inspiring start. If we single out for special praise the captaincy of Hammond, the batting of Paynter, Barnett (126), Hutton (100) and Compton (102), and the bowling of Farnes and Wright, we must not forget the work of the team as a whole in the field. Here at last is a really aggressive and confident England team.

Bradman (51) was challenged fiercely from the moment he appeared. Never did we see the masterful batsman, dominating the perilous situation. He was like a beleaguered city, and Hammond laid siege to him with suitable generalship.

Paynter's glorious innings will long be remembered. Twenty-six 4's, a 6 and a 5 he hit in five and a half hours, and his irrepressible pugnacity, his quickness of foot and swiftness of stroke made his batting delightful to watch.

No player as young as Compton, who is only 20, had made a hundred against Australia. He has matured remarkably since last summer into as likely a player as either England or Australia have produced for many years.

It was a great day's cricket. It is enough to reflect that Australia, with Bradman out, still need 371 runs to save the follow-on. And the turf, in my opinion, is beginning, however slightly, to take spin. What surprises, we may wonder, has this memorable match still in store?

[Despite a magnificent, remarkable 232 by McCabe, made out of 300 while he was at the wicket, Australia followed on 247 runs behind. But hundreds from Brown (133) and Bradman (144 not) saved the day for Australia, whose 427-6 was the highest 4th-innings total in Tests between the two countries, and the 7 100s in the match was a new world Test record.]

County Championship Essex v Kent: 15 July

World record for Fagg: Double 100 in each innings

From Colchester

Arthur Fagg: Unique achievement.

BY scoring a double century in each innings of the match against Essex, the Kent opening batsman Arthur Fagg set up a new world record which even Bradman may find it difficult to surpass.

His figures for the match were: 244 out of 386 in five hours and an unbeaten 202 out of 313 in two hours and 50 minutes. He hit 31 fours in the first innings and 27 in the second. Fagg, who is only 23, has never before scored two centuries in a match.

His performance is all the more remarkable when it is remembered that less than 18 months ago he contracted rheumatic fever while on tour with the M.C.C. in Australia, and was unable to play any cricket at all last season.

Essex and Kent players, as well as the spectators, joined in applauding Fagg on his return to the pavilion when Kent declared at 313 for one. He had not made a false stroke all the time he was at the crease. Essex, needing 393 to win, lost two wickets for eight before lunch, but rain prevented any further play and the match was drawn.

Second Test Last day: 28 June

Bradman's century makes draw certain: Compton's fine batting

By Howard Marshall, at Lord's

THE second Test match ended in a draw at Lord's today, but not before every kind of alarm and excursion had excited us. In the morning, England verged horribly towards collapse, and at lunch, when six wickets were down for 142, an Australian victory was at least possible.

Wicket-keeper Ames, who had a finger of his left hand broken by a riser from McCormick, was caught immediately afterwards, and will be out for at least two Tests. England were in the gravest danger, but Compton (76 not out), playing with the discretion of a veteran, and Wellard (38) staved off disaster, and at 3.30 England were able to declare with their score 242 for four.

Australia, 314 runs behind, had approximately three hours' batting before them, and it was improbable that they would attempt to force victory. Indeed, there were moments when they appeared to be sliding towards defeat. But they survived as Bradman, in a beautiful innings of 102 not out, saw them safely to 204 for six at the close.

On balance, England had the better of the match. After a disastrous start, when McCormick had them at 31 for three, a magnificent Hammond innings (240), a 222 stand with Paynter (99) and another with Ames (186) carried them to the security of 494. Australia were saved by some poor England fielding and a courageous innings, full of quiet excellence, by opener Brown, who carried his bat for 206.

Fourth Test Final day: 25 July

Australia keep the Ashes: Hassett's pluck in tense crisis

By Howard Marshall, at Headingley

BY a quarter past four this afternoon, after amazing cricket, Australia had beaten England in the fourth Test match by five wickets. Never has there been a more nerve-wracking day, and it was a fitting culmination to a remarkable match.

Australian spinner Bill O'Reilly: 10 for 122 in the match.

England could not withstand the venom of O'Reilly and Fleetwood-Smith in the morning, and 10 wickets fell before the luncheon interval for 74 runs. Australia, left to make 105 for victory, were themselves in mortal peril, for Fingleton and Brown were shot out, and then Bradman himself and the great McCabe both fell to young Wright, the Kent leg-break bowler.

Four wickets were down for 61, and it seemed crazily possible that England might win after all, against the odds. But then Hassett (33) drove the nails firmly into England's coffin. Playing with great courage and skill, he attacked the bowling, while heavy thunder clouds rolled up and against the background like the witches' scene from Macbeth. England were inexorably drawn to their doom.

How to explain it? There will be arguments about England's extraordinary collapse for years to come. The wicket certainly played its part, for beyond doubt it greatly helped O'Reilly and Fleetwood-Smith to achieve their triumph. O'Reilly took 10 for 122 in the match, and Fleetwood-Smith seven for 107, and without question this was very fine spin bowling.

The wicket helped the bowlers throughout the match, placing a premium on the true arts of batsmanship. As we should expect, only Hammond (76) and Bradman (103), in their respective first innings, showed true mastery, and this was Bradman's sixth century in consecutive Test matches (all against England), a unique achievement in cricket.

I do not feel that England need be despondent about this defeat, though it means that we cannot regain the Ashes. Our only hope is to win the time-limitless match at the Oval, and make an honourable draw of this intensely interesting series.

First Test Second day: 26 December

Goddard's hat-trick knocks South Africa back

From Reuter, in Johannesburg

A DASHING 97 by B.H. Valentine, who, like P.A.Gibb (93), just failed to get a century, and a remarkable bowling spell by Tom Goddard just before the close, put England in a strong position in the first Test against South Africa at The Wanderers today.

England were all out for 422, having added 96 for the loss of their last four wickets. South Africa made a very promising start and were 160 for two, when Goddard dismissed Nourse (73), Gordon and Wade with successive balls, and they went in at 166 for five.

[South Africa replied with 390 thanks to Dalton (102) and 8th- and 9th-wicket stands of 108 and 97, respectively, with Viljoen (50) and Langton (64 not). Gibb got his century (106) in his first Test, and Paynter completed his second of the match (117 and 106), which ended in a draw.]

Fifth Test Third day: 23 August

Hutton hits out during his historic 364 at the Oval.

Hutton smashes all records: England certain to win farcical Test

By Howard Marshall, at the Oval

HUTTON making his record score of 364 in the final Test match, Bradman being carried off the field with a fractured shin bone, England declaring at the phenomenal total of 903 for seven wickets - these were the outstanding events in one of the most remarkable days of cricket ever played.

That Australia lost three wickets for 117 after tea seemed entirely unimportant. The match is over, to all intents and purposes, and all that remains is to add up the records, among them: Hutton's 364, longest ever innings, at 13hr 20min, highest in 'Ashes' Tests (beating Bradman's 334) and all Tests (Hammond's 336 not), and at the Oval (Bobby Abel's 357 in 1899); Hutton, with Leyland (187), second-wicket record of 382 for England against Australia (Sutcliffe/Hammond 188) and, with Hardstaff (169 not), England sixth-wicket record of 215 (Hammond/Ames 186 at Lord's in June); England's 903, their highest (658-8 dec in June), highest in any Test (Australia 729-6 dec in 1930) and highest in this country (Yorkshire 887 in 1896); and Fleetwood-Smith's one for 298, the most runs conceded in a Test innings.

Records do not make cricket, however, and we can only hope that these fresh ones will prove to be stout nails in the coffin of timeless Tests played on wickets that turn a great game into a farce.

First of all, though, let us praise Hutton for his tremendous exhibition of concentration, endurance and skill. He gave point and purpose to the early hours, for the excitement was intense as, from his overnight 300, he slowly and surely approached Bradman's record of 334. We could almost feel the huge crowd willing him to succeed, and when, with a beautiful square cut, he hit the decisive four off Fleetwood-Smith, a roar went up which must have shaken the Houses of Parliament across the river.

Bradman raced up to shake his hand, and while drinks came out and all the Australians toasted him in the middle of the pitch, the crowd cheered and sang "For he's a jolly good fellow", and cheered and cheered again.

An astonishing scene, and Hutton richly deserved the wonderful ovation. When at last his concentration wavered and he was caught at cover by Hassett off O'Reilly, he had batted for over two days, and hit 35 fours, 15 threes, 18 twos and 143 singles - a prodigious effort.

That Bradman should have slipped and fractured his shin bone while bowling was an ironical commentary on the state of affairs. This was a tragic misfortune for Australia, who have also lost Fingleton with a strained muscle. But even Bradman could not have hoped to stave off defeat, and while we may reasonably be pleased at England's mastery, I cannot believe that any true lover of cricket will be easy in his mind about the conditions in which it was achieved.

[The 'timeless Test' ended next day, the fourth, as Australia, without Bradman (whose bone fortunately was only chipped, not broken) and Fingleton, making little real attempt to prolong the agony, were all out for 201 and 123, and lost by an innings and 579 runs, the biggest defeat in the history of Test cricket.]

1939

3 Jan Queensland wicket-keeper Don Tallon equals a 70-year-old record at Sydney by making his 12th dismissal in the Sheffield Shield match against New South Wales, 9 caught and 3 stumped. The only other instance was by E.Pooley (8ct, 4st) for Surrey v Sussex in 1868. The previous Australian record was 9 dismissals.

24 June England/West Indies Test series begins, the first (and only) played in England with 8-ball overs.

1,3 Jul Hammond, winning the toss for the first time this season, at the 13th attempt, scores an unbeaten 153 of Gloucester's 284 (241 while he is at the wicket) against Kent, for whom his England colleague Wright takes 9-47. On the Monday, Goddard equals the world record of 17 wickets in a match (9-38, 8-68), as Glos dismiss Kent for 120 and 124 and win by an innings and 40 runs. Only Verity (Yorks) and Blythe (Kent) have accomplished this feat before in one day.

4 Jul Sussex, set 428 to win by Northants in just under 51/4hr at Kettering, make them with 25 mins to spare, thanks largely to 232 by George Cox, whose previous 20 Championship innings this season had yielded only 301 runs.

15 Jul Harrow beat Eton at Lord's by 8 wickets, their first victory in this fixture since 1908.

22 Aug E.A.Watts takes all 10 for 67 in Warwick's 2nd innings (0-15 in 1st) as Surrey win by an innings.

22 Aug In the 3rd Test, at the Oval, Hutton (165 not) and Hammond (138) put on 264 runs, a world Test record for the 3rd wicket, Hammond's 22nd Test 100 putting him ahead of Bradman. The Test is drawn, England winning the rubber 1-0. With war clouds gathering, the tourists return home immediately.

1 Sep Verity takes 7-9 as Yorks bowl Sussex out for 33 at Hove. It is his last match for Yorks, as two days later war is declared and there is no first-class cricket for six summers. Only three county matches are left unplayed, not affecting the Championship, and Middlesex finish runners-up to Yorks for the third season running.

TEST SERIES

England in South Africa
E 1, D 4
West Indies in England
E 1, D 2

Third Test Second day: 21 January

South Africa follow on: Paynter's record score of 243

From Reuter, in Durban

ENGLAND are in a winning position in the third Test match. After taking their overnight score of 373 for two to 469 for four, they declared and then dismissed South Africa for 103 at Kingsmead. South Africa scored 73 for one in their second innings.

There was little in the wicket to worry the South Africans, and their collapse was probably due to concentrating too much on defence and to the shrewdness of England's captain, W.R. Hammond, who studied the batsmen's weaknesses and handled his bowling cleverly.

Earlier in the day, Paynter had taken his overnight score of 197 to 243 - a record for these matches, beating the 211 of J.B.Hobbs in 1924. Hammond, who made 120, and helped to put on 242 for the third wicket - only three short of the record of F.E.Woolley and R.E.S.Wyatt - hit four boundaries in adding 21 today. With rain in the air, England went for the runs and scored 96 in 55 minutes before Hammond declared.

South Africa had reached 60 without loss when Edrich, atoning for his batting failures, came on and had Mitchell caught at the wicket for 30. This was the beginning of a bad collapse, South Africa losing 10 wickets for only 43. Farnes (4-29) and Wilkinson (2-12) did most of the damage. In their second innings, Mitchell was still there on 53 when stumps were drawn.

[A splendid, fighting 109 by Mitchell and fifties by Rowan and Viljoen could not prevent England winning by an innings and 13 runs on the third day.]

Fifth Test Tenth day: 14 March

Play-to-finish Test not finished: England need 42 to win but rush to catch boat

From Exchange, in Durban

Ames: At the wicket when the boat home beckoned.

THE play-to-finish Test farce played itself out appropriately when it was abandoned to enable the England team to catch the homeward-bound ship in which their passages had been booked. England, having won the third Test, the only one of the five to be finished, thus won the rubber and avenged South Africa's victory in England in 1935.

After 10 days of record-breaking, heart-breaking cricket, it was agreed between the two captains and the South African Board of Control that the final Test should be abandoned, even though England required only 42 runs to win with five wickets left. All were agreed that, so far as it lay in their power, no such uncricketlike contest would ever be waged between the two countries again.

Rain came so hard at tea that no further play was possible today. The scores at the end were: South Africa 530 (Van der Byl 125, Melville 78, Grieveson 75, Dalton 57; Perks 5-100) and 481 (Melville 103, Van der Byl 97, Mitchell 89, Viljoen 74; Farnes 4-74); England 316 (Ames 84, Paynter 62; Dalton 4-59) and 654-5 (Edrich 219, Hammond 140, Gibb 120, Paynter 75, Hutton 55).

There were records galore, including:

World record fourth innings total - England's 654, beating NSW 572 (1907-08).

World record aggregate - 1,981 runs, beating NSW v S.Australia 1,919 (1925-26).

Longest match - 10 days, beating W.Indies v England 9 days (Kingston 1930).

Record stand in Anglo-South African Tests - 280 (2nd wicket) by Gibb and Edrich, beating Hobbs/Sutcliffe 268 (Lord's 1924).

Both sides made their highest scores against each other.

Hammond and Paynter made a wonderful effort to force a win when they saw the change in the weather, and the England captain's innings was one of the finest of his career. England went so near to winning, with Ames and Valentine at the wicket, that it seems difficult to understand why it was so necessary for them to catch a particular ship home.

It is certain that we shall never see the like of this match again, and while this is a fact that many people will not regret, we shall always look back upon it with a great deal of affection. Without it, Edrich's glorious rehabilitation would have been impossible; the English team would never have had the chance of proving that nothing is impossible, and that the way to face enormous odds is not to hold out a hang-dog bat or to flash a despairing one, but to go about the task with cheerfulness.

County Championship Northants v Leics: 29 May

Northants' first County win in four years gained in two days

From Northampton

AMID scenes of great jubilation, Northants beat Leicester by an innings and 193 runs at Northampton today, and so registered their first County Championship victory for four years - and in two days.

It was a notable day for the county altogether - their first win at Northampton since Leicester were beaten, again at Whitsuntide, in 1933, their first in a match in the county since Warwick were defeated at Kettering in 1934, and their first in a Championship game since Somerset were beaten at Taunton on 14 May 1935.

Northants amassed 510 for eight wickets before they declared with a first innings lead of 376. Brookes, of whom good judges hold a high opinion, played his best innings to date. Always worth watching during his four and a quarter hours' stay, he defended skilfully and hit the loose ball hard, scoring 24 fours.

Leicester's openers put on 60, but after that Northants gradually whittled away the wickets, Merritt taking five for 56, and, with the help of an extra quarter of an hour, they had them all out for 183 to win in two days.

County Championship Glamorgan v Glos: 2 June

Heart-break day for bowlers: Glamorgan's mammoth total

From Newport

ON A pitch described as "the best ever to be prepared in Wales", Glamorgan had little difficulty in saving the game against Gloucester, their score of 577 for four beating their previous highest in first-class cricket - 550 for five against Surrey at the Oval in 1936. And Emrys Davies's 287 not out beat the previous highest individual Glamorgan score - 280 not out by Duckfield, in that same match.

It was not, however, the highest score in the match, for yesterday Walter Hammond - with his 150th century and fourth triple hundred - had made 302 in Gloucester's 505 for five declared, a score that had given them a first-innings lead of 309.

Openers Davies and Dyson, 131 overnight, this morning reached their centuries almost simultaneously, having been together three and a half hours. Dyson made 120, and after he left Davies dominated the cricket. When the game was given up at six o'clock, Davies had defied Gloucester for seven and a half hours and hit 25 fours.

County Championship Yorks v Derby: 24 June

Derbyshire out for 20: Smurthwaite takes 5 for 7

From Sheffield

BRAMALL LANE, scene of many historic encounters, has rarely seen such amazing cricket as was packed into three hours here today. On a rain-damaged pitch, Yorkshire, the champions, were put out in two hours and a half for 83. But even if Yorkshire are down, they are seldom out. They struck back so effectively that in 40 minutes Derbyshire, themselves champions in 1936, were shot out for 20 runs, their lowest total since Lancashire got rid of them for 17 at Old Trafford in 1888.

James Smurthwaite, a 23-year-old bowler from North Ormesby, who has only once played in a County Championship match for Yorkshire before - and then did not bat or bowl - was responsible for the outstanding performance of the day. With the pitch soft on top and hard underneath, he bowled in such deadly fashion that his fast-medium inswingers brought him five wickets for seven runs in four overs, two of which were maidens. Smailes took four wickets for 11 runs, the other batsman being run out.

The sensations had begun when Yorkshire - without England men Hutton, Wood, Bowes and Verity - going in at half-past two, lost half their wickets for 32. And although Sellars, the captain, and Yardley, another amateur, shared in a stand of 30 - the biggest of the day - the brothers Pope, bowling unchanged (Copson was on England duty), carried all before them, George claiming six wickets for 44, Alfred four for 37. In their second innings, Yorkshire made 13 without loss before the close.

[While the absent Hutton was making 196 at Lord's against the West Indies, Yorks still managed to compile 310 (Barber 100) in their second innings. Smurthwaite (0-43) could not repeat his earlier performance, but Smailes, bowling unchanged throughout the match, provided the fireworks, taking all 10 Derby wickets for 47, and with Derby all out for 97, Yorks won by 276 runs.]

Smailes: 10 second-innings wickets.

First Test Final day: 27 June

England beat West Indies by 8 wickets: Headley equals Sutcliffe record

By D.R.Jardine, at Lord's

JUST before six o'clock, England made the winning runs to beat the West Indies by eight wickets. This despite some time lost to bad light, and a century in each innings from Headley's bat. Five other batsmen have performed this feat in Test matches, but Headley joins Sutcliffe in performing the feat twice, and it had never before been done at Lord's.

For England it was a thoroughly satisfactory and encouraging match. The side came up to or exceeded expectations in every department of the game, most notably of all in bowling. Copson, who took five for 85 in the first innings, on his Test début, took four for 67 in the second. Bowes had less success than his bowling deserved. Today he produced a spell which, for art, accuracy and lack of luck, approached being unique. True, he clean-bowled Grant, but the figures of 7o 4m 10r 1w give no picture of the number of times the ball beat the bat, the legs and the wicket. He finished with just the one wicket for 44 runs.

Kent leg-spinner Wright took five wickets in the match, and Verity, with two second-innings wickets for 20 in 14 overs, once more supplied a convincing answer to certain persistent but hardly discriminating critics.

England's batting, after a slow start yesterday, was transformed by a stand of 248 in two and a quarter hours by the young players Hutton (196) and Compton (120). The Yorkshire opener took four hours to reach his hundred, but scored at a run a minute for the remainder of his innings. Compton was even more brilliant, reaching three figures in two hours, a very rapid rate of scoring in present-day Test cricket.

For West Indies, Constantine was disappointing with both bat and ball. Headley, however, with his 106 and 107, proved himself to be among the top three or four batsmen in the world. Unfortunately for the tourists, as with Hobbs and Surrey some years ago, it was a case of 'Headley out, West Indies out'.

The 1940s

South Africa suffer as Denis Compton sweeps a ball to the boundary, the shot that epitomised the cricketing cavalier of the forties.

WITH the outbreak of war in September 1939, international cricket and domestic cricket in most countries was put on hold for more than five years. Who knows how many more batting records the mighty Bradman might have broken in those lost years?

When Test cricket resumed after the war, it was not certain, because of ill-health, that Bradman, now 37, would play again. But he recovered in time to lash 187 and 234 in the first two Tests against the England tourists in 1946-47. Next season, in the twilight of his career, he hammered the touring Indians for six hundreds, four of them in Tests.

When Bradman arrived in England in 1948 for his last tour, in his 40th year, he was no longer regarded as the prime Australian force. But what a farewell tour he had! Fêted at grounds up and down the country, he still gave wonderful value for money: 11 hundreds, 2,000 runs again - for a record fourth tour - and top of the Australian batting averages. If this was decline, it was purely relative.

Coming out to bat for his last Test, at the Oval, he received an emotional ovation from the crowd and the England players. Was there perhaps a tear in his eye when he was bowled by Hollies second ball for a duck? Just four runs would have given him 7,000 in Test cricket and an average of 100.

The Australians dominated the international scene in the late forties, and not only in batting, because they had a matchless pair of fast bowlers in Miller and Lindwall. But if anyone challenged the might of Bradman to reign supreme, it was Denis Compton. Statistically, no one could approach Sir Donald - as he became before the decade had ended. But mere statistics do not tell the story of Compton, the great cavalier. They are incidental to the obvious joy he showed at the crease, a joy and sense of fun he communicated to the adoring crowds who flocked to watch him play.

Compton was a law unto himself. He thrived on taking risks, although in a crisis there was none better - as England found to their relief time and again. But if it's records you want, look no further than 1947, when Compton and Bill Edrich, his partner in crime for both England and Middlesex, rewrote the record books between them. The 'Terrible Twins', as they became known, took an unprecedented toll on the best bowlers in the land during that vintage summer, especially the poor South African tourists. Both beat Tom Hayward's 41-year-old record aggregate of 3,518 runs for a season, Compton scoring 3,816, with 18 centuries, records that have never been approached since. He took 73 wickets with his left-handed googly and 'Chinaman', and fast-bowler Edrich took 67. And when he wasn't playing cricket, Compton was dancing down the left wing for Arsenal, despite a dodgy knee, winning a League Championship medal in 1948.

Outside the traditional strongholds of cricket, another force was emerging - in the West Indies. There were new names to conjure with, the Three W's - Worrell, Weekes and Walcott - batsmen to compare with the very best in the world.

1940

Jan 1940 Maharashtra pile up 798 runs, an Indian record, against Baroda at Poona, Vijay Hazare scoring 316 not out.

4 May 1942 Maurice Leyland (Yorks & England), now nearly 42, making his début for Undercliff in the Bradford League, takes 6-14 against Spen Victoria in 22 balls.

23 Jul 1942 In a match between Sussex and Surrey Home Guards at Lord's, the famous dual international cricketer-footballer Andy Ducat, now 56, is on 29 when, as the bowler prepares to deliver the next ball, he collapses at the wicket and dies.

3 Aug 1942 West Indian Test bowler C.B.Clarke, who did the hat-trick at Harpenden on Saturday, performs the feat again, for the British Empire XI against the Metropolitan Police, taking 10-89 (3-14, 7-75) in the match.

1942-43 A.D.Nourse Jr hits 9 successive sixes, including 6 in one over, and 11 sixes in 12 balls for a South African XI in a match against the Military Police in Cairo, where some of the world's leading cricketers play one-day matches every Sunday.

2-3 Aug 1943 England beat the Dominions by 8 runs in a thrilling match, which includes Denis Compton's 6-15 in the Dominions 1st innings and an attractive 113 from C.S.Dempster (NZ) in their 2nd, as they just fail to make the 360 runs required. Another feature of the match is the dismissal of the West Indian Leary Constantine, brilliantly caught by Leslie Compton leaning back against the pavilion rails.

5 Dec 1943 Vijay Hazare makes 309 for the Rest against the Hindus in the Pentangular Tournament final at Bombay out of a total of 387 - 79.84 per cent of the team score, beating a W.G. Grace record set in 1876.

3 Sep 1944 The Hedley Verity Memorial Match, played at Roundhay Park between H.Sutcliffe's Yorkshire XII and J.Appleyard's XII, captained by Walter Hammond, is stopped by rain when Sutcliffe's XII have scored 129-2 (Hutton 82), but sufficient funds are raised from the 10,000 crowd to endow a bed at Leeds General Infirmary.

1944-45 Rusi Modi (Bombay) sets up a new record of 1,008 runs in the Ranji Trophy tournament.

6-8 Aug 1945 The 4th unofficial Test between England and Australia attracts a total of 85,033 paying customers, a record for a 3-day match at Lord's. Field-Marshal Montgomery turns up on one afternoon and is given a hero's welcome.

1945

England captain Wally Hammond enjoys a day at the races, on leave in 1940.

In England, first-class cricket ceased on Friday, 1 September 1939. But both the government and the services realised that cricket could provide a therapeutic relief from the strain of war, for civilians as well as for servicemen when on leave. Clubs of various kinds took the field - all the armed services and sides such as London Counties, the British Empire XI, the National Fire Service and branches of the Civil Defence. Some of the counties, such as Notts, also fielded teams, and others combined sides. In 1944, England played two one-day matches against a Royal Australian Air Force side, winning them both, and these fixtures led to the five unofficial, or 'Victory', Tests played in 1945.

There was some first-class cricket overseas, in Australia, New Zealand, South Africa, West Indies and, especially, India, where competition for the Ranji Trophy continued uninterrupted and the complete regular programme was resumed at the start of the 1943-44 season. This was a golden age of Indian batting, and the wickets favoured the batsmen.

Among the greatest of these batsmen were the two Vijays - Hazare (Baroda) and Merchant (Bombay) - and Rusi Modi of Bombay. They accumulated some massive scores and broke several records during the war. Denis Compton was posted to India in 1944, and he averaged 87 in first-class cricket, including a double century in the Ranji final, as well as taking a football team round the Allied bases in Burma. His partner-to-be with both Middlesex and England, Squadron Leader Bill Edrich, also broke some records during the war - for missions flown in his Beaufighter - and he won the Distinguished Flying Cross.

In the West Indies, the Inter-colonial Tournament ceased, but first-class cricket, often of a high standard and with some notable record-breaking achievements, continued throughout the war. Among others, the young Frank Worrell began to make a name for himself. In Australia, first-class cricket continued for a couple of seasons, before heavy commitment of troops abroad put an end to regular play.

Varsity Match: 29 June 1942

Cambridge win in last over

From Lord's

CAMBRIDGE beat Oxford at Lord's by 77 runs after a thrilling finish, W.J.H. Butterfield, the Oxford captain, being bowled by the seventh ball of the last over.

Cambridge captain J.D. Matthews won the toss, went in with J.R.Bridger and scored 68. Bridger surpassed his captain's effort with 75, and G.F.Anson made 85.

Cambridge declared at 295 for eight in this single-innings match, and Oxford's early batsmen showed to advantage until a wonderful catch at mid-on by Cangley dismissed Lindsay for 61.

With five wickets to fall at half-past six, play proceeded. Robins, left-hand medium, dismissed three men in an over. Then Matthews put on Austin for the final over, at the Pavilion end, and he bowled Butterfield for 22 to snatch victory. A.F.G.Austin took five for 47, G.L.Robins four for 53.

Barbados v Trinidad: 20 July 1942

Record low in W.Indies: Trinidad bowled out for 16

From Bridgetown, Barbados

DEREK SEALEY of Barbados produced the remarkable bowling figures of eight wickets for eight runs in 6.7 overs at the Kensington Oval as he helped Barbados dismiss Trinidad for 16 runs, the lowest score in the history of West Indian first-class cricket. Only three batsmen troubled the scorers.

The visitors were caught on a pitch badly affected by rain, and were all out in 69 minutes. Sealey's performance included a spell of four wickets in seven balls.

Middlesex & Essex v Kent & Surrey: 3 August 42

Schoolboy takes 3 wickets in first over against county batsmen

From Lord's

MIDDLESEX and Essex, with four wickets in hand, are 17 runs ahead of Surrey and Kent at Lord's, where 25,000 saw a good day's cricket yesterday. And Trevor Bailey, the 18-year-old Dulwich College captain, shocked the big crowd and the Surrey and Kent batsmen by taking three wickets in the first over he has ever bowled in a big match.

Bailey was a late choice for the combined Middlesex and Essex team and, at a cost of three runs, he dismissed such good batsmen as A.C.L. Bennett, J.R.Bridger and L.J. Todd. Bailey all-told took four wickets for 36 runs - better figures than those of the England bowlers G.O. Allen and Morris Nichols.

After Surrey and Kent had scored 193, of which total T.G. Evans made 55, Sqdn Ldr W.J.Edrich and S.M.Brown, the Middlesex players, put their side in a sound position by adding 82 in 50 minutes.

OBITUARY

CAPTAIN Hedley Verity, of Yorkshire and England, died in Italy as a prisoner-of-war on 31 July 1943 of wounds received when leading his company on an assault on a German-held farm-house in Sicily. He was 38. R.C.Robertson-Glasgow described Captain Verity's last courageous engagement in an Obituary in the Wisden of 1944:

"The enemy fire increased, and, as they [his platoon] crept forward, Verity was hit in the chest. 'Keep going,' he said, 'and get them out of that farm-house.' ... They last saw Verity lying on the ground, his head supported by his batman, Pte Thomas Reynoldson of Bridlington. So, in the last grim game, Verity showed, as he was so sure to do, that rare courage which both calculates and inspires."

Verity was the finest spin bowler in English cricket during the 1930s. He was a left-arm bowler (he batted right-handed) of normally slow-medium pace. In his first-class career (1930-39), he took 1,956 wickets at an average of 14.90. He never captured less than 150 wickets in a season, and he took over 200 three times. During his nine years with Yorkshire, they won the County Championship seven times. He played in 40 Tests, taking 144 wickets at 24.37 runs apiece. He will forever be remembered for bowling Australia to an innings defeat at Lord's in 1934, after a week-end's rain, taking 14 wickets for 80 in a day. In what has become known as "Verity's Match", his innings analyses were 7 for 61 and 8 for 43. In county cricket, he twice took 10 wickets in an innings, his 10 for 10 for Yorkshire against Notts at Headingley in 1932 being a world record. His best match haul was 17 for 91, all in one day, against Essex at Leyton in 1933.

Verity was still in his prime when war broke out. The only match still in progress on 1 September, the day Germany invaded Poland, was Sussex v Yorkshire at Hove. In his element on a rain-affected pitch, Verity took seven wickets for nine runs as Sussex were bowled out for 33.

Ranji Trophy Zonal match: 2 Jan 1944

High scoring in Indian cricket

From Bombay

CRICKET continues in India as if there were no world war, and there were plenty of runs over the New Year. The biggest scorers were Bombay, who amassed 735 runs in their first innings against Maharashtra in the Ranji tournament. Their captain, Vijay Merchant, scored an unbeaten 359 in 10hr 40min, and shared a stand of 371 with Rusi Modi, a new Indian record for the sixth wicket. Maharashtra struggled to 298 for nine before conceding the match on first innings.

Barbados v Trinidad: 16 Feb 1944

500 partnership in West Indies

From Bridgetown, Barbados

A new world record for the fourth wicket was set in Bridgetown by Frank Worrell and John Goddard, who put on an unbroken 502 stand. This is only the third 500 partnership in the history of first-class cricket, and beats the fourth-wicket record of Abel and Hayward set up in 1899 for Surrey against Yorkshire at the Oval.

The 19-year-old Worrell, a right-hand batsman who came to Barbados two years ago as a slow left-arm bowler, made 308, while Goddard contributed 218.

Ranji Trophy Final: 1944-45

Compton's 249 not out in Indian final

From the Brabourne Stadium

ENGLAND cricketer and footballer Denis Compton, serving in the British Army in India, hit 249 not out for Holkar in the final of the Indian championship, the Ranji Trophy. But in a high-scoring match, Bombay won by 374 runs.

Compton, who has now scored nearly 1,000 runs this season in first-class cricket over here, was in such commanding form that, had he not run out of partners, Holkar might just have pulled off the most remarkable victory in the history of cricket and scored the 860 runs necessary to win the match.

One Holkar player who will not want to be reminded of his performance in the match was leg-break and googly bowler C.S.Nayudu. Although he was able to include another '10w/m' statistic in his career figures, he achieved the unwelcome world record for runs conceded in a match - 428. His innings analyses were six for 153 and five for 275, and he bowled a record 917 balls.

First Victory Test Final day: 22 May 1945

Sergeant Pepper snatches last-over victory for Australia

From Lord's

AUSTRALIA just managed to force victory by six wickets over England at Lord's in the first of the five 'Victory Tests', when Sergeant C.G.Pepper (54 not out) forced Gover for two off the fourth ball of the last over of extra time. So Australia, led by Warrant Officer Lindsay Hassett, achieved their run chase of 107 in 70 minutes, despite losing Pilot Officer Keith Miller, hero of their first innings with 105, for one.

All-rounder Pepper, who had taken four for 80 when England collapsed from 286 for five to 294 in their second innings, forced the pace in fine style, hitting one enormous six to long-on as Australia made 42 in the last 15 minutes.

The attendance for the three days, over the Whitsun holiday, was 70,000, and 16,000 were there at seven o'clock to witness the exciting climax.

[The series was tied at 2-2, with one drawn. England won the 2nd Test, at Sheffield, by 41 runs, Hammond scoring a brilliant 100, and went one down again at Lord's, where Australia won by 4 wickets despite Hutton's 104 and 69. The 4th Test, also at Lord's, was drawn, Washbrook and Miller scoring hundreds. Finally, at Old Trafford, Cristofani made an unbeaten 110 for Australia, but England won by 6 wickets.]

England v The Dominions: 28 August 1945

Second Hammond 100 fails to save England: Dominions win thriller by 45 runs

From Lord's

THIS great match reached a climax here today as England, despite Hammond's 102, failed by 46 runs to make the 357 needed to beat the Dominions. Hammond, who had scored 121 in England's first innings, was stumped by Bremner for the second time in the match, going for the runs.

The Dominions were captained by West Indian Leary Constantine, in place of Hassett, who was ill and had to withdraw before the start on Saturday. There were eight Australians in the Dominions side, but it was New Zealand left-hander Martin Donnelly who held their innings together on the first day with a splendid 133. Altogether 1,241 runs were scored in the match, including a Lord's record of 16 sixes. Miller scored a superb 185 in the Dominions second innings.

D.V.P.Wright was England's best bowler, taking five for 90 and five for 105, while C.G.Pepper hit a fifty and took seven wickets for the Dominions.

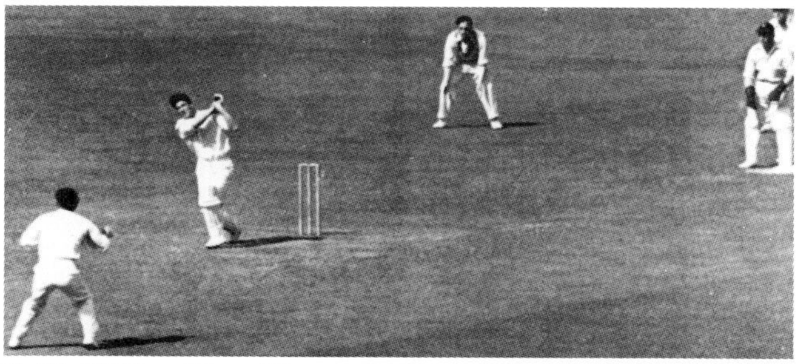

Keith Miller: Magnificent 100 for Dominions

1946

11, 13 May C.T.Sarwate (124 not out at No.10) and S.N.Banerjee (121 at No.11) put on 249 for the Indian tourists against Surrey at the Oval, a 10th-wicket stand second only to the Kippax-Hooker 1928-29 world record and the only instance in first-class cricket of the last two batsmen in the order scoring hundreds.

23 Jul Alec Bedser (England, above) takes 11-93 against India in the 2nd Test, at Manchester, having taken 11-145 in the first Test on his international début.

19 Aug Walter Hammond, playing in the 3rd Test against India at the Oval, becomes the first batsman to reach 7,000 runs in Test cricket.

22 Aug D.R.Wilcox and R.M.Taylor put on 263 for Essex against Warwick at Southend, the highest 8th-wicket partnership in England for 50 years.

26 Aug Yorkshire beat Sussex by 6 wickets at Eastbourne to carry on where they left off before the war and win their fourth County Championship in succession, their 8th in 10 seasons.

14-18 Dec England wicket-keeper Godfrey Evans, on his Test début, concedes no byes during Australia's 659 at Sydney.

TEST SERIES

Australia in New Zealand
Australia 1
India in England
E 1, D 2

Barbados v Trinidad: 6 February

World record partnership in West Indies: Worrell and Walcott put on 574

From Bridgetown, Barbados

THE famous Holmes/Sutcliffe partnership of 555 for Yorkshire in 1932 has been surpassed by two Barbadian batsmen, Clyde Walcott and Frank Worrell, who put on an unbroken 574 runs for the fourth wicket against Trinidad, a world record for any wicket. This stand beats the world fourth-wicket record of 504, also unbroken, set up here two years ago by Worrell himself and Goddard.

Walcott was unbeaten on 314 when Barbados declared at 619 for three, and Worrell had scored 255. The match will go into another (fifth) day, as the last match between the two sides was drawn after four.

[Trinidad, needing 671 to win on the 5th day, made 576-8 (Gomez 213 not, Trestrail 151) and the match was drawn.]

Only Test Second day: 30 March

Lowest ever Test score is recorded

From Reuter, in Wellington

AUSTRALIA beat New Zealand by an innings and 104 runs in the Test match which ended at Wellington, New Zealand, on Saturday.

Australia dismissed New Zealand for 42 in the first innings - the lowest Test score ever - and, declaring after scoring 199 for eight, skittled out their opponents for 53.

Bill O'Reilly's bowling figures for the match were eight for 33.

[This was the first post-war Test anywhere in the world, but newspaper coverage of cricket had not yet caught up with its pre-war comprehensiveness - or accuracy. New Zealand scored 54 in their second innings and Australia won by an innings and 103 runs. It was O'Reilly's farewell Test and his innings figures were 5-14 and 3-19, and it was over in two days. New Zealand's J.A.Cowie took 6-40. What is perhaps most extraordinary about this one-off match was that it was the first Test between these antipodean neighbours - and the last before the 1973-74 season, when they played two three-match rubbers, one in each country.]

County Championship
Warwicks v Notts: 24 July

All ten wickets for Hollies: Bowls out Notts for 135

From Birmingham

W.E.HOLLIES, the Warwickshire slow bowler, took all ten Nottinghamshire wickets for 49 runs at Birmingham today. He is the first player to accomplish such a feat this season.

Perhaps the most remarkable feature of the performance is the fact that no other member of the Warwickshire side contributed directly to the fall of any of the wickets. Seven men were clean bowled by Hollies, the other three falling leg before wicket.

Warwickshire, who had scored 170, led on the first innings by 35 runs, Nottinghamshire being able to total only 135 against the one-man assault of Hollies.

The last time a Warwickshire bowler took all 10 wickets was also on the Edgbaston ground, in 1923, when H.Howell took the Yorkshire wickets for 51 runs.

First Test Second day: 24 June

India XI's big task: Hardstaff's historic 205 gives England the advantage

By Sir Guy Campbell, at Lord's

ON the last day of the first Test match in England for seven years, England will start tomorrow morning in a very strong position. After scoring 428 in answer to India's first innings total of 200, they have taken four Indian wickets for 162.

For this England have Hardstaff, with the dogged and skilful assistance of Gibb, chiefly to thank, for these two won safely through the first two critical hours today, raising the score from 135 to 252 before the latter was out at one o'clock for an invaluable and typically Yorkshire innings of 60.

Hardstaff's not out 205, it is safe to say, will rank among the historic innings in Test match cricket. He scored 163 of it today in 260 minutes, and all the strokes one is accustomed to await and to welcome were there.

The Indian bowling was taxed to the full. but it never got ragged, even in the case of Amarnath, who, one felt, might have been rested at times. And the fielding, in its keenness, dash, enterprise and understanding, was a delight. But, with further support from Smailes (25) and Bedser (30), in particular, Hardstaff gave England a lead of 228.

Merchant and Mankad made a confident start to the Indian second innings, setting about Bowes and Bedser as if they meant to knock off the arrears before stumps were drawn. Bowes had to go off with a pulled muscle, but Ikin broke the opening stand at 67, getting Merchant leg before for 27. Smailes stepped in to take the wickets of Mankad (63) and Modi (21) at little cost to himself, and Bedser bowled Abdul Hafeez for a duck, before Hazare and the Nawab of Pataudi played out time.

[India were all out next day for 275 and England won by 10 wickets, to take what turned out to be a winning lead in the rubber.]

Second Test Final day: 23 July

India defy assault in last 15 minutes thrill

By E.W.Swanton, in Manchester

IN the last quarter of an hour's play in the second Test match between England and India at Old Trafford today, India's last pair survived a thrilling assault by Bedser and Pollard bowling with the new ball, and the match was drawn. No better day's play can be imagined, either to watch or to play in, for all the virtues peculiar to cricket - as we like to think - were well shown.

It will be seen that when England ran out of time she still had 126 runs frozen in the bank. But for the present, we may dwell on the skill seen today by such men as Compton and Abdul Hafeez, Bedser, Mankad, Hazare and Pollard.

Pollard bowled Pataudi, finishing with figures of five for 24 in 27 overs, and Bedser (4-41) polished off the Indian tail to give England a first-innings lead of 124. Compton's chanceless 71 not out on a tricky pitch enabled his captain, Hammond, to declare - in hindsight, too late - at 153 for five, leaving India exactly three hours to save the match.

Within a quarter of an hour, the first three were back in the pavilion. But in the next hour, Modi and Hazare put on 67. After tea, Bedser clean bowled them both, and Amarnath too. He came back after a rest and grabbed three more wickets (7-52), but that last pair, Sohoni and Hindlekar, held out in brave fashion for the most thrilling of draws.

First Test Sixth day: 5 December

Miller joins band of great all-rounders

By E.W.Swanton, in Brisbane

ENGLAND are one down in the rubber tonight, beaten by an innings and 332 runs. The English party is experiencing a reaction after the strain and struggle of battling against Australia's massive first innings total (645) and following on 504 runs behind.

It was Toshack, bowling more accurately today after some public instruction in the middle from his captain and vice-captain, who broke England's two promising stands - that between Hammond and Yardley when England's first innings resumed this morning, and between Hammond and Compton in the follow-on.

There has been no feature of the match more significant for the future than Miller's cricket. In the scorebook, his all-round performance [79, 7-60 & 2-17] compares favourably with that of any player on either side since, and including, the great days of Gregory and Armstrong. Figures are dangerous witnesses (consider Toshack's three for 17 off 16.5 overs in the first innings), but it is safe to say that this match, if it has done nothing else, has introduced to Test cricket a player to take his place among the very best of this generation.

Apart from Bradman (187) and Miller, Australia did not show great class either in batting or bowling. The toss virtually meant the match, and England, though comprehensively beaten, had twice been forced to bat after violent thunderstorms and seem to come better out of the post-mortem than Australia.

Third Test Second day: 19 August

Merchant 'kicked out' at the Oval

From the Oval

INDIAN opener Vijay Merchant looked as if he was set for the duration. The England bowlers never looked like getting him out, but Denis Compton, whose flair for the unorthodox with both bat and ball is well known, found a novel way.

Merchant, who had compiled 128 chanceless runs, went for a sharp single as his partner stroked the ball past Compton at forward mid-on. He was sent back, but seemed to have ample time to return to his crease, when the Arsenal and England left-winger turned on the ball and kicked it at the wicket, running out the dumbfounded batsman by inches.

Followers of Middlesex might remember a similar incident when Joe Hulme, another Arsenal and England winger, performed this rare trick at Old Trafford in 1938.

[India were eventually bowled out for 331, but after England had reached 95-3 (Compton 24 not out), the weather intervened and the match was washed out, leaving England winners of the rubber by 1-0.]

Second Test Fourth day: 17 December

Bradman and Barnes in record Test stand: 405 for fifth wicket

By E.W.Swanton, in Sydney

Bradman and Barnes, resuming this morning on 252 for four, made 405 for the fifth Australian wicket, taking the score to 564 by twenty minutes to six. At that point both, striving ever more greedily for runs, made acceptable mistakes. Their scores were identical at 234. The partnership, a world record for the fifth-wicket, has been exceeded only once before in Tests, by Bradman and Ponsford in 1934.

Tonight, Australia stand 316 in front with four wickets left and a possible ten hours in which to repeat their Brisbane victory. The pitch is taking spin but with few signs of positive misbehaviour.

The innings of Bradman between 1928 and the present tell an eloquent tale of the diversity of his genius. But few chapters of the story, if any, when it comes to be fully written, will throw a truer, more characteristic light on the man than this latest achievement.

In its beginnings, Bradman's innings was a triumph of will power over his aches and pains. Almost as at Brisbane one felt sorry for this frail little fellow engaging the spotlight. Carrying on again this morning with 52 runs to his name, he began once more as an interesting invalid, feeling his way, sometimes beaten but never giving up. Twenty minutes after lunch, he reached his hundred.

By now his assurance was wholly recovered, his limp more of a habit than an inconvenience. Gradually throughout the afternoon, as England's bowlers toiled, the old mastery returned. After tea he devoted himself to the job of pushing on the score with all speed, making 79 in his last 80 minutes at the wickets and hitting the ball to every point of the clock.

Barnes (top) and Bradman running during their stand

Barnes one knows to be a highly accomplished player, and the disparity in class between him and Bradman after tea, when both sought to do the same thing, was the measure of Bradman's greatness.

From the English point of view, yesterday was Wright's day, but today's chief honours belonged to Evans, who replaced Gibb behind the wicket. Nothing in this match has been so astonishing or so welcome as the improvement shown by the Kent 'keeper.

[Australia went on to make their highest score in home Tests against England, 659-8 declared, exceeding their Brisbane total. England made a better showing in their second innings (371), with Edrich (119) and Compton (54) to the fore, but lost their last 6 wickets for 62 and were again beaten by an innings.]

1947

22 Mar Hammond plays his last Test innings, against New Zealand at Christchurch, and finishes with a record 7,249 runs in Tests.

27 Mar Jeff Stollmeyer hits 324 for Trinidad in a friendly match against British Guiana at Port-of-Spain, the highest innings in West Indian domestic cricket.

7 Jun Melville (189) and Nourse (149) put on 319 against England at Nottingham, a world Test record 3rd-wicket stand and South African Test record for any wicket.

18 Jul Leg-break bowler Ian Smith takes 6-1 in 4.5 overs, finishing off the innings with a hat-trick as the South Africans dismiss Derby for 32.

7 Aug Peter (T.B.P.) Smith makes 163 for Essex against Derby at Chesterfield, the highest score by a No.11 in first-class cricket, adding 218 for the 10th wicket with Frank Vigar. His innings includes 3 6's and 22 4's.

9-12 Aug Denis Compton, not content with rewriting the batting records, pulls off a stunning all-round performance for Middlesex against Surrey at the Oval, scoring 137 not out and taking 6-94 and 6-80 as Middlesex win by an innings and 11 runs; he also takes 4 catches. In Middlesex's 537-2 declared, Brown (98) and Robertson (127) put on 211 for the 1st wicket, and Edrich (157 not) and Compton an unbroken 287 for the 3rd in two and three-quarter hours. Both wicket-keepers, Compton's brother Leslie for Middlesex and Surrey's A.J. McIntyre, bowled.

16-20 Aug Bruce Mitchell scores 120 and 189 not out for S.Africa in the drawn last Test at the Oval, and England's Richard Howorth takes a wicket with his first ball in Test cricket.

15 Nov Bradman scores his 100th career 100, 172 for an Australian XI against India (who win by 47 runs) at Sydney, achieving it in only 295 innings, by far the quickest in cricket history.

1, 4 Dec Ernie Toshack takes 5-2 in 19 balls for Australia in the 1st Test at Brisbane and then 6-29, as India are dismissed for 58 and 98 (Australia win by an innings and 226 runs).

TEST SERIES

England in Australia
A 3, D 2
England in New Zealand
Drawn 1
South Africa in England
E 3, D 2

Fourth Test Sixth day: 6 February

Compton and Morris make history - Evans, too

By E.W.Swanton, in Adelaide

THE fourth Test is now a memory, and of all the several records, so far as the Englishmen present are concerned, the most durable is sure to be the heat. Compton and Morris may have achieved by admirable batsmanship two centuries apiece, but in the week's cricket the temperature was consistently the highest scorer.

Compton does not specially need big figures in a Test to emphasise his great talents. Nonetheless, it is a fair mark of distinction to succeed in a strange and unsympathetic rôle. He batted nearly four and three-quarter hours in each innings, almost wholly in adverse times, offered no chance and hardly gave the encouragement of a snick. He batted in the second innings after England's collapse as though he really hated his job, hitting time after time into the deep field and holding his ground to keep Evans from the bowling.

There is a property of Cockney cheerfulness about Evans that makes him almost automatically a good man in a crisis. There was nothing miraculous about his automatic survival from 5.20 p.m. yesterday until lunch today, and it was indeed evidence of how well he was middling the ball when required that he was credited with no run over the record period in a Test match of 100 minutes.

Hammond declared after lunch at 340 for eight, leaving Australia 314 to make in three and a quarter hours. Bradman arrived with one wicket down for 116, and put on 70 with Morris in 42 minutes. But then the attack suddenly faded away. Perhaps Bradman was not especially interested in victory, satisfied to have put the rubber beyond England's reach.

Scores: England 460 (Compton 147, Hutton 94) and 340-8d (Compton 103 not, Hutton 76), Australia 487 (Miller 141 not, Morris 122) and 215-1 (Morris 124 not, Bradman 56 not).

Ranji Trophy Final: 9 March

World record stand in Indian final

From Baroda

VIJAY HAZARE (288) and Gul Mahomed (319) put on a world record partnership of 577 for Baroda's fourth wicket against Holkar in the final of the Ranji Trophy tournament.

This surpasses by three runs the previous highest first-class partnership made by Worrell and Walcott in the West Indies just over a year ago.

Gul Mahomed joined Hazare when Baroda had made 91 for three in reply to Holkar's first-innings total of 202, and the stand lasted 533 minutes. Hazare, who also took six for 85 in Holkar's first innings, batted for 628 minutes.

Vijay Hazare.

County Championship Middlesex v Somerset: 12 May

Young bowler's amazing spell: 5 for 8 in five overs

By E.W.Swanton

MIDDLESEX and Somerset were at one another tooth and nail in this first championship match of the season at Lord's, and at the end of it all Somerset need 75 more runs to win with five wickets standing. The purple patch of a dramatic day in which 23 wickets fell occurred when Tremlett came on for the second time with the Middlesex score 60 for three, and in five overs took five wickets for eight runs.

The pitch was good enough, but really quick for the time of year, and the four whose stumps young Tremlett hit were all late on the stroke and beaten by pace off the ground. Middlesex were all out for 78, and Somerset, after being led on the first innings by 97, went in after tea needing 176 for victory.

[Somerset scraped home by one wicket, Tremlett (19 not out) hitting the winning runs.]

First Test Fourth day: 11 June

Compton, Yardley and Evans save Test for England

By E.W.Swanton, at Nottingham

Three cricketers - Compton, Yardley and Evans - have saved the first Test for England after all, and in so doing have earned much glory and given us a last day of excitement and suspense. The pitch's pacific character right to the last did not encourage an heroic declaration, and to make 227 in two hours and 20 minutes was a proposition which hardly seemed feasible, even against this England bowling.

So Melville made the end as pleasant as he could by batting delightfully once more, and adding an unbeaten 104 to his first-innings 189, though limping painfully.

Compton and Yardley resumed this morning and carried their stand to 237, the highest fifth-wicket partnership for England. Compton went on to his biggest Test innings (163), but Yardley fell agonisingly one short of his century; Evans struck an entertaining 74 in an hour and a quarter and England amassed 551 - the match was safe.

Second Test Second day: 23 June

Great Compton-Edrich partnership: 370 world Test record for 3rd wicket

By E.W.Swanton, at Lord's

Compton and Edrich inscribed their names deep in cricket history in the early part of the day, completing a stand only 12 short of England's highest for any wicket (Hutton/Leyland's 382 at the Oval in 1938), and setting a new third-wicket mark.

They were answered, however, once again by Alan Melville, who needs four runs to complete four hundreds in a row in Tests against England. It was a wonderful performance by the South African captain, and his duel with Wright, as soon as that bowler, around whom controversy is never silent, took the ball about four o'clock, lifted the cricket to a higher plane than anything I have seen since Compton's innings against Amarnath and Mankad on a bad wicket at Manchester last July.

England's innings was monopolised by Compton and Edrich as no two men have monopolised the crease since those partnerships of almost wearisome perfection - to English eyes - between Bradman and Ponsford. The two Middlesex men were together for five and a half hours, and the only flaw was the running between the wickets, which was an almost perfect example of how not to do it. Generally the wrong man called, and when the right man did, he was as often as not sent back.

Edrich went for 189, Compton for 208, his first Test double century bringing his total in three Test innings against South Africa to 436. England declared at 554 for eight, and, thanks largely to Melville, South Africa were 167 for two at stumps.

[Melville duly made his century (117), but South Africa were beaten by 10 wickets. Wright took 5-95 & 5-80, and the Middlesex 'twins' took 7 wickets between them.]

Compton (right) and Edrich going out to bat.

Third Test Second day: 7 July

Edrich and Compton do it again

By E.W.Swanton, at Manchester

ENGLAND's position, only 28 runs behind South Africa with six wickets to fall, is a strong one in the third Test here tonight, and once again the show has been stolen by Compton and Edrich. In a partnership of 228, begun - after Hutton and Washbrook had gone for 48 - when the ball was flying awkwardly, and continuing for 195 minutes, they batted as well as even these two young masters know how.

Edrich is having a run of triumphs at present to which recent cricket history offers few parallels, and Compton brought the number of runs in his last eight Test innings, here and in Australia, to the Bradmanesque dimensions of 894.

Compton's hundred arrived shortly before six o'clock, and when he had batted for 150 minutes. Edrich, stuck still for a while, passed three figures with a string of fours. Compton, hooking once too often, was out for 115, but Edrich stayed to the close, unbeaten on 141.

[Edrich went on to make 191 in 320 minutes and England 478. Despite a brilliant and courageous 115 from Nourse, South Africa made only 267, the last 7 wickets falling in an hour for 50, and England won by 7 wickets.]

Champion County v The Rest: 15 September

Compton and Edrich hit 426 out of 543 total

By E.W.Swanton, at the Oval

MIDDLESEX have established themselves in an impregnable position against the Rest at the Oval by two characteristic and immense pieces of batsmanship by Compton and Edrich, who between them made 426 out of the score of 543 for nine at which Robins declared.

Edrich took his season's aggregate just beyond Tom Hayward's 3,518, after which Compton, who of course had previously done so, reached his 18th century and went on to make 246, his highest score in English cricket. Having retired on Saturday with a recurrence of his knee trouble after adding 138 with Edrich, Compton had his knee strapped up to last the match. He batted a further 170 minutes today for 191 more runs, and, as in several other innings this summer, he began to improvise the most wildly improbable strokes. In one case he tripped over his own feet, fell headlong down the pitch and as he did so flicked Goddard for four to long leg. Perhaps his play was best summed up by the friend in the Players' room, who said he still batted as though he had a lamp-post behind him.

For all Compton's brilliance, it was the soundness and patience of Edrich (180) that had laid the foundations of his side's score. When Middlesex went into the field, Gray had the redoubtable Washbrook and Place for 0 apiece, and when Compton came on, despite his strapping, he had both Howarth and Yardley in one over.

[Middlesex won by 9 wickets, the only county apart from Yorkshire (twice) to beat the Rest in one of these matches. Compton bowled 34.4 overs in the match, taking 6-141. Compton and Edrich, in this last match, concluded their remarkable season, finishing 1st and 2nd in the first-class averages, Compton with 3,816 (avge 90.85), Edrich 3,539 (80.43), aggregates that have never been approached since. Compton's 18 hundreds beat Hobbs's 16 in 1925, and he also took 73 wickets (28.12), Edrich 67 (22.58). Edrich took 35 catches, Compton 31. After Compton in the list of centurions were Edrich and the Middlesex opener Robertson, both with 12. Middlesex won the County Championship.]

County Championship Leics v Middlesex: 14 July

Compton and Edrich again: Middlesex score 637 for 4

From Leicester

W.J.Edrich and Denis Compton scored 272 runs in 130 minutes today in another of those partnerships that are destined to occupy a chapter in cricket history anon.

The Middlesex and England pair, whose feats this season have been almost inseparable, came together when the second wicket fell at 185. Edrich, in overnight, was then nearing his century. He completed it in 150 minutes and proceeded to flog the Leicester bowling for 257. Compton raced to his 50 in 40 minutes and went on to make 151.

Middlesex, who were replying to a Leicester total of 309, declared at 637 for four, and Compton took two wickets before the close, with Leicester still needing 168 to avoid an innings defeat.

[Berry (154) took Leics 17 runs ahead at lunch with 6 wickets and only 80 minutes left, but Middlesex had them out in another 35 minutes for 48 more (Compton 5-108, Edrich 2-37) and the 'terrible twins' knocked off the 66 runs for victory in 7 overs - with 4 minutes to spare!]

1948

1-5 Jan Bradman scores 132 and 127 not out as Australia beat India by 233 runs at Melbourne, sharing an unbeaten 5th-wicket stand of 223 with Morris (100 not).

23-28 Jan Vijay Hazare is the first Indian to make two 100s in a Test, 116 & 145 v Australia at Adelaide, but India lose by an innings, Australia scoring 674 (Bradman 201, Hassett 198 not out).

1 Apr England lose the 4th and last Test match in West Indies and the rubber by 2-0, having gone through a whole tour without a victory for the first time.

3 May G.H.G.Doggart, a freshman at Cambridge, creates a new English record by hitting 215 not out on his first-class début, against Lancs at Cambridge.

15 May The Australians amass a record 721 (all out) v Essex at Southend, 76 more than any team has made before in a day: Bradman 187, Brown 153, Loxton 120, Saggers 104 not out.

21 Jun Capt.J.H.G.Deighton takes the hat-trick for M.C.C. v Cambridge at Lord's, having done it there the previous year for Army v Navy.

22-27 Jul The attendance overall at the 4th Test at Leeds against Australia is 158,000, a record for any match in England. The aggregate of runs (1,723) is also a record.

14-18 Aug Australia beat England by an innings and 149 runs at the Oval for their 4th victory in the rubber, bowling England out for 52 in the 1st innings (Lindwall 6-20, Miller 2-5, Johnston 2-20), only Hutton (30) reaching double figures. But Bradman is bowled by Hollies 2nd ball for a duck. Morris is run out for 196.

10 Sep J.M.Sims takes all 10-90 for East v West at Kingston.

18 Dec B.B.Nimbalkar is left high and dry on 443, just 9 short of Bradman's world record, when Kathiawar concede the match to Maharashtra (826-4) in the Ranji Trophy at Poona. But his 455 stand with K.V.Bhandarkar (205) is a world record for the 2nd wicket.

27-30 Dec Hutton (158) and Washbrook (195) put on a world 1st-wicket Test partnership of 359, as England hit 608 against South Africa in the 2nd Test at Johannesburg.

TEST SERIES

India in Australia
A 4, D 1
England in West Indies
WI 2, D 2
Australia in England
A 4, D 1

County Championship Middlesex v Somerset: 19 May

Compton and Edrich 424 is record

From Lord's

DENIS COMPTON today made the highest score of his career, 252 not out, and with W.J.Edrich created a third-wicket record for English cricket of 424, only 21 runs short of the world record. Edrich hit 168 not out.

They were playing for Middlesex against Somerset, and the record they eclipsed was the 375 of Hearne and Hendren for Middlesex against Hants at Southampton in 1923.

Compton and Edrich shared in so many big partnership last season that they earned the sobriquet of the Middlesex Twins, but this is their first big stand this summer. Compton hit three sixes and 37 fours, Edrich one six and 18 fours. The stand lasted four hours, Middlesex declaring at 478 for two and then taking two Somerset wickets for 21 before stumps.

[Middlesex won by 10 wickets.]

Third Test First day: 8 July

Compton is Test hero, but rain England's only hope

By E.W.Swanton, at Old Trafford

ENGLAND 231 for seven in the third Test here today is a score which can be adequate only if the wind drops and the rain comes, and those whose moral scruples can be submerged by the earnest hope that the rubber is kept alive until Leeds must wish very hard for it.

Compton is felled trying to hook Lindwall.

For the pitch is a beauty and, sad to say, England, to bolster the strength of the batting, have cast away Laker, the bowler, a decision I find it hard to condone.

Once more, fast bowling has shown up the inadequacies of our batting, and once again it has been Compton who has held the innings together. This time he played a hero's part even more spectacularly than usual, for, having come in this morning to face the invariable crisis - this time, 32 for two - he was cut over the head when hooking Lindwall and led bleeding and staggering from the field.

When he returned in the afternoon, England were in even deeper crisis, at 119 for five, but he dealt perfectly well with Lindwall straight away. Evans (34) soon joined him in the most presentable stand of the day, while 75 was added, and at the close Compton was still there on 64.

[Compton continued his heroics, with support from Bedser (37), whom he unfortunately ran out, and played one of his finest innings, 145 not out in England's respectable and unlikely total of 363. But the match was drawn when rain prevented England capitalising on a strong position.]

Fourth Test Final day: 27 July

Australia score record 404 to win Test and rubber

By E.W.Swanton, at Leeds

AT a quarter past six this evening, Neil Harvey hit Cranston past mid-on for four, and Australia had won the fourth Test by seven wickets, and with it the rubber. To achieve this, they made the record score of 404.

Just five hours earlier, Compton had been in the middle of a dangerous spell of bowling from the Kirkstall end of the ground. He had caught and bowled Hassett brilliantly, picking up the ball very low with his left hand when following up half-way down the pitch. Now he lured Morris out of his ground and Evans might have made a stumping, but the ball came awkwardly to the keeper. Changed over to the other end, Compton beat Bradman, who snicked to first slip a chest-high catch which Crapp, perhaps the safest short fieldsman in English cricket, put down. Bradman had then made 22.

We deplored these chances missed, but no emphasis on England's shortcomings must dim the recognition of a remarkable Australian victory. For the first time since the first of all Tests, at Melbourne in 1877, a team had won against a declaration, and in so doing they had scored, for three wickets, only seven runs fewer than either team had ever scored in the fourth innings against the other.

A century by Bradman in a Test generally means an Australian victory, and this was his 19th against England. When his score reached 145, he had made a little matter of 5,000 runs against us in Tests. In his four Tests at Leeds, he has made four hundreds: 334, 304, 103 and now 173 not out. Morris, the other Australian given a 'life', made 182, and the two added 301 for the second wicket.

County Championship Hants v Glamorgan: 24 August

Glamorgan champions: Team of shining virtues

By E.W.Swanton

IT is Glamorgan's championship. By winning the most conclusive of victories at Bournemouth against Hampshire, they have climbed beyond the reach of both Surrey and Yorkshire. Thus the youngest of the 17 first-class counties becomes only the third (Warwick in 1911 and Derby in 1936 were the others) outside those who used to be termed the 'big six' to finish at the top since the competition was extended to more or less its present dimensions in 1895.

The present result is a happy surprise, for there could not have been a more popular success. It is not necessary to flatter Glamorgan in order to praise them. They are deficient in several directions, especially batting. But they have shining virtues, and it is particularly appropriate that these include several of which our first-class cricket stands in need: quickness and 'drill' in the field, slow bowling that couples real spin with control, and that aggressive team spirit which has its mainspring in a strong captain, Wilfrid Wooller, who is himself an outstanding fielder.

The chief credit for Glamorgan's accomplishments this summer must go to Wooller and J.C.Clay, the honorary secretary. Clay, indeed, at the age of 50, has come into the picture in the most dramatic way in the last two matches, with match figures of 10 for 61 against Surrey and now nine for 79 against Hants. By these deeds, he has taken some of the burden from Muncer, whose seven wickets at Bournemouth bring his total for the summer to 150.

Muncer's off-breaks, often helped by Hever with the new ball, the all-round ability of Wooller, Watkins and the veteran Emrys Davies, and several spectacular innings by W.E.Jones have been the principal technical ingredients of their victories. But it was the zeal and fervour behind all this which really tipped the scales, and one's only regret is that the final scenes could not have been enacted at Cardiff before a true Celtic crowd.

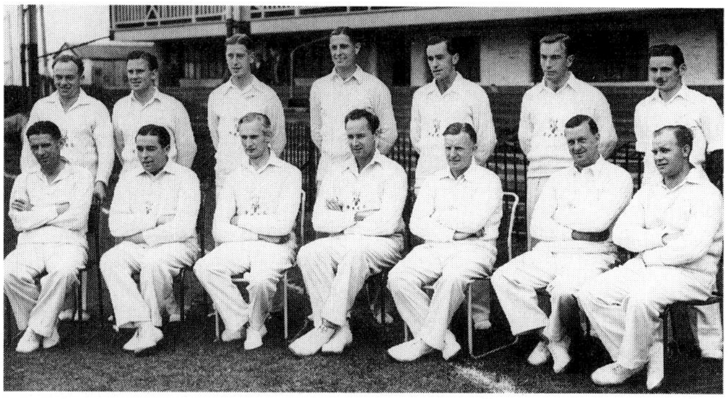

Glamorgan: A great team effort.

MCC Tour of S.Africa: 4 December

Compton's 300 the fastest ever

From Johannesburg

THE classic innings played on Saturday by Denis Compton is still the main topic of cricket conversation here today. He scored 300 out of a stand of 399 with Simpson (130 not out) in 181 minutes when the M.C.C. tourists trounced North-Eastern Transvaal by an innings and 203 runs in two days, winning their sixth victory in seven matches.

Compton, who has never hit the ball so hard, struck five sixes and 42 fours. One six in particular will be remembered. He went down the pitch, made the ball into a full-toss and sent it high into the native stand on the long-on boundary. The distance before the ball hit the ground was probably 110 yards.

It was Compton's fourth hundred in five innings and the highest score of his career. He reached his century in 66 minutes, hit his second in 78 minutes and swiftly made a third in another 37 minutes. Fast-scoring records contain no feat comparable to his performance in an innings of over 200.

Bradman Testimonial
D.G.Bradman's XI v
A.L.Hassett's XI: 7 December

Bradman's last match

From Reuter, Melbourne

DON BRADMAN has played his last innings in first-class cricket - 10 in the second innings of his testimonial match. His side tied with Hassett's. Needing 403 runs in five and a half hours to win, Bradman's team were 402 for nine wickets when stumps were drawn.

On Saturday, Bradman scored an emotional 123 on the ground where he made his first Test appearance 20 years ago. This was his 117th century (including 37 double hundreds). In the Hassett XI second innings, he took a rare turn with the ball and secured two wickets for 12 runs in 1.7 overs. His testimonial realised approximately £A10,000.

[Bradman did play two more matches, and his final career figures were: Innings 338, Not Out 43, Runs 28,067 for an unparalleled average of 95.14.]

First Test Final day: 20 December

England win last-ball Test thriller with a leg-bye

By E.W.Swanton, in Durban

THE most exciting of all modern Tests has ended here in England's victory by two wickets off the last ball of the last over. From the moment when England went in to score 128 to win in two-and-a-quarter hours until Gladwin and Bedser scrambled their leg-bye off the eighth ball of Tuckett's over, the situation grew in tenseness to a pitch where all emotion was drained.

When the over began, with only Wright to come, all results were possible. Off the first ball, Bedser, swinging his bat, gives a nasty high chance to Mitchell at slip from which a single is run. The second is to a length on the leg stump. Gladwin catches it on the rise to send it whistling hard and true just a foot or two over mid-wicket's head, and the ball smacks against the pickets in front of the pavilion.

The third ball Gladwin, swinging violently, snicks for one to long leg. Bedser drives the fourth powerfully to mid-off, who stops it, and an appeal is raised for lbw from the next. Three balls to go, two runs to win.

Bedser prods the next towards cover and these two big fellows lumber precariously but safely across. Scores level. Tuckett gives width to the seventh and Gladwin misses by both time and distance.

One ball to go. Bedser, the backer-up, with scrupulous fairness, keeps his bat in the popping crease until Tuckett's arm comes over. The ball bounces off Gladwin's pads towards square-leg. Another desperate scuffle and Bedser is home with a split second to spare.

The language of Mr Jingle has served before to describe a cricket match and it must do so again. Wonderful match, sir - all heroes - England hitting out - wickets falling - rain falling - light shocking - Mann and Washbrook gallant fellows. Compton a genius, sir, old head on shoulders - this Jenkins, first Test match - Worcester sauce - Yorkshire relish - have it your own way.

Half-hour left, 31 to win - 20 minutes, 18 wanted, Compton bowled behind legs, gliding. What's that, Jenkins caught wicket? - 10 to six, 13 to make - Gladwin missed mid-on by Tuckett, run two - this Gladwin has fight, sir, he'll do it yet, he will.

He has.

Scores: South Africa 161 (Bedser 4-39) and 219 (Wade 63; Wright 4-72), England 253 (Hutton 83, Compton 72: Mann 6-59, A.Rowan 4-108) and 128-8 (Compton 28, Washbrook 25, Jenkins 22).

1949

27-31 Jan West Indies beat India at Madras by an innings and 193 runs, obtaining the only result in the 5-match rubber. Weekes fails to extend his record run of 100s, being run out for 90.

4 Feb Weekes scores 56 for W.Indies at Bombay in the 5th Test, to register a record 7th consecutive 50 in Tests, but is out for 48 in the 2nd innings.

9 Mar Jack Crapp hits 10 off 3 balls to give England a last-minute 3-wicket win in the 5th Test over South Africa at Port Elizabeth and a 2-0 victory in the rubber after accepting Nourse's challenge to score 172 in 95 minutes. Bruce Mitchell ends his Test career with two 50s, and a record South African aggregate in Tests of 3,471 runs.

4 May H.R.H. the Duke of Edinburgh is nominated as President of the M.C.C.

25 Jun Mann declares England's innings closed, to give New Zealand 15 minutes' batting, under the mistaken impression that a declaration on the first day of a 3-day Test is permissible. But the experimental law does not apply to Tests. Fortunately, no harm is done, as NZ score 20 without loss, so no action is taken.

28 Jun Martin Donnelly's 206 for New Zealand at Lord's in the 2nd Test follows his 142 for Oxford v Cambridge in 1946 and 162 not out for the Gents v the Players in 1947 - also at Lord's.

23 Jul Brian Close (Yorks) becomes the youngest England Test débutant, at 18 years 149 days, against New Zealand at Manchester.

29 Aug Yorks beat Glamorgan by 278 runs at Newport to become joint holders of the County Championship with Middlesex, the first tie since 1889. It is the 6th game in a row from which they have taken maximum points.

TEST SERIES

West Indies in India
WI 1, D 4
England in South Africa
E 2, D 3
New Zealand in England
Drawn 4

Third Test
Fourth day: 3 January

Fifth successive Test 100 for Weekes

From Calcutta

EVERTON WEEKES, 24-year-old West Indies cricketer, set up a world record here today by scoring his fifth successive Test century. His 101 in the West Indies second innings against India followed 162 in the first innings.

He began his record run with 141 against England in the final Test in the West Indies last March, and followed with 128 and 194 in the first two Tests against India.

Ranji Trophy Semi-finals: 11 March

Records shattered in Poona: 2,376 runs, nine 100s

From Poona

RUN records tumbled in the week-long Ranji Trophy semi-final between Bombay and Maharashtra at Poona, where the two sides accumulated 2,376 runs between them for the fall of 38 wickets, surpassing the previous record set up by Bombay and Holkar four years ago by 298 runs. Bombay won by 354 runs.

There were nine individual hundreds in the match, which provided the first instance of three players completing centuries in each innings. Maharashtra, set to make 959 runs to win, were all out for 604, a fourth innings total exceeded only by England's 654 for five against South Africa in Durban in 1938-39.

Scores: Bombay 651 (M.K. Mantri 200, U.M.Merchant 143, D.G.Phadkar 131) and 714-8 dec (Phadkar 160, Merchant 156), Maharashtra 407 (M.C. Datar 143, M.R.Rege 143) and 604 (S.D.Deodhar 146, Rege 100).

[Bombay went on to win the final two weeks later, beating Baroda by 468 runs in a comparatively low-scoring match of 1,494 runs. K.C. Ibrahim made 219 and M.M. Dalvi 110 in Bombay's first innings.]

Cambridge Univ v Essex: 7 May

Varsity pair break 59-year-old record

By E.W.Swanton, at Fenners

G.H.G.Doggart and J.G.Dewes have had a field day against Essex. The Fenners pitch is of a notorious and deceptive ease; that among cricketers is of common ground, and the Essex bowling was shown naked to the world by the Australians a year ago. But there is available the most convincing testimony, if it were needed, that these two rising young cricketers played quite remarkably well, scoring at an average rate of 80 an hour and giving only three chances between them, all late in the day.

Their stand of 429 set a new English second-wicket record, surpassing the 398 made by two of the great ones, Shrewsbury and William Gunn for Notts against Sussex in 1890. Speculation, however, as to whether they might beat the world record of 455, set last year in the Ranji Trophy, has been quenched, because D.J.Insole, the Cambridge captain, has declared the innings on 441 for one, and he deserves congratulations for answering what he considers to be the demands of the match and putting figures and records in their place.

County Championship Middlesex v Sussex: 6 June

Day in a lifetime for crowd as Compton hits benefit 182

By E.W. Swanton, at Lord's

For the crowd that packed every inch of Lord's for the second day of Denis Compton's benefit match, it was a day in a lifetime. They sat under a blue sky in the sunshine in their shirt sleeves and blouses, and saw their hero make 182 runs in his own uniquely magnetic way.

He began soberly, launched gradually into his full range of strokes, and, when both his hundred and the Sussex score were left behind, blossomed forth into one of those dazzling exhibitions which are so difficult for the bowler to compete with and so impossible to describe.

Compton's last 82 were made in a few minutes over three-quarters of an hour by a bewildering mixture and variety of the drive, the cut, the hook and the pull, with the delayed wristy drive to either side of cover point as the favourite and most perfect stroke of all.

With his score at 52, Compton had sliced a very wide half-volley from Wood straight into gulley's hands and out again. It was his first and last mistake.

When Denis Compton walked back at last, his brother Leslie walked in, and in the last three-quarters of an hour made a very powerful and excellent unbeaten 59, including some off-drives of a quality not a whit below those we had been enjoying earlier. Where else, as someone remarked, could a man get such value for eighteenpence as he had at Lord's today?

Second Test Final day: 28 June

Test draw provides case for 4-day matches: Donnelly's fine innings

By E.W.Swanton, at Lord's

THE second Test expired painlessly at Lord's this evening. The English players hit the ball in a pleasant carefree way; New Zealand, particularly in the game, toiling figure of Burtt, kept up the dignity of the occasion by bowling and fielding with proper zeal, and everyone relaxed peacefully in the lovely sunshine.

All this followed Donnelly giving New Zealand their one hope of winning by batting in the most attractive way possible in the morning. He added 80 to his score in less than 90 minutes, and thus brought the lead on first innings to 171. Five hours remained when England's second innings opened. But the wicket, which gave such promise on Saturday, had gone into a guileless slumber. The question must be faced as to how this Test series can be brought to the fitting climax of a definite result.

All those who are reluctant to see three-day Tests vanish into oblivion feel a deep conviction that longer matches tend to become a weariness to the flesh. The ideal cricket match of whatever kind includes a brief exchange of risks, and the ideal victory is not one gained by long, protracted siege.

Whether the third Test, at Old Trafford, is brought to a decisive end or not, I feel the fourth should be extended by one day at least. This I realise, in some sort, is a recantation by your correspondent. It seems called for, not as an issue of principle involving the automatic extension of all Test matches in this country, but in the light of the present general standard of bowling, combined with the failure of the cricket authorities everywhere to grapple with the admittedly difficult technical problem of the preparation of pitches.

Donnelly made his runs today with a delightful assortment of strokes and his 200 was only the sixth in Tests at Lord's, following Bradman, Hammond, Hobbs, Compton and W.A.Brown.

Scores: England 313-9 dec (Compton 116, Bailey 93) and 306-5 (Robertson 121, Hutton 66), New Zealand 484 (Donnelly 206, Sutcliffe 57).

[The last two Tests were also drawn.]

County Championship Worcs v Middlesex: 23 July

Robertson 331 in a day: 14 short of record

From Worcester

Robertson: Reached 300 in a day

WITH Compton and Edrich on England duty against New Zealand, Middlesex still contrived to compile 623 runs for five wickets at Worcester on Saturday, thanks largely to J.D. Robertson, who was at the crease throughout the day of 6½ hours in scoring 331 not out. He hit two sixes and 39 fours, and figured in substantial stands with Allen, Dewes, Mann and Robins. The declaration was made at the close of play, although the Press were not informed.

Robertson's innings - his best score, the highest individual score for Middlesex and the biggest score in England since 1938 - has only twice before been surpassed in a day in England. C.G.Macartney hit 345 in rather less than four hours for the Australians against Notts in 1921, and K.S.Duleepsinhji 333 in 5½ hours for Sussex against Northants at Hove in 1930.

[Middlesex won by an innings and 54 runs.]

County Championship Derby v Glos: 5 August

Graveney gets all 10 for 66

By T.H.Evans Baillie, at Chesterfield

With the completion of Gloucester's victory over Derby by 184 runs here today, 24-year-old J.K.Graveney joined the select body of bowlers who have taken all 10 wickets in an innings in county cricket.

This accomplishment of Graveney's in his first season as a regular member of the side was based on common sense, accuracy of high merit, plus whole-hearted cricketing temperament. Graveney, who has a spirited action, bowled slightly above medium pace at a consistent length to a 'spot' at the pavilion end, and exercised the curiously rare quality of bowling at the wickets.

Graveney would be the first to acknowledge his debt to Lambert. With seven wickets down and his side's victory absolutely assured, Lambert, one of the best-class faster bowlers of today, forbore to poach on what had become Graveney's preserves, using his skill to avoid taking wickets or giving away runs.

County Championship Essex v Lancs: 24 August

All-rounder's feat: Bailey takes all ten

From Clacton

T.E.Bailey, the Essex and England fast bowler, took all 10 Lancashire wickets for 90 runs in 39.4 overs. He is the second bowler to achieve the feat this season and the fourth in post-war cricket.

The last Essex player to take all 10 wickets was H. Pickett, against Leicester at Leyton in 1895. Bailey, who played in all four Tests against New Zealand this season, was the first to complete the double of 1,000 runs and 100 wickets.

Lancs were all out for 331, and Essex were 32 for one at the close.

[Nineteen Essex wickets fell the following day and they lost by 10 wickets in two days.]

County Championship Worcs v Surrey: 30 August

Jenkins again does hat-trick

From Worcester

JENKINS, the Worcestershire leg-spinner, who took three Surrey wickets with successive balls yesterday, achieved the feat again today. He appears to be making a habit of doing this to Surrey, his only other hat-trick having been against them at the Oval last season.

The feat is not without parallel in first-class cricket, but it is exceedingly rare, having been performed by Alfred Shaw (Notts v Glos) in 1884, T.J.Matthews (Australia v South Africa) in 1912 and C.W.L.Parker (Gloucester v Middlesex) in 1924.

The fine bowling of Jenkins brought about a remarkable Surrey collapse, and they were beaten by 109 runs. Set to make 217 for victory, Surrey's opening pair scored freely at first, but when the effects of the roller wore off, none of the batsmen could cope with the turning ball. In fact Jenkins and Howorth dismissed the last six with the total unchanged at 107. Jenkins's figures were five for 54 (11-166 in the match).

The 1950s

Australia, without Don Bradman, still started and finished the fifties as top dogs. But in between England enjoyed a period of supremacy such as they had never experienced before.

Yet for England it all started so ominously, well-beaten by West Indies in England for the first time and then crushed in Australia. The turning point came at Lord's in 1953 at the end of June, when a stubborn, fighting stand by Watson and Bailey stopped the rampaging Australians in their tracks - Lindwall, Miller and all - and saved England from impending defeat. Alec Bedser began to match the Australian quickies and England began to believe in themselves under Hutton, their first professional captain, until they finally emerged triumphant at the Oval, where Lock and Laker previewed things to come. It was England's first Ashes success for 20 years.

At the same time, West Indies had emerged as the third cricketing power, to the background of steel bands and the calypso, with 'those little pals of mine, Ramadhin and Valentine'. These two great slow bowlers, emerging seemingly from nowhere, sent England into a spin in 1950, the Three W's - Worrell, Weekes and Walcott - achieved legendary status with the bat, and, after losing at Old Trafford, the West Indies inflicted three crushing defeats on the bewildered home side.

West Indies could not beat Australia, however, losing seven Tests in the fifties and winning only one. But England could. They went from strength to strength, and in Australia it was Frank 'Typhoon' Tyson, arguably the quickest bowler since Larwood, who tore them apart in tandem with Brian Statham. England lost the first Test by an innings at Brisbane in 1954-55, but, with May and Cowdrey emerging as world-class batsmen, they won the next three.

Then came Jim Laker's annus mirabilis, 1956, when even Tony Lock had to take a back seat and watch as his partner performed deeds out of schoolboy fiction and weaved, for both Surrey and England, a seemingly magic spell over the Australians. But, by the end of the decade, with England growing old, Harvey, Benaud, Davidson and the aggressive young O'Neill had put their country back on top again (albeit helped by some bowling of dubious legality).

Youngsters emerging elsewhere as the fifties drew to a close proceeded to dismantle those two great monuments of cricket - the Test and first-class batting records of Hutton and Bradman, respectively. Garfield Sobers of West Indies, with 365, and Hanif Mohammad of the emergent Pakistan, with 499, set the new landmarks that would last even longer than the ones they replaced.

Surrey dominated the County Championship with eight wins in the fifties, including a record seven in a row, before Yorkshire finally made a comeback. Surrey's strength was their bowling - Bedser, Laker, Lock and latterly Loader - but they had an inspirational leader in Stuart Surridge for most of the period, before Peter May, England's finest batsman, took over. In 1950, the number of county matches was increased from 26 to 28, and bonus points for fast scoring were introduced in 1957.

Old Trafford 1956, the magic moment of the fifties: Laker asks the question, all eyes are on the umpire, his finger goes up, Maddocks is out lbw... and Laker has rewritten the record books.

1950

2 Jan Bert Sutcliffe makes 355 for Otago v Auckland at Dunedin, the highest innings in NZ first-class cricket, his 266 stand with W.S.Haig (67) setting a new record for the 5th wicket.

14 Feb In the drawn 4th Test at Johannesburg, John Moroney (118 and 101 not out) becomes the first Australian to make two 100s in a Test against South Africa.

3-6 Mar In the 5th Test, at Port Elizabeth, Australia beat South Africa by an innings, making 549-7 dec, their highest innings in South Africa, with 100s by Hassett (167), Morris (157) and Harvey, whose 116 is his 4th in consecutive Tests and his 8th on tour.

17-19 May On a plumb wicket at Fenners, John Dewes (183) and David Sheppard (227) set a Cambridge (594-4 dec) 1st-wicket record of 343 in 280 mins, the best ever opening stand against a West Indies team, who then proceed to score a record 730-3, including a 350 3rd-wicket stand by Weekes (304 not) and Worrell (160) in 225min, a record for any West Indies wicket in England.

12 Jul Lancs (239) beat Sussex (101 and 51) at Old Trafford in a day, slow left-armer Malcolm Hilton taking 11-50 and off-spinner Peter Greenwood 9-67

12-14 Jul West Indies put on 651-2 on the first day against Leics, a day's total surpassed in first-class cricket only by Australia's 721 against Essex last year. They declare next day on 682-2, with Worrell (241) and Weekes (200) sharing an unbeaten 3rd-wicket stand of 340, only 10 short of their record earlier at Cambridge. They win by an innings and 249 runs.

11 Aug L.E.G.Ames puts Kent on the way to beating Middlesex at Canterbury with 131 (out of 211 in 2hr), the 100th century of his career.

1 Sep Surrey beat Leics by 10 wickets at the Oval to share the County Championship with Lancs, the second tie in successive seasons.

TEST SERIES

West Indies in England
WI 3, E 1
Australia in South Africa
A 4, D 1

Third Test Final day: 24 January

Harvey's great batting: Australia's glorious recovery

By Louis Duffus, in Durban

AUSTRALIA made a glorious recovery in the fourth innings of a thrilling third Test match at Kingsmead today to beat South Africa by five wickets 25 minutes from the time for drawing stumps. They thus won the rubber of five matches with three straight victories.

Battling on a worn wicket against admirably steady bowling by Mann and Tayfield, who between them sent down 73 overs today in sweltering, humid heat, they scored 256 runs while losing only two more wickets. In doing so, they accomplished an unqualified triumph of defensive batsmanship which has done much to mitigate the ignominy of their first innings 75 all out (Tayfield 7-23, Mann 3-31).

They have won from a tight corner, making the 336 runs required, having lost the toss and suffered the whims of weather which had acted against them.

The innings put the stamp of a distinguished batsman on young, modest left-hander Neil Harvey, whose 151 not out, his fifth century of the tour, was a magnificent example of concentration in defence, leading to irresistible attack and culminating in his scoring the winning run after five and a half hours of batting in which he gave no chance.

The Australians' adaptation to a pitch of uneven bounce and which responded to spin was uniformly commendable. Morris (44), Loxton (54) and McCool (39 not out) all rose to the occasion, but the match belonged to Harvey, who has become the outstanding figure of the tour.

County Championship Essex v Glamorgan: 15 May

Bailey 7 for 0, almost unplayable: Innings defeat for Glamorgan

From Brentwood

A devastating spell of seven wickets for no runs by T.E.Bailey, the England fast bowler, enabled Essex to defeat Glamorgan in dramatic fashion by an innings and 114 runs with a day to spare.

Earlier, Essex had gained a first-innings lead of 217 by taking their overnight total of 203 for five to 384. But by the tea interval, Glamorgan had scored 81 for the loss of Davies and Parkhouse, a state of affairs that did not suggest a sensational collapse. However, just 40 minutes afterwards, the Welsh county were all out for the addition of another 22 runs.

In five overs, four of them maidens, and one ball, Bailey got rid of seven of the remaining wickets for three runs, all scored before he gained his first success. No batsman faced him with any confidence on a wearing pitch. He took a wicket with the first delivery of each of his last four overs, and his analysis for the innings read: 11.1o, 5m, 15r 7w. This gave him a match analysis of 10 for 43, so he can be excused his duck in Essex's innings!

Test Trial England v The Rest: 31 May

Laker's 8 wickets for 2 shatters the Rest

By E.W.Swanton, at Bradford

J.C. LAKER, the Surrey off-spinner, took eight wickets for two runs on the first day of the Test Trial at Bradford as the Rest were sensationally bowled out in their first innings for 27 in 110 minutes. No one reached double figures.

Cricketers are divided as to the utility of Test Trials, and there are many who maintain that they are more likely to be a snare and delusion than anything else. This school of thought may well be fortified in their view by the happenings here today. In brief, some of the leaders in their respective departments were able to emphasise their skill, but most of those whose ability really was on trial had the worst possible conditions in which to display it.

Laker, of course, comes into the former category, and his analysis will take its place in the records at the head of the remarkable bowling figures in the history of first-class cricket. Previously, the fewest runs conceded in taking eight wickets in an innings was five - by the great Yorkshireman E.Peate, who performed his feat against Surrey at Holbeck, not many miles from here, in 1883.

Yardley had put the Rest in, and Laker utilised the most helpful possible wicket quite excellently. He spun the ball prodigiously and dropped it on the spot every time. Making due allowance for the inexperience of the batting opposed to him, it was an admirable piece of off-spin bowling. His full analysis was: 14o, 12m, 2r, 8w.

England, with the brilliant Hutton making 85 in two hours, scored 229, and by the close The Rest had reached 27 again, this time for the loss of only two wickets.

[Hollies (6-28) did the damage in The Rest's 2nd innings (113), Laker taking 2-44, and England won by an innings and 89 runs.]

First Test First day: 8 June

Evans and Bailey are heroes of England recovery

By E.W.Swanton, in Manchester

BETWEEN the lunch interval and the close of play on this first day of the first Test match against the West Indies, England's position shifted from precariousness to prosperity in a manner altogether remarkable. A score of 95 for five, made on a most difficult wicket at the additional expense of a suspected fracture of Hutton's right forefinger, had become 312 all out.

If that does not turn out to be a winning score, the cause must surely prove to have been either something very brilliant from the West Indies batsmen or a phenomenal turn in the weather, or a mixture of the two.

This afternoon, Evans and Bailey rescued the situation in a partnership that was worth in all 161 runs, of which Evans's share was an invaluable and scintillating 104. When Evans was out at last at a quarter to five, Hutton reappeared, a hospital examination having disclosed that the worst was a severe and extremely painful bruise.

He hung on literally almost left-handed while Bailey continued to restore England's position, adding 24 more to his original 15. Bailey survived all his tail-end partners to take out his bat in the end for 82 priceless runs. Then, for half an hour, Stollmeyer and Rae fought off the England bowlers to make 17 runs and, more importantly, keep their wickets intact.

The name of Valentine must be joined to those of Evans and Bailey on the honours list. This youngest of the West Indies players, a quite unknown Trinidad cricketer just a few months ago, took the first eight England wickets with his slow left-arm bowling for 104 runs.

He spun the ball sharply from leg and, until he tired, kept a nasty length on the middle and off, so that the batsmen could not often afford the luxury of leaving the ball alone. In all, he bowled 50 overs, 14 of them maidens. Ramadhin, bowling in tandem with Valentine for much of the time, also succeeded in giving the England batsmen severe problems, especially Edrich, and he took the last two wickets.

[England's spinners Berry (9-116) and Hollies (8-133) led England to victory by 202 runs.]

Gentlemen v Players: 26 July

F.R.Brown rescues Gentlemen with 122 out of 131 in 110 minutes

By E.W.Swanton, at Lord's

A MEMORABLE innings was played for the Gentlemen this afternoon by their captain, Freddie Brown. Coming in at No.8, he made 122 out of the last 131 runs scored, bringing the Gentlemen's total to 325, an eminently satisfactory reply to Dollery's gesture in sending them in to bat.

The Gentlemen's effort was the work of three batsmen of Cambridge origin, Dewes (94), Doggart (75) and then Brown, who stole the day with a piece of forcing cricket that enthused everyone, old and young. The more elderly were reminded of how cricket used to be played, before the game's descent to an age of over-sophistication and a dreary philosophy of safety first. And the young now believed their elders at last.

[In a thrilling finish, after Brown had made a challenging declaration, setting them 253 to win in 150 min, the Players needed 36 in 20min with 7 wickets in hand before C.J.Knott's hat-trick left them 10 runs behind, last man Hollies playing out the last 5 balls for an honourable draw.]

Brown heaves Wright to leg.

Second Test Second day: 26 June

Ramadhin (left) and Valentine: Spun England to defeat.

Ramadhin and Valentine bowl England out for 151 on true wicket

By E.W.Swanton, at Lord's

ENGLAND were bowled out today at Lord's by West Indies on a wicket that was true and blameless for 151, which left them 175 behind. With more than three days to go, West Indies took the clearest possible course in batting again and, by the close, the first pair had put their side in a position all but impregnable by increasing the lead to 220.

The first name to be mentioned must be that of Ramadhin. Whatever the future holds for this lithe little man, he may never have Test batsmen at his mercy so completely as he had in today's excellent spell of spin bowling. England's first wicket fell at quarter past one with the score at 62. When the ninth man was out at a quarter to five, they had struggled by methods that were a strain and an embarrassment to watch to 122, and Ramadhin, in 33.3 overs, had taken five for 34. His analysis suffered as Wardle (33 not out) hit out and he conceded another 32 runs.

Valentine's part from the Nursery end was less spectacular, though he kept a perfectly steady length, turned the ball slightly down the hill and took four for 48.

[Walcott made England pay for an early miss and hit 168 not out, adding 211 with Gomez (70) in a record 6th-wicket stand. West Indies declared at 425-6, 600 ahead, and despite a brave 114 from Washbrook, the 'spin twins' Ramadhin (6-86) and Valentine (3-79) bowled England out again to win by 326 runs.]

Fourth Test Fourth day: 16 August

Hutton carries bat in great 202 but West Indies win by innings

By E.W.Swanton, at the Oval

THE West Indies won the fourth and deciding Test here this evening by an innings and 56 runs, with a little more than a day to spare. Thus the rubber is theirs by three matches to one.

For all the extenuating circumstances that may be pleaded for England, West Indies have gained the honours - for the first time in an English season - by better cricket in most of the cardinal respects. Above all, there has generally been a more adventurous spirit about their batsmanship, and England have had no combination of bowlers to compare with Ramadhin and Valentine.

Hutton continued to defy the bowling while wickets fell at the other end, and was unbeaten on 202 when Wright was out after a last-wicket stand of 18 failed to save the follow-on by just 10 runs.

But no one resisted for long in England's second innings, Valentine taking six for 39, Ramadhin three for 38. In the four Tests, these two spin 'terrors' have taken 33 (avge 20.42) and 26 (23.23) wickets, respectively. Worrell, with 539 runs at 89.83, topped the West Indies batting averages.

1951

12 Feb The Commonwealth beat India by 74 runs in the 5th unofficial Test, at Kanpur, to take the rubber 2-0. Jack Ikin (England) finishes top of the Commonwealth Test batting averages with 625 runs at 89.28, having played in all the Tests, as did Frank Worrell (WI) with 445 runs (63.57) and Bruce Dooland (Aus) with 300 (50.00). West Indians Worrell and Sonny Ramadhin finish with most wickets, 18 (avge 33.61) and 15 (28.86) respectively, although Jim Laker's 8 wickets in his only Test cost him 15 apiece.

2 Jul Worcs keeper Henry Yarnold sets a world record with 6 stumpings in Scotland's 2nd innings at Dundee, and, with one catch, equals the world record of 7 dismissals.

16 Jul Hutton makes 151 for Yorks v Surrey, his 100th century, appropriately enough at the Oval, scene of his record Test innings in 1938.

25 Jul Kent fast bowler Fred Ridgway takes 4 wickets in 4 balls against Derby at Folkestone, the first to do so since before the war.

TEST SERIES

England in Australia
A 4, E 1
England in New Zealand
E 1, D 1
South Africa in England
E 3, SA 1, D 1

Fourth Test Third day: 5 February

Hutton's innings a masterpiece, but England's Test fortunes see-saw again

By E.W.Swanton, at Adelaide

LEN HUTTON, with 156 not out, became the first England opener to carry his bat against Australia since Bobby Abel at Sydney in 1892. However, England struggled after taking the last five Australian wickets for 14, and trailed on first innings by 99.

This was not one of England's better days, and there can be no mitigating light thrown on their performance when it is looked at in detail, Hutton excepted. He has batted at his own masterful best on this tour, as I hope these notices have made evident. Nevertheless, he needed an innings such as this, his second century against Australia since the war, to illustrate by figures uncontradictable his present pre-eminence among the world's opening batsmen.

Today he took the full weight of the innings and sustained it by batsmanship that was the nearest possible approach to perfection. On Saturday he had given a stumping chance at 34. This afternoon, when his last partner had arrived, he gave a chance to mid-off. Apart from these incidents, one can remember hardly a scar of any sort. It was a superb illustration of the art and almost faultless, as was his judgement of length, the execution of his strokes and his unremitting concentration.

In so much as no other batsman than Hutton and Morris (206) has yet made 50, it is an extraordinary match. The crowning disappointment, of course, was the prompt dismissal of Compton, glancing Lindwall's fourth ball to the wicket-keeper. His aggregate for five innings in this series is now 31. It is perhaps little consolation to his admirers that other great batsmen have suffered sequences equally mortifying and have 'come again'.

[A début Test century by the 20-year-old Burke gave Australia a comfortable lead and they won by 274 runs on the 6th day. It was England's seventh Test defeat in a row.]

Fifth Test Fifth day: 28 February

England win at last: Bedser, Hutton and Simpson the heroes

By E.W.Swanton, in Melbourne

At last! England's victory by eight wickets in the fifth Test here this evening has altered the whole aspect of the tour as it will be remembered by the players taking part and by those both at home and in Australia who have been following the fortunes of the series.

Moral victories, near things and unlucky breaks are all very well, but each reverse in the three series since the war has made it harder for the English side to break through. Now the reproach is past, and when the comedy of a last over by Hassett, and three premature stump gatherings by the players, had culminated in Hutton making the winning stroke, one sensed the emotion of relief and pleasure among the spectators.

As F.R.Brown, England's captain, observed from the balcony, it would have been even nicer if this had been the match that decided the Ashes. But at least the manner of victory made it clear that, if things had run differently, it could have been, for England won inside four days of playing time on a wicket that played true from first to last and, which is the crux of the matter, after losing the toss.

Thanks to Simpson (156 not out), England gained a three-figure lead yesterday after all, and thanks to Hutton (60 not out to add to his first-innings 79), there was no breathless, palpitating struggle this afternoon for the 95 which were needed to win.

But while these two heroes are being applauded for their part, another name must be added, and it is a matter of personal judgement whether he occupies the chief post of honour. When Alec Bedser got the last Australian wicket today, he brought his number for the series up to 30 (at 16.06 apiece) - joining an illustrious line of great bowlers who have captured 30 or more, including Rhodes, Barnes, Tate and Larwood. In the whole series he was never collared, and his figures in this match - five for 46 and five for 59 - speak for themselves.

First Test Final day: 12 June

South African bowlers gain Test triumph over England

By E.W.Swanton, at Nottingham

AFTER five days' play, in three of which fortunes have fluctuated in the most fascinating way, South Africa won the first Test at tea-time by 71 runs. Since the war they have played three rubbers, two against England and one against Australia, without wining a match, though they have become precious near to doing so several times. The luck has finally turned for them.

Dudley Nourse: Double century for South Africa.

It is only fair to the English side to say that the weather befriended their opponents when England on Saturday afternoon, with Simpson and Compton making hundreds, had climbed almost half-way to the South African score for the loss of only two wickets. The fullest credit must be paid to the well-tried partnership of Rowan (5-68) and Mann (4-24) for getting the most out of the conditions this afternoon. They kept the England batsmen pinned tight to their creases by undeviating length and skilful spin, and only Wardle (30) attempted to collar them as England subsided to 114 all out.

Nourse's gallant 208, played with a broken thumb, was the cornerstone of South Africa's victory, though a word of praise must go to the shrewd captaincy of Eric Rowan, who deputised for him when South Africa fielded.

Fourth Test Third day: 28 July

Peter May is bowled after a fine hundred in his first Test.

Remarkable century début by May

By E.W.Swanton, at Leeds

THE third day of the Test here followed the first two in its general characteristics, the bat again holding a stubborn, unexciting sway on an utterly placid wicket which still gave only the briefest hints of later encouragement for the bowler. In reply to South Africa's 538 (Rowan 236), England have made 325 for three wickets.

Hutton scored exactly 100, but the big happening today was the arrival of another young batsman, Peter May, England in quality as well as in name. Like Lowson (58), he was lucky in having so favourable a setting for his first Test match, and in the encouraging presence of Hutton at the other end. But it is one thing to be given the chance and another to seize it.

To May, of course, must go the palm, and when in the evening he reached his hundred with a handsome straight drive to the boundary off Rowan, the crowd stood and applauded with a warm, prolonged intensity which was an acknowledgment of the virtues that Yorkshire-men especially appreciate in a cricketer.

May is still there on a chanceless 110, and his batting, over nearly five hours of a tense and grilling day, had a steadfast calmness and concentration of purpose remarkable in a young man of 21.

[May made 138, England 505, and the match was a draw before rain put an end to it.]

Third Test First day: 22 December

West Indies on top as 22 wickets fall in day

By Ray Robinson, in Adelaide

IN a sensational first day, 22 wickets fell at Adelaide on a pitch affected by rain seeping under the covers. The Australians are three runs behind with two wickets gone in their second innings, but the new captain, Arthur Morris, has held back his best batsmen in the hope that a sunny week-end will quieten the sportive wicket before the resumption on Monday.

Morris's task has been complicated because he has been given an ill-balanced side to lead. After the usual captain, Lindsay Hassett, had been declared unfit, the selectors sought authority to bring in a player outside the chosen 12 to reinforce their weakened batting. But a minority of members of the Board of Cricket Control present at Adelaide would not take the responsibility of varying an inflexible procedure.

Worrell (6-38), Gomez and Goddard wound up Australia's first innings in two hours, without either Ramadhin or Valentine turning his arm. Weekes, whose 26 in West Indies' 105 was the innings of the day, played a resourceful knock. Valentine took both Australia's second-innings wickets to fall in two maiden overs.

[Australia made 255 (Valentine 6-102), but West Indies won by 6 wickets on the third day.]

Fifth Test Third day: 18 August

Hutton out obstructing the field: Brown once again sees England through

By E.W.Swanton, at the Oval

WHEN time has blurred the memory of a great finish to the last Test, it will be briefly observed that England beat South Africa by four wickets, and the records will show that England won the rubber by three matches to one with one drawn. It may well seem in retrospect quite a comfortable business. But at least the exciting events of the last afternoon are safe - if not for posterity, at least for those who saw the battle ebb and sway from the time of England's going in immediately after lunch to make the 163 they needed, until the moment when Laker made the winning stroke at 20 minutes to six.

What a tossing and turning our emotions underwent in those three and a half hours! Towards three o'clock it all looked so easy for England. Hutton and Lowson had just hoisted the first 50 in capital time and with scarcely a moment's disquiet.

Then within three minutes came the shock of Hutton's extraordinary dismissal on the grounds of obstructing the field - only the fifth such incident in first-class cricket - and the almost unnoticed demise of May, first ball, caught off pad and bat. The South Africans, suddenly seeing a chance of victory, responded with a heightened tautness in the bowling and fielding, which obliged the new batsman, Compton, to struggle for dear life.

When after 50 exciting minutes Compton and Lowson both went their ways, and the score was still only 90 for four, the burden of England's hopes fell once again on the broad shoulders of their captain, Brown. In the 15 minutes between Brown's arrival and tea, the excitement, if possible, grew more intense. Watson was batting like a rock at the other end, but everyone sensed, I think, that, to shift the fortunes of the game, something violent, and therefore hazardous, was needed, especially as Rowan was bowling so well.

In the 20 minutes after tea, Brown and Watson scored 33, 27 of them off Rowan's last four overs. He had been scientifically attacked, and the boot of challenge was now very much on the other foot. The job was nearly done when the faithful Chubb captured first Watson (15) at 132 and then Brown (40) at 151. It remained for Laker (13 not out), the hero of the morning with his six for 55, to make the winning runs.

[The Hutton incident occurred when he made to sweep Rowan, the ball lobbing straight up head-high after contact with his bat and forearm. Not realising he had snicked the ball, he made to strike it away from his stumps, but in so doing prevented wicket-keeper Endean making a catch. It was a correct decision, although the obstruction was not literally wilful as the law demands.]

Second Test Fourth day: 18 December

England have chance of victory: Graveney's big innings

From Bombay

A spell of 70 minutes after tea put new life into the second Test between India and England here today. India, only 71 runs ahead, have lost four second-innings wickets.

Thanks to Tom Graveney's monumental 175, made in eight and a quarter hours of controlled power and concentration, England made 456, only 29 runs behind on first innings. Then Statham, without success, and Ridgway bowled magnificently, the latter capturing the wickets of both openers, before Watson, at the personal cost of six runs, had both the prolific Hazare and Amarnath caught flashing. There is still plenty of good batting left, but England do at least have a chance of winning.

[India were 88-7 before a stand of 71 by Gopinath (42) and Mankad (41) denied England a chance of victory.]

1952

8-12 Feb West Indies and New Zealand meet for the first time in Tests, at Christchurch, West Indies winning a low-scoring match by 5 wickets; Ramadhin takes 9 wickets, Valentine 5.

11 Jun Denis Compton records his 100th century, with 107 for Middlesex against Kent at Lord's.

19-24 Jun Opener Vinoo Mankad hits 184 (out of 270) in the 2nd Test against England, at Lord's, a new Indian Test record, is also top scorer with 72 in their 1st innings, and bowls 97 overs in the match, taking 5-231, but England win by 8 wickets.

25-27 Jun David Sheppard hits 239 not out as Cambridge, set to make 373 at 75 runs an hour, beat Worcs at Worcester by 6 wickets; two University bowlers feature, McGinty for taking 4-0 in 10 balls in the Worcs 1st innings and McCarthy, who is no-balled for throwing.

26 Jul Square-leg umpire Fred Price, former Middlesex wicket-keeper, no-balls Surrey left-arm spin bowler Tony Lock for 'throwing' three times in the match against the Indians at the Oval, the fault seeming to be with Lock's quicker ball.

28 Jul Pakistan are admitted to membership of the Imperial Cricket Conference and accorded Test status.

23-26 Oct Nazar Mohammad is the first player to be on the field for a complete Test match, carrying his bat for 124 (in 8hr 35min) in Pakistan's 331 against India in the 2nd Test, at Lucknow, which Pakistan win by an innings and 70 runs.

16 Nov Hanif Mohammed bats 6hr for 96 in Pakistan's 2nd innings at Bombay, but cannot prevent India winning by 10 wickets.

29 Nov Zulfiqar Ahmed (63 not) and Amir Elahi (47) put on 104 for the last wicket in Pakistan's 1st innings against India at Madras in the drawn 4th Test.

29 Dec Bert Sutcliffe makes 385 for Otago against Canterbury in the Plunket Shield at Christchurch, breaking his own individual NZ scoring record set in January 1950 by 30 runs.

TEST SERIES

England in India
I 1, E 1, D 3
India in England
E 3, D 1
West Indies in Australia
A 4, WI 1
West Indies in New Zealand
WI 1, D 1
Pakistan in India
I 2, P 1, D 2

Fourth Test Final day: 4 January

Australia win Test and rubber: Last pair defy West Indies

By Ray Robinson, in Adelaide

AUSTRALIA beat West Indies here by one wicket in one of the tensest finishes in Test history. Their last-wicket pair were so keyed up that they could not stand still between overs. But they steadied their nerves enough to rescue the match after their captain, Hassett, had thought it lost.

When the last man, angular Bill Johnston, joined the strapping Doug Ring at 222, the Australian innings was lurching towards disaster as three wickets had just toppled for four runs and 38 were still needed to win.

While the West Indies captain and vice-captain, Goddard and Stollmeyer, conferred with the bowlers every over and then some, Ring and Johnston paced about the ends of the pitch like a couple of expectant fathers in a maternity hospital.

Yet in the choice of balls to snatch singles or wallop fours, this pair of tail-enders, picked for their bowling, appraised the situation more coolly than their opponents, whose field-placing was seriously at fault.

Ring made 32 and Johnston seven in the last 35 minutes, leaving poor Valentine to look at the scoreboard in disbelief after his five wickets for 88 in 30 overs had threatened to win the match and keep his side in the rubber.

Earlier, Hassett was Australia's hero as he saw seven partners depart for a combined output of 100 while he compiled a gritty 102 in five and a half hours before Valentine trapped him lbw.

Fifth Test Fourth day: 10 February

India defeat England: Gain first Test victory

From Madras

INDIA deservedly beat England by an innings and eight runs here today to share the honours in the Test series and score their first-ever official Test victory - at the 25th attempt. They played their first match in 1932, at Lord's.

England, 12 for no wicket overnight, needed another 179 to avert an innings defeat, but lost openers Spooner and Lowson in the first two overs. For a brief period, when Robertson (56), Watkins (48) and Graveney (25) were batting, England's hopes rose. But as the ball kept beating the bat, it became obvious that only a miracle could save them.

Indeed, the writing was on the wall as soon as the spinners came on. Off-spinner Ghulam Ahmed did most of the early damage, dismissing four of the seven recognised batsmen, three with the help of short-leg catches.

Vinoo Mankad also took four wickets, giving him match figures of 12 for 108. This great all-rounder, nearly 36, has announced that he intends to retire after this year. He took 34 wickets in the series at 16.97 apiece, the best on either side, and scored 223 runs (avge 31.85).

Monday Cricket Commentary

Hutton to be England's first professional captain

By E.W.Swanton

IT is announced by the selectors that Len Hutton has been invited, and has accepted, to captain England in the first Test against India at Leeds on June 5. Thus has history been made, and a professional appointed, let it be added most deservedly and justly, for the first time since Test matches became the concern of Boards of Control and the Marylebone Club.

It is always a pleasure when distinction comes to a man great in his own sphere, who wears his honours as modestly as a Hutton. It is true, of course, that he is not practised in the mechanics of captaincy, a job requiring a great deal more than may be supposed.

Yet Hutton has always been a thoughtful cricketer whose advice on the field has been readily sought by the present Yorkshire captain, N.W.D. Yardley, and the late captain of England, F.R.Brown, two of the four who have now been responsible for his election.

For myself, I would confess to only one apprehension concerning Hutton's aptitude for the post, and events may well, as I hope, confound it. In his attitude to the broad tactics and strategy of the game, the native caution commonly said to be characteristic of the Yorkshireman sometimes has seemed to his captains and fellow players to cloud his judgment.

We have failed too often against Australia by 'playing safe'. It certainly seems that in the present series the balance of the initiative must come from England, and if our new captain ever errs from an excess of adventure, there is at least one critic who will observe with the most sympathetic eye.

All that one need wish Len Hutton is that he will be as successful and as popular in his job as his predecessor, Freddie Brown.

Len Hutton: New England captain.

First Test Third day: 7 June

India recover after losing 4 for 0

By E.W.Swanton, at Headingley

WHEN India, in a paralysed quarter of an hour this afternoon, lost the first four wickets in their second innings in 14 balls before they had scored a run, it needed the example and fortitude of their captain, Vijay Hazare, to encourage the rest to make any sort of showing. At a quarter past three, with the scoreboard showing the worst start to an innings in the history of Tests, no one would have wagered much on a fourth day's play.

Thanks, however, to a sixth-wicket stand of 105 between Hazare (56) and Phadkar (62 not out), it is not wholly certain that Monday's ending will be a mere formality. At 136 for six, India are now 95 runs ahead, and they have the power to add to their lead. And they should know that in Ghulam Ahmed they have a high-class bowler who might make the gathering of a quite insignificant fourth-innings score a labour and a trial.

There were several notable English performances today. That of Evans (66) was particularly praiseworthy, for the loss of Graveney (71) in the first over put a new load of responsibility on the England wicket-keeper. Jenkins (38) also played his part. But the day's hero was fast bowler Fred Trueman, the 'local boy' making his Test début.

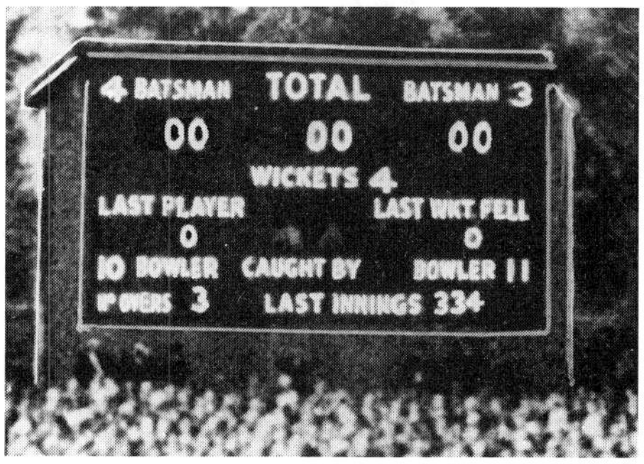

India's innings after 14 balls is depicted starkly on the scoreboard, the worst start in Test history.

Having opened his account in India's first innings with three wickets for 89, he claimed another three in his first eight balls in their second. He had Roy hooking too soon at the second ball of the innings and he was caught at slip. In his next over, after Bedser had dispensed with Gaekwad, he bowled Mantri and Manjrekar with the first two balls. Hazare only saved the hat-trick with a late, involuntary stab, but Trueman got him later in his last short spell, and finished with four for 27 in nine overs.

[Trueman wasn't needed as India added only 29 more runs and England won by 7 wickets.]

Third Test Third day: 19 July

Trueman first English fast bowler to take 8

From Manchester

ENGLAND won the third Test, and the rubber, at 20 minutes past five today, but India's defeat was as certain as anything could be the moment the Manchester weather changed for the worse the night before the match. England declared at 347 for nine, compiled on and off over the three days, with Evans hitting 71 out of 84 this morning in two spells lasting 70 minutes. Then India came and went twice, and lost by an innings and 207 runs.

Trueman, bowling down a strong wind, took eight for 31 as India subsided to 58 all out, equalling their lowest score in Tests (against Australia at Brisbane in 1947). No one can remember an England fast bowler taking eight wickets in an innings before. India's showing in their second innings was little better. This time it was Bedser (5-27) and Lock (4-36) who skittled them out for 82, after Trueman had begun the collapse by having Roy caught for his second duck.

England's close fielding was outstanding, all 14 catches being accepted, many of them in spectacular fashion.

Second Test Final day: 30 December

South Africa beat Australia: First time in 42 years

From Melbourne

ANOTHER outstanding spell of bowling today from Hugh Tayfield inspired South Africa to their first victory over Australia for 42 years, as they won the second Test by 82 runs to level the rubber at one-all. His seven wickets for 81 in Australia's second innings gave him match figures of 13 for 165.

After Endean's marathon 162 not out - he was at the crease for seven and a half hours without giving a chance - Australia needed 373 to win. But when Tayfield destroyed their middle order, taking three wickets in a spell of nine maiden overs, they never looked like getting them.

Tayfield: Outstanding bowling performance.

County Championship
Northants v Essex: 15 July

Three double hundreds at Northampton: Several new records

From Northampton

ANOTHER batsman's dream pitch at Northampton doomed the Northants-Essex match to a draw and provided ideal conditions for several new records to be established.

Brookes (204 not out) and Barrick (211) carried their fifth-wicket stand to 347, beating Northants' previous best of 230 set 41 years ago, and their highest for any wicket, 321 against the South Africans last season.

Barrick, who scored 196 not out against Somerset in his last innings, was the more forceful of the pair, with 33 boundaries in a stay of five and a half hours. Brookes, who held the side together when Essex enjoyed some early successes, had been at the wicket for nine hours when Northants declared at 532 for six, 104 runs ahead.

As Avery of Essex had already made 224 - he added 294 for the second wicket with Gibb (132) - the game produced three individual double centuries.

First Test Second day: 17 October

India's last pair hit record 109: Tough début for Pakistan

From New Delhi

PAKISTAN found it tough going in their début as a Test-playing nation today when India's last pair put on 109 runs to take their first innings score to 372.

Adhikari, 12 not out overnight, advanced to 81 without being beaten and Ghulam Ahmed, in a hurricane innings of 50 in 80 minutes, smacked two 6's and five 4's as they set a new last-wicket record for India in Tests.

At the close, Pakistan were 90 for three, with Hanif Mohammed, the 17-year-old who made two centuries last week against North Zone in the first match of the tour, still there on 42.

[Hanif made 51, but Pakistan were bowled out for 150 and 152 the following day to lose by an innings and 70 runs.]

1953

24 Jan Bruce Pairaudeau makes 115 on his Test début for West Indies against India at Port of Spain, and shares in a 219 stand with Weekes (207) for the 5th wicket.

6 Feb At 17yr 239d, Ian Craig becomes the youngest player to represent Australia; scores 53 in his first innings, against South Africa at Melbourne in the 5th Test (adding 47 in 2nd innings).

12 Feb Neil Harvey (Australia) finishes the series against S.Africa with 834 runs (avge 92.66), 21 more than the series record set by Bradman (1931-32).

1 Apr West Indies compile their highest score in home Tests, 576, against India at Kingston in the drawn 5th Test, all the Three W's making 100s - Worrell 237, Walcott 118, Weekes 109. Running through the last 6 batsmen for 33 runs, Gupte (5-180) and Mankad (5-228) add a little respectability to their analyses.

24 Jul Alec Bedser takes 6-95 in Australia's 1st innings at Leeds to overtake Grimmett's world record of 216 Test wickets.

Bedser: World record

28 Jul Trevor Bailey plays another back-to-the-wall innings for England, 38 in 4hr 20min in the 4th Test at Leeds, to deny Australia the time to win and retain the Ashes.

31 Jul Slow left-armer Bob Berry takes all 10-102 (14-125 in match) for Lancs at Blackpool as Worcs fail by 19 runs to make the 337 they need to win. The last Lancs bowler to accomplish the feat was J.Briggs, also against Worcs, in 1900.

15 Dec South Africa beat New Zealand at Durban by an innings and 58 runs, their first victory at home for 23 years (and first NZ appearance in S.Africa).

TEST SERIES

Australia in England
E 1, D 4
South Africa in Australia
A 2, SA 2, D 1
South Africa in New Zealand
SA 1, D 1
India in West Indies
WI 1, D 4

Fifth Test Sixth day: 12 February

McLean sweeps South Africa to victory: Rubber squared

By Ray Robinson, in Melbourne

INSPIRED hitting by Roy McLean swept South Africa to a six-wicket triumph in the final Test here today and gave them the extreme satisfaction of squaring the rubber at two matches all. Not since D.R.Jardine's side won the Ashes 20 years ago have any international visitors to Australia done better.

McLean, a 22-year-old clerk from Pietermaritzburg, batted with his right eye blackened and scarred from an injury by a ball in the first innings. He came in at South Africa's darkest moment, when the third and fourth wickets had gone in fairly quick succession and 103 more runs were needed to reach the target of 294. Before scoring, he was dropped by the usually reliable Morris at mid-wicket hooking Benaud. Morris then twice missed the left-hander Keith.

Beset by the probing Johnston, McLean decided to eschew caution, and began to hit freely - a policy that made some South African supporters blanch, until they saw the drumbeat of boundaries knock all hope out of the Australians. He hit 14 boundaries in his 76 not out, made at a run a minute, which, with his 81 in the first innings, arguably forms the most brilliant Test double in Australia since the war.

As when England won on the same ground two years ago, Hassett good-humouredly bowled the last over, and when McLean hit his third four in five balls, the patient Keith (40) put his arm around his match-winning partner's shoulders.

First Test Second day: 7 March

McGlew returns to hit record 255 for South Africa

From Wellington

BACK in the side after a month out with a broken finger, opening batsman D.J.McGlew hit 255 not out against New Zealand here, allowing South Africa to declare at 524 for eight. His magnificent knock broke the South African Test record of 236, by Eric Rowan against England at Leeds in 1951.

With A.R.A.Murray (109), he put on 246 for the seventh wicket, another South African record in Tests - exactly double the previous mark of Deans and Nupen against England at Durban 25 years ago. At the close, New Zealand were 80 for one, with Sutcliffe still there on 57.

[New Zealand were twice bowled out for 172, and South Africa won by an innings and 180.]

County Championship Surrey v Warwick: 16 May

Warwick out twice in 2hr 25min

From the Oval

SURREY dismissed Warwickshire twice in two hours and 25 minutes here today, for 45 and 52, winning by an innings and 49 runs. The first Warwick innings, when the wicket was least obnoxious, lasted an hour and a quarter. Their second venture, when it was at its worst, survived five minutes less.

Between whiles, Surrey offered much firmer resistance, but their score of 146 came largely from enterprising batting by Constable (37) and desperate hitting from Surridge (three 6's in his 19), Laker (one 6 in 18) and Lock, who had to retire on 27 when he was hit on the head by a ball from Grove. He was taken to hospital, but is expected to be fit for Surrey's next match this week.

This remarkable victory was engineered by Alec Bedser and Laker. Bedser, using a cross-wind to attack the leg stump, took eight for 18 and four for 17. Laker, who did not bowl in the Warwick first innings, when Lock took two for nine, captured five for 29 in the second innings, including the second hat-trick of his career. A curiosity of the match is that not once did the Surrey bowlers hit the stumps. It was also the first time a match had been completed in one day at the Oval since 1857.

County Championship Somerset v Lancashire: 6 June

Lancs beat Somerset in a day

By Michael Melford

FOR the second time this season, a county match has been completed in a day, as Lancashire beat Somerset by an innings and 24 runs at Bath.

This is only the 13th one-day finish this century, and the 41st since 1831. Somerset, extraordinarily, have been involved six times previously, always on the wrong side, and Lancashire were also their conquerors in 1892, 1894 and 1925.

Last year the square here wore a fierce red hue and the ball turned prodigious distances. Now, though the wicket was relaid during the winter, comes this débâcle, particularly untimely because the match was for the benefit of H.T.Buse. A special meeting of the Somerset executive committee has been called to consider the state of the pitches for the Festival's other two matches.

There is a consoling note in the fact that, between the Somerset innings of 55 and 79, in which Tattersall took thirteen wickets for 69, Buse himself took six for 41.

First Test Third day: 13 June

Another 7 for Bedser: England in strong position

By E.W.Swanton, at Nottingham

AS the world knows, Bedser 'did it again', magnificently, incredibly. His seven for 44 in Australia's second innings reduced them to 123 all out and a lead of only 228. And in the fateful evening period, England endured from five o'clock onwards and made 42 for the loss of Kenyon's wicket.

A matter of 187 runs now lies between England and what would be only the fifth victory over Australia in this country in 40 years. One's feeling on leaving the ground this evening was that England's position was altogether too good to be true. Resuming this morning at 92 for six, England added a further 52 runs, as much as could be reasonably expected, and Lindwall finished with five for 57.

However, the wicket was behaving impeccably, and England had no relief bowling to supplement Bedser and Bailey, who had bowled 82 overs between them in Australia's first innings, when Bedser took seven for 55.

The vital breakthrough came when Bedser had Hassett caught by Hutton for five. Australia were 44 for two, but more importantly they had lost the prop and stay of their batting, and it sowed in Australian minds a distrust of the wicket that was reflected in all that happened subsequently. Only Morris (60) batted with any degree of confidence, and as soon as he went, sixth out at 81, the Australians made what they could as quickly as they could in order to get England in again at all costs.

[The match finished in anticlimax as a draw, heavy rain preventing further play until 4.30 on the last day.]

Second Test Final day: 30 June

Watson and Bailey are men of the hour: Second Test saved

By E.W.Swanton, at Lord's

THERE are excellent cricketers, and there are excellent Test match cricketers, and sometimes there is a great gulf dividing them. It was England's fortune today that there came together in the crisis two men who seemed to grow in stature with the fame of the opposition - Watson, of Yorkshire, and Bailey, of Essex.

They became joined on the last morning of the second Test at 20 minutes to one, after Watson and Compton (33), who had come together last night when England were 12 for three, had withstood the Australian bowling for another 70 minutes. Despite all the bowling variety that Hassett could call upon, and despite the inevitable wear in the wicket, which operated particularly against the left-hander Watson, they declined to be separated until 10 minutes to six, having added 163. By this time, the prospect of an Australian victory, which, when they came together, had seemed just a matter of time, had virtually receded to nothing.

The second hero, Bailey (71), followed Watson (109), the first, quickly into the pavilion, so it still needed another half an hour's resistance - by F.R.Brown, with a forcing 28 out of character with all that had gone before, Evans (11 not out) and Wardle, who safely played the last four balls of the match from Benaud.

Fifth Test Final day: 19 August

Cricket supremacy has passed to England: Elusive Ashes triumph after 20 years

By E.W.Swanton, at the Oval

Compton hits the winning run.

THE FIFTH TEST, which turned sharply England's way when Australia were battling against the spin bowlers yesterday, duly ended in victory here shortly before 3 o'clock this afternoon, that elusive victory which has been awaited ever since D.R.Jardine's side won the Ashes 20 years ago.

The margin of eight wickets was conclusive enough, but the result was not gained without a fight almost to the last ball, between Edrich, May and Compton on the one hand and Johnston, Lindwall and Miller, supported as magnificently as ever in the field, on the other.

Johnston bowled today without respite, until Hassett came on as at Melbourne on a similar occasion in 1951 and again earlier this year against South Africa, to bowl a final comedy over. Lindwall likewise from the Pavilion end kept up a ceaseless fast and accurate attack, apart from five overs from Miller, until he gave the ball finally to Morris, off whom Compton hit the last four needed. It took two hours and 40 minutes of resolute batsmanship to make the final 94 runs, May's wicket being the Australians' only reward.

All this was as it should be, a hard struggle to the finish, and the final scenes were equally fitting, as at the end some 15,000 clamoured in front of the pavilion. Hutton and Hassett obliged with speeches, and the players were cheered on their respective balconies.

It all took one back 27 years to the August evening when for the first time since the First War Australia's colours were lowered in a Test rubber, and the crowd let themselves go as if a reproach had been wiped away.

Then, as now, three rubbers had been won against England, and in 1926 it was universally said that the change in tide would be all to the good of Australian cricket. Again now, after the warning jolt of the drawn series against Cheetham's admirable young South Africans in the last Australian summer, it is established that supremacy has passed to other hands. It will prove to be the spur that has been needed in Sydney, Melbourne and Adelaide, and one can almost savour the unholy relish with which the next M.C.C. side will be received at Perth in October next year.

Scores: Australia 275 (Lindwall 62, Hassett 53; Trueman 4-86) and 162 (Lock 5-45, Laker 4-75), England 306 (Hutton 82, Bailey 64; Lindwall 4-70) and 132-2 (Edrich 55 not out).

Second Test
Second day: 26 December

Bert Sutcliffe hurt: Hits seven 6s

From Johannesburg

LED from the field with an injured head before scoring, Bert Sutcliffe returned from hospital to save New Zealand from following on in the second Test with South Africa here.

The lobe of Sutcliffe's ear was split and the bone behind it injured when he was hit by a ball from Adcock, who was also responsible for hospitalising L.S.M.Miller. Struck on the chest by the South African fast bowler, Miller was coughing blood, but he also returned to the crease.

When Sutcliffe came back, he launched a furious attack on the South African bowling, hitting seven 6's and four 4's in his 80 not out before he ran out of partners.

[Needing 233 to win in their second innings, New Zealand were 75-3, but lost their last 7 wickets for 25 runs, Adcock taking 5-43 to deny them their first ever Test win.]

1954

15 Jan Umpire Burke's wife and son are physically attacked, but fortunately not hurt, after he gives local hero Holt out lbw when 6 short of a début 100 against England at Kingston.

17-23 Mar For the second time the Three W's all score 100s in a Test innings - Weekes 206 and Worrell 167, adding 338 for the 3rd wicket, Walcott 124 - as West Indies amass 681-8 dec in the 4th Test against England at Port of Spain, but England reply with 100s from May (135) and Compton (133) in their 537 and the match is drawn, 1,528 runs being scored for 24 wickets.

10-15 Jun Pakistan's first official Test against England, at Lord's, is ruined by the weather, little more than 8 hours' play being possible.

24 Jul Pakistan's M.E.Z.Ghazali is twice out without scoring in two hours at the crease against England in the drawn third Test, at Manchester.

26 Nov-1 Dec Australia, put in to bat in Brisbane by Len Hutton in the first Test, amass 601-8 dec (Harvey 162, Morris 153) and beat England by an innings and 154 runs.

31 Dec Keith Miller shocks England on the first morning of the 3rd Test, at Melbourne, taking 3-5 in 9 overs with 8 maidens.

TEST SERIES

England in West Indies
WI 2, E 2, D 1
Pakistan in England
E 1, P 1, D 2
New Zealand in South Africa
SA 4, D 1

Fourth Test Second day: 30 January

Tayfield takes six for 13 and New Zealand follow on

From Johannesburg

TAYFIELD, the South African off-spinner, enjoyed a remarkable spell here today, taking five New Zealand wickets in 32 balls without conceding a run. He finished with six for 13 off 14 overs as New Zealand were bowled out for 79 and forced to follow on 156 runs behind.

On a pitch that took little spin, the New Zealanders were completely demoralised by Tayfield's bowling. In their second innings, Adcock took a quick wicket and New Zealand were eight for one at the close.

[Adcock was the destroyer in the second innings, taking 5-45, and South Africa won easily by 9 wickets.]

Third Test Third day: 27 February

Bottles thrown at Georgetown: England can swing Test rubber

By E.W.Swanton, in British Guiana

UNFORTUNATELY, the exciting cricket at Georgetown today was held up for 10 minutes near the end by an outburst of crowd disorder that was not only disagreeable in itself, but very likely prevented England from capturing the last West Indies wicket.

The crowd here has a habit of clapping softly and rhythmically when one or two runs are needed to reach a round figure of some kind. When the partnership between McWatt and Holt had added 98, the applause started, and it rose to a crescendo as McWatt went for the second run that would have made 100. It was a hazardous run, and a fast pick-up and throw to the top of the stumps by May enabled Evans to run out McWatt by perhaps a couple of yards. McWatt, having seen the umpire's signal that he expected, just went on running to the pavilion.

There was quite a pause, and Ramadhin had got to the wicket before a row in one of the public stands behind square-leg was followed by a rapid barrage of soft-drink bottles hurled on to the field behind Menzies, the square-leg umpire. Within a few seconds there were hundreds of them. A few isolated missiles landed on other parts of the field near the boundary, and the uproar became such that there was no question for the moment of the game being continued.

An outburst of bottle-throwing from a section of the crowd holds up the Georgetown Test.

Officials came on to the field as mounted police went to ring off the section causing the trouble. After a parley with the chairman of the British Guiana Board of Control, Hutton waved his team back to their positions and indicated that, bottles or no bottles, play would go on. This decision undoubtedly saved further disorder which, so a stranger felt, might have led to more serious things, so easily are West Indian feelings roused.

Earlier, thrilling batting by Weekes (94), a collapse started by Statham (4-63), and then the eighth-wicket stand between McWatt (54) and the crippled Holt (38 not out) had made the occasion memorable. West Indies, on 241 for nine, are still 194 behind England, and it may be taken that, barring accidents, Hutton will make them follow on.

[West Indies did follow on and, despite another brave knock from Holt (64), lost by nine wickets.]

Fifth Test Final day: 3 April

England win final Test with a flourish: Fighting century by Walcott

By E.W.Swanton, at Kingston, Jamaica

THE Test series was brought to a stylish and becoming end this evening at Sabina Park with a charming piece of batting by Peter May. England's victory by nine wickets made a draw of the rubber with two successes to each side and one match unfinished.

Fast and well as King and Worrell bowled when England batted with just over an hour to play and 72 runs standing between them and victory, May and Watson attacked. The runs were made in a stream of fours, and when the winning hit came 10 minutes from time the spectators expressed themselves with the utmost generosity.

They like to see the ball hit in this part of the world, and altogether the crowd had a memorable last day. The hero from their angle was Walcott. His magnificent hundred (116), painfully made after he had been hit above the wrist by Bailey, was as good as anything achieved in the series for West Indies. Its rival, perhaps, was Walcott's own double hundred in Barbados, an innings likewise of phlegm and courage as well as technical proficiency.

West Indies would have made a longer fight of this match if they had not been deprived of King's bowling half-way through the first innings. But the game was really lost and won by Bailey's bowling (7-34) in the West Indies first innings.

To have squared the rubber after losing the first two matches is an extraordinary achievement, and one in which, to be honest, no English camp-follower could have had the slightest confidence when the team left Barbados. Much of the credit belongs to Hutton, and it was fitting that in the final effort one of his finest innings (205) should play so large a part. He easily topped the England Test averages, with 677 runs at 96.71, while Walcott scored 698 for West Indies at 87.25, in what was a high-scoring series.

Second Test Second day: 2 July

Compton's Test highest foredooms Pakistan: Hanif fightback

By E.W.Swanton, at Nottingham

THE Test wicket at Trent Bridge is of a wonderful ease and trueness, and Compton on the kill is an utterly devastating opponent. As he shows periodically in this phase of his maturity, he can still demoralise and demolish good bowling with strokes both orthodox and improvised at a pace and in a manner altogether unique - one might almost say immoral.

Today all the circumstances conspired to set the stage for one of these Compton performances, and he filled the bill with a degree of success that became literally embarrassing as the weary Pakistan bowlers wheeled automatically away and the fieldsmen chased the hits to all parts of a large, unyielding field.

Beginning at 121 for 2, just 36 runs behind Pakistan's first innings, England by luncheon had reached 262 for 3. At tea it was 495 for 4, and 45 minutes later Sheppard, captain in place of the unfit Hutton, declared at 558 for 6. And after this, Hanif gave a beautiful exhibition of stroke play for 46 not out as Pakistan progressed to 59 without loss, 342 behind.

Simpson (101) completed his hundred this morning, and then for an hour and a half, divided by lunch, the stage was taken by Compton and Graveney, with Graveney (84) the more forceful player in a stand of 154, charming everyone until he was caught at cover, driving.

Compton was now well past his hundred and throwing his bat at the ball. With the patient Bailey (36 not out), who cleverly gave him the bowling, he added 192 for the fifth wicket, of which he scored all but 27. He was finally out for 278, his highest Test innings and also a record for a Nottingham Test, bowled by Khalid Hassan, at 16 years 352 days the youngest ever Test player.

[England won by an innings and 129 runs.]

Fourth Test Final day: 17 August

Pakistan win and share rubber: Bowling too good for England

By E.W.Swanton, at the Oval

PAKISTAN this morning won, by 24 runs, the victory that they had brought near in half an hour's fine bowling last evening. The last four England batsmen, whose task it was to make the 43 more needed to snatch the game from the fire, never seemed likely to do so against the fire and accuracy of the fast-medium attack of Fazal Mahmood and Mahmood Hussain.

So England lost their last eight wickets for 34 runs, the damage done yesterday when they appeared anxious to make the 168 required before the close. Fazal took six for 46 (12 for 99 in the match) and Mahmood one for 32 (5 for 90).

[That England were held in the series was remarkable when the averages are examined: No Pakistan batsman reached 70 in the 4 Tests, Hanif topping the averages with 22.62, a figure exceeded by 5 England batsmen, led by Compton (90.60); Fazal's 20 wickets cost him 20.40 apiece, an average bettered by 4 England bowlers, notably Wardle, with 20 at 8.80.]

The jubilant Pakistan team are cheered off the field after drawing their first series against England.

County Championship Surrey v Worcs: 26 August

Lowest total in Championship match as Surrey win title again

By Michael Melford, at the Oval

SURREY brought the County Championship to the Oval for the third year in succession with a remarkable and historic win over Worcester in two days. In a match that occupied only 4 hours 50 minutes of actual playing time, Surrey's score yesterday of 92 for three declared was enough to give them victory by an innings and 27 runs.

They mopped up the remaining seven Worcester wickets today (Devereux retired hurt) in an hour for only 27 runs. Worcester's second innings total of 40 made their tally for the match 65 for 19 wickets, and meant that only 157 runs were scored in the whole match. This is the lowest aggregate for a completed match ever recorded in the County Championship.

Remarkable, too, are the bowling figures of Lock - 6 for 5 in the match (5.3-4-2-5 and 10-7-3-1). Laker took six for 30 in the match, Bedser five for 19. May made the top score, with 39 not out for Surrey, while only Yarnold reached double figures for Worcester - 14 not out in their second innings.

Thus Surrey reached the climax of a wonderful run of devastating cricket and, as they will be the first to admit, good fortune. The run began on 28 July, when they stood eighth in the table, 46 points behind Yorkshire with two matches in hand. On the wet wickets that have persisted since, they have won eight out of nine matches.

Second Test Final day: 22 December

Tyson and Statham wreck Australia's hopes: Test a triumph for 4 young players

By E.W.Swanton, in Sydney

ENGLAND'S palpitating victory by 38 runs here this afternoon has achieved several things at one stroke. There is no question it has made the rubber. One must go back to 1933 to find the sides approaching the third match all-square in Australia. The match has made a scintillating new reputation, that of Frank Tyson, whose 10 wickets were the reward for as fine a display of sustained speed and stamina as I have ever seen in an English fast bowler. Need more be said than that in half a century only three English fast bowlers have ever taken 10 wickets in a match against Australia?

Again, it has been a victory of the younger generation of cricketers - Tyson, May, Statham and Cowdrey are all under 25. And by winning, Hutton has diverted from himself the onslaught of criticism that greeted the decision not to play Bedser.

When the cricket was continued on this fifth morning, Australia were 72 for two, needing another 153 runs to win. Hutton went on the attack immediately, and although it was Tyson who got the major results, Statham's gallant efforts were almost as valuable. Only Harvey (92 not out), whose magnificent innings set off the frailty of the rest, could resist them.

Tyson accounted for both Burke and Hole in his second, momentous over, in each case beating them with the sheer speed of his yorker. Australia were now 77 for four and they never recovered from this double blow.

Tyson took six for 85 (10-130 in the match), Statham three for 45 (5-128). Melbourne at the New Year will be the focus of all Australia and the whole world of cricket.

1955

1-4 Jan The first official Test played in Pakistan sets the pattern for the series, five dour, defensive draws.

28 Mar England dismiss New Zealand for 26, the lowest ever innings total in Test cricket, to win the 2nd Test by an innings and 20 runs at Auckland. Only Sutcliffe (11) reaches double figures, and the wickets are taken by Appleyard 4-7, Statham 3-9, Tyson 2-10 and Wardle 1-0 (in 5 overs). The feat goes unreported in the English Press, which is in the throes of a long strike.

27 Jun Brian Statham bowls throughout South Africa's 2nd innings (111) for 7-39 in 29 overs to give England victory by 71 runs.

12 Jul Alec Bedser plays his last Test, against South Africa at Old Trafford, taking 4 wickets and finishing with a record 236 in Tests.

26 Jul Trevor Bailey, opening for England, spends 2 hours scoring 8, including 79 minutes without scoring, but South Africa win by 224 runs. It is umpire Frank Chester's last Test, after a record 48.

18 Aug Derek Shackleton, who yesterday suffered in Hilton's hat-trick, takes 8-4 for Hants against Somerset at Weston-s-Mare and then 6-25 in the 2nd innings as Hants win by 264 runs on the second day of a rain-hit match.

26 Aug Surrey beat Sussex by an innings and 8 runs to clinch the County Championship for the 4th time in a row, eventually with 23 wins, 5 defeats and no draws.

29 Oct Imtiaz Ahmed (209) and Waqar Hassan (189) put on 308 for Pakistan's 7th wicket against New Zealand at Karachi, second only to the Atkinson/Depeiza stand for West Indies in May.

TEST SERIES

England in Australia
E 3, A 1, D 1
England in New Zealand
England 2
South Africa in England
E 3, SA 2
India in Pakistan
Drawn 5
Australia in West Indies
A 3, D 2
New Zealand in Pakistan
P 2, D 1

Third Test: Fifth day: 5 January

Magnificent Tyson hero of Test triumph: Australia routed by pace attack

By E.W.Swanton, in Melbourne

THE suddenness and utter completeness of Australia's collapse today, which gave England victory by 28 runs, will rank as a startling curiosity many years ahead. The last eight Australian wickets went down, six of them to the formidable Tyson, for 36 runs.

Tyson and Statham have shown themselves once more, as they did at Sydney, altogether too good for Australia's batsmen when there has been anything in the wicket to tilt the balance.

Tyson's has been the more dramatic part. His analysis in this second innings has never been bettered by a fast bowler in a match between England and Australia. But they have worked essentially in harness as a pair, and each has generally bowled better when his counterpart was at the other end. Tyson has taken 19 wickets in the two matches, Statham 12.

Frank 'Typhoon' Tyson.

The result this morning was virtually resolved after five overs, Tyson having taken the wickets of Harvey, Benaud and Miller. Australia had started the day on 75 for two, needing another 165 runs to win. Now they were 87 for five and in a hopeless position.

In the 13th over of the morning, and after 79 minutes' play, Tyson had Johnston caught at the wicket by the brilliant Evans with a final agile effort, and Australia were all out for 111. This morning, Tyson had taken six wickets for 16 in 51 balls (7-27 in the innings, 9-95 in the match), Statham two for 19 in 48 (2-38 innings, 7-98 match).

Fourth Test Fifth day: 2 Feb

England retain Ashes with great victory: Statham and Tyson again the heroes

By E.W.Swanton, at Adelaide

NINE weeks ago this evening, Australia inflicted upon Len Hutton's team one of the more conclusive defeats of Ashes history by an innings and 154 runs. If anyone on that depressing day at Brisbane had expressed the belief that England would have won the series by the end of the Adelaide Test, he would have been supposed an insane optimist. Yet there it is. The thing has happened, and no Australian doubts that the English victory by five wickets here today is thoroughly deserved.

This fifth day's play was full of excitements, of disappointments, of surging hopes, and long suspense. The bowling out of Australia for 111 appeared to foreshadow a task - the making of 94 runs - to be achieved without any prolonged difficulty. But there came a great piece of cricket by a great cricketer, Keith Miller, who sent back Edrich, Hutton and Cowdrey in 20 balls, leaving England stunned at 18 for three. And when he caught May (26) off Johnston, England were 49 for four, and a collapse was not out of the question.

In fact, there followed a partnership between Compton (34 not out) and Bailey (15) that practically signed and sealed the contract, and by 20 minutes past five the crowd were applauding the first victory by an England side in a series in Australia since 1933.

The turning point of the series, of course, was the fine bowling of Tyson and Statham on the last day at Sydney. And it has been these two, with significant help on occasion from Appleyard and Bailey, who have completed the job. In Australia's second-innings collapse, they took three wickets apiece (as did Appleyard). Of the 66 Australian wickets credited to bowlers in the four Tests so far, Tyson and Statham have taken 43 between them. No more need be said.

Fourth Test Fourth day: 18 May

Record 7th-wicket stand by West Indies: Atkinson and Depeiza bat all day

By Ray Robinson, at Bridgetown

A RECORD seventh-wicket partnership gave the fourth match of this series a surprising twist and kept the Australians in the field all day without a wicket.

Atkinson (215 not out), the West Indies captain, and Depeiza (122 not out), the wicket-keeper, have taken the score to 494 for six in reply to Australia's 668, and are still engaged in a stand that has so far put on 347 runs.

This beats the West Indies seventh-wicket Test record (Headley/Grant, 1934-35) by 200 runs, the world Test record (McGlew/Murray, 1953) by 101 runs, and the first-class record of Ranjitsinhji and W.Newham (for Sussex against Essex in 1902) by four runs.

Atkinson, the more dominant partner, reached his century in a little over two hours, shortly after lunch, and the Australians now began to get worried as none of their bowlers had any effect. Johnson had run through his complete string. Another new ball was taken after tea when the total was 427, and it is doubtful if Lindwall and Miller have ever opened an attack with such defensive fields.

[The stand was broken without addition next day, when Benaud bowled Depeiza; West Indies were all out for 510 and the match was drawn, but not before Atkinson, who made 219, had taken 5-56 in Australia's 2nd innings.]

First Test Fourth day:13 June

Tyson pace earns innings victory for England: South Africa crash

From Nottingham

ENGLAND won the first Test this evening in three and a half hours' playing time by an innings and five runs. With play delayed until one o'clock because of the state of the field, South Africa resumed at 46 for no wicket. The openers took their stand to 73, when Goddard was unluckily run out backing up, Wardle deflecting Statham's throw on to the wicket with his foot. After that, it was nearly all Tyson, who took six for 11 today in 13.3 overs as South Africa crumbled to 148 all out.

No one else derived any help from the wicket, but by sheer speed Tyson contrived to make the odd ball lift. His final spell of 7.3 overs brought him five wickets for five runs as he ripped through the South African defences.

Fifth Test Fourth day: 15 June

Benaud hits Test 100 in 78 minutes: Australia 758-8

By Ray Robinson, in Kingston, Jamaica

AUSTRALIA, who had started off losing their first two wickets for seven runs on Monday, made their highest Test score here today when they passed 729 in the final Test against West Indies.

A hurricane hundred in 78 minutes by Richie Benaud - the third fastest in Test cricket - finally carried them past their record mark. When Benaud was out for 121, Australia declared at 758 for eight, 401 ahead of West Indies.

Australia piled on the runs all day. By lunch, Miller (109) and Archer (128) both had centuries to their credit and the total had been taken to 574 for four. They went on to set a new Australian fifth-wicket record of 220. In the afternoon, Benaud showed no mercy to the tired West Indian bowlers. His innings included two sixes and 15 fours.

It was the fifth century in this mammoth innings as McDonald (127) and Harvey (204) had put on 295 for the 3rd wicket - a record in Test cricket.

[Australia went on to win by an innings and 82 runs on the 6th day, but not until Walcott had set two outstanding Test records with his 110 in West Indies' 2nd innings, becoming the first player to score two 100s in a match twice in one series and the first to hit five 100s in a series.]

Neil Harvey: Double century and Test record 3rd-wicket stand.

Fifth Test Fourth day: 17 August

Laker and Lock clinch rubber 3-2 for England

By E.W.Swanton, at the Oval

A swift, sad South African collapse that began just before one o'clock and was over almost on the hour decided the fifth Test today and established England as the winners of a close-fought and an engaging and exciting rubber - the first ever in England to produce five definite results.

Waite played a very fine innings of 60, which from the first stroke must have suggested to every South African sympathiser present that the 244 required to win was not nearly so steep a mountain as the early successes of Laker and Lock had made it seem.

It was perhaps always probable that, on a wicket on which the ball could be made to turn almost throughout, England would be just the more likely to win. Winning the toss, too, meant a good deal, and England did have the better of the wicket.

Again it was an innings (89 not out) of much character and the intensest sort of concentration by May that gave his bowlers the chance to do the job. Over the series, May has averaged 72 for a total of 582 runs.

South Africa dispatched the England 10 and 11 this morning before May could substantially increase the overnight England score of 195 for eight. Tayfield's final analysis, five for 60, represented an excellent piece of bowling and fittingly capped for him another successful series.

South Africa went in just before noon in search of the largest total of the match. It was half an hour before Laker came on, with Lock 10 minutes later, and they soon had South Africa in the deepest trouble. Some of the desperate strokes the South Africans played suggested the wicket was truly wicked - which in fact it never was. In 15 minutes they were 33 for four, with the Surrey spinners taking two wickets each.

Opener McGlew was still there and, with Waite, proceeded to tide South Africa over any further trouble before lunch. But Lock trapped him lbw two runs later for 19 and South Africa were 59 for five, with virtually all hope gone. Cheetham and then Mansell, the latter for nearly 90 minutes, defended stoutly while Waite pushed the score along, but this was only to delay the inevitable, as Laker (5-56) and Lock (4-62) spun England to their 92-run victory with more than a day to spare.

Third Test Final day: 12 July

South Africa keep rubber alive with thrilling victory

By E.W.Swanton, at Old Trafford

SOUTH AFRICA won a wonderful game this evening by three wickets with barely five minutes to spare, and in so doing breathed new life into the rubber after losing the first two Tests.

The bare facts bespeak the excitement that built up during the afternoon and reached its climax when with 15 minutes left it seemed, almost for the first time, that the incredible might happen and England win after all. Three wickets were left, with 10 runs needed, and Tyson and Lock were bowling as menacingly as they knew.

In an atmosphere of utmost tension, six runs slowly came as the clock moved towards half past six. Then Waite, who had already square-cut Tyson to the boundary, drove him handsomely past the sinister figure of Lock at silly mid-off for the winning hit.

When the day began, England, with six wickets in hand, were 13 runs in front. But at 3.20, with only the injured Evans to come, their lead was a mere 96. "Only" Evans! With a little finger broken in two places, he made 36 thrilling runs in a last-wicket stand with Bailey of 48.

Thus South Africa found themselves obliged to make 145 runs in 132 minutes. Thanks in chief to a brilliant 50 by McLean and a steadfast 48 by McGlew, they got them - just.

Scores: England 284 (Compton 158) and 381 (May 117, Compton 71, Cowdrey 50; Heine 5-86), S.Africa 521-8d (McGlew 104 not, Waite 113, Winslow 108) and 145-7 (McLean 50).

1956

7 Jan Vinoo Mankad (231) and Pankaj Roy (173) set a new world 1st-wicket record in Tests of 413 for India against New Zealand at Madras, beating the Hutton/Washbrook 359 made in 1948 against South Africa, and India declare on 537-3.

9,11 Jun In the first county match held at Stroud, Smales (Notts) takes all 10 Glos wickets for 66, but Glos win by 9 wickets.

26 Jun Gil Langley (Australia) sets a new Test record with 9 dismissals (8ct, 1st) in the match against England at Lord's (2nd Test), including 5 in an innings (a record he shares with W.A. Oldfield) for the 3rd time,.

1-3 Aug As if they haven't seen enough of Laker at the Old Trafford Test, the Australians are at the Oval the very next day to play Surrey again. The first day is lost, but Laker takes 4-41 and 1-17 in a drawn match.

23-28 Aug Having retained the Ashes, England win the rubber with a draw at the Oval in another match badly hit by rain. The third inspirational England selection for a comeback, Compton - after the removal of his right knee-cap last November - makes 94 and 35 not out, and the inevitable Laker takes 4-80 and 3-8 in a match dominated by England. Laker finishes with 46 wickets (avge 9.60), second only to S.F.Barnes (49 v South Africa in 1913-14) in a Test series.

11-17 Oct The first day of Australia's Test against Pakistan in Karachi produces only 95 runs, a record low for a complete day of Test cricket: Australia 80, Pakistan 15-2. Pakistan go on to win by 9 wickets, Fazal Mahmood taking 6-34 and 7-80, Khan Mohammad 4-43 and 3-69.

26 Dec Peter Richardson makes the slowest 100 in Test history - 488min - for England against South Africa in the first Test held at the New Wanderers ground, Johannesburg.

TEST SERIES

Australia in England
E 2, A 1, D 2
New Zealand in India
I 2, D 3
West Indies in New Zealand
WI 3, NZ 1
Australia in Pakistan
Pakistan 1
Australia in India
A 2, D 1

Fourth Test Final day: 13 March

New Zealand gain first Test victory: West Indies out for 77

By Michael Melford

IT is hard to believe that the Test match New Zealand won at Auckland yesterday against West Indies was the first they have ever won since they started playing Tests in January 1929. Crowds flocked to Eden Park on the fourth and last afternoon to see New Zealand clinch victory by bowling West Indies out for 77.

It is ironic that New Zealand should finally attain success in what must have seemed their darkest hour, whereas victory eluded them in other, more prosperous, times.

New Zealand had lost 22 and drew 21 of their 43 previous Tests. And the side that set out for Pakistan last September had as its most recent Test memory the humiliation of being bowled out for 26 by England. All this was forgotten when Cave and Beard completed West Indies' rout yesterday to give New Zealand a 190-run victory.

Scores: NZ 255 (Reid 84; Dewdney 5-21) & 157-9d (Atkinson 7-53), WI 145 (Furlonge 64; MacGibbon 4-44, Cave 4-22) & 77 (Cave 4-21, Beard 3-22, Alabaster 2-4).

Tourist match Surrey v Australians: 16 May

Laker all 10-88 against Australians

From the Oval

J.C.Laker, 34, Surrey's Yorkshire-born off-spin bowler, took all 10 wickets for 88 runs against the Australians at the Oval. He bowled unchanged for 46 overs, 18 of them maidens.

The 'all-10' feat had not been achieved by an Englishman against the Australians since E.Barratt, also of Surrey and also at the Oval, took 10 for 43 for the Players on the first Australian visit to England, in 1878.

To add to the drama, Laker did not want to bowl after tea, having taken four wickets. During the interval, he said to Stuart Surridge, the Surrey captain: "I'm tired. Give me a rest." Surridge replied: "No, Jim. There are more wickets in this Australian innings for you." So Laker bowled on and achieved the performance of a lifetime. Later, Surridge described Laker's performance as "the most wonderful piece of off-spin bowling I have ever seen."

At the other end for much of Laker's 4½-hour spell, Lock toiled away without success, sending down 33 overs at the cost of 100 runs. McDonald, the Australian opener, made 89 and Keith Miller 57 not out. Surrey were 34 without loss at the close in reply to Australia's 259.

[Laker scored 43 in Surrey's 347 (Constable 109), but it was Lock, with 7-49, who was chiefly responsible for bowling the Australians out for 107, Laker taking 2-42, and Surrey, with an easy 10-wickets win, became the first county for 44 years to beat an Australian team.]

County Championship Kent v Surrey: 10 July

Now Lock has all 10: 4 for 0 spell wrecks Kent

By Michael Melford, at Blackheath

IN just under 25 minutes this morning, Lock added the last four Kent wickets to the six he had taken yesterday and joined the 60 other bowlers who have taken all 10 wickets in an innings. His 10 for 54 makes Lock's contribution to Kent's defeat by an innings and 173 runs 16 wickets for 83.

This is the third time this season a bowler has taken all 10 in an innings. Smales did it last month and Lock's team-mate Laker in May, against the Australians. Laker was not playing today.

During most of this very fine piece of bowling, the wicket was by no means impossibly difficult. This morning, however, the ball did turn and lift much quicker, and Lock, fresher now, swept through the Kent tail, taking the four wickets in 19 balls without yielding a run.

Lock: Emulated team-mate Laker.

County Championship Lancs v Leics: 17 July

Lancs win without losing a wicket: Unique achievement

From Old Trafford

LANCASHIRE'S achievement in defeating Leicester at Old Trafford today by 10 wickets without themselves losing a wicket is without parallel in first-class cricket.

Lancashire's opening pair needed to score only 226 runs between them, with six runs coming in extras. Wharton made 87 and 33, Dyson 75 and 31. After rain washed out play on Saturday, Leicester were bowled out yesterday in their first innings for 108, Statham taking four for 32, Hilton three for 19. Lancs then declared at 166 for nought, made in three hours. Leicester made a promising start to their second innings, but lost their last eight wickets for 28 and were all out for 122 (Hilton 5-23, Statham 3-36), leaving Lancashire to make 65 - and history.

Third Test Final day: 17 July

England's Leeds victory makes cricket history

By E.W.Swanton, at Headingley

ENGLAND beat Australia this afternoon by an innings and 42 runs, and made history in doing so, since in nearly 60 years it is their first victory over their oldest enemy on this ground.

Yesterday we had seen some admirable batting by Miller, Benaud and Harvey, keeping Laker and Lock at bay in conditions in which England always expect to enmesh Australia. Today's collapse was due, I suppose, to the ball doing its work more quickly and to Laker's taking charge and proving, in the long run, irresistible.

With an analysis of 11 for 113, Laker joins Washbrook (98) - making his first Test appearance for over five years - and May (101) as England's men of the match. There is little doubt that Laker has reached the full peak of his skill in his benefit year. I have seen him bowl in many Test matches, but never better than he bowled on Friday (5-58) and again this morning (6-55). Lock's results were less spectacular, but it is as a combination that these two are so formidable, just as it was the partnership of Statham and Tyson that destroyed Australia in the last rubber. Lock's seven wickets included Harvey both times, and it must be remembered that today Laker probably had the better bowling end.

Fourth Test Final day: 31 July

Laker takes 19-90: 10-wicket haul completes rout of Australia as England retain Ashes

By E.W.Swanton, at Old Trafford

The only proper formal announcement of the result of the fourth Test is that J.C.Laker defeated Australia by an innings and 170 runs.

Laker followed his capture of nine first innings wickets - itself a record for England against Australia - with all 10 in the second. What is left in the vocabulary to describe and applaud such a tour de force? It is quite fabulous.

Once, just before the First War, S.F.Barnes took 17-159 for England against South Africa in Johannesburg. Other than that, no bowler has taken more than 15 in a Test before, and none more than nine in a Test innings. What is more, in the whole history of first-class cricket, no one has taken more than 17 wickets in a match before.

Laker walks off modestly after his historic performance.

But Laker, in 51.2 overs, has added a 10 for 53 to his 10 for 88 against this same Australian side for Surrey. And in this Test, he has actually taken 19 for 90. His first-innings performance was phenomenal enough, but its merit was perhaps clouded by the deficiencies of the Australian batting, as also by the palaver over the condition of the wicket.

There was no room whatever for argument about his bowling today. He bowled 36 overs, practically non-stop apart from the taking of the new ball, all the time attacking the stumps and compelling the batsman to play, never wilting or falling short in terms of either length or direction. Nor was he mechanical. Each ball presented the batsman with a separate problem. Laker never let up, and neither for an instant could his adversary.

It is, of course, scarcely less remarkable that while Laker was building up new heights of fame at one end, Lock was toiling just as zealously, albeit fruitlessly, at the other. On a wicket on which one famous cricketer captured 19 wickets, the other, scarcely less successful and dangerous, taking one day with the other, in 69 overs had one for 106.

The comparison between the figures is in one sense unarguable evidence of the greatness of Laker's performance. If the wicket had been a natural graveyard for batsmen, it is inconceivable that Lock, even below his peak, even with the other arm tied to his side, would not have taken more than one wicket.

Applause for Laker, but applause too for McDonald, who, in his long vigil - 337 minutes for 89 - rose to the occasion for Australia and fought as hard as any man could do to win his side the respite of a draw. So long as he was in, the odds were still fairly balanced. When he was beaten at last, directly after tea, one of Oakman's five catches in the match, the latter-end batsmen carried on in the same spirit. There was a bare hour to go when Maddox, the No.11, played back and slightly across to Laker, fell leg before, and advanced up the wicket to shake the hero by the hand.

Fourth Test Second day: 27 July

Laker takes 9-37 on treacherous pitch: Australia follow on

By E.W.Swanton, at Old Trafford

TODAY England took a giant step towards retaining the Ashes. They took their score on to 459, bowled Australia out for 84, Laker taking an historic nine wickets for 37, and then captured a further wicket before the close after Australia followed on.

The Old Trafford wicket was awkward, and in spasms treacherous, without being quite the villain the Australian scorecard might suggest. However, the character of the wicket, dusty and lacking grass, was doubly unfortunate in that this Test followed Leeds, where the Australians found the same conditions. From their angle, it must be considered at best a sinister coincidence.

Sheppard, 59 overnight, completed his century this morning, batting nearly five hours in all for his 113, while Evans impudently hit Johnson and Benaud all over the place for 47 in 30 minutes, as 62 runs were added for the seventh wicket.

Australia went in just after 2.30 and made a steady start against Statham and Bailey. With the score at nine, Laker came on at the Station end at 3 o'clock, shortly followed by Lock. Just before four, May changed his spinners round, and as soon as Laker came on at the Stretford end, McDonald (32) was snapped up by Lock at square leg, with the score at 48. The Surrey pair had bowled 18 overs between them before their first success.

Then, for Australia, the rot set in. Laker bowled Harvey at the same score. After tea, Lock had Burke (22) caught by Cowdrey, and well as he bowled this was his only success. It was 62 for three, after which the Australians added only 22 more as Laker swept through the last eight batsmen in 22 balls for a personal cost of eight runs.

[The Rev. David Sheppard, who had given up regular cricket to take Holy Orders, had been a surprise choice, having previously played only 4 innings this season, for Sussex, including a 97 against the Australians. There was very little cricket on the Saturday and Monday because of rain, Australia taking their score to 84 for the loss of one more wicket.]

1957

5 Mar South Africa complete a fine comeback from 2-0 down to square the rubber with England, winning the 5th Test by 58 runs at Port Elizabeth. On a controversial, dead-slow pitch that produces shooters galore, South Africa's 1st-innings 164, in which Endean (70) scores the only fifty of the match, is decisive. Tyson takes 6-40 in South Africa's 2nd innings, and Tayfield 6-78 in England's 2nd, giving him 37 wickets (avge 17.18), a South African record for a series, one more than Vogler against England in 1909-10.

4-9 Jul England make their highest score at home v West Indies, 619-6 dec (Graveney 258, Richardson 126, May 104), then Worrell carries his bat for 191 in West Indies' 372 and O.G.Smith scores 168 in their 367, following on, and the 3rd Test, at Nottingham, is drawn.

29 Jul James Brown makes 4 catches and 3 stumpings for Scotland v Ireland at Dublin to equal the world record for dismissals in an innings.

28 Aug Denis Compton, having decided to give up regular cricket because of continuing knee problems, goes out with a flourish, hitting 143, his highest score of the season, against Worcester at Lord's in his last professional appearance for Middlesex - and he still tops their averages.

TEST SERIES

England in South Africa
SA 2, E 2, D 1
West Indies in England
E 3, D 2

Second Test Final day: 5 January

Wardle puts England 2-0 up: Endean out 'handled ball'

From Cape Town

ENGLAND'S victory by 312 runs was gained here today with shattering swiftness as South Africa lost the last eight wickets of their second innings for 31 runs. Wardle finished with seven wickets for 36 (12-89 in the match). His bowling at Newlands might well have got any side out cheaply, if not perhaps for 72.

Wardle was given the upwind end, which was also the better spinning end, when the fifth day's play began. At the other end, Laker took two wickets for seven runs in 14.1 overs, nine of them maidens, and was also involved in Endean's curious dismissal, the talking point of the day.

Endean spent 40 minutes today without scoring, and was then out 'handled the ball'. He thrust out his left leg to Laker and the ball bounced upwards and might well have fallen on his wicket, when he instinctively removed his left hand from the bat and palmed the ball down - like a hockey player, a game in which he has captained South Africa. When they had recovered from their surprise, Evans and Laker quite rightly appealed, and Endean was given out according to Law 36.

Another curiosity - this is the second Test in succession that England have bowled South Africa out for 72. They now take a 2-0 lead in the series.

May drives the indefatigable Ramadhin to the boundary.

Fourth Test Final day: 20 February

Tayfield's 9-113 earns South Africa victory: England's collapse

By R.A.Roberts, in Johannesburg

SOUTH Africa achieved a victory as famous as their win at Melbourne four years ago, dismissing England here this evening for 214. The last seven wickets fell for 67 to keep the rubber alive by the narrow margin of 17 runs.

Tayfield's nine for 113 (13-192 in the match) was in the end the match-winning performance, and he is the first South African to take nine wickets in a Test innings. But this was a success for South African teamwork, a triumph deserved as it was close.

Looking back on the game in its completeness, one sees the winning of it in South Africa's first innings of 340. That score against England's attack, and in a game involving two suspect batting sides, was inevitably a major contribution.

When Insole (68) and Cowdrey (55) were together in mid-afternoon and the score was 147 for two, a comfortable win for England was in prospect. The subsequent breakdown was a sad reflection on England's present standards, yet they went down fighting, responding to the challenge rather than playing timidly for the draw that would have won the rubber.

First Test Final day: 4 June

England just fail to win fabulous match: May and Cowdrey in 411 stand

By E.W.Swanton, at Edgbaston

THIS has been a fabulous match. A monumental stand by May and Cowdrey, carried on from yesterday, completely turned the game around and left West Indies avoiding defeat in the end by a matter of minutes. May was unbeaten on 285 when he declared, Cowdrey having made 154 in a stand of 411

At noon yesterday, the pair came together, as they did at Sydney three years ago, knowing that only a day-long stand or thereabouts could bring England back into the match, needing as they did still 175 runs to avoid an innings defeat. A day and a half later, West Indies surveyed a scoreboard showing 72 for 7, thanking their lucky stars for an escape from defeat that could surely be measured only in terms of minutes.

Laker and Lock did not have the wicket to bowl on which filled the Australians with dread last summer, but they set the West Indian batsmen a testing problem enough. The root of the collapse this evening was, however, psychological. The change in events, catastrophic from their angle, combined with the long weary spell in the field, made them always like victims. In such circumstances, two hours and 40 minutes can seem an eternity.

May's batting deserves all the superlatives that are part and parcel of a modern Test. His innings is the highest in any Test since before the war, and only four Englishmen have played bigger Test innings: Hutton, Hammond, Sandham and R.E.Foster. As a captain's effort it stands alone. Cowdrey's innings had all the attributes of his captain in an only slightly less degree. They were together eight hours 20 minutes for their 411, - a Test record for the fourth wicket, an England Test record for any wicket.

May declared at 583 for four. The tireless Ramadhin had bowled 98 overs and taken two for 179. The 588 balls he sent down in the innings is a Test record, as is his 774 in the match.

Trueman (2-7) broke through immediately and both West Indian openers were back in the pavilion with only nine runs on the board. From then on it was a backs-to-the-wall battle for the West Indies against the two England spinners, whose bowling analyses - Lock 27-19-31-3, Laker 24-20-13-2 - tell the story. 'O.G.Smith lbw, b Laker 5' does not, for he stayed at the crease for over an hour, an innings as valuable as his 161 earlier, and was not out until the game was safe.

County Championship Northants v Surrey: 7 June

World record seven catches for Stewart

From Northampton

SURREY close-fielder Micky Stewart took seven catches in the Northants second innings today as champions Surrey eased their way to a 10-wickets win. This is a new world record for a fielder other than a wicket-keeper, and only twice before has a keeper caught that many.

Stewart took six of his catches at backward short-leg, one at gully. To stand as close as he does calls not only for remarkably quick reflexes and courage, but also complete faith in his bowlers. Fortunately, these are Laker, Lock and Bedser.

[Surrey took over at the top 4 days later and went on to win their 6th successive title - by a massive 94 points from Northants.]

Varsity Match: 9 July

Records tumble as Cambridge trounce Oxford

From Lord's

CAMBRIDGE completed a record win over Oxford today by an innings and 186 runs, the biggest margin of victory since the fixture began 130 years ago.

It was another triumph for Gamini Goonesena, from Ceylon, the Cambridge captain, who took four for 40 as Oxford were bowled out for 146. Yesterday Goonesena completed his double century, only the fourth in the history of the match, and his 211 is the highest for Cambridge and surpassed only by the Nawab of Pataudi's 238 not out for Oxford in 1931.

His seventh-wicket stand of 289 with G.W.Cook (111 not out), after which Cambridge declared at 424 for seven, is the highest for any wicket in Varsity Match history.

On the first day, O.S. Wheatley took five for 15 as Oxford were bowled out for 92. Goonesena's innings included a 6, a 5 and 21 4's.

Fourth Test First day: 25 July

Loader hat-trick ends West Indies innings: Last 4 go in 4 balls

By E.W.Swanton, at Headingley

ENGLAND, chiefly in the person of Peter Loader, achieved one of the more remarkable feats of bowling here today when they got rid of the strong West Indian batting side for 142.

The light all day was grey and the atmospheric conditions were helpful. Yet when all is said in explanation, it was a great performance, brought to the most exciting possible climax by the Surrey fast bowler Loader. After Trueman had bowled Smith with the last ball of his over, Loader took the wickets of Goddard, Ramadhin and Gilchrist with the only three of the next over. England finished the day on 11 for one, after D.V.Smith was bowled by Worrell for a duck.

Hat-tricks are rare in Tests, and Loader's is only the 12th, the first since before the war and the first in England since 1912.

[Loader took 3-50 in West Indies' 2nd innings and England won by an innings and 5 runs in less than 3 days to clinch the rubber.]

Peter Loader: Test hat-trick.

Fifth Test Second day: 23 August

Lock and Laker rout West Indies for 89: last eight batsmen go for 21

By E.W.Swanton, at the Oval

SOMETHING snapped in the West Indies' will to resist this evening, and in 35 extraordinary minutes their innings collapsed with an utter completeness one can remember seeing equalled only once in a Test match, and that on another surprising wicket last year at Old Trafford, when Australia capitulated to Laker.

Here today, West Indies, after a stoppage of 20 minutes for bad light, continued at 5.45 with the score at 64 for one. Forty minutes later the ninth wicket fell at 89, and since Goddard was lying in bed with a chill, that was the end of the innings.

Earlier, Graveney took his overnight 113 to 161, Evans hit a quick 40 and England were all out for 412. Lock caught Worrell off Loader for four, but Asgarali (29) and Sobers (39) took the score to 68 for one before the remarkable collapse. West Indies' 89 is their lowest in Test cricket. Lock took five wickets for 28 off 21.4 overs, Laker three for 39 off 23.

[West Indies fared even worse the next day, bowled out for 86, only Sobers (42) and Walcott (19 not) reaching double figures. Lock was the executioner-in-chief again with 6-20, as England won by an innings and 237 runs for their third 3-day victory of the series.]

Second Test First day: 20 June

Bailey's 7-44 wrecks West Indies

By E.W.Swanton, at Lord's

TREVOR Bailey ripped through the West Indies batting at Lord's today, taking seven wickets for 44 runs as they collapsed to 127 all out. By the close, after some early shocks, England were seven in front with six wickets remaining.

Among the cricketing arts that have developed, while others have been allowed to fall into decay, is that of using the seam of the ball to encourage it both to swing in the air and to change direction on hitting the ground. Of this type of bowling, Bailey is a master; while of all wickets, Lord's, in fine weather and especially at the start of a match, is ideal for his purposes. Accordingly Bailey controlled events from 12.15 until the West Indies innings ended shortly before 4 o'clock.

With the fast bowlers Statham and Trueman operating in turn downwind from the other end, England bored through the strong West Indies batting in 3 3/4 hours. After a disastrous start - Graveney and May out for ducks - a stand of 95 between Richardson (76) and Cowdrey (39 not out) pulled England up from 34 for three to pass West Indies' score by the close.

[Cowdrey made 152 (his 2nd successive 150), Evans 82 and the 'tail' wagged to take England to 424, and they won by an innings and 36 runs in 3 days, Bailey taking 4-54.]

First Test Third day: 26 December

Inspired Benaud leads Australian fight against follow-on: Heine's 4-37 spell

By R.A.Roberts, in Johannesburg

Slow bowler Richie Benaud led a fine Australian recovery today as they struggled to avoid the follow-on against South Africa's 470 for nine declared. A spell of 4-37 by fast bowler Heine left Australia reeling at 62 for four, but McDonald (75) and then Simpson (60), making his Test début, helped to pull them round, and Benaud is still there with 80. With Davidson (24), he made a mess of the second new ball, and at 368 for seven, Australia should save the follow-on tomorrow.

[Benaud, with 122, duly saved the follow-on, and the match was drawn.]

1958

3 Jan Left-arm googly bowler L.Kline finishes off the 2nd Test against South Africa at Cape Town with a hat-trick, as Australia win by an innings and 141, the only resistance in South Africa's 99 coming from opener Goddard, who carries his bat for 56.

17 Jan Nasim-ul-Ghani plays for Pakistan at Bridgetown in their first Test against West Indies, at 16 years 248 days the youngest Test debutant.

17-19 Mar Sobers makes 125 and 109 not out for West Indies v Pakistan at Georgetown in the 4th Test, so he has scored 599 in his last three Test innings for only once out.

19-21 Jun England bowl New Zealand out for 47 and 74 at Lord's to win by an innings and 148, Lock taking 9-29 in the match.

24-29 Jul England beat New Zealand by an innings and 13 at Old Trafford to become the first side to win the first 4 Tests in England. Lock takes 7-35 in New Zealand's 2nd innings 85.

30 Jul Yorkshire make the following announcement: "The Yorkshire Committee have informed J.H.Wardle that they will not be calling on his services after the end of the season" - the first public sally in what quickly becomes a *cause celebre.* Wardle, a left-arm spin bowler with 102 wickets for England, has a series of newspaper articles due to come out next week criticising the running of the club, its captain, Burnet, and some of the players.

19 Aug MCC announce that, in view of Wardle's Press articles, they have withdrawn his invitation to go with the England team to Australia, because of the "grave disservice" he has done to the game. Wardle admits: "It's my own fault," and, declining offers from other counties, signs for Lancashire League club Nelson.

8-9 Dec Trevor Bailey makes the slowest 50 in Test history, 357 mins against Australia at Brisbane, his 2nd-innings 68 taking 458 mins. Only 106 runs are scored on 9 Dec as England crawl from 92-2 to 198 all out.

12-17 Dec S.P.Gupte takes 9-102 for India in West Indies' 1st innings, but Sobers makes 198 not out, his 5th 100 in 5 Tests, in their second.

31 Dec In the 2nd Test, at Melbourne, England are 7-3 (all Davidson), but they recover to 173-4 by the close.

TEST SERIES

New Zealand in England
E 4, D 1
Australia in South Africa
A 3, D 2
Pakistan in West Indies
WI 3, P 1, D 1

First Test Final day: 23 January

Hanif passes Hutton's time record: Out for 337

From Bridgetown, Barbados

HANIF Mohammed, Pakistan's 24-year-old opening batsman, rocketed to world cricket fame during the first Test match that ended here today against the West Indies. He batted for 16hr 13min, easily breaking the world record for a marathon innings in first-class cricket, the 13hr 20min by England's Sir Leonard Hutton against Australia at the Oval in 1938.

But Hanif failed by 28 runs to beat Hutton's record Test score of 364 in that match. The little Pakistani's innings of 337 was the world's second highest in Test cricket, beating by one run Hammond's score for England against New Zealand in 1933.

Pakistan, who were bowled out for 106 in the first innings and asked to follow on, made 657 for eight declared in reply to West Indies' 579 for nine declared and the match ended in a draw.

Third Test Fifth day: 3 March

Remarkable innings by 21-year-old Sobers: Sir Leonard's Test record goes at last

By Michael Melford

Garfield Sobers made 365 not out for the West Indies against Pakistan at Kingston, Jamaica, a new world Test record. It seems to have been a remarkable innings in a remarkable context. Not only was this vast score his first hundred in a Test match, but it precipitated a unique scene when he made the single to pass Sir Leonard Hutton's record of 364 made at the Oval in 1938.

The crowd of 20,000 in Sabina Park swarmed on to the field and, the West Indies having declared at the useful total of 790 for three, carried the hero to the pavilion. In the tumult they did so much damage to the pitch that the umpires ordered it to be repaired, and abandoned play for the day 55 minutes early.

The tall, left-handed Sobers batted from soon after tea on Thursday until Saturday evening - 10hr 8min, or three hours less than Hutton. At 21, he is seven months younger than Hutton was in 1938. The innings seems to have been attended inevitably by a perfect wicket, and also by a Pakistan attack seriously weakened by injury.

Garfield Sobers: 365 not out

Of the regular bowlers, only two escaped injury, and they suffered the third and fourth most expensive bowling analyses in the history of Test cricket - 0-259 in 54 overs by the fast-medium Khan Mohammad and 2-247 in 85.2 overs by the medium-paced Fazal Mahmood.

All batting feats of this nature are helped by a long occupation at the other end, and Hunte with his 260 obviously played a big part. The second-wicket stand of 446 between Hunte and Sobers is only five short of the record for any wicket in a Test, the Bradman-Ponsford second-wicket stand for Australia at the Oval in 1934.

[Pakistan, with two players unable to bat, were bowled out for 288 in their 2nd innings and lost by an innings and 174 runs.]

County Championship Surrey v Northants: 6 June

Surrey hit for 529 runs: Subba Row scores 300 of them

From the Oval

NORTHANTS took the first points of the season off Surrey in the drawn match at the Oval with a grand total of 529 for nine wickets - and it was Croydon-born Raman Subba Row, the 26-year-old former Surrey player, who set the pace with 300 of them.

Subba Row, in his first season as captain, becomes the first Northants batsman to have reached the 300 mark. He was at the wicket for 9hr 26min and hit 42 fours. Meanwhile, along came Albert Lightfoot - previous highest score 49 - to hit 119 and help Subba Row to add 376 for the sixth wicket, a record for any Northants partnership. When it was broken at 471, Northants had long passed Surrey's first-innings score (378-5 declared).

Between them, they exposed the poverty of Surrey's reserve attack - Laker, Lock and Loader were on duty with England. Although Sydenham had taken three quick wickets to have Northants at 18-3 yesterday, it was left to opening bat Tom Clark to come in with his spinners and three wickets for 48. However, after seven matches, Surrey still lead the county table by 14 points.

Third Test Fourth day: 7 July

Milton hits chanceless century on Test debut: Gloucester opener's 194 stand with May

By E.W.Swanton, at Headingley

THE crowd here, whose enthusiasm has been of late so sorely tried, left happily in the sunshine this evening, having seen England's premier batsman, Peter May, score a delightful hundred. I suppose the Board of Control selectors may have been similarly content, for the last of their choices as opening batsman, Arthur Milton of Gloucestershire, made a hundred also, in his first Test match.

It is seven years since an England cricketer made so auspicious a beginning, and Milton may take it as an augury that the man was May himself, and the ground none other than Headingley. The last Gloucestershire player to do so was W.G.Grace in 1880!

Milton's innings was not set in a triumphal key. He is not that sort of player. But it represented a piece of responsible, competent craftsmanship. He set himself to a purpose, and he achieved it, and it is a long time since one has been able to write that about a professional batsman on trial for England.

Indeed, of all the many who have had the opportunity, it is remarkable that only one other professional batsman whose first-class career has begun since the war ended has made a century for England, and that was Tom Graveney. The number of amateurs in the same category is seven.

Milton is now 30, and in his 10th regular season. He has been slow in maturing. But this is his 20th first-class hundred, and it is certain that the confidence it will have brought him will inspire many more. When May declared this evening at 267 for two, a first-innings lead of 200, leaving New Zealand an hour and a half's batting, Lock breached the innings to the extent of three wickets in 15 balls. New Zealand were 32 for three at the close, the not out batsmen Reid, with but a single boundary to his name, and Sutcliffe, still scoreless after 45 minutes

[NZ were all out for 129 after a long struggle and lost by an innings and 71 runs. Milton, who won one football cap for England in 1952, and like Denis Compton was an Arsenal winger, was the last of the dual internationals.]

County Championship Derby v Hants: 14 August

Leaders Hants crumble to Derby in day of 39 wickets

By Michael Melford, at Burton-on-Trent

THIRTY-NINE wickets fell here in a remarkable day's cricket which ended with Derbyshire beating Hampshire in the extra half-hour by 103 runs. In the process they bowled out the championship leaders for 23 and 55.

Various melancholy records were set up by Hampshire's 23 in the first innings. It was the lowest since 1939 and the lowest ever against Derby. Horton and Barnard were joint top-scorers with five. The biggest stand was six for the seventh wicket, and the innings lasted 16.4 overs. No less extraordinary was the fact that there was not a single bowling change in the match until 6.40 this evening, when Morgan replaced Rhodes and took three Hampshire wickets for four runs in 5.3 overs. During the previous 6hr 40min of play today, and yesterday's 20 minutes, when Derby made eight for one wicket, each side had used only their opening bowlers.

The pitch had had no rain for 20 hours, and a breeze and the hot sun dried it out more quickly than anyone expected. This morning it was as unpleasant as anything I can remember since Trueman and Cowan massacred Surrey one evening at Headingley a few years ago.

Scores: Derby 74 (Heath 6-35, Shackleton 4-36) & 107 (Heath 7-52, Shackleton 3-52), Hants 23 (Jackson 5-10, Rhodes 4-12) & 55 (Jackson 4-16, Rhodes 3-29, Morgan 3-4).

County Championship: 29 August

May leads his Surrey side out at the Oval, champions again.

Surrey champions seven years in succession: Longest run in history of cricket

By E.W.Swanton

The summer of 1958 will be recalled as among the most gloomy within memory. But it will be notable for at least one thing - the victory yet again of Surrey in the County Championship. For this triumph by Surrey is their seventh in a row, and therein they have written a new page of history. Since the Championship was begun in the early 1870s, no county has had such a run.

Once Hampshire's game was rained off, Surrey did not have to bowl a ball at the Oval today against Somerset to retain their title. However, they gained first-innings bonus points anyway, bowling out Somerset, who had already lost two wickets for four runs, for 66 inside the two and a half hours that remained possible.

It is difficult to say anything new in praise of Surrey. The foundation of their strength lies in their bowling, and once more they have won despite the frequent absences of Laker, Lock and Loader and the serious illness of Alec Bedser. On the latter's return, he has been of great value as leader when the captain, May, was otherwise engaged.

Perhaps the main difference between the present Surrey and that of the Surridge days has been in the greater attraction of the batting. May, of course, is a host in himself, and he now sees a fast batting rate as a tactical end, apart from the concrete value of the bonus points, which they have picked up in profusion.

McIntyre, Surrey's reliable wicket-keeper, should be mentioned in this conection, too, hitting well in several games when runs were needed against the clock. And once again, Stewart, Barrington and Lock have set a high standard of catching close to the wicket.

First Test Final day: 10 December

Dashing O'Neill recalls glory of stroke play: Sparkling 71 settles match

By E.W.Swanton, in Brisbane

AN innings of high quality by young Norman O'Neill, on his Test debut, settled the first Test match in Australia's favour by eight wickets this evening. The score was 58 for two when he came in, and the first three batsmen had brought their side to a favourable situation without at all extinguishing England's hopes. This, however, O'Neill proceeded to do in a manner which, at the eleventh hour, lifted the match from the dullest of all ruts.

In a sparkling innings of 71 not out, O'Neill batted in a refreshingly free, confident style for just under two hours. He is a brilliant player, and everyone cannot attempt to bat like him. But all the members of both sides might be the better for the simple reminder that a bowler will only bowl as well as he is allowed to do - even an England bowler of the fifties.

Scores: England 134 & 198 (Bailey 68; Benaud 4-66), Australia 186 (Loader 4-56) & 147-2 (O'Neill 71 not).

1959

1-4 Jan Rohan Kanhai makes 256 for West Indies against India in the 3rd Test, his maiden Test century, and joins Butcher (103) in a 4th-wicket stand of 217, before Sobers hits 106 not out, his 6th 100 in his last 10 Test innings, and West Indies go on to win by an innings and 336 runs.

12 Feb England fast bowlers Statham and Loader are hurt in a car accident which rules them out of the last Test against Australia.

18 Feb Ray Lindwall passes Grimmett's Australian Test record of 216 wickets in the 5th Test against England at Melbourne.

26-31 Mar Having already lost the rubber, West Indies inflict Pakistan's first home defeat in the 3rd Test, at Lahore, by an innings and 156 runs, Kanhai scoring 217. At 15yr 124days, Mushtaq Mohammad is the youngest player to make his début in Test cricket.

9 May Shackleton takes 9-81 for Hants against Glos at Bristol, having taken 9-59 in the same fixture last season.

20 Jun Evans plays his last Test for England, finishing with a world record 219 dismissals (173ct, 46st), way ahead of any other keeper.

19-22 Dec Natal dismiss Border for 16 and 20 at East London, the lowest match aggregate in first-class cricket, N.D.During top-scoring with 9 and hitting Border's only boundary.

TEST SERIES

England in Australia
A 4, D 1
England in New Zealand
E 1, D 1
India in England
England 5
Australia in Pakistan
A 2, D 1
West Indies in India
WI 3, D 2
West Indies in Pakistan
P 2, WI 1

Second Test Fourth day: 4 January

England on verge of second defeat: Query over Meckiff's action

By E.W.Swanton, in Melbourne

ENGLAND collapsed to 87 all out in the second Test here today and Australia need only 30 runs tomorrow, with nine wickets in hand, to go 2-0 up in the rubber. The one thing to take some gilt off Australia's performance was the question mark hanging over the action of fast left-arm bowler Ian Meckiff, who took six wickets for 38.

The day had begun well for England, who mopped up Australia's last four wickets for 26 runs to limit their first-innings lead to 49. In one spell, Statham took three wickets for nought, and he finished with seven for 57. But then England collapsed against the bowling of Davidson (3-41) and Meckiff to their lowest score in Australia for 55 years.

There was, however, a certain unhappiness felt about Meckiff's action by many people on both sides. It could not be said that England were surprised by it, for he has played three matches now against them. Nor should the element of doubt be used as an excuse for some very poor batting.

Pavilion critics are sometimes wrong, and once witch-hunts begin the innocent are often besmirched with the guilty. It is enough merely to record that, as Meckiff came running in with arm seemingly bent at least until the very moment before delivery, there were many members and friends of the Melbourne Cricket Club who voiced their opinions without reserve.

[Australia won by 8 wickets. Meckiff survived until December 1963.]

Meckiff: The controversial action.

Quaid-e-Azam Trophy Semi-final: 11 January

Hanif beats Bradman's world record: Out for 499

From Karachi

Pakistan Test star Hanif Mohammad, 24, hit 499 runs for Karachi in a national championship match here today, beating Sir Donald Bradman's 452 not out, made 29 years ago, the previous highest individual score in first-class cricket.

Hanif, who stands only 5ft 6in and weighs little over 9 stone, ran himself out when attempting a quick single to keep the bowling for the last over of the day. From the scoreboard, which was wrong, he thought he was on 496, and only discovered he had made 499 on returning to the pavilion. He hit 64 fours in his remarkable innings and spent 10hr 30min at the crease. Last year he played the longest innings in first-class cricket, against West Indies.

Coming in after Bahawalpur had been dismissed for 185, Hanif made 25 on the first day, which he took to 255 yesterday, and today he broke the record. Karachi, captained by Hanif's elder brother Wazir, declared at 772 for seven.

[Karachi won by an innings and 479. In a lower-scoring final the following week, Karachi beat Services by 279 runs, Hanif scoring 130 in their 1st innings.]

Fourth Test Final day: 5 February

Australia regain Ashes: Young side with new enthusiasm

By E.W.Swanton, at Adelaide

AUSTRALIA won the fourth Test match here this evening by 10 wickets with an hour and a quarter to spare and so retrieved the Ashes they had surrendered at the less beauteous Oval at Kennington five and a half years ago.

There was a time today, during which Graveney (53 not out) and Tyson (33) were holding up a rather weary Australian attack, when it seemed that England might achieve the minor satisfaction of another draw. The Australian bowling, after three full days in the field, had lost its bite, though the fielding still sparkled. But Benaud at last broke the stand that had lasted an hour and a quarter into the afternoon, and there the resistance ended.

I wrote at the start of the series that the odds were against England, but if anyone had said they were due to win the toss four times running, I would certainly not have supposed they would have gone down 3-0 with one game drawn.

It goes without saying that Australia have well earned their success. While England's strength at first was commonly overestimated, that of Australia was under-valued by people harking back to the abnormal conditions at home in 1956. A much better gauge was Australia's successful tour of South Africa a year ago, when the younger men matured and grew in confidence. Indeed, one of the contrasts between the two sides has been the difference in approach between one, most of whose members are, in the cricketing sense, still coming up, and the other, of whom more than half have left most of their Test cricket behind them.

The Australian batting and fielding have been very much better than England's, and the excellence of most of the English bowling has not compensated for the disparity. Technically Australia have looked the better, and tactically they have not been nearly so quick to go back on to the defensive. Their new captain, Richie Benaud, has knitted them together and kept them keen and happy.

Benaud has also played a major part with both bat and ball, his all-round performance in this match comprising five wickets for 91 and four for 82 plus 46 runs in Australia's first innings.

Second Test Third day: 8 March

Fazal's 12-100 beats West Indies: Pakistan win rubber

From Reuter, in Dacca

PAKISTAN beat the West Indies by 41 runs here with two days to spare, and so take the rubber, having won the first Test in Karachi by 10 wickets. The damage was done by Fazal Mahmood, whose bowling was annihilated a year ago in Jamaica, when he conceded 259 without reward to Sobers and company in one innings. This time he took 12 for 100 in two.

Sobers was top scorer in both innings for West Indies, but with 29 and 45 - a far cry from his 365 in Kingston. In their first innings, Fazal took six for 34 and, helped by teenager Nasim-ul-Ghani (3-4) reduced them from 56 for two to 76 all out.

Needing 214 to win, West Indies never looked like getting them as Fazal completed his second haul of six wickets.

Fifth Test Fourth day: 24 August

England make history by winning rubber 5-0: India lose by innings for third time

From the Oval

ENGLAND mopped up India's last five wickets in an hour and a half this morning and - despite the fighting innings of Nadkarni, 76 in four hours - won by an innings and 27 runs. Thus they win a rubber 5-0 for the first time, something only Australia have done before, at home to England in 1920-21 and to South Africa in 1931-32.

It has been a disappointingly one-sided series, three of the matches being won by an innings, the others by wide margins, too. The Indians have been unable to stretch the successive young England sides put into the field against them. They have had ill luck with injuries to their batsmen, their players are inexperienced, and their captain Gaekwad, apart from lacking experience himself, is perhaps too modest and self-effacing for such a task.

From the English point of view, the Tests have emphasised more than anything else current spin deficiencies on good wickets - and by implication the measure of the loss sustained by Laker's retirement. The chief gain - and it is no mean one - is that the great advance made this year by three youthful batsmen, M.J.K. Smith, Barrington and Pullar, has been consolidated by their successes in the Tests.

County Championship Sussex v Yorks: 1 September

Yorkshire champions after 13 years: Stott and Padgett thrash 141 in 61 minutes

By E.W.Swanton, at Hove

Yorkshire won the Championship here this afternoon thanks to two innings of exemplary hitting by Stott and Padgett. In 61 minutes they scored 141 together, taking their side to the brink of victory. Needing 215 in 105 minutes, Yorkshire got them for five wickets and with seven minutes to spare. Thus they put themselves beyond the reach of Surrey, Gloucester and Warwick, and the prize is theirs at last, for the first time, apart from one tie, since 1946.

Never before have Yorkshire gone more than five years in the wilderness, just as no side had won seven times in a row, as Surrey did. The champions have fought as hard as ever this summer, but May's absence for most of the season was too much of a handicap.

As for Yorkshire, they are to be congratulated with all possible warmth, and in particular their captain, Burnet. When the unhappy domestic events of last summer, namely the 'Wardle Affair', are brought to mind, today's victory will seem all the sweeter to him. From 11th to top is a transition indeed.

The clinching of the title at Hove could scarcely have come in a more exciting fashion. But before today's fireworks the part Illingworth played was immense. Having taken three Sussex wickets for 51 on Saturday, he came in when Dexter had reduced Yorkshire to 38 for three and made 122 in just under five hours to help them to a first-innings lead of 97.

When Dexter and Parkes continued the Sussex second innings today, they had a lead of 46 with three wickets down. In fairness to the chasing counties in the Championship, it would be difficult for Marlar to declare, and when Sussex were eventually out for 311 - Illingworth, again, four for 66 - the run chase was on.

Dexter again made an early breakthrough, dismissing K.Taylor and Close with only 40 on the board. That's when Padgett joined Stott. The stroke play that followed was unforgettable. By the time Padgett was caught at deep mid-wicket for 79, Yorkshire had only to coast comfortably and keep their heads - 34 needed in all but 30 minutes. Marlar had Trueman stumped for 11 and, finally, Stott, caught at long on for 96 made in 86 minutes. It was left to Bolus and, appropriately, Illingworth to knock off the last nine runs.

County Championship
Leics v Glamorgan: 2 June

Maurice Hallam: Rare scoring feat.

Hallam's 71-min 100 sees Leics home: Opener's rare feat

By T.H.Evans Baillie, at Leicester

MAURICE Hallam, Leicester's opening batsman, who is challenging for an England place, followed up his 210 not out in the first innings against Glamorgan with 157 in the second, a rare feat in first-class cricket. His innings included the season's fastest hundred (71 minutes), and he is now only 17 runs away from being the first player to reach 1,000 runs.

His effort put Leicester well on the way to their target of 269 in three hours, after Wilf Wooller had made the third declaration of the match. He gave his only chance when 79, and was not out until Leicester were within 22 runs of victory. They eventually won by eight wickets with nearly half an hour to spare.

[Hallam was first to 1,000 runs two days later, but never won an England cap.]

Second Test Fourth day: 23 December

India's first win over Australia: 14 wickets for Patel

From Reuter, at Kanpur

INDIA gained their first Test victory over Australia today to level the five-match series at one-all. The spinners Patel (5-55) and Umrigar (4-27) took the last seven wickets for 46 (Rorke was absent ill) in 773 minutes, dismissing Australia for 105, their lowest score against India.

Patel finished with match figures of 14 for 124, the best Indian bowling performance in Test cricket, as was his first-innings haul of nine for 69. That was the performance that turned the match, as he captured Australia's eight first-innings wickets for 24 to restrict their lead to 67.

Davidson's fine bowling performance for Australia almost went unnoticed - five for 31 and seven for 93.

The 1960s

The first one-day final: Sussex and Worcestershire battle for the Gillette Cup at Lord's in 1963.

The sixties was a time of change and controversy, rioting and unrest. The decade began with crowd disturbances at Bridgetown and ended with rioting at Hyderabad and Dacca. And in between, there were riots at Calcutta, Kingston and Karachi. In England there were anti-apartheid demonstrations, culminating in the D'Oliveira affair and the cancellation of England's tour to South Africa. The decade also saw the abolition of the amateur status. But the biggest revolution of the sixties was the advent of limited-overs, one-day cricket.

Limited-overs cricket began in England with the Gillette Cup in 1963. There was plenty of opposition to it, but declining attendances in county cricket and falling interest in Test cricket meant that the game needed a shot in the arm, not to mention an injection of money. The Gillette Knock-out Cup was an immediate success, providing an exciting Lord's final in which Sussex beat Worcester by 14 runs in the last but one over. Another limited-overs competition was originated in 1969, a Sunday League sponsored by John Player. South African and Australasian limited-overs competitions were also introduced in 1969.

Sussex and Warwickshire both won the Gillette Cup twice and were runners-up once in the 1960s, and Yorkshire also won it twice, while Lancashire were the first John Player champions. Limited-overs cricket called for its own tactics, and there was criticism that it was detrimental to the traditional qualities of batting and bowling essential to county and Test cricket. It was more important, for example, for bowlers in limited-overs cricket to contain the opposing batsmen than to get them out. As a result, medium-pace bowling just short of a length began to be favoured at the expense of the slow bowler. With the pressure always of making fast runs, the batsman, too, was liable to fall into bad habits, such as the adoption of the angled bat to play shots through the vacant slips area. Only in the quality of fielding did one-day cricket generate any improvement, this in the athleticism in the outfield and in throwing, prime requirements in the saving of runs.

England, having lost the Ashes to Australia in 1958-59, failed to recapture them in the 1960s under the various captaincies of May, Cowdrey, Dexter and M.J.K.Smith. Fifteen of the 25 Tests played were drawn, but Australia's 6-4 superiority in the others was enough to give them winning rubbers in 1961 and 1964 in England and to finish square in the other three. Their winning captains were Benaud and Simpson.

Despite the exploits of fast bowlers Statham and Trueman, who joined in their own personal battle over the world record for Test wickets, England fared badly in Test cricket for most of the sixties, especially at home, suffering two setbacks to West Indies and one to South Africa, and in India in 1961-62 they lost their first rubber on the subcontinent.

Their defeats at the hands of the West Indies, under first Worrell and then Sobers, were comprehensive, and while their bowlers suffered at the hands of Sobers, Kanhai, Hunte, Nurse, Butchers and Co, their batsmen could not cope with the pace attack of Hall, Griffiths and Sobers. But England won back the Wisden Trophy later in the Caribbean, thanks largely to Cowdrey's batting and captaincy, and retained it in England against a declining West Indian side in the three-Test series of 1969. This was an innovation of the sixties - the 'double' tour, in which England entertained two countries in a summer. The first was in 1965, New Zealand and South Africa visiting.

There were several throwing controversies in the sixties. West Indies fast bowler Charlie Griffith had a suspect faster ball, but the chief incidents involved the South African Geoff Griffin and the Australian Ian Meckiff, both of whom had to retire from Test cricket. In 1966, a committee was set up to adjudicate on suspect bowlers in English cricket, and Harold Rhodes of Derby was the centre of intense scrutiny before being allowed to continue his career.

That same summer, English first-class cricket also came under close scrutiny, but the counties were not keen to take up all the recommendations of the Clark report. Yorkshire ruled the Championship roost in the sixties, with six wins, four of them under the captaincy of Brian Close. They had a strong all-round side, an opener, Geoff Boycott, with an insatiable appetite for runs, and arguably the best fast-bowler and spinner in the land in Trueman and Ray Illingworth, respectively. But with Trueman's retirement and Illingworth's departure to Leicester, along with their traditional policy of engaging only players born within the county, they finished 13th in 1969, their lowest ever position. Two counties won their first titles - Hants in 1961 and Worcester in 1964, retaining it the following year. And it was a Worcester player whose name made most of the headlines in the sixties - Basil D'Oliveira, a Cape Coloured from South Africa. A man of great charm and integrity, and a fine all-round cricketer, he found himself the unwitting centre of a political storm and one of the biggest controversies in the history of cricket.

1960

26 Mar Having retired hurt yesterday evening against West Indies off the 5th ball of the last over, on which the players came in with England on 256-3, Ken Barrington is not allowed to resume first thing this morning, the umpires ruling that a new batsman has to go in.

31 Mar M.J.K.Smith (96) and J.M.Parks (101 not out) put on 197 against West Indies in the 5th Test at Port of Spain, an English record for the 7th wicket.

3 Dec Hanif Mohammad (160) and Saeed Ahmed (121) put on 246 against India at Bombay, a new Pakistan Test record for the 2nd wicket, beating their own record of 178 made against West Indies last year.

7 Dec P.G.Joshi (52 not out) and R.B. Desai (85) put on 149 against Pakistan in Bombay, a new Indian Test best for the 9th wicket, beating the previous record by 95 runs.

TEST SERIES

England in West Indies
E 1, D 4
South Africa in England
E 3, D 2
Australia in India
A 2, I 1, D 2

First Test Sixth day: 12 January

Worrell turns blind eye to captain's orders: 11-hour marathon ends in draw

By E.W.Swanton, in Bridgetown, Barbados

THE West Indies fourth-wicket stand between Sobers and Worrell was finally ended here today by Trueman when it had added 399. But the draw, which had been on the horizon for so long, duly came to pass, with the minimum of pressure exerted on the England team.

Today, Worrell fell sadly short of what was required. His failure to respond to the needs of the situation, and indeed to the commands of his captain as signalled from the pavilion balcony, was the more disappointing because it was so unexpected. As vice-captain of West Indies and Commonwealth teams, he has won himself an enviable reputation for his approach to the game. I can only suppose that the tremendous effort involved in his performance, physical and mental, had completely dulled his reactions.

The arithmetic of Worrell's performance is as follows: he batted 682 minutes and hit two sixes and 17 fours. Only Hanif and Hutton have played longer innings, and these were triple hundreds. For a brief spell this morning Sobers had edged his way into the first three in this particular contest. His 226 lasted a mere 647 minutes.

Their stand took West Indies from 102 for three to 501, and Alexander declared on 563 for eight. It was significant that the captain's timing, when Worrell was three short of his double hundred, did not produce a dissenting voice from the knowledgeable crowd. Thus England were required to bat for 2 hours 40 minutes against a balance of 81 runs, which they did, without too much trouble and without losing a wicket.

Scores: England 482 (Dexter 136 not, Barrington 128, Pullar 65) & 71-0, West Indies 563-8 (Sobers 226, Worrell 197 not; Trueman 4-93).

Second Test Third day: 30 January

Riot stops play: W.Indies 98 for 8

By E.W.Swanton, at Port of Spain, Trinidad

Play was halted here this afternoon, and eventually abandoned for the day, when the crowd invaded the pitch after the young Trinidad cricketer Singh had been run out, bringing the West Indies score to the fantastic figure of 98 for eight.

Bottles can be seen in the background as Ted Dexter (centre) and police appraise the situation.

In what the Premier of Trinidad, in his telegram of regret to the M.C.C., describes as 'a disruption', a hail of bottles and beer tins suddenly descended on to the field from the popular corner of the ground. In the absence of any prompt police action, the crowd, which had been jam packed all day, debouched onto the playing area, first in a trickle and then, after an appreciable interval, in an increasing flood.

When the field was thick with people, and not until then, Peter May led his team back to the pavilion. Gradually, police reinforcement arrived - including a mounted section and riot squads armed with steel helmets, fire-hoses and batons - and gained control. But, it was too late, and play had to be abandoned.

During many years of writing about cricket, I have never had a sadder tale to tell, the events at Georgetown on the last M.C.C. tour paling by comparison. There are already various theories as to the cause of the disturbance, although it is perfectly evident that the demonstration was not directed at the England team, nor was it a protest against the run-out, which was a clear-cut decision.

A number of factors might have contributed to the sad events. The crowd - at 30,000, a record for the West Indies - were very closely packed, uncomfortably if not dangerously so. They were downcast at the state of the game - all their heroes gone by lunch, with their side 45 for five on a blameless pitch, and now struggling desperately and stodgily to stop the rot. And there is at least some circumstantial evidence for the theory that a small organised mob of lawless discontents had fomented the trouble, having previously urged a boycott of the Test because fast bowler Gilchrist had been banned from the series after being sent home from India for disobedience.

Whatever the reasons, the police and the authorities missed a vital chance to nip the riot in the bud before it got out of hand. I have often drawn attention to the good sportsmanship of the crowds here at Port of Spain, and it is a tragedy that the happiness and reputation of so many have been allowed to be spoiled by the disgraceful behaviour of a few.

[West Indies were soon out the next day. May did not enforce the follow-on and England won by 256 runs on the sixth day. It was the only result in the rubber. Scores: England 382 (Barrington 121, M.J.K.Smith 108, Dexter 77) & 230; West Indies 112 (Trueman 5-35) & 244 (Kanhai 110).]

Sheffield Shield Queensland v Western Australia: 15 February

Grout sets world records: 8 catches in innings

By Ray Robinson, in Brisbane

AUSTRALIAN Test cricketer Wallace Grout created a world first-class record today by dismissing eight batsmen in Western Australia's first innings, all caught. The Queensland wicket-keeper, 32, was reappearing after illness following the Test tour of Pakistan and India.

The previous record of seven victims was held jointly by four Englishmen, two Australians and a Scot. Grout's feat also broke the record for the number of catches in an innings. He made four off Mackay, two off Allan and one each off Lindwall and Vievers.

Grout, who will keep for Australia in England next year, holds the record for the most catches in a Test innings - six in Johannesburg in 1957.

County Championship Kent v Worcs: 15 June

Kent defeat Worcester (25 & 61) by innings in a day

From Tunbridge Wells

On a brute of a wicket at Tunbridge Wells today, Kent bowled out Worcestershire twice in two hours 50 minutes for 25 and 61 to win by an innings and 101 runs inside a day. The pitch, brown and grassless, never gave the batsmen a chance, and Kent captain Colin Cowdrey afterwards described it as 'disgraceful'.

The Kent seam bowlers Alan Brown and David Halfyard did the damage, Brown taking six for 12 and three for 22, Halfyard four for 7 and five for 20. The only other bowler was Shenton, who took two for 12 in Worcester's second innings.

Commendably aggressive batting by the left-hander Peter Jones (73) had helped Kent reach 187. Worcester went in and lost six wickets for nine runs before four leg-byes put paid to the chance of a record low total. Slade was top scorer with 9, and seven batsmen failed to score.

Put in again, Worcester were 7 for three before Broadbent saved a repeat performance with 22 hard-fought runs in 70 minutes. The extra half-hour was taken, and Worcester were all out at 10 minutes past seven, their second innings lasting 95 minutes.

Third Test Third day: 9 July

No reprieve for McGlew

By E.W.Swanton, at Trent Bridge

BARRING miracles, England have won this third Test, and with it the rubber, needing 24 more runs for victory on Monday with all wickets remaining. But South Africa can take fresh heart from their brave recovery today, after the débâcle of their first-innings collapse yesterday.

Waite (60), his injured hand allowing him a better purchase on the bat than yesterday, batted with all his well-known tenacity and soundness to support the left-handed O'Linn (98) in an admirable partnership of 109 for the seventh wicket.

But the talking point of the day was the unfortunate run-out of captain and opener Jackie McGlew for 45. An accidental collision with Moss, the bowler, prevented him beating a direct throw from Statham, which hit the stumps, and, on being given out, he made for the pavilion without any hesitation. He stopped on being several times called back by Cowdrey. The England captain conferred with the umpires, apparently asking if there was any way that McGlew could stay. But they indicated that there were no grounds on which C.S.Elliott could take back his decision.

Some thought that the umpires could have acted under the Fair and Unfair Play law - but the difficulty here is that nothing deliberately unfair had occurred. It was a highly embarrassing incident, leading one member of the Lord's hierarchy to exclaim rather angrily: "If the Laws don't allow McGlew to have batted on, the sooner they are amended, the better."

[England duly won by 8 wickets.]

Second Test Second day: 24 June

Hat-trick by Griffin as postscript to no-balls

By E.W.Swanton, at Lord's

ENGLAND made a substantial score against South Africa here today and Mike Smith, for the third time in Tests inside 12 months, got out after a fine innings in the late 90s - this time at 99. Yet the position of the game, and the success of the English batsmen, seemed almost subordinated this evening to the astonishing fact that Geoff Griffin, who had been no-balled for throwing six times during the day, came back in his last spell and achieved the hat-trick.

Griffin picked up the wickets of Smith, Walker and Trueman to become the first bowler ever to do the hat-trick in a Test at Lord's, and the first South African to do so anywhere. On the reverse of the ledger stands a tally of 11 no-balls for throwing in this match, all called by umpire Frank Lee, 28 in all so far this summer.

England finished the day on 362 for eight, and I assume a declaration first thing tomorrow.

[England won by an innings and 73 runs. An exhibition match followed the Test, which finished early, and Griffin, who was unable to straighten his right arm naturally owing to a school accident, was persistently called for throwing by Sid Buller, and had to finish his last over bowling underarm. He did not play in Tests again, but completed his career with Rhodesia, mainly as a batsman.]

First Test Last day: 14 December

West Indies force first ever tied Test: Australia lose 3 wickets in last over

By R.A.Roberts, in Brisbane

AN HISTORIC cricket match flared into a stupendous climax here this evening when Australia lost their last three wickets - two of them run-outs - in the final over and were held to a tie by the West Indies. It is the first tie in the history of Test cricket.

Strong men, heroes themselves of countless Test matches, were on their feet shouting themselves hoarse as Solomon's throw hit the stumps and ran out Meckiff off the seventh ball of Hall's final over to end Australia's innings with the scores level.

It was not just the excitement of the finish that had everyone raving about the match. The rival captains, Benaud and Worrell, agreed they had never known a greater game. It was a match of genuine chivalry as well as gripping entertainment.

Australia looked to have the better chance when they began their second innings needing 233 in 310 minutes with the pitch still playing well. Hall, however, turned the match West Indies' way with two wickets either side of lunch and Australia were soon struggling at 92 for six. Davidson and Benaud then swung the game back in a splendid stand of 134 that took Australia to within eight runs of victory with eight minutes left - before Davidson was run out by Solomon.

Hall began the last over with Australia seven wickets down and six short of victory. Benaud was caught and Grout was run out going for the winning run. The scores were level with two balls left as Kline, the last man, came in. He played his first ball to mid-wicket and Meckiff charged down the pitch - but, glory be, Solomon, for the second time in minutes, picked up swiftly and threw down the stumps direct.

Scores: W.Indies 453 (Sobers 132, Worrell 65, Solomon 65, Alexander 60, Hall 50; Davidson 5-135) & 284 (Worrell 65, Kanhai 54; Davidson 6-87), Australia 505 (O'Neill 181, Simpson 92, McDonald 57; Hall 4-140) & 232 (Davidson 80, Benaud 52; Hall 5-63).

West Indies fielders do a dance of delight as Meckiff fails to beat Joe Solomon's throw and the Test is a tie.

1961

13 Jan Hanif Mohammad (62) and Imtiaz Ahmed (135) beat their own Pakistan 1st-wicket record by 10 runs with 162 against India at Madras. It is the 8th record Test partnership for the prolific Hanif.

11 Feb A world record crowd of 90,800 watches the 2nd day of the Australia-W.Indies Test at the Melbourne Cricket Ground.

13 Feb India and Pakistan play out their 12th successive draw in the 5th Test at Delhi. It is to be the last Test between the two countries for 17 years.

29 Apr The season starts with two major experiments for Championship matches, abolition of the follow-on (present rule introduced in 1900) and option of new ball after 85 overs (instead of 75 overs or 200 runs).

31 May South Africa becomes a republic, which means, as they are no longer members of the Commonwealth, they cannot be members of the ICC and their matches with other countries will no longer be classified as official Tests.

13 Jun Subba Row, the 4th cricketer of Indian stock to play for England against Australia - after Ranji, Duleep and Pataudi - like his three predecessors, scores a 100 on his first Test appearance against them.

7 Jul A.J.G.Pearson takes all 10-78 for Cambridge University v Leics at Loughborough, only the 2nd Cambridge player to perform the feat (after S.M.J. Woods, 1890).

11-16 Nov Ken Barrington (151 not out and 52 not out) bats 9hr in the 1st Test v India without losing his wicket.

TEST SERIES

Australia in England
A 2, E 1, D 2
Pakistan in India
Drawn 5
West Indies in Australia
A 2, WI 1, T 1, D 1

Fourth Test Final day: 1 February

W.Indies defied by last-wicket pair: Mackay and Kline save Australia

By R.A.Roberts, in Adelaide

AUSTRALIA achieved their cricket Dunkirk when they saved the fourth Test here against West Indies tonight in a finish hardly less memorable than the famous Brisbane tie. Mackay, after being almost out first ball, batted for three and a half hours, a veritable Horatius, to deny West Indies a victory that for most of the day seemed probable and was almost a foregone conclusion when the ninth wicket fell 100 minutes from time.

But the age-old maxim that no game is lost until it is won applied here, for Kline, clear of eye and brain, stayed with his fellow left-hander throughout this period and saw out time in one of the best last-ditch stands in the game's long and varied history.

What a Test match - and what a series! When Hall dramatically bowled the last ball after two false starts, and West Indies had still failed to take that last precious wicket, though leading by 186 runs, we had witnessed just about everything possible there is to see packed into one rubber. Each side has won once, there has been that tie, and now an equally remarkable draw.

There was just one occasion during the early part of this wonderful rearguard action by Australia's two heroes when the game seemed for a moment to be at an end. This was soon after Kline had come in. Sobers, at silly mid-off, swooped low to pick up the ball from Mackay's bat, off a ball from Worrell, and jubilantly claimed the catch. The West Indies players were about to make for the pavilion when they were stopped in their tracks, as umpire Egar, at the bowler's end, declined to give it - presumably for a bump ball, because it seemed that Sobers clearly caught it.

Reprieved, Mackay went on to score 62, Kline 15, in their unbeaten, heroic stand of 66 to deny West Indies, for whom Kanhai had hit hundreds in each innings, the victory their overall superiority merited, but which a weakened Australia honourably saved.

[At Melbourne, in the 5th Test, Australia won by 2 wickets in another dramatic finish to take the rubber 2-1.]

First Test Final day: 13 June

Subba Row and Dexter save England: Australian bowlers checked

By E.W.Swanton, at Edgbaston

Ted Dexter: Fine 180 held England innings together.

ENGLAND came by their draw today with far less anxiety than anyone could have dared to hope. Australia were defeated in their efforts by two innings of fine skill and character on the part of Dexter (180) and Subba Row (112).

In the conditions that obtained, the Australian attack, with Benaud seriously handicapped, was not sufficient for the job. The two sides will go to Lord's all square, each more than ever aware that its batting is a great deal stronger than its bowling.

Dexter, after his horrible moments yesterday, began this morning like a new man. He was in fine form from the start, and on Subba Row's departure held the innings together and denied Australia the initiative their first-innings lead of 321 had once given them.

Subba Row, completely composed from the start, built up his innings until just before 12 o'clock he reached his hundred with successive fours off Benaud. He added 109 with Dexter, who then put on 161 for the fourth wicket with Barrington (48 not out) before being stumped just before the close.

Second Test Fourth day: 26 June

England's defiant last-ditch fight in vain

By E.W.Swanton, at Lord's

ENGLAND'S bowlers today put up a last-ditch fight that served as a stiff reminder of how, but for batting inadequacies, the game might have gone. Statham and Trueman had Australia, needing only 69 for victory, in dire trouble at 19 for four wickets before the tourists eventually won by five wickets.

The chief criticism of England, who suffered their first Test defeat after 18 unbeaten matches, is that in both innings far too many batsmen, from top to bottom of the order, got themselves out, either doing the injudicious thing or through some latent failure of technique. Barrington's 66 in the second innings was their only fifty.

The Australian batsmen were far less generous. They had to be prised out, and this was as evident today as in the first innings. Statham (3-31) and Truman (2-40) properly earned all the five wickets that came their way as Australia struggled before lunch. And Australia duly found their man in the crisis, Peter Burge (37 not out), who, while Simpson was being put to a horrible inquisition at the other end, defended stoutly and kept the score moving steadily towards victory.

Scores: England 206 (Davidson 5-42) & 202 (Barrington 66; McKenzie 5-37), Australia 340 (Lawry 130, Mackay 54: Trueman 4-118) & 71-5.

Third Test Third day: 8 July

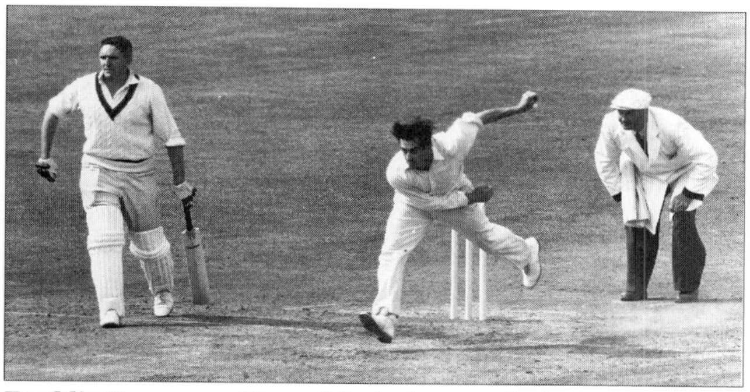

Freddie Trueman: Five wickets for nought in 24 balls.

Trueman again shatters Australian batting: England level series

By E.W.Swanton, at Headingley

FREDDIE TRUEMAN, on his own, albeit controversial, pitch, ran through the Australians this afternoon in a devastating spell of 24 deliveries in which he took five wickets without conceding a run. Australia were all out for 120, and England had little trouble knocking off the 59 runs they needed to win by eight wickets with two days to spare.

England gained their first victory over Australia in eight Tests by more intelligent and, I even think it fair to say, more determined cricket. Further, they had to discount Australia's advantage in winning the toss which, before the start, looked to be the key issue.

Trueman (5-58 and 6-30), for the second time in three days, shattered the enemy ranks, while Jackson, in support, fully vindicated those who had picked him. England, in the two innings, clung on to some fine catches, and Murray again kept wicket admirably. The England batting this time was based on a sensible and flexible appreciation of the situation, and May, on his return to the captaincy, directed operations with a steady and discerning hand.

The only discordant note was the treacherous state of the wicket. The Australians have taken their defeat with their customary good nature, and it was left to May to say that this was a disappointing one for a Test match.

England began the day at 238 for four, one run ahead. But their expected big lead did not materialise, as Davidson (5-63) bowled 14 overs and took three wickets for 9 runs. That England managed a lead of 62 was down chiefly to Lock's 30 in 20 balls, including seven 4's.

Jackson made a quick breakthrough in Australia's second innings, bowling McDonald for one. But Harvey reached his second fifty of the match at around quarter to four and Australia were 98 for two.

At this decisive point, May brought Trueman back to bowl down the hill from the Kirkstall end. The ball old and the wicket slow, Trueman decreased his run by half and his pace by a couple of yards, aiming to cut the ball back from the off. He at once got Harvey with a stopper, and within half an hour the innings had subsided completely, eight wickets going down for 21 runs.

County Championship Hants v Derby: 1 September

Shackleton's 6-39 gives Hants first Championship

By A.S.R.Winlaw, at Bournemouth

IN an atmosphere of much tension, excitement and then rejoicing, Hampshire became County Champions for the first time in their history by beating Derbyshire here today by 140 runs. There could be no more deserving or fitting player to have brought them the Championship than Derek Shackleton, and in a quite magnificent spell of bowling he took six wickets for 39 runs.

He moved the ball away to the slips, brought the ball back, and on a pitch that had hitherto given the seamers no encouragement, he bowled a number of really difficult deliveries.

Derbyshire were set to make 252 to win in 193 minutes, and it was obvious that if they were to get them their first four batsmen would have to succeed. None of them did. Shackleton dismissed all four, and Derby were eventually all out for 111.

Hampshire's win puts them out of reach of last year's champions, Yorkshire, and their triumph owes much to splendid teamwork under the captaincy of Colin Ingleby-Mackenzie. West Indian Roy Marshall and Henry Horton topped 2,000 runs for the third season running, and seam bowlers Shackleton and David White both exceeded 100 wickets.

County Championship Sussex v Leics: 1 September

Another not out hundred for Hallam: Unique feat

From Worthing

LEICESTER opener Maurice Hallam made first-class cricket history today at Worthing when he helped Leicester to a 62-run win over Sussex. His 143 not out enabled Leicester to declare at 256 for two, and in their efforts to keep up the 90 an hour asking rate, Sussex eventually ran out of wickets.

This was Hallam's second hundred of the match and, added to his 203 not out in the first innings, means he hit 346 runs in the match without being dismissed.

Scoring a hundred and two hundred in the same match is a rare achievement, accomplished only by eight other players in first-class cricket. And Hallam is the first to do it without losing his wicket. He is also the first player to do it twice, having made 210 not out and 157 against Glamorgan two years ago.

First Test Final day: 26 October

England win their first Test in Pakistan

From Lahore

AN unbeaten sixth-wicket partnership of 101 here today between Dexter (66) and Barber (39) in 85 minutes finally crushed Pakistan's fight-back and gave England victory with 35 minutes to spare.

Needing to score 208 in 250 minutes, they lost five wickets for 108 before these two came together. This was Dexter's first match as captain, and it was England's first Test in Pakistan. They do not resume the three-Test series until January, after they have completed the Indian part of their tour, including five Tests, in what must be one of the most strenuous programmes ever undertaken by any team.

Second Test Fourth day: 5 December

England regain pride after follow-on against India

From Kanpur

ENGLAND were forced to follow on today against India for the first time in 26 matches over eight rubbers. Hard as Barber (69 not out) and Lock (49), who made his highest Test score, fought this morning, England finished on 244, 223 behind.

However, they have never looked in trouble in their second innings and had wiped off the deficit by the close with the loss of just Richardson for 48.

[England continued batting throughout the 5th day, with Barrington (172), Dexter (126 not) and Pullar (119) making centuries.]

1962

23 Mar The Nawab of Pataudi, at 21yr 77d, leads India against West Indies at Bridgetown, the youngest ever Test captain.

28 Mar West Indies off-spinner Lance Gibbs produces a remarkable spell of bowling between lunch and tea, taking the last 8 Indian wickets for 6 runs in 15.3 overs, 14 of them maidens, as India collapse from 158-2 to 187 all out and lose by an innings. His figures for the innings are 53.3-37-38-8.

5 Apr Frank Worrell (73 not out) and Wes Hall (50 not out) put on an unbeaten 98 against India at Port of Spain, a record last-wicket stand for West Indies, after which Hall takes 5-20 when India bat.

30 Aug Daintes Livingstone (200) and Alan Castell (76) put on 230 for Hants' 9th wicket against Surrey at Southampton.

24 Dec Colin Cowdrey makes 307 for MCC v South Australia at Adelaide, the first triple hundred in Australian post-war cricket and the highest innings ever played by a tourist batsman in Australia.

TEST SERIES

England in Pakistan
E 1, D 2
England in India
I 2, D 3
Pakistan in England
E 4, D 1
New Zealand in South Africa
SA 2, NZ 2, D 1
India in West Indies
West Indies 5

Fifth Test Final day: 15 January

England lose series of disillusionment: India's first rubber

By R.A.Roberts, in Madras

The series of disillusionment for England followed to the last the pattern established at Calcutta, and India's spin bowlers carried their side to victory by 128 runs soon after lunch here today. So an excited, jubilant India took the rubber in no uncertain fashion by two games to none. It is the first time they have won a series against England, the first time they have won two matches in one rubber against a senior cricket country.

Calcutta represented a dramatic turning of the tide for them. Until that match, they had tasted victory against England only once in 27 Tests. Now they have won two successive matches by an aggregate of something over 300 runs. They have proved beyond doubt, now, that under their home conditions England cannot afford to take the field without their best side against them.

India have improved under the selfless guidance of Contractor. Their special ability has been to score heavily in the first innings of each match without fail; and England's weakness has been in failing to stop them doing it. As at Calcutta, the margin on the first innings more or less divided the two teams.

Only Barrington (avge 99), Pullar (84), who unfortunately played in only three Tests, and Dexter (58) made runs in the quantity expected on these wickets against an attack of moderate limits. And, as one feared would happen without Statham and Trueman, England have struggled with the new ball. Manjrekar's 586 runs (eight fewer than Barrington) is a record for India in a Test series.

Scores: India 428 (Nawab of Pataudi 103, Contractor 86, Engineer 65, Nadkarni 63) & 190 (Manjrekar 85; Lock 6-65), England 281 (Smith 73; Durani 6-105) & 209 (Durani 4-72).

Second Test Fifth day: 24 January

Hanif's second 100 does little to brighten stalemate

By R.A.Roberts, in Dacca

HANIF MOHAMMAD (above) duly, almost inevitably, scored his second century of the match here today, but Pakistan's decision yesterday to play for a draw and England's willingness to accept stalemate rendered today's play all but meaningless.

For the record, Hanif added 104 to his first-innings 111, and becomes the first Pakistan batsman to accomplish the feat. As such, he goes into the record books along with such names as Hammond, Sutcliffe, Bradman, Compton, Headley, Walcott, Weekes and Sobers. But, with a draw in prospect, Dexter gave the bulk of the bowling before lunch to his regular batsmen, and it was only when Hanif was in sight of his goal that he brought his recognised spinners to bear.

So when Hanif arrived at his second hundred, out of 198, in 387 minutes, only one or two members of the England side saw fit to congratulate him.

All in all, being one down in the series and winning the toss, Pakistan showed a strange lack of initiative. They both started and finished the match as though they had no faith in making a positive game of it.

Third Test Final day: 7 February

England win series with yet another draw

From a Special Correspondent, at Karachi

IT was probably apt that England's last Test of their exhaustive tour of the subcontinent should end as a draw. Four of the others in their eight Tests against India and Pakistan have gone the same way, and the sad fact is that England have won only one Test match in four months' cricket - the one at Lahore which gave them the series against Pakistan.

Indeed, it is true to say that right to the end the wickets were the winners. With two exceptions against India, they always posed too many problems for an England side boasting only a moderate attack.

Here at Karachi, Pakistan batted through the day to safety, scoring 404 for eight, and only once, in a half-hour spell with the new ball, did England threaten to overthrow them. Dexter pinned his faith in the back-of-the-hand spin of Bob Barber, whose 41 overs was his longest stint of the tour. But it is hard to expect a man to win a Test match when he has had so little practice.

Dexter's 205 in England's innings of 507 boosted his average in the three Tests against Pakistan to 101, while Hanif scored 407 runs (67.83).

Fourth Test Third day: 28 July

Parfitt's 3rd 100 in week against Pakistan: Then Trueman strikes

By E.W.Swanton, at Trent Bridge

Parfitt: scourge of Pakistan

THERE is the essence of pathos in the progress of a Test side that finds itself engaged with manifestly superior forces, and it seems that when one side so palpably needs the luck the other inevitably gets it, as Pakistan found again today against England.

After England had declared at lunch on 428 for five, Pakistan, desperately needing a good start, failed to get it, losing Hanif, their record-breaker, to the second ball of the innings. And when Hanif's younger brother, Mushtaq, arriving next, promptly began to bat with rare brilliance and gusto, and seemed launched on what could have blossomed into a great innings, he was cut short at 55 by a quite hideously good catch by Lock at fine leg off what would have probably been a safe shot to any other fielder in the world.

This morning Graveney was made to work for the last 11 runs of his hundred, and Parfitt followed with his, too. This was the third hundred the Middlesex man has made against Pakistan this week, having already scored two for his county against the tourists in their last game before the Test. Indeed, this was his sixth in his last seven innings against Pakistan.

If it was one of his slowest and least scintillating, it is fair to add that he was not quite himself. A stomach upset is not the happiest condition for playing an innings which may be the making or breaking of his chance of the Australian tour.

When Pakistan went in to bat, on a good wicket, Trueman produced just about his best form of the summer, getting his first two wickets from slip catches off balls leaving the bat, and generally looking lively and penetrative. Knight, in his first Test in England, had two quick wickets, including Mushtaq's, and then Trueman, in one venomous over, snapped up another two to quell a brief revival. At stumps, Pakistan were 127 for six (Trueman 4-37).

[Pakistan followed on, but thanks to 100 not out by Mushtaq in the 2nd innings, and further time lost to the weather, saved the match.]

Fifth Test First day: 16 August

Cowdrey and Dexter hit 248 at 85 an hour

By E.W.Swanton, at the Oval

THE Pakistan bowling has taken some shocking punishment in this series, but today's was among the most relentless and severe. After Sheppard (57) and Cowdrey had made an almost demure opening, putting on 117 for the first wicket, the pace was stepped up in steep progression by Cowdrey and Dexter, who in 170 minutes added 248 for the second wicket at something over 85 an hour.

The batting, on the plumbest and easiest of wickets, was full of style and power, Pakistan supported their limited attack as best they could in the field, and a large crowd in fitful sun and cloud relished the slaughter.

Cowdrey finally went, to a brilliant slip catch by the half-crippled Hanif of all people, for 182. Dexter was still there at the close with 144, and England were on 406 for two.

[England declared at 480-5 (Dexter 172) and won by 10 wickets after Pakistan had followed on, Northants fast bowler David Larter taking 9-145 on his Test début.]

County Championship Yorks v Glamorgan: 7 September

Yorkshire take their 25th Championship

From Harrogate

YORKSHIRE'S Championship victory this afternoon was a comfortable one only on paper. Gained in an atmosphere of Cup-tie tension, their seven-wicket defeat of Glamorgan took them above Worcester to the top of the final table and gave them their 25th title.

Glamorgan never looked likely to build a big enough score to bowl against once Don Wilson, who took 10 for 72 in the match, had broken the back of the innings by catching Lewis magnificently and a few moments later having Walker caught at slip. Yet even the 66 Yorkshire needed seemed quite a target to the faithful crowd when Taylor, their hero of the first innings (67 out of 101), fell to the first ball bowled. As it was, Hampshire, their highly promising young recruit, played a cool innings of 24 not out, and shortly before tea the title was in their grasp for the third time in four years.

For Vic Wilson, whose last season this is, it was, of course, the perfect ending. The first Yorkshire professional captain in 80 years, he has kept a firm, shrewd hand on the reins. Early on, Sharp's batting often held the side together and he made 1,872 runs in the Championship. His slip fielding has been magnificent. Trueman and Illingworth each took over 100 wickets.

Advisory Committee: 26 November

End of the amateur in first-class cricket

By Michael Melford, at Lord's

THE 17 first-class counties decided at a meeting at Lord's to abolish the amateur status. In future all players will be called cricketers.

This historic decision takes the form of a recommendation to the MCC, but there is little likelihood that it will not be accepted. So the amateur in first-class cricket dies after an honourable career stretching back to the Middle Ages of the game.

The ruling will make cricket the only sport, apart from table tennis, in which there is no distinction between professionals and amateurs. One important casualty as a result will be the Gentlemen v Players match, which was first played in 1806.

One does not have to be any sort of a revolutionary to feel that the right decision has been made. The time had come when the successful amateur, by writing and advertising, was making so much money out of cricket, that a form of legalised deceit was being practised. The Counties, however, will have to find the substantial salaries that the best amateurs are now entitled to demand. Equally, the salary list on overseas tours will grow by £4,000 or £5,000.

1963

1,2 May First match in the new one-day Knock-out Competition, Lancs v Leics, the only Preliminary Round tie, runs into a second day because of rain. Lancs make 304-9 (Marner 121) in their 60 overs, and bowl Leics out for 203 (Hallam 106) in the 54th over. Bowlers are limited to a maximum of 15 overs each.

4 May Khalid Ibadulla (Warwick) is given out against Hants at Coventry obstructing the field, only the 9th instance of such a dismissal in first-class cricket.

25-29 Oct Peter Burge makes 283, a record for Queensland, who score 613, but they lose on 1st innings to NSW's 661, Bobby Simpson making 359, the highest score in Australian post-war cricket.

7 Dec Umpire Colin Egar no-balls Australian fast bowler Ian Meckiff four times in an over for throwing, at Brisbane in the 1st Test v South Africa, and captain Benaud takes him off after his one over, spelling the end of his Test career and leading to his retirement from first-class cricket.

21 Dec Sir Jack Hobbs dies, aged 81.

Hobbs: The Master

TEST SERIES

England in Australia
A 1, E 1, D 3
England in New Zealand
England 3
West Indies in England
WI 3, E 1, D 1

Plunket Shield Wellington v N.Districts: 15 January

Reid goes on six-hit rampage - record 15 in 296

From Basin Reserve, Wellington

BEFORE John Reid got to work here today for Wellington, the record number of sixes hit by one player in an innings stood at 11, shared by three players - C.K.Nayudu (Hindus v MCC 1926-27), Barnett (Glos v Somerset 1934) and Benaud (Australians v T.N.Pearce's XI 1953). Reid, during his 296 for Wellington, hit this record for six, as he ran up 15 of them against Plunket Shield leaders Northern Districts.

Wellington went on to make 422, a first-innings lead of 196, and N.Districts are heading for their first defeat this season.

[Wellington won by 10 wickets, but N.Districts won the Shield for the first time.]

Fourth Test First day: 25 January

England's dropped catches let Australia off hook: Landmarks for Statham and Harvey

From Adelaide

ENGLAND dropped at least six catches today and allowed Australia to compile 322 for five wickets at the close, considerably reducing England's chances of taking the Ashes. Harvey was the luckiest beneficiary. Missed four times in his first 26 runs, he went on to play a beautiful innings of 154.

England started well, Simpson caught behind off Statham for a duck with the score on two. This was Statham's 236th Test wicket, equalling Bedser's world record. Illingworth then bowled Lawry at 16, and then the catches began to go down. Twice, from successive balls, Harvey was missed off Illingworth.

O'Neill came in with Australia 101 for three and played a fine innings, with only one difficult chance, when he had scored two. He put on 194 with Harvey, and was out for 100. Harvey, who became the fourth player to score 6,000 Test runs when he had made 61, soon followed. He joins the élite band of Hammond, Bradman and Hutton.

[Statham passed Bedser's record the next day. The match was drawn, as was the last Test, at Sydney, so the rubber was tied 1-1 and Australia retained the Ashes.]

Third Test First day: 15 March

Trueman takes five wickets for world record

By Eric Hill, in Christchurch

WITH his first ball, Freddie Trueman had Playle caught by Barrington and equalled the world record of fellow England fast bowler Brian Statham of 242 Test wickets. He had to wait some time before he made the record his own. New Zealand's score had reached 98 for two before Sinclair, trying to hook Trueman for a second consecutive four, hit his wicket.

New Zealand recovered and were 234 for five, when Trueman struck again. In the last 13 deliveries of 26 overs he summoned the pace and control to take three wickets for one run, completing an analysis of five for 61 and reducing New Zealand to 238 for eight.

[Trueman (7-75) captured the last two wickets and another 2-16 in the NZ 2nd innings to take his total to 250. England won by 7 wickets to take the rubber by 3-0.]

Second Test Final day: 25 June

England 6 runs short with 1 wicket left: Injured Cowdrey needed as last man

By E.W.Swanton, at Lord's

Writing as one whose lasting regret is that he was not at Brisbane for the tie, I have never seen a more exciting culmination to a Test match than this. When the last over started with Shackleton receiving from Hall, Allen at the bowler's end and Cowdrey, plastered from left wrist to elbow, waiting in the pavilion, eight runs were needed for victory.

Shackleton swung prodigiously at the first ball and missed, then took a single for a little tap off the second. Allen played the third nicely to long leg for one.

The next ball was decisive so far as an England win went. Shackleton missed a widish one, which Murray took, and, as Allen charged down to sneak a bye, threw underhand at the stumps. Shackleton was slow to respond, and so we had Worrell taking Murray's throw at the near stumps and beating Shackleton to the bowler's end to run him out.

Colin Cowdrey: Needed in the middle.

Cowdrey thus came in at the safe end, and Allen was content to play the last two balls safely for a draw. So ended a classic game, and a neutral observer, if he could be found, would perhaps say that this was the right result.

In today's cricket, there were two heroes. For West Indies, Hall bowled non-stop fast and furiously, apart from the tea interval, from 2.20 to 6 o'clock, surely an unparalleled feat for a man of his pace. And for England, Close, coming in yesterday when Cowdrey retired with a broken bone, batted with courage and versatility, first withstanding the fast onslaught while he played himself thoroughly in, and in the latter stages taking the battle into the enemy camp in the most exciting way.

Scores: W.Indies 301 (Kanhai 73, Solomon 56; Trueman 6-100) & 229 (Butcher 133; Trueman 5-52, Shackleton 4-72), England 297 (Barrington 80, Dexter 70, Titmus 52 not; Griffith 5-91) & 228-9 (Close 70, Barrington 60; Hall 4-93).

Third Test Final day: 9 July

Inspired Trueman routs West Indies on easy wicket: England win by 217 runs

By E.W.Swanton, at Edgbaston

REVENGE is sweet, and Dexter's side exacted it today in the two crowded hours wherein the West Indies were bowled out for 91, the lowest score they have ever made on a good wicket in more than 30 years of Test cricket against England. I disregard the two innings of 80-odd at the Oval six years ago, because the conditions were highly unfriendly. Here the pitch was true, and the collapse was brought about by some inspired bowling from Trueman which after lunch gave him six wickets for 20.

Trueman took seven for 44 in the innings, in 14.3 overs, and this gave him the admirable match figures of 12 for 119. It was hard to think at Lord's a fortnight ago that Trueman would bowl quite as well again, but today he certainly did. Where the West Indies fast bowlers had been made to look eminently playable by a batsman of the stature (with all due respects) of Lock, who made 56, Trueman found a lift and fire and consistent movement towards the slips that was quite astonishing. There was no disgrace in such a capitulation, complete and swift though it was.

It must afford Trueman some amusement to reflect what was being so widely said about his 'failing powers' two years ago. In two Tests now he has taken 23 wickets for 271 runs.

The game was something of a Yorkshire triumph, since apart from Trueman's achievements the first-innings top scorer was Close, with 55, and in the second it was Sharpe, with 85 not out.

After fighting so even a battle over the first four days, and indeed for most of that time having the better of it, the West Indies must have been acutely disappointed. With the rubber squared and the next Test at Headingley, Trueman for one will be anxious not to descend from the heights in front of his own folk.

Fifth Test Fourth day: 26 August

Worrell leads versatile side to 8-wickets victory and 3-1 win in rubber

By E.W.Swanton, at the Oval

WEST Indies cricket today had its finest hour since the great victories of 1950. That was a 'first time' and so has a special place in history. But in 1950 England were weak. Now, whatever faults can be found in Dexter's side, he has just returned from fighting a drawn series in Australia.

England have been beaten only once in nine years in a rubber on their own grounds. The West Indies have won by three matches to one, a richly deserved triumph. And they can fairly claim at this moment, pending the visit of the Australians to their islands in the spring of 1965, that they are the best-equipped and most powerful side in the world.

The averages tell, so far as the series just ended is concerned, a revealing story. Where England had one bowler consistently effective - Trueman, with 34 wickets at 17.47 - their opponents had four. Where one English batsman averaged more than 40 - Sharpe, with 53.40 in three Tests - the West Indies, again, had four who did so. Significantly, too, Sobers figured in both.

But figures alone do not show how much more versatile and complete was the side that Worrell commanded. Nor do they underline the intangible but invaluable part played by the captain himself. Frank Worrell leaves the scene today a figure of dignity and charm, and withal a great leader of whom Barbados, the island of his birth, and Jamaica, that of his adoption, can be equally proud. I have not known a better series than this in a quarter of a century of reporting. Nor have I known a better captain.

The only disappointment today lay in the inability of the injured Trueman to bowl more than a single over. England needed, especially in Trueman's absence, a quick breakthrough. They failed to get it, and when Rodriguez left after helping to lay the foundations in a stand of 78, Kanhai appeared and played one of the outstanding innings of the series. In an hour and a half of glorious cricket, he and Hunte made 113, after which only the formalities remained for completion.

Scores: England 275 (Sharpe 63; Griffith 6-71) & 223 (Sharpe 83; Hall 4-39), W.Indies 246 (Hunte 80, Butcher 53) & 255-2 (Hunte 108 not, Kanhai 77).

Knock-out Cup Final: 7 September

Sussex win new Knock-out Cup: History in the making

By E.W.Swanton, at Lord's

Gifford: Winner and loser.

A NEW chapter of cricket history was given an exciting and altogether worthy climax at Lord's when Sussex won the first Knock-out Cup. All credit to them, but credit, too, in fully equal portion, for Worcestershire, who over the seven hours of the game fought an even fight and lost finally, with a mere 10 balls to go, by 14 runs.

Where so much has been mediocre this summer, and the weather most of all, it is almost miraculous that both the Test series and this experimental competition should have passed off so well. Often during the play one felt that the rain or the light or both would necessitate the game dragging on until Monday morning. The atmosphere could not have been recaptured. But though Sussex had a wet ball for their last seven or eight overs and Worcester a shocking batting light, the umpires were never called upon to make what would have been an unpalatable and highly unpopular decision.

This 'instant cricket' is very far from being a gimmick. There is a place in it for all the arts of cricket, most of which are subtle ones. That is why the day was so enjoyable, not only for the patriots with their banners and their rosettes 'up for the Cup', but for the practising cricketers, past and present, of all ages and types, who seemed to form the bulk of the 25,000 crowd.

Dexter won the toss and decided to bat. But after an opening stand of 62 by Langridge (34) and Oakman (19), who both fell in successive overs to the left-arm spin of Gifford, only Parks (57) made more than 10, and Sussex were all out for 168, 4.4 of the allotted 65 overs unbowled.

In reply, Worcester really needed an innings of 50 or 60 from one of their four Test batsmen, but it was never quite forthcoming. Sussex used six bowlers, a lop-sided array of fastish and medium-paced men. Buss took three for 39, and Snow three for 13, bowling only eight of his possible 15 overs. Worcester wicket-keeper Booth (33 not out) made a splendid attempt to save the day with a last-wicket stand of 21 - Dexter being forced to spread his fielders on the boundaries - before Carter was finally run out for two.

MCC President Lord Nugent presented the Gillette Trophy and the medals in the presence, on the rostrum in front of the pavilion, of Frank Woolley and Herbert Sutcliffe, who named young Norman Gifford (4-33) as 'the man of the match'.

A sequence study, specially commissioned by The Sunday Telegraph, of Ian Meckiff's action as he opened the bowling for Australia against South Africa at Brisbane in 1963 – he was taken off after being called four times in his first over and never bowled again.

Throwers and Throwing

The first 'throwers' were the bowlers who experimented with the round-arm style in the late 1700s. Tom Walker, who played for the famous Hambledon Club before it disbanded in 1791, was the first to have his action questioned. A Council of the club decided it was foul play, and banned it, chiefly because of the pace of his deliveries. John Nyren, the club's chronicler, said of Walker that he "began the system of throwing instead of bowling".

But it was not until 1816 that the MCC altered the Law on bowling so that it read: "The ball must be delivered underhand, not thrown or jerked, with the hand below the elbow at the time of delivering the ball. If the arm is extended straight from the body, or the back of the hand be uppermost when the ball is delivered, or the hand horizontally extended, the umpire shall call no-ball."

So when the first bowler, John Willes, was no-balled for 'throwing', it was not, as in modern times, for failing to keep his arm straight. And whether or not Mr Willes picked up the habit from his mother or sister, or otherwise - the stories about him are legend - there seems little doubt that he bowled his last ball in July 1822, for Kent against the MCC, leaving the ground in a huff when he was no-balled, never to be seen in a first-class match again.

Round-arm creeps in

But this new style crept in, illegal though it was. Umpires found the Law difficult to apply - the "hand below the elbow" part, anyway - and generally turned a blind eye to dubious bowling actions. After all, batsmen had begun to get the upper hand, 'hitting' the old style of bowling instead of practising the customary cautious defence. Nevertheless, the new style aroused considerable controversy among both players and spectators, and when Sussex fielded a pair of bowlers, William Lillywhite and Jem Broadbridge, who had perfected it, a series of matches was arranged with an All England eleven so that it could be brought into the open and tested against the 'hitters'.

After Sussex won the first two games, one writer, an 'old cricketer', felt their victories had been "undoubtedly owing to a singular novel, and perhaps we may say unfair, manner of bowling, by the over-cast from the arm, instead of the underhand and graceful method of the Old School." And nine of the All England side signed a petition declaring that they would not play the third match unless the "Sussex players bowl fair; that is, abstain from throwing."

However, they did play in the third match, England were dismissed by the "irresistible" Lillywhite and Broadbridge for 27 in the first innings, and Sussex gained a 50-run lead, despite a certain Mr G.T.Knight, who in the words of 'old cricketer', "adopted the liberal system, as it is now called." In any event, All England 'hit' successfully in their second innings and won the match.

It was Mr Knight who was most instrumental in getting the new style accepted, although the controversy rumbled on for another two years before his eloquent arguments finally persuaded the conservative MCC to change Law X to read: "The ball shall be bowled: if thrown or jerked, or if any part of the hand or arm be above the shoulder at the time of delivery, the umpire shall call No-ball." In other words, there were no longer any restrictions on round-arm bowling.

From round-arm to over-arm

The next throwing row erupted in 1862, when the much respected Edgar Willsher, playing for England against Surrey at the Oval, was no-balled six times by, of all umpires, John Lillywhite, son of the old rebel. Indeed, the latter's father William and his partner Broadbridge had continued to champion the new style of bowling (just because it had been legalised, there was no mass conversion on the spot), and they had been joined by a new hero, the massive Alfred Mynn of Kent. Coached as a boy by John Willes, he became the greatest all-rounder of his day, and he revolutionised the game with the tremendous pace of his bowling. It was his success that

Charlie Griffith, controversial West Indian bowler of the 1960s.

produced imitators, and players and spectators ceased to cavil at the height of the bowler's arm. But the Law was not changed again to accommodate this further development until the Lillywhite-Willsher incident, when one umpire decided he could not allow the blatant contravention of the Law even though it was widely, though not universally, accepted. In 1864, by 27 votes to 20, the MCC abolished all restrictions on the height of the hand in delivery, and the gradually contracting Law X now read: "The ball must be bowled; if thrown or jerked, the umpire must call no-ball."

Thus ended the first, long, chapter in the controversy over the bowler's action. Bowling had progressed from under-arm to over-arm, although the former did not die out for many years.

The first throwing epidemic

An epidemic of throwing, or 'chucking' as it commonly came to be called, broke out on the county scene in the early 1880s. There were many complaints that Law X was being infringed by certain Northern players, but the general incompetence, and disinclination to act, on the part of some umpires did not help matters. The tempestuous Lord Harris, captain of Kent (and of England), took it upon himself to wage a concerted campaign against the chuckers. He chaired a meeting of county secretaries at Lord's on 11 December 1883, in which six counties - Yorkshire, Kent, Middlesex, Derbyshire, Notts and Surrey - agreed among themselves not to employ any bowler "whose action is at all doubtful". The counties that declined to sign the resolution were Sussex, Gloucestershire and most notably Lancashire, because they had the most-suspect fast bowlers, Crossland and Nash. After playing at Old Trafford in May 1885, Harris wrote to Lancashire saying he had no alternative but to advise Kent CCC "to decline any further engagement with your club - certainly for this year - and until a more satisfactory state of things maintains." He offered to cede the return match to Lancashire in August. Lancashire found themselves under increasing pressure from other counties, too, and eventually dropped the players in question.

The throwing controversy flared up once more in the 19th century, when the Australians visited England in 1896. Fast bowler Ernie Jones, who won undying fame at Lord's by bowling his first ball in a Test in England right through the beard of a startled W.G.Grace, had a highly suspect action, as did slow bowler Tom McKibbin, who came in for the second Test. Sydney Pardon, editor of Wisden, wrote: "Jones's bowling is to our mind radically unfair, as we cannot conceive a ball being fairly bowled at the pace of an express train with a bent arm." And he denounced McKibbin's off-break as a "continual throw". He felt, however, that is was just as well they passed unchallenged, given the "supine attitude to illegal bowling" in this country, anyway. Jones was no-balled twice on England's next tour of Australia, and subsequently cut down his speed, but McKibbin does not appear to have been called for throwing.

There were a few more instances of bowlers being no-balled for throwing, notably C.B.Fry on three separate occasions in 1898, before the county captains met in December 1900, agreed not to use certain bowlers and drew up a list. This virtually eradicated the problem in England for some 50 years, and there appears to have been little trouble abroad, although a glance at the record books shows that a certain S.Mabarak Ali of Trinidad was no-balled for throwing 30 times in one innings against Barbados in the 1941-42 season.

Curing the second throwing epidemic

The throwing controversy reappeared, however, in the early 1950s and lasted well into the next decade, with Test players from all the leading countries being branded chuckers at various times. The outbreak could so easily have been nipped in the bud had the authorities taken more note of the umpires. Instead, they chose to turn a blind eye, for 'diplomatic' reasons, and the issue became very confused.

In 1951, leading umpire Frank Chester was warned (it was revealed later by no less an establishment figure than Sir Pelham Warner, president of the MCC) that he would receive no support if he called South African fast bowler Cuan McCarthy in the first Test, even though Chester considered McCarthy's action to be unfair. McCarthy, however, played in 15 Tests, but was erratic and expensive.

Tony Lock, on the other hand, was a highly successful spin bowler for England and Surrey. But he had a faster ball that was highly suspect, and he was intermittently called for throwing from 1952, when he was no-balled three times for Surrey against the Indians, to 1960, including two occasions on England's tour of the West Indies in 1953-54. Always on the borderline of fairness, he reverted to his slower style on seeing a film of his delivery taken on the tour to Australia in 1958-59.

The most notorious cases of throwing in post-war cricket, however, were still to come. Perhaps the saddest was that of South African fast bowler Geoff Griffin, who was left with a permanent crook in his arm after an accident at school. He was the first tourist to be called for throwing in England, when, in 1960, his action failed to pass muster in several matches. He had previously been no-balled for throwing a couple of times for Natal, but the 1960 tour finished his career as a Test bowler at only 20.

Shortly after the Griffin episode, the 1960 Imperial Cricket Conference, meeting in London, did much to strengthen the hand of the umpires by clarifying the law with an explanatory note, viz: "A ball shall be deemed to have been thrown if, in the opinion of either umpire, the bowling arm having been bent at the elbow, whether the wrist is backward of the elbow or not, is suddenly straightened immediately prior to the instant of delivery...."

In Australia, they were quick to stamp out the throwing menace, and they averted considerable controversy by leaving their suspect bowlers at home when they toured England in 1961. But their most notorious practitioner, left-hander Ian Meckiff, having been called in Sheffield Shield cricket, was controversially selected for the first Test against South Africa in December 1963 and no-balled by umpire Colin Egar four times in his first over. Richie Benaud had no alternative but to take him off, and he retired from first-class cricket.

Perhaps more controversial was the career of West Indian quickie Charlie Griffith, who with Wes Hall made up just about the fastest and most feared Test attack in the sixties. His action was always under scrutiny, yet he was called only twice in his career, for Barbados against the Indians in 1962 and on the 1966 tour to England, against Lancashire. The latter incident, and the persistent rumblings about his faster ball, unsettled him and he felt constrained to use it more sparingly.

When the MCC set up a sub-committee in 1966 to investigate all bowlers who had suspect actions or had been no-balled for throwing, the Derbyshire seamer Harold Rhodes was the first to be investigated. Although his action was found to be "basically fair", the committee were divided as to whether he did occasionally throw. He continued to be dogged by controversy, likely to be filmed wherever he played and subject to taunts - one batsman came out to face him wearing a crash helmet. Medical tests, including X-rays, suggested he had a 'hyper-extended arm' which created the 'optical illusion' of his arm straightening before delivery, and he was finally given a clean bill of health by the authorities in 1968. But he never added to the two England caps he won in 1959, and, as the throwing epidemic in cricket died out, Rhodes finished his career sad and embittered by his experiences.

1964

11-14 Jan Left-armer R.G.Nadkarni (India) bowls 21 consecutive maiden overs - 131 balls altogether without conceding a run - against England at Madras in the 1st Test, finishing with analyses of 32-27-5-0 in the 1st innings and 6-4-6-2 in the 2nd.

12 Feb Richie Benaud plays his last Test, against South Africa at Sydney, and finishes with 248 wickets and 2,201 runs.

23-28 Jul Bobby Simpson (311) and Bill Lawry (106) put on 201 for the 1st wicket in the 4th Test, an Australian record against England, Simpson's being the highest ever score at Old Trafford and the longest, 12hr 45min, ever played against England. Australia declare at 656-8, England reply with 611, Barrington (256) making his 10th Test hundred, his 1st in England, and putting on 246 with Dexter (174) for the 3rd wicket. The draw is enough for Australia to retain the Ashes.

17 Aug Colin Cowdrey, 93 not out in the 5th Test v Australia, becomes the 7th batsman to complete 5,000 runs in Test cricket.

24 Oct Khalid Ibadulla makes 166 against Australia, the first Pakistani to score a century on his Test début, and shares a 1st-wicket stand of 249 with Abdul Kadir (95), a Pakistani record; in the same Test, Bobby Simpson makes 153 and 115 for Australia.

5 Dec Tom Graveney's 132 for Worcs v Northants is his 100th hundred.

5 & 23 Dec With 100s against South Africa, first Ken Barrington (148 not out at Durban) and then Ted Dexter (172 at Johannesburg) complete a full set of 100s against the other six countries.

TEST SERIES

England in India
Drawn 5
Australia in England
A 1, D 4
South Africa in Australia
A 1, SA 1, D 3
South Africa in New Zealand
Drawn 3
Australia in India
I 1, A 1, D 1
Australia in Pakistan
Drawn 1
Pakistan in Australia
Drawn 1

Fourth Test Third day: 27 January

Barlow and Pollock put Australian bowling to sword: Record 341 stand

By R.A.Roberts, in Adelaide

On the 176th anniversary of Australia's Foundation Day, Goddard's South Africans wrote their own entries in the record book. Their vast score of 595 in nine hours is their highest in any Test, and gave them a first-innings lead of 250. And the stand of 341 in 283 minutes by Barlow (201) and Graham Pollock (175) was the highest for any South African wicket, second only for the third wicket in Tests to the Compton-Edrich partnership (370) for England against South Africa in 1947.

The situation today was ripe for exploitation, after the great work achieved on Saturday evening by the third-wicket pair. They carried on until a few minutes before lunch, when the 19-year-old Pollock was bowled with his head in the air attempting to pull. By then, he had left an indelible stamp upon the minds of all who have watched him here. He is bound to give immense pleasure wherever he plays in the next decade, and it is sad to think that there are countries who may never see him.

Pollock's innings contained 18 fours and three sixes. It says much for Barlow's sense of purpose that he was not left behind in this mammoth partnership. Today, indeed, he scored the faster, though he had more of the strike and certainly his share of luck. He survived numerable snicks that flew everywhere in the general direction of the slips without going to hand. He batted 388 minutes and hit 27 fours.

The later batsmen readily took their cue from Barlow and Pollock, and in the last 45 minutes Simpson and Lawry demonstrated the lasting properties of the pitch by the untroubled way they knocked off 48 of the arrears.

[In Australia's 2nd innings, Pollock's brother Peter took 2-73 and Barlow, with his first bowl of the game, 3-6, S.Africa winning by 10 wickets.]

First Test First day: 21 February

Shaky start for S.Africa after anti-apartheid demo

From Wellington

THE South Africans arrived at the Basin Reserve today for the first Test to be greeted with the news that the pitch had been dug up overnight with a trowel as part of an anti-apartheid demonstration. Fortunately, the damage was not serious, the groundsman was able to stamp the loose turf back into position, and the match started on time.

But South Africa struggled for runs, and when bad light stopped play 20 minutes from the end, they had made 233 for seven wickets, having been pinned down most of the day by New Zealand's accurate bowling.

[The match was drawn, as were both other Tests.]

County Championship: Sussex v Warwick: 8 June

Thomson writes Sussex history with 10-49

By Tony Goodridge, at Worthing

NO ONE plays better on the uncertainty of the batsmen than that doughty warrior Ian Thomson, 35, who has so often come to the rescue of Sussex. Here today he crowned all previous achievements by taking the 10 Warwickshire first-innings wickets for 49 and collecting two more in the second.

Ian Thomson: Exploited the situation.

All told, 22 wickets fell during the day on a pitch that was always suspect although rather grudging in the pace with which it lent its help to the bowlers. Warwickshire, the joint Championship leaders, resumed on 103 for two after Saturday's truncated play. Moved to score as quickly as possible, they had to live dangerously, and Thomson, with his seamers, was just the man to exploit the situation. He started the morning with six consecutive maidens and today took eight for 30. He is the first bowler to take all 10 wickets in a Championship match since 1956 and the first Sussex player since 1899.

Dismissed for 196, Barber and Cartwright making fifties, Warwick proceeded to bowl Sussex out for 120, their seam bowlers Brown, Bannister and Cartwright, with the help of some good close catching, doing the damage. Warwick were 54 for four at the close in their second innings, a lead of 130.

[Thomson took 5-26 in Warwick's 2nd innings (129), but Sussex were dismissed themselves for 23, no one reaching double figures. Bannister took 6-16, Brown 2-7 and Cartwright 2 in 2 balls.]

Fifth Test Third day: 15 August

Trueman takes his 300th Test wicket, Hawke caught at first slip by Cowdrey.

Trueman passes 300-wicket milestone: Four for five off shorter run

By E.W.Swanton, at the Oval

IT was high time this game took an agreeable turn - the series likewise - and today it did so. There was in general something much more positive about the struggle. There was, in some degree, an English recovery – they finished the day 65 behind Australia with eight second-innings wickets standing and Boycott 74 not out. And there was the personal feat of Trueman in taking his 300th Test wicket, the first bowler to do so.

If the thing had been stage-managed, this particular scene could hardly have been more dramatic. Trueman had begun the day with five overs in his most depressing 1964 vein. Delivered from his full run, they had neither control of length nor any deviation from the straight. They cost 25 runs and got Australia off to a flying start: it was Headingley all over again.

Dexter, reasonably enough, then dispensed with Trueman's services until 20 minutes past one. This time he marked out a much shortened run, intending to move the old ball off the wicket. After one uneventful over he found the perfect outswinger - which, of course, is the one that, having moved away, comes back off the pitch - and spread-eagled the dogged Redpath. The next ball also swung away and was obligingly deflected by McKenzie into first slip's hands.

It was now lunch, so everyone had time to speculate not only on the milestone that had suddenly hove into sight but also on a hat-trick. Such a fictional triumph was not to be vouchsafed, but the spectators had nothing to complain about. For at this supreme moment the old magic returned.

First with the worn ball, and then after three overs with the new one, Trueman took the memory back to his best days. Suddenly the rhythm clicked, and it was only a matter of time before the great moment arrived. When it did, Hawke was the batsman, and it was Cowdrey who held his fast-travelling snick.

Parfitt held another, from Corling, as Trueman finished off the innings. From none for 82, his analysis had become four for 87: in seven overs, four for five. If the central character still needed persuading that his future lay in doing more with the ball from a shorter run, this sudden ascent from mediocrity to excellence should have driven home the lesson.

Trueman has been an artist among fast bowlers, with an action as near perfection as makes no matter. It is splendid that he should have reached this goal. And if today's new mood of confidence and peak of form persists, the Australians could well be in for more trouble in their second innings.

[Boycott (113) hit his maiden Test century and Cowdrey and Barrington added an unbeaten 126 for the 5th wicket to put England (381-4) on top, but rain prevented any play on the last day.]

County Championship Worcs v Glos: 25 August

Worcester Champions for first time: 2-hour wait after defeat of Glos

By R.A.Roberts, at Worcester

THE most famous of Worcestershire's 16 victories this season and the fifth in succession came sweepingly and handsomely in the middle of a blissfully sunny afternoon here today when Gloucestershire were beaten by an innings and two runs.

But Worcester and the most fervent of their large family of supporters, clustered around the red-tiled pavilion, endured an agonising two hours before the news they were waiting for came through from Southampton. Their neighbours Warwickshire, the only team with a chance of catching them, had failed. The Championship pennant, won with this triumph, will be flying here next season, Worcester's centenary year.

That they have won the title with three matches to spare is a measure of Worcester's superiority this season. It was appropriate that Kenyon made a hundred in Worcester's innings, as their success is a triumph for his leadership. Another major factor has been the skill and dependability of Tom Graveney, and when these two did not come off, one or more of Horton, Headley or Richardson did.

The venerable Flavell in company with Coldwell, and sometimes Standen, have been the staunch backbone of the faster bowling, while, interestingly, the left-arm 'twins' Gifford and Slade have provided the spin. The lack of an all-rounder should be corrected next season with the qualification of the coloured South African B.D'Oliveira.

[Worcs won their last two games to run away with the title by 41 points. Graveney made 2,271 runs and Flavell took 101 wickets.]

Ayub Zonal Tournament
Railways v Dera Ismail Khan: 4 December

Record first-class defeat: Innings and 851 runs

From Lahore

A farcically unbalanced North Zone fixture, debatably regarded as first-class, ended here today with the defeat of Dera Ismail Khan by an innings and 851 runs in three days. Railways declared this morning on 910 for six, the fifth-highest total of all time. There were centuries from Pervez Akhtar (337 not), Javed Baber (200), Ijaz Husain (124) and Mohd Sharif (106 not).

D.I.Khan were then summarily bowled out for 32 and 27, Afaq Khan taking seven for 14 in the first innings, Ahad Khan nine for seven in the second.

First Test Fourth day: 8 December

England end Test drought: South Africa beaten after 12 Tests without a win

By Michael Melford, in Durban

THESE last few years have been hard times for English cricket, and a Test won is an event to set the bells pealing, even when the fates have smiled down on England throughout with unusual benevolence. South Africa's last seven wickets held out against the English spinners for two and three-quarter hours today, but their side were beaten with a day and a half to spare by an innings and 104 runs.

England would probably have won this match even without winning the toss. But their strength and South Africa's weakness is spin, and this match was played on England's terms. They will not expect another pitch so well suited as this one.

In South Africa's first innings, it was Allen (5-41) who did most of the damage, in their second it was Titmus (5-66). Smith launched his spin pair from the start today and they bowled throughout apart from spells with the new ball by Thomson and Price. Thomson can remember his first Test with satisfaction, and Price, surprisingly, looked faster here than Pollock. England's victory was their first after 12 Tests without one.

1965

5-8 Mar Left-hander Bruce Taylor makes a remarkable Test début for New Zealand v India at Calcutta, scoring his maiden first-class century (105) and taking 5-86 in India's 1st innings.

19-22 Mar Off-spinner S.Venkataraghavan captures 8-72 and 4-80 at New Delhi to help India win the 4th Test against New Zealand and take the rubber 1-0.

30 Mar Pervez Sajjad, having taken 4-42 in the New Zealand 1st innings, has figures of 12-8-5-4 in the 2nd (NZ 79) as Pakistan win the 1st Test by an innings, the only Test to be played at Rawalpindi.

3 Apr Hanif (203 not out) and Majid Khan (80) put on 217 against New Zealand at Lahore, a Pakistani 6th-wicket Test record.

20 May Yorkshire are dismissed by Hants at Middlesbrough for 23, the lowest total in their history, Don Wilson's 7 not out being top score.

2 Jul Walter Hammond dies at his home in Durban, South Africa, aged 62.

20 Aug Alan Rees of Glamorgan is given out 'handled the ball' against Middlesex at Lord's, the first instance of this dismissal in England since 1907.

13 Dec Doug Walters makes 155 against England at Brisbane on his Test début for Australia.

ICC The Imperial Cricket Conference is renamed the International Cricket Conference.

TEST SERIES

England in South Africa
E 1, D 4
New Zealand in England
England 3
South Africa in England
SA 1, D 2
Pakistan in New Zealand
Drawn 3
New Zealand in India
I 1, D 3
Australia in West Indies
WI 2, A 1, D 2
New Zealand in Pakistan
P 2, D 1

Third Test Third day: 4 January

Barrington ignores umpire and takes a diplomatic walk

By Michael Melford, at Cape Town

South Africa won most of the honours in what was a tiresome day's cricket, taking four England wickets for 216. But the match will be remembered for the manner of Barrington's dismissal, which I suppose will earn a place in cricket legend.

One had hoped that the sequence of events that led to last week's disagreeable exchanges had ended, but there was to be one more incident today - fortunately one with a happy ending. Barrington was negotiating the new ball with Dexter after tea, when he sparred at a delivery from Peter Pollock. There was a loud appeal, and Barrington, who had made 49, made as if to walk off. He then observed, evidently with surprise, that he was being given not out, and he halted. But after a moment's pause - no doubt with Friday's incident in mind - he marched off to the pavilion.

Over the rest of the day's play, it might be prudent to draw a veil. South Africa's effort on an unhelpful pitch, and with the temperature in the nineties, was almost entirely defensive. And apart from a vigorous 58 from Barber this morning, England, in reply to South Africa's 501 for seven, set themselves to build a big score at leisure.

Boycott's innings this morning took the early steam out of Pollock, but he did nothing else to help the English cause, making only four singles in 85 minutes. Just as sinister pictures of a marathon occupation by Boycott were beginning to form, he suddenly offered almost his first stroke of the morning and was caught at slip for 15.

Dexter, for a long time tied up by Bromfield, was eventually out for 61, and Parfitt, playing splendidly, was still there at stumps with 44, England having made 240 for four.

[The incident referred to was Barlow's failure to walk when short leg claimed a catch. There was a short exchange of words, and he went on, from 41, to make 138. When he made his 100, there was a pointed lack of applause from the England players, for which there was later an apology. The game ended in a draw, England's captain Mike Smith making 121; both Boycott and Barrington took 3 wickets in S.Africa's 2nd innings.]

First Test: Final day: 8 March

Hall's speed routs Australia: West Indies' first home win

By E.W.Swanton, at Kingston, Jamaica

THE West Indies beat Australia here today by 179 runs, a victory due largely to the superiority of their opening attack, and in particular the sustained excellence of Hall, who took four for 45 in the second innings and had match figures of nine for 105.

This win, gained at the start of the fifth Test series between the two countries, is only West Indies' fourth, their first in a home series. It has been an absorbingly interesting game all through, ruggedly contested yet with good feeling between the sides despite the excitable atmosphere of this cockpit arena of Sabina Park.

Hall has never bowled better, nor has his unflagging spirit been more abundantly manifest. Griffith (2-36) supported him well in spurts without being consistently so fast or so accurate. There was some temporary hubbub when, in the first two overs of his second spell, he was called six times for cutting the front line.

Sobers handled his bowlers well, and, near the end, the crowd enjoyed the crowning pleasure when he himself took the wicket of Philpott, giving him 100 wickets and 4,000 runs in Tests, a matchless achievement.

[Richie Benaud, writing in the Daily Gleaner, stirred up a hornet's nest by accusing Charlie Griffith of being a 'chucker'.]

Fourth Test Second day: 6 May

Australia hurry to 583-2: Openers Simpson and Lawry both hit 200s

By E.W.Swanton, at Bridgetown, Barbados

Simpson (left) and Lawrie: Another record partnership.

THE great partnership between Bobby Simpson and Bill Lawry finally ended today after they had totted up 382, a record for Australia's first wicket by a margin of 149 runs and only 31 short of the world Test record. Australia went on to make 583 for two at the close, a foundation that can hardly fail them.

This is the first time in Test cricket that both openers have scored double centuries. Simpson, who was first out, made 201, bowled by Hall after nearly seven hours at the crease. Lawry, caught by Sobers off Solomon for 210, enjoyed a second-wicket stand of 140 with Cowper, who was there at the close with 102. Lawry had batted nine hours without a chance. It seems a matter tomorrow of the tactical and psychological moment for Simpson's declaration.

[Australia declared at 650-6, Cowper failing to add to his score, but W.Indies made 573 (Nurse 201, Kanhai 129) and the match was drawn after 6 days.]

Third Test Second day: 9 July

Edrich hits ninth 300 in Test history: New Zealand lose cheap wickets

By E.W.Swanton, at Headingley

The Test today went the way that was foreshadowed by the events of yesterday. John Edrich, by taking his score from 194 to 310 before England's declaration, made his imprint on history, after which New Zealand's batting suffered the sort of reaction that a surfeit of runs not infrequently induces among those who have fielded to them, and at the close they were 100 for five.

The England innings was allowed to proceed for all but three hours and a half before, on Edrich passing his 300, Smith brought it to a merciful close at 546 for four. Edrich's was the ninth treble century in Test matches, and the fourth by an Englishman, after Hutton, Hammond and Sandham. It was the third such score at Headingley, the others having been made, need it be said, in more momentous circumstances by Bradman.

A not uninteresting little subsidiary 'record' is that no one apparently has ever before hit so many boundaries in a Test - five sixes and 52 fours. So far as Edrich's wonderful run of scores in first-class matches goes, his total in nine innings is now 1,311, his average 218. When on earth will the luck turn?

Barrington's marathon ended after half an hour this morning, when he had scored 163. The stand between the Surrey pair of 369 was only 13 short of the record second-wicket England partnership of Hutton and Leyland at the Oval in 1938, and is a record for any wicket in England-New Zealand Tests.

[England won by an innings and 187 runs. Titmus took 5-19 in the NZ 2nd innings, including a spell of 4 wickets in 6 balls without any help from the pitch. Edrich was on the field for the whole match.]

Gillette Cup Final: 4 September

Yorkshire triumph in record style: Boycott hitting a revelation

From Lord's

YORKSHIRE beat Surrey in the Gillette Cup final by 175 runs, amassing 317 for four after Stewart put them in to bat. The result was virtually decided by a second-wicket stand of 192 between Boycott and Close, built up with the most brilliant stroke play.

After the solid, relentless rain of Friday, it was quite remarkable that the game took place. But the new drains did their job, the weather forecasters didn't, and the 24,000 capacity crowd had the unexpected pleasure of a warm, dry day under the sun - or at least those who were not of too strong a Surrey persuasion did.

Stewart must be ruing his decision. It is easy to be wise after the event, but is it not better to bat on a wet wicket on a fresh, drying day before the top becomes damaged? And when one cannot start until 12.15 on a bright September morning, is it not certain that the side batting first will have the better of the light?

Surrey were never in the game. Yorkshire won by underlining the traditional values of cricket in a way that did the heart good. Boycott was a revelation. His 146 was the only Knock-out hundred this summer and the highest score in the Cup's three-year existence. He allowed himself a dozen overs for a thorough appraisal of the pitch, scoring half of Yorkshire's 22, and as soon as Close joined him they made a calculated assault on the bowling that took the score to 214 in another 35 overs before Close was out for 79.

Surrey's task of scoring more than five an over was hopeless from the start, and when Trueman (3-31) took the wickets of Edrich, Smith and Barrington in four balls, that was the end of their challenge. For the record, Illingworth took five for 29, but D.J.Insole had no problem in making Boycott Man of the Match.

Second Test Fourth day: 9 August

England well beaten by S.Africa: Triumph for Pollock brothers

From Trent Bridge

SOUTH Africa fully deserved their first Test victory in England for 10 years, by 94 runs, and one can imagine the celebrations tonight in Port Elizabeth, the home place of the remarkable brothers Pollock. Their joint contribution makes a page without parallel in cricket history.

Graham, the batsman, made scores of 125 and 59, while Peter, the bowler, took 10 wickets in the match (5-53 and 5-34).

In addition, Peter contributed 27 runs at No.10 for once out and Graham captured one wicket for six runs in six overs.

For England, the only crumb of comfort today, in what looked like being a thoroughly dismal episode in the English Test story, was the stand after tea between Parfitt (86) and Parks (44 not out). With the score at 127 for seven, England had been batting for 270 minutes on a plumb wicket, with this pair managing only 13 in half an hour. Now they set about the bowling and added 80 in an hour, raising England's hopes, before Parfitt was bowled by Peter Pollock.

[South Africa drew the last Test to win their first rubber against England since 1935.]

County Championship Sussex v Worcs

Worcester retain title in thrilling finish

By Tony Goodridge, at Hove

NEEDING a win to replace Northants at the top of the table and retain the County Championship, Worcester were given a severe fright before beating Sussex at Hove this evening by four wickets with just seven minutes of the extra half-hour to spare.

The manner of their achievement is a proud one, for, little more than five weeks ago, they were ninth in the table with only three wins to their credit. To overtake Northants and Glamorgan, they have had win to 10 of their last 11 matches.

And to win this last match, they had not only to overcome the stubborn resistance of Sussex, especially the bowling of Snow, but had also to contend with the threat of rain, bad light and the pitch.

Sussex's last four wickets today added 80, leaving Worcester to get 132 to win. Time did not seem to be of much consequence, but soon after lunch, John Snow, exploiting a spot on the eccentric pitch, had Worcester struggling at 36 for four. The tension increased when at 70 D'Oliveira, who time and again this summer has rescued Worcester from trouble, was lbw to Oakman.

After tea, Worcester had 85 minutes in which to find 53 runs. Resolutely Richardson (31 not out) and Booth (38) set about getting them, mostly it seemed in singles. Fittingly it was Richardson, who had refused to be stampeded into any rashness during two hours at the crease, who made the winning hit.

Boycott: Gillette record 146.

1966

29 Jan Bobby Simpson (225) and Bill Lawry (119) put on 244 in the 4th Test, at Adelaide, a 1st-wicket record for Australia v England.

1 Mar The Advisory County Cricket Committee, in an attempt to introduce more positive play in the first 2 days of County matches, decrees that each county will play 12 matches (the first game against those sides played twice) with the 1st innings of each side limited to 65 overs, there being no limit to the number of overs per bowler. County committees are to instruct their teams to bowl an average of 20 overs an hour, and polishing the ball will not be allowed - wiping and cleaning to be done under supervision of an umpire.

5 Mar Dick Motz (NZ) hits 22 off an over from Allen against England at Dunedin, a Test record for one player.

15 Mar Colin Cowdrey becomes the 3rd England batsman to score 6,000 runs in Tests, at Christchurch v New Zealand.

15 May First Sunday play in a County Championship match, Essex v Somerset at Ilford, draws 6,000 non-paying spectators and the sale of score-cards, stand seats and collections yields nearly £500.

5 Aug Gary Sobers, scoring his 3rd 100 of the series v England (174) and taking part in a 265 5th-wicket stand with Nurse (137) at Leeds, becomes the first West Indian to make 5,000 runs in Tests and the first player to complete a 5,000r/100w Test double.

23-28 Dec In addition to scoring his maiden Test century (182, including 5 6's, a 5 and 25 4's), and 251 runs in the match, South African wicket-keeper Denis Lindsay dismisses 6 batsmen (all caught) in Australia's 1st innings in Johannesburg to equal Grout's record made on the same ground 9 years ago.

TEST SERIES

England in Australia
A 1, E 1, D 3
England in New Zealand
Drawn 3
West Indies in England
WI 3, E 1, D 1

Third Test First day: 7 January

Barber and Boycott give England great start: Hawke fights back

From Sydney

A late strike by Neil Hawke with the new ball put Australia right back in the third Test here today after Barber's glorious 185 and an opening partnership of 234 with Boycott (84) had placed England in what had seemed an unassailable position.

Hawke's dramatic intervention saw England subside from a dominating 303 for one at about five to five to the less threatening 317 for five some three-quarters of an hour later. At the close, they had falteringly moved on to 328 for five. with Edrich still there on 40, but Barrington, Cowdrey and their captain Mike Smith back in the pavilion. Hawkes figures for his splendidly hostile spell were 8-3-14-4.

But let not these events dim the glory of Barber's innings or of the third-highest opening stand in the story of England-Australia Tests. Barber's part in the English batting effort on this tour has been second to none, but he needed perhaps one outstanding Test innings to establish a position at the top of the tree. Now he has played it. It was his first Test century, and surely will not be his last.

[Hawke finished with 7-105, but Edrich made his 2nd consecutive century (103) and England won by an innings and 93 to go one up.]

Fifth Test First day: 11 February

Barrington to century with a six - again

From Melbourne

THANKS to Ken Barrington (115) and John Edrich (85), England reached a strong position here today after an indifferent start, and by the close were 312 for five. They put on 178 together for the third wicket after England had lost both openers, Boycott selfishly running Barber out and then losing his own wicket at 41.

Barrington played with unaccustomed facility, exuberance almost, with barely a false stroke. The runs flowed, and he reached his hundred, in two hours and a half, by hitting Veivers for a six. No one associates Barrington with sixes, but, remarkable as it may seem, he also reached a hundred with a six on the last tour, at Adelaide. The third wicket made 178 in 178 minutes, and Barrington's share was 115 to Edrich's 62.

England lost Barrington, Edrich and Smith, for a duck, soon after tea, all to Australia's surprise weapon, the medium-paced Walters. But Cowdrey (43) and Parks (29) negotiated the new ball successfully to the tune of 58 in less than an hour and were still there at stumps.

[England made a slow 485-9 declared, before Cowper ground out a monumental 307 in 12hr 7min, Lawry 108, in Australia's 543-8 dec, the match tailing off as a draw, with the 4th day completely rained off. Thus the rubber was shared 1-1 and Australia retained the Ashes.]

Advisory Committee Meeting: 1 March

Suspect bowlers to face season's suspension

By John Reason, from Lord's

THE Advisory County Cricket Committee announced at Lord's last night that a special committee had been set up to adjudicate on bowlers in English cricket who had been either no-balled or reported as having suspect actions. The committee will have the power to suspend a player from bowling until the end of a season.

After one adverse report by either an umpire or a captain, or on the recommendation of a member of the committee, the suspect player will be filmed in at least two matches. There will be no attempt to make the filming secret.

Suspension will not debar a bowler for life, and at the beginning of the following season any suspended bowler will start afresh.

MCC Adjudication Committee: 24 March

Rhodes controversy continues: Committee at odds with top umpire

By John Reason, from Lord's

THE MCC adjudication committee, meeting at the request of Derbyshire CCC to consider the case of fast bowler Harold Rhodes, issued the following statement: "The committee unanimously considered his basic action to be fair, but were divided, on the evidence before them, as to whether or not his action was occasionally suspect. They intend, therefore, to have further films taken and hold another meeting."

By finding Rhodes's action basically fair, the nine (of 13) committee members present are at odds with the country's leading umpire, J.S.Buller. When Buller no-balled Rhodes in Derby's match against the South Africans last season, he clearly considered Rhodes's action to be basically unfair. Rhodes was previously called for throwing in 1960 and 1961.

[Further films of Rhodes's action were taken in June and the committee confirmed their previous statement.]

Rhodes demonstrates his action for the camera.

First Test Third day: 4 June

West Indies thrash England by innings and 40: Sobers supreme

By E.W.Swanton, at Old Trafford

ENGLISH cricket has known several varieties of catastrophe since the mid-fifties, but defeat inside three days, as has just occurred at Old Trafford, is a novelty. It has not happened to an England XI anywhere in the world since Australia beat them at Leeds in 1938 - a matter of 195 Test matches ago.

Congratulations, first, to Sobers and his side, whose win by the margin of an innings and 40 runs by no means exaggerated their superiority in all departments

We have never seen the like of Sobers for all-round virtuosity, and as a fielder not even Sir Learie Constantine, if the memory of my generation is to be trusted, had anything on him. When one thinks of the great 'naturals', Walter Hammond. of course, springs to mind. Jack Gregory, too, and Keith Miller. But take Sobers' performance in this match in all its aspects, his superb batting (161), the fielding including five catches, the holding together of the bowling in the second innings (3-87) in company with Gibbs, in three separate styles as circumstances suggested, to the tune of 42 overs in the day, add the skill and commonsense behind his captaincy - and try to find a parallel. This is the complete cricketing animal.

Scores: West Indies 484 (Sobers 161, Hunte 135; Titmus 5-83), England 167 (Gibbs 5-37) and 277 (Milburn 94, Cowdrey 69; Gibbs 5-69).]

Graveney on the attack.

Fifth Test Third day: 20 August

England's last 3 wickets put on record 361: W.Indies stunned

From the Oval

When Graveney and Murray came together yesterday afternoon, England had lost seven wickets for 166 and were still 102 runs behind on second innings. At the end of another remarkable day at the Oval, West Indies are 135 for four in their second innings and 124 runs from avoiding an innings defeat.

This remarkable turnaround was brought about by the continuation of the eighth-wicket stand, and then another record partnership between the Nos.10 and 11, Higgs and Snow. The 361 runs put on by the last three wickets is a record in Test cricket.

Play continued this morning with England on 330 for seven, Graveney on 132, Murray 81. Graveney began as he left off last night, batting with utter confidence, and it needed a smart piece of fielding from Gibbs to run him out for 165, made in six hours. The stand had realised 217, and although Murray was out shortly afterwards for 112, England, at 399 for nine, were 131 runs ahead and in a better position than even their most optimistic admirers could have wished for.

But there was still more to come - much more. Higgs (63) and Snow (59 not) proceeded to make the first hundred partnership for the last wicket ever achieved for England in this country, 128, only two short of the Foster/Rhodes England record of 1902 - but, then, that was made by a great batsman and a great all-rounder, not two fast bowlers.

Snow, the adrenalin still flowing, then disposed of West Indies' openers with only 12 on the board, both caught behind by Murray, and at stumps the visitors were 135 for four.

[England won by an innings and 34 runs to take some consolation from the series, lost 3-1.]

Clark Committee Report: 19 December

Clark's team opt for two competitions

By E.W.Swanton

AFTER much heart-searching and almost an agony of self-analysis, English first-class cricket approaches the crux. I feel that the impending decision is the most momentous of its kind during my time as a critic. The Clark Committee, chaired by David Clark of Kent, have completed their job, which was to examine the future of County cricket and make recommendations accordingly.

In brief, their chief recommendation is for two separate competitions, in each of which every county plays every other once: the championship of three-day matches, plus another of one-day, for which a title (and a sponsor?) must be found, with seven hours' playing time, under the unvarnished Laws of Cricket.

In the championship, they propose a change in the points allocation. A separate recommendation urges the ICC to recognise one-day matches as first-class.

The committee's findings, which cover several thousand words, outline the diagnosis with commendable clarity and give logical reasons for the cure.

But what now? The plan, yesterday, was put to the Press - which, broadly speaking, did not need much winning over. The cricket writers get more first-hand evidence than anyone else of the need to revise the county system. And I believe that the MCC are strongly behind the plan proposed by the Clark Committee, which, by the way, was set up by the counties themselves.

Yet, despite this impressive weight of opinion, the indications are that the issue, when it is finally put to the 17 counties at the special Advisory meeting at Lord's on January 25, is far from certain.

[The counties rejected the main recommendation by 16 votes to 4.]

First Test Final day: 28 December

S.Africa clinch famous victory: Australia crash by 233

By Michael Melford, in Johannesburg

FROM the depths of 41 for five on Friday morning, and from the dire situation when Australia passed their first-innings score on Saturday with only one wicket down, South Africa climbed gloriously back until with 97 minutes to spare they clinched their first ever home victory over Australia by 233 runs after 64 years of trying.

Today, Goddard, with his six wickets for 53, was their champion, and he left the field this evening on the shoulders of a delirious crowd who were still cheering and singing outside the dressing-rooms an hour later. He was largely responsible for removing the main body of the Australian batting in an extraordinary first 25 minutes this morning when four wickets went down with scarcely any help from the pitch for 15 runs. This paralleled Australia's dramatic collapse in the first innings, when they lost the same four wickets (two to five) for 14 runs

Goddard, of course, is not the only hero of South Africa's remarkable and dramatic victory. There were Lindsay and Van der Merwe, whose seventh-wicket stand of 221 pushed them towards their record second-innings total of 620, Graeme Pollock for a gem of an innings and even the 20-year-old substitute Procter, who finished off the Australians with two catches off Goddard.

Scores: S.Africa 199 (Lindsay 69; McKenzie 5-46) & 620 (Lindsay 182, R.G.Pollock 90, Van der Merwe 76, Lance 70, Bacher 63, Barlow 50), Australia 325 (Lawry 98, Simpson 65) & 261 (Veivers 55; Goddard 6-53).

1967

3-5 Jan The South African brothers Graeme (209) and Peter Pollock (75 not out) make their highest Test scores, at Cape Town, and in the 1st innings put on 85 for the 9th wicket (Peter 41), but Australia win by 6 wickets.

22 Jun England wicket-keeper John Murray takes 6 catches in India's 1st innings at Lord's to equal the world record.

1 Feb MCC confirm the findings of the Advisory County Committee and the Hampshire amendment to the proposals of the Clark Committee - namely, that no alteration to the structure of county cricket be made before the 1970 season.

28 Feb Denis Lindsay (S.Africa) finishes with 606 runs (avge 86.57) in the 5-Test series against Australia, a record for a wicket-keeper.

May Wettest since 1873.

9 Jun Geoff Boycott makes 246 not out at Headingley in the 1st Test against a depleted Indian attack, his highest score and the highest in Tests between the two countries, before Close declares, but is later dropped from the 2nd Test because of his lack of enterprise.

13 Jun India's 2nd-innings 510 is their highest total against England.

31 Jul Hanif (187 not) and Asif Iqbal (76) add 130 v England at Lord's, more than doubling Pakistan's 8th-wicket record (63).

25-28 Aug Ken Barrington hits his 3rd 100 in consecutive Tests v Pakistan, his 142 at the Oval making him the first player to score Test 100s at each of England's 6 Test grounds. He finishes the 3-Test series with 426 runs (avge 142).

26 Aug Fred Titmus (Middlesex and England) completes his 8th 1,000r/100w double, and it will not be done again for 17 years.

26 Dec Sydney Francis Barnes, arguably England's greatest bowler, dies at 94.

TEST SERIES

India in England
England 3
Pakistan in England
E 2, D 1
West Indies in India
WI 2, D 1
Australia in South Africa
SA 3, A 1, D 1

Second Test Second day: 1 January

Riot rules out play: Resumption unlikely

By D.J.Rutnagur, in Calcutta

RIOTING prevented the game between India and West Indies getting under way on the second day. The India Cricket Board of Control met to consider whether the match could continue, but it is likely that the amount of time that it will take to clear up the pitch will rule out play tomorrow, when a final decision will be taken.

The first day's play, twice held up by crowds spilling on to the field, ended with the West Indies on 212 for four wickets. Before the scheduled resumption this morning, there was a problem with the crowd seeking accommodation round the boundaries - apparently more tickets had been sold than there were seats available.

The police mounted a baton charge and the crowd fought back. There were frightening scenes as the police, outnumbered, were forced back, and the crowd burnt down stands and seating.

[The match resumed after a rest day, and West Indies won by an innings to take a winning 2-0 lead in the rubber.]

Tour Match North Zone v MCC Under-25s: 1 February

Brearley lashes 312 in 330 minutes: Young MCC take 514 off Test bowlers

By D.J.Rutnagur, in Peshawar

A MAGNIFICENT undefeated treble century in five and a half hours by their captain, Mike Brearley, saw MCC Under-25 side go a long way today in the process of sweeping through North Zone. By the close they had scored a mammoth 514 for four.

Brearley, whose highest score in first-class cricket was 169 against Combined Services, scored his first 100 in 155 minutes, the second in just over two hours and the third in 51 minutes. He hit 41 fours and three sixes. The only other batsman since the war to score more than 300 in a day was Middlesex opener Jim Robertson, in 1949.

Brearley's first six nearly sent Radio Pakistan off the air, for it missed the commentator's microphone by inches. The second caused havoc in the ladies' stand. Brearley put on 208 for the first wicket with wicket-keeper Alan Knott, who made his first ever senior century with some sparkling shots before he was out for 101 three-quarters of an hour after lunch.

After Buss, Amiss and Fletcher went cheaply, Brearley shared in an unbroken fifth-wicket partnership of 234 in 105 minutes with Ormrod (59), who was forced to play second fiddle while his captain dominated the bowling. Test leg-spinner Intikhab Alam, who plays league cricket in England, took three for 122 but was not the menace we thought he might be, even though the wicket began to turn halfway through the day. At the close MCC were 514 for four, the highest score in a day's play in Pakistan, as was Brearley's innings.

[MCC declared on their overnight score, Hobbs took 6-39 and Hutton finished off North Zone's 1st innings (126) with a hat-trick. MCC won by an innings and 139.]

Fifth Test Fourth day: 28 February

S.Africa complete historic series: 3-1 triumph over Australia

By Michael Melford, at Port Elizabeth

SOUTH Africa defeated Australia by seven wickets this evening with just over a day to spare in this fifth Test match and, by three matches to one, rounded off their very first victory in a series since the countries first met 65 years ago.

When the end came, it was just what the packed crowd would have asked for. Graeme Pollock, Port Elizabeth's own prodigy, was at one end and, at the other, Lance finished the rubber with a towering six. Before the ball had descended high up in the stand, the crowd was on the field and the celebrating of an historic day had begun.

Goddard played another fine innings today, and with three wickets in each innings and scores of 74 and 59 played perhaps the biggest individual part in the triumph.

It was Goddard and Barlow who, by bowling their side back into the first Test on Christmas Eve, tipped the scales towards South Africa for the first time in the series, and it was they who brought off the first decisive coups this morning. Barlow bowled the stubborn Cowper for 54 with his fifth ball, and at the other end Goddard had Martin (20) caught at the wicket. So this obdurate pair were out in 10 balls without adding a run to the overnight score.

The last three wickets, however, added another 71 runs, leaving South Africa 176 to win. Barlow was out for 15, but Goddard and Bacher (40) took the score on apace before Pollock (33) and Lance (28) finished the Australians off. For the record, it is the first five-match series in which a touring Australian team has ever been beaten three times.

Trevor Goddard: Match-winning all-round performance.

First Test Fourth day: 12 June

Pataudi scores third 100 against England as India battle on

By E.W.Swanton, at Headingley

Pataudi in aggressive mood.

IT is no small matter for a Test country such as India to reach their highest score in five tours to England. To have done so after following on 386 runs behind touches the realms of fantasy.

That was the measure of India's achievement today, and all honour to the Nawab of Pataudi, their captain, and to Hanumant Singh for leading their side out of the dark shadows into the bright sunlight of respect handsomely restored.

It was hard to believe as one watched the Nawab that six years ago for all practical purposes he lost the sight of his right eye. He was then 20, and had already established himself at Winchester, for Sussex as a schoolboy, and at Oxford as a cricketer of the highest gifts.

He sees now through the bad eye as through a glass darkly. The loss of focus means that he has not reached quite the dizzy heights that were predicted for him. By determination, by shrewd improvisation, however, he has come to the point of his sixth hundred in his 22nd Test match with an average of 40. It is an uplifting story of handicap surmounted.

The great partnership today was that between Pataudi and Hanumant. In 2hr 40min these two added 134 for the fifth wicket when, if either had failed, all must have been over by tea time. As it is, the game is alive still, and after what has occurred, who will predict the moment of its ending.

Overnight scores: England 550-4dec (Boycott 246 not, D'Oliveira 109, Barrington 93, Graveney 59), India 164 (Pataudi 64) & 475-8 (Pataudi 129 not, Wadekar 91, Engineer 87, Hanumant 73).

[India made 510 (Pataudi 148; Illingworth 4-100) but lost by 6 wickets.]

County Championship Warwick v York: 18 August

Yorkshire booed from field: Close's time-wasting tactics rob Warwick

By Michael Melford, at Edgbaston

Yorkshire clung to the two points that they earn from a draw, but they and their followers are unlikely to look back with pride on the petty, unworthy performance that led to their being booed off the field here this evening. Warwickshire had needed 142 in 102 minutes, and they made a splendid effort to score the runs, finishing only nine short of victory with five wickets standing.

But Yorkshire, running the gamut of time-wasting manoeuvres, bowled only 24 overs in this period. It was a dark, miserable evening of occasional light rain, but no amount of ball-drying could account for this rate achieved by Trueman, Nicholson and Hutton. In the last half-hour, in which Warwick needed 54 runs, only six overs were bowled, and in the last 15 minutes only two.

The Yorkshire and England captain, Brian Close, coming in to instruct the bowler, had just been told by umpire Elliott presumably to 'get on with it' and Jameson had just driven Nicholson over the sight-screen, leaving 24 to get in the last 15 minutes.

Close then had an appeal against the rain promptly turned down, but it got heavier and they went in. It then stopped, and the umpires turned back, with the batsmen, but Yorkshire took longer to reappear, and another four minutes had been used up.

Trueman then embarked on a six-minute over, which included two no-balls and three bouncers. Amiss was out hooking, and A.C.Smith was at the crease long before Trueman was ready to continue. The remaining five minutes was used up with the charade of changing the bowler; Hutton, summoned from a distant quarter, deciding he needed a practice run-up.

Whereupon Yorkshire withdrew through some hostile Warwick members, having apparently been prepared to sacrifice goodwill and reputation for two wretched points.

[There were serious repercussions for Close, who was held entirely responsible. Severely censured by the counties' Executive Committee, who found Yorks guilty of unfair play, he was unrepentant, consequently losing the captaincy of England for the upcoming West Indies tour.]

Third Test Fourth day: 28 August

Asif wins glory with old-fashioned 146: Record late stand makes England bat again

By E.W.Swanton, at the Oval

SOMETHING on the grand scale was required to give a worthy curtain to this summer's Test cricket. At 12.30 such a thought seemed futile indeed. But three hours later Asif Iqbal, the young Pakistani all-rounder, had achieved it. His innings of 146 here today, begun with the board showing 53 for seven and ending on the stroke of the tea interval after the innings defeat had been averted and a new world Test record established for the ninth wicket, was an effort to warm the heart.

It was an innings also to revive the spirits of critics and followers, underlining as it did their belief in the value of a style of play which our modern player-theorists tell us is old-fashioned, and in the more 'scientific' conditions of today, so-called, impossible of achievement.

Asif was magnificent. He begins with a backlift that is high and open, he leans into the ball as he comes forward, and when he plays back he gives himself room by making ground towards the stumps and hits the ball a crisp blow.

Intikhab, the more experienced man, and a good bat in his own right, played the perfect second-string innings, giving only one chance near the end. Asif's innings was chanceless, and the whole partnership of 190 was built at the rate of almost 70 an hour.

It was Close, so often the breaker of partnerships, who brought himself on and induced Asif to push forward, whereupon he was stumped by Knott. Intikhab went next over, bowled by Titmus for 51, and the miracle was over. England scored the 32 needed to win, but not before they had lost two wickets - to Asif, of course!

County Championship
Yorks v Glos: 7 September

Illingworth 14-64 as Yorks triumph: Glos bowled out twice in day

By Henry Calthorpe, at Harrogate

SUPERB off-spin bowling on a turning wicket by Ray Illingworth, who took 14 for 64 in the day, brought Yorkshire to their third Championship title in five years, and to a two-day victory over Gloucester here by an innings and 76.

In the first innings, when Gloucester were all out for 134, Illingworth took seven for 58, and then, when they followed on 175 behind and were out for 99, he had the remarkable figures of seven for six in 13 overs. All his wickets were taken after lunch.

1968

22 Jan Ken Barrington (143) scores his 20th (and last) Test 100, v West Indies in the 1st Test at Port of Spain, reaching a Test century with a six for the third time!

24 Jan An unbeaten 9th-wicket stand of 63 between Sobers (33) and Hall (26), batting throughout the last session on the final day of the 1st Test, deprives England (568) of victory.

23 Feb New Zealand captain Graham Dowling, having made 143 in the 1st Test against India, a NZ record in a home series, makes 239 in the 2nd, at Christchurch, a NZ all-time record, and shares three 100 partnerships.

12-13 Jul In the drawn 3rd Test at Edgbaston, England captain Colin Cowdrey is the first player to make 100 Test appearances and, on scoring 60, becomes the second player (after Hammond) to make 7,000 Test runs. He goes on to make 104, his 21st Test 100.

3-5 Aug Gary Sobers takes 7-69 against Kent at Dover in the 1st innings bowling his left-arm pace, and 4-87 in the 2nd bowling spinners; he then scores the season's fastest century, 105 in 77min.

12 Oct Ken Barrington, 38, collapses at Melbourne (during the Double-Wicket competition) of a heart attack that ends his first-class career (31,714 runs, avge 45.63). In Tests, he scored 6,806 runs (58.67).

19 Oct The 1st World Double-Wicket Championship, played in Australia over 5 rounds in 5 States, is won by West Indies second string, Gary Sobers and Wes Hall.

26-30 Dec Graham McKenzie takes 8-71 (10-159) and Bill Lawry (205) and Ian Chappell (165) put on 298 for the 2nd wicket as Australia beat West Indies by an innings and 30 in the 2nd Test at Melbourne to square the series.

TEST SERIES

England in West Indies
E 1, D 4
Australia in England
E 1, A 1, D 3
India in Australia
Australia 4
India in New Zealand
I 3, NZ 1

Second Test Fourth day: 12 February

Riot stops play in Test: Police use tear gas, Cowdrey struck by bottle

By E.W.Swanton, in Kingston, Jamaica

POLICE used tear gas to break up a riot by spectators which halted play in the second Test match between England and the West Indies at Sabina Park, Kingston, today. Trouble began when the West Indian batsman Basil Butcher was given out to make the score 204 for 5 in the West Indies second innings with 29 runs needed to avoid an innings defeat.

There was uproar and bottles began to fly on to the pitch. Colin Cowdrey, the England captain, was struck on the foot. Cowdrey courageously walked to the boundary fence and appealed for calm. But his move was in vain.

Police carrying plastic shields to fend off the bottles moved into action. Gary Sobers, the West Indies captain, joined the appeals for peace, but both he and Cowdrey had to retreat.

Butcher, beautifully caught behind the wicket by Parks off a leg-glance, had walked before umpire Sang Hue had given the decision, and nothing happened until the next batsman, Holford, had got to the wicket. When Sobers went to the crowd, he told them: "Butcher was out." But those bent on mischief were past hearing.

Cowdrey goes to plead with spectators.

The England team and the umpires reached the pavilion before order was finally lost. The pitch at one moment was being freely run over, and the crowd shouted: "Sang Hue no more." Yet there was no doubt of the legitimacy of the catch. The order to throw the tear gas bombs was given, and the crowd broke in panic.

Play was eventually restarted, with about 70 minutes lost. D'Oliveira finished his fateful over, and at the close West Indies were 258-5, 25 runs ahead, with Sobers on 48.

[Sobers went on to make an unbeaten 113 on the 5th day, declaring at 391-9, and then had Boycott and Cowdrey out himself before England had scored. At the close, England were 19-4, Sobers took the 70min allowed for the riot on an extra day, and England, 68-8, only just held out. Almost forgotten was Cowdrey's 101 on the 1st day, and Snow's splendid 7-49 to tumble West Indies out for 143 in their 1st innings,]

Fourth Test Final day: 19 March

England triumph with minutes to spare: Cowdrey and Boycott lead 78-an-hour dash

By E.W.Swanton, at Port of Spain, Trinidad

England won a victory by seven wickets this evening that had been beyond all human prediction, until Sobers made what, on the face of it, was the most 'sporting' of all sporting declarations. They made 215 in 2hr 42min with eight balls to spare, after a last hour and a half of cricket that maintained a crescendo of excitement from first to last.

Needing 142 in that time, England won thanks to a sparkling stand of 118 between Boycott and Cowdrey, whereof Cowdrey's share was 71 in 75 minutes.

There are various questions that will need a calmer moment to analyse, but writing hot - very hot - on the event, I must couple with the credit to Boycott (80) and his captain an equal measure to the West Indies side for some of the best fielding (though not the best bowling) I ever remember. Also let them be congratulated for scorning any delaying tactics.

Fifth Test Sixth day: 3 April

England's last stand clinches series: Knott & Cowdrey foil W.Indies

By E.W.Swanton, at Georgetown, Guyana

ENGLAND saved the fifth Test this evening and thus won the rubber against the West Indies after a day of hair-raising excitement with the last pair together. That they did so was due to Cowdrey and to Knott.

The captain, who made 82, would be the first no doubt to give pride of place to this splendid young cricketer, who came in when all seemed lost at 12.40, with the scoreboard at 41 for five, and took out his bat for the most valuable 73 runs he may ever make. Men of Kent and Kentish men have done great things for England, but have they ever had a day of such triumph as this?

They came together when England were facing not only defeat but ignominy, and they engaged in a stand that transformed the prospect. When Cowdrey was out 20 minutes after tea, they had taken the score to 168 for six. But there was still 70 agonising minutes left.

Snow lasted 43 minutes for one, using his pads more than his bat before Sobers inevitably had him lbw. Lock, the hero of Monday, lasted this time only seven minutes. But Pocock and then Jones stayed with Knott for the remaining overs.

Scores: W.Indies 414 (Sobers 152, Kanhai 150; Snow 4-82) & 264 (Sobers 95 not; Snow 6-60), England 371 (Boycott 116, Lock 89, Cowdrey 59) & 206-9 (Cowdrey 82, Knott 73 not; Gibbs 6-60).

Second Test Fourth day: 24 June

England fast bowlers rout Australia for 78: 223 still needed to make England bat again

AUSTRALIA were bowled out today in two hours and a half for 78, their lowest score in a Test match since they fell for 58 at Brisbane on a regular gluepot to G.O.Allen's team in 1936.

England, who declared their first innings at the weekend 351 for seven, accordingly have a better chance of squaring the series than the most convinced optimist can have supposed when the proceedings began. In conditions to their liking and sometimes in light unfriendly to their opponents, Brown (5-42), Snow (1-14) and Knight (3-16) bowled most dangerously, and they were excellently supported in the field.

Thus, at the 11th hour and despite the crippling weather delays, the 200th Test between the two countries has made its mark in history after all - irrespective of what happens tomorrow. More time was lost when Australia followed on, and they were 50 for no wicket at the close, still 223 behind.

[With only 150min play possible on the final day, the match was drawn: Australia 127-4.]

County Championship Glamorgan v Notts: 31 August

Sobers hits six 6's in over for Notts

By Arthurian

NOTTS captain Gary Sobers, who also happens to skipper West Indies, achieved the batsman's 'holy grail' at Swansea by hitting six 6's in one over off the unfortunate Malcolm Nash. No one had ever done this before.

The previous record for a six-ball over was 34, by E.B.Alletson, also for Notts, in 1911, but his over included two no-balls. There have been two instances of 32 being scored from a six-ball over, and three players have hit five 6's in an over, Arthur Wellard twice.

It is thanks to an amendment to Law 20, however, that Sobers set the record, rather than being caught off the fifth ball - "a player is not out if the fieldsman, after making the catch, falls across the boundary line". This is just what Roger Davis did after he had pouched the ball on the mid-off boundary. The umpires conferred with Davis before awarding the six.

Gary Sobers: One of the six.

Sobers celebrated by hitting the next ball into the road outside the ground. The crowd rose to its feet, and Sobers, who had made 76 out of 86 in 35 minutes, declared Notts' innings closed at 394 for five.

[In Notts' 2nd innings, Sobers made 72 out of 94 in 111 minutes, and they won by 166 runs.]

Sheffield Shield Queensland v Western Australia: 22 November

Milburn 243 in even time

From Reuter, in Brisbane

COLIN MILBURN, the England batsman playing for Western Australia, tore apart the Queensland attack on the first day of their Shield match, hitting 243 in 234 minutes in an opening stand of 328 with Derek Chadwick - who went on to make 91! Milburn scored 181 between lunch and tea.

[Inverarity and Becker made 100s, WA declared at 615-5 and won by an innings and 75.]

Fifth Test Second day: 23 August

D'Oliveira (158) makes Australia pay - but might imperil South African tour

By E.W.Swanton, at the Oval

ENGLAND piled on the agony today until just after five o'clock, Cowdrey allowing the innings to run its full course before requiring Australia to bat for the last 73 minutes, in which they made 43 for one on what was still an unusually plumb and easy-paced pitch.

England's fine score was made possible today by Basil D'Oliveira, who carried on this morning just as easily and confidently as he had begun last night. He was only fairly successful in the West Indies, which may have caused some to lose sight of the impressive nature of his Test record. In 24 innings, including this one, he has hit two 100s and seven 50s, and acquired an average of 50. For one who habitually bats as low as No.6 in the order these are exceptional figures.

Ironically, however, his fine innings here today may imperil MCC's tour to South Africa in the autumn. It is hardly conceivable now that he will not find a place on merit, when the party is named next Wednesday. And there is a persistent rumour from South Africa that D'Oliveira would not be persona grata.

D'Oliveira and Edrich took their stand this morning to 121 before Edrich was bowled by Chappell for a chanceless 164, made in seven and three-quarter hours. It brought his tally in the series incidentally to within 25 of Denis Compton's 562 in 1948, which is the highest aggregate made by an England batsman in a home series with Australia. D'Oliveira made 158 before he was ninth out, and England went on to a formidable 494.

[Lawry made 135 and Australia 324, before bowling England out for 181, Edrich (17) missing out on the Compton record. Then England, with just 6 minutes to spare, tumbled Australia out for 125 (Underwood 7-50) to win by 226 runs and square the rubber. MCC originally omitted D'Oliveira from the tour party, setting in train the great cause célèbre (see pages 158-9).]

Gillette Cup Final: 7 September

Smith hits Warwicks to rousing victory: Sussex crumple under final assault

By E.W.Swanton, at Lord's

IN SEVERAL respects this curtain to the season at Lord's was more satisfying than anything that had gone before - certainly than any single day's cricket. It was surely the best of the six Gillette Cup finals.

The weather was blissful, the Test pitch extremely good, the sides well matched, with the result in dispute until the close on seven o'clock, and every item of the cricket - to coin a phrase - was razor-keen.

When the Warwick captain, Alan Smith, came in at the fall of the sixth wicket, 60 runs were needed in 13 overs, a higher striking rate than had been achieved by either side all day. Amiss indeed was going very well, but Brown was next in, and with due respect there was not a lot to follow.

Yet Smith, in his characteristic, not to say idiosyncratic, style, so commanded the scene from this crucial moment that the runs came in 10 overs, 39 of them to him.

Scores: Sussex 214-7 (Parks 57, Greig 41; Ibadulla 3-25), Warwick 215-6 in 57 overs (Stewart 59, Amiss 44 not; M.A.Buss 4-42).

Basil D'Oliveira's 100 against Australia at the Oval in 1968 unwittingly sparked a controversy that sucked in prime ministers and parliaments and spawned a movement that fought apartheid for more than twenty years - until it was no longer necessary.

The D'Oliveira Affair

There was always going to be a crisis in the sporting relations between South Africa and other countries as their government became more entrenched in their policy of apartheid, whether or not what became known as the 'D'Oliveira Affair' had brought matters to a head in 1968. Such was the intense feeling of repugnance towards the South African regime, and what it stood for, in so many parts of the world, that it was difficult to see how sporting links with the country could continue to be enjoyed without a great deal of hypocrisy. The issue was, perhaps, clouded by the fact that there were similarly oppressive regimes elsewhere, notably the Soviet Union, but in South Africa the system specifically excluded 'non-whites' from participating in the mainstream of international sport.

Essentially, when Basil D'Oliveira, a Cape Coloured who had qualified to play for England, was first controversially overlooked and then later selected as a replacement in the England party to tour South Africa in 1968-69, the South African government stepped in to say that he would not be acceptable as a member of the team. This not only precipitated the cancellation of the tour, but gave impetus to the movement to isolate South Africa from international sport. The anti-apartheid movement, indeed, succeeded in preventing the planned South African tour of England taking place in 1970, and it was more than twenty years before South Africa again played international cricket.

D'Oliveira - the early struggle

Basil D'Oliveira was born in Cape Town on 4 October 1931. As a Cape Coloured he was prevented by segregation from playing with his white contemporaries, notwithstanding the merit of his performances in minor cricket on the scrubland and matting of Signal Hill, where he once hit 225 runs in 70 minutes and plundered 46 from an eight-ball over.

It would seem that international cricket was a mere pipe dream for this talented young all-rounder, but he always harboured ambitions of playing in England, and in 1958 began a correspondence with John Arlott, whose sympathetic voice he had heard on radio. Thanks to Arlott and Peter Walker, he was offered £450 to play for Middleton in the Central Lancashire League, and that first season had to leave his wife and first child at home. He enjoyed four successful seasons with Middleton, and made his first-class debut with a touring Commonwealth team in Rhodesia.

It was Tom Graveney, on a later Commonwealth tour, who persuaded the unassuming D'Oliveira that he was good enough to play county cricket, and he spent 1964 qualifying for Worcestershire, making a hundred against the Australians. In 1965 he scored six centuries for the county, was the only batsman in the country to make 1,500 Championship runs, and took 35 wickets. He made his Test debut the following season, and soon established himself as England's regular all-rounder.

A catalogue of blunders

The whole D'Oliveira episode in 1968 was a catalogue of mismanagement and blunders by the cricketing authorities and the establishment, while the man unwittingly at the centre of the affair rode the roller-coaster of turbulent controversy with an unwavering dignity that added to his already massive popularity as a cricketer.

D'Oliveira carried the torch for the hopes of his people back home in South Africa, and when, with the pressure very much on him, his form deserted him in the West Indies in 1967-68, there were those who felt he was trying to avoid selection for the following winter's tour of South Africa. Nothing could have been further from the truth, but he failed to recapture his form in 1968 and was dropped by England after the first Test despite top-scoring with 87 not out in their second innings.

It looked, indeed, as if D'Oliveira might have lost his chance of going on the South African tour. Although he hit a rich bowling streak in July, the runs had virtually dried up. But he won back his England place for the fifth Test when opener

D'Oliveira caught and bowled by South Africans at Headingley in 1970 (c. Richards b. Procter), playing for England against the Rest of the World in the series that replaced the South African tour.

Roger Prideaux withdrew at the last minute through illness. This was the turning point. It was D'Oliveira's last chance, and with everything hanging on his performance, he produced his finest Test innings, 158, and then broke a stubborn stand in Australia's second innings to enable Underwood to finish them off and England to square the series. In everybody's eyes, he had booked his place to South Africa - everyone except the selectors, that is.

D'Oliveira's omission caused widespread consternation, with many taking the view that it was a decision made for political expediency. After all, the situation had never been clarified. In 1967, the South African Minister of the Interior had implied that D'Oliveira would not be acceptable as a tourist, but their Prime Minister, Mr Vorster, while emphasising that their internal policy would brook no mixed sporting events, made it clear that visiting mixed teams would be acceptable provided there was no political interference to harm relations between countries or between groups inside South Africa. Did this mean that D'Oliveira would be acceptable? The advice of former British Prime Minister and member of the MCC committee Sir Alec Douglas-Home led the MCC to believe that he would.

The MCC insisted they had chosen the touring side strictly on merit, considering D'Oliveira not for his bowling, which they felt would not be suited to South African wickets (a highly dubious claim), but solely for his batting. In regard to the latter, Prideaux and the young Keith Fletcher were given preference (the omission of Colin Milburn was also a surprise), and the nearest to an all-rounder in the party was Ken Barrington!

The strength of feeling, not only in cricketing circles, against D'Oliveira's omission kept the controversy going. The 'D'Oliveira Affair' was an immediate *cause celebre*. It was front-page news, back-page news, and dominated the leader and correspondence columns of the newspapers. Members of Parliament protested, MCC members resigned and one-time England captain the Rev. David Sheppard led a group of MCC members challenging the MCC's handling of affairs.

Suddenly there was another dramatic twist to the saga. Warwickshire seamer Tom Cartwright had to withdraw through a shoulder injury, and D'Oliveira was named as his replacement - a decision inconsistent with the selectors' reasons for omitting him in the first place. This was all Vorster needed. Within 24 hours he was denouncing D'Oliveira's inclusion: "It is not the MCC team; it is the team of the anti-apartheid movement. We are not prepared to have a team thrust upon us." A week later the MCC, who had in the space of a few days managed to upset first the opponents of apartheid and then its diehard apologists in South Africa, cancelled the tour.

The train of events that followed - the cancellation of the South African tour to England in 1970, the exclusion of South Africa from international cricket - was certainly precipitated by the D'Oliveira Affair. But in retrospect it only hastened the inevitable.

Aftermath

Jun 1969 The Queen awards D'Oliveira the OBE.

Sep 1969 White South African Peter Hain, a 19-year-old engineering student at Imperial College, London, launches the Stop the Seventy Tour Committee.

Dec 1969 Despite the disruption of the current South African rugby tour in Britain, the massive costs of policing it and over 60 police injured to date, the TCCB confirm their unanimous recommendation that the 1970 cricket tour will take place.

Jan 1970 In a Cricketers' Association referendum, 81% of English first-class cricketers are in favour of the 1970 tour. Co-ordinated anti-apartheid attacks on several county grounds result in a shortened tour being arranged, on fairly 'defensible' grounds.

Apr 1970 In a controversial television interview, British Prime Minister Harold Wilson brands the MCC invitation to the South African tourists as "a very ill-judged decision" and encourages non-violent protest against apartheid. The Supreme Council for Sport in Africa threatens the withdrawal of African countries from the Edinburgh Commonwealth Games if the South African tour goes ahead.

May 1970 In an emergency debate in the Commons, Minister for Sport Denis Howell announces a Sports Council resolution urging the Cricket Council to withdraw the South Africans' invitation. South Africa are expelled from the Olympic Movement. The Cricket Council, announcing the decision to go ahead with the South African tour, claim it will be the last Test series between South Africa and England "until cricket is played, and teams are selected, on a multi-racial basis in South Africa". Three days later the Cricket Council cancel the South African cricket tour due to begin in nine days' time (1 Jun), saying they have "no alternative" but to accede to the request made by Mr Callaghan, the Home Secretary.

1976 New Zealand send a rugby union team to South Africa and 22 African nations boycott the Olympic Games. An England youth team is refused entry to Guyana and Jamaica because of South African connections, and a Shell match has to be cancelled when Gordon Greenidge (Barbados) is refused admission to Guyana because he has toured South Africa.

1977 Commonwealth heads draw up the ambiguous Gleneagles Agreement, intended to preclude international competition with South Africa until they practise multi-racial sport at all levels and selection on merit. The South African Cricketing Union (SACU) is formed by the merging of the 'white' and 'black' bodies, but dissidents from the latter immediately form the South African Cricketing Board.

1979 D'Oliveira retires and receives a standing ovation on each of the county grounds he plays on.

1981 The Guyanan section of England's West Indian tour has to be cancelled when Robin Jackman, flown in as a replacement for the injured Willis, is expelled for having played in South Africa. Indian Prime Minister Indira Ghandi intervenes to save England's tour there after the inclusion in the England party of two players, Geoff Boycott and Geoff Cook, who have recently appeared in South African cricket, threatens to abort it. Guyanan batsman Alvin Kallicharran plays for Transvaal and is banned for life by the West Indies Board.

1982 A 'rebel' England side, sponsored by South African Breweries, play a series of matches, including three 'Tests' in South Africa and the players - including Boycott, Emburey, Gooch, Knott, Old and Underwood - are banned from Test cricket by the TCCB for three years. A team from Sri Lanka that tour South Africa are banned from first-class cricket for 25 years.

1983 An unofficial West Indian team, without players vital to future Test sides but including Croft and Kallicharran from Guyana, are the first ever Caribbean tourists to South Africa, creating a furore at home (but surprisingly not so much with the public).

1989 The proposed 'rebel' tour of South Africa by former England captain Mike Gatting and his 'mercenaries' stirs up anti-apartheid demonstrations at home.

The banners are out again, outside Lord's in 1989, protesting against another 'rebel' tour.

Feb 1990 The South African government, under President F.W. de Klerk, lifts the ban on the ANC and other opposition groups, and releases Nelson Mandela from prison. The rebel English tour to South Africa, beleaguered by death threats and pitch damage and harassed by the National Sports Congress, is called off before it is finished, and the second leg due in 1991 is cancelled.

Apr 1991 The United Cricket Board of South Africa is formed by the amalgamation of the South African Cricket Union and the South African Cricket Board, and Dr Ali Bacher becomes the first managing director.

Jun 1991 Apartheid laws in South Africa repealed.

Jul 1991 The ICC sanction South Africa's return to international cricket.

Nov 1991 Return of South Africa to the international fold; they play India in a one-day match at Calcutta.

Apr 1992 South Africa play their first Test since 1971 - their inaugural Test with West Indies, in Bridgetown.

1969

28-29 Jan David Holford (80) and John Hendriks (37 not out) add 122 against Australia at Adelaide, a West Indies Test record for the 9th wicket, and West Indies amass 616 in their 2nd innings to come right back into the match. On the last day, Australia go for the 360 runs, but from 304-3 lose 6 wickets for 29, and are left 21 runs short as the last pair negotiate the remaining 26 balls.

14 Mar Seymour Nurse hits 258 v New Zealand at Christchurch out of a West Indies total of 417, a percentage (61.9) only twice before exceeded in Tests.

17 Jun Rain stops play with 2 hours left on the last day of the County match between Hants and Glamorgan at Bournemouth, and the Hants players leave the ground under the impression the match has been abandoned. Glamorgan stay and, after turning out later for the requisite 2 minutes, are awarded a win by the umpires, a decision later rescinded by MCC, who decide Hants were the victims of a misunderstanding. There had never been any question of a result.

28 Jun John Hampshire (Yorks) makes 107 against West Indies at Lord's on his Test début.

29 Jun R Hutton (Yorks) takes 7-15 in 7.4 overs against Worcs at Leeds in the John Player Sunday League.

27 Jul Somerset captain Brian Langford produces bowling figures of 8-8-0-0 in the JP League, mostly against Essex opener Brian Ward.

25 Sep The 1st India v New Zealand Test starts at Bombay, having been switched from Ahmedabad because of serious rioting there.

20 Nov Gundappa Viswanath hits 137 for India against Australia at Kanpur on his Test début.

TEST SERIES

England in Pakistan
Drawn 3
West Indies in England
E 2, D 1
New Zealand in England
E 2, D 1
West Indies in Australia
A 3, WI 1, D 1
West Indies in New Zealand
NZ 1, WI 1, D 1
New Zealand in India
I 1, NZ 1, D 1
New Zealand in Pakistan
NZ 1, D 2
Australia in India
A 3, I 1, D 1

Fifth Test Fourth day: 18 February

Walters hammers world record as West Indies wilt

By Henry Calthorpe, in Sydney

Walters hammers the West Indies bowling.

AUSTRALIAN Doug Walters became the first batsman in the history of Test cricket to score a century and a double century (242) in the same match when he hammered 100 not out against West Indies today at Sydney. In doing so, he took his aggregate for the series to 696, a record for Australia against West Indies.

The Test had flickered briefly back to life in the afternoon when Australia, who batted again although 340 runs ahead on first innings, lost their first three wickets for 40 against Hall and Griffith. But then Ian Redpath (96 not out) and Walters saw the moment of danger pass, putting on an unbroken 199 for the fourth wicket. At the close, Australia were 579 ahead.

The previous record in a series against West Indies, 650 by Neil Harvey in 1955, had earlier been broken by Bill Lawry, whose aggregate totals 667. But Walters' figures are the more remarkable because he has played in only four Tests and this is only his sixth innings of the series.

[Walters added only 3 more to his record (699, avge 116.50), Redpath (132) made his maiden Test 100 and Australia declared on 394-8, 734 ahead. Sobers (113) and Nurse (137) took the game into a sixth day, but Australia won by 382 runs to take the rubber 3-1.]

First Test First day: 21 February

Ames Test warning: Control crowd or match is off

By Michael Melford, in Lahore

COLIN COWDREY's 22nd Test century and a well-played 54 by Edrich, which launched England on the way to 226 for five, were among the few agreeable events of a chill, uneasy opening day of the series of four-day Tests against Pakistan arranged to replace the aborted South African tour.

The crowd numbered only 10,000, but their behaviour was such that this evening Leslie Ames, the MCC manager, told the Commissioner of Lahore that, unless there was an improvement, England would have to consider whether to continue with the match.

The crowd was generally well disposed to players of both sides, but the occasional violent outbursts of a shouting, chanting mob produced an unpleasant atmosphere for cricket. As soon as the players left the field for lunch, thousands of youths ran across the square, and some invaded the stands. The police offered little opposition.

Aftab Gul, Pakistan's opening batsman, who is a political leader of the students, tried with little success to pacify them. The country has been in political upheaval for some time, and it would appear that the match is being used as an excuse for agitators to cause trouble.

Cowdrey made exactly 100 before he was out next ball, caught off a viciously lifting delivery from Majid Jahangir. His last stroke had put him level with Hammond in the tally of Test hundreds, second only to Bradman, and he needs another 55 runs to become the most prolific scorer in Tests. Nothing could be farther from Cowdrey's mind, however, as the students in the crowd erupted, with wood and fruit flying about, and he departed at a dignified double.

[The match was drawn.]

Third Test: 10 March

MCC home after Pakistan rioters force tour to end

By Michael Melford

At lunchtime yesterday on what should have been the fourth day of the final Test in Karachi, MCC arrived back at Heathrow Airport. The most violent riot of all had caused the match to be abandoned 15 minutes before lunch on Saturday and MCC left for home that night.

This particular demonstration was directed against people watching cricket on a day set aside, only the night before, as one of protest on behalf of teachers. The demonstrators broke into the ground with an ugly, purposeful look that had not marked previous invasions and headed for the pitch.

England at this point had reached 502 for seven after some of the most adventurous batting of the series by Knott and Brown. Knott was within four runs of his maiden Test 100. Brown, however, gauging the mood of the mob, summoned his partner and they raced for the pavilion with the Pakistan players. In no time, the mob had dug up the pitch and then wrecked the main stand.

Armed police soon dispersed the demonstrators, but the match had to be abandoned. MCC manager Leslie Ames had done everything possible to keep the tour alive, but felt it should really have been called off by the Pakistan Board when the team arrived.

First Test Fourth day: 28 July

Underwood (7-32) becomes hero of England victory

By E.W.Swanton, at Lord's

AFTER England's last wicket had added another 39 this morning to set New Zealand the virtually impossible task on this wicket of scoring 362 to win, Derek Underwood exploited the favourable conditions as only he knows how, taking seven wickets for 32 as New Zealand were bowled out for 131.

But New Zealand did not capitulate. In the person of Turner, indeed, they found a man who epitomised calm and skilled defiance. When all might have been over by tea, the eighth wicket lasted nearly an hour, the ninth 45 minutes and the tenth 25. And at the end they had their own hero in Turner to match England's Underwood.

Turner became the 16th man to carry his bat through a Test innings. At 22, he happens to be the youngest batsman on this list, and he is also the only New Zealander: distinction indeed. Turner's special pride must be that he coped confidently, if defensively, with Underwood while compiling his 43 runs, where all of the other recognised bats found him too much for them.

Underwood established his domination with remarkably little positive aid from the pitch, his speed through the air being such that he gave himself little chance of turning the ball. It was enough for the batsmen to think that he was doing so.

Graham Dowling, the New Zealand captain, did, however, feel moved to criticise the pitch and its variable bounce after the match. He said it was too bad to be true, especially at Lord's.

Derek Underwood: England's hero.

John Player's County League Warwicks v Lancs: 24 August

Lancashire become first Sunday champions

By D.J.Rutnagur, at Nuneaton

BEATING Warwicks today by 51 runs for their 12th victory, Lancashire, who still have one match to play, became the first champions of the Player's Sunday League.

Batting first, Lancashire were given a speedy start by Engineer and David Lloyd, but the partnership that really piled the runs on was that between Clive Lloyd (59) and John Sullivan for the fourth wicket. With Lloyd striking four 6's - all of them out of the ground - and three 4's and Sullivan nine 4's, they added 105 in 18 overs, in the Lancashire total of 204 for five.

Warwick lost wickets too regularly to maintain a promising start, and were all out for 153 with 3.1 of their 40 overs unused.

While Lancs were establishing themselves as champions, Clive Radley (Middlesex) was making the new League's highest score, an unbeaten 133 in 40 overs against Glamorgan at Lord's. It beat the 128 not out by the Australian Greg Chappell of Somerset.

County Championship Glamorgan v Essex: 2 September

Glamorgan scrape one-run triumph off last ball

By D.J.Rutnagur, at Swansea

GLAMORGAN beat Essex at St Helen's today by one run off the last ball of the match. No margin could be narrower, and the Welsh county's position at the top of the table heightened the effect of this palpitating climax.

There were three ways in which this thrilling game could have finished as off-spinner Roger Davis prepared to deliver the last ball to John Lever. Glamorgan needed the last wicket to win. Essex wanted three runs to reach their target of 190 in 55min plus 20 overs. And a draw was also possible with the added prospect of Essex (as the side batting second) taking five points if the scores were level.

It was in this tense atmosphere that Lever decided to attempt a virtually impossible second run, having steered the ball down to third man, a part of the field policed by Wheatley, who is not the most agile of fielders.

But with so much at stake, Wheatley moved forward and picked up the ball with commendable speed, and had it in Eifion Jones's gloves with Lever something like four yards out of his ground.

[Glamorgan went on to win their 2nd Championship, after a gap of 21 years.]

Third Test Third day: 18 October

Crowd riot after New Zealand dismiss India for 89

From Reuter, in Hyderabad

A RIOT, which began when India were all out for 89 in their first innings, cut the third day's play by 20 minutes. A section of the crowd stoned police, and one officer was hit. An attempt was made to set a thatched roof on fire, and bonfires were started with waste paper.

After Thursday was washed out by rain, New Zealand lost their remaining wicket this morning without adding to their score of 181. The pitch was supposed to have been cut yesterday, a rest day, but the umpires forgot, and Dowling, the New Zealand captain, was within his rights when refusing to let them compound the error by having it cut this morning.

What effect this had on the Indian batsmen is uncertain, but they collapsed from 21 for one to 50 for nine at tea, Dale Hadlee taking four for 10 and Cunis three for nine. Venkat (25 not out) and Bedi (20), with a brave last-wicket stand of 40, added a modicum of respectability to the score, but a youth coming on to the field to congratulate them was injured by a soldier, and that's when the riot started.

[NZ declared at the end of a slow 4th day (both batting and bowling) on 175-8. With India on 76-7 (Hadlee 3-31, Cunis 3-12) on the last day and some 2hr remaining, another rainstorm stopped play, after which not even the efforts of the barefoot NZ captain to help the motley crew assembled to remove water from the covers could get the match restarted in time.]

Third Test Final day: 11 November

Riot leaves New Zealand victors

From Reuter, in Dacca

BAD light followed by a riot caused the third Test between Pakistan and New Zealand to end in a draw. Thus New Zealand won a series for the first time, with a victory and two draws.

Yet they had looked close to defeat when their second-innings score stood at 101 for eight. Then, daring hitting by Burgess, who carried his bat for 119, and Cunis (23), who helped him add 96 for the ninth wicket, carried the total to 200.

Pakistan, needing 184 to win, had reached 51 for four (Cunis 4-20), with 90 minutes left, when the umpires called the players off because of the light. The crowd grew restive at the delay and invaded the pitch an hour before the scheduled end, and the match had to be abandoned.

The 1970s

The unrest that had plagued the sixties continued into the seventies. Limited-overs cricket proliferated and spread into international cricket, and, in the latter part of the decade, the cricketing world was rocked to its foundations by the intervention of an outside influence in what came to be known as the Packer Affair. For a short time, the breakaway World Series Cricket split the game in two, before a compromise was eventually reached (some would say a 'capitulation' by the traditional cricketing authorities), but cricket has never been the same since.

The attraction of - and the potential profit in - one-day cricket at international level became apparent when 40,000 people turned out in January 1971 at Melbourne to see Australia play MCC in a 40-over (8-ball) match arranged to compensate for the abandonment of the third Test. In the next Ashes series, Australia's 1972 tour to England, a three-match series of one-day internationals was included, instead of the planned sixth Test, for the Prudential Trophy. This practice, with the same sponsors, was perpetuated with all future Test-playing tourist sides in England (except in World Cup years), over two or three matches.

The first cricket World Cup was staged in England in 1975 and, thanks in part to a glorious summer, was an immediate success, producing big crowds, exciting cricket and record takings. The six Test-playing countries took part, with two associate ICC members invited to make up the two groups of four. Fifteen matches (60 overs) were played over 15 days in June, and the tournament was climaxed by a splendid final at Lord's in which West Indies beat Australia by 17 runs. The second World Cup took place in 1979, in England again, with the same formula except that the two associate members qualified through a preliminary competition held in the Midlands for the ICC Trophy. The tournament was another huge success, despite the Packer disruption of world cricket. Australia, especially, and England were weakened by not selecting WSC players (West Indies and Pakistan did). West Indies beat England in the final to retain their title.

Women's cricket meanwhile was holding its own World Cup, indeed upstaging the men's game by holding the first competition in 1973 in England. Staged on a league basis with seven entrants, it was won by England. A second Women's World Cup took place in India in 1978, Australia emerging top of the four competing countries.

A third limited-overs (55) competition was introduced in England in 1972. The Benson & Hedges Cup, which accommodated the 17 counties plus the Combined Universities and two selected minor counties, was based on four groups, or mini-leagues, of five teams which each produced two quarter-finalists for the knock-out stage. The first final was won by Leicester, who beat Yorkshire by five wickets at Lord's.

With four domestic competitions now, there were 38 titles to be won in the seventies, and only four counties failed to pick up a trophy - Derbyshire, Notts, Glamorgan and once-mighty Yorkshire. The decline of the Tykes, although imminent at the end of the sixties, was hard to believe. The county were never far from the headlines, but for the wrong reasons. As Brian Close was relieved of the captaincy in 1970 and Geoff Boycott in 1978, bitter internal feuding split the club into factions, and the playing side suffered.

The most successful county in the seventies was Kent, who won their first County Championship since before the First World War and were successful in every competition, averaging one trophy a year - 3 Championships (including one shared), 1 Gillette Cup, and 3 each of the Benson & Hedges and John Player titles. Leicester won their first ever Championship, in 1975, and also won four one-day trophies.

No cricket competition seemed to be able to survive without outside financial backing, and indeed the ailing County Championship was revitalised by the sponsorship in 1977 by Schweppes. The 1978 competition was for the first time called the Schweppes Championship. Cornhill Insurance had already stepped in to add their name to home Tests.

The Ashes changed hands regularly in the seventies. England regained them in Australia at the beginning of the decade, Australia won them back in the middle, thanks largely to the devastating pace attack of Lillee and Thomson, and then Mike Brearley led England to two comprehensive rubber triumphs in which they won eight and drew two out of eleven Tests, although their record 5-1 triumph in Australia in 1978-79 was against a side far more deprived by the Packer invasion than their own.

In 1979, the Australian Cricket Board reached an agreement with Packer over TV rights, which was what had started the trouble in the first place, and the ICC and TCCB came round, too. The short-lived World Series Cricket, however, did allow the world to see those great South Africans - Eddie Barlow, Graeme Pollock, Mike Procter and Barry Richards - in international competition. At the beginning of the decade, they had inspired South Africa to a 4-0 whitewash of the Australians in what was their last Test rubber before the banishment of the republic from world cricket for over twenty years. Who knows what heights the Springboks might have reached in the seventies had it not been for the unacceptable politics of their government?

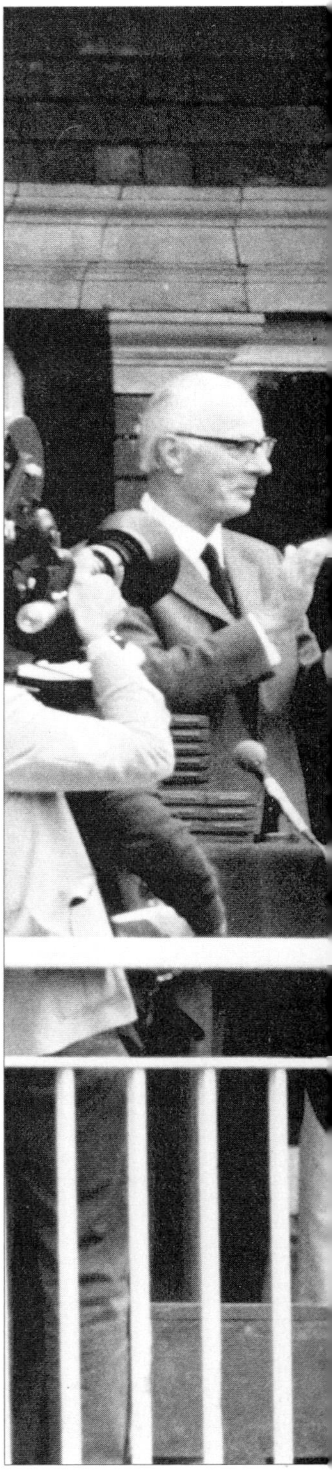

West Indies captain Clive Lloyd is the centre of attention as he holds the second Prudential World Cup aloft, after England's defeat in the 1979 final at Lord's. Most of the England team and some of Lloyd's own colleagues can be seen behind him on the balcony.

1970

6 Jul Colin Cowdrey (64) passes Hammond's world Test record of 7,249 runs in the England v Rest of the World match at Nottingham.

28 Jul Geoff Cope takes 5 wickets in 8 balls for no runs, including the hat-trick, for Yorks v Essex at Colchester.

30 Jul-4 Aug South African Eddie Barlow performs the first Test hat-trick since 1961 (Gibbs for WI v Australia) and equals the feat of M.J.C.Allom (England v NZ, Christchurch, 1930) of 4 wickets in 5 balls when he takes 7-64 for the Rest of the World in England's 1st innings (222) at Leeds. He goes on to take 5-78 in the 2nd innings, and the Rest win by 2 wickets, a 9th-wicket stand of 43 between the two South Africans, Procter and the injured Richards, clinching the series.

Knott is Barlow's first hat-trick victim.

18 Aug Gary Sobers hits the winning runs at the Oval to give his team, the Rest of the World, a 4-1 victory over England. He scores the most runs (588) for either side in the series, with the best average (73.50), makes the highest score (183 at Lord's) and takes most wickets (21 at 21.52).

10 Sep Kent, in their centenary year, and after being bottom of the table on 1 July, win the County Championship for the first time since 1913.

TEST SERIES

England v Rest of the World
RoW 4, E 1
Australia in South Africa
South Africa 4

Second Test Second day: 6 February

Australia stagger to 48-4 facing South Africa's 622: Pollock 274

By Michael Melford, In Durban

GRAEME Pollock's 274, the best innings ever made for South Africa, left Australia struggling today at Durban, the day's play ended with Australia's total reading 48 runs for four wickets.

This, against South Africa's highest total in Tests, 622 for nine declared, is crushing enough. Worse still is that the real damage was done by Eddie Barlow's enthusiastic medium-paced bowling.

Nobody who has seen Barlow bowl would expect him to take three wickets in 10 balls against the best Australian batsmen. But that is now in the scorebook - Lawry, Ian Chappell and Waiters gone for four runs - and with Goddard (1-1) getting Stackpole, a grim battle remains if Australia are to have the slightest chance of forcing a draw.

After Thursday's batting, which almost every English visitor will tell you was the best day's batting he has ever seen, and when Richards (140) made his maiden Test century, an anticlimax was due today. But Graeme Pollock went on with a ready flow of majestic strokes, mostly through the covers, and with Lance (61) put on 200, a sixth-wicket record for South Africa in Tests. Pollock's 274 was made out of 432 while he was at the wicket and included a five and 43 fours.

[South Africa won by an innings and 129 runs, Barlow having a spell of 3-4 late in Australia's 2nd innings to kill off any hopes of a draw.]

19 May

Peter Hain (right) talks with a colleague attacking West Indians playing in England for not supporting the campaign.

S.Africa cricket tour on: Last visit by 'whites-only'

By Guy Rais and Peter Thornton

THE controversial South African cricket tour of England this summer will go on. But the Cricket Council, announcing this decision last night, said it would be the last Test series between South Africa and England "until cricket is played, and teams are selected, on a multi-racial basis in South Africa".

Immediately the decision was announced, Mr Peter Hain, chairman of the Stop the '70 Tour Campaign, said demonstrations would be stepped up. The coming months would see "the greatest show of opposition ever to the tyranny of apartheid".

22 May

Cricket Council cancels tour: South Africans bitter at decision

The South African cricket tour due to begin in eight days' time was cancelled last night by the Cricket Council, who said they had "no alternative" but to accede to the request made by Mr Callaghan, the Home Secretary.

The decision was greeted as "a triumph" by Mr Peter Hain, chairman of the Stop the '70 Tour Campaign, and with bitterness by South Africa, where the Minister of Sport, Mr Frank Waring, said the cancellation was due to "blackmail".

Mr Callaghan wrote to the Cricket Council expressing his "appreciation of the Council's prompt response to the Government's request". In a scathing attack on the decision "forced on" the Cricket Council, shadow Home Secretary Mr Hogg said it was a "classical illustration of the inability of this government to preserve freedom in Britain or maintain law and order".

Mr Billy Griffith, secretary of the Cricket Council, said matches between England and the Rest of the World would replace the cancelled Tests with South Africa.

Fourth Test Final day: 10 March

Hostile Procter's 6-73 completes clean sweep over Australia

By Michael Melford, in Port Elizabeth

BY 50 minutes after lunch at Port Elizabeth today, South Africa had taken the remaining six Australian wickets and won the fourth Test by 323 runs and the series by four matches to nil.

Procter, heavy with 'flu, took four of the wickets and 6-73 in all, which brought his tally for the four-match series to the remarkable one of 26. Again, today, he came on fast and accurate with the new ball and broke up the last Australian resistance.

Before the tour started, South Africa's task had seemed a stiff one. Yet as one looked at the two sides in the nets at Newlands before the first Test, suddenly it all seemed different. On the South African side were five players of world class in Richards, Graeme Pollock, Procter, Barlow and Goddard. What had the Australians to compare with these? On the South African side there were three or four genuine all-rounders, while the Australian batting stopped at No.6.

Procter turned out to be easily the most decisive bowler in the series, and Pollock and Richards confirmed their position as batsmen who would grace any generation. But if there had to be a player of the series, I would plump for Eddie Barlow. He made two centuries, and came on frequently to take the vital wicket, and often the next as well. His enthusiasm and ebullience make him a joy to watch in all he does. I can never remember seeing him drop a slip catch, certainly not in this series, in which he took eight. The South African slip-catching has been the best I have ever seen, but it is Barlow, glasses and all, who gives the impression of infallibility.

The South Africans are looking forward to their England tour as never before.

[South Africa did not play another Test for 22 years.]

First Test Second day: 19 June

Sobers: Innings of pure delight.

Sobers, master of arts, delights Lord's with 147

By E.W.Swanton, at Lord's

There were those last summer who thought they saw signs of a permanent decline in Gary Sobers' cricket. He had played too much. His reflexes had slowed. His eye, perhaps, had lost something of its keenness. The only pity about his performance in the Test at Lord's to date is that the election should have prevented millions from seeing it on their television screens. On Wednesday six for 21; today 147 runs of pure delight.

There has never been a cricketer of such virtuosity. As good as he was, with the added stability of marriage, I believe that, at 33, he may be better than ever. For those of a statistical turn, it is a fact that in the history of Test cricket only a dozen men have taken five wickets or more in an innings and made a hundred in the same match. Now Sobers has done it three times.

Thanks to him, following the fine innings of the South Africans Barlow (119) and Pollock (55), the Rest of the World are in an unassailable position on 475 for six. All that is left is for England to make a struggle of the quality that the occasion deserves.

[Sobers went on to make 183, the Rest made 546 and won by an innings and 80. Sobers took 2-43 in England's 2nd innings, including his 200th Test wicket. Labour lost the election.]

Player's Sunday League Derby v Sussex: 7 June

Ward takes four wickets in four deliveries

By E.W.Swanton, at Derby

ALAN Ward took four wickets in four balls this afternoon on a beautiful fast wicket, M.A.Buss and Graves with the sixth and seventh balls of his first over, Parks and Greig with the first two of his next.

So Sussex were one for four, the one being a no-ball. Thereafter, the left-handed Richard Langridge and Griffith made a brave 76 in 28 overs before Griffith walked out thinking he was bowled, and was promptly stumped. Ward, who had Langridge caught for 41, had final figures of five for 11, and Sussex were all out for 106.

When Derbyshire went in, some handsome strokes by Wilkins (47 not out), Hall and Gibbs saw to it that Ward's famous effort was not in vain, and they won within only 20 overs.

Ward's achievement is the first I have seen in a county match in 43 years, though Gary Sobers took five in five for my side against All-Malaysia on our Far East tour six years ago. No-one before had done the hat-trick in the John Player League, and in county cricket only two men since the war, Fred Ridgway of Kent and Alan Walker of Notts, have taken four wickets with successive balls.

Sheffield Shield Western Australia v South Australia: 20 November

Richards slams 325 in day

By Ray Robinson, in Perth

BARRY Richards, South Australia's South African opening batsman, scored an unbeaten 325 for his state on the first day of their match with Western Australia. It included a six and 44 fours, and was only nine runs short of Bill Ponsford's Australian record of 334 at Melbourne in 1926. Richards, whose second-wicket stand with Ian Chappell (129) was worth 308 and took only 170 minutes, has now scored 693 runs in 28 days, including 224 against MCC.

[Richards made 356 in 372 min, missing by 3 runs Bobby Simpson's highest post-war innings in Australia. South Australia won by an innings and 111.]

Gillette Cup Final: 5 September

Pilling puts end to Sussex hopes

By E.W.Swanton, at Lord's

THE right side won the eighth Gillette Cup Final, as for most of the game it seemed they would. Lancashire fielded most admirably and bowled accurately and intelligently to a well-set field. And when the crunch came, they had a batsman at hand in Pilling.

It was a joy to see how Lancashire captain Bond used slow bowling to help him in the job. Simmons, the off-spinner, had one good wicket, and the promising slow left-armer, Hughes, not the least in the young Lancs galaxy, had 3-31 in 12 overs, the best bowling figures of the day.

Where the occasion fell below expectations was in the general quality of the batting. Michael Buss (42) and Parks (34) played useful innings for Sussex, but the sluggish early run-rate left them struggling to 184 for nine in their 60 overs.

It was not, however, until after tea that we had batting wholly worthy of the scene, when Clive Lloyd and Pilling came together. Fielding together in the covers, they had already rattled the Sussex lower order to the extent of three superfluous run-outs. Lloyd (29) first lifted the character of the batting with several superb strokes before Michael Buss fooled him with a slower ball.

Just as Sussex looked like getting into the game with a chance, however, Pilling showed his nerve and class. In six overs, with Engineer (31 not) settling in quickly, came 30 runs, and the end came fairly quickly after that.

Second Test Third day: 13 December

Greg Chappell (108) and Redpath (159) foil England

By E.W.Swanton, in Perth

A partnership of 219 runs by Redpath and Greg Chappell, in his first Test, restored Australia's fortunes in the most emphatic way after half the side had been got out for 107 at Perth today. It did rather more also, for in its later stages it restored Test cricket as a game that can still be worth watching - just when the record Perth crowd of nearly 23,000 might have been thinking that all the toil and money that have gone into making this ground a new home for Test cricket could have been better spent.

For until young Chappell began to show his natural strokes, there had been long stretches of sterile play. England's 397 had taken 10 hours, and although Ian Chappell had played some fine strokes yesterday evening, he was out for 50 before he got going this morning. Redpath, from his entry at the grisly score of 17 for three, batted with the utmost application and discretion, but the glamour was stolen by his 22-year-old partner.

Greg Chappell's introduction was as torrid as England could make it, and he was content to feel his way, making only a single in the first 40 minutes. Then, in a glorious hour after tea, he went from 48 to 100 and so joined a select company.

[Redpath went on to make 171, Edrich 115 not out for England and the match was drawn.]

1971

2 Jan The 3rd Test between Australia and England is abandoned on the 3rd day without a ball being bowled, and an additional (7th) Test is inserted in the tour programme.

5 Jan Australia beat MCC by 5 wickets at Melbourne in a 40-overs match, the first official one-day international.

14 Jan John Snow (7-40) completes the annihilation of Australia by 299 runs (begun by Boycott with 77 and 142 not), only Bill Lawry (60 not) defying him and carrying his bat for the second time in Tests.

10 Mar India record their first win over West Indies in 25 Tests, by 7 wickets at Port of Spain, despite 35-year-old off-spinner Jack Noreiga having taken 9-95 in their 1st innings.

3 Apr After the first ball of the Transvaal v Rest of S.Africa match to celebrate the 10th anniversary of the Republic, all the players walk off the field and issue a statement to the Press: "We cricketers feel the time has arrived to make our feelings known. We accordingly support our Association in its approach to the Government with the stipulation that merit alone must be the main criterion for selection." The players then return to the field.

30 May In a storm-hit Sunday League match at Old Trafford, Keith Boyce of Essex takes 8-26 in 7.4 overs as Lancs vainly chase a revised target of 98 in 17 overs in farcical conditions.

Oct Australia cancel their South African tour.

TEST SERIES

England in Australia
E 2, D 4, NP 1
England in New Zealand
E 1, D 1
Pakistan in England
E 1, D 2
India in England
I 1, D 2
India in West Indies
I 1, D 4

Seventh Test Fifth day: 17 February

Illingworth leads stricken England side to Ashes triumph

By E.W.Swanton, in Sydney

The Ashes, after 12 long years in Australia's keeping, were recaptured with the minimum of excitement in Sydney today after an hour and a half's cricket with more than a day of the seventh Test to spare. England took Australia's last five wickets for 37 to win the match by 62 runs and the series by 2-0.

The victory is all the more conclusive when it is recalled that England had been put in on a pitch that was helpful to bowlers at the start and grew progressively better, that they began the match without Boycott, their best batsman, and concluded it without Snow, whose injured hand allowed him to bowl only two overs in Australia's second innings.

That the Ashes have been retaken at a heavy and wholly unnecessary cost in terms of sportsmanship should have been evident enough to those who have followed the tour in these columns. But such considerations apart, it is all to the good so far as the ancient series is concerned that, at the sixth time of asking, the supremacy should have changed hands. And Ray Illingworth is to be congratulated on his tactical handling of the side and also on the useful part that his own contributions have made.

An Australian gentleman expresses his dismay to Snow for his aggressive bowling in terms that amuse his fellow spectators.

Snow, of course, has been the chief bowler of the series (31 wickets at 22.83), just as Boycott (657 runs at 93.85) has been the outstanding batsman, while Knott's wicket-keeping has given almost more pleasure than any other item of cricket.

Add the batting of Edrich, Luckhurst and D'Oliveira, and the bowling support provided at various times by Lever, Underwood and Willis, and the sum of it all is a solid all-round performance that Australia could not match.

Scores: England 184 & 302 (Luckhurst 59, Edrich 57), Australia 264 (G.Chappell 65, Redpath 59) & 160 (Stackpole 67)

[On the 2nd day, Jenner was hit on the face ducking into a ball from Snow, who was warned by the umpire for the persistent use of bumpers, and Illingworth protested. The crowd demonstrated against Snow and his captain, who led England off the field, only to return after the umpires threatened to award the match to Australia. Snow took 1-7 in Australia's 2nd innings before breaking his hand on the boundary fence going for a catch.]

First Test First day: 25 February

Underwood (6-12) tumbles out NZ for 65

By Michael Melford, in Christchurch

THE concern felt about the pitch for the first Test in Christchurch has been proved well founded as 13 wickets wickets fell on the first day. New Zealand were bowled out for 65, to which England replied with 56 for three.

When a pitch like this turns up, one spends a lot of time thinking about the ideal bowler to use it and wishing he was present. Today he was, and Derek Underwood duly took six wickets for 12 runs in 12 overs.

Though the outfield, incongruously, was fast, the pitch was damp and soft. It has only thin strips of grass on it and cracks are clearly threatening. The ball followed varying heights for the faster bowlers - Shuttleworth took three for 14 in eight overs - and when Underwood was brought on after 80 minutes, it turned as well, at different heights and paces.

Underwood was in his element. At his brisk pace, bowling at middle and leg as he would on an English pitch of similar type, he fairly raced through the middle and later batting.

A mild thunderstorm during lunch held play up for 80 minutes, but Underwood finished New Zealand off in 55 minutes. When England went in they were soon in trouble to Collinge and Cunis, before Hampshire and D'Oliveira made a start of 31 for three look rather better.

[England won by 8 wickets thanks largely to D'Oliveira's 100, on a pitch still taking turn, and Underwood's 6-85 in the 2nd NZ innings, which took him past the 1,000 wickets mark in first-class cricket.]

Rhodesia v W.Province: 5 March

Procter joins the immortals Fry and Bradman: 6 successive 100s

From Salisbury, Rhodesia

SOUTH Africa and Gloucester all-rounder Mike Procter, in making 254 for Rhodesia in their friendly match against Western Province today, completed his sixth hundred in successive innings, a record held jointly by C.B.Fry of Sussex (1901) and Don Bradman of South Australia (1938-39).

Procter, who accumulated his first five hundreds in five separate matches in the Currie Cup - albeit the 'B' Section, or second division - from November to January, had to wait another two months before his next first-class match. Thanks to Procter's innings and 69 from Gardiner, Rhodesia scored 383 in their first innings against Currie Cup runners-up Western Province.

[Rhodesia won by 7 wickets and Procter did not bat. He scored 22 in his next match.]

Fifth Test Sixth day:19 April

India force draw to clinch series in West Indies: Gavaskar the young hero

By D.J.Rutnagur, in Port of Spain, Trinidad

INDIA clinched the five-match Test series with West Indies when they drew the final Test at Port of Spain, having recorded their first ever Test win over West Indies here in the second Test last month.

The hero of the side was opener Sunil Gavaskar, a 21-year-old university student who became only the second batsman in the history of Tests to score a double century and a century in the same match. Having made 124 in the first innings, he hit 220 in the second to match the feat of Australia's Doug Walters two years ago. Gavaskar batted 8hr 25min, and India were all out for 427.

This left West Indies to get 262 runs to win in 95 minutes plus 20 overs. They went for the runs, but only Lloyd (64) made any real mark. As the wickets began to fall towards the close and defeat became a real possibility, they gave up the chase and at stumps were 165 for eight.

First Test Second day: 4 June

Zaheer's superb 274 sends Pakistan past 600 mark

By E.W.Swanton, at Edgbaston

ZAHEER Abbas again put the England attack to the sword today, taking his score from 159 to 274, a new Pakistan record. At close of play, Pakistan were 602 for seven.

When Zaheer took 14 handsome runs off Shuttleworth's first over of the day, one wondered whether he was going really to cut loose. But it was soon clear that he was content to deal with the bowling strictly on its merits and to deploy his handsome array of strokes as the opportunities presented themselves.

All in all, Zaheer's was a wonderful innings, for which much of the credit must go to Mushtaq for his elder-brotherly guidance and advice at the other end. Mushtaq's third Test hundred came before the great partnership ended - 291 for the second wicket, 45 more than the previous Pakistan record set 10 years ago by Mushtaq's brother Hanif and Saeed Ahmed.

[Pakistan added another 6 before declaring, to enable Asif Iqbal to reach his 100. England, following on, were still 26 behind with 5 wickets left on the last day, which rain curtailed to less than 15 overs. Asif Masood took 9-160.]

Third Test Fifth day: 24 August

Nerve, courage and Viswanath see India through

By E.W.Swanton, at the Oval

AFTER all but 40 years and at the 22nd time of asking, India have won a Test in England, and it gives them the series, too. It still needed an effort of nerve and courage on India's part to make the 173 they required in the fourth innings. When the day began, India, on 76 for two, still required 97. The runs came, with the loss of four more wickets, after three hours of the tensest possible cricket.

The most important innings was the 33 made with the utmost calmness in almost three hours by little Viswanath, at 22, the second youngest player in the match after Gavaskar. Calmness was certainly needed after India's disastrous start this morning when, without a run added, Wadekar (45) was run out.

The fourth-wicket added 48 in 105 minutes before Sardesai was brilliantly caught by Knott off Underwood. England began to exert more pressure, and Solkar made only one in 20 minutes before he lost his wicket. But Engineer and Viswanath made the result certain before Viswanath was out. Chandrasekhar's fine bowling (6-38) on Monday had made the vision possible, but it was indeed a team effort.

Gillette Cup Final: 4 September

Bond's catch sees Lancashire home in great final

By E.W.Swanton, at Lord's

Lancashire beat Kent by 24 runs to retain the Gillette Cup in what was arguably the best of the nine finals so far. They were for most of the time just on top, yet scarcely quarter of an hour from the finish, with Asif Iqbal in full and fascinating command, it looked like the day would be Kent's after all.

Six overs and a bit remained, only 28 more were needed, with four wickets left, and Asif, with 89 to his name, had found in Woolmer a reasonably safe and steady partner. Then came the catch by Bond which settled the matter.

Asif, avoiding Simmons' strong on-side field, made room to off-drive and hit the ball clean and hard, head-high, well wide of extra cover's right. Lancashire's captain, in his 40th year, hesitated a fraction of a second while he sighted the ball in the failing light, then took off and, with a leap that Clive Lloyd would not have disdained, pulled the ball down one-handed as he fell.

Lancs captain Bond and Engineer ('keeper) hold the Gillette Cup aloft.

In a flash, the day had been lost and won, and after seeing the glittering prize so close, Asif must have found Ray Illingworth's inevitable choice of Man of the Match a melancholy consolation.

Lancashire, who chose to bat, must have been satisfied with their score, which owed much to the power of Clive Lloyd (66). The big difference, however, turned out to be the unbeaten eighth-wicket stand between Simmons (28) and Hughes (25), which added 45 in the last six overs and left Kent to make 225, ten more than the highest second-innings score made in a Gillette final. But for Bond, they would probably have done it.

Second World Series match Third day: 11 December

Lillee's speed sends World crashing

By Ray Robinson, in Perth

DENNIS Lillee, of Australia, heads the points for bowlers in the World Series awards, but no points can convey the firing power with which he bowled the World XI to defeat by an innings and 11 runs on the third day at Perth. In taking 12 wickets for 92 against a side well furnished with famous names, Lillee looked like a hawk among hens.

Today, as in his once-in-a-lifetime eight for 29 yesterday which had the World XI all out for 59, the pitch and the batting both appeared to change character for the worse the moment the lean West Australian's long fingers pounded the ball on to the wicket. Nobody else could make the ball leap rib-high from just short of a length at speed that threw timing out of gear.

A third-wicket stand of 107 between Kanhai (118) and Zaheer (51) had given the World XI hope, but an innings defeat loomed closer when a new ball was handed to Lillee at 257 for six, and 22 runs later it was all over.

1972

5 Jan Gary Sobers, 35, completes an innings of 254 for a World XI against Australia, described by Sir Donald Bradman as "probably the best ever seen in Australia".

19 Feb Glenn Turner (NZ) carries his bat for 223 against W.Indies in the 1st Test.

28 Mar West Indies reaches 564-8 in the 2nd innings in the 3rd Test, their highest score against New Zealand.

8 Apr Alvin Kallicharan (W.Indies) scores 100 not out on his Test debut against New Zealand in the 4th Test, at Georgetown.

11 Apr Glenn Turner and Terry Jarvis (NZ) completed a 387 1st-wicket stand against West Indies, Turner compiling his second score of 259 in a week (the first against Guyana). New Zealand's 543-3 dec was their highest score against W.Indies.

20 Apr Gary Sobers (WI) makes his record 85th Test appearance, in 5th Test against New Zealand.

29 Jul England win 4th Test against Australia at Headingley in 3 days to take a 2-1 lead in the series and retain the Ashes whatever happens at The Oval. Derek Underwood, almost unplayable on a helpful pitch, takes 6-45 (10-82 in the match) to pave the way for England's 9-wicket win, although Ray Illingworth's 57 in 4.5 hours is the turning point, and he also takes 4 wickets in the match.

10 Aug Dennis Lillee (Australia) takes 3 wickets in 4 balls in England's 1st innings for the 2nd time in the rubber.

16 Aug Australia win the 5th Test by 5 wickets at The Oval and square the series thanks largely to 5 wickets in each innings by Dennis Lillee, whose 31 in the series is a record for an Australian bowler in England. Rodney Marsh's 23 dismissals in series is also a record. The only hundreds of the match are scored by brothers Ian (118) and Greg (113) Chappell in Australia's 2nd innings.

2 Sep Lancs win their third successive Gillette Cup final, beating Warwicks by 4 wickets with 3.2 overs to spare. Clive Lloyd (12-2-31-0 and 126) is Man of the Match.

9 Sep Troon (170-3) beat Astwood Bank (165-8) by 7 wickets at Lord's in the first final of the Haig National Village Cricket Championship.

12 Sep Warwicks, the only unbeaten county, complete their Championship programme with a win over Notts to claim their 3rd title by 36 points from Kent.

TEST SERIES

New Zealand in West Indies
Drawn 5
World XI in Australia
W 2, A 1, D 2
Australia in England
E 2, A 2, D 1

First Test Fifth day: 21 February

Rowe hits record second century on Test debut

By Henry Calthorpe in Kingston, Jamaica

The Jamaican Lawrence Rowe, who scored 214 in the first innings, became the first batsman to score two separate centuries on his Test debut when he added 33 to his overnight 67 at a run a minute on the last morning. But though West Indies followed this up with some fine leg-spin bowling by Holford, a hundred by Burgess earned New Zealand a draw in the first Test. They finished 104 runs behind with four wickets in hand.

Sobers declared immediately Rowe reached three figures, setting New Zealand to score 341 in 310 minutes. As Holford took four wickets for 35 in 17 overs after lunch, New Zealand slumped from 50 without loss to 135 for five. But Burgess stood firm for just over three hours for his 101, and when he went, Wadsworth and Cunis played through the last hour.

Only two other batsmen have made a double century and a single hundred in a Test - Doug Walters for Australia in 1968-69 and Sunil Gavaskar for India last April - both against the West Indies.

Second Test Fourth day: 26 June

Massie squares the series for Australia: Débutant takes 16 for 137

By E.W.Swanton at Lord's

No Monday miracle here! A greater contrast with the sweat and strain of Saturday could indeed scarcely be imagined as the England last-wicket pair on a balmy summer morning demonstrated that runs were easily come by on this excellent pitch, and Australia then coasted to their inevitable victory.

Massie: Destroyed hopes of a miracle for England.

When, after Gifford and Price had added 30 runs in half an hour, Bob Massie brought things to a close, he made his match analysis 16 for 137 (8-84 and 8-53). This Test will be forever remembered for these figures if nothing else. They are by far the best ever for a Test débutant, the best Australian figures in a Test and the third best analysis in Test history.

Australia knocked off the 81 runs required for their first victory against England in 12 Tests with the loss of two wickets, and the series is squared. There were around 7,000 to see the two and a half hours' cricket on the fourth day, bringing the attendance, including members, somewhere just above 100,000, who paid the largest sum ever taken at a cricket match, around £83,000.

It was a stirring game which, but for the abject English batting of Saturday afternoon, might well have become a classic. In both of England's innings, Dennis Lillee, who took the other four wickets for 140, unsettled the England batsmen with his speed before the prodigious swing of the medium-paced Massie deservedly stole the headlines. But of its kind it was a classic, this 211th Test between England and Australia which must always be known as 'Massie's match'.

Third Test Fourth day: 26 March

Another milestone for Sobers

By E.W.Swanton in Bridgetown, Barbados

West Indies face the fifth and final day's play of the third Test with their backs firmly to the wall, just eight runs ahead of New Zealand and with five second-innings wickets standing. But Gary Sobers and Charlie Davis have already put on 126, and so given their side a chance to escape.

Before a full house of his Bajan countrymen, Sobers on Sunday played superbly. He now has 74, Davis 72. This innings has brought him, in all Test cricket, past the 8,000 mark and so some 500 ahead of his nearest rival in aggregate, Colin Cowdrey. His 8,066 runs have been made in 89 Tests, 84 of them for the West Indies, five for the Rest of the World against England in 1970.

He averages getting on for 100 a Test match. Just throw in 233 wickets, 212 for his country, 21 for the Rest of the World, and you have a statistical achievement - for a man, incidentally, completely uninterested in records and figures - which, as it stands, is unlikely to be surpassed.

These figures are not universally agreed owing to the refusal in some quarters to accept the Cricket Council's definition of the Rest of the World games as unofficial Tests. They are recognised by the editor of Wisden, however, so they are good enough for me. Anyway, those who niggle over the status of those matches have now to acknowledge that after Sunday Sobers has the highest Test aggregate of runs, even excluding the 588 he made in that series.

County Championship: 18 July

Essex crushed by Procter's lbw hat-trick

Mike Procter's match winning performance under scrutiny

By Rex Alston at Westcliff

A remarkable all-round performance by Mike Procter took Gloucestershire to a splendid win over Essex by 107 runs with 12.4 overs to spare at Chalkwell Park, thus consolidating their position as leaders in the Championship .

Without Procter's contribution, the chances are Essex would probably have won the match. The South African all-rounder chipped in with 51 runs and three for 43 in the first innings and 102 and five for 30 in the second. The latter included the rare feat of a hat-trick of lbws while Procter bowled round the wicket to compensate for excessive swing in the cross-wind.

It took Procter 30 minutes to add the 15 runs he needed for his 100. In an innings lasting just under three hours, he hit a six that resembled a golf drive and 13 fours, with the tail helping him to a total of 238, which set Essex to score 245 for victory at around a run a minute.

So he had already put Gloucestershire in a winning position before he embarked on his sensational bowling feat. He trapped opener Saville lbw in his third over, and two overs later came his hat-trick - Edmeades, Ward and Boyce his victims. Essex were 17 for four at lunch, and although they improved after the interval, they never looked likely to hold out.

County Championship: 15 Aug

Pocock takes 7 for 4 as Sussex panic

By Rex Alston at Eastbourne

PAT POCOCK, the Surrey off-spinner, took seven wickets for four runs, including a hat-trick, in his final two overs to deny Sussex victory at Eastbourne. His efforts, plus a run-out off the last ball of the match, left Sussex three runs short with one wicket left.

Incredible is the only word that can be applied to Sussex's failure to win the match and to their losing five wickets in the last over. Set 205 to win in about 130 minutes, they took their score to 187 for one thanks to a second-wicket partnership of 160 between Greenidge and Prideaux. They needed 18 off the last three overs with nine wickets standing when Pocock struck, bowling Greenidge with the first ball and accounting for M.Buss and Parks, too. When he began the last over, Sussex needed five to win with six wickets in hand. But Prideaux, who had completed a first-innings century in the morning, was caught on the boundary off the first ball, and Pocock completed his hat-trick with the wickets of Griffith and Morley. Only a Spencer single off his fourth ball prevented Surrey achieving the impossible, as Pocock bowled A.Buss with his fifth and Joshi was run out off the last ball attempting a second run.

Benson and Hedges Cup Final: 22 July

Leicestershire win first Benson and Hedges final as Yorkshire collapse

LEICESTERSHIRE beat Yorkshire by five wickets at Lord's with eight overs to spare in the first final of the Benson and Hedges Cup, the new League Cup one-day competition.

Despite heavy rain in the early hours of the morning, 18,000 turned out to watch the match, which began on time. Yorkshire struggled to 136 for nine in the allotted 55 overs, which was never going to be enough. They were, however, the only side Leicestershire did not bowl out in a competition they have dominated. In seven matches, no side reached 150 against them, and in the Zonal, five-team league section they were the only side to win all four matches, in addition to which they won an extra point each time for bowling the opposition out (no other side won more than two extra points).

In the B and H format, sponsored for an initial period of two years, the top two sides from each of the sections go through to quarter-finals, played on a knock-out basis. Leicestershire beat Lancashire (135) by seven wickets, and in the semi-finals beat Warwickshire (96) by the same margin.

In the final, Leicestershire's McKenzie took three for 22 in his 11 overs, and Illingworth two for 21 in 10. But the Gold Award for the outstanding individual, chosen by P.B.H.May, went to Balderstone, who hit an aggressive 41 not out for them against his old county. Leicestershire received the top prize of £2,500, to go with the £150 received for each Zonal victory, and Yorkshire, as runners-up, won £1,250.

John Player League: 10 Sep

Kent are champions but Worcs fight to the finish

BEFORE an enthusiastic crowd of 12,000 that tested the capacity of Canterbury's St Lawrence Ground, Kent duly pulled off the John Player League title, though, on a lovely batting wicket against a weakened Worcestershire attack, they might have made easier weather of it.

Worcestershire won the toss and compiled a highly useful total of 190 for 5 in the allotted 40 overs, a bit better than par, perhaps. The left-handed opener Headley was the star, beginning with three superb straight fours off Asif, who took the new ball in the absence of the injured Graham. When he eventually holed out to mid-off off Shepherd, Headley had made 66 out of 107, including most of the 27 made off Underwood's first three overs, against outstanding Kent ground fielding, particularly from Denness, Woolmer, Asif and Luckhurst. Ormrod went on to complete a solid, pleasant innings of 69.

Needing to win to overtake leaders Leicestershire by a point on this last Sunday of the season, Kent began with a flourish, Luckhurst and Johnson scoring 43 in the first eight overs. D'Oliveira, injured in a road accident, was missed by Worcestershire as bowler as well as batsman, while Carter's absence made the faster bowling look thin.

The Kent batsmen could not push along quickly enough to leave the issue beyond doubt, and when Julien, promoted in the order to No.4, stupidly ran Luckhurst (67) out, Kent struggled before Asif (21) and Ealham brought them home in the 38th over, for the loss of five wickets.

However, although 'nerves' affected their play in this crucial match, Kent well deserved to have something to show for their cricket in 1972 - and £2,000 plus a three-week tour in the West Indies is something, indeed.

1973

11 Feb Bhagwat Chandrasekhar sets an Indian record with 35 wickets in a Test rubber. His average in the 5 Tests against England is 18.91.

17 Feb Rodney Redmond (NZ) makes 107 and 56 on his Test debut (his only Test) against Pakistan.

19 Feb Pakistan draw with New Zealand to record their first series win abroad.

29 Mar The third Test between Pakistan and England, at Karachi, ends 45 minutes early because of a dust storm (100 minutes are lost through rioting and field invasions). Three players are out on 99, Majid, Mushtaq and Amiss.

26 Apr Lance Gibbs (West Indies) becomes the first player to bowl 20,000 balls in Test cricket (v Australia, Port of Spain).

9 Aug At Edgbaston, for the second Test, West Indies field 11 players engaged actively in English county cricket.

10, 11 Aug Umpire Arthur Fagg threatens to withdraw at the end of the second day after West Indies captain Rohan Kanhai continues to show dissent over an incident when Boycott is given not out on an appeal for a catch at the wicket. Warwickshire coach Alan Oakman stands for the first over on Saturday before Fagg returns.

12 Aug Kent clinch the John Player League early to retain the title, and win their second one-day trophy of the season, having won the Benson & Hedges Cup three weeks earlier.

23 Aug Kanhai passes 6,000 Test runs.

24 Aug Gary Sobers scores his 26th (and last) Test 100.

25 Aug Bomb hoax at Lord's on Saturday afternoon results in 28,000 spectators being evacuated and the loss of 85 minutes' playing time.

1 Sep Gloucester beat Sussex by 40 runs in the Gillette Cup final to chalk up their first major honour since 1877.

11 Sep County Champions Hampshire draw with Kent at Southampton to finish their programme unbeaten.

29 Dec New Zealand start their first official Test in Australia.

TEST SERIES

England in India
I 2, E 1, D 2
England in Pakistan
Drawn 3
Pakistan in Australia
Australia 3
Pakistan in New Zealand
P 1, D 2
Australia in West Indies
A 2, D 3
New Zealand in England
E 1, D 2
West Indies in England
WI 2, D 1

Second Test Third day: 8 February

Mushtaq & Asif in record 350 stand

A Pakistan record Test partnership of 350 between Mushtaq Mohammad and Asif Iqbal has left New Zealand no hope, other than of saving the second Test match, with two days still to play, reports Reuter from Dunedin.

MUSHTAQ hit 201 and Asif 175 to help the tourists to a monumental first innings total of 507 for six. Intikhab Alam, Pakistan's captain, has announced his intention of declaring, and, for New Zealand, the next two days are likely to be a battle for survival.

The pitch played easily yesterday, but is expected to give the Pakistan spinners more help on the last two days.

Pakistan started the day at 107 for two, and New Zealand's bowlers quickly captured the wicket they dearly wanted when Sadiq Mohammad, the scourge of their attack in the first Test, was bowled by Dayle Hadlee after adding only nine runs to his overnight score.

Mushtaq and Asif were content at first to hit only the bad balls. They scored only three boundaries in two hours, all in the last 30 minutes. But the partnership flourished with a vengeance after tea.

They added 146 in the last hour and a quarter together, before Asif was caught at short leg off a ball from Taylor. He hit 18 fours and a six in his third Test century and personal best Test score. With Mushtaq, he had beaten Pakistan's previous best Test stand – 308, also against New Zealand, at Lahore, 17 years ago – and his country's first-class fourth-wicket stand of 346.

Mushtaq was out one ball after passing his double century. His magnificent innings included 20 fours.

Third Test Third day: 18 February

151 world record stand

BRIAN HASTINGS and Dick Collinge scored 151 runs for New Zealand's last wicket against Pakistan in Auckland to break the longest-standing world Test partnership record.

They thus outstripped the 130 by R.E. 'Tip' Foster and Wilfred Rhodes for England against Australia at Sydney 69 years ago.

Hastings (110) and bowler Collinge, whose unbeaten 68 was his highest Test score, pulled New Zealand from the brink of a follow-on in the third and final four-day Test against Pakistan to a total of 402 and a tie on first innings.

By the close Pakistan were 73 for three and a draw seemed inevitable.

Intikhab's leg-spin brought three wickets in nine balls before Hastings (missed four times) and Collinge (dropped at 35) decided to chance their arm, adding 148 between lunch and tea.

Bruce Taylor's removal of Zaheer in Pakistan's second innings was his 101st Test wicket, a New Zealand record. He later dismissed Sadiq.

Northants v New Zealanders Second day: 31 May

Turner scores his 1,000 runs to join immortals

By E.W.Swanton, and John Mason at Northants

A late cut takes Turner to his historic milestone.

GLENN TURNER has climbed his Everest and Wisden has to add a seventh name on that romantic page which records the scoring of 1,000 runs in May – or, to be pedantic, by the end of May, for, like Tom Hayward, Don Bradman (twice) and Bill Edrich, he was able to start the job in April.

The other three immortals, W.G. Grace, Walter Hammond and Charlie Hallows, scored all their runs in May, W.G. indeed between the ninth and the 30th in that golden year, for him and for cricket generally, of 1895.

This greatest of cricketers needed only 10 innings, while the greatest of all batsmen, Donald George Bradman, in 1938 (when the thing was last done, by him and also by Edrich) batted only nine times and averaged 150.85.

Turner has had the luck to bat more often than his predecessors, 18 times, though in five of these he was undefeated. His average at this moment stands at a splendid 78.30.

On 70 at the end of the truncated first day, Turner needed another 23 runs this morning. Five singles, a two and four fours made up the runs he required, but he spent an uncomfortable hour and a quarter, often tense and nervous, before a late cut, firmly played for four off Bedi, provided the dramatic flourish in what has been the continuing saga of the Glenn Turner Run Machine Show. He went on to complete his century before Bedi finally had him caught by Mushtaq at 111, with his aggregate on 1,018.

First Test Final day: 12 June

New Zealand fall 39 short of historic victory

By E.W. Swanton, at Trent Bridge

THOUGH New Zealand's remarkable resistance continued a while on the fifth day in much the spirit of the fourth, the mountain proved in the end too steep for the later climbers and England came panting home by 38 runs.

There can have been few, outside the England XI, following the game by whatever means, who were not hoping that New Zealand, having got so far, would win this match. After 40 odd years of trying, it would have been poetic justice if the gallant effort of their captain, Bev Congdon (176), supported with such devotion by Vic Pollard (116), had met its due reward.

In the event, their total of 440 was the highest fourth innings ever made in a Test match with the exception of England's 654-5 in the drawn 'timeless' Test at Durban in 1939. It was a remarkable effort in any circumstances, but especially so after their first innings 97, in which Extras was the 'highest scorer' for only the third time in Test history.

It must have been heart-breaking for Congdon, to say nothing of Walter Hadlee, whose two sons, Dayle and Richard, were vitally concerned in the closing stages, to see the victory snatched away when it was clearly within grasp.

England, for their part, as was to be expected of such seasoned cricketers, reimposed their grasp once Pollard was lbw to Greig immediately after lunch. When he was out, after a resistance lasting seven and a quarter hours, New Zealand needed a further 65 runs with three wickets left. But after Taylor went lbw to Snow, England's hero Greig, with 139 in their second innings and seven wickets in the match, finished off the brave tourists by taking the wickets of Dayle Hadlee and Collinge.

Tony Greig, a fine all-round performance for England.

County Championship: 5 July

Cowdrey gets his 100th century

By John Mason, at Maidstone

SHORTLY before 4.45 p.m., Colin Cowdrey, a fraction misty-eyed but smiling broadly, left the field at Maidstone, his 100th hundred safely and sweetly gathered in. His Kent colleagues formed a guard of honour at the pavilion steps.

Kent declared 41 behind Surrey at 326 for five the moment Cowdrey, placing the ball gently square on the off-side, sped through for a single off Jackman to reach 100 – his second century at Maidstone this week.

Nor was Cowdrey's innings – "the last milestone of my career" was how he put it – a poor imitation of the batsman of summers ago. This was brisk (140 minutes, 14 fours), hugely entertaining and of considerable importance to Kent.

Cowdrey, batting at No. 7, a position in itself worthy of comment, was fortunate to be associated on this notable day with Asif Iqbal in their sixth-wicket partnership of 202. In pure cricketing terms, Asif's 119 not out was the better innings.

That, though, is a relative comment only. Not a person on Maidstone's green and pleasant ground would deny that this was Cowdrey's day – the day he became the 16th player to score 100 hundreds – the first since Tom Graveney in 1964, and the third in Kent's history.

First Test Final day: 31 July

West Indies win memorable match: Hayes debut 106

By E.W.Swanton, at the Oval

ENGLAND DID not go down tamely. Hayes' excellent 106 not out and the staunch Hayes–Illingworth partnership salvaged not a little from the wreck of English hopes. But the margin – 158 runs – was in the end conclusive, and in truth it did no more than reflect the West Indian superiority in all departments of the game.

Watching them these last five days, uplifted by their supporters and matching abundant talent with their vast zest for the game, it is hard to credit that the West Indies had not won a Test match since 1969. What is sure is that they can scarcely wait so long for the next occasion for celebration.

England's immediate future, however, is fraught with difficulty. But in Hayes, at least, a new figure of real stature has arrived on the scene. In terms of experience, he is youthful indeed – with only a little more than 50 first-class matches to his name. But, at 26, he gives no impression of immaturity. He moves towards the ball in a way to delight those who remember happier times for England batsmanship, and gets back to hammer the shorter bowling with rare power.

Hayes must thank his captain for the chance of making history by scoring a hundred in his first Test: only four Englishmen have done this since the war, S.C.Griffith, P.B.H.May, C.A.Milton and J.H.Hampshire. Illingworth stayed for two hours for his 40 out of 93 for the seventh wicket, but Hayes was left high and dry as Boyce (6-77 and 11-147 in the match) mopped up the tail.

Third Test Fourth day: 27 August

England crushed by West Indies all-round skills

By E.W.Swanton, at Lord's

NO MIRACLES. The rump of the English batting down to, but excluding, No.11 was disposed of in a couple of hours or a little more. Underwood obstructed for an hour for his 14, and so enabled Fletcher (86 not out) to give the crowd rather better value for their money.

This he did in yet another admirable Lord's innings. But it was a solitary effort against a side that bowled and fielded with a fire and purpose not to be denied, and England's defeat by an innings and 226 runs was by a margin exceeded only once before (Brisbane 1946-47).

Kanhai and his team deserve the warmest congratulations on their first success in a rubber for seven years. On giving reasons for the victory, Kanhai laid stress on the great improvement in the West Indian catching. This is true but, fielding apart, I would ascribe the rejuvenation of the West Indies to three factors, the emergence of Julien, the sudden and unexpected elevation of Boyce to new heights of achievement, and not least to the glorious Indian summer of Sobers.

1974

16-21 Feb Gary Sobers, with 57 runs against England in West Indies' only innings in the 2nd Test, at Kingston, becomes the first player to pass 8,000 runs in Tests. West Indies declare at 583-9, with a 1st innings lead of 230, but England hold on to draw thanks largely to opener Amiss's 262 not out – the next highest 'scorer' was Extras, with 41.

18-21 Feb Sind score 951-7 (Aftab Baloch 428) and beat the questionably first-class Baluchistan by an innings and 575 runs at the National Stadium, Karachi, in the Quaid-e-Azam trophy.

1-6 Mar In the drawn 1st Test against New Zealand at Wellington, Australia's Chappell brothers both score hundreds in each innings, Ian 145 and 121, Greg 247 not out and 133, a total of 646 runs out of 971.

6-11 Mar In the drawn 3rd Test, Lawrence Rowe makes 302, a new record for West Indies against England. Tony Greig scores 148 and takes 6-164 in West Indies' only innings.

24 Mar Ian Redpath carries his bat for 159 out of 346 in Australia's 2nd innings against New Zealand at Auckland.

6-11 Jun England v India, Old Trafford, is the first Test to have provision for extra time at the end of the day if more than an hour is lost (applies on 1st and 3rd days).

21 Jun India's Bishen Bedi takes 6-226 as England compile 629 in the 2nd Test, at Lord's.

24 Jun England dismiss India for 42 in the 2nd innings.

25 Jul In the 1st England v Pakistan Test, at Headingley, a bomb alert delays play for 14 minutes.

8-13 Aug In the drawn 2nd Test, at Lord's, Derek Underwood takes 5-20 and 8-51 against Pakistan.

31 Aug Hampshire, going into their last County Championship game with a lead of 2 points, sit in the Bournemouth pavilion for three days without a ball being bowled against Yorkshire, while Worcestershire, with play possible only on the first day at Chelmsford, take maximum bowling points against Essex to win the title by 2 points.

19 Oct Graeme Pollock scores 222 not out for Eastern Province (373-5, 60 overs) in the South African Gillette Cup against Border.

29 Nov Alan Knott catches Australia's Ross Edwards off Underwood to notch his 200th Test dismissal (185 ct, 15 st).

30 Dec England's Dennis Amiss completes 1,379 Test runs in a calendar year.

TEST SERIES

India in England
England 3
Pakistan in England
Drawn 3
England in West Indies
E 1, WI 1, D 3
New Zealand in Australia
A 2, D 1
Australia in New Zealand
NZ 1, A 1, D 1

Second Test Fifth day: 13 March

Turner the hero as New Zealand at last beat Australia

Reuter report, from Christchurch

NEW ZEALAND completed their first ever victory over Australia, by five wickets at Christchurch. Their hero was Glenn Turner, who became the first New Zealander to score a century in both innings of a Test.

But the historic winning hit came from wicket-keeper Ken Wadsworth, with a boundary. Needing 228 to win, New Zealand, 177 for four overnight, lost the wicket of Jeremy Coney before Wadsworth joined Turner. On a tricky pitch, New Zealand had to struggle for the 51 runs needed on the final day, and they spent an agonising time over the last half dozen.

Turner, 85 overnight, was prepared to wait for the ball he could score from, and slowly pushed his way into the 90s. At 99, he suffered the distraction of Coney's dismissal for 14, with the total at 206. But he reached his century with a boundary cracked backwards of point, after being at the wicket for 240 minutes.

It was a superbly disciplined century, with only a handful of false shots. Turner and Wadsworth edged slowly but surely to their target, and when that was reached, Turner – who had made 101 in the first innings – had scored 110, with Wadsworth on nine. The extent to which Turner dominated the innings is illustrated by the fact that the second-highest scorer was Brian Hastings – who had lost his wicket to the last ball on Tuesday night – with 46.

New Zealand, now one up, go into the third and final Test at Auckland with a strong chance of winning the series.

Benson & Hedges Cup Quarter-final

Young Botham the Somerset hero

By A.S.R.Winlaw, at Taunton

SOMERSET beat Hampshire by one wicket, with six balls to spare, in a thrilling B & H quarter-final, with the Gold Award going to Ian Botham, 18. Going in at No.9 when all seemed lost for Somerset, the young all-rounder scored 45 not out, and won the match with a cover drive to the boundary.

Earlier, Botham (11-3-33-2) had taken the valuable wicket of Barry Richards as Hampshire's first four men all fell with the total at 22. At this point, however, Jesty and Sainsbury hit back with a stand of 95 for the fifth wicket, and eventually Hampshire were all out for 182.

Young Somerset hero Ian Botham, shaken but undeterred after being hit by Roberts.

Then came some rather poor, impatient batting by Somerset, and the match looked lost when they reached only 113 for eight with 14 overs left. All recognised batsmen were out – most of them hitting with heads raised high.

But now came a schoolboy's dream of a match-winning innings. Botham batted, unlike his seniors, with sensible aggression. He and Moseley added 63 for the ninth wicket, profiting at first from some casual Hampshire overthrows, and then from crafty running between the wickets.

Suddenly, with seven overs remaining, Somerset were in with an outside chance. With 38 needed to win, Botham hooked a six, but then was hit in the mouth by a bouncer from Roberts. However, he was quick to take his guard, and with five overs left, only 18 were required. Botham hooked another six, and Somerset were 7 runs short when Moseley was lbw to Roberts for 24.

There were then 16 balls left with the last pair in. Botham contrived to keep the bowling, aided by Clapp's acrobatic dive for a third run, but he played and missed three times in Herman's last over before striking the winning boundary. It was hard luck on Trevor Jesty (79 and 11-2-28-4), but young Botham was the match-winner.

Fifth Test: Sixth day 5 April

England beat West Indies in cliffhanger to tie series 1-1

From Port of Spain, Trinidad

WITH ALL wickets intact, West Indies needed only 196 runs for victory on this last day of the final Test, but more heroics from Tony Greig, who took another five wickets, gave England a dramatic victory by 26 runs with an hour to spare.

It looked easy for West Indies early on, as Fredericks and Rowe, the mainstay of their first innings with a 110 opening partnership, added 33 easy runs to their overnight 30. All Boycott's Herculean efforts – over 13 hours at the crease for 99 and 112 – then seemed in vain.

But then England grabbed three wickets for only two runs as panic began to take hold of the West Indians. First Birkenshaw trapped Rowe lbw, then Greig had Kallicharran caught by Fletcher for his second duck, and Fredericks was run out.

Greig took another three wickets, including the spectacular, diving caught and bowled of the dangerous Lloyd, and Underwood and Pocock chipped in with one apiece to reduce West Indies to 166 for eight at tea.

It looked all over, but stubborn resistance from Boyce (34 not out) and Inshan Ali took the score to 197 before Greig had the latter caught by Underwood for 15. Arnold then bowled Gibbs, and West Indies were all out for 199.

Greig led England off the field with figures of five for 70 to add to his first innings eight for 86, the best England bowling performance since Jim Laker at Old Trafford in 1956.

With 24 wickets in the series at 22.62 apiece, Greig finishes head and shoulders above the other England bowlers and with better figures than any of the West Indians. And his batting average (47.77) edges Boycott into third place for England, with only the splendid Amiss (82.87) ahead of him.

David Lloyd, on the field throughout the last Test, finished with an average of 260 for his two innings in the rubber.

Third Test Fourth day: 8 July

England beat India for loss of two wickets to take series 3-0

From Edgbaston

THE THIRD TEST took its inexorable course as England dismissed India for 216 to win by an innings and 78 runs, with a day to spare, and take the rubber three-nil. This has not happened since the last Indian tour but one in this country, seven years ago.

Only once before in England has a Test been won with the loss of only two wickets, and that was 50 years ago, when England beat South Africa at Lord's. It is a rare occurrence, too, for one player to be on the field throughout a Test match – the feat accomplished by David Lloyd, whose unbeaten 214 in England's first innings set up the win.

Denness, who himself scored 100, declared at 459 for two, having lost the whole of the first day because of rain. India never looked like getting the 294 they needed to make England bat again.

Greig got a couple of wickets in the afternoon, and it was a welcome sight to see him at work in the spinning style on which England's hopes must largely depend in Australia. But, as usual, it was the fast and fastish bowlers – Hendrick, Old and Arnold – who, at a torpid over rate, bored their way through the Indian defences.

Opener Naik put up stern resistance for his 77 before being trapped lbw by Greig. And Mankad (43) was desperately unlucky to go hit wicket when he lost his cap fending off a short one from Old and it fell onto his leg stump.

But the Indian tail soon succumbed, and England's victory was completed in little more than two and a half days' play.

Gillette Cup Final: 9 September

Knott and Woolmer see Kent home in tense struggle

By E.W.Swanton, at Lord's

THE TWO premier sides in one-day cricket fought a grimly tense battle in the postponed Gillette final on a pitch that was always giving the bowlers just a little.

For most of the day Kent kept their heads just in front of Lancashire; but, facing 118, they knew heart-searching moments at 53 for four and 89 for six before Knott (18) and Woolmer (15) saw them home.

The general standard of the batting disappointed, as has been the case often enough on these occasions, with Clive Lloyd, run out for 25, the only man to reach 20. But this was balanced by some marvellously athletic out-cricket by both sides, with Kent perhaps having slightly the edge.

But the highest marks, too, to Lancashire for the fact that they always bowled to attack. This was personified by Wood (17 and 12-5-18-3), who for many of us was the man of the game, though with hot competition from Shepherd, Woolmer and, of course, Knott, whom Brian Close elected Man of the Match amid the usual scenes in front of the pavilion.

County Championship: 27 July

Jameson and Kanhai in 465 stand

By John Mason, at Edgbaston

JOHN JAMESON'S 240 not out for Warwickshire against Gloucestershire was his highest innings in first-class cricket. But this was only one of six records set by him and his partner Rohan Kanhai (213 not out) as they took Warwickshire to 465 for one in 100 overs, having begun after Abberley's dismissal in the first over without a run on the board.

Their partnership beat the world record for the second wicket by 10 runs, and was a Warwickshire record for any wicket. They also established national and Warwickshire records for the second wicket, besides being the first Warwickshire players to score double hundreds in the same innings.

Jameson, in for 310 minutes, hit 34 fours and a six; Kanhai, 30 fours and a six. It seems gratuitous to add that earlier in the week against Lancashire, on the same ground, they put on 231 – small fry!

[Warwicks went on to win by an innings and 61 runs.]

First Test Fourth day: 26 November

India face defeat as Greenidge makes debut 100

By D.J.Rutnagur, in Bangalore

WEST INDIES took a firm grip on the first Test, taking two Indian second-innings wickets for 36 after setting them 386 to win.

Clive Lloyd savaged India's bowlers for 206 minutes in scoring 163, and Gordon Greenidge, run out for 93 in the first innings, made his Test debut century after all.

West Indies declared at 356 for six, and in the last hour of the day Keith Boyce dismissed Sunil Gavaskar and Eknath Solkar, both caught behind by Deryck Murray. India's position is even more dangerous, as Mansur Ali Khan and Farokh Engineer were injured in the field and are unlikely to bat on the final day.

Lloyd's sixth Test century took only 104 minutes, and his chanceless innings contained 22 fours and two sixes. Greenidge, who put on 207 with Lloyd for the fourth wicket in 160 minutes, had 14 fours and two sixes in his 107.

[India were bowled out for 118 and lost by 267 runs.]

1975

14 Jan Andy Roberts (West Indies) takes five for 57 in India's 2nd innings for match figures of 12 for 121 in the fourth Test, at Madras.

23-29 Jan West Indies beat India by 201 runs in the 5th Test, at Bombay, to take the rubber 3-2. Clive Lloyd scores 242 not out in their 1st innings of 604 for six.

30 Jan Alan Knott's 106 not out in the 5th Test is the second hundred by a wicket-keeper in the 219 Tests between England and Australia, Leslie Ames, also of Kent and England, being the only other to achieve three figures (120 at Lord's in 1934).

8-13 Feb Colin Cowdrey plays his last Test, a record 114.

20 Feb Len Baichan (West Indies) scores a hundred (105 not out) against Pakistan at Karachi on his Test debut.

7 Jun England's 334 in a World Cup match against India is the highest in England for a 60-over match.

18 Jun In the World Cup semi-final at Headingley, Gary Gilmour takes six England wickets for 14 and then guides Australia to the 94 they need for victory with the top score of 28 not out after they slump to 39 for six.

16 Jul In the second round of the Gillette Cup, Barry Richards (129) and Gordon Greenidge (177) put on 210 for the first wicket in Hampshire's record total of 371 for four in 60 overs against Glamorgan.

26 Aug Bowler Robin Hobbs, going in at No.9, makes 100 in 44 minutes against the Australians at Chelmsford, the quickest century for 55 years and the fourth fastest ever. He scores his second 50 in 12 minutes off 15 balls, and hits 7 sixes and 12 fours. His runs come in a sixth-wicket stand (two men were absent) of 133 with opener Hardie, who carries his bat for 88, but it is not enough to prevent defeat by 98 runs.

15 Sep Leicestershire, already Benson & Hedges Cup winners, clinch the County Championship for the first time in their 96-year history.

12-16 Dec West Indies beat Australia by an innings and 87 runs at Perth in the 2nd Test, memorable for opener Roy Fredericks' 169 out of 258 in which he completes 100 in 71 balls as he savages Lillee and Thomson; Andy Roberts' 7 for 54 in Australia's 2nd innings; and Lance Gibbs' only wicket, his 300th in Tests.

28 Dec Gary Cosier scores a hundred (109) for Australia against West Indies at Melbourne on his Test debut.

TEST SERIES

Australia in England
A 1, D 3
England in Australia
A 4, E 1, D 1
England in New Zealand
E 1 D 1
West Indies in India
WI 3, I 2
West Indies in Pakistan
Drawn 2

Sixth Test Third day: 10 February

Denness's record 188 gives England 377 lead

By E.W.Swanton, in Melbourne

Mike Denness: Played captain's innings.

IT IS EASY to imagine how disappointing and indeed irritating it must have been since this Test series began to read at home of England's persistent ill-luck. Equally, people must have been questioning the view of those critics on the spot who have maintained that the difference between these sides simply is the presence of Dennis Lillee and Jeff Thomson.

The fact of England's vast score (529) made in the absence of both injured (Lillee after six overs, in which he dismissed Amiss for nought) has served to put the respective virtues in context.

Michael Denness's achievement, especially in the light of his several misfortunes, can scarcely be underlined too strongly. He was the chief architect of the recovery from 18 for two, after Cowdrey had gone, with Edrich (70), Fletcher (146) and Greig (89) in turn playing highly effective roles in support.

By the time he was out shortly after lunch for 188, he had beaten the 173 by A.E.Stoddart in 1894-95, the highest innings hitherto by an England captain in Australia, and topped his own best score.

At one stage, 600 looked on, but Walker mopped up the tail, taking five of the last six wickets for 17 in four overs and a bit, which gave him figures of eight for 143. Thus England's lead was 377.

Australia, whose first innings (152) was wrecked by Peter Lever's six for 38 (four for five in six overs at the start to leave them on 23 for four), fared better in the hour remaining, Redpath and McCosker taking them to 32 without loss.

[Australia reached 274 for three on the fourth day, but despite a defiant Greg Chappell 102 on the fifth, crumbled to 373 all out, and England won by an innings and four runs, their only victory in the rubber.]

First Test Fifth day: 25 February

New Zealand No.11 close to death after deflecting bouncer

From Auckland

EWAN CHATFIELD, the New Zealand No.11 batsman, narrowly escaped death on his Test debut after deflecting a bouncer from Peter Lever into his face. Bernard Thomas, the MCC physiotherapist, and John May, an ambulance man, rushed on to the pitch, and Mr Thomas gave the stricken batsman heart massage and mouth-to-mouth resuscitation before Chatfield could be moved to the ambulance.

Mr Thomas said that Chatfield's heart had stopped beating for several seconds, adding: "It was the worst case I have seen, and I never want to see another."

Lever left the field behind the stretcher weeping, and would not be consoled, though his team-mates tried to convince him that he was not to blame. Nor could the sympathy of New Zealand captain Bev Congdon help. He agreed with the England players that the bouncer was a legitimate weapon to use in the circumstances.

Chatfield and Geoff Howarth, the New Zealand last pair, had carried their overnight stand of 21 to 44 by sound defensive batting, and Howarth had just passed his 50 when the unhappy end came, leaving England victors by an innings and 83 runs.

The blow struck Chatfield on the left temple, and he has a hairline fracture of the skull. He assured the distraught Lever that the accident was his own fault, and is expected to leave hospital tomorrow.

County Championship Essex v Leics: 8 May

Spectacular Boyce hits 100 in 58 min and has 5-7 spell

By D.J.Rutnagur, at Chelmsford

LEICESTERSHIRE felt the full force of Keith Boyce's ability at Chelmsford as the West Indian all-rounder, having registered the fastest Championship century for 38 years – 58 minutes – proceeded to capture five wickets for 25 runs and snap up two slip catches for good measure.

The result of his spectacular efforts, combined with brilliant bowling also from Ray East (4-24), was an unassailable position for Essex. They totalled 300 in 99.5 overs for maximum batting points on a damp turning pitch, and Leicestershire were 60 for nine at the close.

[Boyce took Leicestershire's last wicket with the first ball the next day, and another six wickets for 48 in their second innings gave him match figures of 12-73, but the resolute Balderstone (101) helped Leics hold out for a draw at 207-8.]

Prudential World Cup Final: 21 June

Gritty Australians bow to Lloyd in thrilling final

By Michael Melford, at Lord's

ALL DAY LONG, as the Prudential World Cup final unfolded at 14 overs an hour amid the clank of cans, the honk of horns and other less-than-tranquil visitations of cricket 1975, Australia were on the losing side. But to their great credit they kept going, so that it was always possible that some heroic individual feat might turn the match for them. And when it was all over, just before a quarter to nine, they had lost by only 17 runs.

England supplied a lovely summer's day; West Indies and Australia fought a historic battle; and, though West Indies always looked the stronger side, the 'ifs' that might have brought Australia victory were numerous.

Of these, perhaps the decisive event was when Clive Lloyd, mistiming a pull off Lillee, was missed on 26 by Ross Edwards at mid-wicket, who dived but dropped the ball. If he had held it, West Indies would have been reduced to 83 for four.

In the event, Man of the Match Lloyd amassed 102 runs. With his immense power, Lloyd is a cruel opponent for a fielding side once he gets going, and captains more knowledgeable in limited-overs cricket than Ian Chappell have found it impossible to set fields for him.

With his back foot lifting and drawing back as the bowler bowls, he is astonishingly quick into position for a big man, and he hooked Lillee for six and picked up Walker, then operating round the wicket, for another six with strokes well outside the scope of the ordinary mortal.

Gilmour, bowling straight and moving the ball just enough to make him the most effective bowler for this type of cricket – and perhaps for any cricket in England – finally had Lloyd caught at the wicket. He finished with five for 48. Walker, however, conceded 71 runs without taking a wicket, and West Indies, with difficult catches not being held, scored 82 runs from their last 13 overs. Their total, 291 for eight, is a score no side batting second has yet surpassed to win a 60-over match in England.

If only the Australians, after reaching 81 for one in the 21st over, had not begun to run themselves out. Five run-outs, the first three costing the precious wickets of opener Turner (40) and the Chappell brothers (Ian 62, Greg 15), were evidence of the pressure that Australia were under to keep up the required rate.

Three times the batsmen hesitated, three times Viv Richards threw in accurately, and Ian Chappell, who played so well, became, it is thought, the first batsman to run out his brother at Lord's since Denis Compton did it in the grand manner in 1954 in Leslie's benefit match.

At 162 for three in the 39th over, it needed only Ian Chappell to continue as he was going and for Doug Walters to play the innings which some sparkling strokes appeared to herald. But with the third run-out and a swing across the line by Walters (35), the Australian position began to deteriorate in the soft evening light, until Thomson (21) and Lillee (15 not out) made a last effort of great spirit, mustering 41 in six overs for the last wicket. Inevitably, it was a run out that ended their resistance with eight balls remaining.

Third Test Fifth day: 19 August

Test pitch sabotaged by 'Free George Davis' campaigners

From Headingley

AT 6.50 A.M. on what would have been the final day of an evenly poised Test between England and Australia that promised an exciting climax, Leeds groundsman George Cawthray took off the covers, which had not appeared to be disturbed, and discovered that irreparable damage had been done to the pitch.

Thus the Test had to be abandoned, with Australia – at 220 for three – still 225 runs short of the target that would have clinched the series for them.

With the fourth and last Test, at the Oval, due to start Thursday week and running into September for the first time since 1880, it has been impossible to arrange a Test to take the place of the Headingley match.

The vandalism, which involved digging holes in the wicket and pouring oil on it, was undertaken as publicity for an ongoing campaign to overturn a 20-year jail sentence for armed robbery imposed on George Davis, an East London minicab driver, last March. The campaign was launched in April, and one of the chief organisers, ironically named Peter Chappell, has admitted to ramming a car into the gates of Buckingham Palace and into the front doors of The Daily Telegraph and other newspapers in order to draw attention to the Davis case. Campaigners have also daubed slogans on public buildings and draped a banner across the dome of St Paul's.

[Rain set in at mid-day, so the Test would not have been completed in any case. Peter Chappell was jailed for 18 months in January 1976, the sentence including 9 months for damage to the Headingley pitch and a wall.]

Captains Tony Greig (left) and Ian Chappell inspect the damage to the Headingley wicket.

1976

26 Jan Surinder Armanath (India) makes 124 against New Zealand on his Test debut.

1 Feb Lance Gibbs (West Indies) takes his 308th Test wicket, against Australia in the 6th Test, to beat Fred Trueman's record. He finishes up with 309.

5 Feb Rodney Marsh (Australia) equals the number of dismissals in a rubber with 26 against West Indies, albeit in six Tests.

13-17 Feb Richard Hadlee takes 4-35 and 7-23 against India as New Zealand register their first victory by an innings in Tests.

12 Apr India become only the second country (Australia at Headingley, 1948) to win a Test with a fourth-innings score of 400 or more when they amass 406-4 to beat West Indies at Port-of-Spain.

22 Apr Young Rhodesian bowler Paddy Clift takes 8-17 for champions Leics in MCC's first innings on his Lord's début.

13 Jul West Indies beat England by 425 runs at Old Trafford. Holding takes 5-17 as England succumb to pace in their 1st innings of 71, only Steele (20) and Extras (19) reaching double figures. England's highest scorer in the match is Extras (25) in the second innings (126), in which Roberts takes 6-37. For West Indies, Greenidge scores a hundred in each innings.

14 Jul Herts beat Essex by 33 runs in the Gillette Cup to become the first Minor Counties side to reach the quarter-finals.

31 Jul-3 Aug A badly depleted Middx inflict West Indies' first defeat of the tour, and the only one by a county. Five wicket-keepers are used, Middlesex captain Brearley and then Butcher replacing the injured Kinkead-Weekes, and Findlay relieving Murray for West Indies.

13 Aug Viv Richards, with 291 against England at the Oval, sets a new record of 1,710 Test runs in the calendar year.

4 Sept Northants beat Lancs by four wickets in the Gillette Cup final, the first major honour in their 98-year history.

9 Oct Two notable début achievements in Pakistan v New Zealand at Lahore. Javed Miandad (163), at 19 years 119 days, becomes the youngest ever début centurion and New Zealand off-spinner Peter Petherick, who takes Javed's wicket, follows up with those of Wasim Raja and Intikhab Alam to become only the second player to perform the hat-trick in his first Test.

30 Oct Majid Khan becomes the first Pakistani to score a Test hundred before lunch, and the first player to do so for 46 years.

TEST SERIES

West Indies in England
WI 3, D 2
WI in Australia
A5, WI 1
India in New Zealand
NZ 1, I 1, D 1
India in West Indies
WI 2, I 1, D 1

Fourth Test Second day: 22 April

India declare after fiery Holding burst

By D.J.Rutnagur, in Kingston, Jamaica

FIERY BOWLING by Michael Holding with the second new ball dimmed India's achievement of scoring 178 for one on the first day of the final Test against West Indies at Sabina Park. With two batsmen retired with severe injuries, India were forced to declare at 306 for 6, 15 minutes before the scheduled tea interval, Holding returning figures of four for 82.

Besides Holding's hostile pace, which he sustained through long spells, India's batsmen had to contend with an undulation in the surface of the pitch, which the pace men often hit when they bowled a good length. The sharp lift that Holding and Holder got from this ridge accounted for two dismissals and three nasty injuries.

Gaekwad, who scored an unattractive but brave 81 in seven and a half hours, was struck on the temple and had to retire. Then Patel (14) was hit on the mouth by another rising ball and also had to leave the field.

Patel's injury needed several stitches, and Gaekwad, who was struck over the body, arms and hands innumerable times during his long vigil, was kept in hospital for X-rays.

Viswanath (8) was the third batsman to be injured when he broke a finger trying to play a defensive stroke to yet another lifting ball from Holding. Holding was not averse to intimidating the batsmen with short-pitched deliveries. He bowled bumpers with enough frequency for the umpires to caution him.

West Indies scored 82 without loss before the close.

[West Indies won the Test (and the rubber) by 10 wickets with two days to spare, as India could muster only six men (Bedi and Chandra had injured fingers attempting return catches during the West Indies innings) for their second innings and made only 97.]

England Test trial: 28 May

Underwood and Cope skittle Rest and boost Test claims

By Michael Melford, at Bristol

ENGLAND won the Test trial by 127 runs with seven balls to spare. The Rest were bowled out for 48 – largely by Underwood (15-11-10-4), as formidable as ever on a turner, and a worthy partner in Geoff Cope (14-7-27-5) – on a pitch on which Dennis Amiss had just made 124 not out.

Richard Lumb (13) was the only batsman to reach double figures as England swept through the Rest in an hour and 50 minutes. For six overs, however, the last pair, Miller and Ward, promised to hold out. But David Steele was called up for the penultimate over, and with his fifth ball had Ward caught by Roope, one of a cluster of close fielders.

Fourth Test Fifth day: 27 July

Greig magnificent, but West Indies clinch series

By Michael Melford, at Headingley

WEST INDIES won the fourth Test by 55 runs, and with it took an unassailable 2-0 lead in the series, but defeat is less sour after a magnificent cricket match from which England emerged with much honour and renewed hope.

Several reputations have been re-established or, in Peter Willey's case (36 and 45), founded, not least that of the captain, because Tony Greig's 76 not out, following 116 in the first innings, will go down as one of the great innings that failed.

The honour lies not in running West Indies so close, but in doing so after they had made the morale-breaking score of 330 for two by tea on the first day, and after England's own reply to a score of 450 had stood at 32 for three early on the second day.

There must obviously be disappointment, for of the 204 scored in the last innings, eight batsmen mustered only 14 between them. Only Woolmer (37), Willey and Greig did themselves justice on a pitch that was true enough for 260 to have been comfortably attainable.

Moreover, if the series had been level now, there would have been genuine hope for England in a six-day match at the Oval, especially if the pitch bore any resemblance to the one on which the Essex spinners recently routed Surrey.

One heartening sight was the performance of Willis (3-71 and 5-42), who is the fastest of the current English bowlers. There must have been times, during the months when he has fought against injuries, when it seemed that he might never play first-class cricket again, let alone Test cricket.

Obviously England's Test batting is not yet geared to cope with the fastest bowling. The frequency with which batsmen were beaten for speed around the off-stump showed the difficulty of getting into position in time to play bowling a yard or two faster than is normally encountered in domestic cricket.

Knott in the first innings (116) showed signs of returning form, and Greig played superbly in each innings, scoring all the last 40 runs made from the bat. Ward's nought conceals a worthy piece of resistance lasting 47 minutes during which 46 runs were added for the ninth wicket.

Tony Greig drives Holding.

John Player League

Kent's title with less than half a run to spare

By D.J.Rutnagur

IN A FINISH that the most imaginative writer of fiction could hardly have thought up, Kent emerged champions of the John Player League, the title being decided by the last ball bowled in the competition – at Cardiff. Five counties finished on 40 points, Kent and Essex edging out Leics, Somerset and Sussex by dint of more away wins (five), leaving the whole issue hanging by the slender thread of run rate. The winning margin was 0.428 per over (Kent 4.988, Essex 4.560).

Kent lifted their scoring rate to winning proportions with a spectacular assault on Gloucester's bowlers at The Mote, Maidstone, pillaging 278 runs for five wickets. This devastation, led by Asif Iqbal (106) and Mike Denness, who put on 150 for the third wicket from only 22 overs, prefaced Kent's victory by 123 runs.

Essex, who made the running in the competition for most of the season before fading in the last four weeks, finished in the frame by beating Yorks by 12 runs at Leyton. They scraped through despite being dismissed for a modest 154. John Hampshire then carried his bat for 77, but Yorks collapsed from 76 for one to 142 all out as John Lever and David Acfield took three wickets apiece.

However, neither Kent nor Essex would have been in contention for top place had Somerset not failed so narrowly against Glamorgan or Sussex not been overwhelmed by Warwicks. In fact the possibility of Kent's triumph was deemed so remote that when Sussex were bowled out for 149, the helicopter carrying the trophy and the sponsors' representatives started a futile journey to Cardiff, arriving there as the last dramatic over was in progress.

They were in time to see Somerset No.10 Colin Dredge run out going for the crucial third run that would have given them a tie, two points and the title. The chopper took off again immediately, and proceeded to Maidstone, where Kent were awaiting their awards.

Fifth Test Final day: 17 August

14-wicket Holding brings England a 'darkest hour'

By Michael Melford, at the Oval

ONLY EIGHT bowlers have taken more wickets in a Test match than the 14 for 149 Michael Holding wound up with in the last Test match, and none of those is likely to have done so in such unhelpful conditions. On a dead pitch, at the sight of which most fast bowlers would have winced, Holding bowled England out for the second time, taking 6-57 to add to his first-innings analysis of 8-92. So, with 80 minutes to spare, West Indies won a great Test victory by 231 runs, and the series 3-0.

The damage was done in the first hour, when England lost five wickets for 35, four to Holding in his opening spell. Knott, with Steele and Miller, then fought back for three and a quarter hours, but, in the end, there was too much to do.

The secret of Holding's success was not only that he bowled faster than anyone else, but that he bowled a full length.

At the start of the day, it seemed that England, 391 behind with all second-innings wickets standing, should have been able to bat until the close. But within a few minutes, it was clear that this was going to be one of the blacker days of English cricket. First-innings hero Amiss (203) resumed in the morning with the arm hit on Monday evening heavily strapped, and he was pushing out rather stiffly to Holding's fourth ball when he gave second slip a straightforward catch.

It was Holding, too, in his second spell, who broke England's resistance, knocking out Knott's middle stump as he played forward to a good-length ball on 57. And, appropriately, Holding finished off the innings when he hit Willis on the foot.

First Test Fifth day: 22 December

England win by an innings as débutant Lever wrecks India tailenders

By Michael Melford, in Delhi

John Lever: 10-wicket haul on Test debut

The magnitude of the achievement of Tony Greig's team in winning at the Ferozshah Khotla ground, Delhi, by an innings and 25 runs is most simply illustrated by the reminder that this is only the fifth Test that England have won in India and only the third in five tours since the war. It was also England's first victory under Greig's captaincy.

As John Lever took the last three wickets for three runs in 22 balls, and emerged from a dreamlike first Test match with 10 wickets for 70 and an innings of 53, India were well and truly beaten. Yet England must know that the margin is deceptive, and that this is no time for complacency.

England have certainly looked the better side, as was predicted beforehand, in second-line batting, fast bowling and, especially, fielding. But 80 per cent of their 381 runs were scored by Amiss (179), Knott (75) and Lever. The others have yet to master the best of India's spin attack.

It is unlikely, too, that England would have forced a win without the quick destruction of India's first innings by Lever (7 for 46) and what Sherlock Holmes might have called the Curious Affair of the Changed Ball. Certainly, Lever also swung the new ball on the last morning enough to suggest that the one produced on Saturday night might not be an isolated phenomenon, but the extra humidity and a 9.45 start might have contributed to that.

And what would have happened if Amiss, far from well at the start of the match, had succumbed in England's early disasters (they were 65 for four), or if India had won the toss? The luck, in truth, favoured England, and if it is luck to find umpires in distant lands with much the same interpretation of the lbw law as exists in England, they were lucky in that, too.

In one other way were England lucky. Their brilliant fielding, which deprived India of many runs, would not have been the same without 'Greyhound' Randall, who substituted almost throughout for Amiss, pedestrian by comparison.

The match could not have been played in a better spirit. For the moment, MCC will celebrate joyously, steeling themselves, however, for the second Test, to be played in the huge amphitheatre of Eden Gardens, Calcutta, on New Year's Day.

1977

9 Feb Waheed Mirza (324) and Mansoor Akhtar (224 not out) set a new world record 1st-wicket partnership of 561 (beating Holmes/Sutcliffe, 1932), playing for Karachi Whites against Quetta at the National Stadium, Karachi, in the Patron Trophy tournament. It is the third highest in first-class cricket (although the standard of their opponents is seriously questioned).

18-23 Feb Record extras, 173, in the 1st Test, West Indies v Pakistan, out of an aggregate of 1,398 runs.

4 Mar Colin Croft, in his second Test, takes 8-29 in Pakistan's 1st innings (2nd Test, Port-of-Spain), only the second West Indies fast bowler to take eight wickets in an innings and the equal 12th best bowling analysis in Test history.

1-6 Apr Mushtaq Mohammad scores 121 and 56, and takes 5-28 and 3-69 for Pakistan against West Indies (4th Test, Port-of-Spain).

13 May Tony Greig loses England captaincy for signing with Packer.

12 Jul John Edrich scores his 100th hundred, 101 not out for Surrey against Derbyshire at the Oval.

28 Jul-2 Aug Geoff Boycott (107 and 80 not out) returns for England after 30-Test exile, batting on every day as Australia are beaten by 7 wickets at Trent Bridge.

25-30 Aug England v Australia at the Oval, last Test before World Series Cricket. Alan Knott makes record 65th consecutive (and last) appearance, Geoff Boycott scores 5,000th Test run and finishes with the highest average (147.33) for an Ashes rubber.

29 Aug Ray Illingworth (119 not out) and Ken Higgs (98) take Leics from 45-9 to 273 with a last-wicket stand of 228 against Northants at Leicester.

29 Aug Frank Hayes hits 34 (6,4,6, 6,6,6) in an over for Lancs against Glamorgan off Malcolm Nash at Swansea, the same ground and bowler featured in Sobers' 36 in 1968, but bowling seam instead of spin.

9 Sep The first County Championship to be sponsored by Schweppes is decided on the last day, with Middlesex (holders) sharing the title with Kent and adding it to their Gillette Cup triumph.

25 Nov Packer wins High Court action. The judge, after a case lasting 31 days, rules that players who have already signed contracts with Packer may be considered by Test selectors, and that those cricketers who already have contracts with counties are still entitled to enforce them.

2 Dec First 'Super Test', between WSC Australian XI and WSC West Indies XI, begins at the 77,000 capacity VFL Stadium, Melbourne, in front of 400 spectators, growing to 3,000, while official Test v India in Brisbane draws 9,000.

14-19 Dec Mudassar Nazar (114) makes slowest Test hundred, for Pakistan v England at Lahore – 9hr 17min. Not to be outdone, Boycott (63) takes 4hr 50min for his 50.

First Test Fourth day: 22 February

Last pair rescue Pakistan

From Bridgetown, Barbados

WASIM BARI, Pakistan's wicket-keeper and No.11 batsman, who was rescued by a lifeguard in a bathing incident earlier in the day, turned 'life saver' himself with an unbeaten 60 against West Indies in the first Test. He and Wasim Raja (71), Pakistan's first-innings century-maker, staged a fourth-day rescue of the touring side after a second-innings collapse to 158 for nine, a lead of only 172.

They added a record 133 runs for Pakistan's last wicket, and have set West Indies a target of 306. Pakistan's earlier batting had been laid waste by Colin Croft, 23, a fast bowler making his Test debut. Croft grabbed four wickets – those of Majid Khan, Sadiq Mohammad, Asif Iqbal and Javed Miandad – to turn what had looked an inevitable draw into a seemingly simple win for the West Indies.

Andy Roberts weighed in with two wickets to reduce Pakistan to an unhappy 115 for six at lunch, then took another, following Joel Garner's two successes, to hasten the tourists' collapse. But the two Wasims – and a mammoth total of 68 extras as West Indies' fielding went to pieces – may yet save the day.

[The last day provided more drama as West Indies, with Fredericks (52) and Richards (92) forcing the pace, collapsed from 142 for one to 237 for nine. But Roberts and Croft held out to save West Indies from what would have been their first defeat at Bridgetown since England beat them in 1935.]

TEST SERIES

England in India
E 3, I 1, D 1
England in Australia (Centenary) Australia 1
Australia in England
E 3, D 2
Pakistan in Australia
A 1, P 1, D 1
Australia in New Zealand
A 1, D 1
Pakistan in West Indies
WI 2, P 1, D 2

Centenary Test Fifth day: 17 March

England hero Derek Randall hooks Dennis Lillee for four

England lose but Randall makes a fight of it

By Ray Robinson, in Melbourne

ENGLAND were beaten, as expected, in the Centenary Test in Melbourne. What was not expected, however, was the slender margin of Australia's victory, and Tony Greig, the touring captain, was right to point out that the loss of this one match was outweighed by England's recovery of batting stature.

A thrilling last day recovery, inspired by Derek Randall's 174 – the Notts right-hander's first Test century – swept England to a total of 417 – 11 runs beyond the highest winning innings of any Test. Alas for Randall, Greig and England, it was still 45 runs short of the asking total. So Australia triumphed, as they had in the first-ever Test between the two countries, and by an identical margin.

Yet for seven and a half hours, England had threatened the impossible, clinging to the lifebuoy offered by Randall. England's latest Test hero is slightly built – 5 feet 8 inches tall and 11 stone – yet his strokes skimmed over the Melbourne outfield as smoothly as the Queen's Rolls-Royce.

Randall, forever restlessly fiddling with his cap, maintained his aggressively watchful vigil for the equivalent of a day and a quarter, enabling England to average 3.75 runs an over. Most of his 21 fours were placed through the off field; his cover drives were unexcelled by players of either side.

He went through a difficult time after being felled by a Lillee bouncer, giving partner Amiss some concern. But he recovered, and they carried their third-wicket stand to 166 in 3 hours, before Amiss (64) fell to an in-cutter from Greg Chappell.

There was an incident with Lillee, who claimed a catch off the bat, but Randall pointedly fingered his shoulder. On 161, Randall was given out to a catch by Marsh off Chappell, but the Australian wicket-keeper sportingly had him recalled, indicating that the ball had not carried.

But he was soon to go, pushing forward to O'Keeffe's leg-break and falling to Cosier's bat-pad catch. It was 346 for five. Greig (41) soon went, too, but Knott (42) hit five vigorous fours before he was last to go, lbw for Lillee's fifth victim. Lillee (6-26 and 5-139), Australia's hero, was carried off by his jubilant team-mates. It was the least he deserved.

[It had been a fluctuating match, with Australia, put out for 138 in their first innings, dismissing England for 95, Greig top-scoring with 18. Then Australia's No.7, Marsh, coming in at 187-5, held their second innings together with an unbeaten 110, enabling them to declare at 419-9.]

9 May

35 defect to Packer's TV 'circus'

By Michael Melford

KERRY PACKER, chairman of the Sydney-based television network Channel Nine, said that the following players had signed contracts for the Australia versus the Rest of the World series this winter:

ENGLAND – A.W.Greig, A.P.E.Knott, J.A.Snow, D.L. Underwood.

PAKISTAN – Asif Iqbal, Majid Khan, Imran Khan, Mushtaq Mohammad.

WEST INDIES - I.V.A.Richards, C.H.Lloyd, M.A.Holding, A.M.E.Roberts.

SOUTH AFRICA - B.A.Richards, M.J.Procter, E.J.Barlow, R.G.Pollock, D. Hobson.

AUSTRALIA - I.M.Chappell, I.R.Redpath, R.Edwards, G.S. Chappell, D.K.Lillee, J.R. Thomson, I.C.Davis, R.B. McCosker, D.W.Hookes, K.D. Walters, R.W.Marsh, R.D. Robinson, K.J.O'Keeffe, G.J. Gilmour, M.H.N.Walker, M.F. Malone, L.S.Pascoe, R.J. Bright.

Without firm knowledge of what the proposed unofficial tour of Australia by a team of international cricketers will involve, the Test and County Cricket Board were inclined to see the defection by 35 players, who are reported to have already signed contracts with a commercial television company, as being mainly an Australian affair.

However, D.B.Carr, secretary of the TCCB, said that if the details were as reported: "There are wide international ramifications which will require discussion between all countries concerned. As far as English cricket is concerned it will be, of course, most disappointing to everyone if three or four of our leading players decide to join up with a commercial 'circus' rather than be available to tour with England."

In Australia, the Board secretary Alan Barnes issued a warning that a contract binding a player to a television company might put his career in jeopardy, and this warning was later reinforced at Hove by Len Maddocks, the Australian manager, who is a member of the Board.

Whatever the rights and wrongs of the affair, one cannot blame certain players, especially those on their way out of Test cricket, for feeling that their future lies with the circus. But what kind of future will it be? Professional athletics has been unsuccessful because it lacked the staging that established international events provided. The Test match has always been recognised as the supreme trial between two countries, and whether a synthetic unofficial series between unofficial sides would prosper after the first impact must be in doubt.

It could be, too, that the players themselves, if they forced their Boards to disown them, may lose their glamour. Loyalty is still not an entirely undervalued quality, and cricket followers may not take kindly to players turning their backs on the game that has helped them to the top.

County Championship: 30 June

Turner holds the stage – 141 out of 169

From Swansea

GLENN TURNER, New Zealand's captain, gave a marvellous one-man show for Worcestershire against Glamorgan, carrying his bat for 141 out of 169 – a world record for the percentage of runs scored by a batsman in a complete innings.

He batted for 220 minutes, starting yesterday evening, and hit a six and 18 fours. His hundred was scored out of 128 in 173 minutes, the only blemish coming when he was on 92, Ontong missing a second-slip catch off Nash.

No other batsman reached double figures, the next highest score being seven by Gifford, who figured in a ninth-wicket stand of 57 in 50 minutes which saved the follow-on.

[No play was possible on the third day because of rain.]

B & H Cup Final: 16 July

Gloucestershire romp to victory but fans do them no credit

By Michael Melford, at Lord's

GLOUCESTER easily beat Kent by 64 runs, and provided a fine example of how to make the most of available resources. With the confidence given by Mike Procter's inspiring leadership, they used the talent of their early batting and their fast bowling to assert their superiority at the start of each innings, and there was scarcely a moment all day when Kent came anywhere near to disturbing it.

Man of the Match Andy Stovold (71 and three catches at the wicket) and Zaheer Abbas (70) steered them to 191 for 2 after 45 overs.

When Kent went in facing a total of 237, they managed only 10 runs in the first 10 aggressive overs from Procter and Brain, and lost two wickets into the bargain. For once in Kent's successful limited-overs history, their formidable middle batting capitulated feebly. Brain (7.3-5-9-3) took two more wickets, and Kent were all out for 173 in the 48th over.

Alas, Gloucestershire's supporters did them less credit than their players. At the end, they launched themselves at players and umpires in a way that will have to be stopped before someone is injured.

The trouble is that the only known way, apart from the erection of high fences, is by an appeal for good sense and good behaviour, qualities not nowadays pre-eminent in an out-of-season football crowd that has been sozzling all day.

Fourth Test First day: 11 August

Boycott's century of centuries puts England in charge

By Michael Melford, at Headingley

ONLY THE most macabre imagination could have pictured Geoff Boycott failing to make his 100th hundred on his return to Test cricket at Headingley, and at 10 minutes to six on the first day the feat for which one and all were waiting was duly accomplished.

The day's play thus ended amid tremendous scenes of jubilation, and the fact that England's score stood promisingly at 252 for four, with Boycott on 110, did nothing to detract from them.

Boycott was all but caught at the wicket when 22, but otherwise played with a look of permanence. The Australians appealed at full throttle for a catch at the wicket on the leg side when he was 75, and umpire Alley had to speak severely to the bowler, Bright. Boycott made only five in 45 minutes after tea as he moved on towards the inevitable moment of glory. It was a straight drive to the football stand off Chappell that eventually brought about the historic event.

The ball was not halfway to the boundary when the hero's bat was raised on high, and amid a rare hubbub, small boys were converging on him from all over Yorkshire.

Boycott goes to his historic hundred with a four.

[Boycott went on to make 191, and England, with Botham taking 5-21 in Australia's first innings, won by an innings and 85 runs to clinch the series 3-0 and regain the Ashes.]

1978

4 Jan Indian spinner Chandrasekhar (12-104) takes his second 6-52 at Melbourne to give India their first ever Test win in Australia.

29 Jan Bobby Simpson, at 41 years 360 days, scores 100 against India in the 5th Test at Adelaide.

24 Feb-1 Mar An inspired all-round performance by Ian Botham at Christchurch as England beat New Zealand by 174 runs – 103 and 30 not out; 5-73 and 3-38; 3 catches.

4-10 Mar Geoff Howarth makes 122 and 102 for New Zealand in the drawn third Test with England at Auckland.

17 Mar Graham Yallop (Australia) is the first batsman to wear a helmet in a Test, against West Indies at Bridgetown.

18 Apr West Indies dismiss Australia for 94 (Derek Parry 5-15) to win 4th Test by 198 runs and regain Sir Frank Worrell Trophy last held in 1965.

19 Apr Ian Botham takes a hat-trick for MCC against Middlesex on the first day of the season.

22 Apr Wayne Daniel, back from Barbados only the day before, sets a B & H record with 7-12 in 11 overs for Middlesex against Minor Counties (East) at Ipswich.

2 Jun Chris Old takes 4 wickets in 5 balls against Pakistan at Birmingham in the first Test to be sponsored by Cornhill Insurance.

28-30 Jun Surrey are shot out for 95 and 75 by Kent at the Oval, Derek Underwood taking 4-17 and 9-32.

26 Jul ICC introduce experimental law limiting bouncers to one per over.

28 Jul Tony Pigott, 20, Sussex fast bowler, achieves a hat-trick against Surrey at Hove, never having previously taken a first-class wicket.

24-28 Aug Ian Botham takes 6-101 and 5-39 as England beat New Zealand by 7 wickets at Lord's in 3rd Test.

8 Sep Alan Lilley makes 100 not out for Essex against Notts at Trent Bridge on his first-class début.

16-21 Oct First Test between Pakistan and India for 18 years, at Iqbal Park, Faisalabad, a new Test venue.

14-19 Nov Sunil Gavaskar (111 and 137) makes two 100s in a Test for the second time. Zaheer makes a record 583 (at 194.33) for a 3-Test rubber.

TEST SERIES

Pakistan in England
E 2, D 1
New Zealand in England
England 3
England in Pakistan
Drawn 3
England in New Zealand
E 1, NZ 1, D 1
India in Australia
A 3, I 2
Australia in West Indies
WI 3, A 1, D 1
India in Pakistan
P 2, D 1

England tour of Pakistan: 17 January

Pakistan ban Packer men: avert possible strike

By Michael Melford, in Karachi

THE PRESIDENT of the Pakistan Board made a late announcement that the selectors had been told not to include the three Packer players, Mushtaq, Zaheer and Imran, in the side to play England in the third Test, starting tomorrow. His long statement, which said that the players had been unable, because of their contractual obligations to the Packer organisation, to give an assurance of their future availability for Pakistan, ended a chaotic day, for much of which it had seemed there would be no Test match.

The England team, excluding Ken Barrington, the manager, had spent hours in conference discussing what action they should take if Pakistan did include the Packer players. When the last meeting ended, the new captain, Geoff Boycott, would make no comment. But the fact that no statement was made to the effect that the team were prepared to play in any circumstances suggested that there had been no weakening in the players' stand.

However, the Pakistan Board at the last moment ended its vacillations, helped by a ruling from General Zia, the Chief Martial Law Administrator, and the match was saved.

Fifth Test Final day: 3 February

Australia edge home against gallant India to win series 3-2

By D.J.Rutnagur, in Adelaide

AUSTRALIA, relying on the efforts of an indisposed Ian Callen, wore down India's resistance to win the fifth Test by 47 runs and clinch the rubber 3-2. India, who needed to score 493 to win, and who started the final day requiring another 131 with only four wickets in hand, went down with honour, registering the highest-ever losing score in the final innings of a Test, the previous best being England's 417 in the Centenary Test last year.

Callen, who ran a high temperature last night because of a throat infection, was visited by a doctor in the early hours of the morning. Simpson soon put him on to curb the aggressive intent of stubborn overnight partners Kirmani and Ghavri, and, declining a breather, Callen bowled the old ball out and then continued with the new ball. At 415, he had Ghavri (23) caught driving, and then Kirmani (51) was bowled by Clark.

Prasanna and Bedi added 25 in even time, before Callen made the breakthrough, having Bedi superbly caught by Cosier at second slip. Chandra, the meekest No.11 of all time, lasted six balls before Simpson trapped him with a googly, and India's brave resistance was over.

First Test Fifth day: 15 February

England routed by Hadlee and go down to New Zealand for the first time

By Michael Melford, in Wellington

RICHARD HADLEE duly took the last two England wickets this morning to give New Zealand their first ever Test victory over England, by 72 runs. England, who yesterday needed only 137 in their second innings to win the first Test, but collapsed to 53 for eight, added only 11 more runs. Hadlee took six for 26, and 10 for 100 in the match.

It is not easy to sort out any one reason for England's defeat, and to say that batting alone was to blame would be to oversimplify matters. Nor would it be right to assume that the pitch deteriorated suddenly enough yesterday to justify the fall of 17 wickets after lunch, compared with one in the morning session.

But there were periods when England's fast bowlers, the side's great strength, were disappointingly off target, partly because they were blown off by the wind. Old's marathon feat upwind (30-11-54-6) saved them in the first innings, after Boycott put New Zealand in. And when Willis (5-32) found his rhythm in his splendid second-innings spell of five for 15, his effort, and that of Botham (2-13) and Hendrick (2-16) in support, was all that one had hoped for. Nine wickets in a session for 41 runs is hard to beat.

In England's second innings, the left-arm Collinge proved an ample foil for Hadlee and took three for 35 (6-77 in the match). When Hadlee finally had Willis caught by Howarth at fourth slip, joy was unconfined among the 3,000 spectators – and quite rightly, too, after a 50-year wait. And in looking for the reason that England lost, one should not ignore the fact that the other side did pretty well.

Richard Hadlee, 10-100 in the match.

First Test Fourth day: 5 June

Willis bouncer mars England's easy victory

By Michael Melford, at Edgbaston

ENGLAND won the first Test against Pakistan by an innings and 57 runs, but not in an atmosphere of unqualified satisfaction and goodwill which is desirable on these occasions. The cause of this was a lamentable incident earlier in the day in which nightwatchman Iqbal Qasim was hit in the face by a bouncer from Bob Willis.

Qasim was led off bleeding profusely to have two stitches in the lip. The Pakistan manager, in a statement at lunch, described the bowling as unfair and said that he would take the matter up with the TCCB.

He has, alas, good reason to feel aggrieved. The whole episode tended to devalue the otherwise admirable cricket played by England and performances such as Chris Old's seven for 50 in the first innings, which won him the award for the outstanding player, and Ian Botham's 100 out of 171 in 190 minutes on Saturday – a knock that should have brought home to the watchers the sort of player with whom a kindly fate has now blessed English cricket.

Willis began the day by bowling very fast with a strong wind behind him and with bumpers not reserved for the helmeted Sadiq. No action was seen to be taken by the umpires or by Brearley, though a note to Law 46 in the playing conditions states that "Captains must instruct their players that the fast short-pitched ball should at no time be directed at non-recognised batsmen."

Iqbal Qasim, who batted 10, 9 and 10 in the three winter Tests, qualifies easily in most people's estimation as 'non-recognised', even if he had defended stoutly for 40 minutes. Yet after a time he received a wicked bouncer, bowled to the left-hander from round the wicket. It leapt up to his face, and after a few minutes' treatment on the pitch he retired and did not bat again.

The note endeavours to interpret the spirit of the game, and Qasim is clearly not equipped to defend himself against this sort of ball. The umpires have a duty to intervene, especially in a decade when the bumper has been bowled excessively. But as one who believes that the responsibility lies with the captain, I am afraid that on this occasion, the scholar-captain, like Homer, nodded.

Second Test Final day: 19 June

Botham tears up the record book – and Pakistan

By Michael Melford, at Lord's

THE FALL of Pakistan's last eight wickets for 43 runs this morning, seven of them to Ian Botham, and the loss of the second Test by an innings and 120 runs, looks miserable on paper, but the tourists were up against something out of the ordinary. For no obvious meteorological reason, on a cloudless morning, the ball swung prodigiously, and Botham, in an astonishing piece of bowling, beat the bat with three or four out-swingers an over.

He bowled the full length required with great accuracy, received the best possible help from Taylor, Roope and finally Gooch, and in 13.5 overs took seven wickets for 14. His eight for 34 in the innings is the best analysis by an England bowler since Laker in 1956, and, with his 108 in England's innings, there has never been an all-round performance like this in a Test.

Sobers and Mushtaq came nearest, having twice taken five wickets in an innings in a Test match in which they also made a hundred.

England went out in the morning half expecting to finish the match with spin – after all, Edmonds took four for six in eight overs in Pakistan's first innings 105. The first discovery was that, after an over by Willis (five for 47 in the first innings) from the Nursery end, the wind changed enough for him to switch ends. Botham was thus given the Nursery end, which he prefers, and from which he then bowled triumphantly until the match – and the series – was won seven minutes before lunch.

In the past, Test selectors have been profoundly grateful for all-rounders who have been worth their place in one department and have performed usefully in the other. Ian Botham has played in seven Test matches. He has made three hundreds and a fifty, and has taken five wickets or more in an innings five times. And he is still only 22.

Botham spread-eagles the Pakistan field on the way to his hundred.

County Championship: 1 September

Essex fail by a whisker: Kent are champions

By D.J.Rutnagur, at Southend

ESSEX were held to a draw by Derbyshire in a palpitating finish at Southchurch Park – so Kent are again the Schweppes county champions and Essex must be content with second place. At the end of an exciting match, Essex needed one wicket to win – and keep the Championship open – and Derbyshire were just two runs short.

The scene was set for this high drama of the late afternoon by Essex – badly hindered by rain yesterday – declaring at 190 for five, thanks to a mature and brilliant 84 by Gooch. This left Derbyshire to make 186 in as many minutes, and they made a quick and sound start. But, in mounting the final offensive, they lost five wickets during the last hour – all in a span of 14 overs.

The last over started with Derbyshire needing 13, with the last pair, Hendrick and Mellor, at the wicket. The issue was open even when it came to the final ball, for they could have won if Mellor had hit a six.

1979

2 Jan Sunil Gavaskar (107 and 182 not out for India v West Indies at Calcutta) becomes the first batsman in history to score two 100s in a Test three times.

10-14 Feb Rodney Hogg takes only 1 wicket in the 6th Test but finishes with 41, a record in a series for Australia v England.

23-24 Feb Pakistan wicket-keeper Wasim Bari sets a new Test record with 7 dismissals (all catches) in an innings, against New Zealand at Auckland.

29 Mar Two controversial, unsporting incidents in the 2nd Australia v Pakistan Test, at Perth – fast bowler Hurst runs out Sikander, who was 'backing up', and, in Australia's 2nd innings, Hilditch, at the non-striker's end, picks up the ball to hand it to the bowler and is given out, on appeal, for 'handling the ball'.

24 May Somerset captain Brian Rose legally declares their innings closed at Worcester, after one over, at 1-0 to maintain their scoring rate and ensure a place in the B & H semi-finals. Worcs refund admission money to the 100 paying spectators. (The TCCB later disqualify Somerset for bringing the game into disrepute.)

30 May Australian Cricket Board capitulate to Kerry Packer.

21 Jun Sri Lanka become the first holders of the ICC Trophy, making 324-8 in their 60 overs to beat Canada by 60 runs in the final at Worcester. (The two finalists had qualified to play in the Prudential World Cup.)

11 Aug Mike Procter takes his second hat-trick in successive matches, against Yorks at Cheltenham, the second all-lbw hat-trick of his career (1972).

6 Sep Procter hits the season's fastest 100, in 57 minutes, for Gloucester against Northants at Bristol.

26 Oct Australian cricket returns to the 6-ball over.

7 Nov India beat Australia by an innings and 100 runs at Bombay with a day to spare, wrapping up the rubber 2-0 with 4 drawn for their first ever series victory over the tourists.

14-19 Dec The Test (at Perth) that spawns the immortal scorecard entry 'D.K.Lillee c Willey b Dilley' is notable also for Botham's 11-176, Border's fine 115, Boycott's battling 99 not out (carrying his bat out of 215 as England go down by 138 runs) and Geoff Dymock's match-winning 6-34 in England's second innings – all being overshadowed by Lillee's unsavoury behaviour in trying to use his aluminium bat in the face of objections from the umpires and both captains.

TEST SERIES

India in England
E 1, D 3

England in Australia
E 5, A 1

West Indies in India
I 1, D 5

Pakistan in New Zealand
P 1, D 2

Pakistan in Australia
A 1, P 1

Australia in India
I 2, D 4

First Test Final day: 15 March

Sarfraz shatters Australia with 7 for 1 spell

By Ray Robinson, in Melbourne

SARFRAZ NARWAZ became the first visiting player to take nine wickets in a Test innings in Australia with an astonishing spell of bowling that brought Pakistan victory by 71 runs at Melbourne. The 6ft 3in medium-pacer provided a boy's book finish to the match by claiming Australia's last seven wickets for one run in 33 deliveries.

His innings return of nine for 86 beat the previous best Test bag in Australia, Arthur Mailey's nine for 121 against England here in 1921. It also easily outdid Fazal Mahmood's Pakistan record, seven for 42 against India in 1952.

Australia's first set-back in their chase to make 382 to win came when Graham Yallop, looking at his own stroke behind point, failed to respond to Allan Border's call and was run out by Asif at the bowler's end. But when the new ball was taken in the 72nd over, at 283 for 3, Australia had reduced the leeway to 98 runs, with seven wickets in hand. And Imran, feeling the after-effects of food poisoning, was taken off after two overs.

Sarfraz, off half his usual run, rose to the occasion with accurate seaming either way. He ended the season's best Test stand, 177 by Hughes (84) and Border (105). Border, having made his first Test hundred in 373 chanceless minutes, was the first to go, at 305, and quite extraordinarily the last seven wickets tumbled for five runs.

County Championship: 3 Aug

Procter's hat-trick crushes Leicester

By Roger Malone, at Bristol

SOUTH AFRICAN all-rounder Mike Procter repeated his feat of seven years ago against Essex, when he took the hat-trick in Leicestershire's second innings after scoring a hundred in Gloucestershire's first.

He followed up his fireworks with the bat yesterday with seven wickets for 26, and Leicester were all out for 134. Gloucester easily knocked off the 61 needed to achieve their first Championship win on the benign wicket at their headquarters for three years.

Procter's whirlwind 122 on Thursday caught Leicester by the throat and, with Sadiq's hard-working 137, lifted Gloucester from crisis to comfort. Procter made his hundred before lunch, his complete innings taking only 104 minutes.

Prudential World Cup final: 23 June

West Indies retain World Cup as England lose last 8 wickets for 11

Randall (fourth left) gives England an inspirational start by running out West Indies' prolific opener Greenidge for nine.

By Michael Melford, at Lord's

AN ENGLAND collapse from 183 for 2 to 194 all out, thanks largely to a spell of five wickets in 11 balls from Joel Garner, gave West Indies an easy 92-run win.

Yet it was the early England batting that let them down. Boycott (57) and Brearley (64), although compiling an opening stand of 129, missed their chance against the mild off-spin of Richards and the medium pace of King, and when Boycott was out at 135, nearly 40 overs had been bowled. The younger batsmen were expected to come in and make 152 in 20 overs against better bowling. It was asking for miracles.

In hindsight, however, it was not England's batting that needed strengthening, but the bowling, perhaps by bringing in Miller for the injured Willis. The three bowlers used to fill up the fifth allotment of 12 overs – Boycott, Gooch and Larkins – bowled too short and too near West Indian legs, an area to be avoided at all costs. Their 12 overs yielded 86 runs, and helped to launch the match-winning partnership of 139 between Viv Richards and Collis King (86).

Richards' colourful 138 not out would have won him the Man of the Match award, without the added virtues of his largely unmolested bowling (10-0-35-0) and an improbable catch he took racing along the long-on boundary to dismiss the always dangerous Botham off a well-middled lowish drive.

Schweppes County Championship: 21 August

Essex celebrate their first title after 103 years

By John Mason, at Northampton

ON THE DOT of six o'clock this evening, Essex became County Champions for the first time. Half-an-hour previously, victory by seven wickets over Northants at the County Ground had brought them 17 points - seemingly enough to put them out of reach of all challengers. But were they champions? The remarkable events at Derby meant a nerve-wracking wait of 30 minutes or more for the Essex players before they knew that Worcester had only drawn.

Amid much acrimony, controversy and a series of telephone calls to Lord's, Worcester finished just short of victory over Derby and clearly felt that they had been deprived by well-meaning but misguided advice from the umpires. They were told they had four overs in the 10 minutes remaining in which to get the 25 runs in their second innings to win, and they made 17 in two overs. But a phone call to Lord's by Derby resulted in the decision that the game would be governed by the time available – so it was drawn, and no amount of telephoning on Worcester's behalf could change anything.

Victory over Northants was the 11th in Essex's most successful season in their 103-year history. The operation was a perfect example of the county's team skills that brought them the Benson & Hedges Cup a month ago, the first major competition Essex have ever won. This morning the mechanics of wrapping up the Championship began with Northants 174 for eight in their second innings, a lead of 199. Jim Watts (25 not out) resisted for 50 minutes before losing Tim Lamb, who was Turner's 10th wicket in the match (for 126), and Griffiths.

Essex had five hours to secure the 229 they needed, and Hardie (103 not out) and Denness (51) gave them a fine start with an unhurried partnership of 113. Hardie and Fletcher (39) put on 78 for the third wicket, the latter in his 20th season with the county, the last six as captain. And although Fletcher was out with 19 still needed, Hardie went on to complete his century and stroke the winning runs to give Essex the title with four games to spare.

Fourth Test Final day: 4 September

Gavaskar nearly brings off famous victory for India

By Michael Melford, at the Oval

A Test match long to be remembered finished this evening with India, nine runs short of victory with two wickets standing, drawing a match that for much of an enthralling day had been within their grasp. To win, and square the Cornhill series, they had needed 438 runs, 32 more than any side has made to win in 103 years of Test history.

Yet in the eighth over of the last 20, Sunil Gavaskar, with Chauhan and Vengsarkar in support, had batted so brilliantly that their score stood at 366 for one. Few present will not have wanted India's tremendous effort to be crowned with a historic victory. The mind boggles at the excitement in India, where they were hearing ball-by-ball commentaries.

Ironically, the tide turned just when England really did seem beaten. They had fielded well and missed no obvious catches in the previous seven-and-a-half hours until Botham dropped Vengsarkar on the long-off boundary off Willey. The ball seems to follow Botham, and this time, having a damaged hand, he cannot have welcomed it. But in Edmonds' next over, Vengsarkar uncannily lobbed it to him at midwicket.

At this point, I thought India made a mistake in not sending in the experienced Viswanath in his normal place. He is one of the best players in the world, and he runs well with Gavaskar.

England took their chance, and Edmonds, Willey and finally Botham halted India's triumphant progress. Botham, never out of things for long, bowled the last four overs from the Pavilion end, taking three for 17. Only when Yashpal Sharma was eighth out to him with 10 balls left and 15 needed did England look safe.

Botham, who achieved the 'double' of 1,000 runs and 100 wickets in his 21st Test (beating Mankad's record of 23), was made Man of the Series and Gavaskar, 30 years old and only 5ft 5in, received the match award for one of the finest Test innings in recent years. His 221 out of 389, made almost flawlessly in 8 hr 10 min, was the highest by an Indian against England and the 20th 100 he has made in only 50 Tests, a striking rate second only to that of Sir Don Bradman.

Gillette Cup Final: 8 September

Superb Richards ends Somerset's long, long wait

By Michael Melford, at Lord's

LAST YEAR'S disappointments and a chequered start to this season were easily forgotten as Somerset gained victory over Northants by 45 runs in a Gillette Cup final that seemed to give widespread satisfaction. They were undoubtedly the better side, and anyhow a packed Lord's clearly felt that after 104 years a triumph like this was overdue.

Viv Richards, the Man of the Match, as in the Prudential Cup final, played an innings of 117 perfect in its context in that it tempered expansive brilliance with care and responsibility. From the seventh to the 60th over, he was at one end helping to build a score of 269 for eight which was not unassailable but required something exceptional to beat it.

Allan Lamb's 78, which confirmed him as a still-improving batsman of the highest class, went some way towards providing this, but Northants must have known that they would be outfielded and outbowled, and were no doubt content in the end to have reached this far so early in their reconstruction.

Relying as they did on their early batting, Northants could not afford to lose Larkins and Williams to the towering Garner in his first two overs. The 6ft 8in Barbadian finished with the remarkable figures of 6-29 (5-38 in the Prudential final). In Somerset's innings, Richards' early passage was eased by captain Brian Rose's contribution (41), and the great man was even able to sit back while Botham was making 27 out of 41 in seven overs. He himself stayed on and his story was made.

Now Somerset, not just through this one victory, are a power in the land.

[The following day, Somerset beat Notts at Trent Bridge by 56 runs and, with Kent losing, overtook them to win the John Player League.]

Joel Garner: another towering one-day bowling performance.

Kerry Packer's Circus

The news that rocked the cricketing world in May 1977 came like a bolt from the blue, so well had the secret been kept. It was announced in Australia that 35 of the world's leading cricketers from five countries had signed contracts of up to three years with the Kerry Packer organisation to play a series of specially arranged matches, starting in Australia in the 1977-78 season.

Eighteen of the players were Australian, including most of the team that had just arrived for the England tour. The others came from England - notably their captain, Tony Greig - South Africa, West Indies and Pakistan. It soon emerged that the Packer 'Circus', as the group immediately became known, would be divided into Australia and Rest of the World sides, to be captained by Greg Chappell and Tony Greig, respectively, and would play 54 days of cricket, including five-day Tests, one-day games and three-day matches. Official tours scheduled for this period would surely be thrown into turmoil. England were due to tour Pakistan and New Zealand, Australia to entertain India and then go to West Indies.

But who was this Kerry Packer who had suddenly challenged the traditional institutions of the game and was threatening to turn the cricketing world upside-down? Younger son of Sir Frank Packer, he had, on his father's death, taken over his newspaper and television empire three years earlier. As chairman of Channel 9, one of Australia's five TV channels, Packer had been trying to obtain sole rights to Test cricket. But the Australian Cricket Board (ACB) had twice spurned big offers and preferred instead to sell non-exclusive rights to the Australian Broadcasting Commission for less money.

Packer, then, decided to put on his own 'Tests'. The most remarkable thing, perhaps, about the Packer coup, was the complete secrecy in which the whole operation was carried out. The package was put together by Packer Television Corporation Ltd and an agency called JP Sport, which acted for many leading Australian sportsmen, exploiting their 'merchandising' possibilities. When prospective recruits were approached, they were sworn to the strictest secrecy. There was bound to be considerable opposition from the cricketing authorities, so Packer had already booked the use of grounds not under their jurisdiction.

The news breaks

It was the Australian Cricket Board who received perhaps the biggest shock when the news broke. Not only had 13 of their 17 players currently on tour in England signed up for the Packer circus, but four of them - Chappell, Walters, Marsh and Robinson - were on their sub-committee set up in 1976 to give players a stronger say in running the game, especially regarding financial benefit from team sponsorship. Indeed, Australian cricketers were better off than they had ever been, with endorsements and sponsorship money at an unprecedented high. No wonder the Board were furious. They felt betrayed. But there was little they could do about it, short of cancelling the England tour now underway.

The Cricket Council decided that the England players involved would not be barred from selection for the Ashes Tests. But they instructed the selectors not to consider Greig, England's successful skipper in India, for the job of captain.

Of all those involved in the Packer circus, Greig was the one most bitterly attacked in the media and resented by the establishment. The Cricket Council felt betrayed, and the English Press turned against him, even to the extent of belittling his talents and holding his South African birth against him (an Englishman would not have done such a thing, etc). Tim Rice, in the Sunday Telegraph, wrote: 'Is Greig so short of a few bob that he has to go to these clandestine lengths to make a buck? ... If our handsome ex-captain is prepared to hawk his talents in any market place, would he like a role in Jesus Christ Superstar? ... I may well be able to fix it if he would let me know which part would best suit him.'

Seven weeks after the initial bombshell, the ICC held an emergency meeting and, having agreed that the whole fabric of the game could be "severely damaged" by the type of promotion proposed by Packer, offered to meet him.

Kerry Packer and Tony Greig arrive for the first day of the High Court action in 1977.

Accordingly, Packer, with Richie Benaud and two other associates, met the ICC on 23 June at Lord's. A compromise was almost reached, but when Packer insisted on exclusive TV rights to Australian cricket, the talks foundered. There was no way the Australian representative on the ICC was going to agree to this.

From that moment, the dispute developed into a full-scale war between Packer and the cricketing authorities. Packer had hinted that he would fight against any victimisation of his players, but at a meeting of the ICC on 26 July his warning was ignored. They not only declared their opposition to his programme and withheld first-class status or any official recognition for his matches, but they virtually outlawed the Packer players by the following decree: "No player who after 1 October 1977 has played or made himself available to play in a match previously disapproved by the Conference shall thereafter be eligible to play in any Test match." They also urged individual countries to apply similar sanctions at domestic level.

This was a bad mistake on the part of the ICC, for their actions could be construed not only as an illegal restraint of trade but also as illegally inducing players to break their contracts. The Packer Organisation applied to the High Court for an injunction against both the ICC and the TCCB, and a hearing eventually began on 26 September, the plaintiffs being World Series Cricket and three players, Greig and John Snow (England) and Mike Procter (South Africa). The hearing lasted for nearly seven weeks, at the end of which Mr Justice Slade found that, although the defendants had the best interests of cricket at heart as they saw them, the rule changes banning players from Test and county cricket were *ultra vires*, being an unreasonable restraint of trade, and that the contracts between the Packer players and the WSC were entitled to the protection of the law. The defendants were ordered to pay costs of about a quarter of a million pounds.

The circus begins

Meanwhile, the circus had begun in Australia. Richie Benaud announced at a Press conference that certain innovations would be made, such as restrictions on defensive fields at the start of each game; there would be night games, with a white ball and black sight-screens, and as many as eight TV cameras would be used, among other things, to analyse umpires' decisions. Because of the unsuitability of the grass on some of the grounds being used, special pitches were artificially grown in greenhouses in huge concrete trays and dropped into place in time for the matches. There were to be three teams, Australian, West Indian and World, each with their own 'colours' instead of white, with bonus payments always for winners.

The first season saw extremely sparse crowds for the Packer games, partly because the Australian team were usually outplayed by the other sides, and, although WSC claimed good TV audiences, a great deal of money had to be pumped into the project. By contrast, the official Test series in which Australia beat India 3-2 in a hugely competitive contest attracted good gates and better TV ratings. Only the four floodlit matches in Melbourne (at the Victorian Football League Park) attained the Packer break-even point of a daily 15,000 attendance.

Despite Mr Justice Slade's championship of the professional cricketer's right to work, some Packer 'defectors' met with considerable animosity from their clubs, who felt they were a divisive element, and from their fellow players. England's Packer players were not included in the touring party to Pakistan and New Zealand because they would not be available for all the matches. And when Packer released Imran, Mushtaq and Zaheer in January 1978 to play in the third and decisive Test, the England players threatened not to play. The strike was averted, however, when the Packer players were not selected.

Nor were any Packer players considered for Pakistan's tour of England in 1978, when the England selectors also ignored their Packer men. The Australian Board had put together a completely new squad for their tour to the West Indies earlier in the year, having coaxed Bobby Simpson out of retirement to lead it. But the West Indian Board, fearful that putting out a sub-standard side might have deleterious effects on their already rocky financial position, included their Packer players and won the first two Tests easily. When they then dropped some Packer players to test new blood for their forthcoming tour of India, Clive Lloyd resigned as captain. The other Packer players withdrew, and, unable to guarantee their availability for the Indian tour, were not considered again. This meant that no Packer players were now being considered by any country for international duty.

Packer's second season of WSC cricket promised to be a testing time for principles and resolve. The Packer organisation changed their approach, going down market in a cricketing sense to sell their brand of the game to Australians, and appealing to non-cricket fans with their Channel 9 promotion and presentation. There were lots of gimmicks, from theme songs to free parking. One successful idea on television was to illustrate any cricketing terms used by the commentators, such as off-break or outswinger. Their one-day night matches were particularly successful, and at Sydney Cricket Ground, which Packer had won use of, the attendance for the first floodlit limited-overs game reached 50,000 (albeit with many being allowed in for nothing).

The Australian Board, on the other hand, lost heavily on an England tour for the first time. The 'second-string' Australian team were being hammered in the official Tests, and the Australian fans were shifting their allegiance to their Packer side.

Packer then took his circus to the West Indies, where they were allowed the use of grounds. A successful tour (apart from a serious riot at Georgetown that left a wrecked pavilion) meant that the individual authorities benefited from a share of the gate, and the financially straitened West Indian Board earned a welcome *ex gratia* payment.

During the 1978-79 season, ICC officials twice went to Australia to conduct negotiations with the Packer group to

WSC cricket in 1979, at the Victorian Football League Park, Melbourne.

bring an end to the war. The West Indies, India and Pakistan were particularly anxious for a quick armistice, and it seemed that the obdurate Australian Board was the main stumbling block to peace. Imagine the surprise, then, when news came from Australia on 24 April 1979 that the ACB had struck a lucrative deal with Packer, granting Channel 9 exclusive TV rights to Test and other matches now that their contract with the ABC had expired.

A sudden end to the affair

Packer had won what he had originally set out to get, but at a cost to all concerned, not least to the game itself. But at least world cricket could now continue as before, with the extra sponsorship (such as that of Cornhill Insurance for Tests in England) as security against a repeat of private intervention. When the full details of the Australian deal came out five weeks later, however, they were greeted both inside Australia and overseas with incredulity. The ACB had not only given Packer *carte blanche* with TV broadcasting, but they had also given him a powerful say in the running of cricket in Australia. The first paragraph of the ACB statement was a stunner:

"...the Board has granted PBL Sports Pty Ltd the exclusive right, for a term of 10 years, to promote the programme of cricket organised by the Board and to arrange the televising and merchandising in respect of that programme. For the first three years of the agreement, the Board has agreed that PBL Sports may arrange a contract for the televising of the programme with the Channel 9 network."

There were to be five or six Test matches and an international one-day series (involving Australia and two overseas teams) to be known as the Benson & Hedges World Series Cup, of 15 matches plus a best-of-five final. The Board also agreed to consider favourably the introduction of the 30-yard circle in limited-overs matches, day/night matches and, on an experimental basis, the use of coloured clothing in Benson & Hedges World Series one-day international matches. Astonishingly, too, they agreed to ask the Indian Board to defer their visit until the next season, 1980-81, so that the West Indies could be invited to participate in the 1979-80 programme.

The agreement was, in effect, a virtual capitulation of the Board to a private organisation, to whom they were ceding the promotion of Australian cricket, having already allowed them to make decisions on the clothing, on the rules and, most frighteningly of all, on who would be the next tourists. It was greeted with dismay, and even disgust, by the other countries, who had backed the Board's stand against Packer. However, at the end of June, the ICC had no alternative but to approve the ACB's agreement in principle.

Flawed gospel according to Packer

What have been the long-term effects of the Packer 'revolution'? Writing in The Daily Telegraph during the 1992 World Cup in Australia, some 15 years after that first momentous announcement, E.W.Swanton offered, in passing, some thoughts on the Packer legacy:

"The fifth World Cup has, in many respects, compared ill with the previous four. The opening match set the first, raucous note almost unbelievably with the issue of trumpets to the crowd. All the propaganda tricks have been used throughout by the Australian organisers to whip up the crowds who, many with daubed faces, responded with non-stop noise. This was, indeed, the gospel according to Packer.

"Timings and, to some extent, the rain rules, were devised to suit television by an Australian Cricket Board which the cricket writer Martin Johnson, in a biting phrase, has characterised as 'a minor subsidiary of Channel 9'....And the commentators - as Michael Parkinson remarked, were 'not so much reporting the game as selling it like washing-up liquid'.

"Thirty years ago, when the Gillette Cup was being conceived here, I welcomed it when many were more sceptical, and I certainly do not condemn one-day cricket now of itself. It is a financial necessity and, at its best, such as in the Lord's finals, creates much enjoyment. But it must be kept in balance with the ordinary game in order to nurture the true arts of cricket. It cannot be stressed too strongly that limited-overs cricket never made a first-class cricketer, nor ever will."

The 1980s

Two Somerset stars bestrode the cricketing world in the 1980s - Ian Botham and Viv Richards. Botham, who started the decade in disastrous fashion, leading England in 12 matches without a win, resigned the captaincy after an unhappy tour of the West Indies and a poor start at home against Australia. He then proceeded - by heroic deeds with both bat and ball - to revive England when all seemed lost, and inspired them to grab the Ashes from Australia in the most dramatic Test series of all time. Richards, meanwhile, continued to delight cricket followers as the world's No.1 batsman and helped maintain West Indies as the leading cricketing power.

Imran Khan (Pakistan), Kapil Dev (India) and Richard Hadlee (New Zealand), along with Ian Botham, gave the lie to the theory that modern pressures were such that no one could be expected to be worth his Test place any longer as both batsman and bowler. Moreover, these three great all-rounders spearheaded the rise in standard of their respective countries, who would no longer be treated as the 'chopping blocks' of international cricket. Indeed, in the latter part of the decade, England lost successive home rubbers to India, New Zealand and Pakistan. And although England carried all before them in Australia in 1986-87, they compounded the misery at home with further series losses to West Indies and Australia. Only Sri Lanka were beaten, in the single Test at Lord's in 1988. The Sri Lankans were welcome newcomers to the Test scene, making their début against England in Colombo in 1982 and winning their first Test in 1985, against India. On the down side, international cricket in the eighties was beset by political problems centred on the South African question, with 'rebel' tours, bans and boycotts, and much hypocrisy emanating from all sides.

Only four counties won the Championship in the eighties - Middlesex and Essex three times each, Notts and Worcs, who gained the services of Botham in the latter part of the decade, twice. With the abolition of uncovered wickets in 1980, it became increasingly difficult for young spin bowlers to establish themselves in county cricket, especially with the preparation of 'result' wickets to favour the seamers. The first four-day County Championship matches were played in 1988. Limited-overs cricket continued to inspire negative bowling, with the 'dot ball' the main objective, something often forgotten in the excitement of a close finish.

The 'look' of cricket was transformed in the eighties by the universal acceptance of helmets and visors as standard issue for batsmen, together with a great deal of other protective wear. More controversially, helmets for close-in fielders encouraged much 'sillier' positions than hitherto.

One disturbing trend of the eighties was the increase in bad behaviour on the field, particularly towards umpires. This reached its nadir on England's 1987-88 tour of Pakistan, with Chris Broad's initial refusal to go after being given out at Lahore and captain Mike Gatting's infamous row with controversial umpire Shakoor Rana at Faisalabad.

A familiar sight in the 1981 Ashes series: Ian Botham leads the England appeal as another Australian wicket tumbles - he has just caught Yallop off Emburey. Wicket-keeper Taylor, Gooch and captain Mike Brearley exult in the fall of the wicket that led to Australia's slide from 87 for three to 121 all out in the last innings at Edgbaston, with Botham taking the last five wickets for one run.

1980

15-20 Jan Sunil Gavaskar makes 166 in 593 minutes, the longest Test innings by an Indian and his record 23rd Test hundred, and Kapil Dev takes 4-90 and 7-56 and scores 84 as India beat Pakistan by 10 wickets in the 5th Test at Madras to take a winning 2-0 lead in the series.

31 Jan At Calcutta, Kapil Dev takes his 100th wicket in only his 25th Test, and at 22 years 25 days is the youngest to do so.

3 Feb Kapil Dev scores his 1,000th Test run and is the youngest to complete the 'double'.

5 Mar New Zealand draw with West Indies at Auckland to record their first ever series victory at home.

6-11 Mar The rain-hit second Test between Pakistan and Australia at Faisalabad produces 999 runs for the loss of only 12 wickets. Australia's 617 is the highest Test innings in Pakistan, while Taslim Arif is on the field throughout the match, scoring 210 not out in Pakistan's 382-2, an innings in which every opponent bowled - for the first time this century.

19 Mar A remarkable spell of 5 for 9 off 36 balls by leg-spinner Jim Higgs sweeps South Australia to defeat at Adelaide and allows Victoria to overtake them on the last day of the season and retain the Sheffield Shield.

23 Mar Allan Border (150 not out and 153) is the first player to score two 150s in a Test, Australia v Pakistan, at Lahore.

29 Jul An unbeaten last-wicket stand of 117 for England at the Oval in the 4th Test between Willey (100) and Willis (24) deprives West Indies of a victory that looked probable with England on 92-9.

12 Aug Ian Botham becomes the first English player to do the Test 'double' of 1,500 runs/150 wickets, v West Indies at Headingley.

28 Aug-2 Sep England v Australia Centenary Test at Lord's (drawn) sees umpire Constant assaulted by MCC members after the fifth pitch inspection of Saturday, Boycott score his 7,000th Test run, and John Arlott make his last Test Match Special commentary.

31 Aug Warwickshire beat Leicester to win the John Player League – after finishing bottom the previous season.

22-23 Dec Six Pakistan batsmen are dismissed for ducks, a new Test record, in their 1st innings of the 3rd Test against West Indies, at Karachi.

TEST SERIES

West Indies in England
WI 1, D 4
Australia in England
Drawn 1
England in Australia
Australia 3
England in India
England 1
West Indies in Australia
WI 2, D 1
West Indies in New Zealand
NZ 1, D 2
Pakistan in India
I 2, D 4
Australia in Pakistan
P 1, D 2
New Zealand in Australia
A 2, D 1

B & H World Series Cup First final: 20 January

England pay for vital errors and fail by two runs

By Michael Melford, in Melbourne

ENGLAND lost the first final match of the B & H Series Cup after making a splendid effort to score 216 against the formidable West Indies pace attack on this huge Melbourne ground. But the heartbreakingly narrow losing margin of two runs rubbed in cruelly what might have been but for a few vital errors.

They put West Indies in and removed Richards for only 23. But then Kallicharran (42) was dropped on 26 and King (31 not out) on five.

West Indies were in the process of losing six wickets for 36, including in the 42nd over that of Greenidge (80), who played one of his best innings in Australia. But King launched an assault on Willis, whose last four overs cost 39 runs, and with Garner and Holding he made 20 off the last two overs to boost the total to 215 for eight off their 50 overs.

The West Indies did not drop their catches, and had England at 96 for three. Yet in 10 overs, Willey (51) and Larkins (34) added 56 and were playing very well against increasingly agitated West Indians before both were run out through misjudgement.

The ball seldom reached the boundary, and the running of Brearley (24 not out) and Botham (19) became more desperate, but it just kept England's chance alive. In the last four overs, 28 were needed, after which Botham was caught at mid-on.

With 15 needed off Holding's final over, all hope seemed gone. But Brearley and Bairstow laid about them, ran like furies and Brearley needed four off the last ball. Alas, Bairstow was run out going for the second.

[Two days later, West Indies won by eight wickets at Sydney to take the Cup, Greenidge scoring 98 not out in their 209-2.]

Gordon Greenidge gave West Indies a fine start.

Third Test Final day: 6 February

Botham brightens England's defeat with brilliant 119

By Michael Melford, in Melbourne

IAN BOTHAM'S magnificent innings of 119 not out came too late, but at least it allowed England to finish their Australian programme on a high note. After tea yesterday, the match seemed unlikely to go to a fifth day. In the event, it lasted until the final hour, and the England bowlers made Australia work hard for the first half of the 103 runs they needed.

From the first, the ball was sometimes lifting chest high from Lillee and Pascoe, sometimes scudding along the ground. It was inconceivable that England could hold out. Yet the partnership between Botham and Taylor (32) went on for another 25 minutes to 86, made in 95 minutes, and an innings defeat was avoided.

Underwood found the going too much. But Lever coped remarkably comfortably for an hour and three-quarters while Botham's innings blossomed into something that the 5,000 crowd, admitted at half price, can never have dreamed of seeing.

His batting in Australia has usually been found wanting for footwork and restraint, but now, on 45 when Lever joined him, he rose above the difficulties imposed by the pitch and played some superb strokes with relative safety. He added 70 of the 93 made in the morning as he moved to 100, cutting, late-cutting, timing the ball easily off his legs, driving off front foot and back. He straight-drove the new ball from Dymock two balls before lunch to reach his 100.

Lillee finally broke the stand with a ball that lifted and left Lever sharply after the ninth wicket had added 89. In all, Lillee took 11 wickets for 138, and was named man of the match and of the series.

It was left to Greg Chappell (40 not) to pull together a faltering Australian attempt to score 103, and, after struggling against Lever, he eventually finished the match and the series with some brilliant driving off Underwood.

England's 3-0 defeat was humiliating. Their only consolation, their hope for the future, was the innings played with immense spirit and good sense by the young man on whom England sides of the next decade are likely to be built.

First Test Final day: 13 February

West Indies' good name suffers as New Zealand win

From Dunedin

NEW ZEALAND earned a famous one-wicket victory over the West Indies in an exciting finish to the first Test, but the match was marred by some truculent and unsporting behaviour by the tourists.

Set to score a seemingly easy 104 to win, New Zealand were eventually seen home by their last pair after some magnificent bowling by the West Indies trio of Garner, Holding and Croft had reduced them to 73 for eight. Holding, however, spoilt his performance when he kicked over two stumps in frustration after an appeal for caught behind against Parker was rejected. He was later given a 'talking to' by manager Willie Rodriguez, but not reprimanded.

New Zealand slumped from 40 for two to 54 for seven before the tailenders checked the slide. Hadlee and Cairns took the total to 73 before Hadlee (17) was bowled by Garner. Cairns, who top-scored with 19, and Troup took the score to 100 before Holding had Cairns caught at the wicket, and it was left to the last pair to scramble the four needed, the winning run coming from a leg bye off No.10 Boock.

The West Indies' sporting image was again damaged when Haynes, top scorer in both their innings with 55 and 105, was their only player to attend the award ceremony. Hadlee, whose 11 for 102 was the major factor in New Zealand's win, criticised the West Indies for their lack of good sportsmanship.

Second Test Third day: 24 February

Howarth bats on to 141 after protest

From Christchurch

AN UNBEATEN 141 by their captain Geoff Howarth – his highest score in Test cricket – gave New Zealand a first-innings lead over the West Indies of 20 runs with six wickets in hand at the end of the third day. But he was at the centre of a controversy that saw the West Indians refuse to take the field for 10 minutes after the tea break.

The delay was caused evidently by an unsuccessful demand by the West Indies players for the removal of umpire Fred Goodall. They alleged that he should have given Howarth out when on 68 to a catch behind off Garner.

Howarth, on 99 at the break, reached his century from the first ball he received on the resumption, hooking Holding for four. With Parker (42), who joined him at 53 for three, he took the score to 175 in a magnificent stand, and then batted with Coney to 248 for four at the close.

[Umpire Goodall was the victim of further incidents on the fourth day, alleging that he was sworn at and bumped by West Indies bowler Colin Croft, who also petulantly knocked off the bails when no-balled. Howarth scored only six more, but Coney (80) and Hadlee (103) helped New Zealand to 460. The match fizzled out in a draw as Haynes (122), Greenidge (97), Rowe (100) and King (100 not) piled on the runs in West Indies' second innings.]

First Test Fourth day: 2 March

Iqbal and Tauseef spin Australia to Test defeat

From Karachi

PAKISTAN spin bowlers Iqbal Qasim and Tauseef Ahmed completed their domination of the first Test, bowling Australia to a seven-wicket defeat with a day to spare. Iqbal, slow left-arm, and Tauseef, 20, an off-spinner making his Test début, shared 18 of the 20 Australian wickets that fell during the match.

Iqbal, who had match figures of 11 for 118, took his second-innings haul to seven for 49 as Australia subsided from 90 for six overnight to 140 all out. Pakistan then coasted home at 76 for three.

Ray Bright, the Australian spinner in the same mould as Iqbal, took those three wickets to finish with 10 for 111. Tauseef's figures in his first Test were seven for 126.

Golden Jubilee Test Fourth day: 19 February

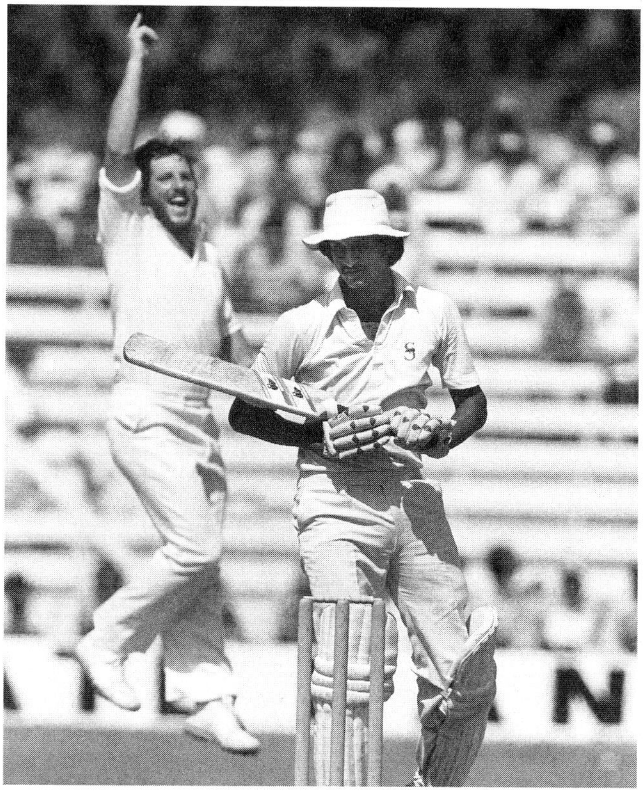

Botham celebrates the fall of Sandeep Patil – one of his 13 wickets and Bob Taylor's record 10 catches.

England end tour on high note

By Michael Melford, in Bombay

ENGLAND'S 10-wicket victory over India in the Golden Jubilee Test with a day and a half to spare provided a cheering end to the three-and-a-half month tour, even if it changed little. It confirmed the frailty of much of England's batting and the uncomfortable extent to which the batting and, still more, the bowling is currently relying on the strength and all-round talents of Ian Botham.

As Gooch and Boycott made the 98 needed to win, the architect of victory was taking a well-earned rest after bowling at one end throughout the Indian second innings. Statistics are not everything, but Botham's record in this match is something out of the ordinary. In more than 100 years of Test cricket, nobody who has made a century has taken more than nine wickets in the same match. Botham took 13.

The last of these, giving him figures of seven for 48 to add to his first-innings six for 58, put another record in the books in the name of Bob Taylor, who had also shared with Botham in the sixth-wicket stand of 171 that turned the match on Sunday. Taylor became the first wicket-keeper to claim 10 victims in a Test. The fact that all were caught, eight off Botham, is another illustration of the nature of the pitch and the unexpected amount that the ball swung under a cloudless sky.

Before anyone dismisses the match as totally one-sided, it is as well to remember that England's answer to India's 242 stood at 58 for five. This was the situation that Botham (114) and Taylor (43) had to repair.

Mike Brearley referred to Botham as a "giant of a cricketer" to be compared only with Sobers.

County Championship: 24 May

Botham breaks record to delight Close

By Michael Austin

IAN BOTHAM, blossoming from controlled aggression into brazen belligerence, hit the first double century of his career, for Somerset at Taunton, to England's delight and the special pleasure of one selector, Brian Close.

When Botham, England's new captain, reached 200 against Gloucester, he achieved a distinction that had eluded Close, his mentor, throughout a 30-year reign in first-class cricket. Close's highest score was 198, but his pupil, with a subtle sense of timing in view of Wednesday's Prudential Cup match against West Indies, swept to a peerless 228, which included 10 sixes and 27 fours.

Botham, making light of a bad back, went to his first hundred in 107 minutes and his second in only 58 minutes. The fourth-wicket stand of 310 with Peter Dennis (98) broke the county record and hurried Somerset to the prosperous regions of 534 for six, which included an almost forgotten, but delightful, innings of 75 by Gavaskar.

First Test Fifth day: 10 June

West Indies dash England hopes in thrilling finish

By Michael Melford, at Trent Bridge

West Indies struggled home 50 minutes after lunch in one of the tensest Test finishes in years to win the first Cornhill Test by two wickets, but only after England had worked their way back into a winning position with a fine exploitation of the conditions.

FROM the moment Bacchus was out to the first ball of the day, it was clear that West Indies, wanting 208 in the last innings, were going to need skill, resource and luck if they were to make the remaining 99 runs. At 129-5, with 79 still required, the odds seemed to favour an England win, but they could not press home their advantage.

One reason was the determination of Haynes, 24, who countered and avoided the moving ball with remarkable adroitness for one with limited experience of English conditions. He had batted five hours for 62 when he was run out two balls from the end. By then, his partner, Andy Roberts (22 not out), who seldom fails in a crisis and was later named Man of the Match by M.J.K. Smith, had made the match almost safe with some judicious hitting.

The other factors that let West Indies escape were two dropped catches and the excessive movement of the ball in the slight haze of a grey morning after a night of rain. It had moved off the pitch throughout the match, but now it often swung and deviated too much to find the edge of the bat. Even at the end of his priceless innings, Haynes was being beaten two or three times an over.

Another reason for West Indies' escape was that England had to rely mainly on two bowlers, Willis and Hendrick, both tiring towards the end. The magnificent Willis bowled 15 overs today for four wickets, 45 runs and umpteen near misses. He took five for 65 in the innings, nine for 147 in the match. But Roberts, who scored the winning runs and took five for 72 and three for 57, was the Man of the Match.

Haynes anchored West Indies' second innings with 62 in five hours.

Second Test First day: 19 June

Magnificent 123 by Gooch: then England lose initiative

By Michael Melford, at Lord's

GRAHAM GOOCH'S First Test hundred, in his 22nd Test match, was well worth waiting for, an innings of the highest class, aggressive but controlled, and made almost entirely against unrelenting pace and accuracy. In the first three and a half hours against the West Indies, he made 123 out of 165, and England, despite having lost Boycott early on, had made as prosperous a start as they have for a long time. But, alas, recession was near.

After Gooch was out, five wickets were lost in the last two and a quarter hours for 67 runs, and the close-of-play score of 232 for seven is not a healthy one on so good a pitch.

Gooch's timing was immaculate, and he hit a six and 17 fours, the bulk of them struck in front of the wicket with the full face of the bat. He was splendidly in command throughout, and gave no chance until he succumbed in only the 50th over to the first of three lbws given by umpire Alley – less culpably than the others, for he was not playing a bad stroke.

He was greatly helped by having a staunch partner at the other end. Though Tavaré contributed only 26 to their second-wicket partnership of 145, he gave the bowlers little hope, and if he was not able to accelerate towards the end of his long innings – 4hr 50min for 42 – well, these are still early and exploratory days for him. His successors were more ambitious and more vulnerable.

[England were all out for 269, and and West Indies' reply of 518 featured a Lord's West Indies record of 184 from Desmond Haynes and a superb 145 from Viv Richards. The loss of some eight hours through rain on the last two days probably saved England from going two down in the series, although Gooch (47) and Boycott (49 not) made spirited efforts to claw back the deficit.]

Benson & Hedges Cup Final: 21 July

Northants scramble home by six runs in tense last hour

By Michael Melford, at Lord's

OF ALL THE LORD'S cup finals of the past 18 seasons, none has had a more remarkable last hour than the Benson & Hedges final that Northants have won this evening by six runs.

The 209 that Northants mustered with difficulty appeared inadequate when Graham Gooch (60) and Ken McEwan (38) were reaching 112 for one in only the 33rd of Essex's 55 overs and making the exercise look supremely easy.

But from the moment that Gooch ended his imperious innings by hitting Tim Lamb hard to the bowler's namesake at mid-on, Essex were in decline. In six more overs they were 121 for four and the match looked very different.

Hereabouts something akin to panic broke out on both sides. Pont charged Williams and survived a stumping chance. Fletcher hit Watts hard to mid-wicket and was dropped. There is nothing like spin to ferment panic, and the admirable Williams by now had the batsmen in all sorts of tangles, bowling Pont in one of them.

Turner drove Williams for the first four in 24 overs and pulled Watts for six, but Sarfraz, coming back for the 51st over, had him well caught by Watts at mid-on, and 47 were still needed off the last four overs.

Yet such was the onslaught by the mighty hitter Norbert Phillip on Griffiths, whose two overs yielded 30 runs, that only 11 runs were needed off the last over. But Sarfraz was well able to cope. He bowled Smith with his second ball, and subsequently avoided the middle of Phillip's devastating bat.

Cook (29) had sustained the first part of Northants' innings, after which Allan Lamb (72), with some brilliant strokes, led a long recovery. He was out at 193 in the 52nd over, but had done enough to win Northants the second trophy in their history and the day's Gold Award for himself. For the Northants captain Jim Watts (22 and 1-30), it was probably the best day in a long and honourable career, and after the match he announced his retirement from cricket.

County Championship: 8 August

Procter (7-60) skittles Worcestershire again

From Cheltenham

MIKE PROCTER'S fiery bowling shredded the Worcester batting line-up for the second time in successive days as Gloucestershire completed a 96-run victory at Cheltenham. The South African all-rounder took seven for 60 with a mixture of pace and off-spin to add to his seven for 16 yesterday, and Worcester subsided to 148, well short of their winning target.

Worcester, it appears, have adopted the role of sacrificial lambs to Procter, who took eight for 30 against them last season and seven for 35 the previous year. After bolstering Gloucester, who had been put in, to 178 on the first day with 73, Procter took seven wickets for nine runs the next morning to send Worcester crashing from their overnight 84 for one to 111 all out.

He made 35 in the second innings, and then took four quick wickets to have Worcester at 29 for four. He rounded off a triumphant performance with the final wicket in his 28th over.

County Championship: 2 September

Brearley's century a fitting seal to title for mighty Middlesex

By A.S.R.Winlaw, at Cardiff

MIDDLESEX became outright County Champions for the seventh time in their 117-year history when they beat Glamorgan by 72 runs at Sophia Gardens. With one match to play, they now lead Surrey by 28 points.

They were led to victory by a magnificent captain's innings of 124 not out from Mike Brearley and, although Glamorgan's batsmen battled away in the best Welsh fighting traditions, the dominant champions eventually won with six overs to spare.

Brearley celebrated in the typical calm delight of beer rather than champagne, and raised his glass in celebration to South African Vincent Van der Bijl, so justifiably top of the national bowling averages with 85 wickets, as "our biggest single factor of all – both on and off the field".

Middlesex, who started the last day at 25 for nought, were able to declare at lunch on 211 for one thanks largely to a stand of 134 between Brearley and wicket-keeper Paul Downton (46). This new first-wicket partnership, established only in the last week of July, has undoubtedly been one of Middlesex's most encouraging features of the season.

With Simon Hughes taking three wickets, Middlesex had Glamorgan at 84 for five, and looked set for a comfortable win with two hours to go. But it needed that undisputed weapon Van der Bijl to return and break the 52-run stand of Holmes and Moseley, and with Daniel and Edmonds mopping up the tail, Glamorgan's last five wickets fell for 26 runs.

Gillette Cup Final: 6 September

Brilliant Butcher rounds off great day for Brearley

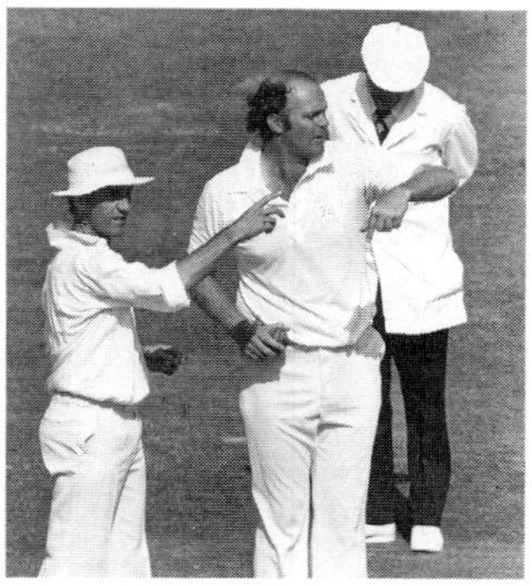

Man-of-the-Match Mike Brearley (left) and Vincent Van der Bijl adjust the Middlesex field to contain Surrey's slog.

By Michael Melford, at Lord's

MIDDLESEX won the last Gillette Cup final by seven wickets with an efficiency that made the occasion at Lord's relatively tame. They and their captain were too knowledgeable for Surrey, and Mike Brearley, unarguably the Man of the Match, had played a well-disciplined innings of 96 not out when the 202 runs needed were made with six overs to spare.

He had put Surrey in on a slow, slightly uneven pitch that changed little during the day. Selvey's 12 overs for only 17 runs, of which six came when Alan Butcher pulled a good-length ball far over mid-wicket, was a big factor in the deepening gloom already cast over the batting by Daniel (2-33) and Van der Bijl (1-32), who later restricted Surrey's final slog. Only Hughes was expensive, conceding 60 runs for his three wickets. David Smith top-scored for Surrey with 50.

Middlesex were well on their way to victory on 121 for three, and needed only about three runs an over. Roland Butcher came in and, with some improbable strokes of eye and timing, made 50 out of the last 80 in 45 minutes, including three sixes over the near on-side boundary and five fours. Off the front foot and back, he made it all look easy, and by expediting the end deprived his currently prolific captain of a third hundred in five days. Brearley was not complaining.

1981

16 Feb Andy Roberts breaks the Test record for runs off a six-ball over by two, scoring 24 (three 6s, a 4 and a 2) off the first five balls of an over from Ian Botham for West Indies v England at Port-of-Spain in the 1st Test.

16-21 Jul Australian wicket-keeper Rodney Marsh breaks the record for dismissals (263) in Tests, and England wicket-keeper Bob Taylor the record for catches (1,270) in first-class cricket, at Headingley in the 4th Test.

13-17 Aug England v Australia at Old Trafford marks a number of records – Tavaré's 78 incorporates the slowest 50 (304min) in English first-class cricket; Border's 123, the slowest Australian Test 100 (373min); Boycott passes Cowdrey's record Test aggregate (7,624) runs for England; Terry Alderman takes his 37th wicket, an Australian record for a series in England – as well as an 86-ball 100 by Botham in a magnificent innings of 118 (123 min) that includes six 6s (Anglo-Australian record) and is made in a 6th-wicket stand of 149 with Tavaré, whose contribution is 28.

1 Sep Alderman takes his record series haul to 42 wickets in the 6th Test, at the Oval.

1 Sep Javed Miandad hits an undefeated 200 out of 311 for Glamorgan against Essex, but runs out of partners 14 short of their target.

14 Nov Lillee (5-18) and Alderman (4-36) bowl Pakistan out for 62, their lowest Test score, as only Sarfraz (26) reaches double figures.

23 Dec Geoff Boycott (105) passes Gary Sobers' record 8,032 Test runs on his way to a record-equalling 22nd Test hundred for England, at New Delhi in the 3rd Test against India.

26-30 Dec Lillee (7-83) passes Lance Gibbs' record 309 Test wickets, at Melbourne in the 1st Test against West Indies, going on to take 10 wickets in a Test (10-127) for a record-equalling 7th time and taking a record 85 in a calendar year.

B & H World Series Cup Third final: 1 February

Chappell's under-arm victory ploy starts storm

By D.J.Rutnagur, in Melbourne

GREG CHAPPELL, the Australian captain, was roundly criticised after instructing his brother Trevor to bowl the last ball of their third World Series Cup final match under-arm – and along the ground – to prevent New Zealand levelling the scores. Chappell's ploy, with New Zealand needing a six to tie the scores, assured Australia of victory and put them 2-1 up in the best-of-five final series.

Brian McKechnie threw his bat down in disgust when Trevor Chappell rolled the ball down the pitch, leaving New Zealand stranded on 229 for eight in reply to Australia's 235 for four. In an angrily worded statement issued in Wellington, Bob Vance, chairman of the New Zealand Cricket Council, suggested the Australian Board should annul the match. Geoff Howarth, the New Zealand captain, described the Chappells' action as "definitely not in the spirit of the game".

The under-arm delivery is legal in Australia, although it was outlawed from limited-overs cricket in England, at the same time as declarations, after the summer of 1979.

Greg Chappell defended his action. "I told Trevor to do it and I told umpire Don Wiser of my intentions," he said. "Wiser then advised Brian McKechnie and his co-umpire."

Earlier, Chappell had been involved in another controversial incident when on his way to making Australia's top score of 90. He skied a ball from Lance Cairns to mid-wicket, where Martin Snedden appeared to hold a brilliant diving catch. Chappell refused to walk, and the umpires told Howarth that they were watching the crease at their respective ends as a guard against short runs.

[Two days later, Australia won the fourth final to take the series 3-1.]

Third Test Fifth day: 11 February

Kapil Dev routs Australia to square series

By D.J.Rutnagur, in Melbourne

KAPIL DEV, the Indian fast bowler, overcame a thigh muscle injury to inspire the tourists to a stunning 59-run victory in the third Test to square the three-match rubber against Australia. Kapil, who was unable to bowl at the start of the Australian second innings yesterday, bounced back to take five of the seven wickets to fall as Australia were routed for 83, their lowest score against India.

Australia, their confidence undermined by the nature of the pitch, which was hopelessly unreliable in bounce, could offer no resistance and were all out 17 minutes after lunch. They had expected the main threat to come from spinner Doshi, but instead they were struck by the brisk pace of Kapil Dev, who finished with five for 28 off 16.4 overs.

Before Kapil Dev went on the rampage in his last nine overs, Doshi achieved the breakthrough half an hour after the start when he beat Kim Hughes with his faster ball. Like Kapil Dev, he bowled unchanged today, very bravely under the handicap of a foot injury, which an X-ray later showed to be a crack in the instep.

Third Test Fourth day: 10 February

India walk-out threat over lbw decision

By D.J.Rutnagur, in Melbourne

THE THIRD Australia-India Test, which seems headed for an exciting finish at the Melbourne Cricket Ground tomorrow, nearly ended with an Indian walk-out when Sunil Gavaskar was given out lbw to Dennis Lillee by umpire Rex Whitehead. The Indian captain, who claimed the ball had taken a thick inside edge before striking his pad, lingered at the crease before ordering Chauhan, his partner, to leave the field with him.

Chauhan followed Gavaskar all the way to the gate in the fence, but when Wing Commander Durrani, the Indian manager, appeared, Chauhan was quickly persuaded to return to the wicket.

Gavaskar's controversial dismissal for 70 ended an opening stand of 165, and India, who had trailed by 182 on the first innings, were eventually bowled out for 324.

Australia, needing to score 143 to win on a well-worn pitch against a depleted Indian attack (Yadav is out and Kapil Dev doubtful), were 24 for three at the close.

Commenting on the incident, Gavaskar said: "I was infuriated at the injustice of it all. Mr Whitehead has stood in all three Tests, and we have lost count of the bad decisions we have had from him."

Kapil Dev, India's five-wicket hero.

TEST SERIES

Australia in England
E 3, A 1, D 2
England in West Indies
WI 2, D 2, Cancelled 1
West Indies in Pakistan
WI 1, D 3
India in Australia
A 1, I 1, D 1
India in New Zealand
NZ 1, D 2
Pakistan in Australia
A 2, P 1

England tour of West Indies: Saturday, 28 February

Envoys in Test battle

By Ian Ball, from Barbados

WHAT has quickly become known as the 'Jackman affair' has resulted in the cancellation of the second Test, due to have started at Georgetown, Guyana, today. But the touring party, after a long wait at Georgetown airport, arrived last night in Barbados to a warm welcome.

Jackman arrived in Guyana on Monday as a replacement for Willis, who broke down in Trinidad. There has been no attempt to hide the fact that Jackman has played in South Africa. Others in the party have spent winters in South Africa, including Boycott, Gower and wicket-keeper David Bairstow, who captained Griqualand West, a South African province, in 1977-78, after the signing of the Gleneagles Agreement.

However, no sooner had Jackman arrived in Guyana, just two days after the England party, than the trouble began. On Thursday, the Guyanese Minister of Foreign Affairs informed the British High Commissioner in Georgetown that Jackman's visitor's permit had been withdrawn, and that the decision to declare him a prohibited immigrant was based entirely on the Gleneagles accord.

The Cricket Council, meeting at Lord's, insisted that it be allowed to pick its Test teams without host governments imposing sudden political restrictions on individuals. The England manager Alan Smith, with support from other Caribbean countries, withdrew the England party.

England tour of West Indies

Test tribute to Ken Barrington

By Michael Melford, in Bridgetown

SEVERAL England cricketers were in tears today as the capacity crowd in the Kensington Oval, Bridgetown, stood in silence to pay tribute to Ken Barrington before the third day's play in the Test began. Barrington, 50, one of England's greatest post-war batsmen and assistant-manager and coach of the touring team, died of a heart attack last night shortly after dining with his wife, Anne, and friends.

Alan Smith, the England manager, said that the players were really shattered: "Ken was one of cricket's most lovable characters, and the boyish enthusiasm with which he bowled at the nets up to Saturday morning did everyone good." Ian Botham, the England captain, said: "To me he was everything. We were very close friends and I used to visit him a lot."

Barrington played in 82 Test matches during a 20-year career with Surrey and made 20 Test centuries, one of them in Bridgetown 21 years ago. He gave up first-class cricket after a minor heart attack in Melbourne, but in 1972 became a Test selector.

County Championship Somerset v Gloucestershire: 16 June

Brilliant Zaheer matched by resolve of Rose

By Gerald Pawle, at Bath

ZAHEER ABBAS, the only batsman in cricket history to score double and single centuries in the same match three times, has performed the feat again. He followed his 215 not out in the first innings with a superb 150, also undefeated, for Gloucestershire against Somerset.

The second effort, in which he shared in a 121 unfinished fifth-wicket stand with Hignell, the last 70 added in 30 minutes after lunch, enabled Gloucester to set Somerset a well-nigh impossible target of 349 to win in 200 minutes. Already handicapped by injury to two of their leading batsmen, Rose and Roebuck, Somerset collapsed, losing their first six wickets for 79.

When the final 20 overs began, they had eight men out for 188. But Rose, who had come in in the emergency at the fall of the last wicket, played an amazing innings stiff-legged of 85 not out, his highest score of the season. Then Roebuck (13), also nearly immobile, appeared as last man and played out the final 14 overs with his captain in an epic last-wicket stand of 45.

Third Test Fourth day: 20 July

Botham: Flayed the Australian bowling in an innings of aggression and quality.

Botham's magnificent 145 brings England back to life

By Michael Melford, at Headingley

ENGLAND were lifted off the ground in an extraordinary day's play in the third Cornhill Test against Australia by the magnificent innings of 145 not out in three and a half hours by Ian Botham and by his stands with Dilley and Old, who joined in flogging the tiring Australian fast bowlers to all parts.

At 135 for seven, 35 minutes before tea, England were still 91 runs short of saving an innings defeat. But Botham and Dilley (56) made 117 in 80 minutes for the eighth wicket; Botham and Old (29) added another 67 in 55 minutes; and Australia, with the last wicket still to take, will need at least 125 in the last innings.

Botham's innings, following his top score 50 out of 174 on Saturday and his six wickets for 95 in Australia's first innings, contained strokes that were classical, rugged and improvised, not all off the middle of the bat but hit with a power that forced seven Australian fielders to the boundary.

The devastation of it all is aptly shown by the statistics. He reached 100 in only 76 balls, and there was a period in which he made 64 runs between 39 and 103 by means of a six, 14 fours and two singles.

When Botham was 32, Bright, in the gully, stuck out his left hand, but the ball was going too fast to hold. This and a hard chance to Marsh off a hook when 109 were Botham's only escapes.

The main assault began with some superb strokes past cover point off the back foot, followed by cuts that were at the boundary before anyone moved, massive driving and a marvellously straight six off Alderman. He lost Dilley, who went to his first Test 50 by flogging Lillee past extra cover, on 252, and Old on 319. Thereafter he kept Willis (1 not out) from strike, hit the last few of his 24 fours with strokes of quality, surpassed his previous highest Test innings, and ran off after playing one of the most memorable Test innings of modern times.

Third Test Fifth day: 21 July

Willis achieves unbelievable with 8 for 43

By Michael Melford, at Headingley

JUST OCCASIONALLY in life the unbelievable does happen. It happened on the last day of the third Cornhill Test at Headingley, when England, who had seemingly been within a few minutes of defeat yesterday afternoon, with Ladbrokes the bookmakers offering 500-1 against them, bowled out Australia for 111 to win by 18 runs.

Ian Botham hauled them up from the depths yesterday, and, having made 149 not out, took the first wicket when Australia batted this morning. But the 130 that Australia needed was very little on a pitch still producing the unpredictable ball but no more often than when they were making 401 in the first innings. Indeed, at 56 for one, Australia seemed to be cruising home.

Then Bob Willis, having switched to the Kirkstall Lane end, began to bowl as straight and as fast as at any time in the long career that has been miraculously extended after injury. He has only once produced better figures than eight for 43, but that was not in a Test match

His inspired spell began 20 minutes before lunch, when he took the first of six wickets in 32 balls for eight runs. It ended 70 minutes after lunch, when he knocked out Bright's middle stump, and England had incredibly levelled the series. Only once in more than 100 years of Test matches has a side following on been victorious – England won by 10 runs in Sydney in 1894-95.

The inspiration today was not confined to Willis, for England threw themselves frantically about the field and, until the last few seconds, held all their catches, the best of them being one by Botham and two by the agile Gatting, while Brearley conducted operations with the unflappability that has coped successfully with numerous tight limited-overs finishes in the past.

With Australia 75 for eight, Bright and Lillee staged a revival, and had put on 35 runs in four overs before Lillee miscued and Gatting, at mid-on, ran and hurled himself forward to take a brilliant catch. There were hearts in mouths as Botham had Alderman dropped twice in three balls by Old at third slip.

Mercifully, it did not matter. Willis produced a yorker, Bright drove over it, and a never to be forgotten Test match was won and lost.

Benson & Hedges Cup Final: 25 July

Richards, Garner make it so easy for Somerset

By Michael Melford, at Lord's

VIVIAN RICHARDS, with the brilliance that is his wont to be at its most devastating on big occasions at Lord's, made sure of Somerset's first Benson & Hedges Cup victory on Saturday as they beat Surrey by seven wickets with 10.3 overs to spare.

Just briefly, around half past three, when Somerset were five for two in reply to Surrey's modest 194 for eight, it seemed that a close tussle might develop. But Richards had other ideas. Within a few minutes it was clear that he was about to respond to what he calls the 'tradition of Lord's', which means that he plays on an altogether loftier, more destructive level than anyone else in this world.

In this mood, Richards makes the length and direction of the bowling largely irrelevant. Wherever the ball is bowled, he is waiting for it with the appropriate stroke. He made his 132 not out off 128 balls in 2 hours 50 minutes.

The five for 14 in 11 overs of Somerset's other West Indian, Joel Garner, with his high arm and awkward trajectory, had cast a fateful gloom over Surrey's early batting. They scored only seven runs in the first 10 overs from Garner and Botham. Only the Surrey captain Roger Knight (92) provided any serious hope, before he finally fell to Garner in the 53rd over.

For Somerset, Roebuck contributed only 22 of the 105 added with Richards for the third wicket, and then they were able to throw in Botham. He, with 37, and Richards made the last 87 in 55 minutes, and Botham gave every indication that his batting at Headingley last week was no flash in the pan.

Fourth Test Fourth Day: 2 August

England snatch victory again as Botham takes 5 for 1

By Michael Melford, at Edgbaston

IT HAS happened again – amid even more hysterical excitement than at Headingley – for there was a much bigger crowd. When all seemed lost, England snatched back the fourth Cornhill Test, bowled Australia out for 121, and won by 29 runs.

Ian Botham was again the hero – this time with the ball. He took over when Australia, needing 151 to win, were, after a bad start, seemingly cruising home at 114 for five. He took the last five wickets for one run in 28 balls. And Australia, who a fortnight ago seemed about to go two up in the series, were 2-1 down.

That England were still in with a chance was due to the 52 runs coaxed from the last two wickets yesterday evening by John Emburey (37 not out). As England found at Headingley, there is a huge difference between having to make 100 and having to make 150, particularly in a fourth innings.

The Australian collapse started when Marsh pulled across a yorker in the second over of Botham's spell, which was being bowled very accurately on a full length. The next ball then came back rather low to have Bright lbw.

Lillee stayed for 20 minutes amid a rare din for a Test match in England, and then drove at a wide ball from Botham, leaving him. Taylor dived a long way, and, having got there, was lucky to hold the ball at the second attempt. Kent, looking reasonably authoritative amid the hubbub, drove across an inswinger from Botham and was bowled.

It took Botham three balls to produce an inswinging yorker to bowl Alderman and, only 12 days after Headingley, history had amazingly repeated itself.

Fifth Test Final day: 17 August

Border makes England wait for Ashes clincher

By Michael Melford, at Old Trafford

ENGLAND won the fifth Cornhill Test by 103 runs, the rubber by three matches to one, and they have retained the Ashes. But, thanks largely to the courageous Allan Border, they needed four and a half hours today to take the last five Australian wickets.

And there were long periods in the freakish situation when an Australian win seemed a genuine possibility. Border held one end throughout, undefeated for 123 after batting for nearly seven hours with the broken finger that he described as "more annoying than paining".

Marsh (47) and Lillee (28) played so comfortably with him on this mild, true pitch that England, with only four bowlers, were sorely tried. Even at the end, the No.11, Whitney, who did not score, held out for 40 minutes, and it was not inconceivable that he would stay another 85 and earn Australia an honourable draw.

Eventually Australia were all out for 402, and a series which has seldom followed a predictable pattern was decided. So only 29 days after England, needing 92 to avoid an innings defeat at Headingley with only three wickets left, were, as it seemed, going 2-0 down in the series, they have taken a winning 3-1 lead.

County Championship
Notts v Glamorgan: 14 September

Hadlee and Hemmings clinch Notts' first title since 1929

By Michael Melford, at Trent Bridge

ALL SORTS of history was made this afternoon at Trent Bridge when Nottinghamshire beat Glamorgan by 10 wickets with more than a day and a half to spare and won the County Championship. This is their first title since 1929, and only the second since their heyday of the 1880s.

For nine days, since their neighbours Derbyshire had won the NatWest Trophy at Lord's, Notts had been the only one of the 17 counties not to have won any competition since the war. That has now been rectified in a remarkable season in which Clive Rice won the toss in the last 10 of their Schweppes home matches. In their first match, Leicester chose to bat, and Rice put the opposition in every time, so Notts batted second in all 11 home matches.

Richard Hadlee spearheaded Notts' title charge today with four for 38, while Hemmings took four for 51. Javed Miandad (75), improvising brilliantly, prevented another débâcle – no-one scored more than 14 in their first-innings 60 (Hadlee 4-18, Cooper 4-25), and Glamorgan's 149 forced Notts to bat again, if only for 30 runs.

NatWest Trophy Final Derbyshire v Northants: 5 September

Derbyshire dash to thrilling win off last ball

By Michael Melford, at Lord's

WHAT MORE could anyone ask after the cricket of the last two months than a last cloudless day at Lord's and victory off the last ball in the most exciting limited-overs final ever played there?

Derbyshire became the first winners of the NatWest Trophy by four wickets after both sides had scored 235. And I suppose that if the competition runs for 50 years, it might never again go to a side who did not score more runs than their opponents in either semi-final or final.

Derby ran a last desperate single to level the scores and win on fewer wickets lost – thanks to the speed of non-striker Geoff Miller and his frantic dive a fraction before the wicket was broken. This was in the half-light at 7.35 p.m., at the end of a day in which Northants had several times been about to put the result beyond reasonable doubt when something went wrong.

Geoff Cook (111), who won the Man of the Match award from Viv Richards, and Wayne Larkins (52) put on 99 for the first wicket after Northants had been put in. But after Allan Lamb (9) was second out at 137, only 98 runs were added in the last 20 overs.

Derby made slow progress, but were 164 for one before Wright (76) and Kirsten (63) were both lbw in the 48th over. Northants seemed likely winners until Sarfraz bowled two fateful overs, Miller (22 not out) pulling a full toss for six in the 57th and the powerful Tunnicliffe (15 not out) clubbing 11 in the 59th. A leg-bye then left Derby to get six off the last over.

A two by Miller, a single, a 'dot' ball, two singles and then Miller's final charge down the pitch as the ball ran a few yards away on the on-side brought the trophy to Derbyshire.

John Wright: Gave Derbyshire a solid start.

First Test Fourth day: 16 November

Lillee kicks Pakistan captain and is fined £120

By Roger Heywood, in Perth

THE CONTROVERSY and acrimony that has plagued the last two series between Australia and Pakistan blew up again in the first Test in Perth when Australian fast bowler Lillee and Pakistan captain Javed Miandad were involved in a disgraceful incident. The clash occurred during the afternoon session, when Miandad played a ball from Lillee to square leg and started to run a single. But before he could complete the run, Lillee wheeled into him.

Miandad brushed the Australian aside with his bat, Lillee spinning round and swinging his arm without making contact. And, although umpire Tony Crafter stepped between the two men, Lillee managed to kick Miandad behind his left leg. The Pakistan captain then raised his bat above his head, appearing to threaten Lillee.

Both umpires later reported Lillee for his behaviour, and also lodged a complaint with Pakistan manager Ijaz Butt about Miandad's involvement. Under Australian cricket's new code of conduct, Lillee's team-mates considered the umpires' report and fined Lillee £120, but declined to suspend him because they felt he had acted under provocation.

After hearing of the fine, Mr Butt said: "If Lillee had been one of my players, he would not play Test cricket again." Mr Butt had complained about Lillee's conduct earlier in the match – his "mimicking, clapping and antics of sitting on the pitch". Greg Chappell, the Australian captain, said: "Javed provoked the incident, and we are very strong in our condemnation."

[Unhappy with Lillee's lenient punishment, the umpires appealed to the Australian Board of Control. Lillee threatened to quit cricket if he was suspended, but when he was – for two one-day matches – he didn't.]

1982

1-6 Jan India v England 4th Test, at Calcutta, sees a record crowd estimated at 394,000 turn up at Eden Gardens; it is Boycott's last Test, for a record 193 innings, 8,114 runs.

14-15 Jan Gundappa Viswanath (222, highest by Indian against England) and Yashpal Sharma (140) share in a 316 stand, the highest for any wicket in Anglo-Indian Tests, and the highest Indian 3rd-wicket.

5-10 Mar Sri Lanka lose their first overseas Test, by 204 runs at Karachi, even though Pakistan field a virtual 2nd XI when the cream of their side refuse to play if Javed Miandad is retained as captain for their England tour.

14 Mar Bruce Edgar's 161 at Auckland in the 2nd Test is New Zealand's highest knock against Australia.

14 Mar Sidath Wettimuny (157) scores Sri Lanka's first Test 100, in the 2nd Test against Pakistan at Faisalabad.

22-27 Mar Pakistan, back at full strength after Miandad agrees to relinquish the captaincy for the England tour, beat Sri Lanka by an innings and 102 runs, Imran Khan taking a record 14 wickets for Pakistan (8-58, 6-58).

24-29 Mar The Ranji Trophy final in Delhi produces the highest first-innings aggregate in first-class cricket. Karnataka amass 705 (4 hundreds, highest Brijesh Patel 124), but lose by 2 wickets to Delhi & Districts, whose 707-8 includes only 2 hundreds (Mohinder Amarnath highest, 185), trophy decided on first innings.

8 May Somerset wicket-keeper Derek Taylor takes a world-record limited-overs 8 catches against Oxford and Cambridge University at Taunton in the B & H Cup.

23 Jun Yorks manager Ray Illingworth, 50, replaces Chris Old as county captain.

9 Jul Ian Botham (208) hits 200 in 268 min off 220 balls against India at the Oval, the fastest double century by an Englishman since Compton against Pakistan in 1954, and, in terms of balls received, possibly the fastest of all time.

31 Aug England's 3-wicket victory at Headingley gives them the rubber 2-1 over Pakistan, with the help of 221 from extras, more than any England batsman scored in the series.

8-10 Sep Yorkshire wicket-keeper David Bairstow takes 11 catches in the match against Derbyshire to equal the world record.

TEST SERIES

India in England
E 1, D 2
Pakistan in England
E 2, P 1
England in India
I 1, D 5
England in Sri Lanka
England 1
West Indies in Australia
A 1, WI 1, D 1
Australia in New Zealand
A 1, NZ 1, D 1
Sri Lanka in Pakistan
P 2, D 1
Sri Lanka in India
1 Drawn
Australia in Pakistan
Pakistan 3

Third Test Final day: 3 February

Garner's 4-5 sets up West Indies win

By Alan Shiell, in Adelaide

ONE OF the greatest Test matches played at Adelaide Oval ended in a five-wicket win for the West Indies – where it could so easily have gone Australia's way. So the West Indies squared the series 1-1 to retain the Sir Frank Worrell Trophy they have held since 1978.

In fairness to the Australians, it was remarkable that they got so close. Lillee's groin injury restricted him to 8.5 overs in the match and both Greg Chappell and Hughes batted with cracked bones, Chappell's in a finger, Hughes' a toe.

All of Australia's good work over the first four days was undone in the morning when their last six wickets sank for a meagre 45 runs off 24 overs in 95 minutes from the resumption total of 341 for four. Garner did most of the damage with the amazing figures of 9-7-5-4.

The West Indies were left to score 236 in 193 minutes plus 20 overs – a formidable target in the last two sessions of a Test – but Clive Lloyd, the captain, hit the winning runs, a four through wide mid-on off Thomson, with only 2.5 overs remaining.

Greenidge (52) and Richards (50) laid the foundations for victory with a second-wicket stand of 100. Lloyd (77 not out) and Gomes (21) consolidated with 62 for the fourth wicket, and Lloyd and Bacchus (27) put the result beyond doubt during an even-time fifth-wicket stand of 59.

Border was Man of the Match for his 78 and 126. Lloyd, magnificent in the crisis and playing probably his last innings in Australia, was chaired from the field by Garner, Holding and Croft.

Inaugural Test
Fourth day: 21 February

Emburey spoils party for new boys Sri Lanka

By Michael Carey, in Colombo

ENGLAND won the inaugural Test match against Sri Lanka at the Saravanamuttu Oval with an ease in the end that probably surprised even themselves. They made the 171 needed for the loss of three wickets, when a far tougher assignment had seemed likely with Sri Lanka starting 152 ahead and only three wickets down.

But Sri Lanka, who surely have done enough in their first match to justify their elevation to Test status, succumbed to the off-spin of Emburey, who took five wickets for five runs in 33 deliveries and finished with six for 33. Betraying their lack of experience, Sri Lanka lost their last seven wickets for only eight runs in 45 minutes that will haunt them for a long time.

England knocked off the runs with little trouble, Tavaré (85) playing an innings of great fluency and selectivity.

'Rebel' tour of South Africa: 3 March

Junior Springboks give Gooch's men unhappy start

From Pretoria

GRAHAM GOOCH'S English rebels made an undistinguished start to their controversial South African trip, struggling to reach 152 for seven declared against the Junior Springboks, who replied with 51 for one on the opening day of a two-day match.

On a dry, placid pitch, the tourists looked anything but international class batsmen, and it can only be assumed that they were somewhat upset by the reports of the general reaction their defiance has caused in Britain. Another factor might have been the size of the crowd, well below the capacity 6,000 expected.

Gooch, who has superseded Boycott as captain on the insistence of the rest of the party, lost the toss and was asked to bat. These two put on 53 for the first wicket. But after Boycott (13) was out, the International XI lost wickets regularly, only Amiss (30) giving any indication of class. The Under-25 captain Kuiper, a seam-bowler, finished with five for 22 off eight overs.

[On 19 March, the TCCB announced a three-year ban from Test selection on the 15 English cricketers in South Africa, of whom only Gooch, Larkins, Emburey and perhaps Les Taylor would have been fairly certain to play Test cricket this summer.

Bearded 'rebels', openers Boycott (left) and Gooch, take the field to start the controversial South African tour.

Benson & Hedges Cup Group match: 25 May

Records crash as Gooch and Fletcher crush Sussex

By Rex Alston, at Hove

RECORDS fell like ninepins as a brilliant exhibition of batting by Graham Gooch and Keith Fletcher sent Sussex tottering to their first defeat of the season. Fletcher, the deposed England captain, hit his first century in a B & H Cup match. Yet, superbly as he played, the Essex skipper had only a supporting role as Gooch finished just two short of 200 in his side's 327 for two – after Sussex had put them in.

Gooch's 198 (five 6s, 22 4s) is the highest individual score in a one-day game in England, and his unbeaten third-wicket partnership of 268 in 39 overs with Fletcher (101) is the highest against a first-class county in the B & H competition. Having taken such a battering, it was no wonder Sussex lost their first six wickets for 75 runs – and the match by 114. Gooch, for good measure, took three for 24 in 4.2 overs.

[Three days later, Sussex beat Kent to qualify for the quarter-finals at the expense of Essex.]

County Championship Lancs v Warwicks: 28 July

Kallicharran and Humpage: 470 stand

By Michael Austin, at Southport

GEOFF HUMPAGE, with an astonishing career-best innings of 254, and West Indian Alvin Kallicharran, who made an unbeaten 230, overpowered Lancashire with an English record stand for the fourth wicket of 470 as Warwickshire reached a total of 523 for four declared at Southport. The previous record was 448, by Abel and Hayward for Surrey in 1899.

Humpage hit 13 sixes, a total exceeded only once in the history of first-class cricket (by John Reid, who struck 15 in a New Zealand provincial match in 1962-63), and the partnership, occupying 293 minutes, was the best for any Warwickshire wicket. Kallicharran's double century was, remarkably, his third this season. He hit 34 fours and, like Humpage, offered only one chance.

Admittedly, the depleted Lancs attack was without the injured Croft and Allott, but McFarlane and Folley had Warwicks at six for two and then 53 for three. A dry and placid pitch belied a green appearance, and a fast and gently sloping outfield rewarded Humpage's pugnacity and Kallicharran's unhurried and deliberate shots, so that Clive Lloyd could merely share the punishment around his seven bowlers. Humpage crowned his day by catching David Lloyd at the wicket off Small, to leave Lancs at 40 for one.

[The match had a most extraordinary sequel: Lancashire declared their first innings at 414 for six, Warwicks were bowled out for 111 (Kallicharran 0, Humpage 21) in their second innings, and Lancs made 226 without loss to win by 10 wickets! Graeme Fowler, using a runner, made 126 and 128 not out.]

The record-breaking Warwickshire pair

County Championship Worcs v Warwicks: 29 May

Turner's 300 has touch of Bradman

By Mike Beddow, at Worcester

A FRIENDSHIP born on the practice grounds of Dunedin, New Zealand, reached total fruition at New Road, Worcester, when Glenn Turner, the Worcester opener, scored his 100th first-class century.

Billy Ibadulla, coach and mentor to Turner while he was studying at Otago Boys High School, appeared from the pavilion carrying two drinks. Each contained tonic water, but one was laced with a large measure of gin. Turner chose the intoxicant, and clearly it was one with special powers, for his remorseless destruction of Warwickshire's bowling, including Bob Willis, the new England captain, brought numerous records for an innings of 311 not out.

It is his highest score of his 18 years in first-class cricket and the highest ever by a Worcestershire batsman. He also becomes the first player to score 300 runs in a day in England since Jack Robertson of Middlesex made 331 not out on the same ground in 1949.

Turner's achievement has a strong link with Sir Donald Bradman. They are the only overseas players among 19 batsmen to have reached a century of centuries, and, of those, are the only ones to have made 300 in a day. Turner's innings took 342 minutes and contained two 6s and 39 4s.

Worcester declared at 501 for one, and Warwicks were 30 for one at the close.

First Test Fourth day: 1 August

Pakistan crumble to devastating spell by Botham

By Michael Carey, at Edgbaston

ENGLAND triumphed comprehensively at Edgbaston in the first Cornhill Test, bowling out Pakistan in 57 overs for 199 to win by 113 runs with more than a day to spare. It was a year almost to the day since their remarkable win over Australia on the same ground. This performance, however, if achieved with a rare facility, was rather more predictable.

Pakistan, needing 313 – a higher score than either side had managed in a match where bowlers were having the better of things – were devastated when Ian Botham took two wickets in his first over without a run on the board. And there was no way back from 98 for seven, although Imran Khan, their captain, whose first innings bowling (7-52) earned him the Man of the Match award, stood firm among the wreckage, top-scoring with 65.

Pakistan's last three wickets managed to add 101, which could be seen as an indictment of some of their earlier batting. And in the final reckoning, nothing tilted the balance of the match more than the record last-wicket stand of 79 between Bob Taylor and Bob Willis on Saturday.

It has been a match of incident and colour from start to finish, what with a century by Randall, the reluctant opener, the record last-wicket partnership, and the bowling of Pakistan's third-choice fast-medium bowler Tahir, who ripped through England's middle order with five for 40.

But Pakistan never recovered from that first over by Botham, who bowled another 20 and took four for 70. Gatting brilliantly ran out Miandad from short leg, and, when Zaheer was fifth out to a reckless stroke during a hostile spell by Willis, there was only going to be one result.

Second Test Second day: 13 August

Mohsin hits 200 but England's position improves

By Michael Carey, at Lord's

MOHSIN KHAN made the first double century in a Lord's Test for 33 years. But England, with assistance from the weather, regained a certain amount of self-esteem and checked Pakistan's progress, restricting them to 428 for eight.

Though a total of this size is still to be made, it is not the one of awesome proportions that Pakistan must have felt within their range, especially with Mohsin's Man of the Match knock. He batted for 491 minutes, faced 383 balls and hit 23 fours, but because of a stoppage for rain soon after lunch was obliged to wait for some four hours for the most priceless run of all, the single he needed to reach 200.

On the resumption, he turned Botham off his legs for a single, and the bowler was the first to congratulate him on becoming the first double-century maker in a Lord's Test since Martin Donnelly's 206 in 1949, only the eighth in 74 Lord's Tests, and the first Pakistani to accomplish the feat. Unfortunately, he was then caught off Jackman without adding to his score.

Mohsin Khan hooks Derek Pringle during his historic Lord's innings.

[Pakistan went on to gain their first Test victory at Lord's and only their second win against England in 35 meetings. They declared on their overnight score, enforced the follow-on, and won easily by 10 wickets after England succumbed in their second innings to the medium-pace bowling of opening bat Mudassar Nazar, who took three wickets in six balls and finished with six for 32.]

John Player League Sussex v Middlesex: 29 August

Sussex romp to first triumph

By D.J.Rutnagur, at Hove

SUSSEX, the early masters of limited-overs cricket, have clinched the John Player League for the first time, becoming the ninth county to win the 14-year-old competition – and they still have two matches to play. They made sure of the title with an emphatic victory over Middlesex, their only remaining rivals, by 23 runs.

Sussex have suffered only one defeat in 14 matches. This kept them marginally behind Middlesex who, with an unbeaten record, headed the table until July, when they were beaten three times in quick succession.

In the crunch match, Sussex decided to bat first, and established an early ascendancy through an opening partnership of 134 between Gehan Mendis, who scored a thrilling century (100), and Ian Gould, formerly of Middlesex. Gould's innings (58) was particularly praiseworthy, for he carried the handicap of a damaged hamstring.

Middlesex, set a target of 229, matched the Sussex scoring rate until Roland Butcher was out for 59. After that, they began to struggle and lose wickets, and were all out for 205 in the last over.

County Championship Somerset v Warwicks: 3 September

Botham races to 52-minute century

By David Green, at Taunton

A remarkable display of hitting by Ian Botham, who reached his century in 52 minutes, comfortably the fastest of the season, carried Somerset to victory over Warwickshire by five wickets.

Botham hit 10 sixes and 12 fours in his 131 not out to take the lead in the Walter Lawrence Trophy for the fastest hundred of the season. In only 40 minutes play after tea, he scored 114 runs, a rate of progress with few parallels in cricket history.

Warwicks started the day at 97 for 8, only 189 runs on, but Lethbridge, who made a career-best 87 not out and Willis (48) batted boldly to add 115 in 70 minutes for the 9th wicket.

Somerset had to make 309 in four and a half hours, a formidable task with the wicket taking spin. They were 57 for three before a splendid and rapid 85 by Richards put them back in the chase. Botham joined Slocombe, who had been playing steadily, and employed the half-hour before tea in careful reconnaissance, scoring 17 runs.

Immediately after the interval he launched himself into a tremendous onslaught, hitting the hitherto tidy off-spinner Sutcliffe for three consecutive sixes over square leg, taking 23 off the over. He took 30 off the next, from the medium-paced Paul Smith, with three on-driven sixes and three fours.

Willis persisted with Sutcliffe, who was again hit for three onside sixes in succession and a four to third man. Slocombe completed a worthy 50, Botham hit Amiss over mid-on, and Somerset, astonishingly, had won with 80 minutes to spare.

County Championship Worcs v Middlesex: 11 September

Middlesex title a fitting end to Brearley's final season

By Michael Carey, at Worcester

MIDDLESEX duly won the Schweppes County Championship at New Road when they obtained the four points they needed by bowling out Worcestershire for 168. Leicestershire, who had pursued them since mid-July, are certain to finish runners-up.

Mike Brearley thus ends his final season as captain of Middlesex on an appropriate high note. Their success owes much not only to his personal brand of leadership, but to their variety of bowling and depth of reserve strength. They were able to cope with injuries, Test calls, and loss of form – notably of Graham Barlow, Player of the Year last season.

With bowlers of genuine pace in Wayne Daniel, Neil Williams and Norman Cowans, plus two spinners of Test quality in John Emburey and Phil Edmonds, they were also well equipped for most conditions encountered during an English summer.

Above all, perhaps, has been Brearley's leadership and willingness to try something different in an effort to make things happen. He assumed the captaincy in a period of turmoil and mediocrity, and led them for 12 consecutive seasons - to four Championships and two Gillette Cups in the last seven.

[Nineties by Butcher and Edmonds gave Middlesex a substantial first-innings lead over Worcester and they ran out winners by 10 wickets, Brearley appropriately striking the winning runs.]

Second Test Final day: 5 October

Qadir's 11-218 decisive

From Faisalabad

AUSTRALIA'S desperate attempt to save the three-match series against Pakistan failed shortly before tea on the final day of the second Test. The tourists, who had begun the day at 176 for four, still needing 157 to avoid an innings defeat, were bowled out for 330, leaving Pakistan victors by an innings and three runs.

The main destroyer was again leg-spinner Abdul Qadir, who mopped up the tail after Marsh was run out for eight, leaving the valiant Ritchie unbeaten on 106. Qadir took seven for 142 in 50.4 overs for match figures of 11 for 218. Pakistan now have a 2-0 winning lead in the rubber following their nine-wicket victory at Karachi.

First Test Second day: 13 November

Alderman injured in pitch invasion

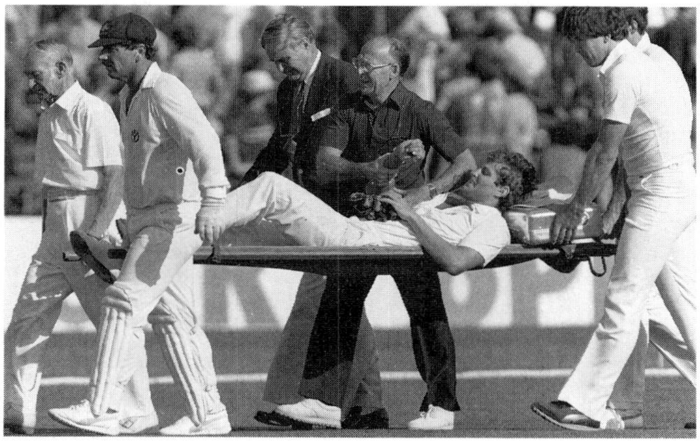

Alderman is stretchered off with a dislocated shoulder after tackling a pitch invader.

By Michael Carey, in Perth

AN INJURY to Terry Alderman, Australia's opening bowler, who dislocated a shoulder in a fracas with a spectator, and frequent outbreaks of violence in the crowd, culminating in 26 arrests, sadly overshadowed everything else in an otherwise worthy second day's play in the first Test between England and Australia at Perth.

England totalled 411, built around Chris Tavaré's marathon innings of 89, and Australia replied with 30 for no wicket, although both their openers had close calls near the end.

Alderman, who was stretchered from the field and taken to hospital in great pain, is expected to be out of action for at least three weeks and could miss the next two Tests. The Australian authorities, however, will not seek England's permission for a replacement bowler for this match. The laws of the game do not normally permit this anyway.

The incident occurred when England, with eight wickets down, hoisted the 400. Some 30 spectators, headed by two waving miniature Union Jacks, started making their way unsteadily towards the middle. When they eventually retreated, Alderman was apparently involved in an exchange of blows with one and chased him. Bringing him down with a rugby tackle, however, he dislocated his shoulder in the process.

While he was carried off, fighting broke out in the crowd, and Greg Chappell led the Australian team off. Willis and Taylor stayed in the middle at the request of the umpires, and they were soon joined by the England manager, Doug Insole, and Phil Ridings, Chairman of the Australian Cricket Board. Some 14 minutes of play was lost – or four overs – before the umpires decided it was safe to resume play. With the concentration of all disturbed, the England innings was soon wrapped up.

Alderman, who returned to the ground in the afternoon with his arm in a sling, explained that he was not retaliating for being hit, but wanted to detain the hooligan for the police.

First Test Second day: 11 December

Ton-up Zaheer emulates Boycott

From Lahore

PAKISTAN batsman Zaheer Abbas chose the first Test against India to record his 100th century in first-class cricket, becoming the 20th player to do so. He is only the third cricketer, after Sir Don Bradman and Glenn Turner, from outside England to accomplish the feat, and the second, after Geoff Boycott, to do it in a Test match.

His 215 was his ninth three-figure score in 53 Tests, his fourth double century. He batted for five and a half hours, hitting two 6s and 23 4s, and lifted Pakistan from their first-day plod of 170 for three towards a total of 485 all out by the close.

Fourth Test Final day: 30 December

Miller-Tavaré double act snatches 3-run win for England

By Michael Carey, in Melbourne

ENGLAND triumphed by three runs in the remarkable fourth Test against Australia – one of the narrowest margins of victory in the history of the Ashes – and now need to win the final Test at Sydney to square the series. It was a juggling act in the slips that finally enabled England to squeeze home in a game that retained its thrilling impact until the final ball.

In the end, with Australia's splendid last-wicket pair only one firm stroke from victory and the field closing in to cut off the single, Thomson edged the 103rd ball of another tension-packed morning to Tavaré at second slip. Into and out of the doubtless clammy palms of the Kent captain it went, but fortunately for him – and his peace of mind for the rest of his days – Miller snatched the ball out of the air, and England were home after 85 minutes of cricket so compelling that a crowd of almost 20,000, admitted free, were often reduced to silence.

As luck would have it, this dismissal was Ian Botham's 100th wicket against Australia and he has now, with 1,000 runs, completed the double against them in 22 Tests, the quickest ever.

While it was gratifying that the all-rounder – who has so often laboured to produce his best in this series – should be involved in a moment that will be savoured for many a long year, it was all made possible by the bowling of Norman Cowans, whose six for 77 earned him the Man of the Match award.

This honour so nearly went to Allan Border (62 not out), as Australia inched their way towards the remaining 37 runs needed this morning to complete an improbable win. Here was another unlikely hero, with only 83 runs to his name in the series. But he had batted with great composure after his understandably diffident start, and latterly scarcely played a false stroke.

England again opted to give him the single in order to tempt the more impetuous Thomson, and in this manner they yielded only four runs from six overs before the new ball became due. Even with the new ball, however, the score crept up, and the stand had reached 70 before Botham finally managed to conjure up enough extra bounce to find Thomson's edge.

1983

24 Jan Mudassar Nazar (152 not out) emulates his father Nazar Mohammad by carrying his bat for Pakistan, against India at Lahore in the 5th Test. No other batsman has achieved this feat for Pakistan.

3 Feb Mudassar hits his third consecutive Test century in the rubber (152), and sets a new series record for Pakistan with 761 runs. This is the 12th hundred in the series for Pakistan, a world record.

4 Feb Imran Khan sets a new series record for Pakistan with 40 wickets.

13 Mar India's Kapil Dev takes his 200th Test wicket, against West Indies in the 2nd Test, and becomes the youngest ever to achieve the 'double' at 24 years 66 days, having passed the 2,000 runs in the 1st Test.

28 Apr Leg-spinner L.Sivaramakrishnan becomes the youngest ever Indian Test cricketer at 17 years 118 days, against West Indies in the 5th Test.

13 Sep Lancashire's Steve O'Shaughnessy (105) hits a hundred in 35 minutes to equal the first-class record of Percy Fender in 1920, albeit off the 'friendly' bowling of David Gower and John Whitaker (Leics) trying to expedite a declaration.

14 Sep India v Pakistan at Bangalore is the first Test in which wides and no-balls are debited to the bowler.

3 Oct Texaco to sponsor next year's three one-day internationals between England and West Indies, replacing Prudential, whose sponsorship ends after 11 years.

29 Oct Sunil Gavaskar hits 121 against West Indies at New Delhi in the 2nd Test, equalling Bradman's record of 29 Test hundreds and becoming the third player to score 8,000 Test runs.

12 Dec Clive Lloyd (161 not out) and Andy Roberts (68) put on 161 together against India at Calcutta in the 5th Test, a new West Indian Test record for the 9th wicket.

29 Dec In the 6th Test between India and West Indies, Sunil Gavaskar breaks India's individual Test scoring record with an unbeaten 236 and becomes the first batsman from any country to make three double hundreds against West Indies. Malcolm Marshall finishes with 33 wickets, equalling Alf Valentine's record for West Indies set in England in 1950 over four Tests.

TEST SERIES

England in Australia
A 2, E 1, D 2
New Zealand in England
E 3, NZ 1
India in Pakistan
P 3, D 3
Sri Lanka in New Zealand
New Zealand 2
India in West Indies
WI 2, D3
Australia in Sri Lanka
Australia 1
Pakistan in India
Drawn 3
West Indies in India
WI 3, D 3

Fifth Test Final day: 7 January

Hemmings frustrated the Australians to compile his best Test score.

Hemmings 95 as England draw and lose Ashes

By Michael Carey, in Sydney

ENGLAND saved the fifth Test with only intermittent alarms at Sydney, though their eighth-wicket pair of Bob Taylor and Geoff Miller had to see out the last 22 overs before England finished at 314 for seven. Australia thus regained the Ashes by winning the series 2-1. But while England's performance was, perhaps, predictably uneven in the face of their remote target of 460, it was eased by an accomplished innings by Hemmings, the night-watchman, who made 95, cruelly short of the second century of his career.

More importantly, he prevailed for 225 minutes, or 60 overs, so giving England the batting substance, in every sense of the word, they might have lacked with the early loss of Tavaré and with little mishaps from time to time at the other end.

Australia collected £46,250 in prize money for the series, England £12,500. Geoff Lawson, with 34 wickets, won the Man of the Series award, and Kim Hughes's innings of 137 won him the Man of the Match award.

First Test Final day: 28 February

Roberts and Richards the West Indies heroes

From Kingston

WEST INDIES secured a thrilling four-wicket victory over India in Kingston, Jamaica, after being set to score 172 in only 30 minutes and 20 overs on the final day.

They achieved the target in the last over, helped largely by Viv Richards, who hammered 61 (four 6s, five 4s) from the 36 balls he received. Earlier, Andy Roberts had taken five wickets for 39 runs, three of them in his first over after tea, on a docile pitch, as India subsided to 174 all out from 168 for six.

Third Test Final day: 8 January

Imran inspires Pakistan

From Faisalabad

PAKISTAN took a 2-0 lead against India when they summarily won the third Test by 10 wickets. Imran Khan was easily Man of the Match, finishing with 11 for 182 as well as scoring a belligerent 117, one of four hundreds in Pakistan's massive first-innings 652.

Imran and Sarfraz destroyed India's second innings. Resuming at 181 for three, India were dismissed for 286 (Imran five for 82), leaving Pakistan needing just seven runs to win.

Sunil Gavaskar, however, carried his bat for a superb 127, including 19 fours, in 437 minutes. It was his 26th Test century, and he now needs just three more to equal Sir Don Bradman's record.

Fourth Test Third day: 15 Jan

Pakistan equal world record stand

From Hyderabad

IN TAKING Pakistan to a mammoth 581 for three declared, Mudassar Nazar (231) and Javed Miandad (280 not out) amassed a third-wicket partnership of 451 to equal the highest for any wicket in Tests, by Australians Ponsford and Bradman for the second wicket against England at the Oval in 1934.

Pakistan then bowled India out for 189, and, with the follow-on 392 runs behind in prospect after the rest day, India face humiliation. Mohinder Amarnath, with 61, and Balwinder Singh Sandhu with a heroic 71 on his début at No.9, were the only Indian batsmen to counter Imran's speed and lift on a perfect batting strip. He took six for 35 in 17.2 hostile overs, and he was supported by his long-time bowling partner Sarfraz Narwaz, who captured three for 56.

[Pakistan went on to win by an innings and 119 runs to take the series 3-0 with two to play.]

County Championship Essex v Surrey: 30 May

Surrey skittled out for 14 after Fletcher's 110

By Rex Alston, at Chelmsford

SURREY were bowled out for 14 when they replied to Essex's total of 287 in the Schweppes County Championship match at Chelmsford, only two runs better than the lowest in first-class cricket – 12, by Northants at Gloucester in 1907 and by Oxford University, batting a man short, against MCC and Ground at Oxford in 1877.

Surrey's innings lasted only 14.3 overs, as Norbert Phillip took six wickets for four in 7.3 overs and Neil Foster, 21, four for 10 in seven. Foster, who had a serious back operation a year ago, was making his first appearance in the senior side since then only because of an injury to John Lever.

Essex had made a poor start to the day (the first day was washed out), losing openers Gooch and Hardie for 27. But they were rescued by captain Keith Fletcher (110) and Ken McEwan (45), as the slow pitch inhibited the pace of Clarke and Thomas.

The heavy roller was used between innings, but this cannot account for Surrey's disastrously feeble batting. Butcher began the procession when he was well caught at the wicket for two. The next six batsmen to depart were out for nought, most of them playing back to Phillip, who kept the new ball well pitched up. Foster disposed of Needham, and Phillip was surprised and delighted to have the dangerous Knight and Lynch lbw.

Clinton, top scorer with six, watched these disasters from the other end before swinging on the leg side to Foster and giving David East a good catch. At eight for eight, Clarke (four) joined Monkhouse (two), and the former avoided a new world low with a wild slog that just reached the leg boundary for the only four of the innings.

[Following on next day, Surrey salvaged some pride, and a draw, Clinton (61 not out) and Knight (101 not out) rescuing them from 18-2 with a stand of 167.]

Prudential World Cup Final: 25 June

Ruthless Indians punish confident West Indies

By Michael Carey, at Lord's

INDIA have won the Prudential World Cup for the first time, beating the holders West Indies by 43 runs, and in the process turning what had seemed a straightforward and predictable final into one of increasing drama and, ultimately, much emotion.

They were put in and bowled out for 183 in 55 overs, which, though not the lowest winning total in a Lord's final, looked highly inadequate against the West Indies batting on a good pitch. Indeed, as West Indies swept effortlessly – a shade too effortlessly perhaps– to 57 for two from only 14 overs, with Richards at his most imperious, it looked as if the anniversary of Custer's Last Stand was to have a singularly inappropriate ending, with the Indians put to flight.

At that point, Richards (33), who had struck Madan Lal for three fours in one over, paid the price either for underestimating the merits of the medium-pacer or for losing his concentration when Lloyd called for a runner. He became the first of three priceless West Indians dismissed by Madan Lal for six runs in 19 balls, falling to a fine catch by Kapil Dev, racing back from mid-wicket. Gomes and Lloyd were also caught, and suddenly West Indies were 66 for five.

With some 41 overs still left and a depth of batting, the holders even then were not necessarily finished. But the ball moved about for bowlers of the pace of Madan Lal, Sandhu, and Binny, and India's out-cricket rose to heights of ruthless efficiency. However, the manner in which seventh-wicket pair Dujon (25) and Marshall (18) applied themselves in adding 43 in 16 overs suggested all was not lost for the West Indies – until Amarnath returned for what was only his second over. He had Dujon playing on, and shortly afterwards had Marshall caught by Gavaskar. Now, at 124 for eight, the Indian fans began their celebrations.

Amarnath, who finished with three for 12 in seven overs, was made Man of the Match, having also scored 26 runs, invaluable in such a low-scoring match, Only Srikkanth (33) and Patil (27) scored more for India.

Amarnath, India's man of the final, hits out.

With Prudential's sponsorship of £300,000 now over, the competition's future will be debated this week by the ICC.

Prudential World Cup: 18 June

Hail to Indian chief Kapil Dev

By D.J.Rutnagur, at Tunbridge Wells

AN ELECTRIFYING 175 not out by Kapil Dev, the highest individual score in World Cup history, kept India in the hunt for a place in the semi-finals. But without his heroism, they would have been trounced in the most humiliating fashion by Zimbabwe.

Instead, India, who lost their fourth wicket at nine, their fifth at 17, and were still gasping for survival at 78 for seven, reached a highly respectable total of 266 for eight, their best ever in the competition. They won by 31 runs, but not before surviving a stirring counter-offensive from Kevin Curran, who made 73.

Kapil Dev's rousing innings, which contained sixteen 4s and six 6s, surpassed by four runs the previous record, set by Glenn Turner for New Zealand against East Africa on an Edgbaston pitch that was far more benevolent than the one at the Nevill Ground. Kapil's unfinished partnership of 126 with wicket-keeper Kirmani – next highest contributor with 24 – is the most plentiful for any country's ninth wicket.

John Player League
Essex v Glamorgan: 17 July

Gooch and Essex break records

By Doug Ibbotson, at Southend

GRAHAM GOOCH, with a devastating 176 off 117 deliveries, not only beat the individual John Player scoring record, but also enabled Essex to establish the highest competition total, when they beat Glamorgan by 56 runs at Southend. Gooch, who struck a six and 28 fours during 126 minutes of controlled mayhem, spurred Essex to 310 for five, to which Glamorgan responded as cheerfully as they could with 254 for four.

The previous highest team score of 307, by Worcester against Derby, had endured since 1975, but the individual record of 162, established by Gordon Greenidge in 1979, had twice been exceeded this season, by Trevor Jesty (166 not out) and Wayne Larkins (172 not out).

NatWest Trophy Second round: 20 July

Gloucester hammer 306 to overhaul Leicester

By A.S.R.Winlaw, at Leicester

GLOUCESTERSHIRE scored 306, the highest second-innings total in limited-overs competition, to beat Leicestershire by four wickets with three balls to spare in a thrilling NatWest finish at Grace Road. Chasing Leicester's total of 302 for five, Gloucester relied – not unexpectedly – on some wonderful batting by Zaheer Abbas. He entered after their first two wickets had fallen for 23 runs and, with aggression rather than his typical artistry, scored 158.

There had been general home surprise when Tolchard elected to bat on a dull, overcast morning, and at 62 for two off the first 20 overs, this was beginning to look like a dubious decision. But then Gower, who had started sedately, was joined by Davison, who attacked the bowling to score 68 out of a stand of 113. Gower went on to compile 138 not out, Leicester's highest ever individual score in the competition.

Zaheer made light of Leicester's safe-looking total, and when he was stumped, at 274 for five, Gloucester needed only 29 off the last 7.2 overs. But with their captain David Graveney lbw for nought, Gloucester began to struggle, and there were only three balls left when Shepherd (25 not out) hit the winning boundary to bring forth a West Country stampede of rejoicing.

Second Test Fourth day: 1 August

New Zealand and 300-wicket Willis make history

By Michael Carey, at Headingley

NEW ZEALAND'S historic first Test victory on English soil duly materialised at Headingley, though a great-hearted spell of fast bowling by Bob Willis played on their jangling nerves before they triumphed by five wickets.

After Gower's unbeaten 112 and a prolonged England innings, Willis took the five New Zealand wickets to fall, which puts him on the 300 mark as the fourth most successful bowler in Test history. But New Zealand, who required only 101, did not need anyone to play an innings of any great length or distinction.

The whys and wherefores of it all will not concern them unduly now the breakthrough has been achieved after 52 years and 28 previous attempts, and the rest of the Cornhill series should be stimulated as a result.

Gower and Dilley resumed for England at 154 for six in a tense atmosphere, just two runs ahead. Dilley always looked vulnerable, and he was caught behind at 190 for 15. England were soon 221 for nine, when Cairns removed Taylor and Willis in the same over. Apart from one mistimed pull, Gower had again played with great selectivity, but he was still eight short of his first Test century in this country since 1979 when Cowans appeared.

On 99, Gower more than once denied himself a single in the interests of the side before completing a thoroughly worthy century in 281 minutes.

Soon after lunch, New Zealand were on their uneasy path to victory, with Willis bowling with such hostility that one ball leapt from just short of a length over both batsman and wicket-keeper for four byes. He beat the bat or found the edge with great regularity.

New Zealand, however, had almost reached their target when he bowled Jeff Crowe for his 300th Test wicket, accomplished in his 81st Test. Botham was finally summoned into the attack at 99, and he immediately obliged with a long hop which Coney pulled to the boundary to seal New Zealand's first Test win overseas since Pakistan in 1969, and only their fifth overall. Cairns won the Man of the Match award for his seven for 74 in England's first innings (10-144 in the match).

Benson & Hedges Cup Final: 23 July

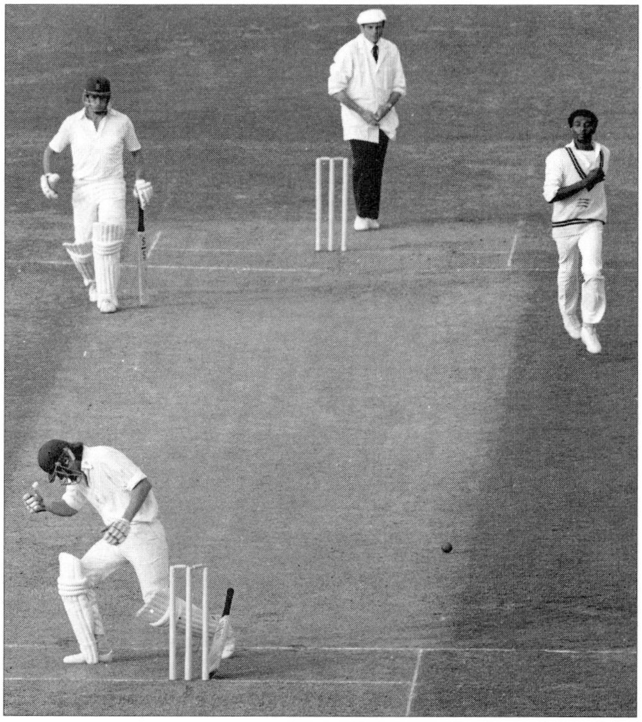

Keith Pont, hit on the helmet by a short ball from Williams, drops his bat and is out hit wicket.

Jittery Essex let prize slip away to Middlesex

By Michael Carey, at Lord's

MIDDLESEX won the Benson & Hedges Cup by four runs in the last over, improbably triumphing in a game that had looked to be in Essex's control all day and was only irretrievable when their last wicket fell at 8.50 p.m.

Essex may well look back and wonder how – at one point 71 for no wicket off 10 overs - they managed to subside to 192 all out, losing their last nine wickets for 65 runs.

In the process, Middlesex's bowling, which had not been highly distinguished at the start, perked up, and whenever the ball was in the air it was caught, which was not always the case during Essex's otherwise disciplined performance earlier. Indeed, they put down four chances of varying difficulty offered by Radley, the Gold Award winner. Without his worthy, much improvised and unbeaten 89, which was made when batting was not straightforward, Middlesex would have finished well short of their eventual 196 for eight.

In a cloudy morning, an hour had been lost for bad light, but when Essex came in to bat, the ground was blessed with warm sunshine. Gooch took 16 off the first over from Cowans, and with Hardie, who hit five fours in his first 17 deliveries, raced past 50 in eight overs. Only 12 had gone when Gooch was caught at the wicket off Williams for 46.

Essex continued to pile on the runs until Cowans caught McEwan (34) athletically off Edmonds at cover. Hardie (49) was fifth out, at 156, caught behind off Cowans. But Pringle and Turner squeezed 29 from the next 11 overs, and at a stage when they needed rather less than a run a ball from four overs, Essex must still have been favourites.

Calmness, though, was not now their strong suit, and after Pringle (16) fell lbw to Daniel, Middlesex finished them off with a run-out and three more wickets from Cowans (4-39), who wrapped it up with the first ball of the last over.

NatWest Trophy
Semi-final: 17 August

Inspired Botham hauls Somerset through to final

By Roger Heywood, at Lord's

IAN BOTHAM, who came back to form for England in the third Test match against New Zealand, snatched victory out of the jaws of defeat for Somerset in the semi-final of the NatWest Trophy at Lord's.

Spurning the possibility of turning his score of 96 into a century, he deliberately played for a tie, which was sufficient for victory over Middlesex, the season's most successful county.

Botham, the captain, took the crease when Somerset were 41 for three. Two wickets then fell cheaply and, at 52 for five, they seemed doomed in trying to reach Middlesex's 222.

But Botham, living up to his best swashbuckling image, took command. Caring little for missing the odd stroke, he changed the whole complexion of the game. With his personal tally on 96 and the team scores equal at 222, many expected him to go for a big winning stroke. But he cautiously played out the last over without scoring - and, with a tied score, Somerset won by virtue of losing one fewer wicket.

Botham said after the match: "Hundreds do not worry me. I worry about wins for Somerset and England."

Somerset now play Kent, victors over Hampshire, in the final.

County Championship
Warwicks v Sussex: 26 August

Imran 6-6 just not enough

By Mike Beddow, at Edgbaston

IMRAN KHAN took six for six and then scored 64 at Edgbaston, but not even his towering all-round play could spare Sussex from a 21-run defeat by Warwickshire.

His best bowling performance in the Championship for five years included the hat-trick as Warwickshire, despite Kallicharran's second century of the match, were humbled for 218, leaving Sussex to make 219 to win in 243 minutes.

A relatively modest target proved to be beyond their limited resources as soon as Imran was caught at silly point off Gifford at 126 for five. Gifford's compelling competitive instincts then inspired Warwickshire to their ninth Championship win of the season.

Imran's astonishing bowling performance involved only 27 deliveries, during which he hit the stumps five times and captured the second wicket of his hat-trick when Paul Smith was given out leg before. Two singles by Kallicharran and a boundary by Gifford were the only scoring strokes in a spell of devastation which, when coupled with his batting, was reminiscent of his heroic effort in the Leeds Test last year.

Imran's performance almost overshadowed Kallicharran's achievement in scoring 270 runs in the match. But the little West Indian ensured that he would not be confined to sideshow status. One over from Waller took him from 87 to 101 before he was left in isolation with an unbeaten 118, including 16 fours and two sixes in 156 minutes.

Yorkshire: 3 October

Boycott (right) and Illingworth, with the John Player Trophy, at Chelmsford last month.

Geoff Boycott sacked by Yorkshire

By Gerald Bartlett

GEOFFREY BOYCOTT, the controversial former England opening batsman, has been sacked by Yorkshire CCC, which has been bitterly divided by the rivalry between him and Ray Illingworth, the captain-manager.

Illingworth, 53, who talked of resigning himself during the summer, has been replaced as county captain by David Bairstow, the 32-year-old wicket-keeper, but will remain as manager. He will cease to play championship cricket.

The decision that Boycott, who is 42, should go after 21 years with the county was taken at a 4-hour meeting of the Yorkshire committee. He was told of the action in South Africa, where he is on holiday.

Mr Ronnie Burnet, chairman of the cricket sub-committee, said: "The committee felt it was time to end the rancour and controversy, and to give the youngsters a chance." Boycott's testimonial arranged for next year would still go ahead, Mr Burnet said.

Yorkshire still face the prospect of a damaging row. Mr Peter Briggs, chairman of a Yorkshire 'reform group', said it would be reconstituted to fight for Boycott's reinstatement.

Boycott scored nearly 2,000 runs last season, but Yorkshire still finished bottom of the County Championship for the first time in 120 years, though they won the John Player League. During his stormy career with Yorkshire, Boycott has often been accused of putting his personal scores before the needs of the team — as this summer, when he was reprimanded for making a slow 140 not out against Gloucestershire. He was made captain in 1972, but was sacked in September 1978. In 1981 he was suspended near the end of the season and banned from the dressing-room after a public clash with Illingworth over his being dropped from a one-day match.

In his career, Boycott has scored 139 centuries, made 44,210 first-class runs and played 108 Test matches for England.

Sixth Test Fourth day: 28 December

Gavaskar takes Bradman Test record

By D.J.Rutnagur, in Madras

SUNIL GAVASKAR, 34, went to the top of the list of Test century makers with an unbeaten 149 against West Indies at Madras, surpassing Sir Don Bradman's record of 29. Gavaskar's 30th Test hundred virtually extinguished West Indies' hopes of a fourth Test victory in the rubber as India, who began the day at 69 for four, advanced to 262 for six at the close, only 51 runs behind on first innings.

Playing his 174th innings in his 99th Test, Gavaskar completed his historic century shortly after India had averted the follow-on and thus as good as made certain of a draw. While the crowd rose to cheer his feat, however, the West Indians stood with their arms folded, an indication that they felt he had an unfair reprieve earlier in the day, when he tried to parry Marshall's second ball, a vicious bumper, which was diverted with some part of his arm to Harper at third slip. Their vehement appeals had been to no avail.

1984

20-24 Jan Against New Zealand in Wellington, Ian Botham scores a hundred (138) and takes 5 wickets in an innings (5-59) for the 5th time - no one else has done it more than twice.

15 Feb The 3rd Test, in Auckland, is drawn, giving New Zealand their first series victory over England.

24 Mar The 3rd Test, in Lahore, is drawn, giving Pakistan their first series victory over England.

4 Jul Warwickshire rewrite the NatWest record books against Oxfordshire at Edgbaston: highest innings, 392-5; biggest win, 227 runs; highest individual score, 206 Kallicharran; highest stand, 197 K.D.Smith (101) and Kallicharran, 2nd wicket. Kallicharran also takes 6-32!

16 Jul Bob Willis, in his last Test, extends his world record of not-out innings to 55 and his record number of wickets for England to 325.

9 Aug Ian Botham is the first player to achieve 3,000 runs/300 wickets double in Tests.

28 Aug Botham takes 5 wickets in an innings for a record 24th time in Tests (against Sri Lanka).

28 Nov-3 Dec India beat England by eight wickets in the 1st Test in Bombay, to end a run of 31 Tests without a victory and extend England's barren spell to a record 13 Tests. Spinner L. Sivaramakrishnan, 18, making his second Test appearance, takes his first Test wickets, 12 in all (6-64, 6-117). Mike Gatting, in his 54th innings, makes his first Test hundred (136). Chris Cowdrey bowls Kapil Dev with his 4th ball in Test cricket, causing his father Colin, listening to Test Match Special in London, to drive the wrong way down a one-way street.

11 Dec West Indies beat Australia at Adelaide to record their 11th consecutive Test win.

TEST SERIES

England in New Zealand
NZ 1, D 2
England in Pakistan
P 1, D 2
West Indies in England
West Indies 5
Sri Lanka in England
Drawn 1
Pakistan in Australia
A 2, D 3
Australia in West Indies
WI 3, D 2
New Zealand in Sri Lanka
NZ 2, D 1
India in Pakistan
Drawn 2
New Zealand in Pakistan
P 2, D 1

Fifth Test Final day: 6 January

Lillee and Chappell bow out in triumph

By Alan Shiell, in Sydney

DENNIS LILLEE was his casual, successful, controversial self until the end, producing yet another match-winning fast bowling effort and an unfortunate tantrum in his Test swan-song, as he captured Pakistan's last four wickets to help Australia to a surprisingly comfortable 10-wicket win in the fifth Test.

After Player of the Series Geoff Lawson (4-48) and Rodney Hogg (2-53) had set up the win, Lillee clinched it by taking four for 22 off his last 58 balls in Test cricket. Australia's openers then needed only 22 minutes to knock off the 35 runs required for a 2-0 victory in the series.

When Lillee led the Australians from the ground at the end of Pakistan's innings, the crowd on the Hill chanted the familiar "Lil-Lee, Lil-Lee..." as a mark of respect on his 70th and last Test appearance.

But Lillee spoiled his chance of bowing out with some grace and dignity earlier by showing dissent at a decision by umpire Mel Johnson, whose refusal of an appeal for a catch at the wicket off Qadir appeared justified by TV replays.

Lillee, 34, finished his record-breaking career with 355 Test wickets (average 23.92), the same number of dismissals as Rodney Marsh (343 ct, 12 st), who emphasised that, although he would be unavailable for the tour of West Indies, he was not retiring from Test cricket.

This match, however, marks the end of an era, for it also heralded the retirement of Greg Chappell, who signed off yesterday with a Man of the Match 182, an epic innings extending over nearly nine hours, and his 121st Test catch, which took him past Colin Cowdrey's record. It was his 24th century in 87 Tests, as he bade farewell in the grandest style.

Second Test Third day: 5 February

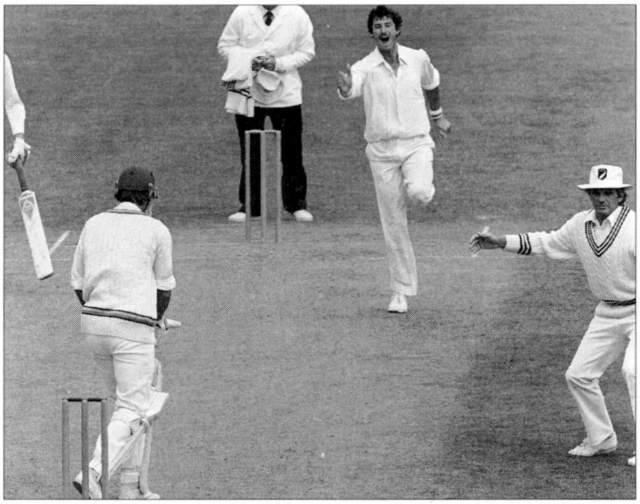

Hadlee has Tavaré caught at the wicket in England's second innings.

England humiliated by New Zealand in three days

By Michael Carey, in Christchurch

ONE of the most remarkable Tests of at least the post-war era came to an abrupt and historic end at Lancaster Park when England were bowled out for 82 and 93, providing New Zealand with their biggest ever victory, by an innings and 132 runs.

It was the first time this century and only the third time in all that England had failed to muster three figures in both innings of a Test. Their demise was so swift, if hardly painless, that the match was over in exactly 12 hours, or effectively two days' playing time. The pitch was condemned by England captain Bob Willis as a "disgrace", and the New Zealand Cricket Council admitted it was short of Test quality. But Willis blamed the England bowling for their defeat.

Hadlee, the Man of the Match, boosted New Zealand's innings (307) with 99 in 81 balls, punishing Botham and Pigott, a last-minute replacement for Dilley, in particular. Hadlee then proceeded to take three for 16 and five for 28, as England's batting crumbled, Randall's 25 in their second innings being the only score over 20.

First Test Fourth day: 6 March

Cook 5-18 as Pakistan scrape home

By Michael Carey, in Karachi

ENGLAND were permitted a tantalising glimpse of what would have been one of the most memorable victories in Test match history before Pakistan overcame them by three wickets in the first Test, at the National Stadium. Pakistan needed only 65 after disposing of more disappointing England batting, but the prospect of a historic first win over England on Pakistan soil did little for the nerves of an inexperienced side, and a series of reckless strokes against the accurate spin of Cook and Marks was the result.

Cook, by taking five for 18, with match figures of 11 for 83, completed a splendid return to Test cricket after some five weeks with almost no cricket at all. At one stage, he had Pakistan at 40 for six, before they struck the winning runs.

When England were batting, only Gower, with two fifties, of England's recognised batsmen seemed able to cope with the mixture of leg-breaks, googlies, top-spinners and flippers produced by Qadir, who took eight for 133 in the match and contributed an invaluable 40 in Pakistan's first innings.

Third Test Final day: 4 April

Australia fall to West Indies pace and go one down

From Bridgetown, Barbados

WEST INDIES, with their fast bowlers in irresistible form, routed Australia for 97 and swept to a 10-wicket victory at the Kensington Oval. Michael Holding (4-24) and Malcolm Marshall (5-42) removed Australia's last six wickets for 29 to set up a resounding win that puts West Indies one up in the five-match series.

Australia, 80 behind on first innings and 68 for four overnight, crumbled in 73 minutes on the final day, and the West Indies openers knocked off the 18 runs they needed before lunch.

Remarkably, at the same time yesterday, neither side had established a first-innings lead. That Australia reached 429 was due mainly to wicket-keeper Wayne Phillips. Coming in at No.8, he struck a belligerent 120, adding 99 for the last two wickets, with Hogg and Alderman contributing three and two not out, respectively. And it was a maiden hundred from Richie Richardson (131 not out) and a fine 76 from Lloyd that then gave West Indies the advantage.

First Test First day: 14 June

Andy Lloyd felled by Marshall on Test debut

By Michael Carey, at Edgbaston

ENGLAND had their problems, not all of which were foreseeable, in the first Cornhill Test, and in conditions that would have assisted any bowlers, let alone those of the West Indies, they were bowled out for 191. Opener Andy Lloyd, 27, making his Test debut on his home ground, was hit on the head by a delivery from Marshall, and was forced to retire during a torrid start.

Lloyd, who had scored 10, twisted away from a shortish ball that rose less than he expected, and was taken to hospital with severe bruising around his right eye and blurred vision, and may be detained for up to 14 days. This left England, in effect, at 20 for three.

Ian Botham, coming in at No.6, took the struggle boldly if somewhat fortuitously to the West Indies, having been dropped at nought, and made 64, only his second half-century against West Indies.

The comfort with which West Indies began their reply suggested it had been a good toss for them to lose. But Willis, who earlier announced that he planned to retire at the end of the season, had both openers, Greenidge and Haynes, leg before, to leave West Indies on 53 for two at the close.

[West Indies amassed 606 and won by an innings and 180 runs. Andy Lloyd suffered severe eye damage that for some time threatened his career. He never played for England again.]

Andy Lloyd is pole-axed by a ball from Malcolm Marshall.

Texaco Trophy First match: 31 May

Richards beats England with majestic 189

By Michael Carey, at Old Trafford

ENGLAND were beaten by 104 runs in the first of three Texaco matches, not so much by West Indies as by Vivian Richards, whose unbeaten 189 was the highest score ever made in a one-day international. It was an innings of much brilliance, especially in its later stages, when, by making 94 out of an unbeaten 106 partnership with Holding (12), he lifted his side to an impregnable total of 272 in their 55 overs.

Starting when West Indies were 11 for two, and needing to overcome problems posed by Miller (3-32) on a turning pitch, Richards faced only 170 balls, hitting five sixes and 21 fours. He also dealt England an insurmountable psychological blow after they had probably had visions of needing only 170 or 180, and they were dismissed for 168 with five overs remaining, Lamb making 75.

Holding took two for 23 in 11 overs, Garner three for 18 in eight, but Geoff Pullar's choice of Richards as Man of the Match was a formality.

[England won at Trent Bridge, but West Indies took the Trophy 2-1 by winning at Lord's.]

Second Test Final day: 3 July

Greenidge 214 gives England thrashing

By Michael Carey, at Lord's

GORDON GREENIDGE made an unforgettable and unbeaten 214 at Lord's to take West Indies to victory over England by nine wickets, giving them a 2-0 lead in the series. With a grandeur that produced a splendid climax to a splendid match, the West Indies in five memorable hours made 344 runs from 66 overs, a fourth-innings target bettered in England only by the 1948 Australians, who made 404 for three at Headingley.

It is only the 10th time that a side has exceeded 300 to win a Test match, and only on four occasions has West Indies' scintillating performance been surpassed. Greenidge and Larry Gomes, whose unbeaten 92 was the product of another composed innings, added 287 for the second wicket, a record for either side in Tests against each other. England's only success was the run-out of Haynes, the first time in nine Tests that West Indies have lost a wicket in their second innings.

Only Bradman and Hammond have made higher individual scores in a Lord's Test, yet Greenidge had to share the Man of the Match award. The adjudicator, Godfrey Evans, set a precedent by splitting it between him and Ian Botham, who scored 30 and 81 and, in West Indies' first innings, took eight for 103, the first to take eight wickets against West Indies in a Test in England. On the basis that such awards should be linked to match-winning performances when possible, Greenidge can feel denied, not least as Botham's magic deserted him when England most needed it.

Indeed, he and Willis, Saturday's heroes, were relegated to the role of yesterday's men in the face of the mighty onslaught, in which Botham conceded 117 runs in 20.1 overs without reward.

Third Test Fourth day: 16 July

Marshall 7-53 underlines England woe

By Michael Carey, at Headingley

ENGLAND unsurprisingly could not prolong their resistance beyond the first 30 minutes of the fourth day at Headingley, and by early afternoon the West Indies had completed an eight-wicket victory in the third Test. This, following similar emphatic triumphs, by an innings and 180 runs at Edgbaston and nine wickets at Lord's, gave them a winning 3-0 lead in the series, the first side to take the first three Tests since the 1921 Australians.

No batting heroics were permitted by Marshall, who took four for 15 in four overs to emerge with seven for 53, his best Test figures – and this after batting one-handed with a broken thumb. Gomes was given the Man of the Match award by Tony Lewis for his unbeaten 104, which kept his side in the game when England were at their most efficient.

Fifth Test First day: 9 August

England's bowlers rock West Indies as Botham takes 300th wicket

By Michael Carey, at the Oval

ENGLAND'S bowlers held sway at the Oval in a manner unprecedented this summer, dismissing West Indies for 190 on the opening day, their lowest total of the series. A disciplined performance was spearheaded by Ian Botham, whose five for 72 took him past 300 Test wickets, and with the ball moving about all day the accurate Paul Allott and impressive Richard Ellison also played crucial roles.

This, coupled with some variable batting, left the West Indies at one point at 70 for six, but Clive Lloyd, though suffering the after-effects of illness, played an innings of much resolution when it was most needed to emerge with an unbeaten 60.

An awkward final session cost England the wicket of Broad while they made 10, but they have set the scene for a highly combative day tomorrow, with much depending on how the extra pace of the West Indies fast bowlers is negotiated, especially early on.

England left out Foster, so that Agnew and Ellison both made their first appearance. Lloyd declared himself fit, won the toss and, contrary to his usual pattern, decided to bat first. While Agnew (0-46) betrayed his understandable nerves with some variations of length and line, Allott (3-25) produced the required accuracy and soon bowled Haynes.

When Botham came on, the West Indies batsmen were beginning to look extremely tentative, and Ellison (2-34) commended himself by not only settling into an accurate groove, but swinging the ball considerably. Lloyd eventually ran out of partners after 202 stoical minutes.

Botham celebrates his 300th Test wicket, Dujon caught in the slips.

County Championship Notts v Warwicks: 27 August

Hadlee achieves rare double

By Doug Ibbotson, at Trent Bridge

RICHARD HADLEE has become the first player since Fred Titmus in 1967 to achieve 1,000 runs and 100 wickets in a season. Having reached the bowling mark against Lancashire at Blackpool last week, he duly knocked off the 21 runs he needed against Warwickshire in an innings of 39, as Notts piled up 350 for six declared in their first innings. It was his 21st match of the season.

The modest but determined New Zealander then confirmed that his successful quest for the double was statistically planned and programmed at the start of the season. It began, he said, as a challenge and developed into an obsession.

The achievement has been attained somewhat ahead of a schedule that did not include the two universities or the touring sides.

"I worked on the need to average 50 runs and 4 wickets a match – 60 wickets at Trent Bridge and the rest, along with most of the runs, in away games. The double century [210 not out] against Middlesex at Lord's gave me a four-match bonus.

"Four months ago, I felt burned out, but the double was a tremendous incentive. Now that it's done, I'm going to relax and enjoy my cricket."

[Hadlee completed the season with 1,179 runs and 117 wickets, topping the first-class bowling averages and taking most wickets.]

Fifth Test Final day:14 August

England 'blackwashed' 5-0 by West Indies

By Michael Carey, at the Oval

ENGLAND subsided to the first 5-0 home defeat in their history in an hour on the last day, and appropriately it was at high noon that the West Indies gunned down the last of the opposition. This whitewash – or 'blackwash', as one banner at the Oval put it – was only the second suffered by England, after Warwick Armstrong's Australians in 1920-21.

Grim reading though these statistics make, they are scarcely a surprise given the respective resources of the two sides. Indeed, it is the West Indies' strength in depth that will be remembered from this series rather than any English shortcomings. They are, by some measure, the best team in the world. Their depth of batting, plus the variety that off-spinner Harper has added to their attack, also makes them comparable not only to any West Indies sides of recent years, but arguably to any Test team in the game's history.

Despite England's fine start to the match, they failed to gain a first-innings lead, and Haynes' 125 in West Indies' second innings of 346 made sure England would struggle. On the resumption this morning, England's last five wickets fell with the minimum of heroics to Garner (4-51) and Holding (5-43), leaving West Indies triumphant by 172 runs.

Ray Illingworth's choice of Gordon Greenidge as the Man of the Series has brought just recognition to a batsman whose contribution to the West Indies has perhaps been overshadowed by the exploits of Viv Richards, Clive Lloyd and the fast bowlers. At 33, Greenidge has probably reached his best over the last couple of years. He topped the West Indies Test averages (81.71) and scored most runs (572), but more than that, he has proved himself the complete opening batsman, capable of performing any role according to the conditions and the circumstances of a game.

Inaugural Test Final day: 28 August

England, held by Sri Lanka, equal worst run

By Michael Carey, at Lord's

ONCE Sri Lanka had overcome the early loss of two wickets, their inaugural Test made its way to the expected draw – a result that left them with the immense satisfaction of a performance that probably surpassed all their expectations, and left England without a win in 12 Tests, a barren spell matched only on two other occasions in their history.

Three wickets fell in four overs later, and Ian Botham, who took six for 90, emerged with a total of 312 Test victims on his last appearance for the time being. Silva became the third Sri Lankan to make a hundred, and Mendis fell only six short of becoming the first batsman since George Headley in 1939 to make two in a Lord's Test. He was caught, ironically, off a Botham off-break.

Sri Lanka, whose impressive first innings of 491 for seven declared (Wettimuny 190) always gave them the upper hand, declared at 294 for seven, 415 ahead, to close what was for them a highly satisfactory first Test match in England.

NatWest Trophy Final: 1 September

Middlesex take cliffhanger off last ball

By Michael Carey, at Lord's

MIDDLESEX won the NatWest Trophy for the first time in gloom that had already gathered, beating Kent by four wickets off the last ball of an increasingly spellbinding final. There have been few better in terms of individual performances, continuing shifts of fortune and, in recent years, commendable crowd behaviour.

Moments of tension came with increasing frequency as Middlesex pursued Kent's total of 232 for six (Chris Cowdrey 58), made on a good pitch after winning the toss, not least after Gatting (37) was out with 108 needed from 19 overs.

As first Slack and then Emburey had illustrated earlier, the slower the bowler the less easily he could be forced on this pitch, and Underwood, with nine overs for 12 runs plus the wicket of Butcher, had produced what seemed a match-winning performance.

But Tavaré removed him, and in the next six overs of seam Radley (67) and Downton (40) made 40 together. They went on to make 87 in 15 overs, a partnership that took their side to the brink of victory. They went within six runs of each other, and it was left to Emburey and Edmonds to make the last 16 at a run a ball, which they did when Emburey, needing a single, hit the very last ball from Ellison through the close field.

Emburey celebrates the winning run in semi-darkness at Lord's, while the zombie-like Edmonds shows the strain.

County Championship Somerset v Notts: 11 September

Essex retain title as Notts fail bravely

By Michael Carey, at Taunton

ESSEX retained the County Championship title, but they were made to wait until the penultimate ball of the season before Notts narrowly failed with a mighty effort against Somerset at Taunton. They lost by only three runs after being required to score 297 for victory from what proved to be 60 overs – and their last pair made 10 of the 14 needed from the final over before a boundary catch ended it all.

Such a memorable climax to a gripping afternoon owed much to Ian Botham's delicately balanced declaration. But the need to maintain a rate of five an over, even on a smallish ground with a fast outfield, suggested that Notts were bound to suffer mishaps. The turning point was the dismissal of Hadlee, the new Britannic Assurance Championship Player of the Season, for 28. With his skipper, Rice, he had put on 40 in six overs, when he lifted Booth high towards the mid-wicket boundary. Lloyds completed the catch before lurching into the advertising boards, and the umpires correctly ruled it fair under Law 32.

While Rice remained, Notts seemed likely winners. But on 98, with 39 required from four overs, he failed to middle a Marks full toss and holed out to substitute Ollis on the mid-wicket boundary. And when the splendid Bore (27), after lifting Marks for six and taking 4-4-2 from the first three balls of Booth's final over, attempted the winning shot with a lofted straight drive, it was Ollis who caught him, too, to end Notts' valiant effort.

So Essex, who beat Lancs yesterday by 10 wickets, won the title by 14 points. They are the first county to retain the Championship outright since Yorkshire in 1968, and the first to bring off the Championship and Sunday League double.

Second Test Final day: 27 November

Aussie captain resigns in tears

By Alan Shiell, in Brisbane

IN A Press conference after Australia lost the second Test to West Indies, Kim Hughes announced his resignation from the captaincy. His voice was filled with emotion as he read his statement, and he could not prevent himself breaking down.

For all the criticism levelled at Hughes's captaincy, his decision still took much courage, because he has loved the challenge and the responsibility despite all-round bad luck. Three times he has moved aside whenever Greg Chappell made himself available and, now the big guns have retired, Australia have drawn two and lost five of the past seven Tests against West Indies, with Hughes scoring only 294 runs at an average of 21. He has not reached 40 in 14 innings.

In a match marred by a running feud between Lawson and Haynes, West Indies won by eight wickets to take a 2-0 lead in the rubber, having won the first Test by an innings and 112 runs. It looks almost certain that vice-captain Allan Border, 29, will take over the captaincy and the very difficult task of turning the series around.

1985

3 Apr Richard Hadlee becomes the first New Zealand player to complete the 2,000 runs/200 wickets Test double during his match-saving innings of 39 not out in the 1st Test against West Indies at Port-of-Spain.

1 Jul In the 2nd Test against Australia, at Lord's, Ian Botham takes 5 wickets in an innings for the 25th time to break the world record held by Sydney Barnes since 1914, and also overhauls Bob Willis's record 325 wickets for England.

3-5 Jul Oxford's Giles Toogood takes 8-52 (10-93 in match) and scores a century (149) in the University match against Cambridge at Lord's.

27 Jul Essex keeper David East takes 8 catches in an innings against Somerset in the County Championship at Taunton to equal Wally Grout's world record (1959-60).

29 Jul Jonathan Agnew (Leics) takes 9-70 in the Championship against Kent, and is no-balled when on a hat-trick and 10 wickets.

21 Oct Javed Miandad (203 not) and Qasim Omar (206) put on 397 for the 3rd wicket at Faisalabad for Pakistan in the first Test against Sri Lanka, the 8th highest stand in Tests.

23 Nov Brendon Bracewell (83 not) and Stephen Boock (37) put on 124 for New Zealand's last wicket against Australia at Sydney.

4 Dec New Zealand win the 3rd Test at the WACA to beat Australia in a series for the first time, 2-1, Richard Hadlee taking 11-155 and finishing with 33 wickets in the 3-match rubber.

Ranji Trophy Bombay v Boroda: 10 January

Shastri hits lightning 200 and six 6s in over

From Bombay

INDIAN all-rounder Ravi Shastri, playing for Bombay against Boroda in the West Zone of the Ranji Trophy, equalled Gary Sobers' record of six 6s in an over on the way to scoring the fastest double century in first-class cricket.

The unlucky bowler was Boroda's left-arm spinner G.Tilakraj. Shastri smote 13 sixes in his 200 not out, before Bombay declared their second innings, to join Greenidge, Humpage and Majid Khan, two behind the world record of former New Zealand captain John Reid. His innings took 113 minutes and he faced 123 balls.

[The match was drawn, but Bombay went on to beat Delhi in the Ranji final, Shastri proving the match-winner with 105 runs and 12-182 in 88 overs of left-arm leg-spin.]

Fourth Test Third day: 15 January

Gatting 207 and Fowler 201 in record mood

By Michael Carey, in Madras

GRAEME FOWLER and Mike Gatting each scored their maiden Test double century in Madras to leave England in an unassailable position in the fourth Test against India with a first-innings lead of 339, five wickets in hand and two days' play remaining.

A total of 611 for five, made from 170 overs, not only reflected the way that England had pursued their objective of grinding India's bowlers into the dust, despite considerable attempts to slow the game down which produced two warnings from the umpires, but also rewrote a chunk of the record books.

In the 108 years since Test cricket began, England had never before had two double century-makers in the same innings. Consider some of the great names who have figured in their 610 Tests, and this evening the toast is Messrs Fowler and Gatting.

It was England's highest score on the sub-continent, where previously no England batsman had scored more than Dennis Amiss's 179 in Delhi eight years ago. The pair put on 241 for the second wicket, an England record against India, and Gatting went on to add another 44 in 33 overs for the third wicket with Lamb (62).

[England declared at 652-7 the next day, Foster took 5-59 to add to his first-innings 6-104, and England won by 9 wickets after India had made them bat again with 412.]

Fowler (left) and Gatting on their way to 200 apiece against India at Madras.

Fifth Test Second day: 1 February

Azharruddin hits third hundred in first three Tests

By Michael Carey, in Kanpur

INDIA'S Mohammad Azharruddin became the first batsman to make a hundred in each of his first three Tests, and there were handshakes all round, with the entire England team involved.

As the England bowlers again toiled at Kanpur's Green Park, India amassed 525 for seven. This, their highest total ever against England, is an accurate reflection of the grudging rewards granted to bowlers of all types so far by this mild pitch. Yet it was not until the final session, when they made 117 from 23 overs, that India were able to produce the momentum needed by a side requiring victory to square the series.

The growing aggression with which Shastri (59), Vengsarkar (137) and finally, and perhaps a little too late, Kapil Dev (41 not out) approached their task suggested that India will not want to bat on after tomorrow's rest day.

[India declared at 553-8, but England avoided the follow-on for the loss of only four wickets, and won the series 2-1, the first side ever to come from behind and win a rubber in India.]

TEST SERIES

England in India
E 2, I 1, D 2
Australia in England
E 3, A 1, 2 D
West Indies in Australia
WI 3, A 1, D 1
Pakistan in New Zealand
NZ 2, D 1
New Zealand in West Indies
WI 2, D 2
New Zealand in Australia
NZ 2, A 1

World Cricket Championship Final: 10 March

Efficient India surge to victory over Pakistan

By Michael Carey, in Melbourne

INDIA won the B & H World Championship of Cricket with scarcely an uneasy moment under the Melbourne floodlights, beating Pakistan by eight wickets after a performance that was typical of the highly efficient way they have played throughout this competition. They have reduced the one-day game to such an art that the elements of surprise and excitement tend to disappear, and this match was theirs from the time Pakistan were contained at 176 for nine from 50 overs, allowing India to pace their way home with 17 balls to spare.

Srikkanth's vigorous 67 earned him the Man of the Match award, and Shastri (63 not out) was named the Champion of Champions, after his third successive fifty, which, allied to his influential bowling, made his efforts a key factor in India's success. His award was a new car, in which he drove his colleagues on a champagne-splashed lap of honour in front of the crowd of 35,296, the highest to watch a game in Australia in which the home country was not involved.

Looking back over the last three weeks, the 13-match competition between the seven Test-playing countries, staged as part of Victoria's 150th anniversary celebrations, has drawn nearly a quarter of a million spectators, and has been successful enough to suggest that the 1991 World Cup could be played in Australia. The tournament, the first of its kind to be played outside England, opened with the thrilling floodlit victory of Australia over England, after which it was dominated by India and Pakistan, who each had smooth seven-wicket semi-final victories, over New Zealand and West Indies respectively.

Third Test Final day: 1 May

West Indies put end to 16-year drought

By Tony Cozier, in Barbados

THE WEST INDIES ended 16 years without a win against New Zealand with a 10-wicket victory in Bridgetown to go one-up in the four-Test rubber. Their last win was in Auckland in 1969, since when the countries have played 12 times, New Zealand winning two and the rest drawn.

When Greenidge hit the winning runs 37 minutes into the final day, it was the first outright result recorded in the eight Tests played in the Caribbean. Victory was a formality as New Zealand resumed on 228 for eight, Coney adding only two to his defiant 81. But the last-wicket pair managed to force West Indies to bat again before Marshall rounded off a fine all-round performance – 4-40, 63 and 7-80 – by catching Smith off his own bowling.

Viv Richards: 322 in a day.

County Championship Somerset v Hants: 24 May

Marshall's 2-4-6 seals Hants' last-over win

By Eric Hill, at Taunton

IN A TREMENDOUS finish to a match of heroic recoveries and wonderful batting containing five memorable hundreds, Malcolm Marshall, needing 10 off the final over from Joel Garner, did it in three balls. He heaved him for a couple, snicked him for four, then slogged a full-length delivery over long-on for a gigantic six to take Hampshire to victory over Somerset by five wickets with three balls to spare – their first win of the season.

So ended a see-saw match in which Botham had revived Somerset's first innings with a remarkable unbeaten 149 out of 193 in 106 balls, hitting six sixes and 20 fours. Then a record eighth-wicket partnership for Hants of 227 by maiden centurions Kevan James (124) and Tim Tremlett (102 not out) earned them a first-innings lead, before Viv Richards enabled Botham to declare at 358 for five with a glorious 186 (10 sixes, 19 fours) in 176 balls.

The declaration, generous on a bland pitch, called for 323 in 26 overs. Botham immediately took a blinding second-slip catch off Garner to remove Greenidge. But a superb 121 in 170 minutes by Chris Smith in a second-wicket stand of 180 in 41 overs with Vivian Terry (83) set up the thrilling finish, Marshall (49 not out) having the final say.

County Championship Somerset v Warwicks: 1 June

Three-ton Richards sends records tumbling

By Eric Hill, at Taunton

AN AMAZING innings of 322 by Viv Richards sent the records tumbling as Somerset, after a shaky start, reached a remarkable 566 for five declared against Warwickshire. It is the highest score in English cricket for 36 years, a career best for the West Indies captain, and a Somerset record, beating Harold Gimblett's 310 against Sussex at Eastbourne in 1948. Richards also became the first West Indian to score 300 in a day.

Richards arrived after Bail had retired following a blow on the helmet from an extremely menacing Small, who immediately had Felton well taken at slip. He began rather sketchily, edging Small several times, was beaten a time or two and, after a flurry of crisp strokes, was struck firmly on the thumb by the aggressive Smith.

This seemed to renew his thirst for runs as he reeled off a seemingly endless array of strokes – glorious, elegant, powerful and outrageous – running his runs rapidly to the very end. He added 122 with Popplewell (55), 174 with Ollis (55) and 183 with Marks (65).

Richards went to his first 100 in 105 balls, his second in another 76 and his third in 63. In all, he faced 258 deliveries, batted for 294 minutes and struck 50 boundaries (8 sixes and 42 fours), a number exceeded only three times in county cricket and nine times in all first-class cricket.

Sixth Test Fourth day: 2 September

Another wicket for the jubilant Richard Ellison.

Glory for Gower as Ashes are won

By Michael Carey, at the Oval

ENGLAND completed victory over Australia with rather more ease than could have been expected in the sixth Cornhill Test, capturing their last six wickets for 58 runs to triumph by an innings and 94 and win an absorbing series 3-1.

From the third day at Edgbaston, England have proved unstoppable with bat and ball, and before lunch David Gower had joined the ranks of England captains who have stood on the Oval balcony celebrating the return of the Ashes – in his case with a replica of the famous urn.

For him, the moment was particularly sweet, coming as it did some 12 months after the annihilation by the West Indies, or, if you like, following suggestions from some quarters this summer that he should resign because of his chequered form. Since those unhappy days, however, he has completed 732 runs in the series and become only the second England captain after Jardine to win both a series in India and regain the Ashes.

He was unsurprisingly named Man of the Series by Tony Lewis, and Gooch collected the Man of the Match award for his 196 after Ellison, with four wickets in eight overs, Botham and Taylor had completed the coup de grace. Gower, whose 351 second-wicket partnership with Gooch was the second highest for any wicket against Australia, joined the illustrious handful who have made three hundreds in a series against them, and remarkably figured in two successive 300 partnerships, a feat only Hutton had achieved before. Yet Gatting led the averages with 87.83.

Botham, who with 31 wickets is now only 12 behind Lillee's record 355 in Tests, returned after his winter's rest to bowl at times as fast as he ever has for England, according to Gower, whose gradual use of him in much shorter stints was also a factor.

But after five other bowlers had fallen by the wayside, the choice of Ellison, who was injured at the start, for Edgbaston proved felicitous. Suddenly England had a bowler who was both penetrative and accurate. He followed his 10 wickets there with another seven at the Oval – all at 10.88 – and was a major factor in England's eventual ascendancy.

Essex sign Border for £30,000

By Neil Hallam

ALLAN BORDER has agreed to sign a two-year contract with Essex thought to be worth £30,000.

The Australian Test captain, however, expressed the concern common to many overseas imports to county cricket that the 'seven days a week grind' of the English summer would make it hard to maintain the sharp competitive edge of his game.

First approached by Essex three weeks ago, Border must now seek formal approval from the Australian Cricket Board

Fifth Test Final day: 20 August

England go 2-1 ahead thanks to Lamb's instep

By Michael Carey, at Edgbaston

ENGLAND overcame their twin adversaries, Australia and the weather, in memorable style at Edgbaston to win the fifth Cornhill Test by an innings and 118 runs with 11.5 overs of a taut and ultimately controversial day remaining. They now lead by 2-1 with one Test left.

After Ellison's remarkable spell yesterday of four wickets for one in 15 deliveries to leave Australia on 37 for five overnight, it looked as if England might be robbed of victory by the elements. But their luck changed abruptly after rain prevented a start until mid-afternoon, for not only did the clouds roll away, but they revealed a silver lining in the shape of a freak dismissal that changed the course of the final session.

This involved the departure of Wayne Phillips (59), caught by Gower when his powerful cut rebounded off Lamb's instep at silly point – he was given out only after the umpires conferred – marking the end of his stubborn 77 stand with Ritchie (20).

From that point, Australia lost their last five wickets for 29 runs in 48 minutes, first to the spin of Edmonds and Emburey and finally to Botham, and were dismissed for 142. Ellison, with 10 for 104, took the Man of the Match award.

So Australia contrived to lose a Test in which they had been placed at 189 for two on the first day, but which had gone remarkably England's way from the moment that Gower – the first England captain to put Australia in two Tests running – ran out Lawson from the first ball on Saturday and followed that with his majestic double century.

NatWest Trophy Final: 7 September

Essex joy, but agony for brave Randall

By Tony Lewis, at Lord's

ESSEX won the NatWest Trophy by one run off the last ball of the match. It was a brilliant response by Notts, who faced a mammoth Essex total of 280 for two in their 60 overs – and 279 for five was just not enough.

If Essex's opening partnership of 202 between Gooch (91) and Man of the Match Hardie (110) took a mighty grip on the game, that of 145 by Robinson (80) and Broad (64) was inspired enough to give Notts an outside chance if some big blows could be struck down the order. Hadlee (22) set off the lash in the tail. Randall (66) then masterminded an astonishing partnership with young Martindale (20 not out) who was playing his first one-day match for his county.

As the good light faded, the countdown began, right to the last over, when Notts needed 18. With ingenuity and brilliant twists of improvisation, Randall started to play beautifully-timed drives off Pringle to the off side. Ten runs were wanted off three balls, six off two, and two from the last ball. But Randall chipped a full-length delivery into the hands of Prichard at mid-wicket. So Keith Fletcher became the first county captain to lead his side to all four titles, and that within seven years.

Second Test Final day: 11 September

Sri Lanka's first win

From Colombo

SRI LANKA have scored their first Test victory, beating India by 149 runs at Colombo in their 14th Test since gaining such status in 1981. Duleep Mendis, the Sri Lankan captain, declared their second innings closed on 206 for three, setting India a 348-run victory target. They never looked like reaching it.

India's captain Kapil Dev was the lone obstacle to Sri Lanka's historic victory as he hit a defiant 78 before being last man out, in the first of the final 20 mandatory overs, having, with Sivaramakrishnan (21), taken India from 98 for seven to 168 for eight.

Sri Lanka's Amal Silva made five catches in India's second innings to become the first wicket-keeper to score a hundred (111 in the first innings) and make nine dismissals in a Test.

Sri Lanka's president Junius Jayewardene witnessed their triumph and declared the next day a public holiday.

John Player League Essex v Yorks: 15 September

Essex clinch title in final over

From Chelmsford

ESSEX retained the John Player League title when they beat Yorkshire by two wickets in a nerve-wracking finish at Chelmsford. An on-drive by the newly arrived Foster off the penultimate ball of the match settled the issue.

Of the other contenders, Sussex maintained their challenge to the end, beating Glamorgan by 93 runs to finish two points adrift.

Although Essex, batting first, had topped the 250 mark in winning their previous two matches, they found that chasing a Yorkshire total of 231 (Sharp 114) was a different proposition, more so when Gooch and Hardie were dismissed cheaply.

They were put in contention again by a third-wicket partnership of 84 in 13 overs between McEwan and Pringle. While Pringle scored 60 from 54 balls, McEwan's parting gift to Essex was an innings of 62, and Prichard, at No.8, weighed in with an invaluable 25.

Essex won eight of their last nine matches to take the Sunday title, the other game being abandoned.

County Championship Warwicks v Middlesex: 17 September

Spinners clinch Championship for Middlesex

By Michael Carey, at Edgbaston

MIDDLESEX won the Britannic Assurance County Championship when, largely owing to the expertise of Phil Edmonds and John Emburey and an accommodating Edgbaston pitch, they defeated Warwickshire by an innings and 74 runs.

The spinners shared eight wickets, and two in four balls by the West Indian quick Wayne Daniel completed the dismissal of Warwickshire for 184 soon after 3.00 p.m., to give Middlesex their eighth win of the season and a margin of 18 points over runners-up Hampshire.

Though the outcome was neither as dramatic nor as prolonged as last season's climax, when the race went to the final ball, it was nevertheless highly satisfactory that the issue remained alive until the last afternoon of the season, which, strange to relate, was a warm and sunny one.

Once Emburey and Edmonds appeared, after seven overs of somewhat variable new-ball bowling, they used it quite magnificently, and there was never a hint that their opponents would escape.

It is Middlesex's fifth Championship in 10 years, their ninth in all, and their first under the captaincy of Mike Gatting, who took over in 1983. Who else, I wonder, has led a Championship-winning side and topped the England batting averages in the same season?

Gifford's middle stump goes flying as fast bowler Wayne Daniel wraps up the Warwickshire innings and completes the title win for Middlesex.

First Test Final day: 12 November

Hadlee completes historic victory over Australia

By Alan Shiell, in Brisbane

NEW Zealand completed their historic victory by an innings and 41 runs at the Gabba, their first in seven Tests in Australia. Having broken the 197 Matthews-Border stand just before the close yesterday to leave Australia at 266 for six by having Matthews (115) caught by Coney, Richard Hadlee took three more wickets this morning, when Australia lost their last four wickets for 67.

Border, the Australian captain, resuming on 106, remained unbeaten on 152. He praised the New Zealanders, and said the Australians seemed to have a mental block about Hadlee, whose match figures of 15 for 123 (9-52 and 6-71) in 52.3 overs was the eighth best bowling performance in Test history.

New Zealand captain Jeremy Coney stressed that the win had come from a team performance even more than from outstanding individual efforts by fast bowler Hadlee and batsmen Martin Crowe (188) and John Reid (108).

First Test Final day: 17 December

Another record for Gavaskar

From Adelaide

SUNIL GAVASKAR became the first player to complete 9,000 runs in Test cricket as the first Test between Australia and India ended in a predictable draw. Gavaskar, having retired hurt twice and made 94 of India's overnight first innings score of 391 for seven, a lead of 10, batted for much of the final day to reach an unbeaten 166 as the touring team ground their way to 520 all out, their highest score against Australia. He achieved the 9,000 mark when he had made 160.

Gavaskar's innings, spanning 551 minutes, was his 31st Test century, and his first since beating Bradman's record of 29 two years ago. With Shivlal Yadav (41), he put on 94 for the last wicket, leaving the Australians only eight overs, in which they scored 17 without loss.

The match will also be remembered for the bowling of Kapil Dev, whose 8 for 106 in the first innings was the best Test analysis by an Indian in Australia and included the last five Australian wickets, which fell for seven runs in 39 balls (Kapil conceding four in 21 balls).

1986

22 Feb Richard Hadlee takes his 300th Test wicket for New Zealand v Australia, Wellington.

17 Mar New Zealand win 3rd Test, at Auckland, and beat Australia in 2nd rubber of season, Bracewell taking 10-106 in match.

10 Jun England lose the first Test to India and David Gower is relieved of the captaincy, giving way to vice-captain Mike Gatting. It is only India's second win in 33 Tests in England.

23 Jun India beat England in 2nd Test to win their first series since they beat England in 1971.

3-8 Jul Sunil Gavaskar plays in his 115th Test, against England at Edgbaston, beating Colin Cowdrey's record. The first innings is his record 200th, and he becomes the first Indian to take 100 Test catches.

29 Jul Dennis Amiss scores his 100th hundred, for Warwicks v Lancs, at Edgbaston.

10 Aug Ian Botham hits Sunday League record 13 sixes for Somerset v Northants in 175 not out (1 run short of Gooch's record).

12 Aug At Trent Bridge, David Gower becomes first English player to be called for throwing as he deliberately 'chucks' his only ball, from which Martin Crowe scores the winning boundary.

5 Sep Derek Underwood takes 7-11 in 35.5 overs, including 29 maidens, as Kent beat Warwicks by an innings at Folkestone.

18 Oct Vengsarkar (164 not) and Shastri (121 not) put on an unbeaten 298 against Australia in the 3rd Test, a series record and an Indian 6th-wicket record. In India's 517-5 dec, Gavaskar (103) makes his 33rd Test century. Shastri finishes with 231 in the rubber for once out, Vengsarkar 186 in two not out innings.

3 Dec Botham catches Boon off the first ball of the Perth Test, to complete the 1,000 run/100 wkt/100 ct treble.

22 Dec India's 676-7 against Sri Lanka at Kanpur is their highest Test score.

TEST SERIES

England in West Indies
West Indies 5
India in England
I 2, D 2
New Zealand in England
NZ 1, D 2
India in Australia
Drawn 3
Australia in New Zealand
NZ 1, D 2
Pakistan in Sri Lanka
SL 1, P 1, D 1
Australia in India
Tied 1, Drawn 2
West Indies in Pakistan
P 1, WI 1, D 1

One-day International: 18 February

Injured Gatting out of Test as England crash to Marshall

By Michael Carey, in Kingston, Jamaica

MIKE GATTING was ruled out of Friday's first Test against West Indies after fracturing his nose as England were beaten by six wickets in the first one-day international at Sabina Park. Gatting, England's most consistent batsman on the tour so far, was struck full in the face, unprotected by his visorless helmet, when he missed an attempted hook against Marshall, the ball then trickling on to his stumps to dislodge a bail.

Although batsmen have been known to return to action remarkably quickly after similar injuries, Gatting's was so severe that immediate surgery was necessary, and England manager Tony Brown said it would be two or three days before the full extent was known.

Wretchedly for both the player and his side, it came at a time when Gatting (10) was coping with the West Indies fast bowling more competently than most, after a lively opening by Patterson (2-17) had reduced England to 10 for two, with Gower adding a fourth nought to his run of low scores.

Gatting is pole-axed by a ball from Marshall which breaks his nose.

Marshall (4-23), appearing as first change, emphasised the West Indies bowling strength by taking four for 12 in seven overs. England's total of 145 for eight, made from 46 overs on a pitch that was variable, though better than its predecessor, never looked adequate. And after an opening partnership of 89 by Greenidge (45) and Haynes (35), the West Indies did not require the services of Richards, who had damaged a hand in the field.

First Test
Fourth day: 27 February

Ranatunga walk-out after heated exchange

From Kandy

PAKISTAN beat Sri Lanka by an innings and 20 runs at the Asgiriya Stadium, but the day was spoilt by ill-feeling on the field. Play was held up for 30 minutes after a heated exchange that resulted in the batsmen and umpires returning to the pavilion.

Arjuna Ranatunga, who top-scored with 33, was given not out when Rameez Raja at forward short-leg appealed for a catch off Tauseef. Ranatunga was subjected to a verbal barrage from the fielders, and protested to the umpires. He then left the field with the other batsman, Roy Dias, followed by the umpires.

After the match, Pakistan's skipper, Imran Khan, said his team felt Ranatunga should have walked: "Test matches have become a serious business, and it is very easy to flare up in the competitive atmosphere."

TCCB Meeting: 6 March

TCCB to act over bouncers

By Derek Hodgson, at Lord's

ANOTHER attempt to limit the use of the bouncer, particularly the infamous 'throat ball', is to be made by the TCCB. They decided at the spring meeting to propose an amendment to law 42 at the summer annual meeting of the ICC, all countries meanwhile being circularised.

In the English proposal, the umpire will no longer have to decide whether the bowling is, as at present, "intimidatory". The amended law would read: "The bowling of fast, short-pitched balls is unfair if, in the opinion of the umpire at the bowler's end, they are either frequent or by their length, line and height, are likely to inflict physical injury on the striker standing upright at the crease. The relative skills of the striker should be taken into consideration."

One of the difficulties of the present law is that the batsmen will not admit they are ever intimidated. An amended law should mean that umpires, theoretically, should take action when the likes of Patterson and Marshall bombard the batsmen as mercilessly as they did England in the first Test match in Jamaica.

Any hopes of radical domestic reform following the recommendations of the Palmer Report received short shrift in a two and a half hour meeting. The suggestions to restructure first-class cricket, reducing the one-day programme, are to be examined by the counties and the Board's public relations and marketing sub-committee, but no alterations can now be made before the 1988 season.

Second Test Rest day: 17 March

Pakistan withdraw threat to abandon Sri Lanka tour

From Colombo

PAKISTAN captain Imran Khan said in Colombo that the tour of Sri Lanka would continue despite an earlier decision by his players to abandon it. He explained that the standard of umpiring in the two Tests had led to a deterioration in relations between the two sides, and on-the-field incidents had brought threats and abuse from spectators.

"However, in the larger interests of the game, and after assurances from the president of the Sri Lanka Cricket Control Board, we have prevailed on the players to continue with the tour," Imran said. "In my entire 16-year Test career, I have not witnessed such vile and obnoxious language and gestures such as were directed yesterday from the so-called VIPs and educated members sitting in the pavilion." He defended Miandad's action yesterday when he rushed into the stand with raised bat after a spectator had thrown a stone at him.

Pakistan resume tomorrow 13 ahead with only one second-innings wicket standing.

[Sri Lanka duly recorded their second victory since earning Test status, by eight wickets, and later drew the third Test to share the series.]

Benson & Hedges Cup Final: 12 July

Brave Kent left in the dark as Middlesex triumph in thriller

By Tony Lewis, at Lord's

MIDDLESEX won an extraordinary cup final by two runs in almost complete darkness and deluging rain, when Kent just failed to get the six runs they needed off the last three balls.

The Gold Award went to John Emburey for his valuable late runs (28), his superbly controlled bowling (11-4-17-0) and his quite dazzling fielding, which included a stunning slip catch to dismiss Kent captain Chris Cowdrey.

However, there were many more heroes – Graham Cowdrey (58) for his exhilarating charge that almost brought Kent victory, Daniel and Cowans for their hostile spell with the new ball that had Kent at 20 for three, Radley (54) for his busy batting and Marsh for his excellent wicket-keeping and his mighty six into the grandstand during the last over.

Kent magnanimously turned down the chance to suspend their innings when, with 84 needed from 10 overs, Daniel was brought back into the Middlesex attack. At the death, Middlesex's fielding was brilliant, and the task of hitting a six off the last ball proved, unsurprisingly, beyond Dilley.

Fifth Test Final day: 16 April

England's luck runs out: another 5-0 humiliation

Michael Carey, in Antigua

AFTER an encouraging start to the day, when England looked like earning a draw for the first time in the series, their attempt to save the final Cable and Wireless Test went horribly awry. In the end, they were bowled out for 170, lost the match by 240 runs, and lost their second successive rubber to West Indies by 5-0.

Though England lost only their nightwatchman Ellison before lunch, four more wickets fell before tea, partly because of a pitch where the ball started to keep testingly low – with the extra pace of the West Indies bowlers a decisive factor.

After Gooch had gone lbw to Holding for 51, England had a slice of luck when Gower, on two, survived a straightforward return catch to Marshall – and two or three lbw appeals from the same bowler were also too close for comfort. Lamb and Gatting – deemed fit to play after just one hour's batting in the previous seven weeks – went for one apiece, bowled by balls that failed to bounce.

Richards' decision to introduce his slow bowler, Harper, for the benefit of Botham (13) brought immediate results as his Somerset colleague dragged the ball on to his stumps. And Harper also accounted for Gower and Emburey to finish with three wickets for just 10 runs in 12 overs.

But the match will be remembered for all time for Viv Richards' record-breaking century yesterday when West Indies needed quick runs for a declaration. He reached his 100 from only 56 deliveries, the fastest in Test history in terms of balls received. It eclipsed Jack Gregory's hundred, made from 67 balls for Australia against South Africa in 1921-22, and Roy Fredericks' more recent one from 71 deliveries for West Indies against Australia in 1975-76.

Richards made his first 50 from 35 deliveries, his second from a mere 21. He hit seven sixes and seven fours in his unbeaten 110, and played one of the finest innings in Test history.

19 May

England bar on Botham after newspaper drug admission

By Guy Rais

IAN BOTHAM, the England and Somerset all-rounder, has been barred from playing in the two one-day international matches against India this weekend following his public admission that he has smoked cannabis. The Test and County Cricket Board has also decided not to allow him to play for England again until his confession has been fully investigated.

The TCCB decision was announced after its eight-man Executive Committee met in secret almost all day [Monday] discussing Botham's admission in a Sunday newspaper that he had smoked 'pot'. The matter will now go before the board's disciplinary committee, and is expected to be considered next week.

Before his suspension, Botham, 30, said he had not smoked a 'joint' since his early twenties. Writing in The Mail on Sunday, in the first person, he admitted that he smoked his first marijuana 'joint' at a party when he was 18, to go along with what others were doing, and that "on other occasions I have smoked simply in order to relax".

Botham, the swashbuckling hero of English cricket, was fined £100 in January after he admitted possessing a small amount of cannabis, found by police at his home in Epworth, Humberside.

The team for the first Test against India is chosen on Friday, 30 May, so Botham's future as a Test player depends on the disciplinary committee's reaching a decision by then. Botham needs only two Test wickets to beat Australian Dennis Lillee's world record.

[The disciplinary committee banned Botham from first-class cricket for two months.]

Botham: banned for two months.

County Championship Gloucester v Somerset: 21 July

Walsh 9-72 and Bainbridge 8-53 as Glos triumph

By John Mason, at Bristol

GLOUCESTERSHIRE, who have never won the County Championship, consolidated their lead as this season's front runners by thrashing Somerset by an innings and seven runs in two days at Bristol. Somerset, dismissed for 147 and 154, were swept aside by Courtney Walsh, who took nine for 72 in the first innings, and Phil Bainbridge, who followed with eight for 53 in the second. Both were career-best returns.

In a remarkable day's cricket, Walsh, having taken six wickets on Saturday, took three more this morning as Somerset, resuming at 85 for six, failed by 11 runs to avoid following on. Walsh was quickly firing away when Somerset batted a second time, but without the same spectacular results.

Enter Bainbridge as first change, a fine batsman – who made 51 in Gloucester's innings and 106 not out as they beat Somerset by eight wickets in the John Player League yesterday – but mostly known as no more than a useful bowler as opposed to a ruthless destroyer. In seven deliveries, he secured four wickets – including that of Viv Richards for a duck – for one run to reduce Somerset to tatters.

Garner (47) thumped six sixes with a muscular swing shortly before tea. But Bainbridge, with the help of Athey in the deep, finally got his man, to lift Gloucester to a handsome lead in the title race.

[Gloucester finished second in the Championship as Essex came from behind to win with something to spare, their third title in four years.]

Second Test Final day: 12 August

England's run of gloom extended as New Zealand go one up

By Michael Carey, at Trent Bridge

NEW ZEALAND won the second Cornhill Test by eight wickets to go one up in the series, and extended England's gloomy sequence of defeats this year to eight in 10 matches.

It was only New Zealand's second win in 32 Tests in this country. Perhaps unsurprisingly in view of that, it was not achieved without the odd anxious moment before their captain, Jeremy Coney, and Martin Crowe completed the task of making 74 for victory.

Not the least remarkable aspect of the result was that New Zealand achieved it without the aid of one lengthy innings from any of their front-line batsmen. They owed much to the resilience of the others, such as Gray (50), Hadlee (68) and Bracewell (110), which illustrated the virtue, temporarily mislaid by England, of simply occupying the crease.

Then there was the incomparable bowling of Hadlee, the Man of the Match, who emerged with 10 wickets for 140, the seventh time he has achieved the feat in Tests, which has put him on a lofty parallel with Lillee, Barnes and Grimmett.

Yet before England were finally dismissed for 230, Emburey's innings of 75, his highest in Tests, offered them a tantalising reminder of what might have been possible on this pitch but for earlier mishaps and contentious hairline decisions.

Third Test First day: 21 August

'Who writes your script?' Gooch asks Botham

By Michael Calvin, at the Oval

Botham spins round in triumph as umpire Shepherd upholds his lbw appeal and Jeff Crowe becomes his record 356th Test wicket.

THE ESSENCE of Ian Botham's contribution to world sport was captured at precisely 12.26 p.m. this afternoon by the smile of disbelief that spread across the face of a blind cricket follower sitting in front of the pavilion at the Oval. His pocket radio merely provided confirmation of what the roar of the crowd had communicated a split second earlier – the England all-rounder had become the leading wicket-taker in Test match history.

Around him at that unforgettable moment, several Surrey members were on their feet, collective incredulity underlined by their laughter. But it mattered little that he could not see the scene. In years to come it will be enough for him to recall Botham's dramatic return and say: "I was there."

The irony is that the hero of the hour, arms thrust towards the heavens in a gesture of triumph, cannot be portrayed adequately in the record book, a one-dimensional statistical summary of talent. Botham's character is better suited to the fiction of the comic book. The lone spectator in the Members' Enclosure who booed him when he came on to bowl at 12.12 p.m. was abruptly ordered by his neighbour to "shut up". Botham's first ball, guided to Graham Gooch by Bruce Edgar, left him with no option but to comply. And Gooch's first words to Botham were: "Who writes your script?"

Very much the modern idol, Botham's approach to practice leaves him open to charges of lack of professionalism. Yet like all great sportsmen, he relishes the pressurised circumstances of individual combat. He broke into a wide grin when Jeff Crowe hooked his 11th delivery for four, and promptly dismissed him with his 12th to beat Lillee's record.

Hitting the seam with unerring vigour, he uplifted England from their doom-laden season by unnerving New Zealand, who finished the weather-hit day on 142 for four, Botham's contribution being three for 36 in 11 overs.

After the match, he graciously insisted that Lillee "will always be a better bowler than me". Asked if he was still the world's greatest all-rounder, however, his prompt reply was "Yeah".

[Botham failed to take any more wickets as a gritty 119 by John Wright edged New Zealand to 287, but, after centuries by Gower and Gatting, he cracked a breezy 59 not out off 36 balls to enable England to declare with an overnight lead of 101. The weather intervened again, however, the match was drawn and New Zealand won their first rubber in England.]

Scarborough Festival: 1 Sep

Rampaging Rutherford hits treble century

By Derek Hodgson

KEN RUTHERFORD, 29, the Otago right-hander, would have kept a computer happy for years at Scarborough today. Batting at No.3 for the New Zealanders against D.B.Close's XI, he hit 45 fours and eight sixes in scoring 317 in 230 minutes off 245 deliveries, the highest ever score by a New Zealander abroad.

His 300 in 219 minutes was the fifth fastest in history and the second fastest in England (C.G.Macartney at Trent Bridge 1921). He had one regret. Taking advantage of North Marine Road's short, straight boundaries, he hit Doshi for four successive sixes, and commented: "I'd have settled for 170 and out if I could have equalled the six sixes of Sobers and Shastri."

First Test Final day: 22 September

India and Australia in second tied Test

By D.J.Rutnagur, in Madras

ON A tension-packed final day at Chepauk, the first Test between India and Australia ended in a tie – only the second time in Test history there has been such a finish.

At one stage, India, set to make 348 from a minimum of 87 overs, needed only 18 to win with four wickets in hand. Then, with Matthews bowling frugally, nerves crept in and the last four Indian wickets went down in four overs, leaving Shastri unbeaten on 48.

A crowd of 35,000 could hardly believe that India had failed to clinch what would have been a famous victory – they were 177 behind on first innings after Australia had compiled 574 for seven, their highest total in India, including 210 from Dean Jones, who needed hospital treatment after batting 503 minutes in intense humidity.

Allan Border had declared at Australia's overnight second-innings score of 170 for five, and the top Indian batsmen all did their bit, with Gavaskar top-scorer with a faultless 90. Shastri levelled the scores with a single off the third ball of the final over. But Matthews trapped an intensely nervous No.11, Maninder, leg-before with the fifth.

First Test Final day: 29 October

Pakistan skittle W.Indies for 53 and go one up

From Faisalabad

PAKISTAN completed a famous victory by 186 runs, dismissing the West Indies for their lowest ever Test score of 53 to go one up in the three-Test series.

Tailenders Malcolm Marshall and Patrick Patterson resisted stoutly for 20 minutes, adding 10 runs to the tourists' overnight score, before leg-spinner Abdul Qadir finally had Marshall caught and bowled for 10 to take his second-innings figures to six for 16.

It was only the West Indies' third Test defeat in their last 37 matches since they were beaten in New Zealand in 1979-80. They then went 27 Tests without defeat until losing to Australia in Sydney in January last year. Their previous lowest score was 76 in Dacca, then part of Pakistan, during the 1958-59 series, which Pakistan won 2-1.

This was a match of extraordinary contrasts. Pakistan spent much of it struggling to avert defeat before winning with almost a whole day to spare. The Man of the Match award went to pace bowler Wasim Akram for his six for 91 in West Indies' first innings and the defiant 66 that so disheartened the tourists in Pakistan's second.

[West Indies (218) won a low-scoring second Test by an innings and 10 runs, and the last Test was drawn.]

First Test Final day: 19 November

England cruise to first-Test win in Australia

By Peter West, in Brisbane

UNFANCIED England really upset the form book with their seven-wicket win in Brisbane, which must go down as one of their most famous Ashes wins. Not only had they suffered humiliating clean sweeps by the West Indies – home and away – and series defeats by both India and New Zealand since their last Test victory, against Australia at the Oval in 1985, but their tour form leading up to this Test has been abysmal.

Most pundits had written England off before this Gabba Test, not least the Australian Press, who had looked on England as a pushover, especially after Australia's much-improved recent showing in India.

England captain Mike Gatting put their success down largely to the fact that all the batsmen made valuable contributions to the score. Botham's 138 was another massive performance from the all-rounder, and Athey's long vigil for 76 in the first innings was crucial.

The bowling of Dilley (5-68) in Australia's first innings and Emburey (5-80) were also major factors, as was the all-round performance of DeFreitas, who took five wickets in the match for 84 and scored 40.

Fourth Test Third day: 28 December

England beat Australia in 3 days to retain the Ashes

By Peter West, in Melbourne

AT 4.39 P.M. on the third day, Man of the Match Gladstone Small caught Hughes at deep square leg off Edmonds and Australia were all out for 194. England had won the fourth Test by an innings and 14 runs to take a 2-0 lead in the series and retain the Ashes. No wonder Mike Gatting and his men were celebrating in Melbourne.

Australia opened their innings at the start 208 behind. They made steady progress to 153 for three, but their last seven wickets – five of them falling to the Middlesex spinners Edmonds and Emburey and two more to needless run-outs – succumbed for a miserable 41 runs. It was the first time England had won a Test match in Australia in three days since A.C.MacLaren's team did so in Sydney in 1901.

Almost everything went famously for England in this game after Gatting won the toss and put Australia in to bat. "I had no qualms about fielding first," he said, "although it was touch and go between Small and Foster to take Dilley's place."

Small, needless to say, delivered the goods. In only his third Test match, his first against Australia, he took five for 48 in the first innings, while Ian Botham, not fit enough to bowl at full stretch, took the other five for 41 as Australia were dismissed for 141. Small, then going in at No.11, contributed a valuable 21 not out to England's 349, and took another two wickets for 40 in Australia's second innings.

Chris Broad, the England opener, acknowledges the reception at Melbourne for his third hundred in successive Tests.

1987

7 Jan Kapil Dev achieves the 3,000 runs/300 wickets Test double.

5 Mar The TCCB announce the appointment of former Surrey and England batsman Micky Stewart as England's first full-time team manager. The Board also announce the reintroduction of covered pitches during playing hours in the County Championship.

8 Mar Pakistani fielders are stoned by an unruly crowd at Ahmedabad in the 4th Test against India, play being suspended for 70 minutes. On their return after tea, six wear helmets.

16-21 Apr Wicket-keeper Brendon Kuruppu defies Hadlee & Co. to score an unbeaten 201 out of 397 dec at Colombo, the first Sri Lankan to make a century on his Test debut. It is the first 200 for Sri Lanka, and he is on the field throughout the drawn match (NZ 406-5). A bomb blast in Colombo claims over 100 lives, and the tour is called off.

18 Jun Deloittes Ratings launched. Vengsarkar (India) tops the batting, Hadlee (New Zealand) the bowling.

6-11 Aug Pakistan, 1-0 up against England, make sure of the series with a first innings 708, the sixth-highest score in Test history. Botham (3-217) concedes an England record number of runs in an innings.

25-29 Nov Eighteen wickets fall on the first day at New Delhi, as West Indies dismiss India for 75 (Patterson 5-24), their lowest score on home soil, and are then reduced to 118-8 themselves.

27 Nov As England career to an innings defeat in the first Test against Pakistan at Lahore, there is a controversial incident in which opener Chris Broad refuses to walk when given out to a catch at the wicket. Gooch eventually persuades him to go, and he is later "severely reprimanded", but both England manager Peter Lush and captain Mike Gatting are scathingly critical of the umpiring, especially Shakeel Khan's, after the match.

14 Dec Allan Border, in his 91st Test, makes his highest Test score (205), and becomes Australia's leading Test scorer, overtaking Greg Chappell's 7,110.

TEST SERIES

England in Australia
E 2, A 1, D 2
Pakistan in England
P 1, D 4
Sri Lanka in India
I 2, D 1
Pakistan in India
P 1, D 4
West Indies in New Zealand
NZ 1, WI 1, D 1
New Zealand in Sri Lanka
Drawn 1
New Zealand in Australia
A 1, D 2

Fifth Test Final day: 15 January

John Bull's brave charge fails: 'Peter Who?' is the hero

By Peter West, in Sydney

AFTER a day when the fortunes of both sides ebbed and flowed in compelling fashion, Australia won the fifth Test by 55 runs with one over remaining. England needing 320 to win, lost four wickets for the addition of 11 runs on either side of the lunch interval. Yet a century partnership between Gatting and Richards had, by the time the last mandatory 20 overs began, left them to make another 90.

But Gatting, four runs short of a magnificent hundred richly deserved, was caught and bowled by Waugh in the second of the last 20 overs. John Bull had led from the front for three and a half hours.

A draw was in prospect when Sleep, in two balls, got Richards and Edmonds with 'wrong 'uns'. Nine more overs remained, and Australia had two more wickets to prise out. Small survived six of these, against the spinners, but in the 18th Reid was recalled and Border took a tumbling catch at slip off the fourth delivery.

The last man, Dilley, arrived with 14 balls left. He scored a couple off the first, and kept out the next. Now Sleep to Emburey, the atmosphere supercharged. He blocked the first five balls, but perished on the back foot, bowled by one that kept low.

It was right that so splendid a contest should have a positive result, and no one should begrudge Australia their joy. After all, England have won the series by two matches to one.

Taylor's two further wickets, allied to his previous six for 78, as well as to two obdurate innings, won him the Benson & Hedges Man of the Match award, which is no bad way to start a Test career. The 'Peter Who?' tag – hung on him because of his surprise selection after only six first-class matches – was dead and buried.

Peter 'Who?' Taylor

Broad, having made three hundreds, won himself four gold goblets, and a gold tray as Man of the Series.

B&H World Series Cup: 22 January

Lamb strikes out for most unlikely victory

By Peter West, in Sydney

ALLAN LAMB struck 18 off the first five balls of the final over tonight to steer England to a palpitating and, at the climax, improbable win over Australia by three wickets. It put England on top of the preliminary table in the Benson & Hedges World Series Cup.

I doubt if many English supporters among a host of 36,463 under the floodlights at the Sydney Cricket Ground gave much for their team's chance when they needed 18 off the last over, bowled by Reid, the fastest and most accurate member of the Australian attack.

With quite remarkable aplomb, Lamb took two off the first ball, four to square leg off the next, and an enormous six to mid-wicket off the third. He then hit the ball into the covers, and there was certainly only one run in the stroke until an overthrow crucially got him back down at the receiving end. One more ball was all that an inspired Lamb required – he clattered it straight to the square-leg boundary.

Following a performance like that, there could be only one man of the match – Lamb 77 not out.

Fourth Test Third day: 7 March

Sunny side up with 10,000

By D.J.Rutnagur, in Ahmedabad

INDIA'S master batsman Sunil Gavaskar, playing in his 124th Test, added to his list of records by becoming the first player to reach a total aggregate of 10,000 runs in Test cricket.

He achieved the feat when scoring 58 of the 63 runs he contributed to India's score of 165 for 3 in reply to Pakistan's 395 in the fourth Test. Pandemonium broke out when Gavaskar, known as Sunny, reached the milestone, and there was a mass invasion of the ground.

The prevalent hooliganism, however, took an uglier turn when large stones were thrown from the cheaper stands at two Pakistani fieldsmen stationed in the deep. The Pakistan skipper Imran Khan signalled all his players to the middle and intimated to the umpires that his team would not resume play until the ground authorities took positive steps to stop the attack on his players.

The game was held up in all for 14 minutes.

Third Test Second day: 13 March

Hadlee and Chatfield skittle West Indies

By Tony Cozier, in Christchurch

NEW ZEALAND exploited an encouraging pitch and indisciplined cricket by the West Indies to take immediate command when the third and final Test started a day late in Christchurch. Richard Hadlee, with six wickets for 50, and the often underestimated Ewan Chatfield, who bowled unchanged throughout the innings for four for 30 from 18 overs, routed the West Indies for 100 in two and three-quarter hours.

The Crowe brothers, Jeff and Martin, then added 94 for the third wicket as New Zealand ended on 117 for 2 to complete a miserable Friday the 13th for the West Indies, whose 1-0 lead in the series suddenly appears most insecure.

After more than two days of rain, Jeremy Coney, who won the toss for the first time, put West Indies in, and Hadlee hit Haynes's off-stump with the first ball of the third over. Nine balls later, Chatfield sent Greenidge's middle stump cartwheeling. Only Richardson (37) reached double figures before a last-wicket partnership of 25 between Gray and Walsh carried West Indies to 100.

[The Crowe brothers extended their stand to 156 and New Zealand made 332 before bowling West Indies out again for 264 (Snedden 5-68). But they lost five wickets before scraping the 33 runs they needed to win the match and tie the series.]

Sheffield Shield
S.Australia v Tasmania: 8 March

Hookes hits 41 4s in 306

From Adelaide

SOUTH AUSTRALIA'S captain David Hookes and wicket-keeper Wayne Phillips set an Australian record for the highest partnership for any wicket when they added an unbeaten 462 for the fourth wicket against Tasmania. Their stand took 299 minutes, occupied 84.3 overs and is the 11th highest partnership in all first-class cricket.

Hookes hit a career-best 306 not out, with 41 fours and two sixes, while Phillips scored an unbeaten 213 as South Australia ran up a massive 643 for three declared in their first innings.

The previous highest partnership was 456, set by Bill Ponsford and Edgar Mayne for the first wicket for Victoria against Queensland in a non-Shield game in the 1923-24 season.

Benson & Hedges Cup
Final: 11 July

Man of the Match Jim Love celebrates Yorkshire's win.

Yorks take B & H final by losing fewer wickets

By Tony Lewis, at Lord's

WITH A mighty flourish by Love and Bairstow with the bat on a sunny evening, Yorkshire announced the fact to the country that they are back in town. Set the target of 245 to win in the 55 overs, they coasted, then fell flat on their faces, staggered up, and finally sprinted.

Their win on the last ball of the day was made of all the best ingredients of one-day cricket. The scores were tied at 244 for six and Yorkshire won on the basis of having lost fewer wickets.

Northants would have known that they were short of 20 runs on a lightning fast outfield. They lost four wickets for 97 before Capel (97) and Williams (44) launched themselves merrily into a partnership of 120, leading their side to a competitive 244 for seven.

Yorkshire's start was splendidly fashioned by Moxon (45) and Metcalfe (47) in a stand of 97. But then they lost three quick wickets. Love and Bairstow, two of the most dangerous batsmen in one-day cricket, came together at 160 for four. They put Yorkshire into the driving seat within the last 10 overs, before Bairstow (24) was run out. Carrick hit two fours before sacrificing his wicket in another run muddle. It was left to Love (75) and Sidebottom to scuttle the four runs needed off the last over.

Third Test Third day 4 July

Imran tears England apart at the seam

By Tony Lewis, at Headingley

A BRILLIANT day for Pakistan – the 300th Test wicket for Imran Khan, an extraordinary claim for a catch behind the wicket, and an England side flapping wildly to get out of the net, all made for fascinating cricket in the third Cornhill Test.

Replying to England's 136, Pakistan scored 353. England, batting again, were immediately enmeshed by a varied and skilled attack and, with three wickets standing, are still 31 behind. Pakistan bowled superbly in what are recognised everywhere as English conditions, the ball seaming and swinging.

There was no pace in the pitch so they had to be accurate. Imran's leadership was tactically sound, but perhaps his outstanding contribution has been to give the side purpose and the will to win from the very first ball.

He also had to play the diplomat, when wicket-keeper Saleem Yousuf was involved in an incident with Botham, whom he claimed to have caught. In fact, the ball dropped from his gloves as he fell. He rolled over on top of it and grabbed it back again, leaping into a jubilant appeal. Botham pointed an accusing finger at him, umpire David Shepherd stepped in between the two men, and Imran had strong words with his keeper.

Earlier, the same umpire gave Broad out, caught at the wicket off a ball that touched his left glove, which was not in contact with his bat at the time. This, of course, should not have been given, and Yousuf's 'catch' was dubious, too. But England were simply outplayed.

[Pakistan won by an innings and 18, Imran taking 7-40 (10-77 in the match).]

Fifth Test Fourth day: 17 March

Pakistan take series despite Gavaskar's 96

By D.J.Rutnagur, in Bangalore

THE VALOUR and classic batsmanship of Sunil Gavaskar in scoring 96 in his last Test under impossible conditions could not prevent Pakistan winning the fifth Test by 16 runs in a tense finish. So Pakistan took the series, the first they have won in India, despite being tumbled out by Maninder (7-27) in their first innings for 116, their lowest score against India.

The spinners Iqbal Qasim and Tauseef Ahmed bowled in tandem for the last three hours of India's innings, which resumed after the rest day at 99 for four. They finished with four wickets apiece (nine apiece in the match), running through India's last five wickets for 49 runs.

Gavaskar's effort will rank with his greatest because of the high degree of skill needed to survive. Turn apart, there were no limits to the evil of the pitch in the matter of uneven bounce. He was out eventually to a ball from Qasim which reared to the shoulder of his bat and had him caught at slip.

[This was Gavaskar's 125th and last Test. He retired with a record 10,122 runs (avge 51.12) and 34 hundreds.]

Fourth Test Final day: 28 July

The draw that left us all exhausted

By Peter Deeley, at Edgbaston

IN A MARVELLOUS finale to what had been for four days a pedestrian Test, England failed by 15 runs - and Pakistan by three wickets – to snatch victory at Edgbaston. So it was the draw everyone had predicted, but one of those games without result that left everyone privileged to watch the final hours emotionally drained, players and spectators alike.

This final day saw no fewer than 17 wickets fall for 276 runs. Compare that with the first four – 998 for two completed innings. That statistic alone tells something of how the balance swung from caution to full-blooded aggression.

By bowling Pakistan out for 205, England were always in the driving seat in the final run chase. That they were ever in such a position was due largely to Foster (4-59), well supported by Botham and Dilley, who each took two wickets. And who will forget Foster's bullet of a long throw which ran out Pakistan's last batsman, Qadir?

In their quest for the 124 runs needed for victory, England faced a task that might have been on in a one-day game. But Pakistan's bowlers, Imran and Akram, had the benefit of being able to bowl both short and wide, a defensive measure that would have been denied them in the lesser competition.

With Gower and Gatting at the crease, England were on course at 62 for three after nine overs. Gatting's run-out, after a mix-up with Athey, was the halting point. Only six runs came off four overs after that, but while Emburey (20) was there hitting to all points (14 off one Imran over, including a six) there was some hope.

But 17 were needed off the final six balls, and run-out disasters – Emburey off the first ball and Edmonds off the third, both with Athey showing unwillingness to back them up – signalled the end, and the game ended with two balls still to be bowled.

County Championship Notts v Somerset: 11 August

Hadlee brilliance puts Notts on top

By John Mason, at Trent Bridge

NOTTINGHAMSHIRE, expertly sustained in times of need by Richard Hadlee and Clive Rice, made a decisive strike for the Britannic Championship at Trent Bridge, where they beat Somerset by five wickets. Victory, their fourth in succession at home, including one at Workshop, took Notts to the top of the Championship, 10 points ahead of Northamptonshire, who have a match in hand.

Hadlee had a hand in everything, a colossal performance even by his supreme standards – 12 wickets for 83 (6-42, 6-41), a dashing hundred (101) and a staunch unbeaten 23 on the last lap after Notts had been in dire trouble.

The Trent Bridge pitch was the x-factor in this match, not that Hadlee, whose withering accuracy and late movement finally destroyed Somerset, requires such assistance. He is too good a cricketer for that.

From an overnight 43 for three and a lead of 30, Somerset, minus the injured Martin Crowe, stumbled to 139, leaving Notts 110 to get for victory. They struggled to 64 for five before Rice and Hadlee joined forces to see them home.

Sunday League Worcs v Northants: 13 September

Record crowd acclaim Worcs league triumph

By D.J.Rutnagur, at Worcester

WORCESTERSHIRE clinched the Sunday League Championship under its new sponsorship, Refuge Assurance, routing Northamptonshire before a record New Road crowd of 6,500.

Save for Botham, the other 10 of Worcestershire's side received a winner's medal for the first time, since it was as far back as 1974 that the club last claimed a title, the County Championship. Worcestershire's only previous success in the Sunday League was in 1971.

Worcestershire's nine-wicket win over Northamptonshire, which required the unhurried getting of a mere 169 runs, was their fifth in a row and, like the last three, also gained by huge margins. In the process, Tim Curtis (69 not out) and Ian Botham (61) put on a century opening stand. But the die had been cast much earlier in the match by Paul Pridgeon (8-1-14-2) and Phil Newport (8-0-24-1), who allowed the Northants innings no foundation.

NatWest Trophy Final: 7 September

Now Hadlee blasts Notts to Trophy victory in Lord's farewell

By Peter Deeley, at Lord's

ON A DAY when the script might have been written in advance for the occasion of his last appearance at Lord's, Richard Hadlee carried Nottinghamshire to a remarkable three-wicket victory over Northamptonshire in the delayed final of the NatWest Trophy.

With eight runs wanted off the last over, bowled by a reluctant David Capel, Hadlee was unluckily involved in the run-out of his partner, Bruce French, from the first ball. But he then more than made amends by hitting the England all-rounder for six over long-off from the second ball and a four to the Tavern boundary off the third for the winning runs.

Richard Hadlee: Lord's farewell script.

Hadlee, 36, ends his association with the Trent Bridge side this season after nine years filled with outstanding performances. But his 70 not out in 61 balls, which won him the Man of the Match award, will go down as one of the most memorable, coming at a time when Notts seemed to be slipping fatally behind in the run-rate.

Northants, the outsiders before the weekend, had started the day as the bookmakers' favourites with their opponents 57 for four and needing 172 runs off the outstanding 29 overs.

With five overs to go, the run-rate had reached more than 10 an over, but the pressure then seemed to get to Northants. Nervous errors in the field turned ones into twos, 21 came from the final two overs of Winston Davis, and although Capel was not feeling fully fit, his captain, Geoff Cook, gambled by bringing him on for two overs at the end. But the 21 runs Capel conceded in nine balls were all that was necessary to bring Notts their first one-day title of any description.

Reliance World Cup Final: 8 November

Australia's victorious captain, Allan Border, carried aloft by jubilant team-mates.

England's run-chase doomed by history

By Peter Deeley, in Calcutta

THE PSYCHOLOGICAL disadvantage of having to chase a set total was once more demonstrated by Australia's seven-run win over England in the World Cup final at Eden Gardens. Australia's bowling was the tighter and they fielded like men possessed.

The setting for the game before an 80,000 crowd, almost the number that Lord's might expect for a five-day Test, was as colourful and exciting as only this frenetic Indian city of 12 million could provide.

Man of the Match Boon (75) and Marsh (24) gave Australia their fifth major opening partnership in this series, 75. The scoring rate dropped as Foster, Emburey and Gooch applied the brakes, but it was difficult to contain the Australians, particularly Valetta (45 not out). The final five overs went for 41 runs, which Gatting acknowledged later was about 20 too many, and Australia finished on 253 for five, a total beyond the grasp of almost all sides batting second in the tournament.

The five-over analyses of Reid and McDermott, each giving away only 17 runs, illustrated the difference between the two opening attacks. Gooch (35) was a prize wicket for O'Donnell. But the mortal stab to the heart was probably Gatting's attempt on 41 to do a reverse sweep off the first ball Border bowled. Coming off the bat, it hit the batsman's shoulder and popped up to Dyer.

Waugh fired in a return which ran out the gallant Athey for 58, and only Lamb offered much resistance after that, with 45 in 55 balls. But like all the later batsmen he was being asked to accomplish the implausible. England needed 75 off the last 10 overs, then 46 off five. DeFreitas kindled a tiny flame with 4-6-4 off three deliveries from McDermott, but in the end the margin was just beyond them. Gallant fighters, but not champions.

First Test First day: 25 November

England bewitched by Qadir's bizarre 9-56

By Michael Austin, In Lahore

ABDUL QADIR, strengthening his claims for admission to the Magic Circle, bewitched, baffled and beguiled England with nine for 56 in 37 overs unchanged, the best figures against them in Test history, as the three-match series began in fascinating style.

England still had the Houdini touch, escaping from 94 for eight to 175 all out as Foster (39) and French (38 not out), following Broad's staunch example (41), shook off the fetters in a ninth-wicket partnership of 57. Pakistan scored 13 without loss in reply.

Qadir's figures for a spin bowler on the first day of a Test match were as bizarre as the under-prepared pitch, the umpiring and the cloistered atmosphere as a crowd of less than a thousand were scattered around the vast terraces.

Qadir's figures were the finest for Pakistan in their 35-year history, and he became the 12th player overall to take nine or more wickets in a Test innings.

[Pakistan made 392 and won by an innings and 87 runs in four days, bowling England out for 130 (Qadir 4-45), their equal lowest score against Pakistan.]

Second Test Second day: 8 December

Umpire accuses Gatting after angry exchange

By Michael Austin, in Faisalabad

SHAKOOR RANA, the umpire, tonight threatened to pull out of the second Test unless he received an apology from Mike Gatting, the England captain, following a war of words just before the end of play. Mr Rana said after the close of play: "I am reporting Gatting to the Test and County Cricket Board, the tour manager Peter Lush and the Pakistan Board for using foul and abusive language. No captain has spoken to me like that before."

Later Mr Rana said he would not take the field tomorrow unless Gatting showed contrition, prompting fears that the whole tour could be in jeopardy.

A productive day in cricket terms for England was especially prosperous for Emburey, who took three for 26 as Pakistan struggled to 106 for five in reply to 292, Broad making 116 in seven hours and Qasim returning five for 83.

In other respects, a more unsavoury saga would be difficult to imagine. It ended with Gatting and Mr Rana exchanging words almost eyeball to eyeball during the final over and being separated by Athey, who ushered away his captain.

Mr Rana, umpiring at square leg, intervened when Hemmings was running in to bowl, because he believed that Gatting was changing his field behind the back of Salim Malik, the batsman. But Gatting, who was fielding at backward short leg, had already informed Salim that he was bringing in Capel.

England's tour management of Mr Lush and Micky Stewart said they had not seen any Test series marred with incidents such as these. *[See feature overleaf.]*

Third Test Final day: 30 December

10-wicket Hadlee is level with Botham

By Alan Shiell, in Melbourne

NEW ZEALAND failed by just one wicket to win the third Test against Australia after one of the tightest and most tense finishes in Test history. So Allan Border won the first of his eight series as Australia's captain. Victory for New Zealand would have squared the series 1-1, but the draw enabled Australia to regain the Trans-Tasman Trophy for their first series win since they beat Pakistan in Australia in 1983-84.

Nevertheless, fast bowler Richard Hadlee, who came so close to clinching victory for New Zealand, equalled Ian Botham's Test record of 373 wickets, taking 10 wickets in a Test for a record eighth time – one more than England's Sydney Barnes and Australia's Clarrie Grimmett and Dennis Lillee.

Australia ended the match with their second innings score on 230 for nine – still 17 runs short of their target – after the last-wicket pair, Craig McDermott and Michael Whitney, had survived the last 30 balls.

Whitney punched the air in jubilation after lasting out Hadlee's final over with a combination of judgement and luck. The 23,859 spectators cheered ecstatically. And Hadlee strode off as the Man of the Match and the Player of the Series.

Tour manager Peter Lush (right) appears to resort to ventriloquism to squeeze an apology out of England skipper Mike Gatting as the affronted umpire Shakoor Rana looks on.

The Gatting/Shakoor Rana Incident

ENGLAND'S three-Test tour of Pakistan in 1987-88 set new lows in on-field behaviour and unprecedented scenes between captain and umpire. Not since the 'Bodyline' tour of England to Australia in 1932-33 had there been such acrimony on and off the cricket field. The much-publicised row between Pakistani umpire Shakoor Rana and England captain Mike Gatting, with its subsequent repercussions, was an incident waiting to happen. And no one, on either side of the affair, came out of it smelling of roses.

Foreboding

England went into the tour with a sense of foreboding. The series earlier in the year in England had not been without incident. Pakistan's voluble manager, Hasib Ahsan, stirred up controversy with almost every mischievous statement he made, particularly with regard to long-standing umpire David Constant.

But the TCCB did not help by refusing the request to replace Mr Constant, even if Pakistan's complaints about him were unjustified. This would make it difficult for the England management to get a sympathetic hearing in Pakistan if they wished to have a Pakistani umpire changed.

The influence of Pakistan's captain, Imran Khan, was seen at Headingley in the third Test, when he reprimanded wicket-keeper Saleem Yousuf for claiming a catch against Botham that had patently been grounded. It had been, perhaps, even more evident at Old Trafford, by Imran's absence from the field. With Javed Miandad in charge, the Pakistan side looked in grave disarray, with many substitutes coming and going, presumably because of minor injuries, and lengthy discussions, resulting in an over-rate of 11 an hour. This provoked comments from the England manager Micky Stewart, but these were answered next day with some brusqueness by Hasib Ahsan, who considered it "improper" and "objectionable" that Mr Stewart should publicly accuse Pakistan of spoiling the image of the game. 'Harmonious' relations were later restored, but when opposing managers allow themselves to get embroiled in public arguments of this kind there is bound to be a mutual lessening of respect.

Apprehension

After England's series defeat at home, Pakistan winning the Old Trafford Test and drawing the other four, the tour of Pakistan was always going to be difficult. Imran Khan had now retired, and Javed Miandad had taken over the captaincy. England were without experienced Test players in Gower, Lamb and Botham.

One was uneasy about what effect the umpiring might have on the England party. The senior players who had been to Pakistan before knew the problems that might crop up, and a cloud of apprehension hovered over them. It was much in everybody's mind that as mild a man as Jeremy Coney had threatened to take his New Zealand side off the field in Karachi three years before.

Almost from the moment that Mike Gatting won the toss in Lahore, England were in trouble. Predictably their tormentor was the leg-spinner Abdul Qadir. Equally predictably there were numerous umpiring errors, and, when Pakistan batted, Miandad was one of the batsmen who steered them into a big lead.

Early in England's second innings came Chris Broad's deplorable refusal to leave the wicket on being given out to a catch by the wicket-keeper. Failure to obey an umpire's decision is an act that strikes at the very heart of cricket, as he doubtless realised later. A large fine was envisaged, but he received only a reprimand, and on the same day the tour manager, Peter Lush, entered the lists with a statement to the Press that was unusually critical of the umpiring.

This opened the floodgates to a diatribe by Mike Gatting that was calculated – or, rather, not calculated at all, because this was Gatting's way – to antagonise the umpires. Without acknowledging Pakistan's superiority in a match in which Qadir returned figures of 13 for 101 and Pakistan won by an innings, Gatting unemotionally developed Lush's theme for 15 minutes from a ringside seat in Gaddafi Stadium.

"It's nice to be able to compete on an even basis, but obviously during this match we weren't competing on an even basis," he began. "When we come to Pakistan, the umpiring always seems to be the same. I've never seen it as blatant as this. I warned the younger players beforehand what they could expect, but until you've experienced it you can't comprehend how the game is played out here. If I were the opposition, I wouldn't be very happy about the way they had won. Still, to them a win is a win, that's all that seems to matter."

The word 'cheat' was never mentioned. But it was as strongly implied by Gatting as in Lush's statement. Of England's 20 wickets, Gatting claimed nine had gone to wrong decisions, all but one by Shakeel Khan, a 35-year-old former first-class player from Karachi standing for the fifth time in a Test.

"Pakistan had three umpires on the World Cup panel, but instead of selecting one of them, they chose an inexperienced one. Why not the best umpires, unless they don't think they are good enough themselves?"

Looking ahead to the second Test, Gatting said: "All I can ask is that we go out and compete. But if the umpiring is the same as here, it doesn't matter what we do – we can't win."

After such a statement, things could only go downhill. And they did.

Enter Shakoor Rana

Immediately after England's defeat in the first Test, the Pakistani umpire with the longest history of Test controversies, Shakoor Rana, was nominated to officiate in the second Test, at Faisalabad. This was a move that turned an already serious problem into an explosive situation. An aggravating factor was that Mr Lush, England's tour manager, was appraised of this development only when shown a Press release about the appointment minutes before it was passed to the Pakistan media.

England were thus allowed no time for objection or even comment, which was especially irritating because Mr Lush had discovered the identity of the umpires for the first Test at 24 hours' notice in a newspaper. He had pointed out this unacceptable situation in a letter to the Pakistan Board, clearly without making much impact

Shakoor had umpired the third Test in Karachi a decade earlier when six leg-before dismissals in England's first innings equalled the Test record. Since then, Jeff Thomson, the Australian fast bowler, had kicked over the stumps after being repeatedly no-balled by Shakoor, whose decision that Anshuman Gaekwad, the Indian batsman, was out to a bat-and-pad catch had led to a confrontation between Gaekwad and the Pakistan team. New Zealand had walked off the field, and stayed off for several minutes at Karachi in 1984-85 when Shakoor rejected an appeal for caught-behind against Javed Miandad. Shakoor's latest controversy was giving out Bill Athey leg-before to a ball which appeared to pitch outside leg stump in the first one-day international at Lahore 12 days previously.

It was hard for the public at home in England, who were accustomed to harmonious relations between players and umpires, to understand how the infamous confrontation between Shakoor and Gatting in the second Test could have happened. But it was certainly a different world in Pakistan, and one in which a feeling of victimisation might build up, with paranoia rife on both sides.

The sinister new habit of siting a microphone by the pitch was always likely to publicise incidents that might normally have passed unnoticed. Now it added to the reprehensible scene that took place on the second evening. England had taken five wickets and were on top for once. They were trying to fit in another over when Shakoor Rana intervened from square-leg, misinterpreting a gesture made by Gatting just after he had had the courtesy to draw the attention of the batsman, Salim Malik, to a change he had made in the field. As Hemmings bowled, Shakoor took it on himself to call 'dead ball'.

When Gatting asked the reason for this, he was apparently met by a shower of abuse and called a cheat. He blew up. One's heart sank as the arms waved furiously on both sides, and the television cameras captured the dreadful sight for all time. Apologies are not freely given on the sub-continent, and the third day's play was lost while Shakoor Rana waited for one from Gatting. Gatting, having been falsely accused of being a cheat, was not inclined to make one unless Shakoor did too.

For a day, the telephone wires between St John's Wood and Pakistan worked overtime. Finally, the message from the headquarters of the English game seemed to be that the tour should continue. That was the effect of the advice given by Alan Smith, the Board's chief executive, in his many conversations with various members of the beleaguered touring party. His advice was reinforced by TCCB chairman Raman Subba Row, who said that he was disappointed by the behaviour of both Gatting and the Pakistani umpire, Shakoor Rana. But when asked if Gatting would be disciplined by the board, Mr Subba Row said: "Any form of dissent is unacceptable, whatever it is. I do not want to allocate any particular blame in any particular direction. That has to follow."

On the rest day in Faisalabad, Mr Lush, having failed to contact the president of the Board of Control for Cricket in Pakistan, Lieutenant-General Safdar Butt, drove to Lahore in an effort to see him. Eventually, Gatting was ordered to make an apology by the TCCB, which he did with a scribbled note on a scrap of paper, and the match resumed too late for England to capitalise on what might have been a winning position.

Reaction at home

General reaction in England within cricket circles was critical of Gatting, though some voices expressed concern also at the standard of Pakistan umpires, and a Conservative MP, Anthony Beaumont-Dark, demanded that the tour be called off and the players return. He said Gatting was wrong to argue on the field of play: "Even bad umpires have to be obeyed. But he would be right to say, off the field, 'We cannot play a game of cricket while we are playing against the umpires as well'."

Television pundit Tom Graveney, the highly respected former England batsman, uncharacteristically stepped right into the controversy. He said he considered that Pakistan had been cheating England at cricket for 37 years. He, too, called for the tour to be ended immediately. He said: "It is just getting worse and worse out there. It was bad enough when I toured in 1951. The feeling between the two teams is pretty disastrous.... The umpiring has been so bad, and I thought England did wonderfully well not to react when Graham Gooch was given out with such a diabolical decision. I have never been in favour of having neutral umpires before, but I think these incidents have been a strong argument for them."

Former Surrey leg-spinner and one-time Pakistan captain and tour manager Intikhab Alam also added his voice to the call for the ICC to reconsider the appointment of neutral umpires. He said: "I have had strong views about this for seven years, and have been advocating neutral observers as well as neutral umpires at all Test matches."

Omer Kureishi, who was Oxford-educated and managed the Pakistan party that Intikhab led to England in 1974, emphasised the view, pointing out the advantage of neutral umpires in the World Cup. He said that "When England play in Pakistan, they don't like our umpires. We have serious misgivings about England's when we go there. It's the same the world over, and umpires from neutral countries would end all this."

The Pakistan Board supported the idea, and had put theory into practice by appointing two Indian umpires for the Tests against West Indies at Lahore and Karachi the previous year. Pakistan were in the minority, however, and declined to continue the experiment because the ICC were against it. Mr Kureishi said pointedly that the only reason he could suggest for this was that the "TCCB live in the 19th century".

Raman Subba Row and Alan Smith flew out to Karachi to repair the damage. In the course of their visit they caused some astonishment by Mr Subba Row's decision to give a sort of hardship bonus of £1,000 to each member of the side. They had certainly had a tough tour and had much to be aggrieved about, but they had allowed themselves to be drawn into reactions that were totally against the best interests of the game and, whatever the provocation, were inexcusable. It was a tour that any one present will wish to forget.

1988

15 Jan Kiran More completes 5 stumpings in an innings (6 in match), for India against West Indies, both new Test records.

27 Feb Mark Greatbatch (107 not) makes a century on his Test début for New Zealand against England at Eden Park.

4 Apr West Indies concede a record 71 extras (b21, lb8, w4, nb38) in an innings, against Pakistan in Georgetown, as they lose their first home Test since Australia there in 1977-78. There are 15 more no-balls scored from.

18 Apr A unique achievement: Peter Bowler makes a century on his début for Derbyshire, against Cambridge University, having scored a hundred on his Leicestershire début in 1986.

21 Apr First 4-day games begin in the County Championship.

30 Jun John Childs of Essex makes his England début at 36 years 320 days.

30 Jul Tony Merrick (Warwicks) takes 6-0 in 10 balls against Derbyshire, including the hat-trick.

4 Aug Graham Gooch becomes England's fourth captain in the rubber against West Indies, after Mike Gatting, John Emburey (2) and Chris Cowdrey.

5 Aug At the Oval, Malcolm Marshall takes his 34th wicket in the series, a West Indies record (extending it to 35 in England's 2nd innings).

8 Aug Derek Pringle becomes England's fifth captain of the summer, deputising on the fourth day for the injured Gooch.

12-13 Nov Richard Hadlee (NZ) takes his 374th Test wicket, against India at Bangalore, to beat Botham's record, and increases his record of 5-wicket innings to 33.

13 Nov Viv Richards becomes the first West Indian to score 100 hundreds, against NSW at Sydney.

26-29 Nov Hadlee takes 10 wickets in a Test for a record 9th time, 5 wickets in innings for 34th.

18 Dec Australia beat England by 8 wickets in the final of the Women's World Cup, at Melbourne.

18-21 Dec In the first Test, at Brisbane, Viv Richards (WI) takes his 100th catch in his 100th Test, and Courtney Walsh takes the hat-trick over the two Australian innings.

TEST SERIES

England in Australia
Drawn 1
England in New Zealand
Drawn 3
West Indies in England
WI 4, D 1
Sri Lanka in England
England 1
West Indies in India
I 1, WI 1, D 2
Sri Lanka in Australia
Australia 1
Pakistan in West Indies
WI 1, P 1, D 1
Australia in Pakistan
P 1, D 2
New Zealand in India
I 2, NZ 1

Fourth Test
Fourth day: 15 January

Hirwani takes début 16-36 as India square series

By D.J.Rutnagur, in Chepauk

NARENDRA HIRWANI, India's new wrist-spinning discovery, yesterday equalled Bob Massie's remarkable feat of taking 16 wickets in his maiden Test as India bowled West Indies out for 160 at Chepauk to win the fourth and final Test. Their 255-run win squares the series 1-1.

Declaring their second innings with a lead of 415 midway through the morning of the fourth day, India bowled out the West Indies, previously beaten only five times in the 1980s, in 156 minutes and 41 overs. West Indies' defeat, the biggest of the six they have suffered at India's hands in 58 meetings, would have been more ignominious but for a daredevil 67 off 62 balls by Gus Logie and some hearty slogging by Clyde Butts, who made 38, including two fours and three sixes.

Hirwani bore the brunt of their onslaught during a seventh-wicket partnership of 61, yet managed to concede a run fewer than Massie in 1972.

The conditions in which Hirwani wrought such havoc were no less favourable to spin bowling than those at Lord's which made Massie's swing unplayable. The West Indies manager Jackie Hendriks, stressing that the ball was bringing up puffs of dust on the first day, described it as "the worst Test pitch I have ever seen".

Bicentenary Test Second day: 30 January

Broad, more in anger at himself, sends a stump flying.

Broad spoils the party again: Should he have been sent home?

By Robert James, in Sydney

ENGLAND opener Chris Broad is in real danger of being sent home if he is guilty of another breach of discipline following today's incident in the Sydney Bicentenary Test. The 30-year-old left-hander, whose 139 was by far England's best score in a total of 425, was fined £500 and warned about his future conduct after knocking a stump flying in the instant following his dismissal.

Broad's heat-of-the-moment gesture happened when, in an attempt to leave alone a lifting ball from medium-pacer Steve Waugh, he deflected it downwards off his forearm. He stood transfixed as it broke his wicket after a gutsy innings lasting seven-and-a-quarter hours. Broad swung his bat at the stumps as he turned for the pavilion, hitting the nearest one hard enough to send it scudding across the pitch.

Broad accepted the fine without demur, acknowledging he had no excuse for what he did. Later, manager Micky Stewart left no doubt that Broad would be sent home from the tour if there was any further breach of discipline.

With his recent record, perhaps he should have been sent home on the next plane. Only the management's mistrust of and indignation at the standard of umpiring in Pakistan saved Broad a similar fine two months ago, at Lahore, when he refused to leave the wicket for upwards of half-a-minute after being given out, in error, by umpire Shakeel Khan.

Then, at Karachi, his reaction to being adjudged lbw to Abdul Qadir made it clear he thought the decision was a poor one, though after seeing it on television, he admitted the misjudgement was his own. Yet, as Stewart volunteered, Broad in every other way is a model tourist.

First Test First day: 3 April

Imran returns to hit West Indies with seven for 80

From Georgetown, Guyana

WEST INDIES crumbled from a promising tea score of 219 for four to 292 all out on the opening day of the first Test against Pakistan at Georgetown. The damage was done by Imran Khan, who finished with seven for 80 as the hosts lost six wickets for 73 in the third session.

Having been persuaded out of retirement by pressure from public, players and, ultimately, the President for this particular assignment, Imran had Haynes caught at the wicket for one. After lunch, with West Indies on 144-3, he had the supremely confident Richardson (75) caught at cover off a slower ball.

Logie reacted with calm and assurance to West Indies' precarious position, and at tea had been batting for 134 minutes for 80. But he became the first of the post-tea victims without scoring further, falling leg before to Abdul Qadir, before Imran swept through the last five batsmen.

[Imran took 4-41 in West Indies' second innings, and Pakistan won by 9 wickets.]

County Championship Somerset v Worcs: 6 May

Hick's unbeaten 405: Best of century

By David Green, at Taunton

GRAEME HICK, the Zimbabwean-born batsman who qualifies to play for England in 1991, became the first cricketer to score more than 400 runs in a County Championship innings this century.

His unbeaten 405 for Worcestershire against Somerset was the second-highest innings in the history of the championship – beaten only by Archie MacLaren's 424 for Lancashire, also at Taunton, in 1895. Hick's innings ended when his captain, Phil Neale, declared at 628 for seven. Neither Neale nor Hick knew how close he was to MacLaren's record score.

Hick made his runs in 9 hours 15 minutes off 469 balls, hitting 35 fours and 11 sixes. It is only the eighth individual innings above 400 in cricket history.

Graeme Hick: Majestic, record-breaking innings.

County Championship Northants v Warwicks: 20 May

Northants snatch win after following on

By D.J.Rutnagur, at Northampton

NORTHAMPTONSHIRE snatched a remarkable six-run win over Warwickshire in the Britannic Assurance County Championship. It was the first time since 1906 that they had won after following on.

Required to score only 119 in the final innings, Warwickshire were bowled out for 112, their last five wickets going down for 14 runs. Three of them, including the crucial wicket of top-scorer Asif Din (48), fell to the off-spin of Williams, but the early damage was wrought by Davis (4-44) and Walker (3-40).

Northants had followed on 245 runs behind Warwicks' first-innings total of 415, yet were able to compile 363 at the second attempt. Warwicks were by no means restricted by pressure of time, nor could the pitch be blamed for their débâcle.

10 June

Gatting sacked 'for damaging cricket's image': Denial of birthday impropriety accepted by Test selectors

By Peter Deeley and Quentin Cowdry

MIKE GATTING was stripped of the England cricket captaincy yesterday after admitting that he took a woman back to his hotel bedroom for a drink the night before he went in to bat to help to save the first Test against the West Indies at Trent Bridge.

The Test selectors made the decision after questioning him about allegations, widely reported this week, that he was sexually involved with the woman. They accepted his denial. But they were concerned at his admission that he had behaved "irresponsibly", said the former England captain, Mr Peter May, chairman of the Test and County Cricket Board selectors.

Gatting had told them that he was celebrating his 31st birthday and invited a woman to his room for a drink, and that for a time they were alone.

Mr May made it clear that Gatting's 'sin' had been to damage the image of the game and the England team. He said: "We like to think it is the greatest honour in the game to play for England."

After being told that he was being dropped as captain, Gatting said he did not wish to be considered for the second Test, which starts next Thursday. The selectors accepted this. Mr May emphasised that the captaincy decision was for one Test only. "It does not rule Gatting out from being captain again," he said. Gatting's immediate successor is thought most likely to be the off-spinner John Emburey, 35, who has been in danger of losing his place because of poor form at Trent Bridge.

Last night Gatting, who is married with two children, issued a statement saying: "I categorically deny allegations of sexual impropriety which have been made against me by certain newspapers. I have instructed my solicitors to commence the necessary action against those newspapers for libel."

Gatting was already under pressure over a chapter on last winter's tour to Pakistan in his autobiography, due for publication at the end of the month. In it he gives his version of the notorious row with the Pakistani umpire Shakoor Rana – and so breaches a contract forbidding him to speak about a tour for two years.

Four other England players have been summoned to Lord's this morning to answer allegations about their part in the Gatting incident at the Rothley Park Hotel, near Nottingham. The England team manager, Mr Micky Stewart, named them as Paul Jarvis (Yorks), Phillip DeFreitas (Leics), Allan Lamb (Northants) and Paul Downton (Middlesex), all of whom had been mentioned in newspaper articles.

NatWest Trophy Sussex v Derby: 22 June

Holding skittles Sussex with world best of 8-21

By Doug Ibbotson at Hove

MICHAEL HOLDING, the former West Indies Test bowler who professes to be some way beyond his best, established a world record for limited-overs cricket when his eight for 21 against Sussex at Hove swept Derbyshire to a six-wicket victory in the first round of the NatWest Trophy competition.

In moving to the top of the NatWest bowling honours list, Holding not only improved on Derek Underwood's eight for 31 for Kent against Scotland last year, but achieved the feat despite nine no balls. Until this season, Holding's figures would have been recorded as eight wickets for 12 runs. Even so, the record in limited-overs cricket is likely to stand for some time – and this against championship opposition.

Holding nowadays modestly insists that he is no longer a truly fast bowler. If this is so, then eight Sussex batsmen were vanquished by some extremely curious off-breaks that flew like shells from the edge of the bat into an arc of catchers between wicket and gulley. Sussex were dismissed for 134 in 46.1 overs, and Derbyshire reached their target comfortably in 17 fewer.

Benson & Hedges Cup Final: 9 July

Swinging Jefferies, as no-ball ends no contest

By Tony Lewis, at Lord's

Match-winner Stephen Jefferies in action at Lord's.

ALMOST fittingly, Hampshire won the Benson and Hedges Cup at Lord's when Derbyshire handed them the winning run, courtesy of a no-ball from Allan Warner. But, in reality, it failed to take anything away from Hampshire's achievement. There was no doubting that they won with a style and certainty which belied the fact that they had never reached a one-day final before.

They shot out Derbyshire for 117, and after proceeding with caution stroked their way to victory with a flourish by seven wickets. Towards the end, Robin Smith (38) played thundering strokes with a heavy bat, his timing precise and his footwork neat. He removed any hope Derbyshire harboured of a mutual collapse, even though Goldsmith held one of the finest catches ever seen at Lord's to dismiss him. Mark Nicholas coasted sensibly at the other end for an unbeaten 35.

Derbyshire's torture began in the morning from the moment Nicholas won the toss and put them in to bat. The problem was not early-morning moisture, because there was little movement off the seam. Swing was the torture – and Jefferies the practitioner.

Stephen Jefferies, the Man of the Match with five for 13, bowling left-arm over the wicket, got the ball to swing into the right-handers or occasionally slanted it across them towards slip. After seven overs he had taken four for 12, extracting the core of the batting talent, Barnett, Bowler, Roberts and Goldsmith. Only Morris (42), who was run out, played a substantial innings.

A South African who plays for Western Province, Jefferies took all 10 wickets in an innings in one Currie Cup match last season. Sometimes, he can be lethargic and ineffective. Today he virtually won the match for Hants.

Fifth Test Fourth day: 8 August

Flag at half-mast as England's fate is sealed

By Peter Deeley, at the Oval

NINETEEN minutes after the tea interval, Gus Logie on-drove Phillip DeFreitas for four and West Indies had won the final Cornhill Test and lifted the Wisden Trophy, for winning the series, by a 4-0 margin.

The flag of the Cross of St George over the pavilion was already at half-mast, as tradition has dictated in these recent years of West Indies domination. They have now won 14 of the last 15 games between the countries.

The West Indies' superiority was quite breathtaking, particularly considering the doubts there were about their continuing supremacy when they arrived in May. The history of England-West Indies contests is getting to the stage where a fifth day is just a contingency against bad weather.

Haynes (77 not out) and Greenidge (77) resumed at 71 for no wicket, with the target 225, higher than the first three innings of the game. Yet neither Viv Richards nor Jeff Dujon, the Man of the Match, was called upon to take a final curtain call as West Indies completed their victory for the loss of only two wickets.

Malcolm Marshall, who was chosen as West Indies' Man of the Series, is, according to Graham Gooch, England's Man of the Series, the best fast bowler in the world by a long way.

NatWest Trophy Final: 3 September

Middlesex keep their cool: Teenager Ramprakash takes the honours

By Tony Lewis, at Lord's

IT MAY well be that the toss of the coin settled the destination of the 1988 NatWest Trophy. Mike Gatting called right and sent Worcester in on a surface loaded with dampness. They scored a modest-looking 161 for nine in their 60 overs, and Middlesex won by three wickets with 27 balls left.

Yet it was not achieved without a brave fight by Worcs, brilliant bowling by Dilley and an instinct for suicide in the Middlesex middle order. The Middlesex success story also included a fine innings by the 18-year-old Mark Ramprakash, who came to the wicket with the score at 25 for 4 in the 13th over and left with three runs needed for victory.

The early part of the match was a nightmare for Worcestershire. In 12 overs, they had struggled to nine for three, and even the prolific Hick was out. It was the seam bowling of Fraser and Cowans that caused the trouble. When Gatting rested them, their figures revealed the grim nature of the batsmen's job: Cowans 9-6-9-1 and Fraser 7-5-9-2.

Worcester skipper Neale grafted them back into the game with a gutsy 64. But all of Middlesex's bowlers were economical, Cowans taking one for 23, Hughes four for 30 and Fraser three for 36.

However, when Middlesex went in, Dilley gave Worcester an inspired lead, taking his sweater for the first time with figures reading 8-3-14-3. Further drama followed when Mike Gatting was run out without facing a ball, and then Slack was also run out. A long partnership between Ramprakash (56) and Emburey (35) at first brought good sense and then a positive move to victory, but not before Dilley (5-29) had accounted for both of them. Geoff Boycott made Ramprakash Man of the Match, but it must have been a close call.

3 August

Now Gatting is fined £5,000 for book

By Peter Deeley

MIKE GATTING, the former England captain, has been fined £5,000 by the Test and County Cricket Board for breach of contract. After a seven and a half hour hearing at Lord's, the Board's disciplinary committee decided he had been guilty of one offence of publishing material without its consent. In a statement, the Board said the size of the fine reflected the "serious nature of the offence". Gatting has 28 days in which to appeal.

The charges arose from the recent publication of his autobiography, Leading from the Front. One chapter, printed under the name of a ghost writer, deals with Gatting's rows in Pakistan with Shakoor Rana, the umpire. England players are under contract with the Board not to write for two years about tours they go on.

The committee said it had taken into account Gatting's previous exemplary record and his great contributions for the good of cricket. "Were it not for these contributions, the fine would have been at least doubled."

County Championship Worcs v Glamorgan: 16 September

Worcs success despite undercover operation

By Peter Deeley at Worcester

WORCESTERSHIRE won their fourth Championship by one point over Kent, beating Glamorgan despite losing 18 overs at the start because of oil on the wicket. Someone had crawled under the covers during the night to pour the greasy liquid on the pitch. Then, after hearing that Kent had beaten Surrey by an innings and briefly regained the lead in the table, Worcester dismissed Glamorgan for a second time in the match – for 103 in the space of 130 minutes – to win the game by an innings and 76 runs.

In the shortened morning session, Worcester's last four wickets added another 43 runs, giving them a lead of 179 – made possible by Hick's majestic 197 yesterday, which helped Worcester to their all-important fourth batting point with 17 balls to spare. Glamorgan saw out the final few minutes of that session, but in the afternoon the home attack were in full stride.

Newport produced one of his most devastating spells of the whole campaign. In 26 balls he collected five wickets for one run as Glamorgan slumped from 58 for three to 80 for nine. A last-wicket flourish produced 23 runs and briefly delayed the end, but it was all over when Leatherdale caught Bastien, appropriately under the shadow of the ground's famous spreading chestnut trees.

County Championship Notts v Yorks: 17 September

Stephenson's double and remarkable all-round feat

By Doug Ibbotson, at Trent Bridge

FRANKLYN STEPHENSON, Nottinghamshire's West Indian all-rounder, climaxed a prolific season for the county in their last match by completing the double of 1,000 runs and 100 wickets – a feat hitherto achieved only by Richard Hadlee, in 1984, since the first-class programme was reduced in 1969.

Stephenson, having already taken 11 wickets in the match, against Yorkshire, to raise his total to 125, followed a first-innings 111 – his first hundred of the season for Notts – by scoring a brilliant 117 (20 fours, two sixes). It brought him a final aggregate of 1,016. He also became the first player since George Hirst in 1906 to score two hundreds and take 10 wickets (4-105, all 7 for 117) in a match.

Alas for Notts, needing 425 to achieve their ninth victory, it was not enough, and Yorkshire cruised to victory by 127 runs.

Franklyn Stephenson, remarkable individual performance.

First Test Fifth day: 20 September

Australia threaten to quit Pakistan tour

By Qamar Ahmed, in Karachi

AUSTRALIA'S tour of Pakistan is in danger of being abandoned after their defeat by an innings and 188 runs in the first Test at the National Stadium, Karachi.

The players, who had a meeting on Sunday after manager Colin Egar, a former Test umpire, had complained to the Pakistani Cricket Board about the state of the pitch and some of the umpiring decisions given by Mahboob Shah, are united in wanting to end the tour.

Allan Border, the Australian captain, said: "I do not believe it is worth our time coming here unless there is a change. The wicket was ridiculous and the decisions given against us were atrocious.

"We were never in with a chance," he added, after his team were bowled out for 116 in the second innings, 90 minutes into the fifth day.

Bobby Simpson, the Australian coach, praised his team for showing discipline on the field. "We did not get one leg-before decision, but Pakistan got six. It seems strange," he said.

The Pakistanis have dismissed complaints about the pitch, saying it was the same for both teams, and Pakistan had managed to score 469 for nine declared (Miandad 211). Intikhab Alam, the Pakistan manager, said his side had won fairly and squarely: "We have outclassed the Australians."

[The Pakistan Board refused to bow down to the tourists' appeal to have umpire Shah removed and he was duly appointed for the second Test. The tour continued, and Australia came close to squaring the series in the third Test.]

7 October

Farce over, as TCCB cancel winter tour to India

By Charles Randall, from Lord's

ENGLAND'S cricket authorities brought an end to the farcical India tour waiting game when they officially called the tour off in London today. It was cancelled after a spell of political shadow boxing with the Indian Board of Control which had lasted for four weeks, since the Indian government's refusal to grant visas to eight of England's 16-strong tour party.

The Test and County Cricket Board announced their decision at Lord's, making India the first full International Board tour to be called off since the South Africans rejected Basil D'Oliveira's selection in 1968.

Alan Smith, the TCCB chief executive, said in a statement: "The TCCB is disappointed that members of its team, which was selected entirely in accordance with unanimously agreed International Cricket Conference rules, should find themselves ineligible for visas to enter India. This is particularly regrettable noting the impending special meeting of the ICC in January."

Second Test Fifth day: 6 December

W.Indies continue Australian cruise

By Peter Deeley, in Perth

THE SKIES are bluer, the sun much hotter and the wickets harder, but the West Indies' voyage around Australia is still beginning to look like a re-run of their triumphal English summer. They are now two up in the series following their 169-run defeat of a home side who are still at least a couple of players short of the quality of their opponents.

The Australian captain, Allan Border, rightly takes some comfort from the big improvement in their showing over the disaster of Brisbane, but he recognised – as did all the England captains in the summer – that it was the relentless pressure of the West Indies' four-man pace attack that was the cornerstone of their success.

Viv Richards, unyielding top-dog that he is, had batted on for 20 minutes in the morning to leave Australia a target of 404 runs (an echo of Headingley, 1948) in a maximum of 85 overs.

That short spell allowed Merv Hughes to collect his 13th wicket in the match, a feat surpassed by only three other Australians, and to sew up the Man of the Match award (5-130, 8-87).

1989

20-21 Jan Tamil Nadu amass a score of 912-6 dec in the Ranji Trophy, including 300s from Venkat Raman (313) and Arjan Kripal Singh (303 not) and a 52-run penalty incurred by Goa.

6 Mar Raman breaks a 44-year-old record by 10 runs, with 1,018 runs in the Ranji Trophy championship.

9 Apr Malcolm Marshall passes Lance Gibbs' West Indies record of 309 wickets, in the Bridgetown Test against India.

4-5 May Franklyn Stephenson takes 13-75 (7-38, 6-37) as Notts beat Yorks by 10 wickets; 32 wickets fall on first day (Yorks 92 and 61-3, Notts 86).

8-13 Jun Having been put in by David Gower, Australia amass 601-7 dec at Headingley and win by 210 runs.

13 Jun Paul Pollard and Tim Robinson put on their second 200 opening stand of the match for Notts v Kent at Trent Bridge, only the second instance in first-class cricket – but Kent win.

24 Jun Harassed England captain David Gower causes a stir by leaving a Press conference during the Lord's Test to attend the theatre.

6 Jul Australian captain Allan Border passes 8,000 Test runs during the Edgbaston Test.

25 Jul Essex are docked 25 points for a substandard pitch (Southend) and it costs them the County Championship.

1 Aug Franklyn Stephenson takes 15-106 (7-59, 8-47) for Notts v Essex at Trent Bridge.

11 Aug Wicket-keeper Warren Hegg equals the world record with 11 catches in a match for Lancs at Derby.

16 Aug An England XI embarrassingly lose to a Holland XI by 3 runs in a 55-over match at Amstelveen (but they later win a 2nd match by 98 runs).

22 Aug Alec Stewart also takes a record 11 catches, for Surrey at Leics.

29 Aug At the end of the 6th Test, Australians Mark Taylor and Terry Alderman finish with 839 runs and 41 wickets, respectively, in the rubber.

15 Nov John Hampshire and John Holder stand for the first time as 'third country' umpires, at Karachi, the first of four trouble-free Tests between Pakistan and India, and Sachin Tendulkar makes his début at 16 years 205 days, the youngest Indian and 3rd youngest ever.

TEST SERIES

Australia in England
A 4, D 1
West Indies in Australia
WI 3, A 1, D 1
Pakistan in New Zealand
Abandoned 1, D 2
India in West Indies
WI 3, D 1
India in Pakistan
Drawn 4
New Zealand in Australia
Drawn 1
Sri Lanka in Australia
A 1, D 1

Fourth Test Final day: 30 January

Born-again Border calms the euphoria

By Robert Steen, in Sydney

ALLAN BORDER tried to cool the euphoria which followed Australia's seven-wicket win over the West Indies in the fourth Test, pleading with his born-again admirers to reserve their hyperbole until after the forthcoming tour of England.

It was half an hour after lunch on the final day that Australia completed their victory. The exultant dressing-room scenes mirrored a profound sense of national relief. But Border, whose unheralded spinning talents turned the tide away from the West Indies after three successive lectures in the brutal science of modern Test success, refused to make any rash predictions.

Border said he recalled all too vividly how another Australian win four years earlier, against another dominant Caribbean combination, on the eve of another Ashes tour, was hailed as a corner turned. Australia duly relinquished the Ashes by a 3-1 margin.

Border, for whom the series had hitherto been rather less than wondrous, topped and tailed proceedings today, initially securing a target of 80 by having Ambrose caught at short leg in the third over, and ultimately sweeping Hooper for the concluding boundary. That first contribution brought his match figures to 11 for 96 (7-46, 4-50). No other Australian captain has taken as many in a Test, and Border himself had never taken five wickets before in a first-class match.

Border, the occasional bowler who took 11 West Indies wickets.

30 January

Amarnath refuses to pay fine

From India

DILIP VENGSARKAR'S troubled reign as India's captain will continue for a tour of the West Indies, but legal and disciplinary problems will influence the tour party selection from a squad of 21.

The latest problem comes with Mohinder Amarnath taking the cricket board to court. He is refusing to pay a fine of £760 after he described the national selectors as "a bunch of jokers" for dropping him, and Vengsarkar was reappointed only after he had apologised for kicking down the stumps following a dispute with an umpire in a local match.

Navjot Singh Sidhu, a batsman accused of beating a motorist to death after a traffic accident, could only tour if a Punjab court lifted travel restrictions, and Maninder Singh, a left-arm spinner, and Manoj Prabhakar, an all-rounder, found their selection in doubt for the New Zealand tour following a brawl during a match.

Third Test Final day: 28 February

Pakistan lay blame on umpires after draw

By Duncan Latham, in Auckland

RIVAL captains Imran Khan and John Wright yesterday joined in the umpiring row after the third Test between New Zealand and Pakistan ended in a draw at Auckland. Pakistan's manager Intikhab Alam had already claimed that "five or six" decisions went against his side. Some, he said, were based on incompetence, others on bias.

After the Test, which left the series a stalemate, Imran accused one of the umpires of being scared to make decisions. He felt incompetence, not cheating, was the cause of the problems. "In my biased opinion – because I wanted Pakistan to win – there were a lot of decisions where we could not see the benefit of doubt that was given to the batsman. The crowd abused us. When we appealed they yelled: 'There go the Paki cheats.' It hasn't been my favourite Test," he said.

Wright criticised Intikhab for his earlier outburst: "I am of the opinion that first you play the game, then there are certain channels where you express your views." He believes neutral umpires should be introduced with the power to discipline players for dissent. However, Wright backed the performance of New Zealand umpires, saying they did the job to the best of their ability.

As for the cricket, New Zealand, having followed on, finished 114 runs behind with seven wickets left. Pakistan's 616-5 dec was the highest in a series with New Zealand, Miandad's 271 the highest individual score and his sixth Test 200. He finished with a series average of 194.50 (only two Tests played). Imran Khan completed the 3,000 runs/300 wickets Test double, and Richard Hadlee broke down with Achilles tendon trouble four short of 400 Test wickets.

7 March

Dexter in at No.1 for a brave new era

By Peter Deeley

ENGLISH CRICKET yesterday found the courage necessary to move the game forward into a new era, with the appointment of Ted Dexter as chairman of a new Test selection body to be known as the 'England committee'. The threatened 'revolt of the rump' by some county chairmen against Mr Dexter's appointment fizzled out – and in the end he was appointed on a show of hands by a substantial majority.

More important than new faces, however, was the acceptance by the 19-strong Test and County Cricket Board of a different structure for finding, developing and keeping genuine playing talent.

The England team manager, Micky Stewart, who expressed his own enthusiasm at his future partnership with Dexter, was probably speaking for most when he said how pleased he was that "the traditional system has changed".

One man who has been given new powers in the shake-up is Alan Smith. As well as continuing to be the Board's paid chief executive, he now has a seat and a say in team selection as an ex-officio member.

Mr Dexter becomes chairman of the new committee, and he and Mr Smith are joined by Mr Stewart and the chairman of the Board's cricket committee, Ossie Wheatley.

When the England committee have chosen the new captain, he will take part in the selection process. But Mr Dexter refused to be drawn on whether he would go for Leicestershire's David Gower, whom he is known to favour.

B & H Cup Quarter-finals: 30 May

Hussain so close to undermining flimsy Somerset

By Charles Randall, at Taunton

NASSER HUSSAIN, a Durham geology undergraduate, hit a pedigree century for Combined Universities, but it was Peter Roebuck, an Oxford graduate, who stepped in to prevent more Benson and Hedges cricket history being written at Taunton.

Roebuck, who scored 102 in Somerset's 55-over total of 252 for six, coaxed the county professionals to a three-run victory by holding a catch and taking two wickets when all seemed lost. Somerset staggered rather than marched into tomorrow's semi-final draw, and the narrow margin reflected the suffocating tightness of one of the great limited-overs matches.

Universities needed 36 off the last seven overs, with seven wickets standing, including Crawley with a broken hand, but Roebuck held a catch at point to dismiss the gallant Longley (49), who had piled on 114 in 16 overs with Hussain, his Durham team-mate.

Roebuck's gentle occasional seamers were then called up in desperation for four overs. Universities needed nine off the final over, with Man of the Match Hussain still in. Six balls and three wickets later, the students had learned a thing or two about cricket. Roebuck's day had begun with 97 before lunch, and his day ended theatrically when Boiling failed to hit the final delivery for six.

Somerset's score was kept under 280 only by the Universities' superb fielding, with Hussain again outstanding. They are the first university side to reach this stage, and Atherton's all-round ability has shone out as a batsman, leg-break bowler and captain.

B & H Cup Final: 15 July

Hero Hemmings' last-ball four grabs the Cup

By Tony Lewis, at Lord's

NOTTINGHAMSHIRE won their first Benson & Hedges Cup with a four struck by Eddie Hemmings off the last ball of their 55 overs this evening, after Essex, who had scored 243 for seven, appeared to be heading for another one-day triumph.

When, in the middle of a tense, sunny evening, three Notts wickets fell for 14 runs in 21 balls, including two in two balls, it seemed their cause had died. But in the end they needed 16 runs to win off the last 12 balls - and four to win off the last ball.

Essex could count on fine performances, especially from Alan Lilley, who came in at four for one and hit an unbeaten 95 in 144 balls, and John Lever, who took two for 43. It was Lever who sent down the last ball, which Hemmings, improbably, square-drove for four even though it pitched on middle and leg.

Tim Robinson (86), the Notts captain, played the most inspired innings of the match. He went to the crease at five for one, then lost Chris Broad, but with Paul Johnson (54) led the fightback with strokes both subtle and brutal.

But when Johnson was bowled off his boot, Randall needlessly ran Robinson out and Franklyn Stephenson holed out first ball, Notts were suddenly 162 for five. Randall (49) and Kevin Evans (26), who had already contributed a valuable two for 28, then put on 59 together in nine overs. The stand kept Notts' hopes alive, and it was left to French and Hemmings to scramble the nine runs needed off the last over.

County Championship Notts v Somerset: 21 July

Historic feat by Cook, but Somerset lose

By Peter Deeley, at Trent Bridge

IN DAYS of old this game, which saw a 78-year-old cricketing record equalled, would have been billed 'Eleven of Notts versus Mr James Cook'. For opener Cook became the second man in history to carry his bat while scoring a hundred in each innings. The irony is that Nottinghamshire won the match, by an innings and 67 runs.

After his 120 not out on the first day, Cook returned to the crease late on the second afternoon and today again saw his team-mates whittled out in demoralising fashion while he made an undefeated 131. In between, Notts made 471 for seven declared.

In the match, Cook batted for nine hours and five minutes and scored 251 out of the 404 Somerset mustered. But at Taunton there should be a searching inquest into the team performance. In the first innings, seven contributed a total of 27 runs; in the second, the last seven added just three!

Jimmy Cook: outstanding feat.

Fourth Test Final day: 1 August

Formalities concluded before the rebuilding

By Peter Deeley, at Old Trafford

THE massive defection of England players past and present to South Africa this winter may have overshadowed Australia's historic Ashes-winning victory. But, as viewed by the England selectors, the clouds that hovered all day above the ground will have been tinged with silver linings. It means that Ted Dexter can now clean the stables of the tired old failures who have brought one victory in the last 24 Tests, without being seen as a hatchet man.

The Australian dressing-room must have viewed the comings-and-goings next door with a certain amount of déjà vu. After all, they have been down the South African cul-de-sac themselves, and it has taken years of rebuilding to reach their present eminence.

Appropriately, the evening sun shone on Allan Border as the captain, surrounded by his colleagues, sat on the balcony enjoying the final, glorious moments. Twice he has lost Ashes series in this country, but the huge margin of Australia's ascendancy - three wins in four - will have wiped away those black images. Soon after David Boon had swept Nick Cook for the four runs that brought victory by nine wickets with 8.1 overs of the final hour remaining, Mr Dexter and David Gower both went to the Australian dressing-room to offer their congratulations.

There are few crumbs of comfort for England in their dark hour, but it cannot be a coincidence that the three men who have performed most ably in this game for the home side have all spurned the mighty rand and made themselves available for England this winter. After Robin Smith's fine hundred and Angus Fraser's honourable three for 95 on earlier days, Jack Russell today produced an epic maiden century (128 not out) and a stand of 142 with Emburey (64) that only emphasised how badly the senior batsmen had performed.

They will provide the nucleus of the new side, possibly under a leader such as Graham Gooch, before the tour of Australia next winter.

2 August

Gatting backhander a knock to Stewart

By Peter Deeley

THE man who comes out with least credit from his inclusion in the rebel tour party to South Africa, announced yesterday, is Mike Gatting, the former England captain, who will lead the side. In recent weeks he first excused himself from England's winter tour to the West Indies for family reasons, then criticised the money he could earn from the one-day tournament in India because he considered the sum "totally unrealistic".

Yet at the start of the season Gatting, 32, had put his name forward as a contender for the England captaincy. Further, when a shoulder injury made David Gower doubtful for the second Ashes Test, the England selectors indicated that Gatting would be their stand-in choice. Micky Stewart, the England team manager, said only last weekend that he would try to convince him to change his mind about his availability for England this winter. These developments must leave Mr Stewart - a man with fiercely patriotic instincts - feeling rather sore.

Gatting's emergence as a force dated from being made vice-captain to David Gower on the 1984-85 tour of India. With Gower's sacking in 1986, Gatting took over and led England on their victorious tour of Australia the following winter. He returned home almost a public hero, and was awarded the OBE in 1987.

He unexpectedly lost a series to Pakistan at home, and narrowly lost the World Cup one-day final to Australia in Calcutta. Then came the infamous 'cheating' confrontation with umpire Shakoor Rana in Pakistan, after which he was most lucky to survive the sack. It required an infelicitous evening with a barmaid for that.

Nevertheless, with Mr Stewart's backing, Gatting at one stage must have thought he still might regain the England captaincy. But with this decision, he has put himself out of Test reckoning for all time.

Openers Taylor (left) and Marsh, still together at the end of the day.

Fifth Test First day: 10 August

Record-breakers heap the agony on England

By Peter Deeley, at Trent Bridge

HUMILIATION heaped upon disaster were England's iron rations today as the Australian opening pair of Geoff Marsh and Mark Taylor entered the record books with Australia's highest-ever Ashes opening partnership. After precisely five hours together, Taylor lofted Hemmings into the empty spaces of the onside for a boundary which passed the previous high-water mark for the first wicket of 244.

That record had been set by Bobby Simpson and Bill Lawry at Adelaide in 1966. Fittingly, both were here to witness the achievement: Simpson is coach of this blossoming Australian side and Lawry is a television commentator. Taylor, who is proving something of a phenomenon on this tour, had already reached his second century of the series to be followed 25 minutes later by Marsh. For both Taylor, 141 not out at the close, and Marsh, undefeated on 125, it was their highest Test score. They now stand only 22 short of the most runs ever scored for the first wicket by either country in these games: Hobbs and Rhodes combined to make 323 at Melbourne in 1911-12. In a remarkable day, the record books also show that Taylor and Marsh are the first pair to bat though a whole day in any Test in this country.

[Taylor (219) and Marsh (138) continued to pile on the agony in a record stand of 329. Australia declared at 602-6 and won by an innings and 180.]

County Championship Worcs v Somerset: 27 August

Hick century makes impossible look easy

By D.J.Rutnagur, at Worcester

SOMERSET were given another reminder today that there is no legislating for the brilliance of Graeme Hick. For after setting Worcestershire the near-impossible task of scoring 300 in 57 overs, they saw the championship leaders reach the target with five balls to spare. Hick remained unbeaten, with 136 off 120 balls, hitting 10 fours and three sixes.

Hick took up the chase in the 16th over, with Worcs on 59 for one. Tim Curtis (84) claimed a shade more than an even share of their second-wicket partnership of 128, which spanned 25 overs. One could sense, though, that the genie would pop out of the bottle at just the precise moment.

At the start of the last hour, with 147 runs needed, the assault began in earnest. With wickets falling at the other end, Hick played with increasing authority. Having taken 68 balls to reach 50, he reached his 100 off only another 20, and went on to win the match with a majestic inevitability.

[Four days later Worcs retained their Championship title, although the eventual margin over Essex, who lost 25 points for a bad pitch at Southend, was only 6 points.]

NatWest Trophy Final: 2 September

Young Neil Smith swats a mighty six in the last over.

Young Smith's six of the best: Warwicks grab Trophy in last over

By Tony Lewis, at Lord's

IN THE gloom of Lord's tonight, Warwickshire, who have had a rampaging second half to the season, won the NatWest Trophy, albeit with only two balls to spare.

Middlesex, for the loss of five wickets, had set them a target of 211 - and they reached it with four wickets in hand. That sounds cool and controlled. It was not. It was frantic, fortunate, yet faintly heroic.

In the pursuit of runs under grey evening skies, Asif Din (34 not out) and Dermot Reeve (42) put on 69 from 94 balls. This helped Warwicks to get to a last-over 'bang'.

When they needed nine off the last five balls, with Simon Hughes bowling, young Neil Smith got a village club to the ball in a wide arc of swing - and the ball disappeared for six over long-off.

It was hard luck on Middlesex. But it is time for the resurrection of Warwickshire. Under Bob Cottam, their coach, and Andy Lloyd, a bright, intelligent captain, they have won this late-season title for the first time since 1968.

It was Lloyd's introduction of his optional sixth bowler, Neil Smith, son of MJK, the former Warwicks and England captain, that stopped Middlesex in their tracks. Not only did he bowl Haynes (50), but he did a fine containing job at a difficult stage, and finished with one for 33 in nine overs. Reeve, too, bowled economically (12-4-27-1) and won the Man of the Match award.

Warwicks struggled from the very start, scoring only 17 in the first 10 overs and losing Moles to Angus Fraser, the only bowler to take more than one wicket in the match (2-30). Cowans (1-23) also kept on top of the Warwickshire batsmen. But when Lloyd (34) helped strike Ellcock for 11 in one over, the impetus began to build up.

Paul Smith (24) struck the unfortunate Ellcock for three successive fours, and Humpage (36) also picked up the tempo. Then came the Reeve/Asif stand, and when Neil Smith (15 not out) went to the wicket, 20 runs were needed off 16 balls. Asif Din paddled the ball and scampered. Smith came and smote. Between them, they clinched an unlikely victory.

Only Test Final day: 28 November

Greatbatch 146 saves defiant New Zealand

By Alan Shiell, in Perth

MARK GREATBATCH claimed a proud place on New Zealand cricket's honour roll with one of the game's greatest innings at the WACA Ground against Australia. The tall, powerful left-hander's 146 not out, a monumental feat of courage, stamina and concentration extending for 10hr 55min, enabled New Zealand to force a draw with Australia in a gripping finish to the one-off Test.

New Zealand finished with a second innings total of 322 for seven, 32 runs ahead of Australia's first innings of 521 for nine declared - made, after being sent in, thanks largely to David Boon's belligerent 200 and Dean Jones's exhilarating 99.

Australia had appeared to be assured of their sixth win in nine Tests this year when New Zealand resumed today at 168 for four, still needing 122 to avoid an innings defeat. An Australian victory looked even more likely when Merv Hughes dismissed Jeff Crowe and Ian Smith with successive balls in the 12th over of the day, and also removed Chris Cairns soon after lunch, leaving New Zealand on 234 for seven.

However, Greatbatch and fellow left-hander Martin Snedden (whose 33 not out beat by one his highest score in 17 previous Tests) defied everything the desperate Australian bowlers could hurl at them for the remaining 48.3 overs in an unforgettable eighth-wicket partnership of 88 in 202 minutes.

Greatbatch had also top-scored in New Zealand's first innings – a 221-minute 76 off 231 deliveries – and he reached his 100 in 7hr 42min, the slowest first-class century ever in Australia *[until overtaken a few days later by G.J. Shipperd of Tasmania]*.

The 1990s

The nineties: Clive Rice leads South Africa back into the fold of international cricket (above), one result of four-day county matches (inset) and farewell to Botham (opposite).

MAJOR innovations and significant events took place in the early 1990s, the most momentous perhaps being the return of South Africa to the international scene after more than twenty years in the wilderness. So, with the granting of Test status to Zimbabwe, the number of Test-playing countries has been dramatically increased from seven to nine.

The number of first-class counties was also augmented, for the first time in over seventy years, the introduction of Durham in 1992 increasing the complement to eighteen. At the same time, the TCCB authorities took positive steps to reform county cricket, and 1993 saw the first County Championship to comprise solely four-day matches – an experiment scheduled for at least two years. The Benson & Hedges zonal rounds were done away with and the format of the Sunday League changed. The most eye-catching innovation, however, was the introduction of 'Packer-like' coloured uniforms – each county vying to outdo the next in garishness – for the Sunday League, although this has not gone down too well with the public.

The Laws of the game have come under scrutiny in more ways than one. Important for scorers – on and off the field – is the change in the penalty for a no-ball, increased to two runs (extras), to be added to any score the batsman makes from the delivery. The introduction in some Test series of a 'third umpire' – off the field, with the TV replay to assist with run-outs and other close decisions – has not found universal approval, although in its own context has apparently worked. A referee has also been introduced for Tests, again off the field, to reinforce the authority of the umpires. And there have been experiments with neutral, or 'third country', umpires for Tests, too.

There has been no lack of argument, on and off the field, the chief controversy being the ball-tampering accusations thrown largely at Pakistan's quickies. Allan Lamb, fined more for trying to expose it than Surrey were for perpetrating it, won his battle in court (or, rather, out of it). But this one seems likely to run and run.

The most sinister trend, however, has been a marked deterioration in behaviour of players on the field, necessitating the above-mentioned, almost panic-induced, experiments with umpiring. 'Sledging, despite its negation of what all cricket – or any other sport – should stand for, was with us long before the nineties, and it's about time it stopped. Neither are ludicrous and clamorous appeals to the umpire anything new, although something must be done about the intimidation of umpires in this respect. But dissent from umpires' decisions, almost unheard of previously, has appeared alarmingly at the highest levels, and to see the authorities pussy-footing around when firm action is essential leaves genuine cause for concern.

Sadly, too, the early 1990s saw the end of many of the great heroes of modern cricket, giants of the eighties all retiring from the game within two or three years of each other: the great all-rounders, Botham and Imran Khan, the great fast bowlers who could also bat a bit, Marshall and Hadlee (will New Zealand ever be the same again?), and the batting idols, Viv Richards and David Gower, the latter in his own charming and affable way but amid clouds of controversy. They leave a huge vacuum in the game, and if cricket is to flourish it has to be filled.

1990

26 Jan Pakistan players refuse to accept umpire Robin Bailhache's direction to captain Ramiz Raja to take off bowler Mushtaq Ahmed after the requisite warnings for following through onto the pitch in the match against Victoria, and manager Intikhab Alam, having been summoned to the wicket, walks off with them. A 'compromise' is reached when Ramiz insists he was unaware of the final warning, and Mushtaq is allowed to continue.

14 Apr West Indies captain Viv Richards climbs into the Press box at St John's, during the last Test, to remonstrate with a journalist about a newspaper article in England, while his side take the field without him.

28 Apr Alan Fordham (206 not) and Allan Lamb (235) put on 393 in 100 overs for the 3rd wicket against Yorks at Headingley, a record stand for Northants.

3 May Jimmy Cook makes 313 not out for Somerset at Cardiff, the highest innings scored in Wales, and is only 9 runs short of Viv Richards' Somerset record when Tavaré declares.

5 May Graham Gooch (215) and Paul Prichard (245) put on 403 for the 2nd wicket against Leics at Chelmsford, a record Essex stand.

10 Jul Sir Richard Hadlee bows out of first-class cricket, having taken 5-53 at Edgbaston in England's 2nd innings, and a record 431 Test wickets; England record their first win over NZ in 7 years and their first home series win against any country since 1985.

27 Aug Graham Gooch finishes with 752 runs against India, a record for a 3-match series.

1 Sep Phil DeFreitas takes 5-26 to help Lancs beat Northants by 7 wickets in the NatWest final and win their second one-day trophy of the season, having beaten Worcs by 69 runs in the B & H final.

21 Sep Hants reach their 4th-innings target of 445 to beat Glos at Southampton with an over and 2 wickets to spare, starting the day at 5-0.

25 Nov West Indies square the series against Pakistan in 3 days and only 180 overs, winning a low-scoring 2nd Test at Faisalabad by 7 wickets.

27 Nov Yorks vote to relax 'Yorkshire only' rule.

6 Dec Durham are invited to become a first-class county.

TEST SERIES

England in West Indies
WI 2, E 1, D 1, Ab 1
New Zealand in England
E 1, D 2
India in England
E 1, D 2
Pakistan in Australia
A 1, D 2
India in New Zealand
NZ 1, D 2
Australia in New Zealand
New Zealand 1
New Zealand in Pakistan
Pakistan 3
West Indies in Pakistan
P 1, WI 1, D 1
Sri Lanka in India
India 1

First Test Third day: 4 February

New Zealand joy as Hadlee takes 400th Test wicket

By D J Rutnagur, in Christchurch

WITHIN a few minutes of Richard John Hadlee's slipping an off-cutter through the gap between bat and pad to rock Sanjay Manjrekar's leg stump this afternoon, the public address system at Lancaster Park came alive to convey to Hadlee, stationed at gulley, a message of congratulation from the New Zealand Prime Minister, Geoffrey Palmer. That was the measure of the great all-rounder's accomplishment – the first player from any country to take 400 Test wickets.

It came on Hadlee's 80th appearance, 26 years after Freddie Trueman made history with his 300th Test wicket for England. The crowd – among them his father Walter, a former New Zealand captain – stood and applauded for three minutes.

The Indians, who followed on 295 runs behind on the third day, forgot their desperate plight and joined in the rejoicing. Their captain, Azharuddin, shook Hadlee's hand as he walked in to bat next, while their cricket manager, Bishen Bedi, rushed out to congratulate him. Later, Mr Bedi said: "I hope Richard is knighted."

Hadlee, 38, who had rocked the foundations of the Indian first innings on Saturday with three for 45, took another wicket before the close, when India stood at 210 for five, still 85 behind.

[Hadlee wound up the Indian innings next day, finishing with 4-69, and New Zealand won by 10 wickets. He became 'Sir Richard' in the Birthday Honours' list.]

'Rebel' English tour to South Africa: 4 February

'Heroic' Gatting lashes out

By Tony Millard, in Pietermaritzburg

MIKE GATTING put the traumas of yesterday's anti-tour demonstration behind him and led his men from the front with a typically belligerent innings of 71 on the second day of the match against a South African Invitation XI.

Gatting's part in yesterday's confrontation, in which he went to meet protest leaders and was subjected to verbal and physical abuse by anti-apartheid demonstrators, was described by Dr Ali Bacher, managing director of the South African Cricket Union and the tour organiser, as "one of the most heroic sporting achievements off the field I have ever seen".

Although Gatting, who with his fellow tourists has incurred a 5-year Test ban, has continued to say that he is in South Africa simply to play cricket, he has willingly met opponents of the tour to hear their points of view.

[The English XI lost the first 'Test' but, as a result of harassment and demonstrations at all the tourists' matches, SACU compromised with the opposition, the National Sports Congress, and cancelled the rest of the tour except for four one-day games. The second leg of the tour, due to take place in 1991, was also cancelled.]

First Test Final day: 1 March

Sun shines down on England's cricketers

By Peter Deeley, in Kingston

ENGLAND took only two hours today to round off their first Test victory against the West Indies for 16 years. After losing the fourth day's play because of rain when the home side were on the verge of defeat, the 20-1 underdogs completed a nine-wicket win in brilliantly sunny conditions at Sabina Park, Jamaica.

The final moments, as England reached the 41 runs they needed, were watched with elation by several former England cricketers, among them Sir Leonard Hutton, Alec Bedser and David Gower. They could look back on a Test England had dominated from the start, having shocked the cricketing world on the first day by dismissing West Indies for 164, thanks largely to Angus Fraser's five for 28 in 20 overs.

Devon Malcolm, on the island of his birth, bowls West Indies skipper Viv Richards.

Lamb was then England's batting hero, with 132, and England led by exactly 200. Then Malcolm, with four wickets, and Small, with three, left West Indies 29 ahead at the end of the third day with two wickets left.

The weather almost saved the home side, but this morning the game started on time. Small soon sent Walsh's middle stump hurtling back some three yards and Patterson was run out. England lost skipper Gooch before Wayne Larkins struck the winning run.

Third Test Final day: 28 March

Deluge prevents England going 2–0 up

By Peter Deeley, in Port of Spain

England, on the verge of their second triumph of the series, could only bemoan their ill-luck in Trinidad when rain swept across the ground at lunchtime with 78 runs needed from their last seven wickets for victory over West Indies. Out of a clear blue sky, a ferocious storm saturated all parts of the playing area.

Play was resumed after an early tea, with 30 overs scheduled, but as a result of delaying tactics by the West Indies and then bad light, 13 remained unbowled, and England, who had lost two more wickets, were still 31 runs short.

It had all started so well in the morning, Malcolm (4-60 and 6-77) claiming his 10th wicket with his eighth delivery to close the home side's innings. The West Indian bowlers then flung everything into a desperate, and seemingly unavailing, counter-attack, sending down 22 bouncers, Ian Bishop unloosing four in the first over.

The introduction of Moseley for the eighth over made England realise they would have to earn their victory. He quickly had Larkins caught at the wicket and then retired Gooch to hospital with a bouncer that had the England captain reeling in agony, with, we learned later, a broken bone in his left hand.

The tension seemed to affect some of the players. Haynes, the West Indies skipper in place of the unfit Richards, and both Allan Lamb and Alec Stewart, who were together at 73 for one when play was stopped, appeared to be engaging in strong verbal debates. As light showers turned to heavy rain just before the lunch interval, Lamb was reluctant to leave the field, but local knowledge showed the umpires' decision to be a wise one.

This is supposed to be Trinidad's driest period of the year, one in which we have already had two one-day internationals washed out. If you ever think of coming here for a holiday, pack an umbrella along with your swimsuit.

Fourth Test Fourth day: 9 April

BBC man angers fans in Barbados

By Peter Deeley, in Bridgetown

Dujon (left) has the ball and Richards begins his 'little jig'.

THE VOICE of Barbados radio station says it has been "deluged" with protests about comments made by the BBC cricket correspondent Christopher Martin-Jenkins concerning the dismissal of England batsman Rob Bailey during the fourth Test on Sunday. Mr Martin-Jenkins told listeners today that he was "extremely sorry" if he had caused offence, adding: "But I cannot apologise for saying what I think is right."

Voice of Barbados relays bulletins from the BBC World Service each day. In one of these, Mr Martin-Jenkins had suggested that umpire Lloyd Barker had been put under pressure by the West Indies fielders into changing his mind and giving Bailey out caught. Mr Martin-Jenkins went on a live talk-in programme today and told his critics: "It appeared to me that umpire Barker changed his mind under pressure from a very orchestrated appeal." But he refuted suggestions by his Barbados interviewer that he was accusing umpire Barker of "cheating".

"I didn't say umpires cheat," he said. "I said players get very close to cheating when they start putting pressure on umpires to change their minds. I repeat again that I didn't criticise umpire Barker. I did criticise the players."

West Indies skipper Viv Richards, the man at whom the criticism was obviously directed, said: "It was a correct decision by the umpire. I heard a noise, I appealed and normally when I do my little jig it is very ceremonial. It means that, hopefully, I am celebrating him [the batsman] being out. But I did not exert any unfair pressure on the umpire."

The leading West Indies cricket writer Tony Cozier wrote in the Barbados Daily Nation today: "At the instant, it [the decision] appeared an umpiring afterthought. Bailey left, indicating it had deflected from his hip, not his bat."

England face a mountain of a task tomorrow, with little chance of success. Set to make 356 to win, they had been reduced to 15 for three at the close.

County Championship Surrey v Lancs: 7 May

Lancashire amass 863, but miss the record

By Charles Randall, at the Oval

LANCASHIRE scored the second-highest total in a County Championship match when they made 863 runs in their first innings against Surrey at the Oval. The total fell 24 runs short of the record of 887 runs made by Yorkshire against Warwickshire 94 years ago.

It was the third-highest team score in home Test and county matches. The highest score remains England's 903 for 7 declared in the 1938 Oval Test against Australia.

Neil Fairbrother, 26, a left-hander, was the principal contributor, hitting 366, which beat by two runs the previous best at the Oval, by Len Hutton in the 1938 Test. He was caught off the last ball before lunch, having batted for 500 minutes and hit five sixes and 47 fours off 407 deliveries. Michael Atherton hit 191 and Mendis 102.

The flatter-seamed ball and the Oval's fast, hard pitch helped Fairbrother up to 12th in the first-class world list of individual scores, though he remains behind Graeme Hick (405) and A.C.MacLaren, another Lancastrian, who made 424 in 1895.

Lancashire reached 745 before their fourth wicket fell, but then suffered a relative collapse.

The match ended in a draw, Surrey having declared at 707 for 9 (Ian Greig 291), which stands as the 10th-highest county match total. When Patrick Patterson chipped a catch to mid-wicket to end the innings, the sides had equalled the best Championship aggregate of 1,570 set by Essex and Kent. Surrey's 80 for one in their second innings extended it to a new mark of 1,650 runs.

Fairbrother: 366.

[On the same day, Essex extended their first innings to 761-6 dec, their highest ever, and the match with Leicester at Chelmsford aggregated 1,530 runs.]

First Texaco Trophy International: 23 May

Greatbatch leads New Zealand to historic victory

By Peter Deeley, at Headingley

NEW ZEALAND showed strength in the face of adversity to accomplish the highest run chase in limited-overs international history — surpassing their own record — and beat England by four wickets with one ball to spare.

Beset by bowling injuries before the start, they demonstrated that their power lay in the depth of their batting. Mark Greatbatch, who is quickly coming to the fore as a player of quality, scored 102 not out, including two sixes, at almost a run a ball. He was instrumental in guiding the side through a difficult patch when they were consistently chasing more than seven runs an over near the end.

The 593 runs scored by the teams equals the highest aggregate in the 18 years of this 55-over competition. Greatbatch won the Man-of-the-Match award over England's Robin Smith, who had earlier scored a fine 128, his first one-day international century, in helping England to a total of 295 for six.

NatWest Trophy First round: 27 June

Records tumble as Rose and Tavaré put Devon to the sword

By D.J.Rutnagur, at Torquay

CENTURIES BY Chris Tavaré and Graham Rose, made with a degree of belligerence that could only be termed violent, led to Somerset's defeat of Devon by 346 runs, the most crushing ever recorded in the 60-overs competition and probably in any form of one-day cricket.

Rose's first century for Somerset (110), completed off 36 balls, with seven sixes and 10 fours, was the fastest, and Tavaré's unbeaten 162, off 130 balls, was his highest, in one-day cricket. Tavaré won the Man-of-the Match award from David Allen on the basis that he took control of the match while there was still some edge to Devon's opposition.

The margin of victory was not the only record to emerge from this one-sided contest. Somerset, who were put in, hit 413 for four, surpassing by nine runs the previous best, also against Devon, by Worcestershire four years ago.

Devon began to lose wickets even before they could contemplate any aggression and were bowled out for a paltry 67, Roland Lefebvre taking seven for 15.

Refuge Assurance League Glamorgan v Somerset: 22 July

Rose and Cook crush records and Glamorgan

By Edward Bevan, at Neath

SOMERSET smashed Sunday League records at The Gnoll today, scoring a massive 360 for three from 40 overs as Glamorgan's bowlers wilted under an onslaught from Graham Rose who scored 148 from only 69 deliveries.

They surpassed the 310 for five scored by Essex, also against Glamorgan, at Southend in 1983, with Rose scoring the fastest 50 (16 balls) and the fastest 100 (44 balls) in the Refuge Assurance League. The margin of defeat by 220 runs was also the highest recorded in the competition, surpassing the 190-run defeat suffered by Northants against Kent at Brackley in 1973.

Rose and opener Jimmy Cook (136 not out) shared a partnership of 223 in 19 overs – another competition record – as Cook passed Viv Richards' record Sunday League aggregate of 579 in 1975. Rose struck eight sixes and 17 fours.

Richards was the only Glamorgan batsman capable of emulating Rose, but after hitting three huge sixes, two off Rose, he was bowled for 36.

First Test Second day: 27 July

Triple centurion Gooch beaten by fatigue on 333

By Peter Deeley, at Lord's

WHEN this extraordinary day had long ended, people were still queuing for a replica scorecard, no doubt to be produced as evidence in years to come that they were at Lord's when Graham Gooch scored his memorable 333, the third highest Test innings by an England batsman.

There can rarely have been more tension in a rather one-sided day's Test play in recent history than that manifested by the near-capacity 20,000 crowd from the moment when the England captain, struggling against physical fatigue in mid-afternoon, finally reached his 300. It happened with the first ball after tea.

From that moment on, Gooch seemed to shrug off the effects of 10 hours at the crease and once more picked up the momentum with which he had earlier destroyed a very average Indian attack. He had his second wind and was now looking at the ultimate prize — Sobers's Test record 365.

He passed Jack Hobbs's 316 for Surrey in 1926 with a six off Shastri, before, on 324, drizzle intervened for a few tense minutes. But nine runs later, Gooch essayed a drive at Prabhakar and the ball nipped back between bat and pad, taking off-stump.

So this son of Leytonstone trudged wearily back up the pavilion steps to the Long Room, dwarfed by walls of applauding admirers, those legs suddenly feeling a good deal more than 37 years old. It was precisely 5pm, and Gooch had been at the centre of affairs since 11 o'clock the previous morning, collecting a mind-boggling 43 boundaries and three sixes along the way - and a host of records.

Graham Gooch, in majestic action during his historic 333.

First Test Third day: 28 July

Azharuddin takes fight to England

By Tony Lewis, at Lord's

A BRILLIANT century by Mohammed Azharuddin, full of natural strokes played without inhibition, sent India racing after England's 653 at Lord's. By the close, India's response was 376 for six, still requiring another 78 to avoid following on.

The innings glowed with fine strokes, and opener Ravi Shastri's fine 100 set the pattern. But the day belonged to his skipper, 117 not out at the close. Azharuddin made good-length, straight balls into blitzing boundaries by meeting them with a flowing bat on the up. His ninth Test century was the fastest scored in this country for nine years. Indeed, it was only one ball slower than Ian Botham's hundred in 86 balls against the Australians at Old Trafford in 1981.

[Azharuddin added only 4 to his score and it was left to Kapil Dev to save the follow-on in dramatic style when, with one wicket left and 24 needed, he obliged with four mighty sixes off four balls from Hemmings. But it was Gooch's match. With 123 in the 2nd innings, he became the first player to score 300 and 100 in the same first-class match and his 456 aggregate was second only to Hanif Mohammad's 499. England won by 247 runs.]

Tendulkar: Brilliant 100.

Second Test Final day: 14 August

Superb Tendulkar century breaks England's hearts

By Peter Deeley, at Old Trafford

TEENAGE wonder, boy prodigy: the superlatives trip off the tongue when it comes to measuring the worth of Sachin Tendulkar's maiden Test century, which steered India to safety this evening.

Yet these descriptions do not do full justice to the quality of the innings. In terms of technique and temperament it might have come from the bat of a man already hardened in the heat of battle, not from a stripling of a boy — no more than 5ft 4in tall — in only his ninth game for his country.

When he was 15, Tendulkar scored a century for Bombay in his maiden first-class innings. At 16, he became the youngest Indian Test player. Now, at the tender age of 17 years and 112 days, he has become the second-youngest century-maker in Test history (after Mushtaq Mohammed), with his 119 not out, compiled during a stay of three and three-quarter hours. When was the last time a youngster still at junior college - where Tendulkar is studying the arts — won a Test Man-of-the-Match award?

When Gooch declared at 320 for four, India needed 408 for victory in 90 overs. Tendulkar came in at 109 for four, but soon India were in deeper trouble, losing their captain and first-innings century-maker (179) Azharuddin for 11 at 127 for five. Victory was out of the question, and there were still 54 overs to negotiate.

Tendulkar had a couple of early close shaves, but only one more wicket fell, Kapil Dev's for 26 after a stand of 56 with the youngster. After that, Manoj Prabhakar (67 not out), in an unbroken stand of 160 in 150 minutes, gave Tendulkar the support he needed to guide India through the final act.

Third Test Final day: 28 August

Gower prospers again as England earn draw

By Peter Deeley, at the Oval

FORM is temporary: class is permanent. The truth of that piece of sporting wisdom came home to us all on the final day of this Test summer as David Gower, emerging from the shadows which have lately obscured his ability, made an unbeaten 157 to save England from defeat and ensure a 1-0 victory in this series against India.

I recall team manager Micky Stewart speaking those words at a time when the hounds were baying for Gower's blood as, for the umpteenth time, he had shown an almost prodigal disregard for his enormous potential with yet another reckless shot. Those who had travelled to this ground to bury Gower instead stayed to praise him, not just for the style and content of his six hours at the crease today, but for the disciplined manner in which he subjugated his will to the needs of his team.

Resuming at 215 for one after following on, still 51 behind India's mammoth 606 for nine declared, England soon lost Atherton. Gower, 32 not out overnight, did not give a hint of a chance today as he studded his six-hour innings with 21 boundaries, compiling substantial stands with Morris (32) and Lamb (52).

The game might have drifted meaninglessly, but the largest crowd for many a year on the last day stayed until the end to enjoy Gower's artistry.

County Championship Sussex v Middlesex: 20 September

Middlesex win the championship race

By Peter Deeley, at Hove

MIDDLESEX swept to their sixth County Championship title in 15 seasons — and jubilant captain Mike Gatting his second for them in six summers — in a race against both Essex, their only challengers, and the inclement weather at Hove today. Sussex once again provided only mediocre batting resistance. Their innings lasted less than 61 overs, the last three wickets being polished off in seven balls as Middlesex eased to victory by an innings and 57 runs.

The end came at 3.22pm with the lowering skies threatening to hold up proceedings. Afterwards, the winners' cheque for £40,000 was handed over by Britannic Assurance, sponsors of the championship. Middlesex's West Indian opener Desmond Haynes won the £1,000 Britannic Assurance award for the batsman of the season, having scored 2,346 runs.

Much of Middlesex's success this year can be put down to the fact that their five top-order batsmen — Haynes, Roseberry, Gatting, Ramprakash and Brown — played in every championship game. John Emburey has also been an ever-present.

Before the season began, some counties had raised the question of double standards over the selection by teams of players ruled ineligible to play Test cricket for England. Sides can only field one overseas 'ineligible', and Middlesex have undoubtedly benefited from the presence of both the debarred Gatting and Emburey as well as Haynes. But against that, it must be pointed out that other sides using 'debarred' players have not reaped any particular benefits.

Sheffield Shield NSW v W.Australia: 21 December

Waugh brothers scale twin peaks

By Michael Coward, in Perth

THE true measure of the new depth to Australian cricket was demonstrated in Perth when Mark Waugh - still to play a Test match - put on another of the extraordinary solo performances which these days are recalled with as much enthusiasm in Essex as they are in New South Wales.

To the unbridled delight of his admirers - and the acute embarrassment of Geoff Marsh, who put NSW in - he scored a career-best undefeated 229. And with his twin brother, Stephen (216 not out), he recorded the highest first-class partnership by two Australians, 464 for the fifth wicket, this against a West Australian attack led by the Test men Terry Alderman and Bruce Reid, who made an impressive comeback in the Brisbane Test after three years out with injury.

The Waughs are the first brothers to score double centuries in the same innings. Lawson's declaration at 601 for four denied them further records, and Western Australia were 131 for two at the close.

[W.Australia followed on 287 behind, but an unbroken 8th-wicket partnership of 242 between Tim Zoehrer (133) and K. MacLeay (102) in 139 minutes saved them from defeat.]

1991

6 Jan Mike Atherton (105) scores the slowest century in Ashes Tests, 424 minutes, at Sydney.

10 Jan ICC vote in match referees for international matches.

6 Mar Viv Richards overtakes Gary Sobers' 8,032 runs to become West Indies' highest scorer in Tests.

22 Apr Dr Ali Bacher is confirmed as the first managing director of the United Cricket Board of South Africa, formed at the weekend by the amalgamation of the South African Cricket Union and the South African Cricket Board.

25 Apr Sanjay.Manjrekar makes 377 for Bombay (855-6 dec) in the Ranji Trophy semi-final against Hyderabad.

2 May Allan Border scores his 9,000th Test run, against West Indies at Kingston.

5 Jul Salim Malik (185 not out) and Nasser Hussain (128) set a new Essex 4th-wicket record of 314 against Surrey at the Oval.

10 Jul ICC sanction South Africa's return to international cricket.

31 Jul The Queen opens the multi-purpose Ken Barrington Centre at the Oval.

7 Aug Derby's fast-medium bowler Dominic Cork takes 8-53 on the second morning against Essex at Derby on his 20th birthday.

16 Aug Jimmy Cook (Somerset) is first to 2,000 runs for the third successive season.

13 Sep Nasser Hussain (196) of Essex chalks up his second county partnership record of the season, 316 for the 5th wicket with Mike Garnham (123) at Leicester.

27 Sep Ian Botham signs a 2-year contract to play for Durham, due to make their Championship début next season.

25 Oct Aqib Javed (Pakistan) sets a new one-day international bowling record with 7-37, including the hat-trick, against India in the final of the new Wills Trophy at Sharjah.

20 Dec Zahir Alam (257) and L.S.Rajput (239) put on a world record 2nd-wicket partnership of 475, for Assam v Tripura at Gawahati in an East Zone Ranji Trophy match.

TEST SERIES

West Indies in England
E 2, WI 2, D 1
Sri Lanka in England
England 1
England in Australia
A 3, D 2
Sri Lanka in New Zealand
Drawn 3
Australia in West Indies
WI 2, A 1, D2

Third Test Final day: 8 January

Gooch's men go down with all guns blazing

By Peter Deeley, in Sydney

ENGLAND'S goal of bringing home the Ashes is now beyond recall, but the manner in which they fought against the odds to stay in the series here reflects credit on a side which until now have, deservedly, earned a poor press.

England did halt a run of successive, heavy defeats, drawing this third Test after a valiant fling at the impossible, pursuing 255 off 28 overs. The sight of David Gower, instead of Atherton, striding down the pavilion steps with Gooch indicated that England were coming out with all guns ablaze. For 68 minutes the pair treated Australia's quick bowlers as if they were one-day trundlers. But, with the field spread wide from the first ball, it demanded something superhuman to achieve a rate of 9.1 runs an over.

Still, Gooch and Gower, in contrasting styles, added 81 in the opening 11 overs, and for the first time in the series Australia were the quarry and not the hunters.

David Gower, 123 runs in England's first innings, reached his Test 8,000 in their second.

Gower (36) was all flowing grace with a minimum of brute force, and when he reached 15 joined the six batsmen to have made 8,000 runs in Tests. Gooch (54) demonstrated his great power by twice hitting Rackemann fully 80 yards over mid-on and mid-off for fours that smashed into the fence on the first bounce.

It could not last, though, and the entry of the spinners quickly brought wickets - four in 24 balls - which put the innings into abrupt reverse. Smith and Atherton, who won the Man of the Match award for his first-innings 105, played out the final half-hour.

It had been a splendid match, with centurions Atherton and Gower (123) answering Australia's 518, and then Tufnell, in his second Test, giving England that slim chance with 5-61. It was Rackemann's 107-minute stay for nine, including an Australian Test record of 72 minutes without scoring, that made England's task in the end impossible.

England's tour: 22 January

Lush not amused at Gower's 'Biggles' prank

By Peter Deeley, in Queensland

TWO England players, David Gower and John Morris, are to be carpeted by tour manager Peter Lush this morning for an unauthorised low-level aerial joyride over the Queensland cricket ground, where their team were playing yesterday.

After batting during the morning, the two slipped out of the ground, donned Biggles-style goggles and climbed into the passenger seats of two veteran Tiger Moth planes at a nearby airstrip.

With some of their team-mates in on the secret — though captain Graham Gooch had not been told about it — the two bi-planes first circled the Carrara ground a couple of times. Then they made a sharp turn coming in between the 200-feet high pylons.

GOWER AND MORRIS ARE INNOCENT-OK

A prank that did not amuse the management: Gower and Morris (inset).

The first plane, with Gower aboard, dropped to within 150 feet of the cricket pitch and flew straight across, casting a shadow before negotiating its way between the pylons at the other end. Down below, Robin Smith, who had just reached his hundred, and Allan Lamb, were almost convulsed with laughter and Smith pretended to shoot at Gower's plane with his bat.

The prank, however, was not treated with amusement by the England management. Mr Lush said he knew nothing about it and appeared taken aback by the news. Micky Stewart, the England team manager, said he had seen "two guys go over in Tiger Moths" and thought they were joyriders. When told who they were, his first response was: "Are you serious? Two of mine?" Both batsmen (Morris made 132) are likely to face a severe ticking-off and a fine.

Fourth Test First day: 25 January

Waugh celebrates his Test baptism with spectacular century

By Peter Deeley, in Adelaide

ENGLAND were like the gambler who wagers his all on a last desperate bid for success — and, but for a breathtaking century by Mark Waugh on his Test début, they might have walked away with the day's honours. With Waugh 116 not out overnight and Australia recovering to 269 for five, however, the tourists' chances of winning this game and maintaining an interest in the series are now receding fast.

Angus Fraser had not totally shaken off his hip problems when the selectors chose to throw him into the fray. And the need for six batsmen meant that Alec Stewart took the gloves for the first time in a Test, relegating Jack Russell to the dressing-room after 20 successive appearances for England.

There should be no criticism, however, of the England selectors for these bold moves. Indeed in mid-afternoon, with Australia, having chosen to bat, reduced to 124 for five, the venture appeared to have paid off.

Then Waugh, replacing his twin brother, Steve, in the side, played what must have been the innings of his life. He altered the course of the day, and possibly the match, after tea, when he scored 95 runs in a session consisting of 29 overs, reaching his century in four minutes short of three hours.

With Waugh still there and Fraser not looking the picture of health at the close, the omens are not good for England.

First Test Final day: 4 February

Crowe and Jones hit world record 467

By Don Cameron, in Wellington

THE FIRST Test between New Zealand and Sri Lanka finished in a flurry of records. Martin Crowe, the New Zealand captain, and Andrew Jones put together 467 for New Zealand's third wicket, a world record Test partnership that beat the previous best, shared by Ponsford/Bradman (Australia 1934) and Nazar/Miandad (Pakistan 1982-83), by 16 runs.

They had come together at 148 for two, when New Zealand still trailed Sri Lanka by 175 runs, and were separated at 615 for three, by which time New Zealand were completely safe from defeat. Their stand was the highest first-class stand by a New Zealand pair and the highest for the third wicket anywhere.

This was the major mark among the records that tumbled during a Test that began with New Zealand being dismissed for 174 on a lively pitch. Aravinda de Silva, the Sri Lankan No.4, had already set a Sri Lankan record with his 267 in their total of 497. Both Crowe, whose 299 is a New Zealand Test record, and Jones (186) recorded their best first-class scores. And when Crowe was finally out, off the third ball of the final over, New Zealand had made 671 for four, their highest total and the biggest in the second innings of a Test.

Duleep Trophy Final: 29 January

Patel attacks batsmen with stump in Indian final

By D.J.Rutnagur, at Jamshedpur

CRICKET suffered the most violent on-field incident in first-class history when Indian international Rashid Patel, a left-arm pace bowler with one Test cap, assaulted two opposition batsmen with a stump during a major domestic final.

Patel attacked fellow international Raman Lamba and his North Zone opening partner Ajay Jadeja as the five-day final of the Inter-Zone tournament for the Duleep Trophy was abandoned amid shameful scenes.

The conflict, in the Keenan Stadium, flared up after a bouncer was delivered at Lamba by Patel, of West Zone, from a long way beyond the popping crease. Lamba, who had been the target of persistent short-pitched bowling, drew away from the wicket and remonstrated with Patel.

Patel then ran to the batsman's end and pulled out a stump. Jadeja, who had followed him up the pitch and warned Lamba of the impending assault, took the first blow on his elbow. Then Patel went in pursuit of Lamba, flailing the stump.

Lamba defends himself against Patel's unorthodox stump attack.

Lamba saved himself from serious injury by using his bat as a shield. The act of physical assault is clearly unacceptable and may spell the end of Patel's career.

The crowd, at a neutral ground in the East Zone, added to the violent scenes by throwing stones, and the match, which was heading for a draw, was abandoned 15 minutes before tea on the last day. North Zone were declared winners by virtue of a first-innings lead – 729 for nine declared against the West's 561.

[Patel got off lightly with a 13-month ban. Lamba was banned for 10 months.]

First Test First day: 1 March

West Indians collapse and suffer injuries in fiery start

By Peter Deeley, in Kingston

THE WEST INDIES lost six wickets for 75 — and had three batsmen taken to hospital — in one of the more extraordinary starts to a Test series, against Australia in Kingston, Jamaica. They recovered to reach 155 for seven by the tea interval, thanks to Dujon (59) and Ambrose (33), and then the injured Logie (77) returned to guide them to the relative respectability of 264 all out by the close

Craig McDermott, who had himself been hit on the head by a bouncer earlier in the tour, was the bowler at the centre of the early dramas. At one stage, he had claimed three wickets for four runs in the space of 13 balls.

There was a steady flow of short-pitched deliveries from the Australian attack, but the injuries resulted from self-induced mistakes on a pitch which made it difficult to play shots with confidence. Haynes badly bruised his foot digging out a McDermott yorker, while Greenidge (collar-bone) and Logie (cut eye) paid the price for trying to play pull shots.

McDermott finished with five for 80, Hughes four for 67, but the honours go to Logie, whose dazzling strokeplay belied both his injury and West Indies' dire situation.

[Australia made 371 (Boon 109 not out), but nearly a day and a half was lost through rain and water that leaked under the inadequate covers as West Indies went to 334-3 (Richardson 104 not out), and the game was drawn.]

Fourth Test Third day: 21 April

Glorious Greenidge 200 proves doubters wrong

By Peter Deeley, in Bridgetown

THE FOURTH double century of Gordon Greenidge's long Test career emphatically quashed all speculation about the possible end of his playing days, as West Indies proved once again that they are still without peers in the game. Greenidge will be 40 in nine days' time, yet here he was batting for just over 10 hours for his unbeaten 209.

His innings has virtually assured West Indies of both this match and the series, as their lead reached 422 with seven wickets still in hand at the close of the third day.

Only two batsmen, Hobbs and Hendren, have scored Test double centuries at a more advanced age, both when they were 41. The Barbadian has struggled throughout this series and, before yesterday, had scored 91 runs in six innings. This was only the second time he had passed 50 in 24 Test innings, yet it brought him his 19th century in 107 appearances for West Indies.

Australia finished in all sorts of trouble, with two substitutes for much of the final session. Moreover, Dean Jones, with one previous Test wicket to his name and nursing a bruised right hand, the stand-in spinner for injured captain Allan Border. Border, who did not field today, is having treatment for the chipped bone in his left thumb.

[Greenidge went on to make 226, and West Indies wrapped up the series with victory by 343 runs.]

County Championship Middlesex v Kent: 1 June

Kent keeper Marsh lands record haul

By Doug Ibbotson

WICKET-KEEPER Steve Marsh could do no wrong at Lord's yesterday, following up his world record-equalling eight catches with a resolute 57 not out to give Kent the initiative in an engrossing tussle against Middlesex.

Marsh shares his wicket-keeping record with the late Wally Grout, who set the mark with Queensland in 1960, and David East of Essex, who caught the first eight Somerset batsmen at Taunton on his 26th birthday in 1985. But, in a grim contest between uncertain batting and the swinging ball, his robust sixth-wicket stand of 97 with Ellison, which enabled Kent to achieve a lead of 231 with five second-innings wickets intact, was just as impressive.

Middlesex resumed at 93 for seven and 13 overs had been bowled before Chas Taylor edged a catch off Merrick. The world record was equalled 25 minutes later when Fraser lunged at Ellison and Marsh, diving to his right, held the catch inches from the ground.

One wicket remained, and only a yard separated Marsh from the ultimate objective when Hughes nudged at Davis and first slip took the catch.

Fifth Test Final day: 12 August

Double celebration at the Oval as England beat West Indies and tie the series

By Peter Deeley, at the Oval

DOWN in the concrete jungle of London SE11, the lion not so much stirred as roared today. A crowded Kennington Oval was reverberating to an England team risen from the Ashes disaster of last winter to share equal billing with Viv Richards' wounded West Indies, the unofficial world champions

At a specially reduced price of £10 a seat, the 11,000 who made up the largest last-day Test crowd seen in many a year had a double event to celebrate. Not only did they witness England's achievement of sharing a series against the Caribbean side for the first time in 17 years, there was the bonus right at the end, for those who believe that legends never die, of Ian Botham hitting the winning run – a four – off the only ball he received.

West Indies had begun the last day on 356 for six, 113 runs ahead and with Richardson still there on 108. He scored only 13 more as Lawrence (5-106) and DeFreitas (2-49) took the remaining four wickets for 29 runs. Tufnell, the first innings hero with six for 25 in 14.3 overs, finished this time with just one for 150 in 46. England lost five wickets in knocking off the 143 runs needed. Man of the Match was Robin Smith for his first-innings 109.

First Test Final day: 10 June

Unsung hero Derek Pringle, arms aloft, has Haynes caught by Smith (left).

England end West Indies hoodoo on a great day at Leeds

By Peter Deeley, at Headingley

WHEN England last beat West Indies in a Test in this country, the captains tossed with a florin, a man was going to the moon and Concorde was a new shape in the skies. That was in July 1969. It has taken a side led by Graham Gooch to break the Caribbean hoodoo 22 years on.

The England captain was himself then a boy of 15. As Ray Illingworth's team beat a West Indies side led by Gary Sobers – also at Headingley – by 10 runs on 15 July, Gooch was in East Africa, sharing a room with John Emburey, one of his team-mates in a touring London Schoolboys party.

In the intervening time, the sides have met 41 times here and in the West Indies. England have won just twice – in Trinidad and Jamaica – lost 25 and drawn 14.

Some 5,000 people witnessed this landmark day, as England reduced West Indies from 11 for one to 162 all out for a 115-run victory. The final moments were greeted with flag-waving, a tin-whistle band and a triumphal conga round the terracing.

As the players appeared on the balcony, there was a special cheer for the hitherto much-maligned Derek Pringle, who took two for 14 and two for 38 and scored 43 useful runs in a low-scoring match. But the gold award went to his Essex and England skipper Graham Gooch for his match-winning second innings 154 not out – out of 252 all out, as Ambrose (6-52) and Marshall (3-58) were scything though his team-mates.

Other English heroes in this memorable match were pace bowlers Phillip DeFreitas, who took four wickets in each innings, and Test debutant Steve Watkin, who collected five.

NatWest Trophy Final: 7 September

Smith revels in big occasion to drive Hants on to pulsating victory

By Christopher Martin-Jenkins, at Lord's

FOR the sixth year running the side fielding first won the NatWest Trophy, but this time there was no question of an early-morning collapse and a one-sided match. Instead, there was one of those pulsating twilight finishes that have become a tradition since Derby and Northants finished with scores level 10 years ago.

Hampshire prevailed to win with only two balls to spare. They thereby set a remarkable record of winning all five rounds of the competition for the loss of only 12 wickets from start to finish.

Robin Smith provided the match-winning surge, revelling once more in the inspirational vibes of Lord's on the big occasion. His 78 took his aggregate from five innings in the competition this year to 331, at an average of 165. This was Hampshire's first success in the trophy, after seven galling semi-final defeats.

Tony Middleton also made 78, calmly surviving the first two spells from Waqar Younis, in company first with Paul Terry, then with Smith. He outpaced Terry in their opening stand of 90 in 27 overs, before running him out, although it took a swift swoop, pick-up and throw from Graham Thorpe, whose 93 would have earned him the Man of the Match award, no doubt, had Surrey got home.

For all Smith's power and range of stroke, Hampshire were still needing 81 off 14 overs when David Gower came in, and was soon trapped leg before by Waqar.

Jonathan Ayling (18 not out) was the hero when the match reached its decisive point — 24 runs needed from the last three overs, with Ayling and Smith together. They made 14 from the first of these, thanks to a fierce cut for six by Ayling. But Smith and then Aymes were run out before Ayling, needing two, tapped Bucknell off his legs to the square-leg boundary.

County Championship Essex v Middlesex: 19 September

Gooch puts seal on summer of success

By Christopher Martin-Jenkins, at Chelmsford

ESSEX, after two seasons as runners-up, won the County Championship today for the fifth time in 13 years.

Twenty-five minutes after lunch on a sunny afternoon at Chelmsford, Neil Foster took the last wicket, his 10th of the match and his 91st in 20 championship games. Middlesex were beaten by the truly crushing margin of an innings and 208 runs and there was still a day and a half of the match to go.

Foster – four for 18 in Middlesex's first innings of 51 and six for 104 in their fighting 307 – led the team off the field. But, appropriately, all Essex's specialist bowlers had a share in the demolition of the county from whom they had taken the title. It is their quality in all departments which makes Essex worthy champions.

Warwickshire have pushed them all the way. But Essex won six of their last seven matches, with a string of high-scoring innings culminating in their 566 for six declared against Middlesex, with skipper Graham Gooch hitting a magnificent 259. The England captain really did put the seal on a summer of success.

Britannic Assurance Challenge Essex v Victoria: 26 September

Downpour leaves Essex 2 wickets from victory

By Charles Randall, at Chelmsford

ESSEX were prevented by rain from inflicting a heavy defeat on Victoria, the Sheffield Shield champions, in their four-day Britannic Assurance Challenge match at Chelmsford. A persistent thunderstorm descended at 1.40 pm with Victoria in a state of rubble, 56 for eight, having followed on 175 runs behind.

At times, Victoria's batting looked little better than novice level against the turning ball. Foster (4-63) reached the 100-wicket landmark with his seamers for the second time in his Essex career with the fifth ball of the day, and took the last wicket, too, leaving Merv Hughes stranded with 60 not out.

Victoria were cleaned up for 168 in the 97th over, but their second innings was worse. They had no answer to the classy, persevering spin of Such (3-7) and Childs (3-19), and were 56 for eight when rain intervened.

One-day International: 10 November

Return of South Africa to the international fold

By Peter Deeley, in Calcutta

SOUTH AFRICA made their long-awaited return to international cricket today, but it was not to be the victorious beginning that they had hoped for: their return to cricket legitimacy was crowned by defeat rather than a fairytale victory.

Instead, India, better versed in the machinations of the one-day world, got home by three wickets to an accompaniment of firecrackers and sparklers worthy of a bonfire night celebration, with the final moments half-obscured by smoke.

In a nutshell, the magnitude of the occasion got to the visitors. Players who had never performed for crowds of more than 35,000 found themselves trapped in a cauldron of noise and passion, heat and frenzy, generated by one of the biggest ever audiences for cricket - officially 90,450 were at Eden Gardens, but the police put it at 95,000.

The visitors' captain, Clive Rice, had been waiting for this day for half his life. Players not known back on the veld for buckling under pressure exhibited signs of pure tension. There was one shining exception: Allan Donald produced the performance of the day with the ball, taking five wickets for 29 runs in 8.4 overs. This was one player who could say later that he had drawn inspiration from the electric atmosphere.

Only Wessels (50) and Kuiper (43) of the South African batsmen made any impression, and only the latter showed the necessary momentum, as they crawled to 177 for eight in the 47 overs sent down by India in the 200 minutes allowed.

Donald, who was much quicker than anyone else on show, had India reeling at 20 for three. But Tendulkar (62), who was lucky to escape a run-out on three, and then Amre (55) steadied the boat, and India won with three wickets to spare in the 41st over.

A historic moment, as Indian captain Azharuddin welcomes South African skipper Clive Rice and his country back to international cricket.

1992

1 Jan Colin Cowdrey is knighted.

10 Feb David Lawrence breaks his knee-cap while bowling for England against New Zealand at Wellington.

30 Apr-1 May Essex's 388-7 and 272-run victory over Scotland are new B&H Cup records.

7 Jun Pakistan's Javed Miandad (153 not out) and Salim Malik (165) set a new series record with a stand of 322 for the 4th wicket against England in the drawn Test at Edgbaston.

26 Jun Mark Waugh (219 not) and Nasser Hussain (172 not) set an Essex 3rd-wicket record of 347 against Lancs at Ilford.

13 Aug Injuries force Leicester to recall BBC cricket correspondent Jonathan Agnew, retired 2 years earlier, for the NatWest semi-final, and his 12-2-31-1 effort helps them beat Essex.

23 Aug Umpires change the ball being used by Pakistan bowlers in a Texaco one-day match at Lord's, no explanation being given, leading to allegations of 'ball-tampering'.

22 Sep TCCB fine Allan Lamb £5,000 for newspaper articles about ball-tampering.

24 Sep TCCB reveal that Surrey have been fined (£1,000 suspended) for repeated ball-tampering.

22 Oct Counties launch their new Sunday League colour strips.

14 Nov Tendulkar (India) becomes the first player to be given out by a 'third umpire' (TV assisted), run out against South Africa at Durban.

1 Dec Over 100 MCC members (less than 1%) force a meeting to debate a motion of no confidence in the selectors, arising mainly from the omission of David Gower from the India tour.

3 Dec Australian captain Allan Border is fined £850 for dissent in 1st Test v West Indies.

9 Dec Sri Lanka beat New Zealand by 9 wickets at Colombo in 2nd Test to win their first series (1-0), in a rubber reduced to 2 Tests after a fatal bomb incident outside NZ hotel induced four players and coach to return home; Tillekeratne's 7 catches in the match equals the Test record for a fielder.

10 Dec Bonus points for four-day county cricket to be gained on 120 overs, and the first batting point at 200 rather than 150 runs.

TEST SERIES

Pakistan in England
P 2, E 1, D 2
England in New Zealand
E 2, D 1
India in Australia
A 4, D 1
Sri Lanka in Pakistan
P 1, D 2
South Africa in West Indies
West Indies 1
Australia in Sri Lanka
A 2, D 1
India in Zimbabwe
Drawn 1
New Zealand in Zimbabwe
NZ 1, D 1

First Test Final day: 22 January

Tufnell guile destroys New Zealand

By Christopher Martin-Jenkins, in Christchurch

THERE has seldom been so dramatic a transformation of a moribund Test match as there was at Christchurch today. Philip Tufnell's brilliant spin bowling made possible England's first victory in New Zealand for 14 years, as he took six of the seven wickets to fall in an hour and 50 minutes after tea to finish with seven for 47.

The game ended 10 minutes from its scheduled close when New Zealand's captain, knowing that a four would save his team, gambled with a lofted drive at Tufnell and skied the ball to wide mid-off, where Derek Pringle took an awkward, swirling catch with the utmost coolness.

"With hindsight," said Crowe, "I should have had a little bit more faith in Chris Pringle." His partner, coming in at No.11 in great tension, had lasted 22 minutes and 15 balls against a combination of Tufnell and Chris Lewis. Had Crowe's shot gone for four, New Zealand would have forced England to bat again, and there would not have been time.

Tufnell, who took four wickets for 100 in New Zealand's first innings, all in a deadly spell of 59 balls for 16 runs, was made Man of the Match.

Benson & Hedges World Cup Semi-final: 22 March

Rain rule clouds England's joy as South Africa miss World Cup final place

By Christopher Martin-Jenkins, in Sydney

ENGLAND'S entry into their second successive World Cup final, the reward for their 19-run win over South Africa in Sydney, was achieved in circumstances of confusion sadly unworthy of so momentous an event. South Africa's outside chance of winning was ended by a mischievously timed shower and the already discredited rules relating to rain interruptions.

It took the gilt off England's gingerbread and ruined what was developing into a thrilling climax, with the odds still favouring the fielding side.

As the rain arrived, however, Brian McMillan and Dave Richardson had scored 10 off five balls from the 43rd over. South Africa, having made a brave assault on England's total of 252 for six off 45 overs, needed 22 to win off 13 balls with four wickets left when the umpires decided it was raining hard enough for them to intervene. Deeming the conditions unfit, Steve Randell and Brian Aldridge, who conducted themselves very well in difficult circumstances, asked Graham Gooch if he wanted to carry on. He, understandably, did not.

Twelve minutes were lost before the umpires decided that play could resume, meaning that two overs had to be taken off — in other words, only one ball remained. South Africa's two lowest-scoring overs had produced only one leg-bye, so their target was reduced by one, to 21 off one ball. A disgruntled McMillan scored one off it and handshakes all round followed. There was nothing wrong with the spirit in which the game was played.

Benson & Hedges World Cup Final: 25 March

Imran's class of '92 pass biggest test

By Christopher Martin-Jenkins, in Melbourne

Pakistan skipper Imran Khan with the World Cup trophy.

SHEER exuberant talents, leavened with a little shrewd experience from the two oldest heads in the team, Imran Khan and Javed Miandad, won the World Cup for Pakistan at Melbourne today. Their 22-run defeat of England was their fifth win in succession in a tournament which had begun most unpromisingly with the loss of Waqar Younis before a ball was bowled and only one win, over Zimbabwe, in their first five matches.

To win against England's strong batting team today Pakistan needed good performances from their three best bowlers, Wasim Akram (3-49), Aqib Javed (2-27) and Mushtaq Ahmed (3-41). Each rose admirably to the occasion after Imran (72) and Javed (58) had paved the way for a late innings assault by Akram (33) and Inzamam-ul-Haq (42) with a third-wicket stand of 139. In a nutshell, Pakistan won because their bowling was more positive and penetrative than England's.

The all-round contribution of Wasim Akram won him the Man of the Match award, but the real match-winner was probably Mushtaq Ahmed, whose dismissal of Hick (17) and Gooch (29) in the 19th and 21st overs of the England innings left those who came after with too much to do. Even so, Neil Fairbrother (62) and Allan Lamb (31) got England back on course towards their target of 250 before Wasim returned for a devastating second spell during which he removed Lamb and Lewis with successive balls. There could only be one result after that.

Only Test Final day: 23 April

West Indian whirlwinds deny South Africans historic victory

By Geoffrey Dean, in Barbados

SCENES of extraordinary jubilation followed one of the West Indies' more unlikely Test victories after Curtly Ambrose and Courtney Walsh destroyed South Africa's second innings with a magnificent display of fast bowling.

Apart from Kepler Wessels (74) and Peter Kirsten (52), no South African got into double figures. The other nine mustered only 11 runs between them out of a total of 148. When Allan Donald, the last man, was bowled by Ambrose, South Africa had lost their last eight wickets for only 25 runs in 20 overs. The West Indies players exploded with relief and charged round the boundary doing a lap of honour in a spontaneous outburst of joy.

Victory by 52 runs for the West Indies in the inaugural Test between the two countries was their 11th in succession at Kensington Oval, Bridgetown, an apparently impenetrable cricketing fortress, where no visiting country has won since 1935.

Yet at the start of play the South Africans, resuming at 122 for two, appeared the more likely victors. Despite the uneven bounce of a pitch criss-crossed with cracks with roughish edges, the ball was 51 overs old and the pace in the wicket had completely gone. Nobody, however, perhaps not even the West Indian players themselves, could have foreseen quite how well Ambrose (6-34) and, in particular, Walsh (4-31), were to bowl.

Walsh's transformation from the first innings was complete. His figures today were 11-7-8-4, and he did not bowl a single bad ball, getting more movement off the seam than any other bowlers at any stage in the match. In taking the wickets of Wessels, Kirsten and Kuiper, the three most experienced South African batsmen, it was he, more than Ambrose, who won the match for West Indies.

Ambrose's consistently excellent bowling throughout the game, in which he took eight for 82 from 61.4 overs, nevertheless earned him the joint Man of the Match award with Andrew Hudson, whose first-innings 163 had seemed to put the tourists in control.

Benson & Hedges Cup Yorks v Kent: 30 April

Tendulkar yorks Lord Hawke's ghost

By Michael Calvin, from Headingley

THE GHOST of Lord Hawke failed to rise from the grave. The Four Horsemen of the Apocalypse apparently felt it inappropriate to arrive as messengers of divine retribution. Instead, Headingley's heretics were free to welcome a small, sleek Indian with a penchant for centuries and silk culottes. Adoption formalities involving Sachin Tendulkar were completed with the minimum of fuss.

They didn't exactly shower rose petals at his feet at 11.32 yesterday morning when, smiling bashfully, he led his new Yorkshire team-mates down Headingley's 20 pavilion steps. A 10-second burst of polite applause, which allowed Tendulkar to mouth a solitary "thank you", was deemed sufficient. They don't get carried away with historic occasions in the land of Geoffrey Boycott and Joshua Tetley.

Both, incidentally, stand to benefit from Yorkshire's employment of the Bombay teenager, whose entry into county cricket marked the end of the 19th century on calendars from Bradford to Batley. Boycott has been a conspicuous advocate of change on the Yorkshire committee. He gladly posed for photographs with Tendulkar, a teetotaller who doubled as a billboard for Mr Tetley's bitter.

Tendulkar then proceeded to claim two Kent wickets in three deliveries with his unheralded medium-paced bowling, but the more widely anticipated treat comes tomorrow when, weather permitting, he will begin the process of convincing domestic cricket's most demanding audience that he is a batting legend in the making.

[Tendulkar was run out for 7 and Yorks lost by 70 runs. He scored 1,070 runs in the County Championship, averaging 46.52.]

India's young Test star Sachin Tendulkar, Yorkshire's first overseas player.

County Championship Glamorgan v Durham: 16 May

Double first for delighted Durham

By David Green, at Cardiff

AT 6.29pm this evening at Sophia Gardens, Simon Brown knocked back Steve Bastien's off stump to secure a first County Championship victory, by an innings and 104 runs, for a delighted Durham side over a somewhat shell-shocked Glamorgan.

Durham, who controlled the match from the first day, when they dismissed their opponents for 224, advanced today from 467 for six to 521 for nine before declaring. It was Durham's highest ever score, and featured hundreds by Larkins (143) and Parker (124).

Needing 298 to make Durham bat again, Glamorgan were soon in deep trouble on a pitch of modest pace but uneven bounce, Botham (three for 47) and the quick left-armer Simon Brown (five for 66) reducing them to 40 for six. Botham also took two slip catches off Brown to dismiss James and Richards, the second an astonishing effort, for he dived far to his left from second slip to hold a fast-travelling edge with his left hand.

Tony Cottey resisted stoutly to make 112 not out, but once Botham came back to dismiss the stubborn Watkin, the end came quickly.

TCCB Meeting: 19 May

Four-day format gets TCCB vote

By Christopher Martin-Jenkins, from Lord's

According to Alan Smith, chief executive of the Test and County Cricket Board, delegates at today's momentous meeting at Lord's left with a determination to be positive about the reformation of county cricket for which a majority of them had just voted. A slender majority of only 11 to 8 with one abstention must in all truth, however, have left many wondering if they had done the right thing.

From 1993, and for at least the next two years, the County Championship, which apart from one experimental season after the First World War has been a three-day game since the competition took formal shape in the 19th century, will comprise 17 four-day matches, each county playing the others once

The Benson & Hedges zonal rounds will disappear, depriving the home clubs of an average of £5,000 a game, and the Sunday League will change from a 40-over Sunday afternoon bash to a competition of 50-over matches, starting at noon or soon afterwards.

The package had been recommended by a working-party chaired by Michael Murray of Middlesex, and to have achieved agreement on such sweeping changes reflects considerable credit on the way he and his colleagues have gone about their business.

Second Test Fourth day: 21 June

Pakistan keep their nerve: England lose on golden day of 17 wickets

By Christopher Martin-Jenkins, at Lord's

THE 25,000 at Lord's this evening were treated to a finish no less exciting than the one here in 1963 when all results were possible as the last over began. Time on this occasion, however, was of importance only to those hoping for a result by the close of the fourth day.

Pakistan, setting out an hour after lunch to make only 138 to win the second Test and go one up in the series, were 41 for four by tea and 95 for eight 22 overs later. On a golden evening, the last act of an intense and unpredictable drama began when Waqar Younis walked out to join his fast-bowling partner, Wasim Akram, with 43 runs still needed and 11 overs of the day to go.

With Akram playing coolly for the most part and with great authority, and Waqar trusting his eye to drive when the ball was up to him, Pakistan were finally carried to a two-wicket victory by their unbeaten ninth-wicket stand of 46.

An extraordinary day had seen the fall of 17 wickets. It should be made plain that the pitch itself could not begin to explain the fact that, with Alec Stewart's shining exception (69 not out), no England batsman could score more than 15 in their second innings. Only Stewart (74) and Gooch (69), indeed, had been able to go past 30 in the first. Stewart's achievement in carrying his bat for the four hours of England's second innings was only the seventh instance by an Englishman and the first time at Lord's.

Third Test Fourth day: 6 July

Gower record overshadowed by Pakistan row with the umpire

By Christopher Martin-Jenkins, at Old Trafford

WITH David Gower (73) happily playing one of the leading roles, England went most of the way towards saving the third Test at Old Trafford, batting with much determination throughout a day of flawless sunshine to make 390.

That was the central fact of a day which ended sadly in frayed tempers and an enquiry by the referee, Conrad Hunte, into clear breaches of the ICC's code of conduct by Pakistan's captain, Javed Miandad, and fast bowler Aqib Javed.

Thanks in part to Pakistan's poor slip-catching, England saved the follow-on. Gower achieved his cherished England run-scoring record during a scintillating morning's cricket in which England added 123 runs against attacking fields, and determined lower-order batting reduced Pakistan's first innings lead to 115.

The innings was prolonged until 6.20, by which time some Pakistan tempers had become lamentably frayed. Umpire Roy Palmer, reasonably enough, told Aqib to cool down and pitch the ball up after he had hit Devon Malcolm, England's short-sighted No.11, on the helmet with a bouncer delivered from well over the popping crease.

Miandad sided with, rather than trying to mollify, his young fast bowler, who would have been much better off trying to hit Malcolm's stumps. An over later he did, but first Aqib delivered a second successive bouncer, causing Palmer to no-ball him under the one-bouncer-an-over rule.

Miandad and Aqib remonstrated angrily with Palmer, whose more experienced fellow-umpire, David Shepherd, was obliged to walk up and order play to continue. Mr Hunte appears to have little option but to take some action against them tomorrow.

Fourth Test Fourth day: 26 July

Calm Gower levels series for England

By Christopher Martin-Jenkins, at Headingley

ENGLAND'S six-wicket victory at 5.45pm this afternoon preserved Headingley's reputation for the dramatic and Pakistan's for volatility. It was the 11th Test in succession here with a positive result, and by squaring the series it has set up a potentially epic final Test at the Oval next week.

England, needing only 99, were faltering at 65 for four, with Mushtaq Ahmed bowling his leg-breaks, googlies and top-spinners with wonderful skill and accuracy. But David Gower, a member of the last England side to beat Pakistan exactly 10 years ago on this very ground, was in calm residence, and Mark Ramprakash, who had made three ducks in his previous Test innings, stayed with him while the remaining 34 runs were scored.

One of Neil Mallender's eight wickets (for 122) in only his second Test.

Graham Gooch had battled it out with Gower in a tense second-wicket stand of 34 and added a precious 37 to his first-innings 135 after Salim Malik (82 not and 84 not) had again played with the finesse of a true virtuoso to keep his side in the game.

A weekend full of dramatic changes of fortune, with Neil Mallender taking five for 50 in Pakistan's second innings, played to the end on the emotions of the players and spectators, and tested two experienced umpires to the full. Television's slow-motion replay showed clearly that, when he had scored 13, Gooch was run out by two feet, but umpire Ken Palmer, with only his eyes to rely on, gave him not out.

And Gower had made seven, and England 49 of the 99 they required, when Pakistan appealed passionately to Mervyn Kitchen for a catch behind the wicket off Mushtaq Ahmed. When it was given not out - and this time the replay was inconclusive - another young Pakistan cricketer disgraced himself. Referee Clyde Walcott's subsequent action and his statement were exemplary, but the young members of the Pakistan team simply have to understand that petulant dissent is odious in cricket.

First Test Final day: 22 August

Sri Lanka blow chance of famous Test victory

By Mike Coward, in Colombo

AUSTRALIA scored an improbable 16-run victory over Sri Lanka in an extraordinary Test at the Sinhalese Sports Club ground. The Sri Lankans, who had been within sight of a famous win for the previous four days, lost their 10 second-innings wickets for 88 before a dumbfounded crowd of 10,000.

It was a fantastic conclusion to a Test match which rivalled the astonishing comeback by the West Indies against South Africa in Barbados earlier this year. Sri Lanka, required to score 181 from a minimum of 58 overs for their most significant victory in 10 years of Test cricket, were 105 runs from their target, with all wickets intact, when extrovert off-spinner Greg Matthews dramatically changed the course of the match.

Matthews' dismissal of Rochan Mahanama (39) precipitated an astounding collapse. He took four for 76 and Warne three for 11 while, of the three centurions in Sri Lank's first-innings 547 for eight declared, only Gurusinha (31 not out) made any impact.

Only Test Second day: 19 October

Zimbabwe's Houghton crafts historic century

By Peter Deeley, in Harare

DAVID HOUGHTON, the Zimbabwe captain, completed his country's maiden Test century shortly before the close this evening, and ensured the newcomers will avoid defeat in their first game at the top.

Coming in 30 minutes into the morning session, when Zimbabwe were 199 for four and India looked to be finally gaining the ascendancy, Houghton showed enormous discipline, reining in his natural aggression until the final session, when the visitors were looking weary after two days in the heat.

Zimbabwe finished on 406 for five - by some margin already the highest total by a side in its first Test innings - with Houghton unbeaten on 110 and the left-handed Andy Flower, elder brother of Grant, who scored 82 yesterday, on 55.

[Houghton (121) and Flower (59) extended their stand to 165, Zimbabwe made 456, but India saved the follow-on and the match was drawn.]

Houghton, Zimbabwe's captain, during his historic 100.

Second one-day international: 9 December

Wessels accused of striking Kapil

By Peter Deeley, in Port Elizabeth

INDIA'S 'friendship tour' of South Africa degenerated into a public slanging match after angry exchanges on the field during the second international tonight.

Amrit Mathur, India's tour manager, accused the home captain Kepler Wessels of deliberately striking Kapil Dev with his bat. South African team manager Mike Procter said the Indians were guilty of bad sportsmanship. And Ali Bacher, managing director of the United Cricket Board of South Africa, rebuked Mathur for prejudging the case against Wessels.

Round two takes place this evening in Johannesburg, when match referee Clive Lloyd delivers his report to Dr Bacher on incidents which soured South Africa's second consecutive six-wicket win in the seven-match series.

It all began when India, dismissed for a paltry 147 on a substandard pitch, were fighting to get back into the game. Kapil's fifth over found Kirsten – the non-striker – straying out of his crease. Three times before on this tour, the bowler has warned the same batsman for the same infringement, and this time Kapil did not hesitate — he whipped off the bails and successfully appealed.

Local umpire Cyril Mitchley gave Kirsten out, but the batsman stayed for some time, arguing with fielders and umpire, maintaining he had not been given a warning.

Two balls later, Wessels' bat appeared to collide heavily with Kapil's shins, and the Indian needed treatment before he could continue.

[Match referee Clive Lloyd fined Kirsten £240, but the case against Wessels, who claimed the clash was not deliberate, was "not proven". Mr Lloyd complained that South African television had not been able to supply him with the relevant replays.]

First Test First day: 13 November

Wessels' second maiden 100 holds South Africa together

By Christopher Martin-Jenkins, in Durban

AFTER losing the toss and the wicket of Jimmy Cook to Kapil Dev's first ball of the match, South Africans must have wondered if by starting their first Test for 22 years on Friday the 13th they had not tempted providence too far.

Not Kepler Wessels. Playing the ball late and close to his body with a technique as tight as a Yorkshireman on holiday, South Africa's admirably disciplined captain held his side together against intelligent Indian swing bowling on a pitch with an all too rare combination of pace and even bounce.

In the end, India, with four wickets for the spinners, found success in a way they had hardly intended. By dismissing Wessels for 118 half an hour before the end, and having Omar Henry caught at slip in the final over, they finished the day with the advantage, having South Africa at 215 for seven.

But the day belonged to Wessels. From the moment he steered the second ball of the morning past gully for four, his hundred was an innings notable for character, concentration and a wide range of strokes. He batted four hours, 20 minutes for his fifth Test century. Only 13 other men have played Test cricket for two countries, but he is the first to score a hundred for them both.

10 December

No-ball penalty to be worth two runs

By Christopher Martin-Jenkins, at Lord's

NO-BALLS in first-class and one-day cricket next season will produce two extra runs rather than one. What is more, they will be in addition to runs scored off the bat.

For the first time in English cricket, a six scored off a no-ball will gain a side eight runs. This was the most significant of several changes to the playing conditions for next season agreed at the two-day winter meeting of the Test and County Cricket Board at Lord's.

The two extras will apply to all types of no-ball. Batsmen will be credited only with runs scored off the bat, but the two-run penalty will count against a bowler's analysis.

In future, also, beamers – all balls passing above a batsman's shoulder height – will be regarded as no-balls, not as wides. Again, therefore, the penalty will be two runs, not one.

Third Test Fourth day: 29 December

Donald sets up S.African Test triumph

By Peter Deeley, in Port Elizabeth

SOUTH AFRICA duly accomplished their first Test win for more than 22 years by the comfortable margin of nine wickets with a day and five minutes of this third Test to spare. However, their hour of glory was almost stolen by one of the game's older boys, Kapil Dev, who in an epic one-man rearguard action threatened to turn the match on its head, despite being in acute pain with an injured hand. He had come in with India 27 for 5, and, during four and a half hours at the crease, scored 129 out of 188 runs, giving India an improbable lead of 152.

Ranking equal in achievement was Allan Donald's seven for 84, giving him his best overall return in Tests of 12 for 139. On a slow pitch, Donald, the Man of the Match, has proved after only four appearances for South Africa that he is worthy of the 'world-class' label.

South Africa knocked off the runs for the loss of one wicket, and Wessels was still there at the end on 95.

Prominent in the after-match celebrations were team manager Mike Procter and Ali Bacher, MD of the United Cricket Board, members of the side that beat Australia on this same ground in March 1970 – after which the country went into purdah because of apartheid. It has been a notable rebirth.

1993

5 Jan Needing 127 to beat Pakistan at Hamilton in a one-off Test, New Zealand are bowled out for 93 by the rampant Waqar Younis (5-22) and Wasim Akram (5-45); 'Extras' top-score with 22.

30 Jan- 1 Feb West Indies retain the Frank Worrell Trophy, beating Australia at Perth by an innings and 25 runs by lunch on the 3rd day. Curtly Ambrose, International Cricketer of the Year, is Man of the Series and, for his devastating 7-1 spell in 32 balls in Australia's 1st innings (119), Man of the Match (match figures 7-25, 2-54).

28 July Lancashire opener Mike Atherton, 25, is appointed England's new captain.

9 Oct Wicket-keeper Paul Kirsten takes 7 catches in an innings for Griquas against W.Transvaal to equal the S.African record for dismissals - originally set up by his father Noel (6ct, 1st) in the 1959-60 season.

25 Oct The record for the highest individual score in S.Africa (Eric Rowan's 306 in 1939-40), having been broken first by Terence Lazard, with 307 for Boland against W.Province (19 Sep) in a pre-season match belatedly accorded first-class status, falls again to Daryll Cullinan, who makes 337 for Transvaal on the last day of a Castle Cup match against N.Transvaal.

13 Nov David Gower, 36, controversially omitted from the upcoming England tour of West Indies, announces his retirement from the game to the dismay of cricket lovers everywhere.

18 Nov Sarfraz Nawaz abandons his libel action against Allan Lamb in the 'ball-tampering' case.

29 Nov NZ suffer heaviest Test defeat, out twice for 161 (each time in 292 mins) as Australia beat them by an innings and 222 at Hobart.

7 Dec TCCB decide to scrap the England committee, with international selection to be the responsibility of a separate committee comprising chairman (still to be chosen), England's manager and captain, and two new elected members. The Sunday League will revert to 40 overs next season, with fielding restrictions for the first 15 overs scrapped.

21 Dec ICC announce £1.1m sponsorship by National Grid of panel of international umpires from the 9 Test-playing countries, all Tests to be umpired jointly by one panel and one home official for initial period of 3 years.

Third Test Fourth day: 5 January

Lara joins the elite with glittering 277

By Phil Wilkins, in Sydney

BRIAN LARA, in an unforgettable exhibition of uninhibited West Indian batting, became the highest scorer in West Indies-Australia Tests with his 277 at the Sydney Cricket Ground today. The 23-year-old left-hander, 121 not out overnight, played supremely well in only his fifth Test for his maiden century at this level, with cover drives and clip shots forward of square-leg a feature of his 38 boundaries.

Lara, run out for 277.

Even a 15th Test century by Lara's batting partner and captain, Richie Richardson (109), with whom he added 293 for the third wicket in 303 minutes, paled in comparison. Richardson described Lara's innings as "breathtaking".

The Test appears certain to end in a draw tomorrow. The West Indies are still trailing on the first innings, having reached 488 for five in reply to Australia's 503 for nine declared. Lara's 277 was the highest innings in Australia since Bob Cowper's 307 against England in Melbourne in 1965-66 and the fourth-highest by a West Indian in Tests. Just when he had set his sights on Sobers's record 365, Lara was run out by a brilliant piece of fielding from Damien Martyn.

[West Indies made 606 and the match was drawn.]

Fourth Test Fourth day: 26 January

Bizarre Walsh strike gives W.Indies unique one-run victory

By Phil Wilkins, in Adelaide

WEST INDIES gained a unique place in the record books when accurate fast bowling brought them an historic one-run victory over Australia in the fourth Test. The victory was the narrowest in the 115-year history of Test cricket, although two Tests have been tied.

A fluctuating match was finished in four days with no side making more than 252. Australia, set 186 for victory, were 74 for seven, but were taken to the brink of success by Test newcomer Justin Langer (54) and a last-wicket stand of 40 between Tim May (42 not out) and Craig McDermott (18).

With one scoring stroke separating the two teams, McDermott attempted to sway out of the path of a rising delivery from Courtney Walsh, only for the ball to strike the peak of his helmet and deflect against his batting glove for the catch at the wicket to Junior Murray.

Jubilant, ecstatic West Indian players embraced and snatched stumps, some even falling to the ground in disbelief after a triumph that levelled the series, with the final Test starting in Perth on Saturday.

Curtly Ambrose took 10 wickets in the match and gained the Man-of-the-Match award as well as fulsome praise from both captains.

Second Test Final day: 15 February

England lose by an innings as India take series

By Christopher Martin-Jenkins, in Madras

INDIA duly won the second Test and with it the series, the Charms Cup and the adulation of a fair proportion of the country's population of 862 million. It took 10 overs and one ball for the spinners to capture England's last two wickets this morning.

England managed to make 21 more runs before Devon Malcolm's dismissal completed India's biggest ever victory over England, by an innings and 22 runs. Sachin Tendulkar was Man-of-the-Match for his formidably brilliant innings of 165 in India's 560 for six declared.

The last time India beat England twice in a row was in 1986 at Lord's and Headingley, resulting in the deposition of David Gower and the slightly reluctant accession of Mike Gatting. What musical chairs the three G's have played in the strangely mercurial last decade of English cricket. Now it is Graham Gooch's turn under the cloud which never seems to leave England captains for very long. Gower looks on smilingly as a contented television commentator, biding his time perhaps. Gatting frowns and thinks wistfully back to his triumphant tour here under Gower eight years ago. Gooch can only look forward to the third and final Test in Bombay starting on Friday.

Chris Lewis was out for 117 after adding only nine runs today to his brilliant century, driving when not quite to the pitch of a ball from Anil Kumble and giving him a return catch for his worthily acquired sixth wicket of the innings.

TEST SERIES

England in India
India 3
England in Sri Lanka
Sri Lanka 1
Australia in England
A 4, E 1, D 1
India in Sri Lanka
I 1, D 2
India in South Africa
SA 1, D 3
West Indies in Australia
WI 2, A 1, D 2
Pakistan in New Zealand
Pakistan 1
Australia in New Zealand
NZ 1, A 1, D 1
Zimbabwe in India
India 1
Pakistan in West Indies
WI 2, D 1
South Africa in Sri Lanka
SA 1, D 2
New Zealand in Australia
A 2, D 1
West Indies in Sri Lanka
Drawn 1
Zimbabwe in Pakistan
P 2, Z 1

Gatting, victim of first-ball sorcery from Warne.

Only Test Final day: 18 March

Now England lose to Sri Lanka

By Christopher Martin-Jenkins, in Colombo

THE one-off Test was very much in the balance at the Singhalese Sports Club this afternoon until Hashan Tillekeratne, coming in with Sri Lanka teetering nervously at 61 for four on a turning pitch and needing 75 more to win, played another cool and boldly positive innings to give his side a five-wicket victory.

With Arjuna Ranatunga (35), Sri Lanka's sole survivor from their first Test against England 11 years ago, Tillekeratne (36) added 69 for the fifth wicket to make sure that there would be no repetition of the collapse which prevented their expected victory against Australia on the same ground last August.

Tillekeratne was Man of the Match and has now scored 194 against England in two games without being dismissed. He was there when, four balls after tea, Sri Lanka gained their first success in five Tests against England and their fourth in 43 Tests overall.

England bowled better in Sri Lanka's second innings today, but it was too late. They lost the match by failing to make the first innings total of over 450 on an ideal pitch which would have allowed them to dominate it. Instead, they suffered their fourth defeat of the winter and their fifth in the last five Tests.

Scores: England 380 (Smith 128, Hick 68, Stewart 63) and 228 (Emburey 59), Sri Lanka 469 (Tillekeratne 93, P.A. de Silva 80, Mahanama 64, Ranatunga 64, Hathurusinghe 59) and 142-5.

First Test Second day: 4 June

England face fight for survival after Warne's big turning point

By Christopher Martin-Jenkins, at Old Trafford

FROM the moment that Shane Warne, the ebullient young leg-spinner from Victoria, ripped his first ball past an astonished Mike Gatting midway through the afternoon, England looked mentally and technically defeated in this first Test. They ended the day 87 behind Australia's 289 with eight wickets down.

Warne's devastating power of spin upstaged further impeccable off-spin bowling from Peter Such, whose six for 67 was the best first analysis by an England bowler since J.K.Lever's seven for 46 in Delhi in 1976. By the close, Such was batting, and with a spirit which brought an eccentric and entertaining end to an old-fashioned day dominated by spin.

If Such's success owed as much to the soaking to which the pitch was exposed on Sunday as to his exemplary accuracy, Warne's was purely the product of the tremendous tweak he imparted on the ball. That first delivery dipped in the air to land outside Mike Gatting's leg stump and spun back with the speed of a cobra to strike the off.

Warne may not have as good a googly as Mushtaq Ahmed or the accuracy of Anil Kumble, but one knew as Gatting departed in frowning confusion that England, always vulnerable against good wrist-spin, were going to be in trouble.

County Championship Glamorgan v Middlesex: 2 July

Richards and Dale share stand of 425

By Edward Bevan, at Cardiff

VIV RICHARDS, determined to end his first-class career on a high note, and Adrian Dale, in no way overshadowed by his more illustrious partner, both hit double-centuries in an unbroken fourth-wicket stand of 425 as records tumbled at Sophia Gardens.

On a remarkable day, when batsmen and statisticians prospered, only one wicket fell as Glamorgan declared at 562 for three, before Middlesex replied with 129 for one. Richards was unbeaten on 224 from 357 balls in 417 minutes, with four sixes and 28 fours, while Dale hit a career-best unbeaten 214 from 455 balls in 526 minutes, with 22 fours. Their partnership was the seventh best for the fourth wicket in all first-class cricket, and the seventh highest for any wicket in championship history.

It was also a Glamorgan record for any wicket, surpassing the previous best of 330 between Alan Jones and Roy Fredericks against Northants at Swansea in 1972.

Richards showed during his chanceless innings that the power and timing is as delightful and merciless as ever, while Dale, on reaching 212, became the second player — his team-mate Hugh Morris was the first the previous day — to pass 1,000 runs for the season.

Unless the pitch at Sophia Gardens deteriorates during the remaining two days, however, their efforts are unlikely to be rewarded with a victory over the championship leaders.

[Middlesex, with centuries from nightwatchman Emburey (123) and Gatting (173), went on to gain a 22-run first-innings lead and then bowled Glamorgan out for 109, Tufnell taking 8-29. They won by 10 wickets to go 30 points clear in the County Championship.]

Third Test Final day: 6 July

Resurgent England run into brick wall

By Christopher Martin-Jenkins, at Trent Bridge

ENGLAND stopped the rot and the Ashes are still at stake, but in the end the pitch was too good and the bowling not quite good enough. A seventh-wicket stand of 87 by Steve Waugh, whose Test place had been in some jeopardy, and the 22-year-old giant Brendon Julian finally thwarted England after they had taken six wickets before tea.

Five days ago, no doubt, England would have settled for the draw which keeps the series alive. Having come so close to a greater prize, however, the final act was an anti-climax after Graham Thorpe's 114 not out and his unbeaten stand of 113 with Nasser Hussain had set up the opportunity to go all out for the win. But to have competed throughout the game and finished in the ascendant after seven successive defeats against four different countries represents a most welcome improvement by the reshaped England side.

Thorpe's hundred arrived with a bold hook in Julian's second over of the morning. He is 23 and the 14th England player to make a century in his first Test.

Setting Australia 371 to win in a minimum of 77 overs, England took only one wicket before lunch, and in such fast-scoring conditions a repeat of Headingley 1948 was not out of the question.

Instead, on a bright and blustery afternoon, five more Australians were dismissed, three to Andrew Caddick in an 11-over spell for 16 runs, before Waugh and Julian played the 30 overs away.

Benson & Hedges Cup Final: 10 July

Cork guides Derbyshire to rare peak

By Scyld Berry, at Lord's

UNTIL the advent of one-day cricket, an identikit photograph of a Derbyshire batsman would have been a dogged defender eschewing all strokes on a seamers' greentop. But their successors veered so far to the opposite extreme that at Lord's the total they set for Lancashire was the third highest in a B & H final by a side batting first, and was eventually enough by six runs.

Where once the 'Peakites' scorned the attractions of the off-side ball, they went for it today with some abandon. At first the results were disastrous, as they subsided to 66 for four in the 16th over. But the pitch was so good that the policy ultimately paid off, and along the way this final developed into the most entertaining for several years.

To have lost four wickets, and yet to continue scoring at more than four runs an over, was a considerable feat by Derbyshire in which their opponents' fielding played a part. For half an hour Lancashire's fielders went to pieces, and this was just the encouragement that comparative novices like Tim O'Gorman (49) and Dominic Cork (92 not out) desired.

Dominic Cork.

To their stand of 109 from 28 overs, O'Gorman contributed a sweetly-timed pick-up for six, and Cork some dogged running between wickets in spite of a hobble. But his most remarkable feat was to move a yard to the off-side and flick Akram's penultimate ball to fine leg for four.

Apart from making their fine recovery, Derbyshire fielded better and, with one exception, took their catches as the pressure told on their opponents. Atherton made 54 off 143 balls, Speak 42 off 79, but after a 70-minute break for rain from 6pm, Lancashire had to score 112 from 17 overs, 43 from five, and 21 from the last two.

Gradually the resistance was squeezed out of them, for all the stroke-play of Neil Fairbrother, their captain. Proving again that he is the best one-day batsman in the country, Fairbrother (87 not out) kept his side in the chase in fading light. But, having to score 11 from the last over, he could manage only a single off the first two balls. Then DeFreitas was caught, and although Fairbrother survived a TV replay on a run-out appeal, he could not deny Derbyshire their first B & H Cup.

Fourth Test Fifth day: 26 July

Gooch quits after England defeat

By Christopher Martin-Jenkins, at Headingley

GRAHAM GOOCH resigned the captaincy of England's cricket team today after Australia had beaten his team by an innings and 148 runs at Headingley. Taking the last of England's six remaining wickets only 40 minutes after lunch, Australia thus won the series and retained the Ashes.

Gooch had been appointed for the whole series, but his decision came as no surprise after England's eighth defeat in nine matches. Announcing his decision he said that the side needed "someone fresh. It's right and proper someone else should have a go." The new man to lead England in the fifth Test at Edgbaston next week will be named as soon as Mr Ted Dexter, chairman of the England committee, has convened a meeting.

Leadership did not come naturally to Gooch, but he would have looked altogether more impressive if he had been blessed with match-winning bowlers. He is a decent and likeable man and a batsman who has played some brilliant, and several great, innings. Of his 34 games in charge, England have won 10, lost 12 and drawn 12. Gooch has left with his head held high, and he should console himself with the fact that his has been an honourable reign.

Scores: Australia 653-4 dec (Border 200 not, S.Waugh 157 not, Boon 107, Slater 67, M.Waugh 52), England 200 (Gooch 59, Atherton 55; Reiffel 5-65) and 305 (Stewart 78, Atherton 63).

Women's World Cup Final: 1 August

England celebrate ladies day at Lord's

By Charles Randall, at Lord's

CASH-strapped women's cricket in England might be on its uppers, but after a magnificent World Cup final win at Lord's the game must soon be on its up-and-uppers. Batting first, England made 195 for five. New Zealand were all out for 128. It was a comprehensive victory against a side that beat them 10 days ago. New Zealand might justifiably claim to be the tournament's best side, but England won when it mattered.

The first World Cup took place in 1973, two years before the men's version, with a concept founded on charity, in the form of a sizeable donation by the millionaire Sir Jack Hayward. Little has changed. This tournament was rescued by the Foundation for Sport and the Arts, chaired by Tim Rice, when the hoped-for commercial backing melted away.

It was England captain Karen Smithies who settled the issue with her slow-medium bowling, taking one wicket for 14 off 12 overs. England's other key players were Jan Brittin, whose 48 took her past the 1,000 World Cup runs mark, and Carole Hodges, who produced an innings of 45 in her last international match. Jo Chamberlain, the powerful left-hander from Leicester - the nearest to a female Botham - won everyone's admiration with 38 off 33 deliveries, a wicket, a catch and an important run-out; enough to win her the player-of-the-match award. Thanks mainly to Chamberlain and the nippy running of Barbara Daniels (21 not out), England took 71 runs off the last 10 overs, phenomenal scoring for women with full-sized boundaries to contend with.

The New Zealanders pushed along ahead of the asking rate until Suzie Kitson held a diving slip catch off Kirsty Bond's sliced drive. At 51 for two, this was the turning point, for New Zealand's runs dried up, Chamberlain's direct hit ran out the prolific Diane Hockley, and their final chase petered out.

Jo Chamberlain hits out for England.

Sixth Test Final day: 23 August

England outplay Australia and celebrate their first Test victory for 13 months

By Peter Deeley, at the Oval

Angus Fraser: Winning comeback.

ENGLAND have ended a run of defeats without equal in their Test history, beating Australia by 161 runs on the final day of the last Test. They did it with less than an hour to spare, and Michael Atherton, the captain, was immediately confirmed as the man chosen to lead the side in the West Indies this winter.

England had gone 11 games since their last Test victory, against Pakistan 13 months ago. They had gone 19 matches since their last success against Australia. It was in Melbourne on 28 December 1986 that Mike Gatting's team won by an innings and 14 runs. And no member of the current England side was then playing.

Three fast bowlers who had not played for England before during this summer were instrumental in their victory, sharing all 20 wickets. Angus Fraser of Middlesex, who returned after two and a half years out of international cricket with serious back and hip injuries, captured eight, with Derbyshire's Devon Malcolm and Glamorgan's Steve Watkin taking six apiece.

Fraser was named Man of the Match, while Graham Gooch — who handed over the captaincy two games ago to Atherton — was chosen England's Man of the Series by Australia's coach, Bobby Simpson, who described him as being "head and shoulders above any other England batsman". Australia's Man of the Series was their 23-year-old leg-spinner Shane Warne, who took 34 wickets. He was nominated by Keith Fletcher, the England team manager, who said of him: "He is the best player of his type I have ever seen."

More than 10,000 people crowded into the Oval to see the dying moments, but were frustrated for a long time by Australia's tail-end batsmen, until Fraser took the last wicket on the stroke of 5.15pm — fittingly that of Warne.

NatWest Trophy Final: 4 September

Memorable Warwick fightback prises trophy from Sussex grasp: Records tumble in last-ball victory

By Scyld Berry, at Lord's

IT WAS, of its kind, as brilliant a match as this summer has seen. In the course of it Sussex were inspired to the highest total in any domestic cup final in the last 30 years - 321 - and yet Warwickshire matched them run for run to win the NatWest Trophy by five wickets off the last ball.

On a prime surface for batting, centuries were scored by David Smith (124) for Sussex and Asif Din (104) for Warwick, only the eighth and ninth in both sorts of cup finals combined. Yet Dermot Reeve (81 not out) was perhaps even more effective in piloting his side to the verge of victory in a stand of 142 with Asif Din, the Man of the Match.

For Warwick to have had the self-belief to win after such a mauling in the field was an amazing achievement, and again after losing both their openers by the fifth over. But they gradually began to defy gravity and common expectation. What chance they had was kept alive by Paul Smith (60), and his robust stroke-play. Sussex's weakness lay in their ground fielding, particularly around the boundary, which turned numerous twos into fours and helped Warwick keep their rate always above four an over.

Whittling the target down, Warwick needed 139 off 20 overs, and 46 off five, as they kept up with Sussex neck and neck. It was heroic stuff. Off the last over, Warwick had 15 to make. Reeve drove the first for four, the next for two, the third for two more, thanks to another Sussex misfield.

Seven needed off three, but six would do if not another wicket fell. Reeve slogged another four and took a single. So there was Twose left in the darkness, with one run to win. It was his first ball and he got enough bat on it, with all the fielders clustered, to slice it over cover.

An epic finish to one of the best of one-day games.

Second Test Fourth day: 10 September

S.Africa's historic victory as Sri Lanka crumble to defeat

By Neil Manthorp, in Colombo

SOUTH AFRICA sealed their first Test victory on foreign soil since 1965 when they crushed Sri Lanka before lunch in Colombo. The victory margin of an innings and 208 runs was the biggest in their history.

Once again they were indebted to their fast bowlers. Left-armer Brett Schultz, who finished with nine for 106, was the obvious Man of the Match despite Cronje's 122. He made the breakthrough in the second over of the day, getting one to lift on Arjuna Ranatunga. Sri Lanka were five down and the rest was easy.

South Africa are a young and enthusiastic side. When Peter van der Merwe's team beat Mike Smith's England side at Trent Bridge 28 years ago, only four of the 1993 team had been born.

Axa Equity & Law League Kent v Glamorgan: 19 September

Richards bows out by leading Glamorgan to Sunday crown

By Christopher Martin-Jenkins, at Canterbury

GLAMORGAN sealed the best season they have had since they won the championship in 1969 by getting past Kent's 200 for nine in the 48th of their 50 overs in front of the biggest crowd at Canterbury since the days of Knott and Underwood. As if by popular, indeed divine, command, Vivian Richards ended his career by being at the crease when the second of his adopted counties won a match which kept everyone guessing until Tony Cottey, tiny and quick, shared with Richards in an unbroken fifth-wicket stand of 60.

In keeping perhaps with the type of cricket, Cottey's winning runs, after a splendidly confident innings of 33 not out, came from a top edge over the wicket-keeper's head. Nor was Richards' 46 a vintage innings. He had some uncomfortable early moments against the extremely fast young Anglo-Australian Duncan Spencer.

But the means did not matter so much to him nor to the wonderfully spirited hordes of Welsh supporters who had made the long journey to watch the fortuitous climax of a controversially reshaped Sunday competition. At the start of this final match, the two counties had identical records — 12 wins, two defeats and two no-results.

Hugh Morris's cheerful captaincy and positive, consistent batting has had much to do with the Glamorgan success story this year. His punchy innings of 67 today, which took his Sunday total this season to 737, a record for the county, put them on the road to victory.

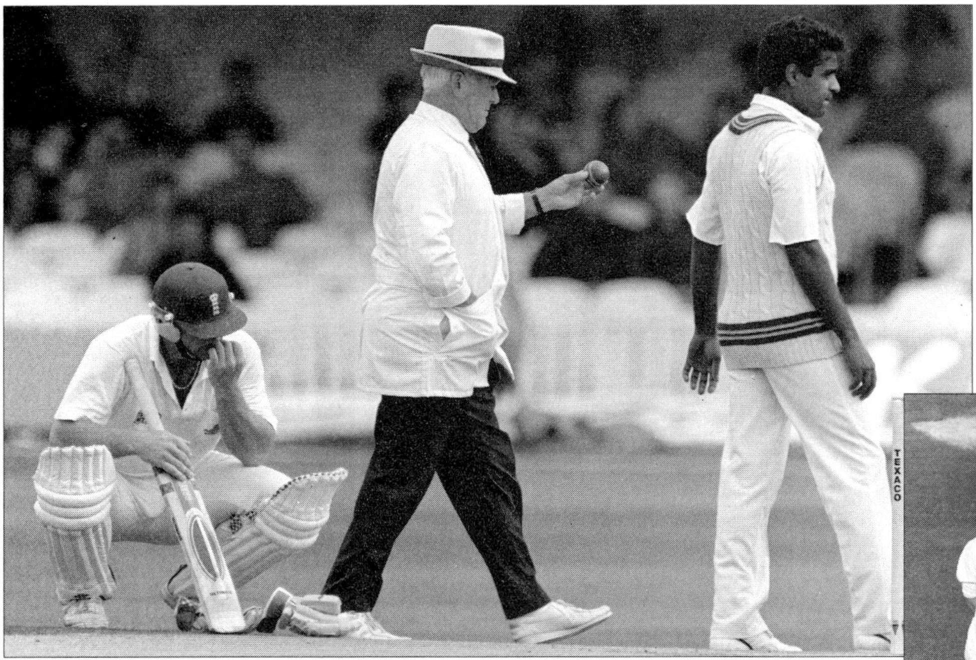

Umpire Ken Palmer examines the ball during the Texaco Trophy one-day international at Lord's between England and Pakistan in August 1992, the match that was a focus of the Sarfraz-Lamb court case the following year. Robin Smith (left) gave evidence in the hearing (although there is no significance in the fact that he is biting his nails!).

Imran Khan: Practitioner of reverse swing.

Ball-Tampering

On 18 November 1993, former Pakistan Test bowler Sarfraz Nawaz abandoned his High Court libel action against the England batsman Allan Lamb, his one-time team-mate at Northants. But that was by no means the end of the affair. The accusations of ball-tampering, which had been whispers and rumours before Lamb's controversial exposé in the Daily Mirror in 1992 — the subject of the case — were now well and truly out in the open. Not only that, but there were also allegations of an attempted cover-up by the Test and County Cricket Board.

The thrust of Lamb's newspaper article was that Sarfraz had shown him how to doctor a ball when they played together at Northants, and that this illegal ball-gouging technique was passed on to Pakistan's 1992 attack and used to make deliveries swerve prodigiously. Sarfraz, 44, agreed to drop his action when it became clear that Lamb was not accusing him of doctoring the ball. In fact Lamb, 39, acknowledged that he had never seen Sarfraz cheat throughout his career.

But Sarfraz's part in the affair was really a side issue. The most damning evidence in the case was given for the defence by leading umpire Don Oslear, who told the High Court of ball-tampering during the Lord's one-day international between England and Pakistan in August 1992.

An umpire's evidence

Mr Oslear, who was the reserve umpire for the match, said that the ball had been changed, but the TCCB decided not to disclose the reason — that it had been tampered with. He flatly contradicted the explanation given at the time by the Pakistan team manager, Intikhab Alam, that the ball was replaced because it was hammered out of shape. Mr Oslear also accused the Pakistanis of scouring the ball during a previous match, at Headingley. The action was discontinued before Mr Oslear was due to be challenged on his evidence.

Other evidence for the defence had been given by England batsman Robin Smith, 30, who told the court that the Pakistanis doctored the ball throughout the summer. Further evidence was due to have been given by Ian Botham when the action was dropped.

So what! says Imran

The case had been followed closely in Pakistan, where the country believed its sporting honour was on trial. It involved some of the most serious allegations of cheating ever levelled against a cricket team. The accusation was aimed at three players in particular — Wasim Akram, Waqar Younis and Aqib Javed — who were said to have used their nails to roughen the ball. The effect was to induce 'reverse swing', making the ball almost unplayable.

Former Pakistan and Sussex captain and all-rounder Imran Khan, writing in The Daily Telegraph two days after the case, claimed that: "Ball-tampering, one way or another, has gone on since cricket has been played." He said that lifting the seam with the finger-nails to get extra movement off the wicket, though illegal, was a common occurrence — "almost every seamer did it" — yet he had never seen a bowler reprimanded by an umpire for doing so. He also explained the phenomenon of 'reverse swing', something virtually unheard of in England until the alterations in the cricket ball made it possible after 1981, in certain conditions, and then, after further reduction of the seam by the TCCB in 1990, "quite common in county cricket" (see Box).

Official cover-up?

Christopher Martin-Jenkins, also writing in The Daily Telegraph, was more concerned with the part played by the authorities - the TCCB and the International Cricket Council (ICC). He pointed out that they "distanced themselves from the High Court dispute even as Lamb's solicitor was alleging an official cover-up and calling for more open government of the game." He quoted TCCB chief executive Alan Smith's statement explaining that "the Board's principal concern has been, as always, to support its umpires and, in particular, to preserve the confidentiality of its reporting systems with them and the finality of their decisions".

Mr Smith, he asserted, did not comment further about the fining of Lamb by Northamptonshire (£2,000) and the Board (£6,000, reduced on appeal to £4,500) for the breach of his contract which his articles for the Daily Mirror involved.

Smith had been accused in court by the umpire, Mr Oslear, of taking the decision not to inform the press of the reason for the ball being changed. However, the former TCCB media relations manager Ken Lawrence provided the inside story of the events that took place off the field during the one-day international in question. Also writing in The Daily Telegraph, he exonerated Alan Smith from any blame. Both Lawrence and Smith, apparently, had learned at lunch that the ball had been changed by the umpires (John Hampshire and Ken Palmer), and agreed that the Press had to be told. A short statement was prepared and given to match referee Deryck Murray, the former West Indies Test wicket-keeper. And it was Murray, presumably constrained by the fear of legal action and other repercussions, who issued the singularly unhelpful statement at the time that the ball had been changed, without saying why.

Further analysis by Martin-Jenkins of the behind-the-scenes action is worth recording:

"Alan Herd [Lamb's solicitor] claimed that the TCCB had been obstructive. They were 'very concerned about protecting the image of cricket, yet every conceivable effort was made to ensure that we did not see the ball'. He said players he had contacted had been frightened to speak publicly for fear of breaching their contracts. 'The Board,' he said, 'claimed they were not directly involved, but it depends on your view of "directly". They made every effort to make sure people did not come forward.'

"Apart from re-opening old wounds, the court case has confirmed that the ball was changed at Lord's on 23 August 1992, because of the umpires' suspicion that it had been damaged illegally. Oslear, who will be 65 before the 1994 season begins and is therefore likely to be left off the list of first-class umpires, said in court that it had been made clear to the Pakistan team manager, Intikhab Alam, that the ball was being changed on the orders of the match umpires because of a transgression of law 42.5. ('no-one shall ... alter the condition of the ball'), not, as Intikhab subsequently stated, because it had gone out of shape. Two immediate questions arise. Why was it necessary for there to be sensational newspaper revelations by Lamb, and a subsequent libel case, for the facts to emerge and 'official' history to be rewritten? And why was such official obfuscation deemed to be supporting and upholding umpires who had taken a legitimate decision — belatedly it seems in view of the court allegations by England players — that ball-tampering had been going on all season? The ICC officials concerned were clearly terrified by the prospect of legal action by Pakistan. I understand, also, that the umpires, anxious to avoid a fuss so late in the tour, told the referee that, although they were changing the ball, they would not be giving their reasons in their match report. Murray's view, therefore, may have been that cricketing justice was served, in that Pakistan would not be gaining an unfair advantage, but that he was in no position to take action if nothing was to be reported officially.

"Certain truths need repeating: that ball-tampering is no greater cricketing crime than seam-lifting, which has been endemic in the game at all levels for decades; that if certain Pakistani bowlers are, or have been, pioneers in the dubious art of ball-tampering, they are not the only ones to have tried it; that Pakistan have in Waqar Younis and Wasim Akram — and formerly had in Imran Khan — brilliant exponents of the fast, swinging yorker with an old ball; that these men would have been emulated by other bowlers of their own and other nationalities if only they had possessed the necessary skill; that batsmen defeated by swinging deliveries of full length have less reason to complain about the broken spirit of the game than those whose bones have been broken by bouncers; and that, despite all this, the law is explicit and needs to be enforced.

"Happily, there is evidence that this is happening. The greater vigilance insisted upon by both the ICC and the TCCB since last August has resulted in only one further instance of ball-tampering, when Transvaal were given a suspended fine for picking the seam."

Reverse swing

(from Imran Khan's article in The Daily Telegraph, 20.11.93)

On the subcontinent, although there are exceptions, especially in Pakistan, the atmosphere during a cricket season is dry, and the wickets have barely any grass on them. As a result, lifting the seam or applying substances on the ball to enhance orthodox swing — the two illegal, but almost accepted, methods used elsewhere — are pretty ineffectual. In these conditions we have this phenomenon that was, until recently, unheard of in England - reverse swing. In other words, instead of a ball swinging the orthodox way — i.e. opposite to the shine — it swings with the shine.

Because of the rough outfields and grassless pitches, the balls lose their shine quickly and the leather gets scuffed up. By applying a lot of sweat and shine on one side and leaving the other side rough, the ball will swing towards the shining side. It is nonsense to say reverse swing can only be obtained by ball-tampering. On certain rough outfields and dry pitches, by the time a fast bowler comes back for his second spell, the ball is rough enough for reverse swing. In Australia, because of the nature of the wickets, which become dry and rock hard by the fourth and fifth days of Test matches, even during the first spell the ball gets so roughed-up that it takes reverse swing. In 1976 at the Melbourne Cricket Ground I saw Dennis Lillee, in the second innings, moving the ball with the shine with great devastation. A couple of years earlier, Max Walker, whose home ground was the MCG, wrecked the West Indies in Guyana with reverse swing. Even earlier, Freddie Trueman had written in his book about this occasional anomaly when the ball swings with the shine.

Reverse swing was unknown in England until 1981, when the TCCB made changes in the balls. Before then, with the much bigger seams — and on wickets that were never as bare or as hard as in Pakistan or Australia — it was virtually impossible to produce reverse swing. Moreover, the lush green outfields preserved the ball even when it was 100 overs old. Only in August, during dry spells, could I bowl reverse swing.

After 1981, suddenly the ball began to swing much less in the orthodox fashion and the leather somehow tended to get scuffed up much quicker. From mid-July to the end of August, when the outfields and the squares became well worn, I regularly used reverse swing after the ball was 40 to 50 overs old. Of course, I had to tell my Sussex colleagues — much to their bemusement — to preserve the rough side rather than the shining side.

In August 1982, on a rough Lord's square when Pakistan were playing England, the ball got scuffed up within a few overs. While we were bowling reverse swing, the English bowlers were unable to get any movement at all. There was some innuendo of ball-tampering after the match even then.

The thing about reverse swing is that not everyone can do it. One must have the ability to swing the ball in the first place. Secondly, it takes a while to perfect the delivery, as the ball is gripped and released differently. In 1990 in England, the seam of the ball was further reduced by the TCCB, and since then reverse swing has been quite common in county cricket.

Can of worms

It did not take long for further revelations to come to the surface. On 21 November, the day after Martin-Jenkins' piece, Scyld Berry and, in Adelaide, Geoffrey Dean told Telegraph readers of sensational confessions by the New Zealand team currently playing South Australia Down Under:

"The New Zealanders yesterday joined in the revelations. Their acting captain, Ken Rutherford, admitted that their medium-pacer, Chris Pringle, had tampered with the ball during the tour of Pakistan in the autumn of 1990. 'We experimented after we noticed that the old ball was swinging extravagantly for Pakistan. We roughed up one side of the ball in the nets before the third Test at Faisalabad and the ball started to swing an extra half a metre.' Pringle took seven wickets for 52, and 11 in the match.

"The New Zealand tour manager, Ian Taylor, confessed on the team's return home that Pringle had tampered with the ball during the third Test. He also accused the Pakistanis of having doctored the ball by damaging the surface during the series, in which Waqar Younis took 29 wickets at only 10 runs each."

Index

Players, first-class counties and competitions featured in match reports, photographs and (from 1945) diary of the year are listed here. Photographs are indicated by a duplicate page reference.

ACKNOWLEDGEMENTS FOR ILLUSTRATIONS

Allsport 245
Allsport/Shaun Botterill 230 (main), 239
Allsport/Chris Cole 238
Allsport/Mike Hewitt 243
Allsport/Joe Mann 244
Allsport/Adrian Murrell 186-7, 205, 207, 209, 212, 220, 230 (inset), 236 (top), 236 (bottom, inset), 246 (top), 247
Allsport/SportStar 237
Associated Press 160
Barnaby's Picture Library 84
BBC, Cardiff 157
Colorsport 88, 90 (both), 92 (right), 93 (both), 94 (left), 96, 97 (right), 98, 100, 101, 122, 154, 171, 196, 210, 213, 241
Daily Telegraph 231
Patrick Eagar 159 (right), 162, 163, 168, 170, 172, 173, 175, 176, 178, 179, 180, 181, 182, 183, 184, 185, 188, 189, 190, 191, 192, 193, 194, 195, 198, 199, 200, 201, 204, 206, 208, 211, 214, 215, 216, 217, 219, 222, 223, 224, 225, 226, 227, 228, 229, 232, 233 (both), 234 (both), 235, 236 (bottom, main), 240, 242, 246 (bottom), 248, 249
Patrick Eagar/Jan Traylen 202, 203
David Frith Collection 74 (bottom), 105, 107,
Hulton-Deutsch Collection 66-7, 74 (top), 80, 104, 109, 112, 117 (left), 123, 125, 133, 138, 139, 158, 164 (right), 166,
Roger Mann Collection 59, 61, 64, 68, 69, 72 (both), 75, 76 (top), 77 (both), 83, 108, 111, 113, 136-7,
Popperfoto, 82, 92 (left), 94 (right), 97 (left),
Press Association 71, 218
Bill Smith 161, 169
Sport & General 118, 119, 124, 131, 132, 141, 142, 143, 144 (right), 145, 151, 152, 153, 155, 164 (left), 167,
Sporting Pictures 174
Sunday Telegraph 146
Syndication International 126, 147 (all),
Warwickshire CCC 197 (both)
Yorkshire Post 121 (top)

Other photographs from the NS Barrett Collection.